# Edgar Cayce's Story of the Bible

## Edgar Cayce's Story of the Bible

Edgar Cayce, the twentieth century's most astoundingly accurate prophet, had the psychic gift of being able to put himself into a state of self-induced trance. In this state, Cayce, a man of little formal education and not scholarly by temperament, predicted such future events as the discovery of the Dead Sea Scrolls and the development of the laser beam. He was also capable of diagnosing illnesses that were beyond the knowledge of contemporary physicians—often for people thousands of miles away.

But outstanding among all his accomplishments as a clairvoyant, mystic and prophet was his ability—through psychic readings as well as in his life teachings—to make the Bible live!

Here are Edgar Cayce's profoundly magnificent revelations about God's love, reincarnation, humankind's spiritual role, and the true meaning of the Bible.

# Edgar Cayce's Story of the Bible

### Robert W. Krajenke

**A.R.E. Press** • **Virginia Beach** • **Virginia**

A.R.E. Press
215 67th Street
Virginia Beach, VA 23451-2061


ISBN 13: 978-0-87604-703-3

Cover design by Christine Fulcher

DEDICATED WITH APPRECIATION AND GRATITUDE
TO RICHARD COPELAND
*Whose generous donation made this new edition possible.*

# Contents

*Foreword* ............................................................................................................ *ix*

*Author's Preface to the Single Volume Edition* ..................................... *xi*

*Introduction* ................................................................................................ *xv*

**PART ONE: *From the Birth of Soul's to the Death of Moses*** ....... xxvii
Chapter 1:  In God's Mind a Spiritual Creation ............................. 1
Chapter 2:  The Coming of Adam .................................................. 17
Chapter 3:  The Fall of Man ........................................................... 35
Chapter 4:  Cain and Abel: Hostile Brothers ............................... 43
Chapter 5:  The Deluge: Division and Dissent ............................. 59
Chapter 6:  The Tower of Babel ..................................................... 77
Chapter 7:  Abraham, Isaac, and Jacob ........................................ 81
Chapter 8:  Joseph: Forerunner of the Christ ............................. 109
Chapter 9:  Exodus ........................................................................ 117

**PART TWO: *From Joshua to the Golden Age of Solomon*** ............. 195
Chapter 10:  Joshua, the New Leader ............................................ 197
Chapter 11:  The Book of Judges ................................................... 245
Chapter 12:  The Book of Ruth ...................................................... 259
Chapter 13:  Man Crowned King .................................................. 267
Chapter 14:  The Birth of a Prophet .............................................. 273
Chapter 15:  The Story of Saul ....................................................... 291
Chapter 16:  King David .................................................................. 323
Chapter 17:  The Golden Age of Solomon .................................... 349

**PART THREE: *From Solomon's Glories to the Birth of Jesus*** ........ 367
Foreword: World Affairs and the Bible                                        369
Introduction: The Coming Is from Within                                  371
Chapter 18:  Solomon's Sins .......................................................... 375
Chapter 19:  Jeroboam, King of Israel ........................................... 385
Chapter 20:  Elijah and Elisha ....................................................... 413
Chapter 21:  Bad News for Judah .................................................. 431
Chapter 22:  New Light ................................................................... 441
Chapter 23:  Good King Hezekiah ................................................. 447
Chapter 24:  The Lost Tribes and the New World ........................ 461
Chapter 25:  Judah in Babylon ...................................................... 473

Chapter 26: Liberation ............................................................................ 489
Chapter 27: Return from Bondage ......................................................... 497
Chapter 28: The First Return .................................................................. 505
Chapter 29: The Second Return ............................................................. 523
Chapter 30: The Third Return ................................................................ 555

Epilogue ................................................................................................ 577

The Relevance and Significance of Edgar Cayce's Story of the Bible Today ............. 583

Appendix: Edgar Cayce's Bible Class Notes and Lectures ........................................... 585

Index ................................................................................................... 601

# Foreword

*Out* of the thousands of individuals who received readings from Edgar Cayce, several hundred people were told that they had incarnations in biblical times.

From early childhood, Edgar Cayce was a devout Bible student and began teaching Sunday school, using the standard orthodox literature, while still in his teens. He continued this practice throughout his life. Many are still living who remember his outstanding ability as a Bible teacher, most of whom never knew him as a psychic or in any other capacity than as a teacher.

A few years before Edgar Cayce died he was persuaded by members of several local A.R.E. Study Groups, to teach a weekly interdenominational Bible Class starting with the Book of Genesis and going straight through the Bible.

As a child, Edgar Cayce had determined to read the Bible through in a year, by reading three chapters each weekday and five on Sunday. After doing this he decided to read more chapters each day until he could catch up to his years of age. After reaching that point he continued to read the Bible through each year, until—when he died at the age of sixty-seven—he had read the Bible through sixty-seven times!

The Tuesday Night Bible Class, as it was called, wanted Edgar Cayce to incorporate in his teaching not only his own knowledge of the Bible but his understanding of the concepts presented through his psychic readings. The members had already been exposed to some of these concepts through their study of the lessons "in soul development" contained in Books I and II of *A Search for God*.

Having been Edgar Cayce's secretary since 1923, I was asked to take down in shorthand and transcribe the Bible minutes from these weekly discussions.

Robert Krajenke has shown extraordinary insight in paralleling Edgar Cayce's comments on the Bible, and blending them with the quotes from the Life readings having to do with Old Testament characters.

It has long been my belief that Edgar Cayce's greatest contribution to this age was his making the Bible come alive for so many people. I saw this happen during his lifetime. Since his death I have seen it even more.

Edgar Cayce loved the Old Testament. He used to say often that without the Old we would not have had the New; without Abraham, Moses, David, we would not have had Jesus.

Now Robert Krajenke, through his discernment and compilation of Edgar Cayce's statements both in the conscious and psychic state, is perhaps again making the Bible live for the many who will read these pages.

Gladys Davis Turner (1905–1986)

# Author's Preface to the Single Volume Edition

Edgar *Cayce's Story of the Old Testament* was originally published in the 1970's in three separate volumes. This new edition merges those three volumes into one. This seems worth noting. As we depart the astrological influences of the Piscean Era and migrate into the energies of Aquarius, we see a movement toward Oneness manifesting in social, political, religious and spiritual movements throughout the planet. The unity of three as one aptly expresses the core truth at the heart of all major spiritual traditions—"Hear O Israel, the Lord thy God is One." It is often said that we humans are spiritual beings having a physical experience, not physical beings having a spiritual experience. We are made in the image of God (Gen. 1: 26). As God is One, all parts of us—body, mind and soul—are designed to cooperate and move in harmony, all being expressions of One. And so it seems that the joining of the original three volumes into one is an outward expression of this same energy that is uniting people and toppling and reforming the old, rigid and elitist hierarchal power structure. As around the world, so we find within ourselves this same impulse of rebirth and renewal for which Scripture and the wisdom teachings are designed and dedicated to assist us in our discovery and examination of ourselves and the nature of the Divine. All is One—present to assist each of us in our return to wholeness and harmony with God, Nature, and our fellow beings.

Edgar Cayce was a marvelous teacher of spiritual wisdom. His love of the Bible is legendary, and the wisdom and lessons he drew from it have touched, changed, and motivated countless people to experience their own lives and challenges from a spiritual perspective. "We do not learn by reading the Bible as history," Mr. Cayce said, "but by living it."

While portions of the Bible story are literal historic events and people that is only one level of a multilevel book. Edgar Cayce understood the importance of our Scripture, from the first of Genesis to the last of Revelation as a continuous story of our soul's journey through the earth. Somewhere in that story, as we seek to awaken a more conscious understanding and relationship to the Divine, we find ourselves in the characters that represent or manifest some phase or aspect of our present state of development. The prologue to the story begins offstage, before the foundations of the earth were laid. The Cayce readings tell us our first existence was as spiritual beings in the spiritual world. We moved in consciousness out of the oneness and awakened in a state of separateness in the density of matter. We still and always will retain the essence of the divine image of original creation: a creative, conscious spirit with the ability to direct our energy as we choose, and learn to live with the results. With Adam the stage is set. The actual story begins with his fall and loss of the all-supplying abundance of the Garden. In the flesh, who hasn't experienced loss and betrayal, temptations and separation, weakness and strength, confusion and clarity as we experience our lives wherever we find ourselves. All that was lost to the first Adam is regained and restored by the second Adam, Jesus, whom the readings tell us is the same soul, who through many incarnations in the earth, regained his full sonship with his Source. Jesus the man becomes Christ the power, and a true Elder Brother who will, through the Holy Spirit, guide us step by step on our own path back to the oneness and perfection of the Whole. It is our destiny to find our way back to the all-supplying Garden to eat from the Tree of Life in unity with the One, no longer lost or deceived by a dual-minded, self-created ego lost in the bewildering knowledge of good and evil.

Again, I take this opportunity to express my gratitude to Mr. Richard Copeland for his generous gift, and the enthusiasm and support of Kevin Todeschi, Executive Director and CEO of Edgar Cayce's A.R.E., for making made this new Three as One edition a reality. They also have provided me with a much valued and welcome opportunity to include additional material from the records of Edgar Cayce's popular Bible Class lessons.

It is my prayer that in this One volume you find assistance and wisdom to lead you to ever greater expressions of love and unity, which are found in the divine image that you are.

Robert W. Krajenke, Virginia Beach, VA

# Introduction

*The* Bible is a Book of Life, and all Life comes from God. What we find in Scripture we see manifested in our lives every day. Unless we can experience the validity of the concepts presented to us, we have no basis for understanding their merit or meaning. We believe the Bible because we can experience its truths. It is possible to experience everything written in the Bible, Edgar Cayce said, and that is why the Book is holy, and why it comes from God.

Jesus quoted what the psalmist already knew—that we are all gods in the making. (John 10:34; Psalm 82:6) We are gods because we possess a soul. It is the soul that is the Image of God, the readings tell us, and not the physical body. For Edgar Cayce, the Bible was an inspired record, the word of God written by men as they were moved by the Spirit. And what inspired them? Cayce asked. Their souls! We are all potential Christs, and as the Spirit moves through our souls, we can write, read, and live in the same consciousness as the saints and prophets of the past.

The approach of Edgar Cayce is based on application and experience. His interpretations have the unique and vital quality of making the Bible "come alive."

A number of people who knew Edgar Cayce feel that the greatest contribution he made in their lives was to re-awaken them to the Bible. Since his death, many who have studied his psychic legacy have carried the same conviction.

A study of the Cayce interpretations, correlated with regular reading of the Bible, can increase the dimensions of our own humanity as well as make the Divine more real. The following are a few examples from the clairvoyant discourses of Edgar Cayce regarding the Bible:

(Q) What present printed version of the Bible gives the nearest to the true meaning of both the New and Old Testaments?
(A) The nearest true version for the entity is that ye apply of whatever version ye read, in your life. It isn't that ye learn from anyone. Ye only may have the direction. The learning, the teaching is within self. For where hath He promised to meet thee? Within the temple! Where is that temple? Within! Where is heaven on earth? Within! Meet thy Savior there . . .

There have been many versions of that which was purposed to have been written, and has been changed from all of those versions, but remember that the whole Gospel of Jesus Christ is: "Thou shalt love the Lord thy God with all thy mind, thy heart, and thy body, and thy neighbor as thyself." Do this and thou shalt have eternal life. The rest of the book is trying to describe that. It is the same in any language, any version.                                        2072-14[1]

For there be many misinterpretations, poor translations, but to find fault with that thou hast and not used same is to make excuses that you haven't it as it was given . . .                                      281-20

For much might be given respecting that ye have that ye call the Bible. This has passed through many hands. Many that would turn that which was written into the meanings that would suit their own purposes, as ye yourselves oft do. But if ye will get the spirit of that written there ye may find it will lead thee to the gates of heaven . . . Read it to be wise. Study it to understand. Live it to know that the Christ walks through same with thee.                                             262-60

But study and know thy relationship to the Creator. No better handbook may be used than the Scripture itself.                        1966-1

---

[1]The numbers following verbatim quotes identify the case number as it is cataloged at Edgar Cayce's Association for Research & Enlightenment, Inc., Virginia Beach, Virginia; www.edgarcayce.org.

The concepts presented in this book are drawn from the clairvoyant readings of Edgar Cayce. A secondary source is the commentary and philosophy he expressed in his weekly Bible class.

Edgar Cayce had the psychic gift of being able to put himself into a self-induced trance. While in this state, Cayce was completely unconscious, yet able to discourse at length on any subject which was asked of him. Although a man of little formal education, and not scholarly by temperament, while in this sleep-like condition, Cayce had access to unlimited information. These discourses are called "readings."

The accuracy of many of the readings can be ascertained because they related to the diagnosis of physical ailments, often for people hundreds or thousands of miles away, whom Cayce had never met or seen.

Still other readings contained intimations of the future which have been confirmed by the passage of time. The readings anticipated such events as the discovery of the laser beam and gave vivid descriptions of an Essene community before the discovery of the Dead Sea Scrolls.

The approach to Life taken by the readings, with its emphasis on dreams, meditation, and small group dynamics, is clearly a harbinger of many recent developments, and several decades ahead of the interest now shown by psychologists, theologians, and social therapists. In many ways, the readings' view on the nature of Man and the possibilities in Life are still far ahead of the conclusions and implications drawn by these modern practitioners.

The readings also discussed reincarnation and dealt with it in a specific framework compatible with Judeo-Christian ethics. Indeed, reincarnation aids in clarifying many of the enigmatic and mysterious statements made throughout Scripture.

The framework, philosophy, and logic of reincarnation, as explained by Edgar Cayce, give a consistent picture of God's Love and also offer an acceptable explanation of Jesus' life and development as the Savior. It was the result of many incarnations in the earth in which all the trials and errors of the flesh were experienced and overcome by the soul's yearning to be One with God.

Perhaps what is most inspiring and encouraging about a Bible with reincarnation in it is that we may find ourselves as part of the story, as many who obtained readings from Edgar Cayce did.

The discourses which deal directly with reincarnation are called "Life readings," and were given for individuals who requested them. They described influences from previous incarnations which were directly affecting the present life of the individual.

In many instances biblical incarnations were given and, in this volume, became a primary source of information. All extracts from the readings are verbatim quotes.

Cayce said the source of his information came from the knowledge and memory stored in the subconscious mind of the individual for whom the reading was given. If this is correct, and his descriptions of past lives accurate, the Life readings are as close as we can come to actual "eye-witness" accounts. These readings are a unique and fascinating record of the thoughts, the emotions, and the effects of circumstance upon the consciousness of individuals who were present when the Old Testament history was being lived.

Almost all the readings which Cayce gave show the influence of the Bible, yet few readings were devoted exclusively to Scripture.

The "364 series" (those readings beginning with the number "364") contains 12 discourses devoted to the history of Atlantis and the symbology of Genesis. The 281 series contains 65 discourses dealing with healing prayer and a study of the Revelation of St. John. The 5749 series was obtained by Tom Sugrue for his philosophy chapter in *There Is a River*, and contains some of the best exposition of the Cayce philosophy paralleled with Christian theology and the tenets of other religious beliefs. The 262 series of 130 discourses deals with the principles of spiritual growth, and forms the basis of the "A Search for God" ecumenical study group program of the Association for Research & Enlightenment, Inc.

These series contain the best material for interpreting a clairvoyant's view of the great themes and questions which are raised in Scripture, such as the nature of God and His relationships to Man; the purpose for life in the earth, and why Man loves and why he suffers; Good and Evil, Karma and Grace, Free Will and Predestination.

The second source of Edgar Cayce's interpretations of the Bible is the record kept in his Tuesday Night Bible Class which he conducted during the last four years of his life.

Edgar Cayce was born and raised in a Fundamentalist tradition. In the early days, his career as a psychic offered him no major theological difficulties. He was able to diagnose physical ailments, and the people recovered when his recommendations were applied. His strange gift seemed to be simply a manifestation of God's Love.

But as his work continued and his fame grew, requests began coming in from a variety of people in widely scattered environments, and concepts such as reincarnation and astrology began appearing in his discourses.

Cayce, who never recalled a word he spoke in trance, was troubled by the presence of these unorthodox concepts. For a long time he debated if he should continue giving readings. Yet the conflict was finally resolved. "No one seemed to be getting hurt," he observed, "and the readings are still doing good." Thus, God's Love was still working in mysterious ways its wonders to perform. And it caused Edgar Cayce to think, to study the readings, and to discuss them with those who were close to him. As Cayce matured and developed, his unconscious statements became fully integrated into his conscious philosophy.

Although a lifelong Bible class teacher, his Tuesday Night class, coming at the end of his life, represents some of his most developed perceptions.

The Bible was not studied as a history or past fact. The lives of the Bible characters and the conditions which surrounded them were studied as relative conditions, stages of development, or planes of consciousness which were applicable in the present. Not only were the great accomplishments studied, but also the faults and failures, in order to make the Bible characters more real and understandable.

The main objective of the study was to gain a better concept of the Bible and its personal relationship to each individual, and to determine which truths were applicable in daily life.

No claim is made that the Bible class quotes reflect the actual words spoken by Edgar Cayce. Indeed, what was recorded was often the consensus of opinion following a group discussion over which Cayce presided. In presenting these quotes, I have felt free to edit and rework the material in order to present it as succinctly as possible.

It was Edgar Cayce's intention to review all the material upon completion of the study and make any necessary additions or changes before allowing publication. He died before the study reached its conclusion. Thus, the Bible notes have never been widely circulated.

Edgar Cayce taught a Bible class almost all his life. The notes that appear in this preface and the appendix come from a yearlong series of talks (Jan 4, 1939–Jan 2, 1940) requested by members of the original *A Search for God* study group. The request to Mr. Cayce was to compare lessons emerging from the study group readings (the 262 series) that were dedicated to spiritual development with the wisdom he found in his much loved Bible. He agreed, stating his purpose would be to make the truths practical for the group and for all those who seek to apply them. They are meant for us, as well.

Gladys Davis, Edgar Cayce's lifelong secretary, recorded each of the talks in this series. Rather than being verbatim, like the trance readings were, these transcriptions preserve the ideas and wisdom he shared, and also give us the flavor of the man as a conscious and enlightened teacher.

(Note: some editorial liberties have been taken with the existing notes for a fuller, more organic presentation of the insights and spiritual philosophy he expressed. RWK.)

## A Way of Looking at the Scripture— and Seeing Ourselves in It

### (Notes from Edgar Cayce's Bible Class)

*The* story of the Bible all through is the story of a *human* body. Each character then representing some characteristic of a body—each phase of an existence or consciousness is depicted in some one or another character and so on so the whole thing is our own selves depicted for us in the lives of others.

Let us not think of the characters, in our study of the Bible, as merely historical figures, but rather as individuals who passed through an experience not unlike our own.

Through the Old Testament characters we may see the individual developing through various stages to reach the perfection which Christ represents in our lives. We see ourselves in such characters evolving from purely materialistic through the mental into the spiritual life as shown in Christ—in whom we may completely know ourselves to be what we are and what we shall be, by His grace.

When we measure the Old Testament characters by the standard of the Christ, we see many faults and shortcomings; but we must remember that they were only developing toward the Christ Consciousness, just as we are today, and they did not have the Christ Pattern fully outlined for them as we have now.

Their lives were also of a very complex nature, as is ours today. An example is in the parable of Lazarus and Dives (Luke 16:19-25) When the leper Lazarus died, he went to Abraham's bosom. We can't conceive of this being literal. It must be a consciousness or an experience through which the individual soul passes. Abraham represents *faith*. We must have faith, but faith must be part of our experience before we know we have faith. Similarly we find that other characters represent various portions of our own development, characteristics, we might say, that are within our own natures.

Unless we as individuals can experience that which is written in the Bible is ourselves, we cannot say we believe what is says.

## *From Genesis to The Revelation—an Overview*

For students of the Edgar Cayce readings, the two key books of the Bible are Genesis and The Revelation. "Unless you understand The Revelation," Cayce once said, "you can't understand the Bible. And you can't understand The Revelation until you understand Genesis."

*In The Beginning God created the heavens and the earth.* (Genesis 1:1)

Genesis begins with a simple premise. God is Spirit, and Life both in the heavens and of the earth, in all its phases and expressions, is a manifestation of that power.

God is. God was. He ever shall be. With God there is no beginning. Then, to what does "The Beginning" refer?

The earth is just one aspect of God's total creativity. Our planet is just a mote in our solar system, and our solar system is a speck in a larger system, which in turn is only a part of something even greater—a universe within universes!

"The Beginning" is not a description of God's first creative act, nor even of His most important. "The Beginning" describes that creation in which Man—God's child—finds himself.

According to Edgar Cayce, the purpose of Genesis was to keep in the mind of man a memory of "The Beginning."

> . . . for as is seen, that as is given [in Genesis] is the presentation of a teacher of a peoples that separated for that definite purpose of keeping alive in the minds, the hearts, the soul-minds of entities, that there may be seen their closer relationships to the divine influences of Creative Forces, that brought into being all that appertains to man's indwelling

**as man in the form of flesh in this material world.**          364-5

Additional information in the Cayce readings states the substance of Genesis was drawn from extant, ancient manuscripts, and from information Moses obtained while in deep states of meditation. Other references indicate Joshua, Moses' aide, possessed psychic powers and assisted in the interpretation of both the psychic and historical materials.

Moses, as the author of Genesis, was attempting to give an all–inclusive description of Creation and the place man had in it.

Genesis affirms Man was created in the Image of God, which the readings interpreted to be the soul, not the physical body. Man, according to Edgar Cayce, was first a celestial being in a spiritual world. Only through a Fall, a rebellion in heaven, did man become a material being. The spiritual estate was lost to the flesh.

Moses was recounting the evolution of God's Spirit in the earth, telling the story in a highly condensed, symbolic language through which the finite mind of the Israelites could grasp an understanding of infinite happenings.

Just as Genesis preserves a past memory, The Revelation points to potential consciousness.

**And then The Revelation . . . is a description of, a possibility of, thy own consciousness, and not as a historical fact, not as a fancy, but as that thy own soul has sought throughout its experiences, through the phases of thy abilities, the faculties of the mind and body, the emotions of all thy complex . . . system.**          1473-1

The Revelation is the restoration of John's consciousness of himself as a spiritual being. The first eleven chapters of The Revelation deal with experiences through dream and meditation regarding the purification of John's body and subconscious mind. The remaining chapters show the affects. The flesh no longer binds him nor limits his consciousness. John obtained that state promised by The Christ—"a memory before the foundations of the world." John was conscious of that estate he shared with God "In The Beginning" as a soul before the world was made, or Genesis was written.

Between Genesis and Revelation is the history of a nation, the first of which we have a record, who chose One God and experienced everything that is possible to be experienced in this earth. There were other groups who believed in one God, but only the chronicles of the Jews present a complete and continuous history, with the good and the evil, the beautiful and the immoral running together. It describes their beliefs, and what they did about them. From Genesis to Revelation there is presented a complete pattern of man's experience in the earth. The pattern visible throughout the Bible is a viable one through which all men can obtain that condition realized by John.

When was "The Beginning?" It was when consciousness began, as seen from this answer from the question:

**(Q) When did I first exist as a separate entity?**
**(A) . . . the first existence . . . was in the Mind of the Creator, as all souls became a part of the creation. As to time, this would be in the beginning. When was the beginning? First consciousness!** **2925-1**

Man's first awareness was spiritual. Man's first existence was as a celestial being in God's Mind. God is Spirit, and Man, in His image, was a spiritual creation.

Many are the Cayce readings which strongly and beautifully affirm that the gift of Free Will is inherent in this creation, and is the birthright and heritage of each soul.

God desired companionship, and in His desire moved in spirit and brought co-creators, heirs to the Kingdom—the Sons of God—into existence.

All God's creations follow fixed laws and will always be that which they were set to be in the beginning, except Man. A star will never be a moon, nor a moon a rose, nor a rose a man. Only Man can—and did—rebel against God, and thus altered his destiny.

The consciousness of the Light was followed by chaos. In Genesis 1:2, Darkness covers the face of the Deep. What is deeper than God? or darker than sin? This verse indicates the condition which resulted as souls began to misuse and abuse their birthright of Will, and first occurred in spirit, before the earth was made.

The loss of the First Consciousness, or Divine Awareness, was the result of rebellion. The spirit of selfishness is symbolized in Lucifer, Satan, the Devil, and the Serpent. They all are one—spiritual rebellion.

Separated from the source of Light and Love, many of the Sons of

God became oblivious to the purpose for which they were created. The Father knew if they continued in their activities, ultimately they would deteriorate all their spiritual glory and power, and efface their own existence.

The truest utterance in all Scripture, which Cayce stressed, is "God does not will that any soul should perish." (2 Peter 3:9)

The earth was first an expression of God and not intended as a place of habitation for souls, yet it became the place of opportunity through which these spirits could realize their separation. The pain, the adversity and suffering of material existence would eventually awaken within the soul the unquenchable desire to return to God. The parable of the Prodigal Son is a model of this experience.

Throughout its long stages of evolution, souls were fascinated with the material creation, and tempted by the possibilities in it for expression and experience. Unspeakable conditions began to manifest as a result of their interference with natural laws. Much of mythology, with its monsters, centaurs, harpies, gods, and heroes, consists of memories of this earliest, pre–Adamic history.

Because God is love, and wills no soul perish, a divine plan was instituted. In order to establish a standard, or means of comparison by which these souls, entrapped in their own distorted thought–creation, or ego–projections, could measure themselves against perfection, God made himself manifest through the creature called Adam, or Man.

The Divine Image appeared in physical form through Adam who was the prototype for a race which appeared in the earth in five places at once. Sons of God, who were still in spiritual surroundings and conscious of the Light, chose to take on the form of Man, and entered into the earth and began a ministry of love, education, and healing to their brothers.

The soul whom we know as Jesus was the leader and director of this movement, and is the one we know as the first Adam.

The work of the five lines of the Adamic race was nothing less than the resuscitation of imperfect man and the regeneration of his fallen consciousness, a work which still continues.

The Fall of Adam is representational of the fall in flesh of the perfect race. They also were tempted by the possibilities for experience in a material world. Eventually they lost the consciousness of their spiritual ideal and purpose for entering the world. From time to time great leaders arose to remind them that the kingdom they were seeking was a spiritual one and not earthly.

It was over two hundred thousand years between the first experience of Adam and the last as Jesus. Other lives in the Old Testament of this soul include those as Enoch, Melchizedek, Joseph, Joshua, and Jeshua, high–priest following the return from Babylon. An incarnation as Asaph, choirmaster at the time of King David, is intimated. The readings suggest other incarnations as well—a total of 33. In all of them, the Master–soul contributed the knowledge of "The Lord, Thy God, is One" to all religions.

# *Part One*

## From the Birth of Soul
## to the Death of Moses

*And is there a nation on the earth like thy people Israel, whom God saved to be a people for himself and to make him a name and to do for him great and notable deeds upon the earth, as he had done in former days for thy people whom thou savedst for thyself out of Egypt, a people whose God thou art?* (2 Samuel 7:23)

For the universe, God, is within. Thou art His. Thy communion with the cosmic forces of nature, thy communion with thy Creator, is thy birthright! Be satisfied with nothing less than walking with Him.

**1297-1**

**1**

(Genesis 1)

# In God's Mind a Spiritual Creation

**The earth's sphere, with the creation in the mind of the Creator, has kept its same Creative Energy, for God is the same yesterday, today, and forever . . .**                                                                              **900-340**

**Hence we find the evolution of the soul, as has been given, and as is manifest in the material world, took place before man's appearance, the evolution of the soul in the mind of the Creator, not in the material world.**                                                                              **900-19**

Genesis 1, according to Edgar Cayce, is the description of a *spiritual* creation, occurring within the Mind of God. All things first originate in Spirit, the readings proclaim. Material existence is a shadow, or reflection, of spiritual patterns. Material evolution is a reflection of a process of God's consciousness as He directed the manifestation of His spirit in materiality.

**The earth and the universe, as related to man, came into being through the Mind—Mind—of the Maker . . .**                                                  **900-227**

**Mind is ever the builder. For in the beginning, God moved and mind, knowledge, came into being—and the earth and the fullness thereof became the result . . .**                                                              **5000-1**

"God's Mind" is a creative energy—a conscious and intelligent force composed of Love, Harmony and Beauty, and is omnipotent and omnipresent.

According to the interpretation in the Gospel of St. John, the Light which was in Jesus was the same Light out of which the world was created.

> . . . Would that all would learn that He, the Christ–consciousness, is the Giver, the Maker, the Creator of the world and all that be therein.
>
> 696-3

The following indicates how early in the process of Creation souls became fascinated and tempted by the possibilities for their own expressions and experiences.

> When the earth became a dwelling place for matter, when gases formed into those things that man sees in nature and in activity about him, then matter began its ascent in the various forms of physical evolution—in the mind of God!
>
> The spirit chose to enter (celestial, not an earth spirit—he hadn't come into earth yet!), chose to put on, to become a part of that which was as a command not to be done! 262-99

It was this spirit in rebellion that later was represented by the serpent.

> Remember, as given, the earth is that speck, that part in creation where souls projected themselves into matter, and thus brought conscious awareness of themselves entertaining the ability of creating without those forces of the spirit of truth.
>
> Hence, that which has been indicated—that serpent, that Satan, that power manifested by entities that . . . through Will separated themselves. 5755-2

## "And Darkness was upon the Face of the Deep"

(Q) In relation to the Oneness of all force, explain the popular concept of the Devil, seemingly substantiated in the Bible by so many passages of Scripture.

**(A) In the beginning, celestial beings. We have first the Son, then the other sons, or celestial beings, that are given their force and power. Hence that force which rebelled in the unseen forces (or in spirit) that came into activity, was that influence which has been called Satan, the Devil, the Serpent; they are One. That of rebellion.** 262-52

Hence, "darkness was upon the face of the Deep." This represents the spirit of ignorance, selfishness, the loss of the Divine Awareness which resulted when the Sons of God separated themselves from the Creator.

As the above readings affirm, this occurred in spirit, before the earth was made. The earth, as written, was "without form and void."

**As has been given, error or separation began before there appeared what we know as the Earth, the Heavens, or before Space was manifested.** 262-115

**"And the spirit of God Moved upon the Face of the Waters"**
**In the beginning, when chaos existed in the creating of the earth, the Spirit of God moved over the face of same and out of chaos came the world—with its beauty in natural form, or in nature.** 3976-8

The following reading reaffirms the concept which has already been advanced. The creation of matter was first only an expression of God. But it became a source of self–indulgence and selfish expression as His Sons and Daughters began to project their individual and personal influences into it.

**For the spirit of God moved and that which is in matter came into being for the opportunities of . . . His Sons, His Daughters. These are ever spoken of as One.**
**Then came that as sought self-indulgence, self-glorification; and there was the beginning of waning among themselves for activity—*still* in Spirit.**
**Then those that had made selfish movements moved into that which was and is Opportunity, and there came life into same.** 262-114

Thus, in the reading's view, the earth was not created out of a Void or from Nothingness. Rather, His spirit moved over the chaos and rebellion, and from these diverse elements He created Balance and Harmony, and established the foundations of the World.

The World became a place of "Opportunity" through which souls could begin to realize their separation from their spiritual surroundings.

> **As given from the beginning, by becoming aware in a material world is—or was—the only manner or way through which spiritual forces might become aware of their separation from the spiritual atmosphere, the spiritual surroundings of the Maker.**
>
> **What has been given as the truest of all that has ever been written in Scripture? "God does not will that any soul should perish!" but man, in his head–strongness, harkens oft to that which would separate him from His Maker!**                                    **262-56**

Apparently, "The Spirit of God moved upon the Face of the Waters" is correct as a description of the first phase of the material evolution of the earth. As it moved through the Mind of God, its first appearance was as "mist" or vapors.

> **. . . those portions as man looks up to in space, the mists that are gathering—what's the beginning of this? In this same beginning, so began the earth's sphere.**                                    **900-340**

The following is Cayce's description of the entire evolutionary progress:

> **First that of a mass, about which there arose the mist, and then the rising of same with light breaking over that as it settled itself as a companion of those in the universe, as it began its natural (or now natural) rotations, with the varied effects upon the various portions of same, as it slowly—and is slowly—receding or gathering closer to the sun, from which it receives its impetus for the awakening of the elements that give life itself, by [the] radiation of like elements from that which it receives from the sun.**                                    **364-6**

How long did this evolution take? How long were the Days of Creation? Seven days? Seven years? Or seven million years or a trillion years? Vast epochs of Time are involved in which spiritual awareness became a material consciousness.

Time is a relative concept devised by man as a means to measure and understand his own experiences. Yet, as Cayce states in one reading, one minute experiencing the consciousness of God is more real and enduring than a thousand years of experience among the carnal-minded

With the creation of the earth and souls willfully projecting into it, we find two important statements made by Edgar Cayce.

The first is his affirmation that the earth was a separate creation from souls, and not intended as a habitation for them.

**The earth and its manifestations were only the expression of God and not necessarily as a place of tenancy for the souls of men, until man was created—to meet the needs of existing conditions.** 5749-14

Cayce's other statement defines the real dwelling place—the universe!

**For the universe was brought into being for the purpose of being the dwelling place of the souls of God's children—of which birthright this entity is a part.** 2396-2

## "And Dry Land Appeared"

As the earth evolved, continents appeared and oceans formed. The Sons of God experienced each phase of development.

Two states of consciousnesses were being expressed: those who were "Sons of Darkness," who were becoming more and more selfish and material-minded, and those who were still "Children of the Light," who were experiencing the cycles of evolution through the Light and in harmony with God's Patterns.

It is necessary here to follow out the activities of the Sons of Darkness, in order to establish our premise.

As these souls took on form and shape, great civilizations evolved over the continents. These beings possessed great mental and spiritual powers, and warfare—a reflection of the spiritual pattern—began between the two groups.

The readings admonish us not to confuse our flesh bodies of today with the bodies of Man in the very early history. They were soul-bodies then, Cayce states, "light" bodies which "were not so closely knit in matter." (281-42)

Lecturing to his Bible students, Cayce described the condition thus:

"These beings were male and female in one; they were images (in spirit) of that God-spirit which moved and brought Light into being. Consequently, they also had the ability to push out of themselves, or to divide into various manifestations. They began to do this for their own selfish gratification, or for the propagation of their own selfishness, rather than for the glory of their Creator.

Unless we can get a glimpse of such a state existing in the earth, it will be impossible to understand the necessity, later, of God creating a perfect man, through which all souls might return to their original source."

"And God Said, Let There Be Light" (Gen. 1:3)

A characteristic of Cayce's interpretations is that all phases of Scripture are related to states of consciousness which are directly experiential. Thus, "Let there be Light" can be experienced through an awakening to the perfection of the godhead within. The verse also relates to "First consciousness," and the creation of souls.

For in the beginning, God said, "Let there be light." You are one of those sparks of light, with all the ability of Creation, with all the knowledge of God. 5367-1

When Jesus spoke of himself as "The Light" it was in reference to this Light of Genesis.

Begin and read Genesis 1:3, and see that is to thee *Light,* the light of men, even that One who is the Christ-Consciousness. 3660-1

This verse was of central importance to Edgar Cayce. One of his Bible class students recalls his stating that the rest of Scripture was an attempt to explain, "And God said, Let there be Light."

Apparently the First Consciousness of souls not only partook of the awareness of "The Lord thy God is One," but also "love of neighbor as self":

The *spirit* moved—or soul moved—and there was Light (Mind). The Light became the light of man—Mind made aware of conscious existence in spiritual aspects or relationships as one to another.          1947-3

## The Divine Image

In Genesis 1:27 it is written, "God created man in His own image." God is Spirit, and therefore the image is spiritual. According to Edgar Cayce, the Divine Image is the soul of man, the Mind and Spirit those aspects of Man which are god-like, individual, and eternal.

For the image in which man was created is spiritual, as He thy Maker is spiritual.          1257-1

For the soul was made in the image of the Creator, to be a companion with that influence which is constructive, which is creative.     1232-1

For as each soul—not the body but the soul—is the image of the Maker, so with the awareness of the soul-consciousness there may come the awakening to the realization of the soul's relationship with that universal consciousness, as is promised in Him.          2246–1

. . . the soul remains ever as one. For it is in the image of the Creator and has its birthright in Him.          1243-1

This describes the state of man "In The Beginning."

Man in his former state, or natural state, or permanent consciousness is soul. Hence in the beginning all were souls of that creation, with the body as of the Creator—of the spirit forces that make manifest in using same in the various phases or experiences of consciousness for the activity.          262-89

These two extracts indicate the nature of these pre–Adamic creations:

Some brought about monstrosities, as those of its [that entity's] association by its projection with its association with beasts of various characters. Hence those of the Styx, satyr, and the like; those of the sea, or mermaid; those of the unicorn, and those of the various forms—these projections of what? The abilities of the psychic forces (psychic meaning, then, of the mental and the soul) . . .          364-10

. . . there . . . were those who were physically entangled in the animal kingdom with [the] appendages, with cloven hooves, with four legs, with portions of trees, with tails, with scales, with those various things that thought forms (or evil) had so indulged in as to separate the purpose of God's creation of man as man—not as animal . . .   2072-8

## The Pre-Adamic World

Although the mating of the Sons of God with the Daughters of Men is considered a post-Adamic experience, Cayce used this verse many times to describe events occurring many thousands of years before Adam.

*And it came to pass, when men began to multiply on the face of the earth, and daughters were born unto them,*
    *That the sons of God saw the daughters of men were fair; and they took them wives of all which they chose.* (Genesis 6:1-2)

The lust described above was only one form of indulgence. Yet, in essence, it captures the spirit of the whole Rebellion.

. . . as a spirit [man] pushed his individuality into matter and began to express or manifest *personal* influence—for self, for ease, for comforts, for those things that would enable the individual entity to, in matter, lord [it] over others.                                   1448-2

The following reading is a direct interpretation of the meaning of "Sons of God," and "Daughters of Men."

(Q) Explain the "Sons of God—Daughters of Men—Sons of Man."
(A) . . . the influences of those souls that sought material expression pushed themselves into thought forms in the earth. And owing to the earth's relative position with the activities in this particular sphere of activity in the universe, it was chosen as the place for expression . . .
    Then, as those expressed they were called the Sons of the Earth—or Sons of Man.
    When the Creative Forces, God, made then the first man—or God-man—he was the beginning of the Sons of God.
    Then those souls who entered through a channel made by God—not

> by thought, not by desire, not by lust, not by things that separated
> continually—were the Sons of God, the Daughters of God.
>
> The Daughters of Men, then, were those who became the channels
> through which lust knew its activity; and it was in this manner then that
> the conditions were expressed as given of old, that the Sons of God
> looked upon the Daughters of Men and saw that they were fair, and
> *lusted!*                                                    262-119

Cayce found in the history of Atlantis the literal, or historical, basis
for his interpretations of Genesis.

The existence of Atlantis is still a highly speculative and controversial question, yet evidence mounts which supports the view that it once
existed. Yet the readings make reference to a Lemurian civilization,
which antedates Atlantis. They also allude, rather obscurely, to civilizations called Da, Og, and Oz.

Although some remnants of this distant history can be found, it appears material science will never be able to definitely prove their existence. As the readings state, souls were not so closely knit in matter then,
and thus these civilizations were more as "mental" or "thought-form"
experiences.

The only records which remain exist on the ethers of Time and
Space—the Akashic Record, the source from which Edgar Cayce drew all
his information. This record can be read by anyone who, through spiritual development, achieves attunement to the universal forces.

> Then through Mu, Oz, Atlantis—with the breaking up of these—why,
> *why* no records of these if there were the civilizations that are ordinarily
> accredited to them by the interpreting of the records made by entities
> or souls upon the skein of what? Time and Space!
>
> But he only that has recognized Patience within self may indeed
> make the record as an experience in the consciousness of any.
>                                                    262-115

In a Life reading, Cayce was able to trace back the origin of a young
man's homosexual tendencies to a pre–Adamic experience. The entity
then had manifested as an androgynous "thought-projection."

> . . . we find the entity was in the Atlantean land and in those periods
> before Adam was in the earth. The entity was among those who were

then "thought–projections," and the physical being had the union of sex in the one body, and yet [was] a real musician on pipes or reed instruments. **5056-1**

The following describes another pre–Adamic experience, and suggests the nature of the spiritual and mental climate prevailing.

. . . in the Atlantean land the entity was the time–keeper for those who were called things, or the servants, or the workers of the peoples, and the entity felt latent and manifest, as in the present, the wanting to reform, to change things, so that every individual soul had the right to freedom of speech, freedom of thought, freedom of activity.

For to the entity, even in those periods of man's unfoldment (for this was before Adam), the entity found during its activities the desire to improve, to make better those environs for the workers of that period. That alone brought into the entity's consciousness of man's position, the need of a pattern.

And the entity saw, the entity felt the need of God's hand in what evil, or Satan, had brought in the earth. **5249-1**

Although the events in Genesis took place amidst the thriving civilization of Atlantis when many of the characters and creatures of mythology inhabited the earth, the writers of Scripture are not concerned with the details of history. Their sole concern was centered on the Light of Genesis 1:3 and its manifestations in the earth.

Distortions and variations of the Light—such as giants, talking serpents, and later, the pagans—are acknowledged when necessary to the narrative, but never a subject by itself to be discussed, described, or otherwise dwelt upon.

The writers were concerned with the perfection of God. It is the Christ-Light and its development that is followed throughout.

He, that Christ-consciousness, is that first spoken of in the beginning when God said, "Let there be light, and there was light." And that is the light manifested in the Christ. First it became physically conscious in Adam. And as in Adam we all die, so in the last Adam-Jesus, becoming the Christ—we are all made alive. **2879-1**

## *The Six Days of Creation*

Although the "dark side" of Creation has been dwelt upon in the preceding, it is necessary in order to establish an essential part of the Cayce philosophy—the conditions which made necessary the coming of Adam and the later raising up of the nation Israel.

From the Beginning, souls were involved with materiality at all different levels, from the highest to the lowest, from the lightest to the darkest. Cayce is unique in his interpretation of the Six Days of Creation as the evolving consciousness of those Sons of God who were projecting into materiality and experiencing it through the Light.

The Six Days describes the manner in which God directed the manifestation of His Spirit in materiality. It is the evolution of those Images first formed in Spirit.

The first Day arose from the recognition of the Light after a period of Darkness, or separation.

**Do study creation, man's relationship to God. What is light, that came into the earth, as described in the 3rd verse of Genesis 1? Find that light in self. It isn't the light of the noonday sun, nor the moon, but rather of the Son of Man.**                    **3491-1**

Time began through a consciousness of separation. In God's Mind there is no division. All is One.

**"Let there be light," then, was that consciousness that Time began to be a factor in the experience of those creatures that had entangled themselves in matter; and became what we know as the influences in a material plane . . . Hence, as we see, the divisions were given then for the day, the night; and then man knew that consciousness [which] made him aware that the morning and the evening were the first day.**
**262-115**

**Or, as illustrated, the Day becomes the first day of the consciousness of separation from the forces [from] which the power, or the activity, is in action . . . Darkness, that it had separated—that a soul had separated itself from the light. Hence He called into being Light, and the awareness began.**                    **262-56**

The Second Day reflects the consciousness which was caused by the division of Spirit. The earth, as it took form, divided into two great forces, Water and Earth—Mind and Matter! More awareness is developed on the Third Day. An interesting concept is seen in the following:

> Water, as manifest, [is] the beginning of life. Over large bodies of water, then, do many men of many lands learn that [which] is hard to be understood by those on land . . . Hence, many are given to dwell near large bodies of water, where sands and sea, where much comes that may not be touched by hands, may not be seen with the human eye, but is felt in the heart and trains the soul.
>
> Wonders are often given as to why the restlessness of waves causes quietness from within. The answering of that from within self to the far call of the Spirit, of "God moved over the face of the waters and dry land appeared"; that man in his coming might make manifest the varied forms of the expression of God in his universe. 900-465

As the earth began to move out of itself into its various manifestations, there came the awareness of the powers of reproduction, and the "seed within the seed." Genesis describes God's creations as "after its kind" and that He saw that "it was good." This distinguishes them from the selfish creations which were neither "good" nor "after its kind," which was the Spirit of God.

> Each thought, as things, has its seed, and if planted, or when sown in one or another ground, brings its own fruit; for thoughts are things, and as their currents run must bring their own seed. 288-29

The notes from Edgar Cayce's Bible class record these comments about the seed of Genesis and its Significance.

> "We can make a pattern of everything in nature, but we can't make it reproduce. We can't give it life. The seed of all vegetation is within the earth, because the power to reproduce was given to it by the Spirit from the beginning.
>
> "The first principle was that God moved out of Himself. Consequently everything created has the seed within itself and creates by moving out of itself. Life in all its forms is God, and has the power within for its own reproduction."

On the Third Day, the spiritual force in natural elements is recognized.

**(Q) What are "the forces of the natural elements"?**
**(A) Fire, earth, air, water. These are the natural elements in the physical plane, and—as the forces of these have the influence—as the spirit of the air . . . The Spirit of each! see?** **288-27**

On the Fourth Day the Solar System was recognized as the source of particular forces and powers which could be used "for signs and for seasons."

**In the beginning, as our own planet, earth, was set in motion, the placing of other planets began the ruling of the destiny of all matter as created, just as the division of waters was and is ruled by the moon in its path about the earth; just so in the higher creation, as it began, is ruled by the action of the planets about the earth.**

**The strongest power in the destiny of man is the sun, first; then the closer planets, or those that are coming into ascendancy at the time of the birth of the individual; but let it be understood here, no action of any planet or any of the phases of the sun, moon, or any of the heavenly bodies surpasses the role of Man's individual will power—the power given by the Creator of man in the beginning, when he became a living soul, with the power of choosing for himself.** **254-2**

**For, remember, all of these planets, stars, universes, were made for the *entity* and its associates to rule, and not to be ruled by them, save as an individual entity gives itself to their influence.** **2830-2**

When the earth brought forth its Life—the creations of the animals, of sea, sky and land—we have the Fifth Awareness, or state of consciousness.

The Sixth Day brings forth the creation of Man, and the soul partook of both spiritual and physical awareness. The sixth state is the level of the god-man.

Two interpretations of Genesis 1:27 are possible, and both of them are correct. It is an indication of the birth of the soul. It is not part of the earth creation. The animal is the highest order of that evolution. Man is a separate creation in itself, and was first created in spirit.

The second view is that, because of the need for a perfect man, once the earth had evolved to its completeness, then the physical pattern for the body of man—or his soul—was imaged in God's Mind. Thus, Genesis 1:27 is a harbinger of the physical creation in Genesis 2.

> . . . the preparation for the needs of man has gone down many, many thousands and millions of years, as is known in this plane, for the needs of man in the hundreds and thousands of years to come.
>
> Man is man, and God's order of creation, which he represents even as His Son, who is the representative of the Father, took on the form of Man, the highest of the creation in the plane, and became to man that element that shows and would show, and will show the way, the directing way, the Life, the Water, the Vine, to the everlasting, when guided and kept in that manner . . . 3744-4

When the earth evolved to the point where all the necessary elements were present for sustaining life in this form, we have the advent of Adam, and the coming of the Sons of God.

> Man was made in the beginning, as the ruler over those elements as . . . prepared in the earth plane for his needs. When the plane became . . . such [that] man was capable of being sustained by the forces and conditions as were upon the face of the earth plane, man appeared not from that already created, but as the Lord over all that was created, and in man there is found that in the living man, all of that that may be found without in the whole, whole world or earth plane . . . the soul of man is that making him above all animal, vegetable, mineral kingdoms of the earth plane. 3744-4

> And, remember, man, the soul of man, the body of man, the mind of man, is nearer to limitlessness than anything in creation. 281-55

On the Seventh Day, God rested.

> Sure, it is indicated that He rested on the 7th day—to take stock, or to let His purpose flow through that which had been made, that it might be perfected in itself. 3491-1

The Seventh Plane could be considered as one of contemplation and review. All that which was destined for manifestation in the earth plane had been perfected within itself, in the Mind of God.

Now His Spirit flowed into these creations, giving them Life:

**(Q) Please explain the statement in Genesis, "In six days God made the heavens and the earth and rested the seventh day."**

**(A) . . . When it is considered (as was later given, or written even before this was written) that "a thousand years is as but a day and a day as but a thousand years in the sight of the Lord," then it may be comprehended that this was colored by the writer in his desire to express to the people the power of the living God—rather than a statement of six days as man comprehends days in the present. Not that it was an impossibility—but rather that men under the environ should be impressed by the omnipotence of that they were called on to worship as God.          262-57**

## 2

**(Genesis 2)**

# The Coming of Adam

*And all the trees of the field were not yet in the ground, and every herb of the field had not yet sprung up; for the Lord God had not yet caused it to rain upon the earth, and there was no man to till the ground.* (Genesis 2:5; Lamsa translation.)

Chapter 2 begins with the actual manifestation in the earth of those spiritual images fashioned in chapter 1.

In Genesis 1, God divided (in His Mind) the waters, created the seas, imaged the trees, herbs, and fruit; yet Genesis 2 recounts, " . . . no plant of the field was yet in the earth . . . for the Lord God had not caused it to rain." Man was created spiritually in chapter 1 and given dominion over the earth, but in the second " . . . there was no man to till the ground."

Clearly, two different creations are recounted there.

The readings assure us that Creation is not yet finished. It is still unfolding, an ongoing process. Perhaps even today, all the things which God has intended for this plane have not yet "sprung up."

*But a powerful spring gushed out of the earth, and watered all the face of the ground.* [Genesis 2:6]

The above verse is also taken from the Lamsa translation. This rendering suggests a dynamism lacking in the King James, Edgar Cayce's Bible, which reads, " . . . there went up a great mist from the earth."

A correlation between a passage in the Book of Job and several Edgar Cayce Life readings reveals a great hidden meaning in this 6th verse.

Water is symbolic of the source of Life in the earth, and is the first materialization of spirit.

> **As is known of all, water is a necessary element in the material forces for the sustaining of life in the material plane; hence this element is often called the mother of creation. How does water, then, supply that which nourishes in this material plane? Being made up of elements in itself that are the essence of that which may truly be called spiritual in itself, it gives that association or connection between the spiritual forces acting in the material elements of the earth, or material forces; hence in entering in the kingdom of the Father is knowing and following and being those elements that supply the needs of that which builds in the material plane towards the continuity of the spiritual forces manifest in the earth. So one enters, then, through that Door with the Savior, that brings that necessary force in the life of others, and in saving others saves self. How came the Son of man the Way that leads to perfection in heaven and in earth? In overcoming the forces in nature and in earth, by giving of self for others; hence becoming the Savior of others becomes the Son and one with the Father.**                                      **262-28**

The "powerful spring" suggests a definite and dynamic action of the Spirit; because of its textual relationship, it is also interconnected with the coming of Adam.

But what action is being symbolized here?

In Job 38 (reading 262-55 states Job was written by Melchizedek, one of the early incarnations of soul who later incarnated as Jesus), the Lord, speaking to Job, states "the foundations of the earth were laid" when "the morning stars sang together, and all the Sons of God shouted for joy."

In the Life readings, Cayce was able to trace for several individuals an initial experience with the earth which dated from this period "When the Sons of God came together," and is the same event described symbolically as "a powerful spring gushing from the earth."

> **. . . in the beginning, when all forces were given in the spiritual force,**

and the morning stars sang together in the glory of the coming of the Lord and the God to make the giving of man's influence and [the] developing in the world's forces [this entity was there].　　2497-1

. . . when the earth's forces were called into existence, and the Sons of God came together, and the sounding of the coming of the Man was given, . . . this entity was there.　　234-1

This was the dynamic action of the Spirit!

[This entity was] in the beginning, when the first of the elements were given, and the forces set in motion that brought about the sphere . . . called [the] earth plane, and when the morning stars sang together, and the whispering winds brought the news of the coming of man's indwelling, of the spirit of the Creator, and he, man, became the living soul. The entity came into being with this multitude.　　294-8

Two individuals were told they had been spiritual messengers of this cosmic event.

. . . in the days when the Sons of God came together to reason in the elements as to the appearance of man in physical on earth's plane . . . this entity was among those chosen as the messenger to all the realm.
　　137-4

. . . the entity was in the beginning, when the Sons of God came together to announce to Matter a way being opened for the souls of men, the souls of God's creation, to come again to the awareness of their error.
　　The entity then . . . was among those *announcing* same.　　2156-2

The origin of the "chosen people" began with entities such as the following who chose to make "heaven's forces" manifest through "the creature called man."

When the forces of the universe came together, upon the waters was the coming together of the Sons of God. The morning stars sang together. Over the face of the waters was the voice of the glory of the coming of the plane for man's indwelling.

When the earth in its form became a place, and afterward able to be an abode for the creature called man, this entity chose that through this manner, it, that entity, that part of the whole—would—would—through these creatures—make manifest heaven and heaven's forces through these elements. 341-1

The coming together of the Sons of God created an impression on one soul which has sustained it through the eons that followed.

. . . when the Sons of God came together to announce the coming of man's dwelling on the earth plane. This then . . . has ever been the indwelling force through–out the ages . . . of the love of the Creator. 2553-8

A close associate of Edgar Cayce's was told in his reading:

. . . when souls sought or found manifestation in materiality by the projection of themselves into matter—as became thought forms—and when this had so enticed the companions or souls of the Creator, first we had then the creation in which "God breathed into man [God-made] the breath of life and he became a living soul," with the abilities to become godlike.

Hence we find the first preparation or estate, or manner in which those souls might through material manifestations acclaim—by the living, by the being—that which was and is and ever will be consistent with the purposes of creation—was given into the estate of man.

The entity was among those first who through those channels came into consciousness awareness of the relationships of the material man to the Creative Forces; that came into material activity during the early portions of man's *consciousness* of being an independent entity, or body, in a material existence. 2157–20

Adam and his descendants represent those who entered in the earth through the Mind of the Maker, or in accordance with the pattern out-lined in Genesis 1.

The earth and the universe, as related to man, came into being through the Mind—Mind—of the Maker, and, as such, has its same being much as each atomic force multiplies in itself, or as worlds are seen and being

> made in the present period, and as same became (earth, we are speaking of) an abode for man, man entered as man, through the Mind of the Maker, see? in the form of flesh man; that which carnally might die, decay, become dust, entering into material conditions. The Spirit, the gift of God, that man might be One with Him, with the concept of man's creative forces throughout the physical world.     900-227

Cayce constantly reiterates, "Mind is the Builder." The Sons of God, as they entered the earth, were attuned, influenced, animated by the spiritual mind of the Creator.

> For, was not the physical being made from all else that grew? For, of the dust of the earth was the body–physical created. But the Word, the *mind*, is the controlling factor of its shape, its activity, from the source, the spiritual–the spiritual entity.
>
> Thus there are within the abilities of each soul that ability to choose that as will keep the body, the mind, the portion of the spirit, attuned to holiness—or oneness with Him.     263-13

Those who entered with this awareness found in themselves that ability to "subdue the earth."

> . . . "Subdue the earth." For all therein has been given for man's purpose, for man's convenience, for man's understanding, for man's interpreting of God's relationship to man. And when man makes same only a gratifying, a satisfying of self, whether in appetite, in desire, in self motives for self-aggrandizement, self–exaltation, these become—as from old—stumbling blocks. But he that hath put off the old and put on the new is regenerated in the new Adam, and last Adam, in the Christ.
>
> And as many as have done so may find in themselves that knowledge of His presence abiding with them; so that things, conditions, circumstances, environs, no longer become stumbling blocks—rather have they become stepping stones for the greater view wherein they each may gain at least in part first, gradually growing in grace, in the understanding to know those glories, those beauties God hath prepared for them that know the way of the Cross with the Christ as the Good Shepherd.
>     262-99

Those souls who entered with the Light entered in harmony with the natural elements of this plane.

> And, as was given, be thou wise—not in thine own conceit, but in the
> wisdom of the Lord, and subdue the earth: or making these . . . coordinant
> with that which is in thine own body, mind, and soul.
>
> For, when the earth was brought into existence or into time and
> space, all the elements that are without man may be found in the living
> human body.
>
> Hence these in coordination, as we see in nature, as we see in the air,
> as we see in the fire or in the earth, make the soul, body, and mind one
> coordinating factor with the universal creative energy we call God.
>
> 557-3

## Adam

In Genesis 1, God said, "Let us make man"—creation by Divine Fiat,
or through the Word. In Genesis 2, God "formed" Adam[2] (or "man," as in
the King James and New American Catholic translations). The suggestion here is a manipulation of materials and an action in Time.

Most liberal interpreters agree "man" and "Adam" carry the same
meaning, indicating the origin of mankind, and not an individual. Yet
the Cayce readings show that both a literal and symbolic meaning apply. Adam represents a race,[3] but is also an experience of one soul—the
first Adam, who, through his incarnations in the earth, became the Savior of man, the last Adam—Jesus who became the Christ.

> When there was in the beginning a man's advent into the plane known

---

[2]Lamsa translation.

[3]Unlike archeologists and other scholars who look for a physical race identified
through blood lines, bone structure, and other physical features, the Adamic race
which Cayce describes is one of Spirit whose members are identified by a common
mode of thought and action.

> . . . who is Israel? . . . Israel is the seeker after Truth. Who may this be? Those
> who put and hold trust in the fact that they, as individuals, are children of the
> universal consciousness or God! 5377-1

> . . . the greater meaning of the word—Israel those called of God for a service
> before the fellowman. 587-6

For those who seek are indeed Israel, and Israel indeed is *all* who seek; meaning not those as of the children of Abraham alone, but of every nation, every
tribe, every tongue—Israel of the Lord! That is the full meaning of Israel.

2772-1

as earth, and it became a living soul, amenable to the laws that govern the plane itself as presented, the Son of man entered the earth as the first man. Hence, the Son of Man, the Son of God, the Son of the First Cause, making manifest in a material body.

This was not the first spiritual influence, spiritual body, spiritual manifestation in the earth, but the first man—flesh and blood; the first carnal house, the first amenable body to the laws of the plane in its position in the universe. 5749-3

After man was formed, God "breathed into his nostrils the breath of life; and man became a living soul." This is similar to the seventh day of creation when, the images being formed, God rested and allowed His spirit to flow into the pattern, animating His creation.

The following suggests new insights into this verse.

(Q) Please explain, "He breathed on them, and saith unto them, Receive ye the Holy Ghost." (John 20:22)
(A) . . . As the breath of life was breathed into the body of the man, see, so breathed He that of love and hope into the experience of those who were to become witnesses of Him in the material world.
(Q) Does this verse have reference to the beginning as Adam?
(A) In the same manner of beginning, yes. 5749-10

. . . as the breath, the ether from the forces [that] come into the body of the human when born breathes the breath of life, as it becomes a living soul, provided it has reached that developing in the creation where the soul many enter and find the lodging place 3744-4

The following suggests a state of cosmic consciousness.

(Q) [Explain] the Holy Breath?
(A) . . . As we say, the All-Seeing Eye of God, the All-Seeing Eye of self can only be attained when in attune to God. And when attuned, he hath breathed the Holy Breath on the activity of the entity. 2533-8

The place of manifestation for this new race, and the individual soul of Adam, was in "a garden eastward in Eden."

"Eastward" is the direction of the sun. Thus the location of the garden symbolizes a condition close to the source of all life. Both Man and the

Garden were projections of the God–consciousness.

"Eden" is not important as a place, but as a condition, an expression of consciousness by souls in the earth. It was the material experience of many and a record of it has been left in all parts of the world.

> *And out of the ground the Lord God made to grow every tree that is pleasant to the sight and good for food; and the Tree of Life also in the midst of the Garden, and the Tree of Knowledge of Good and Evil.* (Genesis 2:9)

The Garden is a literal truth, an actual state and condition of the world at one time, but is also symbolic of man's body. Later the body is referred to as "the Temple" by teachers such as Jeremiah, Paul, and John. Jesus referred to his own body as "The Temple." (John 2:21) But in the beginning it is called "the Garden."

The existence of the Tree of Knowledge indicates the probability from the beginning of the perfect man's separation from the Source. The Father–God was aware of the possibility, yet did not know if, how, or when it would happen until the soul, by its own choice, caused it to be so.

We recall at this point that Joshua was aiding Moses in the composition and interpretation of this myth.

The two Trees are reflected in the two principles he later voiced in his great statement, so often quoted in the readings:

> *There is set before you good and evil, life and death, choose thou this day whom you will serve. As for me and my house, we will serve the Living God.* (Joshua 24:15)

These two principles of spirit still exist, as they did in the beginning. A soul can choose consistently to eat from the Tree of Life, and thus maintain his connection to the Source; or use his existence to experience the things of the world in a manner which gives him knowledge, yet results in separation and eventual death of the Spirit within.

Death does not come in a moment, or even in an epoch, but if the soul continues to sin, continues 'to eat', then it reaps its karma from the laws of cause and effect.

It was six hundred years before Adam died.

**And again He has said, as He showed the way, as He fulfilled in giving His life, "In the day ye eat thereof ye shall surely die." Yet the tempter said, "Not surely die," for it may be put off; and it was—six hundred years—and yet death came, the pangs of the loss of self.** 3188-1

## A Soul Group

*And a river went out of Eden to water the garden, and from thence it was parted, and became four heads.* (Genesis 2:10)

In verse 10 we again return to a water symbol—the river with four heads. Rivers in the natural world have one head and part into tributaries. Thus, this river is unlike any in the earth, and must be symbolic of a spiritual influence entering the earth. This river is the same as the "powerful spring" of verse 6.

Adam was a god-man, the first to enter the earth at one with, or through, the Light. He entered as a living soul, manifesting the spiritual image in Genesis 1.

The readings declare that Adam (the soul who later became Jesus) did not enter alone. Many of the Sons of God who "shouted for joy" when the morning stars sang together came with him. 144,000 is the symbolic number—which may even be literal as well—of those who participated in this movement.

This influx is what is really meant and symbolized by the four-headed river.

**When the earth brought forth the seed in her season, and man came in the earth plane as the lord of that in that sphere, man appeared in five places then at once—the five senses, the five reasons, the five spheres, the five developments, the five nations.** 5748-1

**Man, in Adam (as a group; not as an individual), entered into the world (for he entered in five places at once, we see—called Adam in one, see?) . . .** 900-227

The following again calls to mind the existence of the "dark side" of creation and speaks of the decision made by the soul we know as Jesus, who became the Christ.

**Then, as the sons of God came together and saw in the earth the**

unspeakable conditions becoming more and more for the self-indulgence, self-glorification, the ability to procreate through the very forces
of their activity, we find that our Lord, our Brother *chose* to measure up,
to earn, to *attain* that companionship for man with the Father through
the overcoming of *self* in the physical plane.                 262-115

(Q) What is the explanation of "The Lamb slain before the foundation
of the world?" (Revelation 13:8)
(A) . . . As the Master gave, 'Before Abraham was, I AM—before the
worlds were I AM." Hence, when there came the necessity in the realm
of the spiritual home for the coming of the Lamb into the earth for its
redemption, the Truth, the Light, the Offering was made. Hence the
expression as given . . . Then, when we comprehend we realize there is
no time, no space, and that the divinity of the man Jesus was perfect in
his own activity in the earth. For, it was offered even from the first.
                                                              262-57

Adam, who later became Jesus, manifested in the Atlantean environment. The other points of entry are listed in the following.

(Q) Was Atlantis one of the five points at which man appeared in the
beginning, being the home of the red race?
(A) One of the five points. As has been given, in what is known as
Gobi, India, Carpathia, or in that known as the Andes, and [what is]
known as in the western plain of what is now called America—the five
places.
    In their presentation, as we find, these—in the five places, as man.
(Let's get the difference in that as first appeared [as thought-forms] in
what is known as Atlantis, and that as man appearing from those
projections in the five places—and, as has been given, from their environ
took on that as became necessary for the meeting of those varying
conditions under which their individualities and personalities began to
put on form)—one in the white, another in the brown, another in the
black, another in the red.                                     364-9

This simultaneous projection is the explanation offered by Cayce as
to why similar Creation myths and legends of the Fall are found in all
parts of the world—it was all happening at the same time!

(Q) The center or beginning of these projections was in Atlantis?
(A) Was in Atlantis. Hence we have, as from the second incarnation there—or the story as is given in Judaism doesn't vary a great deal from that of the Chaldean; neither does it vary at all from that [which] will be discovered in Yucatan; nor does it vary a great deal from that as from the older ones of the Indian (East Indian, of course—as it is from the present).                                        364-9

A later reading in this 364 series asked this pointed question.

(Q) Why was the number five selected for the projection of the five races?
(A) This, as we find, is that element which represents man in his physical form, and the attributes to which he may become conscious from the elemental or spiritual to the physical consciousness. As the senses; as the sensing of the various forces that bring to man the activities in the sphere in which he finds himself.
(Q) Did the appearance of what became the five races occur simultaneously?
(A) Occurred at once.                                        364-13

The course of the five rivers is outlined and the lands they water are described. This description is included, not to pinpoint a definite location, but to make it all-inclusive. The Spirit was moving as one big stream of consciousness, manifesting in every possible way as part of man's new abode.

The river Pishon circled the land of Havilah, "where there is gold." (Genesis 2:11) Gold is one of the basic forces within man that produces or allows consciousness. Gold is the connecting link between mind and body. The presence of gold helps make this symbolic picture all-inclusive.

There are elements in the earth from which, to which, every atom of the body responds. Here we find that silver and gold are those necessary elements that are needed in body when mind has been attuned to Creative Forces for helpful influences.                    3491-1

The following is a description given by Cayce of the earth's surface at the time of the five projections.

In the first, or that known as the beginning, or in the Caucasian and Carpathian, or the Garden of Eden, in that land which lies now much in the desert, yet much in mountain and much in the rolling lands there. The extreme northern portions were then the southern portions, or the polar regions were then turned to where they occupied more of the tropical and semi-tropical regions; hence it would be hard to discern or disseminate the change. The Nile entered into the Atlantic Ocean. What is now the Sahara was an inhabited land and very fertile. What is now the central portion of this country, or the Mississippi basin, was then all in the ocean; only the plateau was existent, or, the regions that are now portions of Nevada, Utah, and Arizona formed the greater part of what we know as the United States. That along the Atlantic board formed the outer portion then, or the lowlands of Atlantis. The Andean, or the Pacific coast of South America, occupied then the extreme western portion of Lemuria. The Urals and the northern regions of same were turned into a tropical land. The desert in the Mongolian land was then the fertile portion . . . The oceans were then turned about; they no longer bear their names, yet from whence obtained they their names? What is the legend, even as to their names?          364-13

From a Life reading, we find another indication of this projection.

. . . we find the entity was in the Egyptian land, the Indian land, the lands from which most of those came for one of the branches of the first appearances of the Adamic influence that came as five at once into the expressions in the earth, or the expression in that now known as the Gobi land.          1210-1

There were also other centers that were developing. For in the projections they began as many, and in creating influences they began as five—or in those centers where crystallization or projection had taken on such form as to become what was called man.          877-26

The soul whom we know as Adam, and later as Jesus, we know by other names through his subsequent incarnations in the earth. His Old Testament lives include those as Melchizedek, Enoch, Joseph, Joshua, and Jeshua. The readings state before this soul had an earthly name, his name as a soul, or celestial being, was Amilius.

**These [the Sons of God] were all together [in spirit] in Amilius. They were material bodies as came in Adam.** **288-29**

*And the Lord God took the man, and put him into the garden of Eden to dress it and to keep it. And the Lord God commanded the man, saying, "Of every Tree of the garden thou mayest freely eat:*
*But of the Tree of Knowledge of Good and Evil, thou shalt not eat of it; for in the day thou eatest thereof thou shalt surely die." (Genesis 2:15-17)*

In the 9th verse, the existence of the Tree of the Knowledge of Good and Evil was acknowledged; in the 17th verse, as the Sons of God enter into the earth, they are told definitely what their relationship to this "Tree" should be.

Failure to heed the warning will result in the same loss of understanding and awareness as the spiritual darkness which preceded the creation of the earth.

**For that purpose came He into the earth . . . that there might be completed that as He had given, "In the day ye eat thereof, ye shall surely die." In the day thou sinnest, ye have destroyed, then, that something in thine consciousness that must be paid, that must be met in thyself.** **3028-1**

*And out of the ground the Lord God formed every beast of the field; and every fowl of the air; and brought them unto Adam to see what he would call them. (Genesis 2:19)*

According to a Cayce reading, this verse contains a hidden meaning.

**Hence, it is given in thy writings of Scripture (although in a hidden manner, ye may observe if ye will look) how Adam named those that were brought before him in creation. Their *name* indicates to the carnal mind their relationships in the sex condition or question.** **5747-3**

The desire for companionship is innate in God, and was the first cause for the creation of souls. Souls, created in the Image of God, carried the same desire.

**The story, the tale (if chosen to be called such) is one and the same. The**

apple, as "the apple of the eye," the desire of that companionship innate in that created, as innate in the Creator, that brought companionship into creation itself. Get that one!                                         364-5

With the evolution of the animal kingdom, souls began using various phases of animal life as the negative force for their projections. At first this had occurred spiritually, through the creation of thought-forms. Eventually, as these thoughts became more crystallized and hardened through the living power which had been projected into them, they became living creatures and began to populate the earth—a mixture of thought-forms and animal life. Great monstrosities evolved, and many other sordid and unnatural creatures which were eventually eliminated at the time of the Flood.

It is interesting to note that verse 19 of the King James translation, when the animals are brought before him, is the first reference to Adam by name. Until then he is referred to solely as "the man." The Lamsa translation refers to Adam throughout. The Catholic New American Bible uses "the man" exclusively.

Liberal theologians claim Genesis is a symbolic account of the evolutionary events in the history of mankind, created from speculations of early man once consciousness had evolved. "The man," or "Adam," is the personification of the entire human family. Some say Moses was aware of other forms of human life, but that he represented the highest order, the most advanced, and his account is not about mankind in general, but only of his race, or superior order. The Humanist scholars assert man evolved from the lower forms of life, and was not "created."

The Fundamentalists assert literally man was a spontaneous creation of God, and did not evolve. They also claim that man is literally descended from two original parents, Adam and Eve.

According to the Cayce readings, a great deal of Truth is found in both positions, but neither one has "all the truth." There is evolution, and man's physical frame was modeled after the highest of the primates—the great ape. The ape was used as a pattern. But the soul, with its consciousness and creativity, improved even upon that form. Thus man appeared. There was a set of first parents, a literal Adam and Eve. But they are also symbolic of all the "first parents" in all the five lines of the Adamic race, and were the highest order of the many varied forms of soul-life that were manifesting.

Adam's search for a helper, or "helpmeet," suggests a larger pattern.

The Life readings show that many Sons of God came in with Amilius (or Adam) as helpers.

One woman asked in her reading:

**(Q) In Atlantis, was I associated with Amilius? If so, how?**
**(A) One as projected by that entity as to a ruler or guide for many, with its associating entity.** 288-29

Many of the "trapped" souls had hooves, scales, fins, etc., as portions of their material bodies. One of Cayce's Bible class students was told in her reading:

**This entity was the companion of that beginning of activity in the Atlantean land. Thus, not as a mother of creation . . . but as an advisor to those who would change in their form of activities; or the attempts as later expressed in the entity of being rid of the appendages of materiality.** 2454-3

This was the beginning of the effort to get souls to disengage from animal associations.

**The land was among those in which there was the first appearance of those that were as separate entities or souls disentangling themselves from material or that we know as animal associations. For the projections of these had come from those influences that were termed Lemure, or Lemurian, or the land of Mu.**

**These then we find as the period when there was the choice of that soul that became in its final earthly experience the Savior, the Son in the earth dwellings, or of those as man sees or comprehends as the children of men.** 877-10

Perhaps in verse 19, when the King James changes the general term "the man" to the specific "Adam," we have a switch in focus from the collective and representational race experience to the specific, singular, and unique experience of Adam, the soul who later became Jesus. Amilius (or Adam) was the leader of this whole movement and it was through his choice that the sex issue or question was settled.

The question before Adam was how he could produce or propagate one of his own kind, or species, in the earth.

Instead of turning to the animal kingdom, Adam drew upon the spiritual resources within himself for the propagation of his "helpmeet."

*And the Lord God caused a deep sleep to fall upon Adam and he slept; and he took one of his ribs . . . and the rib, which the Lord God had taken from man, made he a woman, and brought he, unto the man.* (Genesis 2:21)

The "deep sleep" indicates a state of meditation.

**These are, as seen, the records made by the man on the mount [Moses], that this Amilius—Adam, as given—first discerned that from himself, not of the beasts about him, could be drawn—was drawn—that which made for the propagation of beings in the flesh, that made for that companionship as seen by creation in the material worlds about same.   364-5**

Adam, we remember, was "a living soul." He was not encased in the dense, flesh frame of man today.

**Yea, but the individual of that period was not so closely knit in matter.
281-42**

As a body of "light" or energy, he was able to control its shape by the nature of his thought.

**As to their forms in the physical sense, these were rather of the nature of thought-forms, or able to push out of themselves in that direction in which [their] development took shape."           364-3**

All souls were created in the beginning as both male and female; or, more accurately, neither male nor female as we understand the terms today. The soul itself has no sex, but has both positive and negative energies. As it comes into materiality, it takes on either the positive or negative pattern, according to its development and the purpose to be accomplished.

The time came when Adam (as a race) had to be divided into positive and negative forces. This division was necessary in order for the Adamic race to propagate perfect physical bodies through which the entrapped or "lost" souls could manifest and gradually find their way back to the Source. This form of reproduction had to be accomplished through kindred beings—souls—and not the animal kingdom.

Thus, when the deep sleep fell on Adam (the individual), he took on the active, positive, male force.

> " . . . He breathed into him the breath of Life and he became a living soul." As the sleep fell upon him, and the soul separated—through the taking of man's portion—and He becoming a portion of man.   282-3

> . . . then—from out of the self—was brought that as was to be the helpmeet, not just [the] companion of the body.   364-7

Eve was created to complete and complement Adam's positive or male expression.

> How received woman her awareness? Through the sleep of the man! Hence intuition is an attribute of that made aware through the suppression of those forces from that from which it sprang, yet endowed with all of those abilities and forces of its Maker.   5754-2

This does not mean Adam split or divided his soul, nor that Eve was an inferior creation. Both were complete entities, entire souls, and, as the above indicates, were "endowed with all those abilities and forces of [their] Maker."

Adam was able to project out of his own body the negative substance through which another soul, by suppressing its positive, could manifest.

Perhaps the closest analogy we have to the creation of Eve from the body of Adam is in the claim made by spiritualist mediums who are able to produce disincarnate spirits at their séances. This materialization is done, the medium states, from an ectoplasmic substance which he is able to project from his body while in a meditative state. The discarnate moves into the ectoplasmic field and molds it according to his own features, to be recognizable to those at the seance.

The creation of the body of Eve, drawn from self and not the animal kingdom, was a spiritual procreation, an immaculate form of conception. The indication is that the descendants of Adam were practicing this manner of propagation up to the time of Noah and the Flood. After Noah, the knowledge was generally lost, but restored (or brought to mind again) through the Virgin Birth.

Were this turned to that period when this desire, then becomes consecrated . . . again in the virgin body of the mother of the Son of man, we see . . . that even that of the flesh may be—with the proper concept, [the] proper desire in all its purity—consecrated to the living forces as manifest by the ability in that body so brought into being, as to make a way of escape for the erring man.                                    364-6

Uniting the opposing forces, the positive and negative, male and female, and bringing them into a creative balance and stabilizing our relationships with our "opposites," becomes the way of returning and reuniting with the Oneness of Spirit.

(Q) Is the destiny of woman's body to return to the rib of man, out of which it was created? If so, how; and what is "the rib"?
(A) With this ye touch upon delicate subjects, upon which much might be said respecting the necessity of that union of influences or forces that are divided in the earth in sex, in which all must become what? As He gave in answer to the question, "Whose wife will she be?"
     In the heavenly kingdom ye are neither married nor given in marriage; neither is there any such thing as sex; ye become as one—in the union of that from which, of which, ye have been the portion from the beginning.
                                                                              262-86

# 3

## (Genesis 3)

# The Fall of Man

...we see the creation of the world, as the awareness of these influences that have become enmeshed, entangled into matter; that they are seeking they know not what.

For that desire to procreate in self, or to hold to selfish interests, has grown—grown—until it *is*—what did He give?—*the prince of this world, the prince of this world!*

Know that He who came as our director, as our brother, as our Savior, has said that the prince of this world has no part in Him, nor with Him. (John 14: 30)

Then as we become more and more aware within ourselves of the answering of the experiences, we become aware of what He gave to those that were the first of God's projection—not man but *God's* projection into the earth; Adam and Eve.

And then in their early day they were tempted by the prince of this world, and partook of same.                                                    262–115

The readings are very definite about the cause of Adams Fall. Sin came into God's Creation through the misuse of the God–Force at the sexual level. This was the real temptation, the "forbidden fruit" offered to Eve.

The apple, then, that desire for that which made for the associations that bring carnal-minded influences of that brought as sex influence, known in a material world, and the partaking of same is that which brought the influence in the lives of that in the symbol of the serpent, that made for that which creates the desire that may be only satisfied in gratification of carnal forces, as partake of the world and its influences about same— rather than of the spiritual emanations from which it has its source.

Will control—inability of will control, if we may put it in common parlance.                                                                      364-5[4]

Perhaps the Serpent made Eve aware of that mysterious substance which was now the home for her soul—her own body, undefiled and unexplored.

*And when the woman saw that the free was good for food, and that it was pleasant to the eyes, and a tree to be desired to make one wise, she took of the fruit thereof, and did eat, and gave also unto her husband with her; and he did eat.* (Genesis 3:6)

Cayce's thoughts on Conception and Childbirth are worth noting here. The readings placed great emphasis on the ideals and purposes of the parents toward sexual union, conception, and childbirth. Their mental and spiritual ideals can exert a more powerful influence on the unborn child than the physical forces of heredity and environment. A long series of readings, part of the 281 series devoted to the book of The Revelation, investigated such desire . . . is phenomena extensively. The conclusion of this series is succinctly stated in the following:

(Q) It is the spiritual activity within the body of the parents, or the lack of it, that determines the influence predominant in the life of their child. (A) This is true.                                                                     281-54

There are many examples in Scripture—and they win be commented upon throughout—where the spiritual preparation of the parents resulted in the birth of children who became the great leaders and examples for Israel.

---

[4]Although the symbol of the serpent covers all activities which keep souls out of attunement with God, the present interpretation will center on its manifestation as carnal desire. This is not the only interpretation, but one that is practical and applicable. Of course "carnal desire," as spoken of in the reading, is not limited to sexual lusts, but with all activities that use spiritual energies for gratifying of material urges.

The neglect of these activities produced Israel's great sinners and stumbling blocks. And the first example of this is Cain.

Eula Allen, in her Creation Trilogy,[5] suggests that Cain was actually fathered by a Serpent-being who seduced Eve. Literally, the serpent could have been a crystallized thought-form of a soul. Eve could easily have been beguiled into listening to this handsome being who was already wise in the ways of the world, and knew exactly how to present himself to her.

The following thoughts are taken from the Edgar Cayce Bible class notes.

> "No doubt that one who tempted Eve presented himself in a very beautiful and desirable way, so that Eve believed him and forgot, for the moment, God's commandment which, apparently, she had received second-hand from Adam. The serpent (so-called) seemed much more real to her.
>
> It's the same today. Unless we constantly seek guidance from within, we are apt to be led into temptation by the things of this world."

Was Cain propagated through the serpent—or fathered through the self-indulgence of our first parents? In either case, Cain is clearly the result of The Fall, the first creation of the created.

The serpent is the earthly form (and first manifestation of evil mentioned in Scripture) of that spirit which rebelled in Heaven, still working to undermine God's plan for reuniting His children with Him. Adam and Eve, until they fell, were one with the consciousness of God.

> **It was the eating, the partaking, of knowledge; knowledge without wisdom, or that as might bring pleasure, satisfaction, gratifying . . . Thus in the three-dimensional phases of consciousness such manifestations become as pleasing to the eye, pleasant to the body appetites. Thus the interpretation of the experience, or of that first awareness of deviation from the divine law, is given in the form as of eating of the Tree of Knowledge.**
>
> **Who, what influence, caused this, ye ask?**
>
> **It was that influence which had, or would, set itself in opposition to**

---

[5]*The Creation Trilogy,* A.R.E. Press, Virginia Beach, VA; an extensive and thorough study of Genesis and Creation.

the souls remaining, or the entity remaining, in that state of at-onement

815-7

## *A Pattern for All*

The Fall in Eden symbolizes the experiences of the twin-souls Adam and Eve, yet it also represents the pattern for all the Sons of God who entered with them.

Man, in Adam (as a group, not as an individual) entered into the world (for he entered in five places at once, we see—called Adam in one, see?) and as man's concept [came] to that point wherein man walked not after the ways of the Spirit but after the desires of the flesh, sin entered— that is, away from the Face of the Maker, see? and death then became man's portion, spiritually, see? for the physical death existed from the beginning; for to create one must die . . .          900-227

This universal pattern is reflected in this Life reading which describes a temptation similar to Eve's.

. . . the entity was in the Atlantean land, during those periods of the early rise in the land of the sons of Belial as oppositions, that became more and more materialized as the powers were applied for self-aggrandizement.

The entity was among the children of the Law of One that succumbed to the wiles—and it may be *well* interpreted in that answer recorded in Holy Writ—"Ye shall not surely die, but it is pleasant for the moment, and for the satisfying of longings within."

Thus did the entity begin to use spiritual forces for the satisfying of material appetites.          2850-1

*And the eyes of them were opened, and they knew that they were naked . . . And they heard the voice of the Lord God walking in the garden in the cool of the day; and Adam and his wife hid themselves from the presence of the Lord God amongst the trees of the garden. (Genesis 3:7-8)*

Both Adam and Eve became self-conscious, aware that the appetites of their bodies were at variance with the desires of the spirit. The new consciousness brought fear.

> . . . with these changes coming in the experience of . . . Adam and Eve, the knowledge of their position, or that as is known in the material world today as desires and physical bodily charms, the understanding of sex, sex relationships, came into the experience. With these came the natural fear of that as had been forbidden, that they know themselves to be a part of but not of that as partook of [the] earthly, or the desires in the manner [of those] as were about them, in that as had been their heritage.                                                                364-6

Apparently, the temptation and Fall were part of the Divine Plan, a necessary experience which had been foreseen by Amilius while in the spiritual state.

> . . . as the first begotten of the Father, [who] came as Amilius in the Atlantean land and allowed himself to be led in ways of selfishness.
>                                                                                  364-8

The Fall also involved a clairvoyant experience for Adam.

> (Q) When did the knowledge come to Jesus that He was to be the savior of the world?
> (A) When He fell in Eden.                                                 2067-7

The God-Force became sexual force, or carnal force, in the Garden. The destiny of Adam, after the Fall, was to restore and demonstrate the full potential of man's creative energies in the flesh. This was realized through the Immaculate Conception of Mary (who had been Eve) and in the life of Jesus through his ministry and especially his Resurrection, the ultimate triumph over the physical.

This reading was devoted solely to the sex question.

> Yes, we have the question here regarding sex and sex relationships . . . This has been the problem throughout man's experience or man's sojourn in the earth; since taking bodily form with the attributes of the animal in which he had projected himself as a portion of, that he might through the self gain that activity which was visualized to him in those relationships in the earth.
> Hence slow has been the progress through the ages. And as has been seen, and as may be gained by a study of man's development, this . . . has

ever been a problem before man.

    This is ever, and will ever be, a question, a problem, until there is the greater spiritual awakening within man's experience that this phase biologically, sociologically, or even from the analogical experience, must be as a stepping stone for the greater awakening; and as the exercising of an influence in man's experience in the Creative Forces for the reproduction of species, rather than for the satisfying or gratifying of a biological urge within the individual that partakes or has partaken of the first causes of man's encasement in body in the earth.   5747-3

The different natures of Cain and Abel may reflect a change in Adam and Eve concerning the purposes for sexual union. Cain was rebellious, self–indulgent, and unruly. Abel sought the approval of his Creator. Seth, the third son, is the beginning of a nation dedicated to God and to the proper uses of the creative energies which Man had been given.

Train him, train her, train them rather in the sacredness of that which has come to them as a privilege, which has come to them as a heritage, from a falling away, to be sure; but through the purifying of the body in thought, in act, in certainty, it may make for a people, a state, a nation that may indeed herald the coming of the Lord       5747-3

## The First Adam and the Last Adam

For *all* that ever was and ever is to be learned is [that] "The Lord thy God is one"—*one* . . . No matter in what clime, under what name, all must come to that as was from the beginning. For, know that He—who was lifted up on the Cross in Calvary—was . . . also he that first walked among men at the beginning of man's advent into flesh! For He indeed was and is the first Adam, the last Adam; that is the way, the truth, the light!       2402-2

(Q) What was meant by "As in the first Adam, sin entered, so in the last Adam all shall be made alive"?
(A) Adam's entry into the world in the beginning, then must become the savior of the world, as it was committed to his care. "Be thou fruitful, multiply, and subdue the earth!" Hence . . . Adam, the first Adam, the last Adam, became—then—that that is given the power over the earth, and—as in each soul the first to be conquered is *self*—then all things,

> conditions and elements, are subject unto that self!　　　364-7

The story of the Old Testament is one of evolution—spiritual, mental, and physical. The growth in attitude from the self-centeredness in the first Adam to the spiritual directions of the Last is demonstrated in the following:

> Let's draw comparisons of man made perfect through experience, and man *willfully* being disobedient.
> In the first, we find man listening to those influences which were at variance to God's way. Then in the temple, even at twelve, we find the perfect man seeking, asking, and answering as to man's relationship to God . . .
> Draw the comparison within thyself as to those experiences indicated in the 1st, 2nd, and 3rd of Genesis and those in the 2nd of Luke—where we find our pattern, our lesson . . . one willfully seeking to know the relationship to the Creator, or the answer, "Know ye not that I must be about my Father's business?" How different from that other, "The woman thou gavest me, *she* persuaded me, and I did eat!"　262-125

The following indicates a similar evolution In Eve, who listened, but did not weigh the words of Satan or their implications.

> . . . seek not for knowledge alone. For, look—*look*—what it brought *Eve*. Look rather for that wisdom which was eventually founded in she that was addressed as the handmaid of the Lord, and who "pondered those things in her heart," as to how and why Gabriel would speak with her.　　　　2072-10

The life as Jesus completed the cycle and established the pattern for all men. The soul again was purified and spiritualized, yet, by having passed through the earth and overcome it, he had control over all his soul's forces. Thus, the Savior.

> . . . Hence, as Adam given—the Son of God—so he must become that [one who] would be able to take the world, the earth, back to that source from which it came, and all power is given in his keeping in the earth that he has overcome: self, death, hell, and the grave even, became subservient unto Him through the conquering of self in that

made flesh; for, as in the Beginning was the Word, the Word was with God, the Word was God, the same was in the beginning. The Word came and dwelt among men, the offspring of self in a material world, and the Word overcame the world—and hence the world becomes, then, as the servant of that [one who] overcame the world.                    364-7

How, why, where was there the need for there to be a resurrection? Why came He into the earth to die, even on the Cross? It has been, then, the fulfillment of promise, the fulfillment of Law, the fulfillment of man's estate[6]: else why did He put on flesh and come into the earth in the form of man, but to be One with the Father; to show to man his (man's) divinity, man's relationship to the Maker; to show to man that indeed the Father meant it when He said, "If ye call I will hear. Even though ye be covered with sin, if ye be washed in the blood of the Lamb ye may come back."

Then, though He were the first of man, the first of the sons of God in spirit, in flesh, it became necessary that He fulfill all those associations, those connections that were to wipe away in the experience of man that which separates Him from His Maker.

Though man be far afield, then, though he may have erred, there is established that which makes for a closer walk with Him, through that one who experienced all those turmoils, strifes, desires, urges that may be the lot of man in the earth. Yet He put on flesh, made Himself as naught—even as was promised throughout, to those who walked and talked with God.                    5749-6

---

[6]Genesis 3:15. "That man can completely overcome evil"–he fulfilled the promise and showed the way.

# 4

## (Genesis 4)

# Cain and Abel: Hostile Brothers

*The* greater significance of Scripture lies not in depicting external history, but in what the outward events represent to the inner man. The rupture between Cain and Abel depicts an ever present condition in man.

> It has been understood by most of those who have attained to a consciousness of the various presentations of good and evil in manifested forms, as we have indicated, that the prince of this world, Satan, Lucifer, the Devil—as a soul—made those necessities, as it were, of the consciousness in materiality; that man might—or that soul might—become aware of its separation from the God Force.
>
> Hence the continued warring that is ever present in materiality or in the flesh, or the warring—as is termed—between the flesh and the devil, or the warring between the influences of good and evil      262-89

The development of the Adamic race was an attempt to crystallize the thought-form projections into God's manner of expressing the Spirit. However the attempt failed. As these five races entered, they began to take on forms that would gratify and satisfy carnal desires.

With the fall and ensuing entrapment and loss of spiritual consciousness in a material world, more souls, or spirit, continued entering this dimension as a "balancing factor" to the spirit of self-indulgence which was leading many of the Sons of God astray.

> **(Q) What was meant by the Sons of the Highest in Atlantis and the second coming of souls to the earth, as mentioned in a Life reading given through this channel?**
> **(A) In this period or age, as was seen—there is fault of words here to project that as actually occurs in the formations of that as comes about! There was, with the will of that as came into being through the correct channels, of that as created by the Creator, that of the continuing of the souls in its projection and projection—see? while in that as was of the off–spring, of that as pushed itself into form to satisfy, gratify, that of the desire of that known as carnal forces of the senses, of those created, there continued to be the war one with another, and there were then— from the other sources (worlds) the continuing entering of those that would make for the keeping of the balance, as of the first purpose of the Creative Forces, as it magnifies itself in that given sphere of activity, of that [which] had been given the ability to create with its own activity— see? and hence the second, or the continued entering of souls into that known as the earth's plane during this period, for that activity as was brought about.** 364-7

Perhaps this "continued entering" by the Sons of God as a balancing factor to avert complete separation through self–indulgence is what is meant when Enoch prophesied, saying, "Behold the Lord comes with ten thousand of his saints." (Jude 1:14)

Their effect as teachers and ministers is shown in the fact that by the time of Seth's son Enos, "men began to call upon the name of the Lord." (Genesis 4:26)

The above reading continues:

> **Let's remember that as was given, in the second, third from Adam, or fourth, or from Amilius, there was "In that day did they call upon the name of the Lord"—is right! and ever, when the elements that make for littleness, uncleanness, are crucified in the body, the Spirit of the Lord, of God, is present! When these are overbalanced, so that the body (physical), the mental man, the imagination of its heart, is evil, or his purpose is evil, then is that war continuing—as from the beginning. Just the continued warring of those things within self as from the beginning;**

**for with these changes as brought sin into the world, with same came the fruits of same, or the seed as of sin, which we see in the material world as those things that corrupt good ground, those that corrupt the elements that are of the compounds of those of the first causes, or elementals, and pests are seen—and the like, see? So does it follow throughout all creative forces, that the fruits of that as is active brings that seed that makes for the corrupting of, or the clearing of, in the activative forces of, that being acted upon.** 364-7

To the Israelites, Babel was the place where God divided mankind into various nations. (Deuteronomy 32:8) However, the first indication of the fragmentation of the original unity is in Genesis 4, with the murder of Abel and the flight of Cain and Cain's marriage to an unknown outside group.

Cayce indicates these events were taking place 500,000 to 50,000 years before Moses! (877-26)

**. . . in the Atlantean land when there were those divisions between those of the Law of One and the Sons of Belial, and the offspring of what was the pure race and those that had projected themselves into creatures that became as the sons of man (as terminology would be) rather than the creatures of God.** 1416-1

The following reading discusses the divisions that were taking place. Cayce uses the terms "Sons of Belial" in the reading, but they represent the same activity as "The Children of Cain." Cayce told this person he had been "firstborn of the sons of men":

**When the first of life in flesh form appeared in the earth's plane, this entity was among those making the first appearance in the form of man, or when the development reached such that the universal forces then created the soul man. The entity was among the firstborn of the sons of men.** 4609-1

In the second influx came the Sons of the Highest as bearers of spiritual knowledge. Some were giants, and were sought out by those of the first creation. The reference to "first dwellings" indicates a service also.

When there was the second coming of souls into the earth's plane, this
entity was among those who gave the first dwellings for groups. The
entity was of giant stature, and was of those who were called Sons of the
Highest, for there came many of the first role that were sought by those
peoples. This was before the day of the Flood.                    2802-1

The following is a significant reading which defines the separation
between the Sons of God and the issues which polarized them:

Hence we find there had been the separating into groups (as we would
call them) for this or that phase of activity; and those that were against
that *manner* of development.

   The Sons of Belial were of one group, or those that sought more the
gratifying, the satisfying, the use of material things for self, *without*
thought or consideration as to the sources of such nor the hardships in
the experiences of others. Or, in other words, as we would term it today,
they were those without a standard of morality.

   The other group—those who followed the Law of One—had a
standard. The Sons of Belial had no standard, save of self, self-aggrandizement.                                                         877-26

The descendants of Seth kept to the heritage of Amilius, or Adam.
Cain is symbolic of the followers of Belial.

A form of non-sexual conception—represented by the creation of Eve
from the rib of Adam—was practiced by those souls who were of the
Law of One. Through their unity with the Spirit, the innocent and pure
in spirit could enter into the earth plane through the channels they
established. The Sons of Belial, who were indulging in sexual or carnal
forces, were attuned to a more material consciousness. Their spirit had
become polluted through their activities in the earth.

Then we find the entity, now known as or called [877], was among the
children of the Law of One; entering through the natural sources that
had been considered in the period as the means of establishing a family.
However, they were rather as a group than as an individual family.

   For those who were of the ruling forces were able by choice to create
or bring about, or make the channel for the entrance or the projection
of an entity or soul, as the period of necessity arose.

   Then such were not as households or as families, like we have today, but rather as groups.

Their *standard* was that the soul was given by the Creator or entered from outside sources *into* the projection of the *mental* and spiritual self at the given periods. *that* was the standard of the Law of One, but was *rejected* by the Sons of Belial.

But this entity, [877], is the one whom we are to follow in the present; as for its application of those innate tenets, that are a portion of the aroma of the innate being, as it were, or the influence that is as the rate of vibratory force of the entity in its relationships to the universal activity or vibratory forces.

These are the abilities to which the entity may attune self, through all the various phases of its application in those directions in other experiences.

But that was among the first entrances, or the second entrance of the entity *from* the without, into that form which became encased as an entity, an *individual* body, see?                    877-26

Later it is recorded that Noah "was pure in his generation," which probably refers to this spiritual manner of producing offspring.

## Earliest Developments—The Animal Nature and the Ego

As perfect men separated from the unity and oneness of Spirit, individual awareness, or the ego, evolved. The impact of this was the fragmenting of the Sons of God into scattered groups and clans.

As they moved further and further away from their first estate as spiritual beings, they became dependent upon the material world, rather than the God-Within, for protection, sustenance, and knowledge. This reading speaks of that development:

In the first, then, we find the necessity of now supplying its own foods, its own protection, its own activities for amusements, for developments, for its associations one with another, and—as given—then selfishness, and the desire to excel, the desire to place self as in control of, in the supervision of, those things or others about same, gradually developed households, groups, clans, masses, then originally—or eventually—in that known as various groups, houses, or nations.                    364-12

The murder of Abel by his self-centered and ego-conscious brother,

Cain, is a record of this early development.

Unruly Cain is a personification of that Fallen Spirit which fathered all the divisions and separations between man.

> **With man's advent into the world, then personalities, individualities began to find expression in subduing the earth, and man—with his natural bent—not only attempted to subdue the earth, but to subdue one another; and the result was the differences of opinions, the various sects, sets, classes, and races.** 3976-8

The extent to which man became involved in the animal world, or materiality, is suggested in a symbolic way, when it is recorded, "God made for Adam and his wife coats of skin." (Genesis 3:21) This verse might possibly signify the flesh body which gradually became an encasement for the soul.

> **As to their forms in the physical sense, these were much rather of the nature of thought-forms . . . As these took form, by the gratifying of their own desire for that as builded or added to the material conditions, they became hardened or set—much in the form of the existent human body of the day . . .** 364-3

The coats of skin also signify the self-awareness that resulted from abuses of the physical body, which became a part of an actual evolutionary development, as many of the Sons of God changed their diets from herb and seed to meat.

> **As for the dress, those in the beginnings were (and the Lord made for them coats) of the skins of the animals. These covered the parts of their person that had become, then, as those portions of their physiognomy that had brought much of the desires that made for destructive forces in their own experience, and these then were of those about them that were given as meat, or used as same—that partook of the herbs.** 364-11

Those who had partaken of the animal forces now needed the meat of the animal to sustain their physical bodies. The vegetarian diet was kept by those who had not mixed or indulged, and was the manner imaged by God (Genesis 1:29) for the souls in the beginning.[7]

> These were those same herbs that the seed were to have been for food
> for the man in self, and only those that partook of same may be called
> even clean—in the present day . . . for these carry all the elements in
> their natural state. Little of minerals should ever be the properties within
> the system, save as may be taken through the vegetable forces, save
> where individuals have so laxed themselves as to require or need that
> which will make for an even balance of same.          364-11

Those who "remained clean" and those who indulged in "desires that
made for destructive forces" are symbolically represented in Cain and
Abel.

The concept of Sacrifice, which is integral to their story, was also an
evolutionary concept at this time, kept by those whom Cayce termed
"The Sons of the Law of One."

> . . . in the latter portion of the experience of Amilius [or Adam] was the
> first establishing of the altars upon which the sacrifices of the field and
> the forest, and those that were of that [which] satisfied the desires of the
> physical body were builded.          364-4

The concept of sacrifice was an attempt by those souls who were still
spiritually attuned to create a mode of worship which would aid others
in re-establishing their relationship to God. The real sacrifice was dis-
engaging from animal involvements, as is seen in the following from a
Life reading.

> The entity was among the children of the Law of One, those that were
> the sons of men, yet of the daughters of the Lord—or those who had
> become purified of those entanglements in the animal forces that
> became manifest among many.          1066-1

---

[7]The ideal diet recommended by Cayce included "fish, fowl, and lamb," with proper
combinations of vegetables, either cooked or raw. Cayce never advocated vegetari-
anism as a universal diet. Apparently because our physical bodies, over many incarnations, have become dependent upon and conditioned to meat as an energy source.
To suddenly deny meat to the body could cause great harm. In order to preserve and
maintain balance, health, and stability, the return to the Genesis diet must be gradual.

Sacrifice was an attempt to lead souls to the realization that they must sacrifice the animal, or carnal desire, or the self–centered earthly ego, which they had builded within themselves.

**For, He has given, no sacrifice is acceptable save as of the desires of self to be one with Him.** 531-5

## The Vocations of Man

Genesis places Cain as the father of those who are in the world. He is the ancestor of the first practitioners of man's three principal vocations: agriculture ("And Adah bare Jabal: he was the father of such as dwell in tents, and of such as have cattle," (Genesis 4:20); the arts ("And his brother's name was Jubal: he was the father of all such as handle the harp and organ," (Genesis 4:21); and science, and warfare ("And Zillah, she also bare Tubal–Cain, an instructor of every artificer in brass and iron, " (Genesis 4:22).

**With these developments came then the gradual infection of the use of elements from without for protection, as implements with which to protect themselves, which began with the use of fitting stone, iron, brass, copper, and those elements known in the present as instruments of warfare, or of building, or of preservation of the various emoluments of individuals. Hence we had also those for ornamentation of the body, ornamentation of the abode, ornamentation of the various surroundings that had to do with the individuals in their various sets, classes, or groups.**

**These made for such as dwelt in groups in homes or cities, while others made for those as of following the field, or those as of the hunters, or those as of the agriculturists, or those that had herds, and their various necessities that followed with these.** 364-12

Just as the descendants of Cain obtained their vocations through their dependency upon the earth, the children of Seth were to practice man's other vocation: religion. They were to be guided and sustained by that which came from Within, and to live in the manner as the spirit directed.

**To what uses, then, did these people in this particular period give their**

**efforts, and in what directions were they active?**

**As many almost as there were individuals; for, as we find from the records . . . To some there was given the power to become the Sons of God; others were workers in brass, in iron, in silver, in gold; others were made in music, and the instruments of music.** 364-10

The great geniuses of today, whether in the arts, science, agriculture, or religion, reflect the manner in which they, as entities—as souls—partook or developed in the beginning. Their "genius" is the result of a continued involvement with their vocation over many incarnations.

## They Were There

One of the most significant factors of the Edgar Cayce Life readings is in the weight and support they give to a literal approach to the Bible. Cayce stated almost all portions of Scripture can be interpreted on three levels: literal, metaphysical, and spiritual. But for any level to be valid, it must be practical and applicable and able to be coordinated with the others and be "as one, even as the Father, *Son*, and the Holy Spirit are one." (281-30)

In other words, a literal level must be consistent with our understanding of mental processes and coordinant with spiritual truth as well. Failure to interpret its three–fold meaning is to deny the Bible its intrinsic wholeness. In some mysterious way, to acknowledge as factual those stories which have previously only been studied symbolically, or allegorically—or dismissed as fantasy or unenlightened primitive mythology—is to restore with added depth the indefinable sacredness of this Book of Life. A good example is found in the Tree of Life, with its significance on both a symbolic and literal plane.

The Tree of Life is found at the beginning and the end of the Bible, in Genesis and Revelation. In Genesis, Man loses the Tree of Life because of his fall. In Revelation, Man regains his access to the Tree. Symbolically, both trees represent the same principle.

**(Q) What is meant by the tree of life with its twelve kinds of fruit that yielded her fruit every month and the leaves of the tree for the healing of the nations? (Revelation 22:2)**

**(A) That as the tree planted by the water of life; that is, as the sturdiness of the purpose of the individual in its sureness in the Christ; and the**

leaves represent the activities that are as for the healing of all that the individual activities may contact, even in material life. And that it is *continuous*, as by month, as for the purpose, as for the activities.

**281-37**

However, in the actual Garden everything was literally pure and pristine, a reflection of those images conceived in the mind of God. Thus, everything, even the trees, carried spiritual meanings.

In 1944, an Iowa housewife was told preceding an incarnation in Egypt as one of the handmaidens who discovered Moses in the ark (Exodus 2:5), she had been near Eden.

. . . we find the entity was in the early, early days, when there was the garden called Eden. There we find the entity was among those who looked on the activities of the mother of mankind. The entity then was among the "things"[8] and yet was touched in person, was touched in heart, and sought to know the meaning of same, for it saw then fruit, leaves, trees, which had their spiritual meaning in peoples' lives.

**5373-1**

The relationship to this suborder ultimately became an issue between the Sons of God, dividing them into two camps.

A young Unitarian widow was told of her experience in Atlantis.

In that sojourn, then, we find that [the entity as] Assen-ni was of the children of the Law of One; with the Children of Belial as the negative influence or force among the children of men.

And there was the realization by Assen-ni that those who had been born were, through no fault of their own, being used as creatures for exploitation; and that through the very influence and power of the Children of Belial the Creative Energies were being used for destructive purposes—or as cloaks behind which their activities might be carried on.

**1007-3**

The Cain and Abel story and the question it raises, "Am I my brother's

---

[8]The "things" referred to in the above were also described as "automatons" in other readings. These were creatures which were the result of the mating of the Sons of God with the Daughters of Men. (Genesis 6:2; reading 281-24)

keeper?" may be drawn, in part, from the conflicts of this period. The patriarchs of the Bible drew upon the same source to face similar problems as the children of the Law of One thousands of years earlier. The above reading continues:

Thus those disintegrations were brought about that were so well given in the injunctions later written in the admonitions to Abraham, to Jacob, to Moses, to Elijah, to Joshua, to all the children of promise–of which we have records.

**And if the entity will interpret the admonitions of Moses, much of that which is the inner basic principle of the entity may be found.**

**1007-3**

## The Descendants of Cain

Two of Cain's ancestors appear in the Life readings.

In a reading given for a seven–year–old girl, a very interesting reference is made to Tubal–Cain (Genesis 4:22) as "the first son to become perfect to become an associate with those of other activities." Could this mean that the children of Cain had adapted themselves to the world yet still held a sufficient measure of the Light which enabled them to associate with the mixture races whereas the Adamic race was supposed to keep itself separate from the world?

The daughters of Eve are mentioned as well:

**Before that we find the entity lived in that period when there were those in the land of the inter-between, or that between the lands then of Eden—that was between the Euphrates, or where the Red Sea, the Dead Sea now occupy—was the entity's dwelling land.**

**There we find the entity was an associate and a companion of one Tubal-Cain, the first of the sons that had been made perfect to become an associate with those of other activities in the earth.**

**The entity withdrew, and made for those activities that brought about that which is the cry of those that are wounded in body, wounded in spirit, wounded in soul.**

**Then in the name (as would be called) Su-Su-Lu, though it was a trying and a testing experience, the entity gained. For the entity made overtures to those of the daughters of Eve (in person—that Eve of the garden, that Eve who made for the activities). Though the entity then**

was the seventh, tenth generations, it made overtures in person—in the age at those periods.

In the present experience we will find the entity seeking the association, desiring the association of those much its elder. Not that the periods of its own childhood, not that the periods of the recreation and all developments are not a portion of it, but periods when the tales, the counsels, the imaginations of those of elderly years are sought by the entity.

Do not forbid, but do direct. 1179-2

Cain's progeny also appear in a reading for a young boy, thirteen years old, an invalid since birth. He was told his condition was karmic and originated during the time of Lamech (Genesis 4:19–24) The reading closes with an indication of the harmful effects the descendants of Cain had upon this entity. Truly was this the line that caused God "to repent that man was made." (Genesis 6:6)

. . . we find the entity was in the period when there were those changes in the sons of Tubal-Cain, when Lamech made for those choices of the first beginnings of when man as man partook of those things that made for the multiplicity, or when polygamy began among those peoples. [Genesis 4:19] This brought to the entity during the experience that of disorder, disturbance, the unfavorable expressions of many about the entity; and bringing those experiences that have builded for disorders in the experience. 693-3

Lamech's actions can be viewed as a continuation of the effects from the negative spirit manifested in Cain.

## Adam Reincarnated: Enoch

And Enoch walked with God, and he was not for God took him. As [were] many of those in those first years, in this land, this experience.
364-10

Enoch is also one of the incarnations Cayce attributed to Jesus in his development as The Christ. The readings also suggest, as in the above, Enoch is representational of many in the earth at that time who had retained their spiritual and mental attunement and were not fully enmeshed in matter.

Man in his natural state, the readings have said, is soul, or spirit. Although not much is stated about Enoch in the Bible, the readings do give a few illuminating references. Enoch acted as a prophet who sought to give warnings about the impending Deluge.

**Read the Scripture pertaining to the days of Noah, the law proclaimed by Enoch (found mostly in Jude and in the early chapters of Genesis).**
**3653-1**

**. . . Enoch as he warned the people.** **3054-4**

He bestowed blessings and recommendations as well as warnings.

**Again it was manifested in Enoch, who oft sought to walk and talk with that divine influence; with the abilities . . . to find self in the varied realms of awareness, yet using the office of relationships as a channel through which blessings might come, as well as [through which] recommendations and warnings might be indicated to others.** **2072-4**

The possible extent of Enoch's activities is suggested through a tradition that links his name with Hermes. Hermes, for long ages, has been considered the architect of the Great Pyramid of Cheops. Manly Hall, in his Encyclopedia of Mosaic Heremetics, Rosicrucian Symbolic Philosophy, in his commentary of Hermes states that many investigators believe Hermes is the same entity whom the Jews refer to as Enoch.

Enoch, in reading 5749-14, is included as one of the major incarnations in the development of the soul who became the man Jesus. Occasional references in other readings indicate Jesus had an incarnation in Egypt under the name Hermes. Further information in the readings, parallel with traditions maintained by the Jews, will strengthen the view that these, Enoch and Hermes, are one and the same.

## *Pyramid Builders*

According to the Edgar Cayce readings on the prehistorical period of ancient Egypt, the high priest, Ra–Ta, and Hermes directed the construction of the Great Pyramid at Gizeh.

**Then with Hermes and Ra . . . there began the building of that now**

**called Gizeh . . . that was to be the Hall of the Initiates of that some-
times referred to as the White Brotherhood.          5748-5**

**(Q) What was the date of the actual beginning and ending of the
construction of the Great Pyramid?
(A) Was one hundred years in construction. Begun and completed in the
period of Araaraatt's time, with Hermes and Ra.
(Q) What was the date B.C. of that period?
(A) 10,490 to 10,390 before the Prince [of Peace] entered into Egypt.
                                                            5748-6**

The meaning of the word *Enoch* is initiator. The Edgar Cayce information on the Great Pyramid definitely states its purpose was to serve as a
hall of initiation.

Another tradition which would link Hermes and Enoch is found in
the Kaballah.

Josephus in his Antiquities of the Jews (quoted in the Kaballah) states
there is a legend that Adam was forewarned of the Flood. Seth, Adam's
surviving son, erected two pillars on which he inscribed the keys to the
science and philosophy taught by Adam. Enoch, who also knew of the
impending Deluge, became concerned that the knowledge would be
lost through this calamity. Therefore he constructed an underground
temple with nine vaults. In the final vault were the two pillars upon
which, in allegorical symbols, the secret teachings were preserved.

A similar activity is ascribed to Hermes by Edgar Cayce.

The readings show the constructor of the Great Pyramid, Hermes,
designed a secret room known as The Hall of Records, which is as yet
undiscovered. In this, according to Edgar Cayce, are placed the ancient
teachings of the Law of One as well as a history of Atlantis. Thus we
have "a parallel between this activity of Hermes and the vaults dug by
Enoch.

This question relates to the Hall of Records:

**(Q) Give in detail what the sealed room contains.
(A) A record of Atlantis from the beginnings of those periods when the
Spirit took form or began the encasements in that land, and the
developments of the peoples throughout their sojourn, [together] with
the record of the first destruction, and the changes that took place in the
land; with the record of the sojournings of the peoples to the varied**

activities in other lands; and a record of the meetings of all the nations or lands for the activities in the destructions that became necessary with the final destruction of Atlantis; and the buildings of the Pyramid of Initiation; [together] with who, what, where would come the opening of the records that are as copies from the sunken Atlantis . . . 378-16

# 5

## The Deluge: Division and Dissent

*The* division and conflict between those Cayce called "Sons of the Law of One" and the "Children of Belial" intensified as it progressed. It began thousands of years before Adam, and has continued into the present.

When the serpent was cursed in Genesis 3:15, he was told that his posterity and that of Eve's would always be at war with each other, and that hers would ultimately triumph. This is a spiritual law, Cayce states. Those who do good and have the ideal of brotherly love and service to God will always be opposed by and in conflict with those who are motivated only by selfish ends, material gain, and sensuous gratification.

In the days of Noah, this conflict brought world-wide destruction:

> . . . we find these as the Sons of the Creative Force as manifest in their experience looking upon those changed forms, or the daughters of men, and there crept in those pollutions, of polluting themselves with those mixtures that brought contempt, hatred, blood-shed, and those that build for desires of self without respects of others' freedom, others' wishes—and there began, then, in the latter portion of this period of development, that [which] brought about . . . dissenting and divisions among the peoples in the lands.                          364-4

One of the issues which divided the Sons of God (or Adam) and the Sons of Belial (or Cain) was their relationship to the suborder of "things" or automatons—creatures which were a result of the mixture of the Sons of God with the Daughters of Men. The "things" were Sons of God who were cut off from the spiritual consciousness, and trapped in imperfect and incomplete forms. The Sons of Belial cultivated them, and used them for the rendering of certain tasks—slaves of the powerful.

**(Q) What is meant by automatons who labored in that experience?**
**(A) They were the offspring of the Sons of God with the Daughters of Men, or vice versa.**                                                    **281-44**

The Bible describes much of the spiritual awareness of that period.

*And God saw that the wickedness of man was great in the earth, and that every imagination of the thoughts of his heart was only evil continually.*
*And it repented the Lord that he had made man on the earth, and it grieved him at his heart.* (Genesis 6:5-6)

The following interpretations help clarify its meaning.

**The heart, of course, here referred to, is not the physical organ, but the purpose, the desire that is to be attained.**                    **2283-1**

**. . . for, as has been said, "repent that man was ever made." Why? "For the purpose and intent of Man is to satisfy earthly desires of the flesh rather than that of the manifesting of My Spirit in [the] earth's plane."**
**139-9**

More detail is supplied in the following:

**With the continued disregard of those that were keeping the pure race and the pure peoples, of those that were to bring all these laws as applicable to the Sons of God, man brought in the destructive forces as used for the peoples that were to be the role, that combined with those natural resources of the gases, of the electrical forces, made in nature and natural form the first of the eruptions that awoke from the depth of the slow cooling earth, and that portion now near what would be termed the Sargasso Sea first went into the depths. With this there again came that egress of peoples that aided, or attempted to assume control, yet carrying with them all those forms of Amilius, that he gained through**

**that as for signs, for seasons, for days, for years. Hence we find in those various portions of the world even in the present day, some form of that as was presented by those peoples in that great development in this, the Eden of the world.**                                    **364-4**

Cayce indicates that the Flood as we know it through the Old Testament was in actuality the second of three great catastrophies which destroyed Atlantis—or Poseida:[9]

**. . . before this we find when the ruling force of Poseida was before the gates of the mighty waters that in ages back submerged this plain.**
**4228-1**

The negative activity of this period, and the destruction which followed, established a symbol, or pattern, which has forever held true in man's experiences.

**For as has been given from the beginning, the deluge was not a myth (as many would have you believe) but a period when man had so belittled himself with the cares of the world, with the deceitfulness of his own knowledge and power, as to require that there be a return to his dependence wholly—physically and mentally—upon Creative Forces.**
**3653-1**

Atlantis was convulsed by three separate destructions which occurred over a long period of time—thousands of years! The second destruction is the one we know as the Deluge.

Symbolically, Noah represents the activity of all the Sons of Light who, through their attunement with Creative Force, or God, took warning of the impending disaster, made adequate preparation, and escaped, settling in all parts of the world.

**In the latter portion of same, we find as cities were builded, more and more rare became those abilities to call upon rather the forces in nature to supply the needs for those of bodily adornment, or those of the needs to supply the replenishing of the wasting away of the physical being; or**

---

[9]See Edgar Evans Cayce, *Edgar Cayce on Atlantis.*

hunger arose, and with the determinations to set again in motion, we find there—then Ani,[10] in those latter periods, ten thousand seven hundred (10,700) years before the Prince of Peace came—again was the bringing into force that to tempt, as it were, nature-in its storehouse-of replenishing the things—that of the wasting away in the mountains, then into the valleys, then into the sea itself, and the fast disintegration of the lands, as well as of the peoples—save those that had escaped into those distant lands. 364-4

## Methuselah

If the geneology in Genesis 5 is literal then Methuselah was alive at the time of the Deluge. The readings show the lifespan in those days was indeed incredible.

The days upon the earth then were counted in the tens, the fifties, and the hundreds, besides the days or weeks or years in the present. Or, the *life* existence of the entity, as compared to the present, would be years instead of weeks; or, in that experience to live five to six to seven hundred years was no more than to live to the age of fifty, sixty, or seventy years in the present. 1968-2

Cayce described in a Life reading for a prominent brain surgeon and metaphysician an experience as "the eighth from Adam." This could mean that the surgeon (1851) had been Methuselah. As a descendant of Adam, he, too, was concerned with the study, interpretation, and preservation of the records made by the children of the Law of One in Atlantis and preserved by Enoch.

Again we find the entity, before that, was in the Egyptian land during the very early periods.
For the entity was the eighth from Adam, and in the days of the exodus and the periods of understanding through those activities; journeying more from what is now the Chaldean than the Egyptian land, though spending many of the periods in the activities through which the records were set as for things that were, that were to be—these become

---

[10]Ani is mentioned several times in *Myths and Legends of Ancient Egypt* by Lewis Spence.

a part of the study of the entity throughout those periods.

Hence oft the entity may lose self in those things that are found there. For, as that was the interpreting of the earth as it was, as it is, as it is to be, so came those activities to preserve same for the seeker to know his relationships to the past, the present, and the future, when counted from the material standpoint.

And as the entity sought in those experiences to make time and space, as well as patience, the realms that express the universality of the Force called God, so may *this* become in the present experience that in which the entity may excel—in giving assurance to those who seek their closer understandlng of the relationships one to another.        1851-1

The Bible says God repented he made man. (Genesis 6:6) Edgar Cayce interpreted this to mean a change in heart and a new plan for man's salvation. The following comments are taken from the Bible class record:

"To repent means to change the mind because of regret or dissatisfaction. God decided to give man a new opportunity, or a new method, for saving himself. Because man was so wicked, God cut his life span to 120 years. The only hope for man to extricate himself from the flesh was to die at a younger age, and get a new start by being reborn. This was God's way of making man aware of a new opportunity. How terrible it would be today if we kept living for thousands of years!"

This reading compares man's lifespan then and now:

What was the length of life then? Nearly a thousand years. What is your life today? May it not be just as He had given, just as He had indicated to those peoples, just as He did to the lawgiver, just as He did to David— first from a thousand years to a hundred and twenty, then to eighty? Why? Why? The sin of man is his desire for self-gratification.

What nations of the earth today vibrate to those things that they have and are creating in their own land their own environment? Look to the nations where the span of life has been extended from sixty to eighty-four years. You will judge who is serving God. These are judgments. These are the signs to those who seek to know, who will study the heavens, who will analyze the elements, who will know the heart of man, they that seek to know the will of the Father for themselves answer, "Lord, here am I, use me, send me where I am needed."

3976-29

## *Noah*

The Deluge is both symbolic and literal. Noah was also an actual entity.

In a noteworthy Life reading, a four year old child was told he had been Thomas Cambell, founder of the Cambellite movement, Elisha the prophet, and the ancient patriarch of the Deluge:

> For, before *that* the entity was that one to whom was entrusted man's advent into the world—Noah!
>
> For this we find those weaknesses. Then, not as one refraining from those, but beware ever of any strong drink or fruit of the vine passing the lips of *this* entity—through these early periods, especially.      2547-1

Although Noah was found naked and drunk in his tent after the Deluge, before the Flood it is written he and his family were "perfect in their generations." (Genesis 6:9) Noah and his family still adhered to the tenets of the Law of One. They had not yet "broken the faith"—as this one had:

> Before that we find the entity was in the Atlantean land during those periods when there were the separations of the peoples from the high and the low estates of the varied developments that were in that period of man's experience in the earth, when there were the Sons of the High; or as given in Holy Writ, "The Sons of God looked upon the Daughters of Men."
>
> The *entity* was among the Sons of God, yet looking upon the Daughters of Men and making of self in those associations those periods when faith was broken with others, and when there was the belittling of the tenets and the truths in the *powers* that had been given among those peoples for the manifesting of that which would cleanse their souls that they might be one with the Creative Forces in this *material* world and in the spiritual forces also.                                    518-1

Noah and his group, no doubt, refrained from mixing with the creatures who were combinations of the thought–forms projected by the

SONS of Belial and the descendents of Cain.

> They were perfect in their day and generation. As individual entities they had chosen virtue in every form in relationship to things, conditions, and personalities in the earth. 3653-1

> The eight souls were saved for a definite purpose—to preserve the consciousness that had been brought into the earth through Adam and the followers of the Law of One, and to continue the spiritual and mental evolution of mankind.
> For the entity was among those eight souls saved for a definite purpose, and brought that influence in the earth that is today that source from which spiritual and mental advance has been kept toward that more commonly termed the more civilized groups or individuals. 2627-1

Cayce's commentary to the Bible class follows:

> "Noah is the next man after Enoch who walked with God. So God chose him as the channel through which His new method would be used. It is indicated that at the time of the Flood, Noah was the only man living who had come down in a direct line from Seth without contamination through intermarriage with the thought-form projections. All flesh was polluted. Only Noah and his family were allowed to have a part in the New Dispensation."

Although it is written Noah was perfect in his generations, we have evidence later (Genesis 9:21-25) he was not perfect, mentally or spiritually. Even though he had come down in a perfect line, his anger and resentment at Ham show he was not free from sin. This also shows how powerful our own anger can be in its effect upon others. Noah's anger produced a curse on all Ham's descendants. Our own words and actions create similar conditions. They bring fruits after their own kind.

Cayce continues:

> "The Bible says, 'There were giants in those days.'
> "Many of the myths which have been handed down to us are based on truth from the beginning. With the intermarriage among the various projections of the physically strong, no wonder there were giants. They

had superhuman ability, but lacked spiritual awareness. They were intent upon increasing their physical strength without taking thought to its
spiritual source.

"Noah's sons must have married their own close relations. All others
were contaminated—or mixtures."

A literal reading of the Bible indicates the Flood covered the southern portion of Europe, western Asia, and northern Africa. Yet in the
eastern portion of Asia, in South America, Egypt, and Yucatan, myths
have been preserved about a great flood and the salvation of one family.

Did the Flood really cover the whole face of the earth, as stated in
Scripture? Or did similar experiences occur within all the five races at
different periods?

The readings predict the discovery of ancient Atlantean records in
Egypt and Yucatan which will reveal the answers to these questions.

How did Noah gather all the animals? The Bible class records show
an interesting comment made by Cayce: "Animals are much closer to
God in spirit than we are. They sense any great change that is imminent. Perhaps they came to him."

## In the Ark

An interesting group of readings follow involving entities who were
with Noah on the ark. Cayce began this reading for a young Kentucky
housewife by commenting:

**What an unusual record—and one of those who might be termed as
physically the mothers of the world! For the entity was one of those in
the ark.**

**In giving the interpretations of the records here, we find that there
is much from which to choose. But these we choose with the desire and
purpose to be the means of help to the entity in better fulfilling those
purposes for which it has entered the earth's plane in varied periods of
its experience.**

**For the entity has appeared when there were new revelations to be
given. And again it appears when there are new revelations to be made.**

**May the entity so conduct its mind, its body, and its purposes, then,
as to be a channel through which such messages may come that are
needed for the awakenings in the minds of men as to the necessity for**

returning to the search for their relationship with the Creative Forces or God.

Will this entity see such again occur in the earth? Will it be among those who may be given those directions as to how, where, the elect may be preserved for the replenishing again of the earth?

Remember, not by water—for it is the mother of life in the earth—but rather by the element fire.

As to whether or not the entity will be among those in the earth when the changes again come, will depend upon the entity's preparation of self.                                                                                3653-1

Cayce described for her experiences in Lemuria, the period of the Judges in Israel; in the Holy Land during the time of Muhammad; and in the South during the War Between the States, as well in the era of the Flood.

He told her she had always been in the earth during times of great change and when new revelations were being made. Edgar Cayce described her experience during the Deluge thus:

Next we find that the entity entered in those periods when the littleness of man had come up as a stench before the throne of mercy and grace, or the Creative Forces.

The entity was among the peoples not of the lineage of Noah, but of those later known as the Hittites. Then the entity gave expressions to that same experience that was materially manifested in Mu, and the entity—as the wife of a son of Noah—became among the eight souls in the ark, in the preparation and in the endurance thereof, and in those experiences gained in the activities through the earth's influence.

The name then was Maran. From that sojourn there is much experienced in the present in the entity's liking of the history of the early ages of man, of those experiences that are the promptings for the souls and minds of individuals, rather than the material things.

At times the entity is berated by others for being rather in that mind of "Don't care" than in that of a practical, everyday life.

Hence the entity is a "sensitive." Read the Scripture pertaining to the days of Noah, the law proclaimed by Enoch (found mostly in Jude and in the early chapters of Genesis). Here is one entity who may write, not automatic but rather inspirational writing, shutting itself away and attuning itself by very distant music, and especially bells. For, under such

an inspiration—not as a means of doing other than attuning the inner
self—the entity may write inspirationally of things pertaining to mental
and spiritual aspects of individuals grasping for attunement to the
divine.                                                                  3653-1

## The Family of Japeth

Through a series of readings members of a New Hampshire family
discovered they had all known each other in the ark. The New Hampshire man (2726), a dairy farmer, was told he had been Japeth and that
his present wife (2425) had been his wife.

Japeth's wife, Rezepatha, was pregnant when she entered the ark and
gave birth during the deluge. The child which was born to them was
also reincarnated in the present, but not a part of their family and,
indeed, unknown to the farmer or his wife.

A nurse which the family had hired to watch over their children was
told in her reading she had been her mistress' mother during this early
period of history.

This interesting story begins with the father—Japeth:

**Before that we find there was the experience of the greater period of
development for the entity in the material world.**

**For we find the entity, as the son of Noah, chose the better way for
transmitting in fact, in activity, to his peoples after the sojourn in the ark,
not only the needs for the establishing of homes but of home altars, and
the uniting of those home altars in a group, a nation, a national activity.**

**The name then was Japeth. In the experience the beauty of the
companionship, of the entity's activities, not only before but after the
period of preparation and throughout the sojourn, found its expression
and activity in that channel through which the hope of the world did and
has Come again.**

**Thus in the present may the entity, with those associations, those
companionships, bring—has brought—an activity which may add to that
harmony in the material world, that will again *sing*—as the entity did
through that period of activity—the realm of the infinite made manifest
in man's heart, man's purpose, man's joy.**

**Leave aside, then, those things that would easily beset, knowing thy
purpose and thy ideal, thy *ideal*—physically, mentally, spiritually. Know
that all that takes place or that takes form in the mind is prompted either**

by the spirit of truth or the spirit of rebellion. Which *will ye* choose?

Know the ideal, then, must be as was manifest in Him, who gave, "If ye love me, ye will keep my commandments—and I will come and abide with thee." That promise is in spirit, is in truth.

Hence those as this entity may bring, with its companionship—as did bring, as did keep the home fire bright to the altar of the Lord—may bring again to man, in those activities in the earth, that of a joy. Not easy from the material angle, unless that ideal is held aloft in spirit, in mind, in material things.                                                    2627-1

His present wife was then his companion in the ark:

Q. What have been my associations in the past with, first, my wife, [2425]?

A. The greater experience, the greater advancement is in that innate or soul urge from that period in the ark.                           2627-1

His wife's life was described as follows:

Before that the entity was in that activity when there were those preparations for changes being wrought in the relationships of Creative Forces with the sons of men.

The entity was among those, or that one chosen by Japeth as the companion in the ark.

With [the] relationships to that activity, the entity finds within self the visions of changes, in the relationships that are again soon to be established by and through the elements themselves in their dealing with men and Creative Forces or God's Laws.

The name then was Rezepatha.                                2425-1

An English nurse, who had been employed to watch over the couple's young children, was told in her reading that she had been Japeth's mother-in-law—and had helped prepare her daughter Rezepatha for the responsibility she was to bear.

Before that, during the early activities when there were those preparations for the preserving of man's activity in the earth—the entity was the mother of that entity who was the companion of Japeth, when there were the preparations of the ark.

The entity was that one who contributed to those abilities for that
daughter who in her associations brought to the earth the line of
activity, the purposes to hold to love as well as purpose.

The name then was Lapeth.                                    2625-1

The nurse then asked about past life connections, first with the wife:

(Q) What has been my former connection with the following and how
may I best help them in the present? First, [2425]?
(A) Oft there have been the associations. The greater was in the
experiences when the entity was the mother of that entity now known
as [2425], during those periods just before what is called the Flood . . . In
the present, as has been and may be gathered from paralleling the lives,
not only of the offspring in the present—there may be brought that
consistency of purpose, that beauty of living for a purpose.
(Q) Mr. [2627]?
(A) In the experience that has been indicated—the period of the
Flood...
(Q) Should I continue making my home with [2425]?
(A) By all means!                                            2625-1

Three years after this series of readings, a middle–aged Pennsylvania
stenographer was told in a previous life she had been the child of Japeth
and Rezepatha.

Before that we find the entity was in the land when there were those
preparations that man would not be wholly destroyed but how that the
Father-God warned Noah to build the ark and to gather his sons and
their families. The entity was one born in the ark during those periods,
for the wife of Japeth, the son of Noah, was heavy with child, and it was
born during those periods in the ark.

The entity knows, then, the escape, knows the way innately, and that
it is only through the hands, the arms of God. Keep that eternal. Do give
that to thy fellowman.                                       5367-1

The youngest child of the New Hampshire couple was told he was
among the first–born after the Deluge:

Before that the entity was in the earth in the early periods of man's activity, when there were children born to the sons of Noah.

The entity was among the first of the groups born in the earth after the deluge or Flood and the resettling in the lands of that period.

Then in the name Pelus, the entity was among those who made rules, laws, and regulations for activities under which there was agreement by the various groups of its own peoples, in their separations, as to the records of how there were to be the settlings and where and what would be the privileges of individuals.

Thus we find those activities leading to the needs for the entity being first mindful of the health, then the opportunity in the training for law and public service.                                          5008-1

## Japeth's Prayer

Following his descent from the ark, Noah made an altar and sacrificed. He must have been moved to do something in order to show appreciation for being saved. After the sacrifice, and the promise given to him through the rainbow, Noah began to till the fields. (Genesis 9:20) Included in this answer is an insight into some of the problems and conditions which faced Japeth and Noah as they left the ark. The young farmer asked:

(Q) In farming, what should my emphasis be on?
(A) Each product is to supply certain elements to the body of man; not by man's changing same, but that purpose the Creator gave it as food, as a supply to man's physical need *in* even a changing world. Thus the stress should be upon each product being given *its* opportunity for fulfilling its mission in relationship to man; or the study of the soil as to how *better* to produce grasses, vegetables, fruits, berries, or the like; or to supply the elements in the animal kingdom—as of the pig or the *cow*; that its flesh, its milk, may have those elements *necessary* for supplying to men that which has its spiritual value and not in a cantankerous or a diffusing manner. For, as man assimilates in the mind, so it assimilates in the spirit. That is why the entity in its experience with its associates when leaving the ark, found it necessary for taking these things into consideration—as to those very necessary elements.                      2627-1

In closing his reading, Cayce recalled a prayer for 2627 which indicates Japeth's realization of his relationship with God:

Let thy meditation oft be that even as ye did upon the hills in Ararat:
"Lord, Thou art Maker of heaven and earth. Thou hast preserved Thy
servant for a purpose in the earth. Thou hast given me, today, opportunities. Help me, O God, to choose the right way; that I may ever be a
channel of blessings to others, pointing the way ever to Thee."
We are through for the present                                    2627-1

## The Beginning of the Rainbow and End of the Thought-Forms

The following is an interpretation of the meaning of the rainbow in
Genesis 9:12–17. It signifies a state of consciousness arising from a period of trial and testing which has been successfully met.

. . . the promises of the Divine that were and are written in the rainbow
of the sky, when the cloud has passed, are the same as written in the lives
of individuals that they, too, who are in the closer walk with the
Creative Forces, may see their sign, their colors, and *know* whereunto
they have attained in *their* relationship with Creative Energies or God.
                                                                  1436-2

No matter what man may bring upon himself in a material sense, he
can rely on God's laws and promises to remain the same.

The Flood resulted in the cleansing of the earth. The negative, spiritually polluted thought–forms which had been created by the Sons of
God were destroyed in the Deluge. The cataclysm marked the end of an
era. Abraham starts the new.

Thence we find the entity passing through those experiences becoming
rather aware, with the sons of those activities in the experiences when
all thought–forms in matter were put away—through the experience of
Noah.                                                             257-201

Apparently the Deluge marked the end of the centaurs, satyrs, cy-
clops, harpies, and mermaids, and the other creatures who are now
preserved in the mythology of the world.

Some brought about monstrosities, as those if its (that entity's) association by its projection with its association with beasts of various characters. Hence those of the Styx, satyr, and the like; those of the sea, or

**mermaid; those of the unicorn, and those of the various forms—these projections of what? The abilities in the psychic forces (psychic meaning, then of the mental and the soul . . .)**                    **364-10**

Not all the thought-forms partook of the animal. Cayce described many as entangled in the plant and mineral kingdoms as well. These too were destroyed.

**. . . those who were physically entangled in the animal kingdom with appendages, with cloven hooves, with four legs, with portions of trees, with tails, with scales, with those various things that thought-forms or evil had so indulged in as to separate the purpose of God's creation of man, as man—not as animal . . .**                    **2072-8**

The Egyptian sphinx is a monument to these pre–Deluge creations:

**These may be seen in a different manner presented in many of the various sphinxes, as called, in other portions of the land—as the lion with the man, the various forms of wing, or characterizations in their various developments. These were as [the] presentations of those projections that had been handed down in the various developments of that which becomes man—as in the present.**                    **5748-6**

Many souls, like Noah, were manifesting the higher awareness. They heeded the warnings, made adequate preparations, and escaped the destruction.

## The Foundation of a New Age

The exodus from Atlantis carried souls both East and West—into Egypt and Yucatan, and other parts of the world.

The Sons of God, who had entered with Adam, projecting into five parts of the earth at once, established great civilizations. The activities in the Egyptian civilization are most vividly described in the readings. Both Sons of God—the descendants of Adam—and the surviving thought-form races migrated to these centers.

The work of the Sons of the Law of One—or descendants of Adam—was concerned with maintaining and developing a record of the God-consciousness in the earth. They were also concerned with getting the earth–bound entities to relate to mental, spiritual, and physical patterns that would re-establish their relationship with spiritual forces.

> Before that the entity was in the Egyptian land when there were those preparations for purifying the body and those activities that enabled men to put away [the] appendages, that man in the experience inherited through the pushing of spirit into matter to become materially expressive—and thus [had] brought the necessity of man being materialized in the earth as the perfect body in Adam [in the beginning].
>
> 3333-1

Following are a few brief descriptions of the work that was being done in Egypt.

> . . . there arose the needs for the Temple of Sacrifice, where entities, individuals, might offer themselves for the purification of their bodies, that they first might be channels through which there might come entities, souls, manifesting in the earth with the entire activity of body, mind, soul . . . And with these expressions there were those who chose the activities that were set in motion for the purifying of their bodies, that there might be the purifying of physical conditions which had been and were being affected by the emotional forces, or the carnal influences about them in the experience.     281-43

Cayce described the Temple of Sacrifice as the equivalent of a modern day hospital, where surgery was performed to remove the appendages— such as scales, hooves, claws, and horns—from the thought–form bodies.

> The passage of individuals . . . through the experiences in the Temple of Sacrifice was much as would be in the hospitalization, or a hospital of the present day, when there have become antagonistic conditions within the physical body, such as to produce tumors, wens, warts, or such.
>
> Magnify this into the disturbances which were indicated or illustrated in conditions where there was the body or figure of the horse, or the head of the horse with the body of man; or where there were the various conditions indicated in the expressions by the pushing of spirit into physical matter until it became influenced by or subject to same. Such influences we see in the present manifested as habits, or the habit forming conditions.

> Then there are, or were the needs for the attempts to operate, as well as to adhere to diets and activities to change the natures of the individuals, that their offspring, as well as themselves, might bring forth that which was in keeping with—or a pattern of—those influences in which there were *souls* or spirits with the idea, or ideal, of seeking light.
>
> For, how is it termed in the record? That the heart and purpose of man is to do evil! 281-44

A highly developed form of spiritual, and psychological counseling was done in the Temple Beautiful, also in Egypt.

The Temple of Sacrifice was a physical experience, while the Temple Beautiful was rather of the mental, in which there was the spiritualization—not idolizing, but crystallizing of activities or services to a special purpose—or specializing in preparation for given offices of activity.

> Hence from same has arisen a great many of the signs, the symbols, the various influences that have had and may have a part in influencing peoples and individuals . . . toward activities for greater expansions, greater developments. 281-43

> In the present when evil has taken hold, it forms itself into those influences that are called habits, or inclinations, or intents; and it is necessary to eliminate these from the purposes and aims and desires of individuals.
>
> So were the experiences through those activities in the Temple of Service of what is known as the Temple of Sacrifice; sacrificing self that the spirit, the purpose, the love of God might be made manifest through the individual. 281-44

When the holocaust was over, a new era in the evolution of man began. Temple services such as in Egypt laid the foundation. The physical pattern brought with the Adamic line was now firmly established. No longer would great monstrosities or unusual mixtures be created. The era of occult projections (via mind and spirit force) was over. All souls who desired to enter the earth's plane had to manifest through the natural channels provided through the sexual union of man and woman.

The sex-force, which had tempted man and led to his entanglement in matter, would have to be purified and creative in order to lift him out.

A new phase of development follows the Deluge. If the pre–Deluge era relates to the period of establishing physical evolutionary patterns for man, the ensuing period relates to the building of Mind, or mental awareness. Only through a purified Life-force enlivening the mind of man and his senses could a higher awareness be developed—as the recipient of this reading was counseled:

> **Think no evil, speak no evil, hear no evil, and as the Truth flows as a stream of life through the mind in all its phases or aspects of same, so will it purify and revivify and rejuvenate the body.**          **294-183**

Just as the ideal pattern for the physical body was established, or evolved in the phase preceding the Deluge, the following cycle relates to the development of the perfect Mind.

> **For, that which leads to the Christ is the Mind. And the mind's unfoldment may be that indicated from Abraham to the Christ.**
> **281-63**

But before Abraham, there is Babel.

# 6
## (Genesis 11)

## The Tower of Babel

As the Sons of God multiplied in the earth, the size of their groups increased, and they eventually became nations.

> Thus when man began to defy God in the earth and the confusion arose which is represented in the Tower of Babel—these are [the] representation of what was then the basis, the beginnings of nations. Nations were set up then in various portions of the land, and each group, one stronger than another, set about to seek their gratifications.
>
> **3976-29**

The developments represented in Genesis 11 occurred over many thousands, if not millions of years, and originated in pre–Adamic civilizations. Moses, in order to present an easily grasped and comprehensible picture, told his history as a continuous, chronological sequence. Actually the events symbolized in Cain and Abel, the Flood, and the Tower were occurring simultaneously and were overlapping events. These stories depict the same phenomena, told from different points of view—the loss of the spiritual consciousness and its effect upon the Sons of God.

> . . . commenting upon the subject *Destiny of the Soul:* As man finds himself in the consciousness of a material world, materiality has often,

in the material-minded, blotted out the consciousness of a soul.

**262-89**

Before Babel, the whole world "spoke one language with few words." (Genesis 11:1)

**The disruption of communications of all natures between men is what? Remember the story, the allegory if ye choose to call it such, of the Tower of Babel.**                                   **5757-1**

Edgar Cayce's Bible class lessons contain several thoughtful conceptions. The following is a composite of the presentation:

"Were the people conscious of evil while building the Tower? They must have been aware of doing something that deep within themselves they knew was not necessary to do. They felt they had to rely upon their own physical abilities to build material defenses against another disaster. They were acting in direct opposition to the promise that there would no longer be any wholesale destruction by Flood.

"They were afraid of being scattered, and the very thing they hoped would prevent it actually caused it to happen.

"Because they were of one mind, to build in the material, God saw the power of their united imaginations could and would—build such a barrier that they would never find Heaven.

"As they built, they became aware of God. The Spirit entered into their consciousness and changed their attitude toward the work. No wonder they became confused.

"God's laws are such that their own material building began to confuse them. It is the same today. We can go so far in the material and no further. We defeat our own selves.

"Their concept of Heaven was a place high up. They were looking outside of themselves for it. They were about to start the whole process of thought-form creation all over again. They had to realize, through long ages of suffering and learning obedience (just as we must) that the real building of the Tower is within the individual, not outside. The preparation must be within."

The time arrived, even in the Adamic line, when the people no longer wholly believed in spiritual truths or universal law. They began to worship their own physical abilities, their own individual prowess and powers, and began to act independently of the Spirit. Once this pattern was established, trouble and tribulation resulted.

Yet man in his greed, in his own selfishness, has set himself so oft at naught by the very foolishness of his own wisdom.

> For the soul had understanding before he partook of the flesh in which the choice was to be made. The choice, or the road, or the path, once taken, then the end thereof was (and is) tribulation, toil, misunderstanding. And this expression came into such measures that there arose the periods when man came as one and said, "We will build, we will go to now and make those conditions that will prevent any such confusion again among men."
>
> And then came the diversity of tongues and confusion arose. For the very selfishness of man had brought [about] this confusion, this defiance to a God of love, of mercy, of patience, in such a measure that He gave that expression, "There is nothing beyond the scope of man's ability unless he misinterpret his brother's words."                    262-96

In a subsequent reading, a clarification was asked:

> (Q) Please explain . . . what is meant by "any such confusions" referred to when it was said, "We will build, we will go to now and make those conditions that will prevent any such confusions again among men." Why did they think a Tower would help?
> (A) The Tower was after the flood. This is very simple—to reach above. Why do you build houses? Why do you build boats, those things that become "above the flood"? It was just the same! Same concept—that it might reach even to that which would not be destroyed by flood again.
>                    262-99

If Cayce is correct, this entity was an ancestor of those who erected the Tower:

> Before that the entity lived in the earth during those periods when the peoples were separated that prepared for the preserving of the activities in the earth.
>
> The entity was the son of Ham (Canaan) that laughed at the weakness of the grandfather [Genesis 9]. Thus the entity was one of

those who occupied the ark, or was in the ark during that period.

After the journeys in the ark, the entity set out activities in definite conditions for the establishing of groups in various portions of the land.

Thus things that have to do with mechanical things are innately of interest. And the entity gathers those peculiar things or oddities about itself in one respect or another.

As to the abilities of the entity in the present . . . the application of self should be in writing of the peculiarities, the oddities of various groups and in their manner of worship in various portions of the earth.

3345-1

In this Life reading we have a record of activities around the Tower of Babel. It indicates the pattern is still the same today:

. . . the entity was active when there were those first separations of the sons of those who were saved at the periods when the ark settled upon Ararat, and when the divisions arose just before the activities in the Tower of Babel.

We find that the entity attempted to create the better relationships with the various groups of individuals, and those who sought to make for disturbances that brought dissensions among the sons of Noah.

For the entity attempted to carry on those tenets and conditions which had been presented by his grandfather Noah in that period. Yet the entity was overridden by those of power, might, and position. Hence latently, though he may find expression in overactivity, we find the entity feel himself a little bit beneath that he attempts to gain.

The name then was Jeurepth.                          2460-1

# 7

# Abraham, Isaac, and Jacob

*According* to the Cayce readings, Melchizedek (Genesis 14) is the next appearance of the soul who had been Adam and Enoch—the soul who had chosen as his path of destiny to be the leader and savior of mankind, and later fulfilled it as Jesus, when he became the Christ.

In John 8:56–58, when the Jews were questioning Jesus, he responded, "Your father Abraham rejoiced to see my day; and he saw it and was glad." Jesus also told them, "Truly, truly, I say to you, Before Abraham was, I am."

If Jesus is harkening back to his experience as Melchizedek here, then Genesis 14 records, in a few brief lines, one of the most significant meetings of all mankind.

*And Melchizedek brought out bread and wine; and he was the priest of the most high God.*

*And he blessed him, and said, "Blessed be Abram of the most high God, possessor of heaven and earth.*

*And blessed be the most high God, which hath delivered thine enemies into thy hand."* (Genesis 14:18–20)

Abram not only rejoiced to see the "day" of this high priest, but also paid tithes. Abram was able to recognize the Living God manifesting in

81

Melchizedek. He had the same insight, apparently, that Peter did at a
later date!

*Jesus said to them, "Who do you say that I am?"*
    *Simon Peter answered, saying, "You are the Christ, the Son of the*
*Living God." (Matthew 16:15-16)*

With all the nations, after Babel, turning to gratification and power, it
became necessary for a new nation to be raised. Abram is the father of
this people, a new nation dedicated exclusively to being *God's People.*

> . . . or as in the priest of Salem in the days when the call came that a
> peculiar peoples would proclaim His name . . .                      364-8

This nation was to be used for the renewing of the mind of man,
restoring his memory through spiritual discernment.

> . . . a peculiar people, set aside for a purpose—as a channel through
> which there might be the discerning of the spirit made manifest in flesh.
>                                                                  2879-1

> Thinkest thou that the grain of corn has forgotten what manner of
> expression it has given? Think thou that *any* of the influences in nature
> that you see about you—the acorn, the oak, the elm, or the vine or
> *anything*—has forgotten . . . ? Only man forgets! And it is only in His
> mercy that such was brought about. For what was the first cause?
> Knowledge—knowledge! What then is that cut off in the beginnings of
> the Sons of God? Becoming entangled with the daughters of men, and
> the Daughters of God becoming entangled with the sons of men! As in
> Adam, they forgot what manner of men they were! Only as he lives, [as]
> he manifests that life that is the expression of the divine, may man begin
> to know *who*, where, what and when he was!                  294-189

Peter and Abram share several features in common, and reflect a
universal spiritual pattern. As a result of their spiritual development,
both men had their names changed: Peter to Simon, and Abram to
Abraham. Their spiritual perceptions established them as the first patriarchs, or fathers, of their "church."
    Peter's realization of the Christ in Jesus established him (or the aware-

ness itself) as the "rock" of the New Testament church.[11] Perhaps Melchizedek bestowed a similar blessing on Abram. Abram's awareness was the foundation upon which the Old Testament was built.

The discernment of the Spirit manifesting in the flesh is the base, or cornerstone, for this spiritual movement which began after Babel and the dividing of the nations, the foundation succeeding generations could return to and enlarge upon, building an ever-expanding body of souls attracted to each other for a common purpose.

> . . . for as given of Old, no soul can say that Christ is come of God save the Holy Spirit convict him of that statement.  262-72

Just as Abram was able to see Melchizedek as the Son of a Living God, Melchizedek was able to recognize in Abram the elements of spirituality and worldliness that would establish him as the leader of this new movement. In the following Cayce puts forth a simple, far-reaching concept which in its application can be a working principle for all.

> Nations were set up then in various portions of the land [after Babel], and . . . set about to seek their gratifications. Very few—yea, as ye will recall, it even became necessary that from one of these groups one individual, a man, be called. His ways were changed. His name was changed.
>
> Did it take sin away from the man, or was it only using that within the individual heart and purpose and desire even then, as man throughout the periods of unfoldment put—in his interpretation—that of material success first?  3976-29

Abram's desire for material success was a principal motivation, but he had the willingness and the wisdom to let the Spirit direct him in the fulfillment of his ambitions. Perhaps Melchizedek tutored him in this awareness and coached him in harmonizing his material desires with their spiritual source.

The earlier chapters of Genesis have been symbolic accounts of the Adamic race as a whole. With Abram, the book begins to focus exclusively on the development and history of a particular people. Yet this

---

[11]See 262-87.

people remain a symbol of mankind. As a struggling, seeking, oft-cursed, oft-blessed race, they are a microcosm of Humanity in its search for God, manifesting all the potential within for good and evil.

## Melchizedek

**These become hard at times for the individual to visualize; that the mental and soul [bodies] may manifest without a physical vehicle.**

**987-4**

Perhaps one reason why Melchizedek was able to impress Abram was that this high priest, like Adam and Enoch (and many of the so-called Eastern masters today) was a "living soul." Melchizedek was not a flesh man. It is written of him:

*Neither his father nor his mother is recorded in the genealogies; and neither the beginning of his days nor the end of his life.* (Hebrews 7:3)

Thus, he was "a living soul."

**For as He hath given, "The earth, the heavens will pass away, but my words shall *not* pass away." Know that the soul, the psychic forces of an entity, any entity, any body, are . . . eternal—for they are without days, without years, without numbers . . .**
**1376-1**

Cayce described the three primary appearances of Jesus—Adam, Enoch, and Melchizedek—as "in the perfection" (5749-14) and distinguished them from the later ones which were "in the earth"—Joseph, Joshua, Jeshua, and Jesus. It is also written of Melchizedek that "he is a priest forever." (Psalm 110:4, Hebrews 7:17)

In his resurrected body Jesus is "without days or years" and once again High Priest "after the order of Melchizedek."

**Though He were the *Son*, know that there was the lonesomeness, the fear of those influences that beset those He loved. Yet, knowing He hath entered into that glory, becoming the high priest of His people, they that seek Him daily, and having sat down on the right hand of the Father, then through Him ye have that promise, "Lo, I am *with* thee." 531-9**

## The Offices of High Priest

Just as Abram began the line which eventually resulted in the ultimate incarnation in the flesh of the Son of the Living God, Edgar Cayce
told a woman that in a very distant and ancient age, she had begun
activities and established a line which made the appearance of
Melchizedek possible. Although Melchizedek's genealogy is not known,
Edgar Cayce said that in prehistoric Egypt [884] had been his great-
great-grandmother:

> . . . we find the entity was in what is now known as the Egyptian land,
> during those experiences when there were those being sent as the
> emissaries for the peoples in the various lands; where there had been and
> were the attempts to correlate the teachings of those in various portions
> of that eastern land.
>
> The entity was among those that aided in the establishing of that in
> the Persian land, which later became as the tenets of that people from
> whom—many ages later—Melchizedek came. And the entity finds that
> when this is said within its inner self there is a response which makes for
> an opening of the greater promises from within: M-e-l-c-h-i-z-e-d-e-k,
> the great-great-grandson of the entity, who came as without days, as
> without father or mother, yet as in [the] desire of the entity that—as
> Sususus—created or begun the condition through its efforts.
>
> For it brought into the associations of those with whom the entity
> labored that which would make for peace, harmony; glorying in the
> acceptance of the truths from the Infinite—as it may express itself in the
> finite minds of men.                                              884-1

If Cayce is correct, one of Melchizedek's greatest contributions to the
spiritual development of mankind was the creation of the Book of Job,
a religious allegory, a pattern of man's experience in the earth:

> (Q) Was Jesus, the Christ, ever Job in the physical body? . . .
> (A) No. Not ever in the physical body . . . For, as the Sons of God came
> together to reason, as recorded in Job, who recorded same? The Son of
> Man! Melchizedek wrote Job!                                      262-55

Another body of teaching initiated by Melchizedek was later used to
found the School of Prophets, which eventually became the Essene

Community to which many of the early Christian Jews belonged, including Mary, Joseph, and Jesus.

> **Hence the group we refer to . . . as the Essenes . . . was the outgrowth of the periods of preparations from the teachings of Melchizedek, as propagated by Elijah and Elisha and Samuel.**          **254-109**

Thus the teachings of Melchizedek are not only the basis for much of the Old Testament wisdom, but the Christian philosophy as well.

Melchizedek's blessing of Abram in Genesis 14 provides another example of a spiritual service:

> **. . . Melchizedek, a prince of peace, one seeking ever to be able to bless those in their judgments who have sought to become channels for a helpful influence without any seeking for material gain or mental or material glory . . .**          **2072-4**

## Father Abraham

Abraham, Isaac, and Jacob were the first patriarchs and set the examples. All the later prophets, seers, and writers of the Old Testament refer to the experiences of these three men. God *spoke* to Adam, *walked* with Enoch, and *talked* with Noah, but only with the coming of Abraham, Isaac, and Jacob did man's concept of God become a personal thing.

On February 19, 1939, a fifty-four-year-old beauty salon manager obtained a Life reading. In this very touching extract from it, Cayce describes the influence Abraham and his family had upon her.

> **. . . the entity was in that land when there were those activities in which the chosen of the Lord, as recorded, were making for those activities which later brought about the dwellings of him called father of the faithful.**
>
> **The entity then was among the daughters of Heth from whom Abraham purchased the land near Socoh. [Genesis 23] The entity was acquainted with that patriarch, though—as considered in those days—of an unknown people; yet through the activities viewed by the entity as to same there was aroused that which brought a longing for a knowledge of a something of which the entity had heard.**
>
> **For the manner in which Abraham, Isaac, and Sarah—and even Ishmael—**

were in the care of their own brought the love of a home; yet to the entity—as in the present—seeking rather the knowledge of that city not built with hands, but rather that eternal in the heart and soul of those.[12]

Hence we find again those abilities of ministering, of teaching—not as proclaiming but in *living,* and in the quietness of the conversation, being able to give that which awakens within the minds and hearts of others that search for that which the entity finds in its emblem—the lamb and the lotus, in purity that touches even to the lips of God.      1825-1

On May 2, 1935, a young writer was told of an early life and Abraham's effect upon her:

> . . . when there were the settlings of the land, when first the land of promise came to be a portion of Abraham's or Abram's and Sarai's activity. The entity was then among the daughters of Heth, of those peoples in that land, in the name then Beloi, and was very closely associated with Sarah, Abraham, Lot, and those people that settled in those plains of Abraham. And the entity's daughter became then the leading among those that made for the combinations of the peoples of Isaac's son and those of the Canaanite land.
>
> In the experience the entity gained, for it proclaimed many of those tenets or lessons or philosophies, or activities—as would be called in the present—as to establishing the relationships with individuals, and what became as the Creative Forces or that philosophy of life as pertaining to the Creative Energies as given out by Abraham during the period. The entity proclaimed same to the peoples roundabout, and made for the closer companionships with those first leaders of those people set apart for an activity in the earth.      846-2

A Jewish businessman was told when Abraham went out from Ur, he had accompanied him. A love of travel and adventure is a result of that experience.

---

[12]Revelation 21: " . . . there is then the new Jerusalem." For as has been given, the place is not as a place alone but as a condition, as an experience of the soul. Jerusalem has figuratively, symbolically meant the holy place, the holy city . . . the ark of the covenant in the minds, hearts, the understandings, the comprehensions of those who have put away the earthly desires and become as the *new* purposes in their experience, become the new Jerusalem, the new undertakings, the new desires. (281-37)

. . . before this we find in the Promised Land to those peoples who came up from Ur, and the entity was among those who served that leader, ruler, or patriarch, and gave much and required much at the hand of those about the entity in that day. Then the name was Shouel, and the urge as is seen—the desire of travel, and the urge of profit in traffic, for this, as is seen, is the greater influence in the present experience in earth's sojourn. 2855-1

A twenty-year-old stenographer was told that Abraham had had a decided influence upon her in an earlier incarnation as one of his grandchildren.

. . . the early portion of those activities with Abraham, known as the father of the faithful. And the entity then was acquainted with those activities, being the daughter of Ishmael-Temah by name. And, being associated and acquainted with those activities and influences, the entity was among those who brought many of the changes in the affairs and activities of the peoples during that experience.

The entity held to rather the tenets of Abraham, as well as the knowledge of the activities of Isaac. 1709-3

These readings spoke of the influence of Abraham upon others. The following suggests an influence which may have strengthened Abraham himself—*his mother!* On January 30, 1930, a fifty-three-year-old housewife, a Theosophist, was told that following a life in Egypt, in 12,500 B.C., she had incarnated in India.

The entity then was among those when there came the destruction of the peoples in the valleys by those who *would* make rule from the hills. The entity then [was] among those who were *conquered* in body, but not in mind—and little by little the entity, through that experience, brings to bear such influence, such a condition, as to bring the peoples who would become the rulers in accord with the mental and the spiritual *builders* of that land, and of the house came Abraham. In the name Terahe. Not the father, but the mother. 115-1

## Abimilech

On October 18, 1934, a thirty-four-year-old physicist of Christian background was told he had been Abimilech, whose story is recorded in Genesis 20:

> The entity then was in the name Abimilech, or the ruler of those people in the lands that lay between the Egyptian and Syrophoenician lands. The entity then gained, even through those experiences and associations. Yet from those very activities there were brought those desires on the part of the entity, Abimilech, to bring to the knowledge of those who were as servants—or those whom the entity served in the capacity of the king of that land—that "he that would be the greatest among all would be the servant of all." While the entity had much in its experience and through that sojourn, that in the material and the moral life in the present would be questioned, yet the purposes, the aims, the desires, the activities were rather as the growth throughout that sojourn.
>
> And the abilities of the entity in the present to apply same are in the innate influences that impel and make for a growth in the *soul*, or in the *entity*—which is the combination of all its experiences with its soul also—that may make for not only the material but the mental and spiritual growth that comes to a greater and better knowledge, understanding, of those things in the earth. 699-1

As the above reading affirms, Abimilech was a spiritually-minded man. (Genesis 20) Unlike Pharaoh, who was awakened only through a series of plagues (Genesis 12), Abimilech was warned through a vision of the deception which Abram had practiced on him. Abram's presenting Sarah as his sister previously in Egypt had not only protected them, but had established him, via Pharaoh's gifts, as a wealthy man.

Perhaps he and Sarah agreed to practice this deception everywhere they stopped, or when they felt it was needed.

> . . . as indicated in the law of the Book, the life of the man Abraham was not beautiful, yet that faith which motivated same is beautiful, and the memory and of the children of faith we find beautiful. 4035-1

Edgar Cayce's Bible class lesson was a hard look at Abraham and his rationalizations to Abimilech.

> "Abraham's excuse was he did not feel God was in that place or among the people. He had become so used to thinking of himself as being a

chosen one, he forgot to look for the good in others. He depended, rather, upon his ability for slyness and trickery.

"Abraham's actions, first with Pharaoh and then with Abimilech, are hard for us to understand. We can only say that he was very human. Even today, no matter how old we are or what our circumstances may be, we are constantly attempting to justify ourselves. Usually we are looking for the easiest ways to 'get by.'

"We might even say Abraham was just practicing another good Jewish trick, and getting a lot of money out of these people. The Philistines were as wealthy as the Egyptians.

"Still, if we think of the experience as something we can apply in our own lives, it would represent our attempts to justify ourselves in material things.

"Abraham felt he had a special interest in God not shared by others. Many feel that way today. They feel they are especially gifted and have a right to the best of everything. This is true. Each individual has a right to be best in life, but only in harmonious co-operation with others, and not at their expense.

"Abimilech reproved Sarah for taking his gifts to Abraham. He felt they were not deserved because they had taken advantage of him."

## A Forced Issue

Even though Peter was able to recognize the Christ and was established as the head of the new Church, it became necessary, a very short while later, for Jesus to rebuke him. (Matthew 16:22-23)

**The falling in and out of attunement is found in even the greatest ones in Scripture. They represent humanity in all its phases. And Abraham is no exception.**

**For remember, though he walked in many ways contrary to God's edicts and laws, Abram's try was counted to him for righteousness.**

**3129-1**

On October 18, 1941, a fifty-six-year-old missionary nurse was told in her Life reading that she was a witness to one of Abraham's contrary ways:

**. . . the entity was in the land of Ur, when there were those journeys of**

**that one called. The entity was among those of that household, who knew and understood, and who made administrations for the welfare of Abraham and Sarah. The entity knew of those choices when there were the attempts on the part of man to force an issue with God. How oft ye find in thy experiences today that there are those same attempts on the part of individuals to tell God how they desire health, position, to be well spoken of.** 2608-1

In Genesis 15, Abraham, at ninety–seven, is told by God he would have a natural heir, a son. In Genesis 16 Sarah, who had been barren all her life, urges Abraham to conceive the promised heir through Hagar, her personal slave.

"This," Edgar Cayce remarked, "was another instance where woman tempted man to try some other way than the one outlined by God. And Abraham, although called 'Father of the Faithful,' was willing to listen. Sarah was anxious. She wanted Abraham to receive the blessing which had been promised. So, she decided to help things get started."

"This is the way we are," Cayce continued. "If we plant a seed today, we dig it up tomorrow to see how it is growing. Patience is the greatest lesson—to wait upon the Lord." As soon as Hagar conceived, she looked with contempt on Sarah. And Sarah became disturbed and angry.

The seed which had been planted bore its own fruit—this is the first instance in Scripture of jealousy and hatred between two women.

Cayce concluded the Bible lesson with the thought:

"Sarah, no doubt, realized she had sinned, and for that reason, took it out on Hagar. Most of us will try and blame someone else, when we really know within ourselves that we are at fault."

Fearful of Sarah, Hagar fled into the wilderness. In a psychic experience in the desert, she was told by an angel that her child would be " . . . a wild ass of a man, his hand against every man and every man's hand against him."

This child was Ishmael, from whom the Arab nations trace their descent.

## Isaac and Ishmael

On October 16, 1940, Edgar Cayce used the following illustrations in a psychic discourse on the endocrine system of the human body:

> When Abraham and Sarah were given the promise of an heir through which the nations of the earth would be blessed, there were many years of preparation of these individuals, of the physical, mental, and spiritual natures. Again and again it is indicated as to how they each in their material concept (watch the words here, please, if you would understand) attempted to offer a plan, or way, through which this material blessing from a spiritual source might be made manifest.
>
> Hence we find as to how the material or mental self-misunderstanding, misconstruing the spiritual promises—offered or *effected* channels through which quite a different individual entity was made manifest; and through same brought confusion, distress, disturbance one to another in the material manifestations.                281-48

It was Sarah's impatience in waiting for the fulfilling of God's promise which resulted in Ishmael's birth. When her spiritual development matured, the promise was fulfilled. Isaac was conceived!

> Yet, when the last promise was given, that even in their old age there would be given an heir, we find that when Sarah thus conceived there was the development of a body physically, mentally, and spiritually so well-balanced as to be almost etheric in his relationships to the world about him, when the material manifestation had grown to maturity.
>
> Here we find, then, that mind and matter are coordinated into bringing a channel for spiritual activity that is not exceeded in any of the characters depicted in Holy Writ.
>
> When, then, were the characteristics, the activity of the glandular system as related to that individual entity? We find that there was a perfect coordination in and through the whole period of gestation, and the fulfilling of the time according to the law set in motion by the divine influence that was the directing force of both parents through the period.
>
> We find also that throughout the period of gestation the activities about the entity, the mother, were such as to *influence* the entity yet unborn, in patience to a degree not manifested in any other of the patriarchs. While the physical conditions made manifest in the body during the growth into manhood were affected by *material* laws, there was not the changing or deviating whatsoever from the spiritual through the mental.

Hence we find that illustration of what may be termed the individual ideally conceived, ideally cherished and nourished through the periods of gestation . . .

What, then, were the developments of that ideally conceived entity as related to the study here of the endocrine system?

First, the individual was one conceived in promise; with the desire, the purpose, the hope—in the act *of* conception—to bring forth that which had *been* promised. Hence the ideal attitude of both parents in that individual case.

Hence as given, first the pineal, the cranial, the thymus . . . then the gradual development of those influences which brought a goodly child; one subject to the care of both parents—by natural tendencies from conception; bringing into materialization that one worthy of being accepted and of *receiving* the promise beyond *many* of those who were of the seed of Abraham.                    281-48

With the birth of Isaac, Sarah ordered Hagar and Ishmael's banishment. The Bible class notes offer some interesting and perceptive commentary:

"We wonder how Sarah could have been so cruel. She had been the one who had brought Abraham and Hagar together. However, this is a good lesson in human nature. Usually when we obtain something which is for us perfection, we want to rid ourselves of everything that reminds us of imperfection.

"Ishmael was a constant reminder to Sarah of her lack of faith in God. She wasn't big enough to meet her own sin, and bring up Isaac at the same time. No doubt this is why God favored the banishment of Hagar and Ishmael. He knew what each person was capable of accomplishing, and that they would have to work out their shortcomings together at another time. Everybody has to meet his own self eventually. The most important thing then was to create the proper environment for Isaac, who was to mean so much to the world. If Hagar and Ishmael had remained, perhaps it could not have been done."

## Abraham and Edgar Cayce

The past and the present combine in this experience. On February 12, 1932, Edgar Cayce had the following dream:

"I thought I was with Mr. and Mrs. Lot and their two daughters running out of Sodom when it was raining fire and brimstone. What had been called, "She turned to a pillar of salt" (Genesis 19:26), because she looked back, was that they really passed through the heat which came from the fire of heaven, and all were tried as by fire. I got through the fire."

On April 1, a reading was given to interpret the dream. The reading stated that Edgar Cayce actually had been one of the messengers (Genesis 19:1, 15, 16) who had been sent to warn Lot and the citizens of Sodom. Evidently Edgar Cayce was one of the three who had spoken to Abraham beforehand. (Genesis 18)

> In this particular vision, this is rather as an experience through which the body passed with those at the period; for the body then, the entity, was one that accompanied these bodies in this experience, and in the present must and will pass through—in the mental attitudes that are being assumed as respecting the body and activities—much as those bodies in that experience. As to whether [Cayce] is to remain in that of the escape, as then, or is warned as respecting the outcome of the individuals seen, depends upon the attitude, and activities in the physical of the body through these trials; for they [the trials] will be as of by fire.[13] 294-136

On April 2, the following day, a subsequent reading was given to interpret the above references. Although the dream related to a past life experience, it was attempting to communicate a message about the present. Edgar Cayce felt the dream pertained to the apparent necessity of leaving Virginia Beach, the place where previous readings had indicated he should settle.

After financial support was withdrawn from the Cayce Hospital and it closed at the onset of the Depression, Cayce faced a severe dilemma. Three homes into which he had moved were sold, necessitating further moves. Then he was unable to find a place to live.

In that as given of Lot, there was the choice by Lot as to whether this experience would be among the peoples in the city or those of the

---

[13]1 Corinthians 3:15.

plains, or of those of the hills. The life was chosen rather among those, and companionship of these, of the city, which—in common parlance— "turned out bad!"

> In the correlating with the life of Edgar Cayce, Virginia Beach was chosen rather by those sources through whom the information comes; and while the experience is as the attempt on the part of individuals and a group to make same so unpleasant as to cause much the same attitude as was forced to and through the life of Lot—but Lot's experience was besought by a just man—Lot sought little for himself, save as to the gratifying of that as had been builded about same. So, as correlating the experience, then, of the leader or director at the time, and the experience as is in action of the *physical* manifestation of the body, rely rather upon those sources or channels through which such information and direction has come.
>
> Believest thou that thou has contacted, do contact, those sources from which good may come to self or to others? Then act in that way and manner, irrespective of the attitude or actions of others.     294-137

This reading expresses some of the pressures and problems confronting Edgar Cayce, but also gives us a rare view of the nature and character of Lot. It is noted Lot sought little for himself, except gratification. Understanding this self-indulgent strain in an otherwise godly man gives us the basis for a possible interpretation of his daughters' incestuous actions (Genesis 19:31-35). If he didn't have it within him, they could not have seduced him.

"After his escape from Sodom, Lot refused to go with the angel to the mountaintop," Edgar Cayce commented and observed. "The mountaintop represents the place where man communes with God—or, where self must be met and seen in light of the Divine. Evidently Lot was not prepared to do this. He had been saved because of the prayers of Abraham, but even Abraham's prayers could not keep Lot from having to meet himself." Lot chose rather to go to "a little city" (Genesis 19:20), perhaps to commit his same follies, but in a "smaller" way.

Evidently Lot's wife shared the same weakness as her husband, as this reading indicates:

> As the trust, the hope, the faith is manifested by the patience day by day, does there become the more awareness in self's own inner consciousness

that all is well with Him; knowing that if the Lord is on thy side, who may be against you? Trust, and do that thou knowest to do, acting as the Spirit moves within—and look not back; remember Lot's wife.

262-25

(Q) In the reading of August 7, please explain what is meant by "Look not back; remember Lot's wife."
(A) Looking to the front ever, for as one looks towards the light, the shadows fall behind and do not become stumbling blocks to individual development. Thoughts are things, and while the past that is passed may be used as stepping-stones to higher things, looking back causes one to stumble, even as Lot's wife looked upon that left as longing for those satisfying elements that made for the carnal, rather than the spiritual life.

262-28

## Abraham and the Power of Prayer

Edgar Cayce often referred to Abraham's intercession for Lot and the other citizens of Sodom and Gomorrah as demonstration of the power and potential of prayer. (Genesis 18:17-33)

As has been given, however, that which has prevented and does prevent the whole of civilization becoming a turmoil is the attempt of those who have the ideals of the Prince of Peace at heart! And as of old, the prayers of ten may save a city; the prayers of twenty-five may save a nation—as the prayers and activities of one may! But in union there is strength!
Then if that purpose would be kept, it must ever be kept in mind that we are our brother's keeper.

1598-2

. . . where there were ten, even, many a city, many a nation has been kept from destruction.

3976-8

The prayers of the righteous shall save many. "Where two or three are joined together in one purpose, I am in the midst of same." The combination, then, of both—for the supplication is putting self in that attunement to the forces as manifest in the growth, the development, of spiritual forces as are manifested in the material world.

136-45

Why then the turmoil in the world today? They have forgotten God!

Not that it is merely a karmic condition of a nation of a people; for know ye not that the prayer of one man saved a city? Think thou that the arm of God is shorter today than in the days of yore?             3976-25

. . . even as Abram or Abraham—"If there be fifty, will it not be spared?" "O, if there be ten faithful, will it not be spared?" Then the hope of Europe depends upon *you* in your own home *today!* In not the same way, but the same manner as did the life of Lot, or of the other peoples in Sodom and Gomorrah. [World Affairs Reading, January 15, 1932]
3976-8

Though we may look upon, or feel that that which was given to Abram— as he viewed the cities of the plain and pleaded for the saving of same— was an allegorical story, or a beautiful tale to be told children—that it might bring fear into the hearts of those that would have their own way—may it not come into the hearts of those now, today, wilt thou, thine self, make of thine own heart an understanding that thou must answer for thine own brother, for thine own neighbor! And who is thine neighbor? He that lives next door, or he that lives on the other side of the world? He, rather, that is in need of understanding! He who has faltered; he who has fallen even by the way. He is thine neighbor, and thou must answer for him!             3976-8

## *Abraham and Isaac: The Sacrifice*

This lesson is taken from the Bible class notes:

"What is meant by God 'tempting' Abraham? In James 1:13 we are told, "Let no man say when he is tempted, I am tempted of God; for God cannot be tempted with evil, neither he tempteth any man. We understand from 1 Corinthians 10:13 that God does not *allow* us to be tempted beyond our abilities, but with every temptation prepares a way of escape.

"The temptation, then, is not from God, but a result of a cause and effect law which has been set in motion. Our temptations come from our own deviations from spiritual laws in the past.

"In the case of Abraham, it would seem the sacrifice of Isaac was a supreme test, rather than a temptation. Yet it is impossible to conceive of God singling out one individual for testing or tempting, just to see what he will do. Certain opportunities were presented to Abraham as a result of natural cause and effect laws.

"When Isaac was born—almost a physical impossibility, considering their ages—it must have seemed a miracle to Abraham and Sarah. Abraham must have been thoroughly convinced of God's ability to do anything. His faith was so great he was willing to sacrifice Isaac, knowing God could and would restore him if his son was to be the channel through which all the nations of the earth would be blessed."

Good being from the all good, or as He gave there is none good save God—then that which would be good for an individual might not be to another godly; and thus it would be sin to that individual. Thus Righteousness versus Sin becomes again a personal application of the individual's awareness of God's purpose.

> For, as many be illustrated: to the workaday mind of today, Abram's offering of Isaac would appear foolish, yet—as stated—it was counted to him as righteousness, not sin.
> This, then, is a personal application of the awareness that is in the consciousness of the seeker after God.          262-128

In the symbolic, or metaphysical sense, the offering of Isaac, like the slaying of Abel, is a foreshadowing of the sacrifice of the Christ.

> What, then, is this faith that is indicated? This one knows, when one becomes aware of same; yet may never put it into words nor tell another by words—or acts even—as to what that consciousness of faith is. Yet we may see the shadows of same in what faith has prompted in the experience of others, as it is so well expressed in the seventh of Hebrews, or as given in that God so had faith in man as to give His Son *himself*, to die—*in* the flesh; knowing that man must come to the realization—and would—that he, too, must often crucify that of material desire within himself, if he would glorify his better self, or if he would prefer his brother above himself. Or, even as a man, Abraham, the son of faith, the author of faith, offered—or was willing to offer—his only son, his physical heir; knowing that there *must* be a purpose from that inner voice as to that command.          2174-2

The conclusion to this Bible class lesson is provoking and dramatic:

"Taking all the biblical references regarding temptation into consideration, we must believe this was a very crucial period in the history of mankind. This was Satan's opportunity to deceive Abraham into destroying his own son, and thus thwart God's plan of salvation. Abraham's faith was so great in what he believed to be God's command, Satan was thwarted instead. Through faith, Abraham was able to behold the other sacrifice.

"We can try and delude ourselves by saying there is no evil. If we believe in the record laid down for us, we must realize that Satan is abroad in the earth, seeking to add to his side all who listen to him. It is only those who have faith in God, as Abraham did, who can escape him.

"There comes a time of supreme testing to each soul—Abraham and Isaac, Jesus in the mount."

## The Sons of Isaac

Sarah, Rebekah, and Rachel all had the same experience. They had to wait many years before they gave birth to their sons. Other women were fruitful, and they were barren for most of their lives. Why was this? Were they not the chosen channels through which the line of Judah was established, and through which the Prince of Peace was eventually to come? Those who are to fulfill the promises of God must first prepare themselves through patience, humility, prayer, and supplication. They must fist become worthy to receive such a blessing.

Throughout history, the great spiritual leaders have come in answer to prayer and preparation, and through the need expressed by individuals and groups.

The Cayce information on ideals and purposes toward conception and sexual union are extremely significant in this day and time of world turmoil. Millions of people in the earth today seem to have no greater impetus than to fight one another, and to put selfishness and greed above love and service.

This is a continuation of the Edgar Cayce reading on the endocrine gland system, regarding the birth of twins to Isaac and Rebekah:

**Then we have that illustration in the sons of Isaac, when there were those periods in which there was to be the fulfilling of the promise to Isaac and Rebekah. We find that their *minds* differed as to the nature or character of channel through which there would come this promise**

[Genesis 17:3-8]; when, as we understand, there must be the cooperation spiritually, mentally, in order for the physical result to be the same. *Here* we find a different situation taking place at the time of conception, for *both* attitudes found expression. Hence twins were found to be the result of this long preparation, and yet two minds, two opinions, two ideas, two ideals. Hence we find that *here* it became necessary that even the *Divine* indicate to the mother that channel which was to be the ruler or that one upon whom would be bestowed the rightful heritage through which the greater blessings were to be indicated to the world, to humanity, to mankind as a whole. [Genesis 25:23]

Hence we find two natures, two characteristics—physically, mentally, spiritually. Here we find what might be termed a perfect channel again and with same a testing—not only of the parents themselves but of the individuals that were begotten under those conditions in which the promise was as clear to them as it had been to Abraham. Here we find, as indicated, there was *not* a union of purpose in those periods of conception. Hence we find both characteristics, or both purposes of the individuals, were made materially manifest.

What then, ye may well ask, made this difference in the characteristics of the individuals; conceived of the same parents, under the environ or the law from the body of the one; with such a different characteristic made manifest as they grew to maturity?

As indicated, the first cause—that purpose with which the individuals performed the act for conception to take place, or under which it did take place. *That* is the First Cause! And the growth of that conceived under the same environ, through the same circulation, through the same impulse, was such that—when gestation was finished—one was of the nature or characteristic of the mother, the other was of the nature of indifference with the determination of the father; one smooth as the mother, the other hairy, red, as the father in maturity; and their characteristics made manifest were just those examples of the variations. Though conceived at once, born together, they were far separated in their purposes, their aims, their hopes; one holding to that which made body, mind, and soul coordinant; the other satisfying, gratifying the appetites of the physical and mental without coordinating same through its spiritual relationships to the progenitor or those conditions and environs from which they each drew their desires, their hopes, their wishes.

Do ye think that one received a different instruction from the other?

Each received the same, yet their reaction, their choice of that in the environment made physical characteristics that varied in their activity.

Why were the characteristics such that one desired or loved the chase, the hunt, or the like, while the other chose rather the home, the mother, the environ about same? Were these depicted in the very physiognomy of each individual? When they had reached that period when the *choices* were made, these were manifested. But when did they begin? What gland developed this characteristic in one and not in the other? The cranial and the thymus receiving the varied vibration, one brought harmony—not fear but harmony—with caution; the other brought just the opposite, by this "stepping up" in the rate of vibration. Or, if we were to study these by numbers, we would find one a three, the other a five, yet conceived together . . .

Hence we find there the various forms of manners in which there is illustrated those characteristics that made for individual activity, that *prompted* the carrying on of that through which the channel of hope might be made manifest.                    281-48

Another example regarding twins can be seen in the story of Tamar and Judah in Genesis 38. Because Judah failed in his promise to secure a husband for his widowed daughter-in-law Tamar, she disguised herself as a harlot and sat at a roadside, waiting for Judah to pass.

Judah failed to recognize his daughter-in-law behind her disguise, and went in to her. The result of this union was a set of twins, one of whom became the ancestor of King David and, later, Jesus. Is this a case of the two ideals at the time of conception finding expression? Cayce states in the following Life reading that Tamar's purposes were in keeping with God's will. Apparently Judah's were only for self-indulgence:

Before that we find the entity was in that now known as or called the Palestine land, during those days when the sons of Jacob sought for companions; and to one of the sons of Judah (Er) the entity, Tamar, became the companion.

Owing to the *willfulness* and the sin of Er, he was taken.[14] There was

---

[14]When this entity asked Cayce to describe the karmic relationship she had with her present father, Cayce responded, "He was Er, the husband in that experience. And is there a wonder that there are those disturbing forces in the material relationship in the present. Leave these with the Lord!" (1436-2)

the command or the seeking that there be the fulfillment of the law of the day; and Judah—in an unknown way—failing, yet the entity sought for that as would keep the issue of the body, and went in unto her own father-in-law; and bore two sons, one becoming then later the father of the fathers of Joseph and Mary—the parents of the Master.

There the entity was condemned, yes; yet her purposes, her desires were reckoned with by the God of mercy as being in keeping with His will and His ways.

Hence there is brought into the experience of the entity again the joys of knowing the Lord hath given, "Thy will, my will, are one with the Creative Forces."

And there is reckoned through the ages, then, that ye became as one that chose to do above the ways of men when the voice of man rose above thine own sex.

Hence in the experience, judgments are not taken away—if the entity will trust rather in the *Lord* than in the judgment of men, or the children of men.

For God is the same yesterday, today, tomorrow—yea, forever; and they that come unto Him in *humbleness* of heart, seeking to know His face and His way, may indeed find Him.                    1436-2

This Life reading (1436-2) is one of the most interesting of all the Life readings in the Cayce files. In her next incarnation, Cayce states she was "the woman taken in adultery." (John 8:3–11) A remarkable similarity can be discerned in these two events when viewed in this connection.

## Jacob's First-Born

The following extract is from a Life reading in which a thirteen-year-old child was told that following an incarnation with Lamech (Genesis 4:19) he had been Reuben, the first-born child of Jacob and Leah.

Before that we find the entity was among the first–born of Jacob and Leah, and making for the expressions that in the beginning brought much that was in accord with the callings into an activity where these might have brought the blessings upon the activities in the sojourn. Yet when the desires of the flesh entered, and the associations with those things and about those peoples that had been as an expression of intolerance to those peoples, the entity made for the associations that brought disorder, discontent within those of its own household and those of its people in that experience and that expression.

These made for again those activities that have brought in the present the necessity of the awareness of the spiritual awakening within—the expression and experience of the entity. 693-3

As a youth, Reuben was a promising child. As he grew older, influences around him began to stimulate and awaken desires and emotions that were a portion of his former incarnation (from the time of Lamech). In Genesis 35:22, it is written he had sexual relationships with Bilhah, his father's concubine.

The deep affront that Jacob felt this to be is evidenced in Genesis 49, when the dying Jacob delivered his final words to his twelve sons. He cursed Reuben for defiling his bed, and prophesied he would never have pre–eminence. Reuben was "unstable as water."

Edgar Cayce's Life reading for 693 shows how prophetic Jacob's words were. The record shows a pattern of deteriorating expressions throughout his incarnations. In the present life the child bore the heavy karmic burden of a severe form of epilepsy with multiple seizures, partial paralysis, and, in a broken home, was the bed–ridden dependent of a mother who did not want him.

## Joseph and Benjamin: Sons of Jacob and Rachel

Jacob labored seven years to wed Rachel, and was deceived by her father, Laban, who married him to his eldest daughter, Leah. Jacob contracted for another seven years and married Rachel. While Leah and his two concubines delivered ten sons, Rachel was barren. The long delay strengthened their love. When Rachel finally conceived, their first child was Joseph, the first physical incarnation of the soul who had been Adam, Enoch, and Melchizedek.

... the same soul-entity who in those periods of the strength and yet the weakness of Jacob in his love for Rachel was their first-born Joseph. 5023-2

A child of Love! A child of love—the most hopeful of all experiences of any that may come into a material existence; and to some in the earth that most dreaded, that most feared. 5755-1

The following discusses Joseph, and is a continuation of the discourse on the effects of the attitudes of parents on their unborn child. Apparently the superior attitude Joseph evidenced toward his brothers (Genesis 37) stemmed from the dominant mood of Rachel throughout her pregnancy.

> Then, with Jacob and Rachel we have the material love, and those natures in which the characteristics of material love were thwarted. Yet in the very conception of same—though under stress (for there is held here by the mother the desire to outshine, as it might be poorly said)—we find a goodly child, one with all the attributes of the spiritual-minded individual; partaking of both the father and the mother in the seeking for a channel through which God might be manifested in the earth. And yet the entity had those physical attributes that brought into the experience of individuals those things that were reflected in the mind, in the movements and activities of the mother throughout the periods of gestation—when the entity had grown to manhood.          281-48

The reading also describes the variation between Joseph and his younger brother Benjamin, and supplies the additional note that Benjamin was later Saul, first King of Israel. Reading 5148-2 indicates the same soul had also been Seth, the third child of Adam and Eve.

> Also from the same attitude taken by those parents when the second son, Benjamin, was conceived—what were the varying characteristics here? The material love was just as great, the satisfying of material desire was completely fulfilled; yet it lacked that desire to *bring* such as was wholly a channel through which the *spiritual* was to be made manifest. But it was a channel that *eventually* brought the material made manifest in Saul, an incarnation of Benjamin.          281-48

## A Friend of Jacob's

Edgar Cayce's opening comments in reading 3851, a Life reading for a thirty-eight-year-old Jewish interior decorator, were:

> This is the fellow who fixed all the stakes for Jacob when he changed all the cows, you see, from spots and those that were roan.          3581-1

The story which Cayce refers to is found in Genesis 30:25–43.

Before that the entity was in the Holy Land in the days when Jacob labored for the daughters of Laban, during those periods when the helpers of Laban chose rather to become helpers of Jacob.

The entity was among those who aided in preparing the places of feeding for the cattle when Laban had set up such and such conditions under which divisions would be made of the cattle or goods.

Thus those things having to do with wood, with blemishes, marks, spots, and things in wood are all of special interest to the entity. Today they may be called other names, but the entity finds that woods of gum and other solid woods that are known for their particular marking are of particular interest to the entity. And in themselves they carry a meaning that is not explained in the entity. But consider, such markings may even control the dispositions of people, as they did the animals. How truly the Lord is one, and moves in mysterious ways His wonders to perform among men. Ye say peculiar interpretations? But it's one.

The name then was Raoul. The entity journeyed to the Holy Land with Jacob. The entity was particularly interested in the happenings to Jacob when he wrestled with the angels. For the entity was one of those who looked after the son of Jacob when there was fear of the brother Esau, and remember there was only one of that particular group of sons in that particular period—Joseph. And the name means much to the entity in the present.                      3581-1

An intimation of a deep friendship is suggested in Cayce's response to the following question of 3581:

(Q) What have been my past relationships and what are my present responsibilities with . . . Rosalyn?
(A) In the Holy Land you were very close—yes, companions, and you were very close to Joseph, to Rachel, to Jacob.                      3581-1

## The Only Daughter

Little is known of Dinah, Jacob's only daughter. Her story is told in Genesis 34. Historians dispute its authenticity as a historical fact. The story is viewed rather as an amalgam of many incidents, an allegory of the tribal warfare of that patriarchal age in which women were often

defiled by invaders and revenged by their kin. Jewish scholars also question the historical validity of the Books of Ruth and Esther, suggesting
they, too, are allegorical in nature. However, the Edgar Cayce readings
strongly suggest that in all three cases a historical interpretation is valid.
A twenty-four-year-old doctor's receptionist was told she had been
Dinah in a previous existence:

> . . . we find the entity was in the Promised Land, during those periods
> when there was the building of that which was and is a mighty influence
> in the relationships of man to Creative Forces.
> There we find the entity was among the children of Jacob, and the
> daughter in that experience—one among twelve sons; and she whom
> Shechem sought, and over which much turmoil to Levi and Simeon was
> brought, owing to the conditions which arose through those activities as
> they journeyed in that land from the Arabian.
> The entity gained and lost; and there are those experiences that arise
> accordingly in the present, from the activities in that sojourn—as to its
> relationships to individuals, owing to the social status, and owing to
> those conditions which arise in the activities.
> Hold fast to that which is the purpose, and the promise. Remember,
> thou hast the promise within thine own self; and it is not as to who will
> descend to bring a message, or who would come from over the sea that
> ye might hear or know. For, Lo, He is within thine own heart, thine own
> consciousness. In thine own body has He promised to meet thee.
> As ye have experienced the awareness of the arousing to healing,
> know that He *is* life.[15]
> Then the name was Dinah.                                    951-4

Although Dinah is generally lost to history, the Edgar Cayce reading
traced her progress both before and after her tumultuous experience as
Dinah. In the previous life she had been in prehistoric Egypt, at the time
of Ra-Ta, the high priest. She was one of his daughters, and served in
the Temple Beautiful . . . "for the preservation of those activities in which
there was to be rather the pure strain of the pure blood." Cayce said she
rose to power in the Temple Beautiful, but "united" with the influence of

---

[15]She had been healed of arthritis by following advice in her three previous
readings.

the Atlanteans "that brought the children of Belial's seeking for self-indulgences."

Her rape by Shechem and the bloody retribution by Simeon and Levi could possibly have been karmic in nature, a result of this Egyptian life.

## *Jacob's Ladder*

The ancient ladder symbol which appears in this dream makes it particularly outstanding.

(Q) [asked by Miss 993 in 281 series] Please interpret the following dream which I received a few days before Christmas: I was climbing a ladder and as I approached the top I became conscious of one round being out of the ladder at the top. It was with great difficulty that I continued to climb at this point Thankful to say, I was able with my finger-tips to reach the top. It took all my strength to pull my body up it. Those who were following back of me seemed to have no such difficulty, and one of the group made that remark. There was an answer by one already there, that as I made the climb I had laid the last round in the ladder.

(A) Both prophetic and profound in this experience of the body-consciousness with the soul's experience. That the ladder represents the Way is evidenced, as has been given in interpretations for those that visioned even the ladder to heaven upon which there ascended and descended the angels of light. In that the rung was missing and that self had to make the effort to attain the top makes for those experiences oft in the mind's consciousness of many, that others that self considers as having an easy way do not become confronted with those hardships as is felt at times are experienced by others. But rather as the voice that came from above, when the self had made the way easier for those that would ascend by the experiences of self, that "I *am* the way," knowing that He made of Himself no estate that others through Him might have access to the Father. And as the voice of those who cry the way is easier that thou hast made the last rung, for us; and as there is the cry from above, "Well done," there should come that peace within self that thine work of thine hand is acceptable in His sight. Be not unto vainglory, but rather in that happiness that passeth understanding in knowing that the work of thine hands is acceptable in His Sight. **281-19**

Cayce again referred to the ladder when another woman, Mrs. 1158, requested a Life reading:

> As to the appearances in the earth, the one stands so far beyond the others—as indicated—that they become rather of little note; yet they each have their influence as a lesson, as a stepping stone upon the pathway. Or rather as that vision that was given of old—yea, which has been, which will become a vision to thine self—of that ladder upon which the rungs of life become here and there the pathway upon which the angels of mercy, light, patience, understanding, brotherly love, descend and rise again. As thou in thine experience has seen the ladder with the missing rung, know that such missing rungs are to be placed by not that as a service as duty alone; rather as the service of love, that ye may be even like Him.                                                    1158-2

## The Promise to Jacob

In Genesis 32:24–28, Jacob wrestled with the angel, and was given the name of Israel. Later, on his deathbed, he prophesied to his son Judah that the scepter of Israel would not depart from his descendants.

> (Q) What should be understood by the statement [Genesis 49:10], "The scepter has not departed from Israel"?
> (A) Israel is the chosen of the Lord, and that His promise, His care, His love has not departed from those that seek to know His way, that seek to see His face, that would draw nigh unto Him. This is the meaning, this should be the understanding to all. Those that seek are Israel. Those that seek not, have ye not heard, "Think not to call thyselves the promise in Abraham. Know ye not that the Lord is able to raise up children of Abraham from the very stones?" So Abraham means call; so Israel means those who seek. How obtained the supplanter the name Israel? For he wrestled with the angel, and he was face to face with the seeking to know His way. So it is with us that are called and seek His Face; we are the Israel. Know, then, the scepter, the promise, the love, the glory of the Lord has not departed from them that seek His face.          262-28

# Joseph: Forerunner of the Christ

*Throughout* the story of Joseph, the writer keeps emphasizing that God was *with* Joseph. However, it was the God in Joseph which did the works. His great ability at dream interpretation was simply the natural expression of the Divine Within going out to meet the needs and circumstances of the moment. God is in all and "with" everyone who seeks to do His bidding.

Joseph is the first *physical*, or flesh, incarnation of the soul who had been Adam, Enoch, and Melchizedek—three experiences which Cayce described as "in the perfection" (5749-14). Why, when he was a "living soul" with mind and Spirit attuned to the Creator, did he enter into the chaos of the earth plane, taking on a body of emotions and physical drives and desires that could, would—and did—separate him from this Oneness? As the Savior, it was necessary for him to undergo all the experiences of man:

> . . . would that all would learn that He, the Christ Consciousness, is the Giver, the Maker, the Creator of the world and all that be therein! And ye are His, for ye are bought with a price, even that of passing through flesh as thou, that He might experience and know all thy thoughts, thy fears, thy shortcomings, thy desires, the dictates of the physical consciousness, the longings of the physical body. Yet He is at the right hand,

is the right hand, is the Intercessor for ye all. Hence thy destinies lie in
Him.                                                                    696-3

Cayce listed the life of Joseph as among the seven major incarnations
of the Christ-consciousness in the development of the man Jesus.

The weaknesses of the flesh are evident in some aspects of Joseph's
life. He inherited his mother's attitude of superiority. This is reflected in
Joseph's relationships with his brothers. He expected them to be humble
before him. His ego also shows when, in Genesis 42, he accuses his
brothers of being spies. He must have felt a bitterness and vindictiveness, and wanted to retaliate for some of the suffering they had caused
him.

The divine is more apparent in Joseph than his weaknesses. The following Life readings show Joseph's influence on several entities and the
spiritual awakenings this association created within them. Truly do they
show and anticipate Joseph's development as the Savior and Redeemer,
able to bring all who follow Him back to their spiritual source.

An elderly Protestant woman, an authoress and lecturer was told:

. . . the entity was in the Egyptian land, in that period when there were
the preparations for the peoples of another land entering—or the days
when Pharaoh of that period was aroused to activity by the voice of
Joseph, the wanderer in that realm.

There we find the entity was among the daughters of that Pharaoh—
in the name Kotapet.

In the experience the entity gained much through not only the
mental application of those tenets of that messenger who came to save,
as it were, a people as well as himself, but—as that entity was the
messenger of the living God among those in a disturbed world—the
entity caught that vision of the universal love as might be exemplified in
the relationships of a people, of a nation—and not as in self-indulgence
or self-aggrandizement for the passing appetites, or for those things
that made for the laudation or the enslavement of any that material
blessings might be in the experience of a few.

Hence we find again the entity giving of self in giving the expressions
of mercy and grace among a people disturbed by those activities which
had been as of a race consciousness in that sojourn.

In the present from the experiences in that sojourn, then, we find the
great abilities in giving in word, in messages—that may be a part of the

> mental consciousness of the many—those things that will bring universal peace, universal love within the hearts and the realms of those who may take heed by the mental experience of this entity.          1837-1

A middle–aged Christian Scientist was told she had been among the princesses of Egypt. Influenced by Joseph's teachings, she devoted herself to teaching the lower caste, or classes.

> . . . the entity was in the land now known as the Egyptian, during those periods when there was the understanding gained by the ministrations and activities in the days when Joseph ruled in that land. The entity then was among the princesses of Egypt, and of that king who made for the establishing of that closer relationship to those who had chosen to serve the living God, rather than to serve their own selves.
>
> For the entity was acquainted with and oft associated with Joseph, the incarnation of Him whom the entity later served so well in Thessalonica! There the entity gained through the experiences in aiding those who were of the low degree or caste to become acquainted with the forces and powers that brought the greater comprehension and activities of the people in that sojourn.
>
> Hence we will find in the present experience a lesson in the life of Joseph that is nowhere else gained in the writing of the Old Testament.
>
> Then the entity was in the name Zerlva.
>
> In the present application of self in respect to the lessons, the innate forces gained there, it is seen that there are the abilities to question with those who are seeking here and there for a greater comprehension of what the experience in materiality is all about—that which will give them, as then, an insight into the fact that it is the practice of the principle of patience that gives the development. For as He gave, "In patience ye become aware of your souls."          1825-1

A follow–up reading for this entity supplies another page in Edgar Cayce's story of the Old Testament:

> Mrs. Cayce: You will have before you the life existence in the earth plane of [1825] . . . and the earthly existence of this entity in Egypt as Zerlva, a princess of the king's household that established closer relationship to those who had chosen to serve the living God. You will also give a fuller explanation of the entity's experience there, and of her associations

with Joseph and the knowledge of the truth and accomplishments gained there . . .

Mr. Cayce: In those periods when there had been the raising of Joseph from the keeper in the prison to a place of authority close to the king, then the entity—Zerlva—was a princess of the second wife of the King of Egypt in that period. His name is given here in the Exodus itself.

The entity in those periods was acquainted with the family of Joseph's wife; and thus became a worshiper of the one God.

After the famine and the restoration of the princess and the princes of Egypt, and the high priests of the various groups or cults, the entity then interested self in the activities of those peoples that sought gold and silver, and the gems that became a part of the regalia of the princess and prince of the Egyptian people, and that became a part of those things sought that were loaned to the children of Israel when they went out of Egypt. [Genesis 15:14; Exodus 3:21-22, 12:35–36]

This early period, though, was some several hundred years before this gold was turned to the Israelites by the Egyptians. But it was a portion of this same gold that was loaned to the children of Israel when they were led out.

The princess cared for those records that were kept for the peoples during that period, and became one loved not only by her own people but by the sages or older members of the household of the children of Israel. For it was the Israelites that the entity used for or entrusted with the activity of the mining of its holdings in the upper portion, or the southernmost portion of Egypt, in the hills and the mountains there.

1825-2

The city of Heliopolis—or On—was a great Egyptian center of culture and learning. Joseph married the daughter of the high priest of this city, and thus was in a position to be exposed to and represent the very best in the arts and schooling of this flourishing civilization. This city later became known as Alexandria. A teen-age Jewish girl was told in her reading that she had been the daughter of the high priest, and wife of Joseph:

. . . the entity was in the land now known as Egypt, when there were those turmoils that arose with those activities just before the periods of the famines in the land.

There the entity was that one whom Joseph chose as the companion, of all the peoples that were a part of his experience—the daughter of the high priest of Heliopolis.

Thus we find that the entity came under those tenets, those truths which were so much a part of her companion.

In the experience the entity gained throughout; in the abilities to make adjustments for the peoples of various beliefs, various activities—that brought peace and harmony throughout the sojourn in that land.

With the entrance of Joseph's father, the entity then—Asenath—studied what had been a part of the customs of the early patriarchs—Isaac, Abraham—who had been those who had brought such satisfaction, such an awareness.

Hence, as has been first indicated, the deep convictions of the spirit as may make alive in materiality are innate in this entity; and, with deep meditation, these may be aroused to mental *and* material activity in the entity's relationship to others—as a helpful influence to all.     2444-1

Everyone who came in contact with Joseph was influenced by him. With the arrival of Jacob in Egypt, carrying with him the legends and teachings of his ancestors, perhaps Pharaoh and others began to realize the real source of Joseph's abilities. An elderly Protestant widow was told she had been in Pharaoh's household during the time of Joseph. The reading speaks of a new teaching, or understanding, introduced to the people.

. . . the entity was in the Egyptian land, during those periods when there were those uprisings, when the activities and changes were wrought by the entrance and the raising of Joseph to position in the land.

The entity then was of the household of Pharaoh, who brought things to pass by the activities in that land. Thus we find the acquaintance with a new religious force, the new undertakings by peoples, and the variations between the spirit of an activity and the reality in physical manifestation (which is so seldom understood), or between the corporal and the spiritual.

In that experience the entity made manifest much of judgment, much of kindness, much of patience, and brought those activities that made for the greater expression, greater expansion, greater understanding through those trying periods of those peoples.

The name then was Tekla. The entity rose in authority and in power, and throughout the period of its experience in all the earth there were economic, social, religious developments for all those peoples.

In the present we find that power, might—by position, by association—should never be abused, but used to the glory of the Creative Force as prompted the entity through that experience.          2612-1

The interpretations of the names of Joseph's two sons (Genesis 41:51–52) indicate how deeply he felt the suffering and outrage of his slavery and bondage. His anger is also shown in his accusation of his brothers as spies. Yet, as the following reading suggests, the deeper motivations in his relationships with his brothers was to return good for evil. Joseph tested his brothers. By concealing his identity and making all the trouble he did before revealing himself, his brothers had time to realize they were meeting their own sins. (Genesis 42:21)

The condition of the inner-man is reflected outwardly in weather patterns, climate changes, and other aspects of the environment. This concept, found in the Cayce readings, is supported by many passages in the Bible. In the following, a suggestion is made that the seven years of famine were karmic in nature, a reflection of the sins of the people. A Quaker teacher, and student of metaphysics, was told:

> . . . the entity was in the Egyptian land, during that period when there were sore distresses being brought about by the sins of the peoples—and when Joseph was in the land.
>
> There we find the entity was among the daughters of Pharaoh who ruled in that experience; coming in contact with Joseph and Joseph's interpretation of a living God.
>
> This aroused in the experience of the entity, as Princess Teheru, the longing for a greater understanding, greater interpretation, as material blessings were shown. And the tendency for the entity to turn these into such became a stumbling block.
>
> Yet, as there were those expressions of activities in which there were material blessings, there was love manifested. When there was given that understanding to the Princess as to how Joseph had made himself known to his brethren, and thus had asked Pharaoh—through the pleadings of the entity—that he might seek his father in his old age, and to his brethren give good for evil, there came another awakening to the entity in those experiences when there were such activities that the peoples brought those forces into the founding of what may indeed be called the Society of Magicians. This was founded, not for that purpose

into which same has been turned, but by the offices of this entity.

Again, beware of that which holdeth not wholly to the spirit of the Christ, as it may be made manifest in the lives and hearts of men everywhere. 2067–1

Joseph's abilities as a dream interpreter came through his attunement with the divine, or God within him. The other magicians attempted to decipher dreams through patient study of the known laws and rules. Because Joseph was attuned to the Highest, he was able to succeed when the others failed.

One entity was told he was one of the magicians in Pharaoh's court:

. . . the entity was in the Egyptian land, during those periods when there were the activities in which the land was ruled by an unknown entity—through unusual circumstances—which brought to the experience of the entity the unusual experiences.

For, the entity was among the magicians of Pharaoh's court during the period of Joseph's rise to power, and through those periods in which there was the consummation of the changing to the various conditions that arose in might and power through those periods. This brought that temperament, that tendency latent and manifested, for the questionings of powers, influences, and forces that direct human experience.

The name then was Tep-Lepan. The entity gained, the entity lost; gained during the periods of deeper thought and meditation, lost in the period of grudges, the period of attempt to apply necromancy as related to the magic, or the reasonings. 2386–1

## The Death of Joseph

And Joseph took an oath of the children of Israel, saying "God will surely visit you, and ye shall carry up my bones from hence."

*So Joseph died, being an hundred and ten years old; and they embalmed him, and he was put in a coffin.* (Genesis 50:25-26)

According to the Bible class lessons, Edgar Cayce believed Joseph had foreknowledge about his descendants going into bondage. This premonition, Cayce said, may have been Joseph's reason for the oath, which requested his body be kept with them. During the forty years in the wilderness, the children of Israel carried Joseph's body with them, although no mention is made of those who had the responsibility of caring for it. This was four centuries after Joseph's death.

If his kinsmen had taken his body to Canaan immediately after his death, as they did with Jacob, perhaps the Egyptians would not have allowed the Israelites back into Egypt to settle—and history might have been changed.

Apparently Joseph knew that his body would be a protection for his people.

# Exodus

*From* the time of Joseph until Moses there had been no noteworthy happenings to confirm the covenant which had been made with Abraham. The first chapters of Exodus, with background, details, and significant events in the early life of Moses, lead up to the renewal of the covenant. Through Moses God affirms the eternal contract He has made between Himself and His people—Humanity!

Not only is the covenant renewed through Moses, but it is enlarged upon, with the addition of definite roles, regulations, and laws which must be followed. New prophecies and promises are added. Many of the events throughout Exodus are the fulfillment of prophecies which have already been made.

As one through whom the covenant was being renewed, Moses had to become a "living" example of the power and presence of the God he worshipped. He not only had to receive and record the law, he also had to comprehend its significance and be able to interpret it for those he had to lead. In order to have this understanding, he had to live in accord with all that came through him as a divine channel.

In Egypt, as in every other country at that time the people worshipped idols, statues, and other physical objects which represented attributes and activities of their gods. For the Egyptian, the serpent was the god of wisdom. The bull represented strength. The hawk and the eagle governed mental superiority. Everything that was necessary for material existence was represented by some figure. They were worshipped by those Egyptians who were seeking to manifest the particular attributes or aspects embodied in that god.

When Moses approached Pharaoh and asked that his people be given their freedom to worship, Pharaoh wanted to know what their god was like. He assumed it would be represented in some definite, concrete material form.

Moses was challenged with the task of bringing the Hebrews, once again, into the realization that their God was a living God, one whom they could worship in spirit, and who would answer prayer. In this crucial period in Israel's history, Moses established a new relationship between man and God. Before this, the people always worshipped the God of their fathers. The people never prayed, "Our God—My God," but always to the God of Abraham, Isaac, and Jacob. Moses established a means by which God can be approached directly, and thus become more personal to each individual.

Edgar Cayce felt that the new identity of God as Jehovah was like a sign to the people. The name made Him more personal, just as the name Jesus does for the Christian. Throughout the Exodus, the Hebrews began to feel, experience, and comprehend the awareness of the presence of the divine in their lives. Jehovah became the most endearing word by which they could refer to this all-powerful, unseen, creative force manifesting through them. The covenant which had been made to Abraham, Isaac, and Jacob began to be more real to them.

This promise, Edgar Cayce said in one of his Bible class lectures, was renewed in Jesus, who said he would bring into remembrance *all* things, even from the foundations of the world. Just as it was necessary for the Hebrews then, he taught, it is the responsibility of the individual today to make that promise real in his own life.

## Joshua: An Aide to Moses

The first five books of the Bible are called the Torah by the Jews and represent the most significant portions of their Scripture. Although traditionally attributed to Moses, Edgar Cayce suggests that Joshua may have had a great responsibility in formulating these concepts. Only by accepting the incarnations Cayce attributes to the development of Jesus do we have the basis for understanding the following:

... from the very first of the Old Testament to the very last even of Revelation, He is not merely the subject of the book, He is the author in the greater part, having given to man the mind and the purpose for its having been put in print.　　　　　　　　　　　　　　5322-1

Adam entered the earth to be the savior. Enoch was a prophet, and, if the traditions and legends are accurate, dedicated himself to preserving records of the Law of One. Melchizedek wrote the Book of Job, and was the author of teachings used later by Samuel and Elijah in founding the School of Prophets.

Joseph initiated the first period of bounty and favor for Israel as a nation. After his death, the period he instituted gradually deteriorated into bondage and servitude. After the passage of four hundred years, this soul then reincarnated as Joshua and was instrumental in leading Israel out of Egypt into the Promised Land of Canaan, for the second material kingdom in their history.

Although "writings of Joseph" are mentioned once in the Cayce readings, nothing is known about them. Yet, they must have influenced, or have been assimilated into portions of our Scripture.

Two readings refer to Joshua as the "interpreter" and "mouthpiece" for Moses. Reading 364-5 states Genesis was compiled from existing, ancient records and from information obtained by Moses through deep meditation. Joshua no doubt aided Moses in understanding the meanings of the old manuscripts and interpreting those experiences while in altered states of consciousness. It is quite possible both Joshua and Moses were psychic and clairvoyant.

It is twice recorded that Joshua accompanied Moses when he went to commune with the Lord on the mountaintop (Exodus 24:13) and in the tabernacle (Exodus 33:7). Only Joshua was permitted to do this. Not even Aaron, Moses' own brother, was allowed to accompany Moses.

In the light of these possibilities, Joshua becomes one of the most outstanding and significant characters of the Old Testament.

## The Birth of Moses

Four-hundred-year cycles play a recurrent part in the spiritual history of Israel When the book of Exodus opens, the four-hundred-year period of captivity foretold to Abraham is nearly completed. Four centuries have passed between the death of Joseph and this soul's rebirth as Joshua. An identical time span occurs between his last Old Testament incarnation as Jeshua, the high priest at the time of the rebuilding of Jerusalem, and his birth as Jesus.

Throughout the later history of Israel, it will be seen that the prayers of the people in times of distress or servitude have resulted in the incarnation of a great leader. Moses is the first of these figures, and the one who dominates the entire Old Testament. Many other great leaders will follow, who always arise when the people have returned to dependency on God.

The details of Moses' birth and his being set adrift on the Nile, to be discovered by the princess, are a familiar story to all of us. However, in a reading for an Iowa housewife, who was told she had been a hand-maiden to this princess, Cayce supplied additional facts. Note the touch-ing detail about the lilies.

> **Before that, we find the entity was in the Egyptian land when there were those beginnings of the preparations for the coming of the lawgiver. The entity was among those of the maids to the princess of Egypt, and the individual who waded into the river to bring the little ark or bassinet ashore with the babe in same. About the babe were lilies, which is a portion of the symbol, and it is a gentle reminder of the law given by the entity [Moses] whom the servant or maid brought to this princess. These should be reminders and thus keeping the law. For the law of the Lord is perfect and it converts the soul as application is made in same through patience. The name then was Abatha. 5373-1**

The orthodox interpretation has always been that the child was im-mediately taken into the Egyptian court and raised as an Egyptian, with the child's mother hired as his nurse. Yet the following reading, given in 1944 for a woman from Pennsylvania, indicates the child was not raised as an Egyptian for the first several years, but in his own home, among his own people. Several members of the Egyptian household accompa-nied the child, and, like this maiden, were exposed to the spiritual in-fluences in that home.

> **Before that, we find the entity was in the land when there were these who gathered about the ark which had been placed in the Nile. The entity was then a maid to Pharaoh's daughter and one who was given the privilege to be in the household of Moses' mother during the rearing of**

the babe who became the lawgiver to the world. For this is the basis of the activity. Thus the entity, in the name then Tanai, heard the prayers, not only of Jochabed, but Miriam, as this entity saw the child grow and knew that for which it was destined, that there were those forces, those influences such that indeed the soul of each entity is a corpuscle in the body of God.                                                                       5367-1

Another woman, a Christian service volunteer in her present life, was told she had been an instructor to Moses. The reading also suggests an exchange of ideas and information between the Egyptian teachers and the Hebrews:

Before that, the entity was in the Egyptian land, during that period when there were the preparations for those activities which brought about the return of the children of promise to the Promised Land.

The entity then was in the household of the Pharaoh, and in the name Tahi. The entity encouraged those activities and aided in the instruction of Moses as not merely an Egyptian but from the associations with Jochabed, the entity learned from the scribe Ezakiai [?] of those promises that had been made to the saints before Abraham, Isaac, and Jacob.

These became a part of the entity's experience. And when there were the journeyings from the Egyptian land, the entity was among those who went with Moses, Aaron, and Miriam; the entity being a close associate of Miriam through those periods of journeying, and strengthened the hands of those who aided in preparing the way.                        2574-1

The sympathy and understanding of many highly placed Egyptians is further evidenced in this extract:

Before that, the entity was in the earth during the period when there were those preparations for the journeying of the people of promise from the Egyptian land, in that period when the Pharaohs were in authority over that people.

The entity then was the daughter of Pharaoh, and a sister of Bithiah who nurtured and brought up Moses as her son. This daughter was not mentioned in Holy Writ, yet she wielded a power for good in those periods, even as did Bithiah.

The entity aided in changing the edicts by the influence it wielded

over the overseers and the counselors to that Pharaoh; thus lightening,
in a great extent, the burdens of those people.                    2550-1

## *Moses Slays an Egyptian*

And it came to pass in those days, when Moses was grown up, that
he went out among his brethren, and saw their oppression; and he saw
an Egyptian beating a Hebrew, one of his brethren of the Children of
Israel.

*And he looked this way and that way, and when he saw that there was
no man watching, he slew the Egyptian and hid him in the sand.* (Exodus
2:11-12)

Using this episode as it is presented in the Bible, Cayce and his Bible
students drew the following conclusions:

"According to Egyptian law, Moses should not have taken the
Hebrew's side. This incident shows his sympathies were entirely with
the Hebrews. Moses had a violent temper. This is indicated in many instances throughout his life.

"Although he was trying to help them, the Hebrews resented it and
taunted Moses with their knowledge of the slaying. This is the attitude
of many today who are in trouble and yet resent any interference.

"Who told Pharaoh about the slaying? It must have been one of the
Hebrews, someone who had no more understanding of Moses' purposes
than the one who disputed with him. To the Hebrews, Moses was an
Egyptian. They did not know he was one of them, who wanted to help
his people. Perhaps they thought it was a personal malice ,which
prompted Moses to kill the taskmaster. He did it so quickly, in a fit of
temper, the Hebrews never knew the real reason."

Just as Cayce suggested to his Bible class, perhaps the real reason for
this murder has never been known or understood. The version we have
in the Scripture is framed in such a way that it highlights Moses' love
for and involvement with the Hebrews. Yet a different story of this same
incident is told in a Life reading given for an attractive twenty-year-old
woman:

Before this, we find the entity was in that period when many changes were brought to a people throughout the world.

The entity then was in that land now known as Egyptian, during the period when the princess Hatherpsut (the entity's mother) was in power; and the entity's name was Sidiptu, hence a sister of that leader Moses, the lawgiver of Israel.

During the reign of the mother, the entity was associated with those people later despised on account of the love (physical) that the mother found in association with a peoples.

And the entity was then pledged to one of the leaders of Israel, in the house of Levi; and being despoiled by an Egyptian, it was *this* one that the brother, Moses, slew, hence causing that disruption which brought— at the latter period of the mother's and the entity's sojourn in the land— a *new* pharaoh to the *ruling* of the peoples; this one coming then from the mountain or southern land of an almost divided land over this incident in the entity's experience.

While the entity may be said to have gained and lost, gained and lost through the experience, under the tutelage of those peoples with whom the brother was associated—as did the entity's mother—much understanding was brought of the legends of a people that had been called for a particular service.

*This* is noteworthy of interest, then, in the entity's experience in the present; that to the entity, one that has had an experience that deals with the universal manifestation of a spiritual or unseen power is sacred to the entity.

Hence another reason for precaution in self, as the developments come—and will come, if there will be the application of self in the mysteries of the unseen that may come for self.

And it is well that self, when contemplating and meditating, surround self with the environs of an oriental nature; for the dress itself should ever be rather the robes or loose clothing about the body. There should ever be something that is *old*, something that is plaid; something that bespeaks of either the scarab, bull, or serpent; with the perfumes of the East.

But know that these are but those things that will make for the arousing of the *inner* self, and *not* the force that *arises*; rather a *material* element for the *producing* of same.

And the abilities from the experience of the entity in Egypt may be brought forward in the present, in aiding to give much to peoples that seek for the development of self and of their relationships with the Creative Forces and their relationships to their fellow man.

For, the wisdom of Hatherpsut may be in the entity in the present experience as a builder in a mental, a commercial, or a material way.

The spirit of the mother in that experience, then, may *yet* aid and guide in the present; *beautiful* in body, *beautiful* in mind in the experience, yet turned the world upside down!                355-1

The Edgar Cayce readings admonished many individuals to be either hot or cold—good or bad—but *be* and *do* something. God can work with desires and emotions, no matter at what level, as long as they are in action. But He cannot work with energies that have become static or lukewarm. (See Revelation 3:14–16.)

Although the anger that resulted in the taking of a life cannot be condoned, the necessity to flee took Moses to a place where there could be the further unfolding of his own consciousness, and of his destiny. The flight from Egypt took Moses to the land of Midian, where he married into the household of Reul, a priest of that land. (Exodus 2:15–22)

The Eastern sages have a saying that "when the pupil is ready, the teacher appears."

Reul is also called Jethro, an honorary title connected with his office as priest. Reul is also referred to as a prince of Midian, and the Midianites were descendants of Abraham. Jethro must have been well versed in the lore, legends, and teachings concerning Abraham. He no doubt was familiar with the prophecy in Genesis 15:12–15, concerning the years of bondage.

Now that this period was nearly over, we wonder how the priest interpreted the strange events which led an Egyptian prince of Hebrew blood to his tent. Perhaps Reul had already been prepared through dream or vision and recognized Moses as the channel through which the prophecy of deliverance would be fulfilled. As a shepherd, alone in the midst of nature for long periods of time, Moses had ideal conditions in which to absorb the teachings of his father-in-law, and to meditate upon his destiny. While his people in Egypt "groaned under their oppression" and began to build the desire to be free, Moses was preparing himself for the part he was to play.

## The Burning Bush

The burning bush that appeared to Moses appeared in a vision to a member of Cayce's original Search for God group. The interpretation which Cayce gave to her can be applied equally as well to Moses:

> **(Q)** Please explain the experience I had on the morning of July 17, in which I saw a pyramid of smoke over my head and then a burning bush within. What do these symbols mean?
> **(A)** The awakening to that as must be a portion of the experience necessary for the full cleansing, the full awakening to the possibilities that lie within.
> How hath He given that ye shall be purged? Even as by fire. This, to be sure, is emblematical; that thy service may rise as sweet incense from the altar of service in thyself. So long as ye look upon a service done, a good deed, as a lesson, as a duty, as a service, so long are ye subject to same.
> When to do good is the joy, when to deny self is a pleasure, then thou wilt know the *I AM* is awakened within. 262-85

Like this woman, Moses had to be brought to the point where there could be an awakening to the purposes for which he had entered into the earth, and to realize the "possibilities" within that would aid him in fulfilling that purpose. At the time of his vision, Moses was handicapped by fear and doubts. He felt unable to lead the people because they did not know him, and hindered as a spokesman because he was a stutterer. But as he applied himself, he outgrew his limitations and gradually became aware of the "I AM" within.

Perhaps Yahweh, or Jehovah, was such an endearing and an oft invoked name, because of the effect the sound vibrations had upon the conscious and subconscious minds. It was the word which Moses heard during his experience of inner awakening. The combinations of the letters and the phonetic sound of a word, which Cayce suggested to one individual to stimulate an inner awakening, is very reminiscent of the "I AM THAT I AM," or JEHOVAH, heard by Moses—and carries the same significance!

> **(Q)** Give meaning and pronunciation of the word J-A-H-H-E-V-A-H-E.

(A) Java; meaning the ability within itself to know itself to be itself and yet one with, or one apart from, the infinite; to be a part of that realm of helpers; to know self as a part of and in that realm where the angels are, or in that realm of the individuals who have been, who are, with the Announcer, the Lord of the Way, and who have attained the consciousness of the Christ-within.                    2533-8

## A Discussion

The Bible records a dialogue between Moses and God:

*And Moses said to the Lord, "I beseech thee, O, My Lord, I am not eloquent, neither heretofore nor since thou hast spoken to thy servant; for I am a stutterer and slow of speech."*

*The Lord said to him, "Who has made man's mouth? or who makes the dumb, Or the deaf, or the seeing, or the blind? Is it not I, the Lord?*

*Now therefore go, and I will be with you, mouth and teach what you shall speak." And Moses said to him, "O, My Lord, send I beseech thee, by the hand of whomsoever thou wilt send."*

*And the anger of the Lord kindled against Moses, and he said to him, "Behold Aaron, your brother, the Levite. I know that he is a good speaker, and also behold, he will come forth to meet you, and when he sees you, he will be glad in his heart.*

*And you shall speak to him and put my words in his mouth; and I will be with your mouth and with his mouth, and will teach you what you shall do."* (Exodus 4:10-15)

Actually, these issues, such as the power of God, Moses' limitations, and Aaron's usefulness, could have been debated by Moses and his kinsmen. The following was given to a middle–aged Lutheran minister:

**Before that, we find the entity was in the land of the high hill, but much different than is presented by the name alone in the present. For the entity was among those who aided, studied, disputed with Moses when he had had his vision that he must return to Egypt for the relieving of the pressure upon the chosen people. Not because of any particular thing, save their desire, their search, their one ideal in the fact of a living God that might be touched with the infirmities of the human experience.**
                                                    **5159-2**

In another reading, Cayce says Moses was "slow to comprehend" (5276-1) the message of the burning bush. However, through the convictions brought about during that vision and from the understanding derived from study and debate with his kinsmen, Moses was ready to commit his purpose into action. Willing as his spirit was, he applied it with misunderstanding.

When there had been fulfilled that preparation, or a part preparation of material knowledge of Moses, he set about to put into activity that purpose for which he had come into the earth. Yet materially he chose an error, a sin, in establishing the righteousness of his fellow men. Thus a full period was required—as of earthly righteousness or earthly knowledge—to undo or to coordinate that [which] was to be a working principle of righteousness versus sin. *Then* he was *called*; as was Paul in his persecution of the church, conscious of a purpose but *active, doing* something *toward* an activity which by education to him (physically) was correct, yet sin.

He, too, was called and directed. So, too, may each individual be active in principle, in purpose, being sincere, being direct. Thus may the individual gain the greater working knowledge of that which is righteous, versus that which is sin.

Then, let each be not slothful, not putting off, not unmindful that ye must be up and doing, working, BUSY at that which is to thee, *now, today,* that as thy conscience directs thee to do; in sincere, direct manner. And ye may be sure He counts that try as righteousness; and the sin that may appear to self or to others is but upon the reverse—which is righteousness.                                          262-126

Once we realize we have a purpose, or a "calling," we should not let fear or ignorance hold us back. If we begin to apply what we know we are supposed to do, guidance, direction, and further enlightenment will follow. Using Moses as an illustration, Cayce points to this spiritual law in the following:

(Q) In what way may I best attain my ideal?
(A) In the applying of self day by day in every way, that thou knowest, that makes a personal application of that thou knowest to do, without questioning of the morrow; for the morrow has its evils and its goods, sufficient unto self. Today is! Use that thou hast in hand. So does the

awakening come. Even as called by God to lead a people, as was Moses, a shepherd, and the flocks in Moab. Use what thou hast in hand, for the ground whereon thou standest is holy! Do thou likewise!    262-13

Perhaps, instead of establishing a concept of racial superiority, the more spiritually correct attitude would have been an expression of universal brotherhood in which no race or special group was favored, as is seen in the following:

(Q) What should be the attitude of this country toward the refugee problem as it relates specifically to the Jewish people? Please explain their problems.
(A) They are like every other individual. *Their* problems, so long as *all* are considered, is one. If they themselves become secular or become tyrannical in their nature, then this—too—will become a problem in America.
     The attitude toward the refugees—they that entertain those who are without home, or hungry, may entertain the Lord himself. For "As ye do it unto the least, ye do it unto thy Maker." That should be the attitude, ever. But *live*, each soul, in such a manner as to implant not the bigness of the individual but the love of God made manifest among men!
     These are problems not only, then, of the Jewish peoples, but of those of every cult, or every "ism" or "cism." For remember the first principle—*all* are equal before God!                3976-24

## Pharaoh's Hard Heart

Oft will it be learned by the study of phenomena of a people's action, that seemingly all forces in the universe are used to bring about that which is good, for it has been said, "I will harden the heart of Pharaoh, that he will not let my children go." Through this same seed came the Son of Man, and through these same trials through which the forefathers passed, the burdens and sins of the world were laid upon the Son.
     Then, through the trials, the temptations, the besetters of evil from within and from without, may any work that is His [God's] be expected to grow, and in that manner become polished bright, and a shining light unto the world.                254-31

Why did God harden Pharaoh's heart? The power of a living God had to be impressed upon the minds of the people. Several hundred thousand people had to be convinced that the plagues and miracles conjured by Moses were not merely magician's tricks, but actually manifestations of God's power, and a result of Moses' attunement. The Egyptian magicians were students of metaphysical laws. Either through feats of materialization, or thought–control over the minds of others, they could make sticks turn into snakes, or have grains of sand change into lice or fleas. The magicians were versed in all the possibilities contained in the manipulation of three dimensional laws. Yet Moses and Aaron were able to go beyond these feats because they were attuned to an infinite source of Creative Energy.

A gifted leader is able to sway throngs of people to respond to great causes, but it takes faith in a spiritual ideal—not just a belief—for individuals to keep their attention and efforts consistently and persistently focused in one direction.

If the people believed Moses was merely a better magician than the Egyptians, there would not be sufficient devotion to carry them through the trials once they achieved their freedom. They had to believe that God was speaking through Moses, and that Moses was manifesting His power. Moses later tried to teach the people that they, too, could attune themselves to God and that He would speak to them. In essence, Moses was telling them that all the magic could be theirs if they would attune themselves to God and use it for His purposes.

Most of us are like these Hebrews, Cayce explained. Human nature does not change. We believe in God, but every time a hardship or difficulty arises, we falter in our beliefs.

Just as human nature stays the same, so do the magic and miracles of that period—we merely call it by other names. Today scientists are still working with three dimensional concepts and understanding. And what is it they discover? Just another way of using God's laws. Their discoveries may be used for the glorification of the Spirit in the earth, or result in the destruction of everything that is good, including the best that is within us.

Unless the Pharaoh's heart became "hardened," there never could have been built a great desire in the people to follow Moses. The increasing manifestations of the great power he was united with was essential in building that desire. All the things which happened then were necessary to raise the morale and consciousness of the people who had been slaves for several hundred years.

A teacher to Moses learned much as she watched the changes in the hearts and minds when Moses returned and set the people free. In 1942, this entity was a widow, a nurse, and a student of Unity, but in the past . . .

> . . . the entity was in the Egyptian land, when there were those peoples making preparation for the sojourning from there. The entity was among the children of those peoples who saw that activity; being then a maid to Pharaoh's daughter that discovered the babe, Moses, that saw the unfolding of that life in the varied environs, that heard much of the cries of those peoples as through those years their tasks were made harder and harder.
>
> It may be said that the entity was a teacher, in a manner, to Moses; and thus the wisdom of old is of special interest to the entity. Ritualistic activities of mind and body to bring effects within same find a deep something within the entity.
>
> The name then was Zeruba. The entity gained the greater in the mental and spiritual unfoldment in the experience, as it watched, as it meditated upon the happenings as the entity grew older and watched the unfoldment of those who were in authority and as these things changed in their relationship to the material happenings.
>
> Thus lands, nations, various peoples, and their problems as peoples and individuals are of interest. Thus the entity is innately something of a historian, as well as mentally and manifestedly in mind. These abilities may be used to material advantage if the spiritual purposes are in keeping with that which is ever creative, as manifested in the Son.
>
> 2851-1

How did Moses feel as he returned to Egypt? He had obtained a very high state of consciousness through his experiences in Midian, under Jethro's tutelage. Now the knowledge he obtained demanded application. This is a law the readings constantly pointed to—"Knowledge not applied is sin." Moses had foreknowledge of the slaying of the first-born, and knew he had to prophesy this to Pharaoh if he refused to release the Hebrews. Moses certainly believed in the divinity of his mission and the fact of God's protection, for what he was called to do was almost certain death under the laws of the state.

With his first confrontation with the Pharaoh, Moses had every right to believe the prophecy about his heart was correct. Pharaoh reacted the way men who have held absolute power have done through the ages. His religion or philosophy made him the most important figure in the earth, and kin to the divinities of heaven. Pharaoh was not ready to change this concept for another which might alter his opinion of himself.

## The Plagues

The basis for a later experience as a helper to Joan of Arc, Cayce told this young lady, is found in her life as an assistant to Moses and a witness to those many miraculous deeds.

> Before that the entity was in the Egyptian land, when there were those preparations for the exodus; during those periods when the lawgiver was active in bringing the awareness or consciousness to the pharaohs of that period.
>
> The entity then was of the household of that assistant to Moses—that is, of Aaron's household; not as a daughter or as a relative, but rather as a helper in that preparation needed for those periods of activity. Hence, as is experienced by the entity, there is latent within self a constant looking for divine or outside interference with activities of individuals or groups, and rarely does the entity look to same for itself. Yet know, as the lawgiver gave, it is within self. For, thy body is indeed the temple of the living God, and there He meets thee.
>
> The name then was Ceclia. 2936-2

Another reading tells us:

> Magicians then were not merely sleight of hand performers, or presti-digitators, or those who worked mysteries, but rather they were—as would be termed today—the lawyers, or the students of laws of *every* nature pertaining to the ruling and directing of the subjects of a kingdom or of a household. 2386-1

Because the magicians of Egypt were versed in the arts of reproducing phenomena, they could easily duplicate Aaron's feat when he cast down his staff and it turned into a serpent. (Exodus 7:8-11) The Egyptians, as Edgar Cayce points out, were schooled in all magic—or laws—up to a certain point. But the ability—or attunement and purpose—of

Moses and Aaron enabled them to transcend that level of material knowledge.

*For they cast down every man his staff and they became serpents; but Aaron's staff swallowed up their staffs.* (Exodus 7:12)

Perhaps it was a flash of intuition, or an inspired moment. There is a tradition, as Churchward points out,[16] that this confrontation was between the minds of Aaron and Moses and the priesthood. They were both schooled in occult sciences, and thus able to raise the level of their vibrations beyond that of the Pharaoh or any other person present. A mass hypnotism resulted in which these people were compelled to see things as they were imaged by these masters. Because of the attunement of Moses and Aaron, and the spontaneous creativity that seems to earmark much of God's action, they created an image which the magicians were not able to surpass.

On the second of August, 1939, a theatrical technician who listed his religious preference as "practicing the Golden Rule" was told he had been a magician in Pharaoh's court. An aptitude for "new ideas" stems from that life.

**Before that we find the entity was in the Egyptian land when there were the persecutions, when the kings had forgotten Joseph.**

**There we find the entity was among those of the household of the pharaohs of that experience; and yet favoring the teachers because of the dreams, the visions, the interest in the magical things of that day. These brought to the entity much disturbance, and yet—as was experienced in the latter part of that sojourn—even with the departure of the children of Israel—the entity became more and more an adept in soothsaying; bringing to itself much of power and much of the ability to direct the lives and affairs of the many.**

**These then may in the present bring activities or abilities to direct many, especially in those things as would have to do with the creating of new ideas as for conveniences in the home, the office, or the store. These are activities through which the entity may gain the greater, the designing in woods or metals. These are the channels for expression for the entity.**

**But, first learn to govern self. Learn patience, learn mercy, learn judgment. Get understanding, and abuse it not. And when these are**

---

[16]James Churchward, *The Children of Mu* (New York: Paperback Library).

**applied in the experience, we will find those abilities in those directions such—as indicated—as to bring harmony, peace, and understanding; and greater success materially, socially.** **1974-1**

The following reading suggests the plagues of Egypt may have been a result of the life style of the Egyptians:

**Consider the days of old, these are not foolish! When there were the families that produced upon the farm, how much better not only were the lives of the individuals but the character of the product—and there were not half so many pests to deal with!**

**And whence came they? From the same place that the flies and the fleas and the grasshoppers came to plague Egypt.** **470-35**

A commentary on the ten plagues of Egypt was made by Edgar Cayce in his Tuesday Night Bible Class. This was not delivered in the trance state of his readings, but as a series of evening lectures:

"The judgments of God or Egypt were called plagues. We will consider each one in its proper order.

"First, the Nile is changed into blood. We might say the ten plagues are symbolical of the various stages of evolution. In our study of creation, it has been considered that physical evolution emanates first from water. Man must spiritualize his creative impulses. In the last stage (the slaying of the first-born) it is only possible through the shedding of blood for redemption; in other words, sacrificing the individual life blood for the ideal. The pattern was shown to us through Jesus. Individually, we have our own shedding of blood to do. Not physically as He did, but in giving up our own purposes for His.

"Symbolically, the 'first-born' of any situation, from Cain on down, seems to represent the selfish impulses that brought about our involvements in materiality. What is the *first* reaction in a situation? Does it bespeak of self's spirit or the Christ's? The plagues remind one of Jesus' teaching, 'There is no remission of sin save through the shedding of blood.' It is only through tribulation and sacrifice that we shed selfishness from our activities.

"The second plague was the visitation of frogs. (Exodus 8:1-5) Frogs were particularly worshipped by many Egyptians, especially in the king's household. They were considered a great delicacy, and raised as food for the court. This visitation showed the Egyptians that the Israelites' God had the power to raise instantly that which took the Egyptians great care and time to produce.

"The third plague—the infestation of lice (Exodus 9:16)—demonstrates God's power to create living creatures, or insects, from an unnatural source. Lice are blood sucking insects, and would first have appeared upon the bodies of individuals or animals. Therefore, the Egyptians could not say the lice 'just happened' because of the unusual filth conditions. It could be said, however, that the lice were a natural result of the water having been turned to blood. The very moisture in the ground, if it were blood instead of water, would have made a natural breeding ground.

"In the fourth plague we find the first difference in the Egyptians' feelings toward the children of Israel. The Egyptians were beginning to realize that the Hebrews were favored by a divine influence. (Exodus 8:30-32) Pharaoh was willing to permit the children of Israel to rest from their labors a few days and make sacrifices to their God. But Moses could not accept this. He knew he had to get the people out of the land entirely and away from the Egyptian influence.

"The fifth plague (Exodus 9:1-7) was striking at their source of supply. The disease on the cattle and the other beasts of burden was hitting at their pocketbooks.

"We notice after the third plague that the children of Israel were not afflicted as were the Egyptians. They seemed to be immune after that plague. Perhaps this indicates the Israelites had become so in tune with Moses' purpose that such things did not come near them. Today we still hear of people who believe that if they hold the proper mental attitude mice, flies, mosquitoes, or any other kind of pest will not bother them.

"It has been indicated that the fifth plane of consciousness is the highest an earthbound consciousness can attain. This is interesting in the light of the sixth plague (Exodus 9:8-12) being the first the Egyptian magicians could not duplicate. It is also the first time these magicians could not immunize themselves from the plague's effects.

"Boils usually come from a condition of the blood. The blood had become susceptible to boils because of conditions resulting from the previous plagues. However, the children of Israel were immune. Possibly they were receiving guidance on how to keep their blood purified. We know that when we are sincere in our efforts, the next step is always shown us.

"The plague of the hailstorm (Exodus 9:13–35) was the first plague in which the choice of the individual became the governing factor. With the forewarning of the hail, every individual had the opportunity to choose if he would believe in the power of the God of Moses', or trust in Pharaoh's protection.

"This was the first time Pharaoh repented and admitted that he and his people were wicked. Human nature has not changed much from that day to this. As soon as things returned to normal, Pharaoh returned to his old ways.

"The plague of locusts is covered in Exodus 10:1–20. After the hail, the Egyptian people knew they should heed the warning about the locust. The people wanted Pharaoh to let Moses and his people go. They pleaded with Pharaoh. But Pharaoh could not concede. He had been taught from his birth that he was a god and all powerful. It was difficult for him to acknowledge his slaves' God was more powerful than he. It is also stated over and over again, 'God hardened Pharaoh's heart.' Perhaps this indicates this particular ruler was working out his own destiny, according to what he had built in the past.

"Pharaoh admitted his guilt again. Yet he went back on his word. It is hard to conceive of an individual who would not be completely overcome after being shown such things repeatedly in such a dramatic manner.

"Exodus 10:21–28 relates the ninth plague, Darkness. This plague signifies the spiritual darkness of an individual who continually refuses to recognize or use the light that is offered.

"Moses would not accept Pharaoh's conditions. When Pharaoh, in his wrath, told Moses not to try and see him again, Moses said, 'Thou has spoken well.' Thereafter, Moses dealt directly with the people.

"Smiting of the first-born, the tenth plague (Exodus 12:29–30), produced greater suffering than all the others.

"Before the last plague, Moses was divinely led to prepare his people for their departure from Egypt. He knew the tenth plague would be the final one. The Israelites were to cleanse their bodies by eating certain specially prepared foods. Their doors were to be marked with the blood of the sacrifice. God knew which were the believers, but this act gave the people a chance to express and show their allegiance.

"After the death of all the first-born, the Egyptians were glad to lend the Israelites anything they had, just to be free of them. The Lord had told Moses beforehand that his people would not leave empty-handed.

"Even when he told Moses to leave, Pharaoh asked for Moses' blessing. Evidently he now feared Moses and in awe of his power. Perhaps he wanted assurance Moses would not continue to call curses on him. Then, the Egyptian people, too, almost demanded that Pharaoh humble himself before Moses. This shows the power a people may exert, even under a monarchy. If sufficient pressure is created, the people *can* demand their rights. They were afraid that if Pharaoh did not accede to Moses' wishes, all would be dead. Also, the other plagues had not touched Pharaoh personally. The people had suffered because of their ruler's stubbornness. They were forced to work harder to keep him supplied with all things which he was accustomed to having. Consequently, the tenth plague, which took his first-born son, touched him for the first time."

A woman was told her interest in metaphysics and mysticism was a result of her Egyptian incarnation at the time of the plagues:

Before that the entity was in the Egyptian land, during those periods when there was the exodus of the children of promise from the land.

The entity was among the household of the pharaohs of that period. Hence all of the mysticism as wrought by that people, as well as the magicians of the own people, was a part of the entity's experience.

Thus, we find the entity *innately*, as well as manifestedly, is drawn to activities of the nature in which all such influences are a part of the experiences of individuals.

The name then was Zeta-Elda; and the entity gained. For though there were trials and sorrows, the activities innate brought the thought of—and the attempt to correlate—the relationships of man to man, with the relationships of man to the eternal influence. This brought great development, and abilities in the experience of the entity that may be applied in the present in an analysis of self and of that which forms the impetus for activities in the lives of others.      2185-1

A poignant note is added in the following. Evidently, the last plague, the slaying of the first-born, touched her personally:

(Q) Have I been associated in any past life with my son Junior, if so, when, where, and how?
(A) As we find, the son was the brother in the Egyptian experience, and was among those taken when the death angel passed over.
Learn what *that* means also, as it may be analyzed, as to the

experiences that have been a part of thy present relationship. How many sorrows, and yet joys and variations of same, in this relationship!

Joy may come out of same, if self holds to self–analysis and determinations.                                                        2185-1

## Freedom!—"The Metaphysical Pattern"

The Edgar Cayce readings insist that, because man has been endowed with free will as a spiritual birthright, nothing but the nature of his desires binds him to any condition. If we listen to the mouthpiece of God within (Exodus 6:9), instead of our own miseries and bondage, we can leave our "Egypt" anytime.

> As an individual in any experience in any period uses that of which it (the soul or entity) is conscious in relation to the laws of Creative Force, so does that soul, that entity, develop toward—what? A companionship with the creative influence!
>
> Hence karma, to those disobeying—by making for self that which would be as the tower of Babel, or as the city of Gomorrah, or as the fleshpots of Egypt, or as the caring for those influences in the experience that satisfy or gratify self without thought of the effect upon that which it has in its own relation to the first cause! Hence to many this becomes the stumbling block.                                        5753-1

We need only sufficient desire, and enough faith to begin to trust to those ever expressive soul forces within, to be guided from experience to experience as we develop an ever–expanding mental–spiritual–physical consciousness. Remember Cayce's statement that the Bible, from Abraham to Christ, is a pattern of mental unfoldment.

> Hence, all that manifests in the material world is a shadow of that which is of mental or spiritual import. As to whether or not each division in mind, matter, becomes sufficient to be indwelling, or an at-onement with the Creative Force, is dependent upon the application of the purposes and desires of such force in its material association in materiality . . .
>
> Then, the knowledge of the existence of such is the mental process. But the *application* of the source of each of these—as a premise in the experience—is that there is the willingness—of that which is the spirit, at

an at-onement with the First Cause, or God, or Creative Force—to be used . . . to produce that as the Creative Force would have signified or manifested in a material world—or constant desire, purpose, will, to be at an at-onement with the Creative Forces in its associations, in its dealings, in its relationships to its fellowmen.       **1861-4**

This extract reiterates that the pattern of mental unfoldment is molded through *service,* "the willingness to be used to produce that as the Creative Forces would have manifested in a material world," and through the seeking after truth, "the constant desire to be at an at-onement with Creative Forces." These are the desires that will lead us out of the thrall of the appetites, the senses, or the ego. But the first step toward freedom leads into the wilderness. Psychologically, once we decide to leave the narrow world of a habitual consciousness, we must confront the subconscious, the repressed and hidden areas of our mind.

"Mind is the factor that is in direct opposition to the Will," Cayce tells us. (3744-1) Like the complaining children of Israel, the old habit patterns, the conditioned thinking, our familiar and unquestioned attitudes and responses, will scream out with desire to return, to go back. Any step forward entails new responsibilities, new obligations. Often, we feel we would rather be bound in servitude, free from responsibilities.

This is our wilderness period. We cannot cross the Jordan into the Promised Land, where there are more battles to be fought, until the conflicting aspects of self are brought under the spiritual function of the Will. When we have the courage to take the responsibility for the *whole* body—spiritual, mental, and physical—raising it from servitude to service, we begin our Moses structure, another phase in that pattern "from Abraham to Christ."

## The Red Sea

The pharaoh within us, until weakened and humbled by the "shedding of blood," would keep the spiritual energy represented by the children of Israel, suppressed, using it for his own desires—to build his monuments and storehouses (Exodus 1:11). Once we can release this energy, and are willing to follow it, the intuitive soul forces within will lead us back to at-onement and The Promised Land, where we become " . . . with power temporal, power mental, power spiritual . . . Sons and Daughters of God . . . joint heirs with Him to the Crown of Glory." 262-36

The crossing of the Red Sea is an emblem, or symbolic expression of the move into a new state of consciousness.

Q. Please explain the Master's statement to Nicodemus, "Ye must be born again."
A. When Nicodemus asked, "How can such things be?" the rebuke came in His answer, "Art thou a teacher in Israel and knoweth not these things?" Or, that all must pass under the rod, even as was given by those teachers that as Moses and the children passed through the sea they were baptized in the cloud and in the sea; as an example, as an omen, as a physical activity of a spiritual, a physical separation from that which had been builded in their experience as the sojourn in Egypt . . . Oh! that all would gather more of that understanding that the soul is a body and the physical is the mere temple, the mere shell, the mere material manifestation of that which may not be touched with hands! For it appears that we must be born again that we may dwell in those mansions not made with hands—but are prepared for those that have washed their robes, their bodies, their souls in the blood. For, ye are ones that may know the truth, if ye will but manifest in thine own experiences that ye have learned in thine meditations with thine God.
Ye must be born in flesh, in spirit again, that ye may make manifest that ye have experienced in thine own soul! 262-60

The water of the river in Eden that divided in four heads was symbolic of a spiritual force entering in the earth. The water of the Red Sea indicates a cleansing, or baptism, as seen in this dream interpretation given by Edgar Cayce for a Jewish stockbroker:

Q. [Dream] Voice: "Now the water is come to wash it all away." I replied, "Aw, it has not. Why we aren't even finished our triangular battle."
A. In this is seen rather that of the spiritual forces as come from the superconscious forces to the subconscious in the representation of the deeper lesson as is to be gained from that as has been often given of old, "All shall be saved so as by water," see? for as the Children of Promise passed through the Red Sea and were all baptized unto Moses, in the Cloud and in the Sea, the lesson then is as of the cleansing of the physical forces to that pure water, that, as is given, to be the work of spiritual

forces, or as is seen again as cleansing with the waters, see? for this becomes necessary in the putting away of those that so easily beset, coming nearer unto that perfect understanding of the spiritual laws of the God manifest in the physical world. 900-132

Whenever we have obtained a separation (or salvation) from destructive forces, we should give thanksgiving. The experience should elevate us into a state of consciousness symbolized by a song of rejoicing, such as this one, the Song of Moses:

*He is mighty and glorious, the Lord Jehovah has become our savior; he is our God, and we will praise him; our Father's God, and we will exalt him . . .* (Exodus 15:2)

Miriam also rejoiced:

*The Miriam the prophetess, the sister of Aaron, took a timbrel in her hand; and all the women went out after her with tambourines and with timbrels. And Miriam answered them, "Sing to the Lord, for he has triumphed gloriously; the horse and his rider he has thrown into the sea."* (Exodus 15:20-21)

The date of the following reading, July, 1924, shows it to be among the first Life readings given by Edgar Cayce. A characteristic of these early readings is their briefness, no matter how notable or interesting the past experience may have been. This reading, for a young Jewish woman, suggests she may have been Miriam, the sister of Moses:

On the one before this, we find in the land of the Promise, where the children came again to the land of Promise from the bondage, and in this entity then we find the sister of the leader of the peoples who were brought from the land, and in this entity then [Moses] were the people led in the praise of Jehovah in the deliverance from the land. (Exodus 15:2, 20-21)

In this present we find the attraction to the hopes of the peoples' return to this Promised Land, and of the peoples again giving the message as of [the] promise to the world, as it will give. 2497-1

The young woman was also told she had been among the Sons of

God who were influences in the creation cycle of Genesis. His final comment to her was:

> Give then of self, putting this in the lives and in the hearts of all, only the spiritual forces and the soul development goes to Jehovah.   2497-1

## *Rebellion*

In the flight from Egypt, the 600,000 men, with their families, household goods, livestock, and all the things they "borrowed" from the Egyptians, must have extended over a large area. In the wilderness of Zin, they were able to group together as a congregation for the first time. Since their numbers were so vast, it was impossible for Moses to have direct personal contact with most of them. Perhaps most of them had never heard him speak. His pronouncements were probably relayed by other people, increasing the chances of misinterpretations and distortions of the original messages.

A young Jew, unemployed at the time of his reading, was told that in past experiences he had been a gambler in the American West, trained gladiators in Rome, and was a trumpeter in Jerusalem at the time of Ezra. He also had been one of those leaders in the Exodus who, through selfishness, rebelled, and brought destruction to the people.

> Before that, we find the entity was in the land *now* known as or called the Egyptian, when there were those activities in the preparation of a people to be delivered under the leadership of the sons of Levi.
>
> There we find the entity was among the relations and friends of the *mother* of Moses and Aaron; and the entity—though among those who were in bondage—was raised to one as a leader in the Exodus.
>
> The entity there gained something of the purposes of creative forces with the children of men, using same in corrective fields—as Zephaniah; and yet in the wilderness turning same to self again—which brought destructive forces into the experience.
>
> But lean ye heavily upon the tenets of old, and the voice which ye heard in the pronouncements throughout those experiences there.
>
> The entity, of course, was not among those who reached the Promised Land, but knew of the faults, the fancies, as well as the judgments of those through that period of thirty-odd years of journeying in the wilderness.

> In the present experience, turn again to those counsels in the
> application of thyself and thy abilities in the present day relationships
> with others.                                                 1881-1

Shortly after the congregation assembled, the winds of rebellion began to blow.

*And the whole congregation of the children of Israel began to murmur*
*against Moses and Aaron in the wilderness;*
*    And the children of Israel said to them, "Would that we had died by*
*the hand of the Lord in the land of Egypt, when we sat by the pots of meat,*
*and when we did eat bread to the full; for you have brought us forth into*
*this wilderness to destroy the whole assembly with hunger." (*Exodus
16:2-3)

Two months after the experience in the Red Sea, the real enemy of
the Hebrews emerged. (Exodus 16:3) Until now, it had been an external
one, the Egyptian oppressors. But now the one that is *within* emerges.
This enemy is much more deadly than their former oppressors, who fed
and clothed them. The spirit of the Hebrews themselves could keep
them embroiled in turmoils and forever wandering through a wilderness.

## *Manna*

*Then the Lord said to Moses, "Behold, I will rain bread from heaven, for*
*I will prove them, whether they will keep my laws or not." (*Exodus 16:4)

This entity, a niece of Aaron's, was both a helper and a rebel in the
wilderness. A credence of legendary events stems from this life. Before
that we find the entity was in the land now known as the Egyptian,
during those periods when there was the cry of the people going up
before the Throne of Grace because of the hardships as put upon them;
for their burdens were heavy in those days.
    The entity then was among these peoples, again of that one chosen
as the priestly tribe, when the law by the leader—by the lawgiver—was
given later in the holy mount. But the entity aided in carrying out those
periods of purifications during those days when there was the making for
the hardening of the heart of the leader and the setting in the minds of

those children of the chosen ones as to the purposes for which they as a people were being called forth.

Then in the name Estrada, the entity was a niece of Aaron, the mouthpiece for the lawgiver. The entity gained and lost during the experience. For as there were the preparations, so did there come—during the periods in the journeys beyond the Red Sea—those periods of wonderment and rebellion in the experience of the entity.

Yet oft in the present the entity has felt that she has in some manner been a portion of many of those things that are recorded that others call but legendary tales. To the entity their truth may be made to mean, and does mean, much more than to many—if it will be let itself turn within.

872-1

The memory and influence from legendary events remains with another entity who had been an Egyptian at the time of the Exodus:

Before that we find the entity was in the land now known as or called the Egyptian land, when there were those periods following the Exodus of a peculiar people.

There again we find the entity among those peoples who sought for the comprehending of the activities in other lands.

And we find the entity aiding in the preparation for ways and means of the day for associations and connections by physical activity and associations.

Hence the preparations and manners of travel—and yet ships and waters are a part of the experience, as have been the experiences of the entity in its dreaming or day dreaming—the visions of the things or conditions that would influence men and nations in their activity toward those things as were handed down in manners such as even legendary folklore or legendary powers as attributed to individuals for their own development, but the greater for the release of influence or power for their fellow man.

The name then was Hep-Su-Tun. 1782-1

In *Worlds in Collision*, Dr. Immanuel Velikovsky advances a scientific reason for the physical manifestation of manna. In the following, Cayce gives us an interpretation of mental and spiritual manna. If they so chose, the children of Israel could partake daily on all three levels.

Remember, as He said to His disciples, "I have food, I have strength ye know not of." In giving of His strength to the woman at the well, it brought that heavenly food that satisfied the soul, that makes the growth, that brings the at-onement, yea, the atonement to the soul. And this ye may have, if ye will apply thyself in the better, yea in the broader sense. For those are thy stepping-stones. Do not let them become stumbling stones. 540-18

. . . as each entity under a given name makes its correlating of that it does about the Creative Forces in its experience, it is coming under those influences that are being fed by the manna—*which is a representation of the universality as well as the stability of purposes in the Creative Forces as manifested to a group or a nation of peoples.* [Author's italics]

So it becomes that as the Master gave, "Ye shall not live by bread alone, but by every word that proceedeth from the mouth of the Father."

That indeed is the holy manna which each entity, each soul in each experience must make a part of its mental and spiritual self. 281-31

One of the hardest lessons to be learned is the lesson of thanksgiving. Being thankful for whatever occurs to us keeps a way open, through our trust and humility, for the mental, spiritual, and physical "manna" which will be supplied each day sufficient for the need.

It is well that ye be reminded, then, of how—in those periods when there were the preparations in the lives and experiences of a peculiar people, under unusual circumstances, in extraordinary environments— they were reminded, not in their days of plenty but in the days when each day they were given only sufficient for that day, that periods were to be, should be, set aside when thanksgiving was to be a part of their activity—their remembrances for all the joys, the sorrows, the disappointments, the hopes that were and might be theirs if—*if*—they would but hold to those promises; relying—as it was necessary in those days, those hours, for a complete dependence—upon the bounty of a merciful Father, who had a purpose in the bringing out, in the edifying, in the directing.

And today, as ye look back upon those experiences, ye—*too*—find thyselves chosen. Have ye chosen Him? For as was given then, "If ye will be my people, I will be thy God." This is a universal experience, then. To each soul gathered here, to each soul throughout the land, to each soul as may be in all lands: *"If ye will be my people, I will be thy God!"*

3976-21

## Joshua's Love

Early in the trek, we glimpse a deep personal experience of Joshua, the soul who later became the Christ. It was events like these, the early death of his betrothed, that helped shape the destiny of his soul as he underwent all the experiences of man in the earth. On June 16, 1944, a nineteen–year–old Jewish girl was told:

> . . . the entity was in the Egyptian land when there were the activities in the preparations for the exit from Egypt to the favored land, the people through whom was chosen the hope of the world.
>
> The entity was then the close friend of Joshua. Yes, one of those to whom Joshua was engaged, as would be called in the present, and of the daughters of Levi, not the same as Moses and Aaron but rather of Korah. There we find the entity beautiful, lovely, beloved of Joshua and yet weak in body, because of conditions under which the entity had in a portion of its experience labored, and thus weak-lunged, passing away during the period of the journey to the Holy Land.
>
> But to have been beloved of Joshua was sufficient to have builded, into the personality, that individuality of the entity, that which still makes the entity beloved of all who know the entity best, loved by all its companions, it associates, just as in those experiences with the great leader who was to carry the children of promise to the Holy Land.
>
> The name then was Abigal. 5241-1

Two years before the above reading, the parents of an eleven–year–old boy obtained a reading for their son. They were told the boy [2779] had been the brother to this girl and a friend of Joshua's. A hint of the suffering and tragedy of his sister's death, in that life, is expressed in the following, as Cayce describes the boy:

> One that is at some periods as a tyrant in self, and yet so tender, so gentle, so understanding as not to be able to see the least thing suffer. And a real proof of this, as may not be experienced in any other association would be for the entity to come in contact with an individual suffering in the last stages of what is called T.B. or consumption; for

through such there might be seen even a flare-back to the period of the greater manifestation and awakening of this entity in the material plane.
2779-1

That life of great manifestation and awakening was described as follows:

Before that the entity was in that land when there were those prepara-tions for the journeying of the children of promise from the Egyptian land; when the leaders Moses, Aaron, and Hur brought about those experiences.

The entity then was of the same age and an associate of Joshua, who became the spiritual leader even to Moses in the interpreting of his experiences in the activities through that journey; as well as the com-panion of Joshua.

For, the entity then was the friend of Joshua, being the brother of the girl whom Joshua loved, yet who on the journey—before the wedding—died of tuberculosis. Thus that innate feeling, the entity will find, may be expressed in hearing of, reading of, *any* persecutions; and especially of the suffering of those from tuberculosis.

The name then was Jarael. The entity experienced turmoils through that sojourn. Yet, when there were those experiences after the hard-ships and the early portion of the journey, when there were those meetings between Moses in Mount Sinai, Joshua's interpretation to Jarael brought the greater spiritual concept—and aroused much of the entity's experience in the material sojourn before that.

Then the entity gained and became as a leader, as one who—with many of its associates or companions in the present—may, with some direction (dependent upon the suggestion made), become *again* as a leader and a director in this material experience. 2779-1

Some Jewish scholars claim that the real complainers among the chil-dren of Israel were not the Hebrews, but Egyptian "hangers on" who followed Moses. They were the ones who were in disfavor in their own land, and used the opportunity to escape their fate by joining with Moses. Most of the children of Israel, the Jewish commentators feel, had faith and did not question Moses' guidance. They were familiar with the concept of God as Spirit. The Egyptians, who were used to having mate-rial forms as images to worship, needed constant reassurance that help could always come from unexpected and unforeseen sources. They needed the miraculous to make them realize the Israelite God was to be experienced rather than seen.

The Life readings indicate Egyptians did accompany Moses, and many Egyptians, even those in authority, were favorable to the Hebrews.

> Before that the entity was in the Egyptian land when there were those of the children of promise leaving the cities of Egypt.
>
> The entity was an Egyptian—not of the people of promise, or of the Jews—as they were even called then, or Hebrews—but the entity was favorable to those. For, the closer friend of the entity was the associate of Joshua—who was so ill when they left, or when they were preparing for the leaving, and who died on the way.
>
> Then the entity was in the name Shalmahr, and the entity was among those close to those in authority and power in the land. For the entity's companion and its associates were in rule over those people, though the entity was favorable—as indicated—to the Jewish or Hebrew women, especially. 1635-3

These remarks were made by Edgar Cayce in his Tuesday Night Bible Class:

> "Moses and Joseph married the daughters of Egyptian high priests. No mention is made of Joshua's marriage. Although the physical lines of Joseph and Moses were not the channels through which promise of Christ's coming was fulfilled, their spiritual influence and teachings far surpassed those who did keep to the pure physical strain. Evidently Joseph and Moses came into the earth to perform the tasks they did. It was not important to them or to the future welfare of their people that they conform to the letter of the law. Yet for others, it seems very important that they obey the law physically. A thing is right for one person and not right for another—depending upon the ideal or purpose for coming into materiality. There are times when individuals are not required to keep to the letter of the law. It is always necessary—and possible—to seek to show *ourselves* approved unto God and His purposes."

Joshua did marry, as this brief comment from a physical reading indicates:

In the mental and spiritual body, keep in self the ideals that were set by self in much of its [the soul's] association through the various periods in the earth; as was seen especially as the wife of Joshua—as a close association with the Master: "Let others do as they will or may, as for me and my house, we will serve a Living God."                573-1

A request for a Life reading was made, but circumstances intervened, and it was never obtained.

## Jethro's Contribution

Moses encamped at Sinai, at the mountain where he had the burning bush experience. When Jethro, his father–in–law, knew where Moses had settled, he came to see him with Zipporah (Moses' wife) and his two sons.

Jethro was a descendant of Abraham and Keturah, and was familiar with the form of worship and sacrifice taught by Abraham.

Edgar Cayce, reading for an elderly Protestant businessman, saw in his soul's experience several lives where he had significant roles in great spiritual, moral, and political movements. He had been in the colonies at the time of the American Revolution, and had participated in all the discussions with the great leaders about separation from England. In a Roman incarnation before that, he had, as a powerful Caesar, helped spread the empire. And before that, he had been Jethro, Moses' father–in–law:

. . . we find the entity was among the princes of Midian, or a Prince of Midian—Jethro, the father-in-law to Moses; and to him was given the abilities to counsel with the elders of the peoples who gave not only the ordinances as to material conduct of the elders but much as pertained to the manners of preparation of sacrifice.

For the entity then was not only as a counselor to that people who became as leaders to the world because of their religious forces and influences but to those who came to many another land.        1266-1

When Jethro appeared, he saw Moses bogged down from morning to evening, judging all the controversies and complaints of the people. Jethro was able to make wise use of his abilities to "counsel with the elders." He aided Moses in establishing the appointment of seventy men who were to be chiefs over thousands. They were to carry out all the detailed matters, and leave Moses free for more important things.

With all his ability and guidance, Moses needed the practical suggestions made by his father-in-law. The Lord uses everyone who is willing to be used. No man could do what Moses had to do unassisted. As a priest, no doubt Jethro was divinely guided.

The following readings belong to several of those elders who were selected at that time.

Hur was one of those chosen. Hur is an important figure who is twice mentioned in Scripture. He stood with Moses and Aaron on the mountain top, upholding Moses' arms, while Joshua led the Hebrews in their first battle against the Amalekites. (Exodus 17:10)

Later, when Moses and Joshua went on the mountain to commune with God, Aaron and Hur were left in charge of the congregation. (Exodus 24:14) Hur's grandson was the craftsman Bezaleel, who supervised the construction of the Tabernacle (Exodus 31:2)

In 1943, Edgar Cayce told a Danish executive he had been that gifted leader:

> Before that, the entity was in the Egyptian and Palestine land, when the first counselors were selected for Moses, Aaron, and Joshua and those that led the people to the Promised Land.
>
> Then in the name Hur, the entity carried forward those activities in a manner bespeaking the keeping of a well organized effort on the part of the many groups, and even the personalities to be dealt with, even as indicated in Moses and Aaron and Miriam as well as Joshua and the sons of Korah and the rest of those leaders at that period.
>
> Study those tenets also especially in Exodus 19:5. There is the basis, my friend, of those things in which ye may excel.          3435-1

A young woman requested a Life reading and was told she once had been Hur's daughter, and evidently made positive contributions:

> . . . the entity was in the Egyptian land, when there were those preparations being made for the journeying from the land.
>
> There the entity was in the household of Levi, and a recorder—as would be termed today, or a helper—to Moses and Aaron; but the companion—or the daughter—of Hur.

> In the experience the entity became acquainted with much that had to do with the ways, means, and manners of controlling groups, and those who find fault with the interpreters of the law as well as those who interpreted the attempts of the Creative Force to bring the consciousness into the lives of individuals of His purpose with man.
>
> There the entity became something of a politician, as would be termed today, as well as an instructor in the ways of those who would keep their own household intact.
>
> Then the entity was in the name Shebeth, and the entity gained much that may be applied in the present in that of teaching, or in analyzing individuals or individual problems. Apply these abilities in the spirit of creative energies, not as for self nor for the gratifying of some appetite of body or of mind—mental.            2796-1

Her present husband had been associated with her twice before, in experiences with Israel:

> (Q) When, where, and how have I been formerly associated with my husband?
> (A) In Egypt, as in association with Hur; as in the Promised Land in the activities there. Not very good friends in the one—very close in the days of David.            2796-1

Of the "able men" which Moses chose (Exodus 18:25–26), there was one who did not always make wise judgments. Cayce saw in the soul of the person a deep urge for atonement and penance, in part stemming from this experience.

> Before that we find the entity was in the earth during those days and periods when this chosen people from the Egyptian land journeyed toward a land of promise, and when Moses chose the seventy elders that were to be judges among thy brethren.
>
> The entity then was of the household of Reuben, chosen as among those that acted in these capacities; in the name Eleasiah.
>
> In this capacity, judgments were not always the best. And when those days came when Beth-Korah made for rebellions, we find the entity was among those not called but who gave his counsel, being moved by the promptings that had been in the experience through the very associations of those experiences in the mount.

Thus we find those changes coming over the entity then, and the later days were spent in what has often been felt within self; whether it is to be an atonement, at-onement, or penance.

Choose rather the living way, that ye may how Him. For God hath not mocked man, but the premises have ever been, "When ye call, I will hear" if ye are in earnest; if ye are in doubt—fear has crept in!

1238-1

## The Encampment at Sinai

When the Lord told Moses he would speak to him on the mount, He gave Moses and the people three days to prepare themselves for the visitation. (Exodus 19:9-11) Perhaps three days has no symbolical or special significance, but it did give everybody an opportunity to prepare themselves. Many did not make the preparations and consequently were not allowed to participate:

*And it came to pass on the third day in the morning that there were thunders and lightnings and a thick smoke appeared upon the mountain and the sound of the trumpet exceedingly loud; so that all the people that were in the camp trembled.* (Exodus 19:16)

The thunder and lightning left a deep impression on this soul.

. . . before that the entity was in the Palestine land as a companion to Miriam, who aided in directing spiritual precepts, yea in the tenets of the law that Miriam's mother and brethren gave to those peoples.

The days at Sinai brought misery, brought strength, brought power. And the entity is still afraid of thunder and lightning, yet such has its attraction. The Lord is in the storm, for He is the Lord of the storm also.

The name then was Shushan. The entity was among the daughters of Aaron, and thus one of the household and understanding of the priesthood. 3659-1

And the whole mountain of Sinai was smoking because the Lord descended upon it in fire; and the smoke thereof ascended like the smoke of a furnace, and the whole mountain quaked greatly.

*And when the blast of the trumpet sounded long and grew louder and louder . . . the Lord came down upon Mount Sinai, to the very top of the mountain . . . and Moses went up.* (Exodus 19:18-20)

This reading creates a vivid picture of a literal, historical happening:

Draw a comparison, my son, as to what has been given you. Does this not stand much in that same position as illustrated in those days when the people waited? Though they had seen the Lord Jehovah descend into the mount, they had seen the mount so electrified by the presence of the God of the people and ohm of the Omnipotent to such an extent that no living thing could remain in the mount or on same, save those two who had been cleansed by their pouring out of themselves to God, in the cleansing of their bodies, in the cleansing of their minds. And yet they tarried only a few days, their cry to the leader was, "We know not what has become of this man. Show us another way. Why cannot we return rather to the gods of the Egyptians. Make thou one that shall lead us, for we know not what has become of this man." (Exodus 32:1]

Thou hast been shown a way, a perfect way, whereunto thou mayest cleanse thyself, thine body. Why seekest thou to find another god that may lead thee, that is made whether of gold, stone, wood, or what not? Why not be patient my son, and prepare thine self that thou mayest in the very spirit of truth manifest the perfect way. Not a fault in thee, no. Thine overanxiety, or—as was expressed by another teacher—the very zealousness of thine self may eat thee up and destroy the real value of that thou mayest be in thine zealousness trying to do! Oft has it been given, "Stand ye still and see the glory of God." Let *Him* have his way with thee, that thou mayest indeed know thou art guided step by step with His ways.

Then, as to the healing or the aid, if thou workest together, let *Him* guide; not thou seeking through another channel, or even this channel, to do other than He has prepared—or the ways He would prepare thee for the best thou mayest do.                    440-16

Edgar Cayce brought out the following points in his discussions with the Bible class:

"The burning mountain was also the place where Moses saw the burning bush. The mountain was charged with electricity. The people then knew a constructive side of electricity that we have lost today. Those who did not know the laws of it could easily be destroyed, just as one could today.

"The vibrations were raised so high, that those who were not attuned could not stand it. The area was "roped off" to prevent sudden death to those who might accidentally overstep the boundary. Moses led the people in a period or meditation, or a devotional, to better prepare them for what they were about to witness. All the people could hear the thunder and see the lightning. Perhaps some even sensed the meaning of it. But only a few could hear the voice.

"Even with the three days of preparation, the priests were not able to go into the mountain with Moses and Aaron. Either they were not sufficiently attuned, or completely sanctified. To be in an attitude of prayer, or going through certain forms of purification externally is not enough. Our *lives* must be in accord with what we are seeking. We must be attuned to those vibrations which are necessary for receiving spiritually. This is what Jesus meant when he told us to ask in His name—not to ask just with words, but by living our lives as He lived his. If we do that, we can ask and it will be done."

## *The Ten Commandments*

The following commentary is taken, once again, from the records kept of Edgar Cayce's weekly Bible class:

"It is well to picture in our minds how the Ten Commandments were given and who was with Moses at the time. The rest of the Bible is written around this chapter. Even the Sermon on the Mount, given by Christ, is just an extension of it.

"'Thou shalt have no other gods before Me.' No individual is to be considered before God. This is probably the most violated command of them all. We do not consider ourselves idol worshippers, but it is hard not to think first of ourselves and our own wishes above all else.

"This is our great trouble today, as individuals and as a nation. We want what we want. *We want* to be all power. *We want* to hold on to all the *material possessions* we have, regardless of everything else. Can we say, 'Thy Will Be Done,' and mean it, when our desires and material possessions are at stake? Jesus said if we try and save our life, we shall lose it. It behooves us to heed this commandment, to try and practice it in our daily life.

"Notice the first few commandments pertain to our relationship to God. The rest are about our relations with our fellow man.

"The second commandment: a graven image could be anything to which we have so much importance as to be all encompassing for us. It might be position, fame, money, prestige, or any material desire that outweighs our desire to be a channel for God's manifestation and glorification.

"Non-Catholics feel it is sinful to make a statue of the Virgin. Orthodox Jews feel Christians are disobeying the second commandment when they worship Jesus as the Christ. Yet they look on the patriarchs and prophets of old as messengers of God and examples to follow. There is a difference between an object you worship and an example you live by. Jesus promised a day would come when we would worship God in spirit and truth. Until we reach that state of consciousness, we will need constant reminders before us to help us reach the goal we are striving for.

"What is meant by 'a jealous God'? It is necessary at times to use certain words to convey certain meanings. Jealousy was and is a thing that is understandable. Perhaps this is only another way of saying, 'What ye sow so shall ye reap.' It indicates certain laws are set in motion according to our actions, which bring about definite results.

"Visiting iniquities of the fathers upon the children of the third and fourth generations was refuted by some of the later prophets. Ezekiel disavowed the proverb that the sour grapes eaten by the fathers would set the children's teeth on edge. He stated each soul was accountable for his own sins. The theory of reincarnation might explain how a soul might come back into the third or fourth generation of its own strain to materially reap what it had sown.

"The third commandment: Jesus said we should not swear by the temple, for that is where God lives. If we say harsh things against others, perhaps it is the same as taking God's name in vain. We all are divine in Him.

"The fourth commandment: an individual must decide for himself how he can best keep the Sabbath. The Sabbath was intended as a day of rest, in which appreciation could be shown for the blessings of the week. Our manner of doing this depends upon our purpose and what we consider showing appreciation. Rest does not mean just sitting and holding our hands. More often it means a change in the way you think. Whatever we feel is right, we should live up to it.

"There are seven centers in the endocrine system of the body. These centers are centers through which spiritual impulses enter into the physical body. They act separately and collectively. They must coordinate if we are to remain balanced. It has been indicated by some, that it is absolutely necessary to give a seventh of our time to serious contemplation of our spiritual natures, else we cannot keep a balance.

"The fifth commandment: 'Honor thy mother and father; that thy days be long upon the land which the Lord Thy God has given thee.' To honor your parents is to think of them before yourself, showing them preference. This is the first commandment with a promise. If you truly honored your parents and respected them, you probably would desire to live longer, and your life would be in keeping with the purpose you had in entering this life.

"'Thou shalt not kill,' the sixth commandment. Jesus told us that we can kill with anger. In fact, to kill 'one's spirit' with anger, a harsh word, pessimism, or any other form of negativity is a violation of this commandment. We are meant to be constructive and creative, not destructive. We should not destroy what we cannot give.

"'Thou shalt not commit adultery.' According to Jesus' interpretation, the seventh commandment refers not only to the physical act of adultery, but to any thought which would contaminate or separate us from the purity and spiritual unity for which we are striving.

"The eighth, ninth, and tenth commandments are self-explanatory. We must remember that there are 200 extremes in the material sense of the law, but not according to the spirit of the law as given by Jesus. In Him the extremes meet."

A newspaper woman was told she was one of the first who heard and applied those new commandments.

**For the entity was among those that journeyed from Egypt to the Holy Land, when there were those chosen to act in the capacity of the judges in the various tribes.**

**The entity in the name Abarther, of the tribe of Asher, was among the first to comply with those judgments at Sinai, when the records and the laws were given to those peoples in the particular land. The entity kept those judgments through the period, being among those that were also helpful to Joshua before the entering into the Promised Land.**

**The entity was not among those who entered in, but those who paved the way for helpful forces during those preparations for same. This gives**

the entity in the present experience very peculiar ideas concerning political favors, but it will be hard for the entity to be a machine person. Yet it will be necessary in the experience, if the entity would comply with the rules, especially in those areas from which it may seek such honors. Change rather the ideals of thy constituents, and you'll mean much as their representative.                                                    3486-1

## The Tabernacle

Along with the ten commandments and the laws and ordinances which Moses received at this time, he also was given the perfect pattern for the tabernacle of worship for the living God. According to Cayce, every facet of this tabernacle has a spiritual, mental, and physical relationship to the body of man. The body is the temple, the readings stressed.

Another newspaper woman, a Christian Scientist, learned in the wilderness the meaning of the temple:

Before that, the entity was in Egypt when those peoples entered into the Holy Land, now called the Jewish or Hebrews.

Then the entity was among those selected to be in charge of those activities that dealt with the preparation of the temple in the wilderness, or the tabernacle that eventually became the temple.

And, as the entity has learned in the present, the body is indeed the temple, and that the pattern given in the mount is that pattern of the individual entity or self as it is set up and hedged about, and yet is the place where man meets his Maker.

The entity then became one well grounded in those tenets and truths, the weaknesses of the material needs oft overshadowing the entity, yet in those periods of the close walk with the leader who entered into the land there was brought peace and harmony into the experience.

Then the name was Elded.                                                    3129-1

Many people were required to execute the minute directions and details outlined in Exodus 25–27. Cooperation between the tribes was necessary, because all tribes were involved. A six-year–old Ohio boy was told he had been a craftsman from the tribe of Dan:

> Before that, we find the entity was in the land now known as the Holy Land when the peoples journeyed from Egypt to the Holy Land.
>
> The entity was among those who aided some of the sons or children of Dan to prepare the mechanical things for the carrying of the tables, the altar, candlesticks, and those things which were to be used by other individuals.
>
> The entity was then in the name Eijalu. In the experience the entity gained the more, and with the application of self came knowledge and power within self to control influences about the entity.       5153-1

Psychologically, the work demanded they recognize a state of perfection. That discipline still remains with this particular entity, who was also of the Danites.

> Before that, we find the entity was in the periods when there was the journeying from the Egyptian land to the Promised Land and when there was the choosing of the individuals who were to prepare the various elements which were to be used in the hangings in the preparations of the tabernacle in the wilderness. The entity was then of the tribe of Dan and in the name Segualar prepared the cloth which was the first veil between the Holy of Holies and the Ark itself. [Exodus 26:31-33]
>
> Thus the desires latent in self to be superlative in its work, to be honored in the office to which it may be assigned or to which it may be aspiring. But know there are those applications of such in which they must be made tenable judgments between individuals.       5392-1

The directions for the completed tabernacle are both symbolic and literal. The intricate anatomy of our physical bodies represents a reflection of a spiritual pattern, which we can find within ourselves. The symbolic relationship between the body and the temple is drawn here:

> The entity finds self a body, a mind, a soul. These are as the shadows which were indicated in the mount by the outer court (the body), the inner court (the mind), and the still more holy of holies (the soul).
> 2067-1

> (Q) Is the temple here the physical body?
> (A) Rather the mental in which is the pattern as of the tabernacle; or the holy mount—or that as set by a unified service of the body-mind, the

body-physical, the body-spiritual; that vehicle that is without nails (as was the tabernacle as a pattern), not bound together, yet a covering, a place, an understanding for a unified activity with Creative Forces, or the power of God. The veil without, the holy within, and the holy of holies—knowing that there must be the cleansing, there must be the purifying, there must be the consecration. All of these are as patterns, they are as conditions, they are as experiences for each and every soul. (Q) Is the court referred to the body apart from the spiritual centers? (A) As indicated, rather is it as the environ without—the body-physical and mental within for its sacrificial forces, and then to the spiritual force within as to the holy of holies.                                                      281-32

The inner relationship to the outer pattern is further discussed in this psychic reading:

In the expressions as shown in the tabernacle, in the orders as given for its construction—the size, the shape, the measurements, the figures above the holy of holies, the directions of the colors as indicated for the hangings, the manner in which each board was to be set, the manner in which each skin was to be used or dyed—these were not only for the physical protection but for the expressions that would come in the experience of individuals that took the service of worship there as being a thing within themselves. Hence became material, emblematical, and the experience of the application of same in the worship there became as a living thing in the experience of the individuals.                        338-4

In the book of The Revelation, much of the symbolism is based on Old Testament experience. The Revelation was closely investigated by friends of Edgar Cayce, and many psychic readings were given in order to interpret it correctly. Through the series of readings known as the 281 series, they discovered how much of the Old Testament patterns and symbols relate to forces within the perfect structure of man.

## Symbology of Two

And you shall put the mercy seat on top of the ark; and in the ark you shall put the testimony that I shall give you.

. . . and I will commune with you from above the mercy seat, from

*between the two cherubim which are upon the ark of the testimony . . .*
(Exodus 25:21-22)

The two cherubim have a strategic position in the place of communication. Perhaps these two angels have the same metaphysical significance as the two witnesses in Revelation 11:3. The two witnesses were
interpreted by Cayce (281-33) as representing motivations which arise
from outside the physical being—the astrological, or mental, influences—
and the emotional forces which are produced from incarnations in the
earth.

**These then are the witnesses. The innate and the *emotional*; or *the
spiritual-mental*, the *physical-mental*; the subconscious, the
superconsciousness.**                                            **281-33**

Could these two cherubim—"above the mercy seat" represent the
same two forces?

## *Symbology of Ten*

*Moreover you shall make the tabernacle with ten curtains of fine twined
linen, and blue and purple and scarlet material; with cherubim, the
workmanship of a craftsman shall you make them.* (Exodus 26:1)

The symbology of ten is suggested in the following:

**(Q) What was meant in a previous reading by this statement: "For he
that sings, he that sees, he that speaks, he that hears well is especially
gifted of God; and not only has the one or the two but the five talents
that may be made into such measures, by the choice of the entity, that
he may be ruler not only over the five senses but the ten kingdoms in
God's own way"?**
**(A) It was meant what was said. Just as that indicated in the parable of
the talents by the Master. He that used the five talents was given more.
He that uses the five senses—as of speech, of song, of hearing, to the
*glory of God* is given the ten to use or to rule over—as was the man with
the talents.**                                                  **622-7**

If these curtains represent the ten senses of man, then the veils are an appropriate symbol. This shows they are still "behind the veil" and hidden from all but the Seeker.

## The Mercy Seat

*And you shall make a mercy seat of pure gold, two and a half cubits long, and a cubit and a half breadth.*

*And you shall make two cherubim of gold, of cast work shall you make them on the two sides of the mercy seat.* (Exodus 25:17-18)

. . . that ye *are*—that of good—rises ever as an incense, sweet before the throne of mercy . . . that which has been kind, gentle, patient, merciful, long suffering in self's experience during a day, rises before the throne of the mercy seat within self to that of an incense of satisfaction.

**281-30**

The mercy seat was a symbol to help the people understand what they were to expect of God. They didn't understand it then, and too often we don't today, Cayce told his class. God is Love, and in His Love is kindness, patience, and understanding. We will never know the meaning of mercy until we understand God's mercy to us. The best means of obtaining this awareness is to practice showing mercy to others.

Mr. Cayce's thoughts on these aspects of temple symbology were delivered to his Tuesday Night Bible Class as follows:

"To have our bodies and minds conform to the same pattern as the temple outlined in Exodus, it is necessary to do certain things uniformly and with the proper attention to detail. But not so ritualistic as to forget the spirit or purpose behind the rite. The daily ritual should remind us of the necessity to make our lives in accord with our spiritual purposes.

Some part of our day should be dedicated to meditation, to entering into the holy of holies within ourselves. We should prepare ourselves for this communion with the highest forces known. We need to make a habit of doing those things each day which will keep us in remembrance of the fact that the body is the temple. *There* He has promised to speak with us."

These thoughts are given by the unconscious Cayce on entering into the holy of holies within self:

For as [was] given of old, how oft must that associate of the entity [have] been lonely; that man of God who waited long upon the mount, [who] gave to those peoples of old those commandments as from Jehovah Himself? Lonely? Yes, in the physical sense; but that as he gave stands ever as the judgment of man to his Maker, "There is set today before thee good and evil, life and death. Choose thou." Thus has it come to all who waited then with him, and as his successor gave, "Let others do as they may, but as for me and mine, we will serve a *living* God."

With that attitude, with that purpose, with that intent in the dealings with thy fellowmen, there will come a peace, a harmony, and an understanding that—as has been given—is not known by those who seek not to do His ways. 1238-3

For, "My spirit beareth witness with thy spirit" is an immutable, an unchanging law. And again, the heavens, the earth may pass away, but His laws shall not pass away.

Hence, in thy seeking, find that answer; not as from something without, but from opening the door of thy own consciousness to the promises that are sure in Him. For ye will find that as the pattern which was shown in the mount to Moses, as well as the greater pattern in the temptations to Jesus upon the mount; in that indeed as He was lifted up, He draws all men (and this means women also) unto Him. 2067-1

Do stay close to the Ark of the Convention, which is within thee!
5177-1

Keep that as indicated. Let the strength of self not be wavered by advice of the many; but turn to the within, knowing that the *power* lieth there!

For when ye enter into the holy of holies, in thine own self, there ye may find *strength* that is beyond compare of man's physical abilities.
1752-1

*And you shall erect the tabernacle according to the right pattern thereof which I have shown you on the mountain.* (Exodus 26:30)

## Aaron's Breastplate

*And Aaron shall bear the names of the sons of Israel in the breastplate of judgment upon his heart when he enters the holy place, for a continual memorial before the Lord.* (Exodus 28:29)

Each precious stone in Aaron's breastplate carried the vibration of the tribe it represented. The messages from God pertaining to each tribe were interpreted by Aaron according to his understanding of the emanations from the stones.

**Well that the entity have the stones or minerals about self when in periods of meditation; or in those periods when it may find itself more easily attuned to the influences that may use the body, either in the healing forces that flow through—through its attunements, or through the visions and the associations of the entity . . .**       **688-2**

A warning was given regarding stones:

**These do not give the messages. They only attune self so that the Christ Consciousness may give the message. Listen to no message of a stone, of a number, even of a star; for they are but servants of the Lord and Master of all—even as thou.**       **707-2**

In Babylonian mythology, certain gods were messengers to mankind, and wore upon their breasts "Tablets of Destiny." Through these stones the people could inquire of their gods for yes and no answers to questions concerning their destiny as a nation and the fate of their kings. This is an interesting parallel with the Israelites. Aaron, as high priest, and the spokesman for Jehovah, and the breastplate was used exclusively in matters concerning the king or nation. Perhaps, in earlier days, the use of stones as a means to attune to a higher consciousness was very widespread.

**Each element, each stone, each variation of stone, has its own atomic movement, held together by the units of energy that in the universe are concentrated in that particular activity. Hence, they come under varied activities according to their color, vibration, or emanation.**       **531-3**

## Urim and Thummin

*And you shall put in the breastplate of judgment the Urim and the Thummin; and they shall be upon Aaron's heart when he enters before the Lord.* (Exodus 28:30)

Urim and Thummin have been interpreted in a variety of ways, from "purity and perfection" (Lamsa) to "revelation and truth" (Jewish Encyclopedia).

Certainly the high priest had to strive for "purity and perfection" in his heart in order to receive "revelation and truth." This is applicable for us in the present. The true importance of Urim and Thummin is that they were aides, a helpful means through which the priest could attune his consciousness to the Divine.

(Q) Is there any likelihood at the present time of developing a machine based on the action of the electro-magnetic cell, which may assist in securing direct communication as done by Aaron and Moses—and many others—with Urim and Thummin?

(A) Find in self that as Hatherpsut put to self, in knowing who should be chosen—yet the trouble arose. Do not make the same mistake, that the vibration is the force—but that which impels same from the Creative Force. Such machines are claimed to be made. Some do, some do not, create the right vibration. Too oft does there enter in those personalities of those seeking.

Then, in self, find the way to aid; and call again on Ra-Ta, and on Hatherpsut—they are as Urim and Thummin, a channel only.   355-1

Hence intuitive force is the better, for in this there may come more the union of the spirit of truth with Creative Energy; thus the answer may be shown thee, whether in Urim, in Thummin, in dream, in numbers, in whatever manner or form. For He is the strength of them all, and beareth witness in thee and through thee—if ye but do His biddings.   261-15

A Michigan housewife [987] had once helped prepare the legendary breastplate. When Cayce viewed her record in the psychic state, he saw her love of God symbolized by a golden cord which ran through all her experiences from the beginning of time. The cord represented the central desire of the soul, and served as a link which connected all her experiences into each other. Her present life could be her last earth experience, Cayce told her, unless she chose to enter again on a mission, or a service, for God. Her activities in the Wilderness helped build that consciousness, and are described as follows:

> Before that we find the entity was in that land, that period, when the chosen people were being given upon the holy mount the manner of their exercise in the temple, or in the service before the tabernacle.
>
> The entity then was among the daughters of Levi, and those chosen to make the vestment of the priest. And to the entity, because of its own abilities, there was given the preparation of the setting of the breastplate and the putting of the stones thereon, and the preparation of the Urim and Thummin for the interpretations of the movements that came upon the high priests in the holy of holies to be given to his people in or from the door of the tabernacle.
>
> Then in the name Henriettah, the entity's activities were in a high force equal to the cousin Miriam. Throughout the experience, the entity gained; for it reasoned with Nadab and Abihu; it counseled for Korah, yet did not allow self to become entangled in any of those influences that would have made for the rise to the position of fame. Rather did the entity choose to remain as one in the background that there might be given the greater understanding to that mighty people as they stood in the presence of the I AM that had brought them to the holy mount.
>
> In the present from that sojourn, those things pertaining to the mysteries of the temple, the mysteries of numbers, of figures and those things that have their hidden meaning, become as a portion of the entity. Yet oft does there arise that sudden change as to the fearfulness of people giving too great a power to such things that would lead them astray; as they did in the experience of the entity in the wilderness.
>
> 987-2

## Strange Fire

**Know then that the force in nature that is called electrical or electricity is that same force ye worship as Creative, or God, in action.  1299-1**

Free will is as powerful as electricity, and can be a force for evil or good, depending on our use of it. Through their knowledge of the Godhead and its energies, and the vibrations they raised in worship and devotion, the Hebrews could electrify a mountain, part the sea, or make water spring from a stone. Misuse of this tremendous force resulted in death, as it did for Nadab and Abihu.

This reading makes use of the symbol of "strange fire" which Nadab and Abihu offered on the altar of the Lord. (Leviticus 10:1)

> Many having lost sight of the purposes, the ideals, have presented strange fires upon the altars of truth. These are necessarily blinding to those who would remain, even in the straight and narrow way. Be not blinded to those conditions that easily beset each individual, yet there must ever remain that loving care, that perfect differentiation between those [who] would build for constructive influences in the lives of those who would associate themselves in carrying forward that of truth, that is life itself, as is set in Him who has ever presented a way for a more perfect relationship between the Creator and the creature.   254-52

*And there went out fire from before the Lord and devoured them and they died before the Lord.* (Leviticus 10:2)

> Remember the pattern in the mount, in self, in the physical body, in the mental body, in the spiritual body. *That* is the mount! So long as there is perfect coordination in the mount, all things work together for the *good* of the mount. When there is the rebellion in the mount, then there is disconnection, destruction, disconcerted effort, and the coordination—the cooperation of activity—is made awry. Hence death in the physical ensues, by the disintegration, through disconcerted action, through the *incoordinated* action—and this mental, and physical, and spiritual.
>
> So, in overcoming all He set that as the Throne, or the mercy seat that is within the temple, as the pattern, as in the mount . . . "I will arise and go to my Father, in Him, through him. *I will! I will!*   282-36

The subject of this reading was a young Jew who listed his beliefs as "non-orthodox":

> Before that the entity was in the earth during those days when the peoples were returning from the Egyptian land to the Promised Land.
>     The entity was among those of the household of the sons of Levi, and close to the sons of Aaron; being then a companion to one of those

destroyed because of offering strange fire—Abihu—then in the name Ashua.

With those periods of turmoil that arose within itself, the entity found dissension; yet becoming later the companion of Ithamar's son, the entity brought the bettered conditions when there came the periods of preserving and maintaining for those of the priesthood a unity of activity in their temple service, directing in the separating of each group for definite services.

In the present from that experience we will find that those engaged materially in such activities as a service in temple, or in teaching, or in directing of the spiritual life, will be particularly attracted to this entity; though the entity will hold such afar off. It would be well to consider same during the twenty-sixth and twenty-seventh years in this sojourn, for in those periods the entity should think of marriage.     1204-3

In this reading, we find the *wife* of Nadab:

Before that we find the entity lived in the earth during those periods when there were the preparations for the journey to the Promised Land.

Again the entity was in one of the families of the Levites, nigh unto the household of the leaders in that experience; being in the household of those who were then friends, neighbors, and associates of Jochebed, the mother of Moses.

These associations with the mother brought the entity into close association and activity with Miriam and Aaron, during those periods that the entity Moses joined closer with the activities and relationships with his own people.

During the period of [the] sojourn through the wilderness, the entity then became nigh unto the priesthood again; becoming then the wife of Nadab, one of the sons of Aaron made the high priest.

With the destruction of these in the Wilderness of Zin because of their offerings of strange fire on the altar, it brought to the entity the widowhood which made the longings for the changes that were gradually wrought by the activities with the sons and the daughters of Jethro, those that joined themselves later to the activities.

And the sons then of the tribe of Judah became the protectorate to the entity during the rest of its experience in that sojourn . . .

In the present these make for conflicting influences at times in the experiences of the entity. Yet join into the services in the tabernacle, for these mean much to the entity. 325-63

Mrs. 325, the wife of Nadab, in her present incarnation was the mother of Mr. 257, for whom the following reading was given.

> Before this the entity was in the land where the peoples were become the separate and distinct people, and was of the priesthood of that people, and in that time was he one of those offering strange fire upon the altar.
>
> As to these conditions as brought in the present sphere, we find first:
>
> Those that bring the entity's soul and spirit forces close to the worship of the Jehovah, yet holding itself ever afar from giving of its best, or of its first self, to these natures.
>
> In the second that of the strength of the elements necessary for the insight, yet with the first giving that peculiar bend to the insight as not understood by self or others. Hence, the mighty force of will to know self, and understand self, if it would make the best in the present plane.
>
> 257-5

There is an interesting parallel between the present Mr. 257 and his life as Nadab. Mr. 257 was a personal and long time friend of Edgar Cayce, and was one of the key men upon whom the responsibility fell for establishing the A.R.E. Through this friendship, he could fulfill the vital role he had neglected as Aaron's son.

The following reading was obtained by Mr. 257 for guidance in respect to his role in furthering the work of Edgar Cayce. The karmic implications of his present condition are drawn by Cayce. At the reading's conclusion, Mr. 257 is put on notice that his responsibilities are an opportunity—and a necessity—to cleanse himself of the egoism that led him astray as Nadab.

> (Q) Should [257] plan to devote his entire time to the work as he planned and how can he accomplish it now?
>
> (A) Rather not as he has planned. Let him prepare himself as God has planned. Be a channel of blessing, not tell the forces nor God how to do His work . . . Rather be that channel through which individuals may be given an opportunity to approach the throne itself, and cast not thine pearls before swine nor so conduct thine own self that thine good is evil-spoken of nor thine evils are good-spoken of . . .

As conditions of the material natures clarify themselves, as they will, do not mix material conditions with spiritual forces. Do not attempt to serve God and mammon. Do not serve thine neighbor with one hand and draw from his pocket with the other. Rather let thy yeas be yea and thy nay be nay, knowing that [what] is given for the increase is from the Giver of all things.

(Q) From whom came this beautiful message?

(A) From self. Oft has this very condition confronted self, as to whether to be able to put on again those royal robes, and to prevent from offering the strange fires on the altars of the throne, has come to the self; and would the entity, the soul, be again associated in that love that makes for purity before the throne, the decisions in the flesh must be made.

(Q) What can [257] further do in his daily life to show himself more approved unto the Giver of these gifts?

(A) Study to show thyself approved unto God, avoiding the appearances of evil, knowing that as the acts of thine going-ins and coming-outs are that reflection of the God ye would serve; if that God be money, power, position, fame, these must reflect in . . . the life [and] the acts of self. Will those forces be manifested as were made manifest as of old, when Abraham [was] called to go out to make a peculiar people, a different nation, so again may the body bear that call as when offering in the temple, that "Mine people have wandered astray," yet in the little here, [in] the world there, the precept and example, they may again know Jehovah is in His holy place.

(Q) Who was [257] during that period of Abraham?

(A) Walked with Abraham.

(Q) Is the name given?

(A) One who stood at the tent when the call was that as given, "I will make of thee a strange nation." Not in the flesh. Later in the flesh as was seen when the body [257] offered strange fires on the altar in the word of mouth in that [which] led many astray. *Now the body [is] given the opportunity in this experience to make for a cleansing of that experience.* [Author's Italics]                                                  5502-3

In rabbinical literature, two opposing views are taken concerning Nadab and Abihu. One views the brothers arePrometheans who purified themselves and made the supreme sacrifice to bring Divine Fire into the congregation. Less romantic (and more nearly correct, according to the readings for Mr. 257) is the other which holds the brothers were consumed by their own self-esteem. They considered themselves superior to Moses and Aaron and were jealous of their leadership. They also felt they were too good to be married. This entity learned a great lesson from Nadab and Abihu's intemperance.

> Before that the entity was in the Egyptian land, being among those journeying from Egypt to the Holy Land. There the entity was among those associated with the high priests, for the entity was then the wife of Abiathar. The relationships to Aaron and to Nadab brought unusual experiences, when there were the activities first setting up the service in the tabernacle. From these lessons the entity, then Abijah, found the necessity of being convinced within self, and of keeping in what may be termed the straight and narrow way.
>
> These periods brought to the entity the extreme disturbance through a portion of the sojourn, and again those activities that set the entity as one in authority throughout that period of journeying through the wilderness; aiding in the choosing of those helpers to Abiathar, as well as the other sons of Eleazer who led in those activities after the happenings in the wilderness.                    3416-1

## Who Were the Enemies?

*And it came to pass, when the ark set forward, Moses said "Arise, O Lord, and let them that hate thee be scattered; and let thy enemies flee before thee."* (Numbers 10:35)

> Ye have no enemies. Let this ever be within thine own heart: Do *right* in self, and that which is thine own can not, will not be taken from thee. Those who try such are enemies to themselves. Look not upon them as enemies to thee. Feel sorry for them for their misconstruction of right.
>                                                                 3250-1

Moses prayed that *God's* enemies be scattered, not his own. The Bible gives no indication who the enemies were. Was it an external enemy—something perceived from afar? Or was it his own people who bore a spirit at enmity with God's? Shortly after this prayer, several more rebellions occur. In one, the issue was meat. (Numbers 11) In another, a personal issue was provoked by Miriam and Aaron, his own brother and sister, over Moses' marriage to an Ethiopian.

## *An Opportunity to Enter*

After a three day journey, Moses was told to select individuals, in whose judgment all Israel had confidence, to spy out the Promised Land.

After forty days they returned, bringing fruit from the land and a good report. They said the land flowed with milk and honey. The cities were fortified, and " . . . we saw giants, the descendants of giants; and we were in their sight like grasshoppers." (Numbers 13:33)

The giants were the remnants of those beings who had entered into materiality outside the line of Adam.

> In the matter of form, as we find, first there were those projections from that about the animal kingdom, for the *thought* bodies gradually took form. These took on *many* sizes as to stature, from that as may be called the midget to the giants—for there were giants in the earth in those days, men as tall as (what would be termed today) ten to twelve feet in stature, and in proportion—well proportioned throughout.    364-11

If this is true, then we can understand why it was necessary for this line to be destroyed, and why Joshua (who had been Adam) had the responsibility to do so. Once they were slain, and their race extinguished, they would have to reincarnate through those channels which were the result of the creation of Adam. Their souls then could begin on the upward process of evolution. God had promised the children of Israel these tribes would be destroyed. He promised them possession of the Holy Land. Now they were being tested as to whether they were willing to stand on those promises.

> Before that the entity was in the land when there were those activities during the journeying from Egypt to the Promised Land. Though the entity was not among those who reached the Promised Land, he was among those who were the defenders of those causes to which the two [Joshua and Caleb] were engaged who reported the ability of the group—or Israel—to enter in at once.
> The entity was also of the tribe of Aaron, or of Levi; but not of those that were ever active in the temple—more as those that cared for the temple activity.

Thus the entity was acquainted with those conditions which had to do with the preparation by Moses, by Joshua, by Aaron, and by those in authority, as to the manner in which the groups were to be formed in their march.

Thus certain routine, certain activities always become a part of the entity's experience; the desire that right things be in their right place, and that right things should follow in a consecutive way or manner. These become as latent and manifested experiences for the entity.

The name then was Shem—of the brethren of Moses and Aaron; of that group dedicated for a special service in activities in that direction.

Keep the faith, then, as well indicated there. For those who seek are indeed Israel, and Israel indeed is *all* who seek; meaning not those as of the children of Abraham alone, but of every nation, every tribe, every tongue—Israel of the Lord! That is the full meaning of Israel.

In the present, then, we find that there may be that systematic use of those tenets as superscribed there by the lawgiver himself—these may be well applied in the present.                                                            2772-1

But the men who went up with him said, We are not able to go up against the people; for they are stronger than we.

*And they brought up to the children of Israel an evil report of the land which they had spied out, saying the land through which we have gone to spy out is a land that devours its inhabitants; and all the people that we saw in it are men of a giant stature.* (Numbers 13:31-32)

Cayce opened his reading for a young dramatic arts teacher [3463] in a most unusual manner, saying, that the entity was someone who "will either make something so unusual as to almost startle the world, or he won't amount to 'a hill of beans'!" In order to make this contribution, Cayce said the young teacher must gain confidence in himself, by having confidence and trust in the purposes of the divine. Thus he could make amends for many shortcomings in past lives.

Before that the entity was among those journeying to the Promised Land, among those peoples chosen to spy out the land, and was with the leaders who returned with the good report.

The entity was persuaded by the greater number that there was not the ability to conquer or to overcome. The name then was Japin. The entity lived through that experience regretting the rejection of those convinced within self by the Holy Spirit [of] God, just to be on the popular side for the moment. The entity again and again regretted the declaration that the optimism of Caleb and Joshua was foolhardy.

Thus in the present there may be the warning, Do not reject that thou knowest in thine heart, mind, and soul to satisfy a moment of gratification, of being popular, or being upon the popular side. But know that self is right, and that it is in keeping with the divine within self. For there is within each soul, each entity, that image of the Creator—if there is the attuning of the self, the ego, the *I AM* to the divine—which may enable nothing to hinder the entity from accomplishing, attaining any position of power that is the desire of the heart. But use it aright. Forget not the declaration made by him whom ye rejected that led those people into the Holy Land, "Let others do as they may, but as for me, I will serve the living God."           3463-1

In Atlantis, [3463] was among the children of the Law of One, but joined with the Sons of Belial and "brought death, destruction, sin, and ugliness in many, many ways." He turned away from a ministry of education through love, kindness, and patience to gratify selfish desires, and rejected all warnings given by the spokesmen from the holy sources. By supporting Caleb and Joshua in their favorable report of the Promised Land, and uniting with those who were convinced by the Holy Spirit, he had an opportunity to correct those weaknesses which had begun in Atlantis.

His lack of confidence has been a result of a failure to stand firm and has remained a pattern in succeeding lives, although he did gain spiritually as a martyr in Roman times. He was warned by Edgar Cayce, if he turned from the way of truth and light to gratify self's desires and vanities, 'Woe be unto the entity, not only here [in this life], but in those experiences to come.'

This particular reading supports the hypothesis that many of those who were with Moses in the wilderness were the Sons of God who had come with Adam in the beginning, but had fallen away from their spiritual purposes. The Wilderness period gave them the opportunity to reestablish their relationship to God, which they either accepted or rejected.

*Then all the congregation was in commotion; and lifted up their voices and cried; and the people wept that night.*

*And all the children of Israel murmured against Moses and against Aaron; and the whole congregation said to them, "Would God we had died in the land of Egypt! Or would God that we had died in the wilderness!*

*Why has the Lord brought us into this land, to fall by the sword that our wives and children should be prey? We were better off when we dwelt in Egypt." (Numbers 14:1-3)*

For two years the children of Israel had been listening to Moses and Aaron preach. They had gathered the commandments of God under which they were to live. They heard all the prophecies. As slaves, they were used to having others make decisions. Now they were forced to make one themselves. Had they sufficient courage and faith to face the adversaries God had promised them they could subdue, they could have entered and taken possession of the Promised Land. Fear ruled. They rejected God's promises. Thus a long period of wandering began.

## *Korah's Rebellion*

Throughout the years of wandering, Moses was plagued by one rebellion after another. The people grumbled when their stomachs were empty, and complained when thirsty. Even Aaron and Miriam rebelled when Moses married an Ethiopian woman. Still other rebellions occurred when factions, such as Korah's, began to question Moses' authority and his right to be their leader.

*Now Korah, the son of Izhar, the son of Kohath, the son of Levi, and Dathan and Abiram, the sons of Eliab, and On, the son of Peleth, sons of Reuben, started a faction.*

*And they rose up before Moses with certain of the children of Israel, two hundred and fifty chiefs of the assembly, who at that time were men of renown;*

*And they gathered themselves together against Moses and against Aaron and said to them "Is it not enough for you, seeing all the congregation are holy, every one of them, and the Lord is among them; wherefore do you lift up yourselves above the whole congregation of the Lord?" (Numbers 16:1-3)*

A missionary woman, whose husband had become an alcoholic, was told:

**Before that the entity was among the chosen people journeying to the Holy Land. The entity was among, close to, the sons of Korab, that one who rebelled; not Korab, but the son of Korah—Zipohar.**

**The entity in the present is again meeting self in the condemning of others, for, again the pattern is the withdrawal from companionship because of unbelief, unfaithfulness.**

**In that experience the entity suffered in mind, gained in principle and in the patience that will yet be tried as by fire.**          3179-1

There is more than one instance when individuals questioned Moses' authority. Even after the miracles they had seen him perform, they disputed whether God had really chosen him or not.

*And Moses spoke to Korah and to all his company and said to them, "In the morning the Lord will show who are his, and who are holy; and he will cause them to come near to him; and those whom he has chosen will he cause to come near to him.*

*This do: Take for yourselves censers, you Korah, and all your company;*

*And put fire into them before the Lord tomorrow; and it shall be that the man whom the Lord chooses, he shall be holy; this is enough for you, O you sons of Levi."* (Numbers 16:5-7)

We must constantly make tests within ourselves as to which is God's way. As long as we are not fully convinced by the Spirit, there is always the possibility of being deceived by others, or the subtleties of our own egos. But if we truly are sincere, we can bring it all before God—and by this test and the results, know which is the true path, pattern, spirit, or leader to follow.

**The test should be as within self. For read thoroughly, analyze the admonitions given by the lawgiver after his experience of the period of activity in the earth—one and twenty years had the entity been given to giving the law, the moral law, the penal code, the marital law, relationships of all kinds. Know indeed the knowledge is latent within.**

                                                                5377-1

Edgar Cayce speculated with the class"

"It seems to us that if we had walked across the sea on dry land we never could forget it. But when we look at ourselves and think we have come a long way, we realize that perhaps we are not much farther advanced in many ways than these people. Often we vow to ourselves that we won't do so and so, then we forget it before the sun goes down."

This entity sided with its family through duty, and was able to gain spiritually.

Before that, the entity was in the lands when there were the journeyings from the house or land of bondage to the free land, or to the land of promise.

The entity then also was of the lineage of the Levites, but of the Korah tribe, being among the daughters of the sons of Korah.

In that experience the entity gained, and yet held to its duty to its father and mother, which brought destructive experiences in the activities of the entity in its youth, though the entity was not destroyed when those of the household of Korah were destroyed. However, resentments were builded in a manner that found expressions again, without due consideration to the spiritual experiences of the entity.

Thus the necessity in the present—for the *truth* of spiritual life and spiritual processes as related to the material *and* mental forces—for the entity returning to a physical, mental, and spiritual understanding in order for there to be a normal balance.

The name then was Ashbahel.                                                    2153-3

This entity learned a lesson from Korah, and also gained spiritually.

Before that, we find the entity was among those peoples who journeyed from the Egyptian land to the Promised Land.

The entity was among those who were of the sons and associates of Korah, but not of the Levites who were destroyed. Being young in years during the experience, the entity learned a lesson, and became among those who joined with the Gershonites as the keepers of moneys, or the records of same, until there was the division of the lands in the Promised Land.

Hence, we find the entity in the present is one that may be a very good statistician, or datastician, especially as to things pertaining to the working of or working with things made of wood—as varnish or finish, of form, or shape, or molds, of things that would have to do with ornaments for same.

For as one of the Gershonites, though of course, as indicated—of the kinsmen of Korah—the entity gained throughout that experience; and was close to the elders as they established their activities in the Promised Land.

Hence, there is the great desire for knowledge pertaining to those who are in high places—the innate urge to be *true* to all influences, and yet—as it were—seeing the shady tradings of those about the entity, the upper hand as taken because of weaknesses of some character or nature in the associates or friends or the activities with others; but be not tempted by same.

The name then was Ajlon.                          1950-1

*And Moses said, "Hereby you shall know that the Lord has sent me to do all these works; for I have not done them of my own mind.*

*If these men die the common death of all men or if they be visited after the visitation of all men, then the Lord has not sent me.*

*But if the Lord make a new thing, and the earth opens its mouth and swallows them up with all the things that belong to them, and they go down alive with all that belongs to them into Sheol, then you shall know that these men have provoked the Lord."*

*And when Moses had finished speaking these words, the ground split asunder under them;*

*And the earth opened its mouth and swallowed them up with their households and all the men who were with Korah and all their goods.* (Numbers 16:28-32)

This woman was among the faction who were "swallowed up."

Before that we find the entity was in that land now called the Egyptian, during those periods when there was the Exodus of the people from that land going into the Promised Land.

The entity then was among the daughters of Aaron, that was the teacher with Moses the leader, the son of Egypt that with his peoples chose to carry those things forward. The entity kept well into the teachings in those experiences. And when there were the rebellions when the sons of Korah were destroyed, the entity had turned rather to those things that bespoke of the adding to, even as the brethren had done, when Nabad and Abihu offered strange fire. The entity offered strange fire in those things that became an abomination in the days of Korah, and the earth swallowed up the household of Abazeal the daughter of Aaron. For in that experience did the troublesome things that make for the aggrandizement through position and power, the aggrandizement of selfish interests, bring those things of defiance to the lessons and tenets and applications of extremes in a material world.

In the present, we find from the experience innately, the periods of rebellions that arise. Hence, the necessity of those injunctions that have been shown: learn ye patience! Bear ye one with another and thus wholly fulfill the laws of love, for these are they whose feet shall walk in the pathway of light and lead many aright. Go not after the strange paths that lead into destructive forces even as Korah.         683-1

*They, and all that belonged to them went down alive into Sheol, and the earth closed upon them, and they perished from among the congregation.*

*And all Israel that were round about them fled at the cry of them, saying "Lest the earth swallow us up also."*

*And there came out a fire from before the Lord and consumed the two hundred and fifty men that offered incense.* (Numbers 16:33-35)

This reading raises the question, just how did they die?

Before that, the entity was active in that period when there were the journeyings from Egypt to the Promised Land. And the entity was among those who defied the leader, who set in question as to whether those authorities were only given to one individual or not, and not answered, though as the record is given, destroyed; but not in the way and manner as would be indicated by that character of record presented, but as in the fact of the self being allied with those that did defy—*not* God, but the authority of a man.

In that experience the entity followed close with the true tenets of truth, that the law is a universal consciousness and is applicable in the experience of each soul that seeks the truth in his relationship to the Creative Forces, or God—an influence within and without, that must answer by the manner in which ye apply same in your relationships to others.

**Thus the questions as to the sincerity of individuals or groups—this oft becomes the measuring stick of the entity in the present.** 3031-1

This entity, a Jewish male, sided with Joshua and Moses in the dispute.

Before that, we find the entity was among those peoples born in the wilderness during the journeying of the children of promise to the Promised Land—during those days when there were disputations as to those activities of Korah.

We find the entity standing close with those of Joshua, Aaron, and Moses to the defense of the activities through those experiences of the purifying of body for the dedicating of same for a service in the activities of the peoples as they journeyed.

There we find the entity gained, throughout that experience; being one that upheld those tenets, those principles, those ordinances as were proclaimed during those experiences.

And from that experience, those abilities to bring quietness out of dissension, the abilities to quell those activities that would become mob activity, those abilities to counsel with those who are individually sad hearted, come as a natural activity of the entity.

The name then was Shulzar. 1856-1

Desire is fire, and it purifies. As long as we create a desire to be at-one with God, no matter how many rebellions or complaints we make—no matter how many diversions we insist upon in our wanderings—eventually we will achieve the object of our desire. A state of peace and unity with God and man. It is a law. As long as there is the constant desire, and striving, there will be the achievement, and "forty years" shall come to an end.

## The Stumbling Block at Meribah

*And there was no water for the people to drink; and they gathered themselves together against Moses and against Aaron.*

*And the people quarreled with Moses and with Aaron, saying, "Would God that we had died with the death with which our brethren died before the Lord." (Numbers 20:2-3)*

Edgar Cayce's comments to his Bible class were simple and prag-matic on this lesson:

"When they needed water, they blamed Moses instead of turning to God for guidance and direction. Each time Pharaoh refused to let the people go, Moses didn't doubt what God had already told him. He went back and asked God what he should do next. If his people had followed Moses' example, things would have been much different."

*And Moses and Aaron gathered the congregation together before the rock, and he said to them, "Hear now you rebels; out of this rock we will bring forth water for you."*
*And Moses lifted up his hand and struck the rock with his rod twice; and the water came out abundantly.* (Numbers 20:10-11)

More lessons were drawn for his students:

"Because of all their complaining and backsliding, Moses must have felt very superior to the rest of the people. He said 'Must *I* give this rebel-lious people water to drink?' One of the hardest lessons to learn and manifest is humbleness of spirit, especially when one is in the position of authority. With all his abilities, Moses had not conquered himself. He took unto himself the glory of giving the water."

**For these are at those periods when . . . there *must* be the *disseminating* or the giving away of the egoism of self. Consider as an example in thy study of same, the servant Moses. For these become as may be found even for and from that record as ye have, the stumbling block at Meribah.**                                                                **281-29**

The following commentary suggests Moses' transgressions at Meribah may have been the breaking of the first commandment.

**(Q) Can [257] receive donations from people he has introduced during the past years?**
**(A) Provided [257] presents same as a service to mankind, and not as "I accomplish so much for so much." Let the body-mind, the body-consciousness, gain this lesson: that "I must be made one with the I AM," rather than the I made to appear as the representative of the I AM, see?**

For let that mind be in you which was in Him as he gave those lessons as were written upon the tables of stone—for this begins with the first and the greatest commandment of all: set not self in seeking or in obtaining, or in any manner set self beyond or a judge of any man's, or of any individuals, or of any ideas above and beyond that first set, "Thou shalt love the Lord thine God with all thine heart, thine mind, and thine body!" 257-20

## Another Detour

*And Moses sent messengers from Rakim to the King of Edom, saying, "Thus says your brother Israel, you know all the trouble that has befallen us;*

*How our fathers went down into Egypt and we have dwelt in Egypt a long time; and the Egyptians oppressed us and our fathers;*

*And when we prayed before the Lord, He heard our voice and sent an angel, and has brought us forth out of Egypt; and behold, we are in Rakim a town in the uttermost of your border;*

*Now let us pass through your land"* . . .

*But Edom said to him, "You shall not pass through my border, lest I come out against you with the sword."*

*. . . and Edom came out against them with a strong force, and with a strong hand. Thus Edom refused to give passage through his border, wherefore Israel turned away from him.* (Numbers 20:14-18, 20-21)

Isaiah proclaims we must make straight a path in the wilderness. This could be interpreted from a metaphysical point of view to mean the establishment of a pattern of activity that leads us directly to God. We must travel through the depths of our own subconscious minds to build that highway that will establish a permanent connection with the superconscious forces. As we seek to make a straight highway through the subconscious to these higher forces, often we may uncover pockets of suppressed, rebellious energies which create long detours.

This inner pattern is represented externally in Numbers 20, when the Edomites would not let Moses pass through their lands. Thus they could not go "straight" in their journey, but were forced to take a detour of endless, barren miles.

Two of those Edomites are represented in the following:

Before that the entity was in the land where the activities were carried on, when the children of Promise passed through the land that they were forbidden to pass through, save with permission.

For the entity was among the descendants of Esau. Thus one that looked to the products of the field, and the abilities to use the mountainside in the interests of those things pertaining to mining, herding, though then as a leader.

The name was Jared. The entity took advantage of a group. Hence, expect a group to take advantage of thee! For what ye measure, it must be, it will be measured to thee. For ye must pay every whit that ye measure to others. And this applies in the future as well as in the past. Do ye wonder that your life is in such a mess!

From same in the present, then, ye will find things pertaining to spirituality, a search for truth, coming nigh unto thee, even as then. Do not disregard same in the present. Lay hold on same. Seek Him while He may be found.                                                    3063-1

In the one before this we find in that land when the peoples were returning to the Promised Land. The entity then among those who hindered their return through Edom, and of the Edomites. Then in the name Gibdden, and the entity gained and lost in this period—gaining in that of the manner of the entity's service, losing in being of the oppressive disposition, or using will force in that direction against self's own judgment.

In the urge from same is seen that the entity uses those conditions of religious force and position in an erroneous manner, for rather than preparing self to meet the needs of same, attempts to bend same to meet the needs of present day conditions.                        2676-1

## An Intimation

And the Lord sent fiery serpents against the people, and they bit the people, so that many people of Israel died.

Therefore, the people came to Moses and said to him, We have sinned, for we have murmured against the Lord and against you; pray before the Lord, that he take the serpents away from us. And Moses prayed for the people.

And the Lord said to Moses, Make a fiery serpent of brass, and set it upon a pole; and it shall come to pass that everyone who is bitten by a serpent, when he looks upon it, shall live.

*So Moses made a serpent of brass, and set it upon a pole, and it came to pass that if a serpent had bitten any man when he beheld the serpent of brass, he lived.* (Numbers 21:6-9)

Edgar Cayce saw in Numbers 21 an intimation of Christ's death on the cross. This reading gives the basis for Cayce's insight:

**Get a hold upon self. Read, study, to know by heart, that given, "In my Father's House are many mansions. Were it not so I would have told you, for I go to prepare a place, that where I am ye may be also, and I—if I be lifted up—will draw *all* men unto me. Even as Moses lifted the serpent in the wilderness, and he that looked was healed from within—he that looketh on me, as I am lifted in that consciousness of the individual that the soul hangs upon that clarifying of the life from *all* forces of the material forces, may be lifted up and enlivened from within." 4757-1**

The readings insist we have the power to heal ourselves, if we will only believe the power lies within.

Eventually the brazen serpent became a stumbling block, just as any symbol that is abused and misunderstood.

## Balaam

In Numbers 22, the children of Israel are very close to the Promised Land. They are encamped on the east side of the Jordan, opposite Jericho. Balak, the king of the Moabites, was afraid they intended an invasion of his domain. As a protection, Balak sought out Balaam, a famous psychic of the time, in order to have a curse pronounced upon the Israelites.

Balak believed if Balaam pronounced a curse, the very worst misfortune would fall upon Israel. Balaam was a prophet, who was possibly schooled in the lore of Egypt, Persia, and cults further eastward. He also was acquainted with the worship of God as proclaimed by the Israelites from the time of Abraham.

Balaam must have valued his psychic abilities, for he wasn't intimidated by Balak. He told Balak he could only say what God allowed him to say. He wouldn't attempt to sway the message to suit Balak's desire. This indicates Balaam recognized the power he had came from a higher source over which he had no control. No doubt he hoped the information he received would be favorable to Balak because it would bring great material gains. But he knew not to force the issue—else it would be to his own undoing, and the riches would mean nothing.

At night, Balaam received a message from God—perhaps in a dream or through the trance state:

> *And God came to Balaam at night and said to him, "If these men have come to call you, rise up and go with them; but only the word which I shall say to you, that shall you do."*
>
> *So Balaam rose up in the morning and saddled his ass and went with the princes of Balak.*
>
> *And God's anger was kindled against him because he went; and the angel of the Lord stood in the way for an adversary against him.* (Numbers 22:20-22)

This is one psychic's commentary on another: Edgar Cayce's Bible lesson follows:

> "Did God go back on his word? If He told him to go, why did He send the angel to block the way? Was He angry? Perhaps Balaam was so anxious to go, because of the possibilities for material gain, that he misinterpreted God's message. Often we persuade ourselves we are doing the right thing when we are not, because we are so intent on having our own way."

> *And when the she-ass saw the angel of the Lord, she lay down under Balaam; and Balaam's anger was kindled, and he stuck the she-ass with a staff.*
>
> *And the Lord opened the mouth of the she-ass and she said to Balaam, "What have I done to you that you have struck me these three times?"* (Numbers 22: 27-28)

Cayce comments to his Bible class:

> "Unless we count the serpent in the Garden, this is the only reference in all Scripture to an animal speaking. Many animals are very close to the universal consciousness and can sense and see things man does not. When the ass spoke, Balaam answered it in a most natural way. Perhaps he didn't realize this was a genuine psychic experience. When he real-

ized what was happening, he fell on his face, possibly fainting and losing consciousness."

In a reading for an astrologist, Cayce found:

> . . . the entity was in that land wherein the children of promise entered
> on their journey to the Promised Land—in Midian. The entity was among
> the daughters of the prophet that was called to curse Israel and was
> spoke to by the beast as well as warned in those experiences.
> These brought the entity to a better interpretation and to the study
> of the laws recorded through the activities of those peoples.
> In the latter portion of its sojourn the entity sought activities that
> brought better relationships, before there was the full destruction of
> those peoples that hindered. The entity joined then with those that
> made terms later in the Promised Land.
> The name then was Elzjah.                                    3356-1

Evidently this astrologer was also involved in spiritualism as the following question infers.

> (Q) Was Odenatus of Palmyra, who is now Meah "over there," my true
> mate?
> (A) The true mate was the one that was in the Midian experience, when
> there had been the acceptance of those activities in the Promised Land.
> It was not Odenatus but Demetrius that was the brother of Odenatus.
>                                                              3356-1

## Balaam Succumbs

Although he failed in his effort to have Balaam pronounce a curse on
Israel, Balak evidently was able to bribe Balaam to devise an ingenious
plan which resulted in the death of thousands of Israelites.

In his commentary on Balaam, Edgar Cayce suggested Balaam's ea-
gerness for material gain may have been the reason the Lord rebuked
him after giving Balaam permission to go with the men of Moab. Cayce's
view probably originated from two sources—his own insight into human nature, and two New Testament references, 2 Peter 2:15 and Jude
1:11.

Revelation 2:14 refers to Balaam as the one "who taught Balak to cast a stumbling block before the children of Israel to eat things sacrificed to idols and to commit adultery."

This suggests Balaam had a part in enticing the Israelites to participate in the sensual pagan rituals of the Midianites.

*And Israel abode in Shittim, and the people began to commit whoredom with the daughters of Moab.*

*And they invited the people to the sacrifices offered to their gods, and the people did eat, and worshipped their gods.*

*And Israel joined herself to Baal-peor; and the anger of the Lord was kindled against the children of Israel.* (Numbers 25:1-3)

The spell of these self-indulgent attractions drew many thousands of Israelite men into the Moabite camp where the laws and moral code established by Moses were wantonly disregarded.

The whole of Israel seemed threatened by this mass defection. In a moment of righteous indignation, Phineas, the grandson of Aaron, stayed the plague in a most dramatic manner. Zimri, a respected leader and prince of Simeon, had entered the tent of a Moabite woman, Cozbi. Phineas followed him, and thrust his spear through both of them while they were engaged in the sexual act. The people were stunned by the example made of these two. The fear of God rose in them, and they returned to their priests, listened to their counsel, and refrained from the temptations offered by Moab.

According to our present standards, Phineas took upon himself a great responsibility, killing two people in the name of God. Yet this decisive act was exactly what was needed to restore order and to prevent the complete dissolution of Israel.

Does it seem fair that two should bear the punishment for the sin of thousands? Apparently the soul of Zimri gained from that experience by being used as an example:

**Before that the entity was among the children of promise, as they journeyed from the Egyptian land to the Promised Land.**

**The entity was a prince among his own people, but one whose activity was of such a nature as to cause Eleazar to act to stay the plague among those peoples, in the matter of the entity's associations with the Midianite woman.**

**In the experience, we find that the entity in the early portions was *so***

*well* thought of as to be called a prince among his peoples—a judge, a counselor to his brethren—among those who were chosen as leaders. Yet the entity allowed self-indulgence, self-gratification, to so overcome all of those purposes, all of those longings of so many, as for the entity to do that which brought (even for the moment's gratification) such disturbing conditions among those who sought the right way.

Then, in thy experiences of the present day, choose thou rather God's way. Take Him, His principles, His directing influence into account, as ye counsel with those of thy brethren, those of thy neighbors. And who is thy neighbor? He to whom ye may be an aid, a help today—whether he be in the chair beside thee or upon the other side of the globe—he is thy neighbor.

So live, then, as to present thy own body a living sacrifice, as ye did unknowingly in that experience; for ye stood *between* destruction of life; giving thy life, even in such an act; not purposefully. But *purposefully now,* in intent of mind and heart and soul, ye *must* do *good*; and not "do others" in the way that brings discouragement, disheartening, discouraging forces or disturbances.                               2052-1

The subject of this reading was a thirty-six-year-old New York attorney. In a subsequent reading, the young lawyer asked for guidance pertaining to his marital problems. He had lost interest in his wife and wanted to marry another woman. He claimed he loved both women, but in different ways, and did not want to hurt either of them.

The reading gave specific advice, and also revealed this was a karmic situation arising from that Old Testament experience. His present wife had also been his wife then, and the "other woman" had been his Moabite sexual partner.

As the entity innately has experienced, these individuals represent a definite activity taken by the entity in its experience in the earth plane among the princes—or the prince of his peoples in that experience in which there was allowed self-indulgence, self-gratification, owing to the beauty physically of that individual who now would appear *physically* superior to that other duty and obligation which is a part of the entity's present experience.

And to allow such influence in the present to cause the discarding, the irreparable activity, would bring not only degradation but a continued consciousness of wrongdoing, and fear would creep in. And, so far as the mental and spiritual life of the entity is concerned, it would prove degrading to the entity. . . .

As regarding spiritual and *mental* conditions, there is only *one* course for the entity, and that is to discard *any* relationships with [Mistress] other than of a purely helpful nature from the social angle.

There needs to be the closer relationships with the entity whom *this* body, *this* entity so belittled in that experience in which there were the needs for the priest to disregard the laws and to stay the plague of self-indulgence among those peoples.

Thus, putting away that individual who caused these will be for the betterment of self, for the development of self and that individual, as well as building for those relationships which may bring spiritual, mental, *and* material blessings to the entity—through the closer relationship with [Wife] who was the companion in that experience.

In analyzing these conditions—to be sure, entanglements have come about, but these must be settled within self. Just as the consciousness has caused uncertainty, so will the correct spiritual and mental decision bring harmony and peace—and give *better* activities in the experience of this entity . . .                                                                  2052-3

In his communications with Edgar Cayce, the young man related that his wife had been unfaithful to him. Cayce felt, in the light of the above reading, that his wife carried a hidden urge to defy and hurt him, just as he had disgraced and humiliated her when he fornicated with the Moabite woman, breaking the law of Moses which forbids associations with any outside the tribe of Israel. The lawyer also described that his wife's love was in the form of dependency on him. This was exactly the kind of love he needed, Cayce advised. By having the proper attitude of love and protectiveness toward her, he would be able to make up for his past experience with her.

It was also pointed out to him that any sexual relationships with the other woman, whether legally married to her or not, would always carry with it a consciousness of sin. In the subconscious mind of both, there would always be the memory of their being used as an example of immorality.

## Another Example

Perhaps more than Zimri and Cozbi were slain. This reading speaks of actions by Eleazar, the father of Phineas. The entity sought to learn about a companion who had been destroyed, and gained a concept of morality, the reading states, "experienced by few."

> **Before that the entity was in that land when there were the journeyings of a chosen people to the land of promise.**
>
> **In those experiences when there was the full destruction of the Midianites with the activities in a portion of the land the entity was in the household of those in authority—in the name then Heloise. The entity sought to know all of those happenings to those that had attempted to hinder, as well as the outcome of the destruction of a companion with the Israelites by Eleazar.**
>
> **These have brought, do bring a concept of relationships in morality to the entity in a manner that is experienced by few. These, though, make for abilities of the entity to write, or to draw conclusions from the happenings that might be applied in the experience of many, if the entity were to apply such in those directions.**               **3345-1**

## War on Midian

The wrath of Moses was kindled against the Midianites, and he ordered their complete destruction. Only the virgin women and small female children were spared.

The material gain which Balaam received from Balak gave him only short pleasure. He is listed among the dead in the ensuing campaign (Numbers 31:8).

Edgar Cayce's Bible class commentary follows:

> "The Midianites were almost entirely destroyed. The young ones, who could be trained as servants, were kept. All the older ones, who might lead others astray, were put to death. This was the result of their attempt to undermine the morals of Israel. The way the Midianites lived, and the means they resorted to, made all this necessary.
>
> "Even before he left Midian, Moses was told the day would come when all those who were not then serving the Lord would be destroyed. The same is true today. Any nation, any group of people that utterly disregards God will someday be destroyed.
>
> "Apparently it was not possible for Israel to be in the world but not of

it, as Jesus tells us to be. God has always recognized man's weaknesses. The opportunity to reach God is constantly given to man, but if man continually disregards it, then the natural laws of cause and effect will wipe him out and force him to begin all over again. Physical destruction is merciful in this sense. The Midianites not only disregarded their opportunities to get closer to God, but they became a stumbling block to the elect."

In this reading, Cayce counsels a former Midianite in the ways of Israel:

Before that we find the entity was in the land when there was the passing of the peoples known as the Hebrews through the wilderness.

There we find the entity was among the daughters of Midian, and acquainted with and in sympathy with those activities of those peoples in many ways. Yet with the destructive forces that came about through wars (as is manifested in the adverse forces of Mars), we find that wrath, anger in the minds of others has driven the entity oft to do and be in the present—as through *those* experiences—that which it of itself chose not, because of the *fear* as created by the wrath of many forms in the experiences of those with whom the entity was thrown.

The name then was Abijah.

In the present experience, again we find the abilities in many directions, the abilities of comprehension, the activities in which knowledge may easily become a part of the entity's experience. The application is not always so easy. But if the entity will turn to those forces and influences from which all power arises—knowing the *sources* of that ye believe, as *well* as what ye believe—then ye may be enabled to enact and to carry *on* in a way and manner that will become more self-assertive, not as with *selfish* motives, but for the good of the *purpose* for which the entity seeks expression and manifestation in and throughout this experience.                                                                 1752-1

A Michigan housewife was told she had been a Midianite and yet was not slain:

Before that we find the entity was in the Holy Land when those peoples were journeying there. The entity was among the Midianites who consorted with the peoples led by Moses and Joshua.

There was a reckoning, as others were in authority. Yet the entity found that which answered to a something within and gained through that experience, for being spared to journey with the sons of Manasseh into the Holy Land.

The name then was Jeluen. 5231-1

Apparently 1752 and 523 were among the 32,000 Midianite virgins who were spared. (Numbers 31:35)

## The Death of Moses

Why was Moses not allowed to enter the Promised Land? This question has occupied many minds. The clairvoyant readings of Edgar Cayce suggest that it was a natural result from cause and effect law.

This interpretation is based upon the answer which Cayce gave when asked which material would best parallel the "A Search for God" Study Group work:

The Bible is the best parallel, especially the admonition by Moses after he had finished all of his own egotism and had come to realize that there was not to be the experience in self for the enjoying of that which had been builded, owing to that weakness of selfishness. That's the last chapters of Deuteronomy, of 30th on. 262-100

Apparently Moses knew for most of the forty years that he would not enter the Promised Land. (See Deuteronomy 1:37, Numbers 20:12, and Deuteronomy 3:23–27) By the end of his life, Moses was able to realize and accept that it was something within him, his own selfishness, which prevented him from entering. He expressed two great indications of spiritual maturity—honesty with self, and detachment from results.

Chapter 30 of Deuteronomy indicates the consciousness which Moses had evolved. The key passage is found in verses 11–14 (King James translation):

*For this commandment which I command thee this day, it is not hidden from thee, neither is it far off.*

*It is not in heaven, that thou shouldest say, "Who shall go up for us to heaven, and bring it to us, that we may hear it, and do it?"*

*Neither is it beyond the sea, that thou shouldest say, "Who shall go over*

*the sea for us, and bring it unto us, that we may hear it, and do it?"*
  *But the word is very nigh unto thee, in thy mouth, and in thy heart, that*
*thou mayest do it.* (Deuteronomy 30:11-14)

In this reading Cayce draws a lesson for Moses' development:

> . . . and yet there have been and are periods when confusions arise and
> when some individual expression has drawn off the entity to seek its
> activity, even as Moses turned aside to see the bush on fire and yet was
> not consumed.
>
> So the entity, as in Moses, finds itself slow in making comprehension
> until he had been through those experiences of even being in the
> presence of the divine, having given to man the outline of the law, and
> of how man in his relationship to God, in his relationship to his fellow-
> man, in his relationship to himself could say, as must the entity learn,
> "Say not who will descend from heaven to bring a message, for lo! the
> whole law is expressed, is manifested, is indicated within one's own
> consciousness." For the body is indeed the temple of the living God and
> He hath promised to meet thee there.
>
> Open thy consciousness and let it ever be . . . not merely in words,
> but in purposes, of hopes, of desires . . .                          5276-1

The inwardness and great significance of this verse is further discussed in the following.

> Thus, as the lawgiver interpreted, "Lo, He is within thee." Man's
> discerning of that he would worship, then, is within self; how that he, the
> individual entity, makes manifest in his dealings daily with his fellowmen
> that God is, and that the individual entity is—in body, in mind, in soul—
> a witness of such; and thus he loveth, he treateth his brother as himself.
>
> Such an admonition has in man's interpretation oft put God, the
> mighty, the Lord, as far away. And yet he recognizes, if he accepts this
> admonition of the lawgiver, that He is within self.
>
> This is more clearly demonstrated and interpreted in the words of the
> Master himself, "In my Father's house are many mansions," many
> consciousnesses, many stages of enfoldment, of unfoldment, of bless-
> ings, of sources. And yet God has not willed that any soul should perish,
> but has with every temptation, every trial prepared a way of escape—or
> a way to meet same; which is indicated here by the Creator, the Maker

of heaven and earth and all that in them be. 2879-1

## The Body of Moses

A very enigmatic verse appears in the New Testament concerning the death of Moses:

*Yet Michael, the archangel, when contending with the devil about the body of Moses, did not dare to bring railing accusation against him, but said, "The Lord rebuke thee." (Jude 1:9)*

The war over Moses' body is an illustration of the real conflict that goes on within the soul.

**While there may be in the experience of the entity much of earthly fame, much of earthly fortune, these abused will turn again and demand flesh for flesh, and these become—as it were with [Michael]—disputing with Satan over the body of Moses.** 1406-1

Shortly after physical death, the soul undergoes a period of transition, or "inter-between" state, in which there is the movement from a material to a spiritual consciousness. In the after-life, the Cayce readings declare, our three-dimensional consciousness is absorbed by our subconscious mind which becomes the conscious mind of the soul.

In the subconscious mind there are programmed in psychic patterns the energies which have prompted all our thoughts, acts, and deeds while on earth. "To be absent from the body is to be present with the god (or gods) you have worshipped," the readings both promised and warned.

Moses was present with the two great forces he expressed in his life. The Devil represents the energies of self-will and egoism which would retard his development and hold his consciousness in the earth. Michael represents the protection and defense inherent in Moses' spiritual development, and would aid the soul in its evolution in new dimensions of consciousness.

The warring over (or within) the body of Moses was to determine the direction his soul would go in its experiences in the after-life.

**(Q) Are angels and archangels synonymous with that which we call laws**

of the universe; if so, explain and give an example.

(A) They are as the laws of the universe; as is Michael the lord of the Way; not the Way but the lord of the Way, hence disputed with the influence of evil as to the way of the spirit of the teacher or director in his entrance through the outer door.                    5749-3

No doubt the symbolic clash between Michael and the devil was over each soul, but people who are leaders are especially subject to these contending forces.

(Q) Why is Edgar Cayce surrounded by such wrong vibrations and entities in this great work?

(A) For there has been the continued battle with those forces as Michael fought with over the body of Moses. He that leads, or *would* direct, is continually beset by the forces that would undermine. He that endureth to the end shall wear the crown. He that aideth in upbuilding shall be entitled to that that he builds in his experience. He that faltereth, or would hinder, shall be received in the manner as he hinders.   2897-4

Moses demonstrated a way, and it was the best which had been shown. But it was not perfect—for selfishness had entered. Consequently, there were questions. And whenever a question is present, Satan is at hand.

Cayce saw in the life of Jesus a demonstration of the perfect Way, and one in which there was no question.

This counsel to a Jewish philanthropist who had interested himself in Cayce's Christ-oriented philosophy indicates Michael will defend all those who give service through a spiritual ideal.

Even as Michael in the way defended from the wicked one the body of the lawgiver of thine people, mine people, even as this mighty Lord of thy Way defended him may he defend thee in the ways thou goest, if thou will only keep thy hand in the Master's hand.        900-428

## The Bones of Moses

The bones of Joseph were carried with the Israelites until the passing of Joshua, and served as a focus for protection and inspiration. Yet the burial place of Moses was never revealed. The people were not allowed to know this. They would have made a shrine of his tomb, and thus jeopardized the whole purpose of his life. Moses had dedicated himself to the worship of God as *Spirit*. At the tomb, the people would be worshipping Moses—the man—rather than the Spirit which inspired his teaching, enlightened his mind, and directed his life.

The Promise in the Christ is "That where I am there ye may be also." This is the Promised Land for all who seek that estate we had with the Father before the world was. True understanding is found in knowing we are at-one with God.

Hence, the individual who aided man in setting forth laws, rules, or regulations—or who is known as the lawgiver—gave expression to that which, if it is wholly understood in the consciousness of an individual, puts before him all the problems and yet the answers to same, day by day.

Then, as he gave, it is not who will descend from heaven to bring you a message, or who will come from over the seas or from without to make you aware; but lo, the whole answer is within thy own consciousness. For, as ye become aware of this in thy relationships, there is the realization within self of that spiritual awareness which may enable self to *do* that which is ever the constructive exercising of the will in materiality, for: today there is set before thee good and evil life and death; choose thou.

That factor of the spiritual self, or of the soul (the will), then enables the individual to cooperate with that spirit, that truth, that fact which has ever been set before man: "If ye will be my son, I will be thy God"; "If ye call, I will hear"; "Behold, I stand at the door and knock; I will enter, if ye ask."

Then, these are not mere sayings! They are *facts*, truths, life itself! but the individual is not made aware of same through the material things nor material-mindedness; rather through spiritual-mindedness, as to purposes and activities of the soul in its lessons, its tenets that it has carried through its expressions in the earth.       **1797-3**

# *Part Two*

## From Joshua to the
## Golden Age of Solomon

*Now therefore write this song for them, and teach it to the Children of Israel; and put it into their mouths; this song will be a witness for me against the Children of Israel.*

*For I will bring them into the land which I swore to their fathers, a land that flows with milk and honey; and when they have eaten and are full and live in luxury, then they will go astray after other gods and serve them, and provoke me and break my covenant.*

*And when many evils and troubles have befallen them, this song shall be read before them as a witness; for it shall not be forgotten out of the mouths of their descendants; for I know their inclination and all that they do here this day, before I have brought them into the land which I swore to their fathers.* (Deuteronomy 31:19-21)

**Self-glory, self-exaltation, self-indulgence becometh those influences that become as abominations to the divinity in each soul; and separate them from a knowledge of Him. For thou art persuaded, for thou knowest from thine experience, nothing may separate the soul of man from its Maker but desires and lusts!**                          **1293-1**

# Joshua, the New Leader

**For without Moses and his leader Joshua (that was bodily Jesus) there is no Christ!** ***Christ*** **is not a man! Jesus was the man; Christ the messenger; Christ in all ages, Jesus in one, Joshua in another, Melchizedek in another; these be those that led Judaism! These be they that came as that child of promise as to the children of promise; and the promise is in thee, that ye lead as He has given, "Feed my sheep."** **991-1**

History provides only scant information about Joshua. Although he is considered a second Moses, he is mentioned only as "the son of Nun" from the tribe of Ephraim. No other family history is given. As an Ephraimite, Joshua was descended from Joseph, and thus was his own ancestor.

Like Abraham and Jacob, Joshua's name was changed when he entered into service under Moses. He was originally called Hoshea, which means Salvation. (Numbers 13:8,16) Joshua was the general who, in Israel's first battle, defeated the Amalekites. (Exodus 17) He was Moses' faithful servant and guardian of the Tabernacle. (Exodus 24:13, 33:11) He was a zealous and faithful defender of Moses' reputation as a prophet. (Numbers 11:28)

He is famous for two miraculous victories, at Jericho when he crumbled the walls with trumpets and shouting (Joshua 6), and at Gibeon when he commanded the sun and the moon to stand still. (Joshua 10)

Moses acknowledged Joshua as one "filled with the spirit," and in a simple ceremony, laid hands on him and gave him supreme command over Israel. (Deuteronomy 34:9) Joshua's duty was two-fold: to conquer the land and to apportion it to the tribes.

The power of God was with Joshua as it was with Moses. While at floodtide, the waters of the Jordan parted for Joshua, and Israel crossed into Canaan dry-shod, carrying with them twelve stones from the river-bed which, when placed at Gilgal with the Tabernacle and the Ark of the Covenant, became Israel's first memorial and holy place in the Promised Land.

Later Joshua moved the Tabernacle and the Ark from Gilgal to Shiloh and established his headquarters there. Joshua put all the laws of Moses into writing, and at the end of his days, gathered the people at Shiloh and drew them into a voluntary, free-willed covenant with God. He died at the age of 110.

This is the outline of Joshua's life presented in the Bible. The few personal features about this man are vivid and consistent. The Edgar Cayce readings add several new details about Joshua which help fill out the picture.

From reading 3188 we learn that Joshua was, like his predecessor Moses, "oft a lonely, lonely man—as man." Although Joshua was the most outstanding of the sons of Nun, reading 1737 tells us many of that house were adept as spiritual counselors.

The Bible gives us only selective details and events which the chroniclers remembered or considered important. Archeologists reconstruct their story from the enduring but mute artifacts they unearth. The Cayce readings bring out the less tangible and subtle aspects of the past, such as describing intra-personal relationships and those perishable and fragile memories which are preserved only by the person who experienced them, as in reading 3509. From it we learn that Joshua had a nephew who was awed by the stories told about the wilderness and who rendered valuable service to his uncle.

Edgar Cayce's comments to his Bible class complete our picture of Joshua.

"Nothing is indicated about Joshua having any special training, merely that he was a man Moses trusted. He is spoken of as his minister and servant. Whenever Moses received any instruction, Joshua was always at hand—not the 'mouthpiece' as was Aaron, but rather as the hand of

Moses. He remained in the tabernacle with Moses for long periods of time. Perhaps Joshua was the channel through which Moses received much of his information.

"When we consider it from this angle, Joshua might be considered one of the strongest characters in the Old Testament.

"Joshua didn't have an educated background. He wasn't as learned as Moses. There must always have been a number of people who were ready to remember that. Consequently, it was necessary for Joshua to be imbued with courage and self-confidence in his ability to succeed.

"We might say he was 'the man of the hour,' the only one who could take over where Moses left off.

"Joshua was perhaps eighty years old when the first mention is made of his being old and stricken. [Ch. 13:1] His life had been rugged, quite different from Moses. Joshua had been a slave in Egypt whereas Moses had been raised as royalty during his early life and didn't have to undergo the same hardships. Consequently, even at the early age of eighty years, Joshua was beginning to appear old. Apparently he was able to rejuvenate himself though, for he lived to be 110."

Edgar Cayce's belief in Joshua's abilities to rejuvenate himself stemmed from personal experience. Throughout his life Edgar Cayce demonstrated amazing recuperative powers. A dramatic illustration of his ability is described by Hugh Lynn Cayce in *Venture Inward*. On the verge of pneumonia, Edgar Cayce willed himself back to health in the space of a few minutes. His own Life reading indicated he had doubled his life-span in prehistoric Egypt through self-rejuvenation.

## Joshua and the Holy War

These in the earth activity were much alike [Joshua and Jesus] not as combative, as in the warrings, but in spirit and in purpose, in ideals, these were one . . . Thus may ye use the Son of Man, Jesus, the Master, as the ideal in the present and find a new meaning—if there is the studying and the paralleling of the life of Jesus and Joshua. 3409-1

In a culture which accepts warfare and combat not as necessary evils, but as a noble profession and an honored vocation, Joshua is an ideal type: the devout warrior, prepared by youthful service to command as a man who earns through his masculine vigor respect and honor in his old age; a man who combines strength with gentleness, ever looking for and obeying God's commands, and with simplicity and innocence wields great power calmly and with unswerving aim directs it to the accomplishment of a high, unselfish purpose.

Yet this ideal picture is questioned sharply today by those who look to Jesus' example of pacifism and brotherly love. It is Joshua's very reputation as a religious warrior that causes him to be questioned. Racial and religious differences have occasioned more wars and bloodshed than any other problem throughout man's history. And to modern thinkers, Joshua seems to be the epitome of the ardent advocate of the holy war. How could the All-Merciful Father of Jesus be the same God who could sanction and bless a war of extermination? It appears to be the lowest form of religion when a leader uses God's name as an excuse to invade a land and wrest it from its native people by destroying men, women, and children. Joshua seems to be the antithesis of Jesus. Yet, as the readings tell us, the same soul, who as Joshua was so zealous and vigorous in conducting this war, later, as Jesus, taught us to love our enemies, to turn the other cheek, and went unresisting to his own crucifixion.

Perhaps no single feature of the Old Testament is more abhorrent to modern man, or presents a greater stumblingblock to understanding, than the incessant and implacable effort by Israel to exterminate its enemies.

Yet in this complex and controversial arena, information in the Edgar Cayce readings and the understanding he expressed in his Bible class offer some valuable illumination and insights which are helpful in grappling with Joshua's holy war and its purpose.

The first premise Edgar Cayce calls us to accept is the Oneness of all force, and that God is an active influence in the lives of individuals. In a lecture to the A.R.E. study groups, he said:

"Do we believe the stories in the Bible that tell us God commanded the children of Israel to destroy this or that people? Isn't it the same today? We have a Christian nation founded upon that very thing. Our forefathers came over here and destroyed a people because something told them they must worship God according to the dictates of their own conscience. What told them? Wasn't it the same spirit force? It is the same spirit force that moves into the earth and acts upon individuals, that same *power* which has given to men their development—whether they crawled up out of the ocean or were made complete in the beginning. It is the same power and force that we worship as the All-Powerful God, that has left for us its evidence in the lives of men and women everywhere."

## *Joshua and a God of Love*

The readings assure us that God never changes. Down through the eons His Spirit is the same, one of peace, love, patience, and mercy. But Man in his separation from God has conceived Him to be many things. The needs and development, the purposes and understanding of an individual, a group, a state, or nation often determine the color and form which God is given.

> **What is thy God? Where is He, what is He . . . How personal is He? Not as Moses painted a God of wrath; not as David painted a God that would fight thine enemies; but as the Christ—[who presented Him as] the Father of love, of mercy, of justice.** 262-100

The idea of a war against nations was first expressed by Moses. A war which was to continue "from generation to generation" was pronounced against the Amalekites. (Exodus 17:14–16) He also commanded the Israelites to "blot out" the Amorites, the Hittites, the Perizzites, the Canaanites, the Hivites, and the Jebusites. (Exodus 23:23; Deuteronomy 7:1, 20:17) Thus Joshua inherited these commands and was under solemn ban to carry them out. Yet the question must be asked, was this really God's Will, or Moses' own concept?

Before Moses there is an absence of exclusiveness in Israel's destiny. The covenant with Noah included "every living creature of all flesh." (Genesis 9:15) God's first promise to Abraham was that through him "all the families of the earth shall bless themselves." (Genesis 12:3) The promise is repeated to Jacob almost word for word: "by you and your descendants shall all the families of the earth bless themselves." (Genesis 28:4) Nor did Jacob consider violence particularly meritorious. He was appalled by the vengeance of Simon and Levi (Genesis 34), and on his deathbed prayed, "Simon and Levi are brothers; weapons of violence are their swords. O my soul, come not into their council; O my spirit, be not joined to their company; for in their anger they slay men . . . " (Genesis 49:5–6)

The law of Moses contains many peaceful, universal, and democratic patterns. "An eye for an eye" was not a code of revenge, but a law by which the poor and powerless could get justice from the rich and mighty.

The readings indicate when Moses began his mission he was only partially awake, or aware, and that he chose an error, or "sin" in establishing the righteousness of his people. (262-126) This created misunderstanding, the reading states, and required a full period of earthly experience to undo. (True righteousness is exemplified by the publican in Jesus' parable in Luke 18:10-14, according to reading 262-125.)

The spirit of nationalism which Moses engendered in his people drew out their vigor and heroism, but also created a strain of sectarianism, intolerance, and narrow–mindedness which eventually had to be overcome. These attitudes went full cycle at the time of Jesus and reached their tragic conclusion with the complete destruction of Jerusalem in 70 A.D.

The angry God which Moses gave Israel, superior in battle, jealous, possessive, and vindictive, yet abounding in mercy to those He favored, was perhaps the only God Israel needed and could understand. This God ensured fear, confidence, and loyalty in a faltering people who might not have been inspired by a God of universal purposes and peace.

Moses took a people who had been slaves for four hundred years into the Wilderness. If for no other reason than for survival, a nationalistic and martial spirit had to be raised. Although it was nationalistic and self–centered, the idea that Israel was the most righteous race chosen by a superior War–God enabled the Israelites to marshal their energies and secure their place in a hostile world. The genius of Moses was to give his people a concept of God which spoke to their particular needs and condition.

Israel eventually outgrew this consciousness. Even through the time of David, the Israelites prayed to a God of War. Only after the decline of the kingdom after Solomon and the rise of the prophets did Israel look for a God who could save and restore rather than conquer.

And, as the readings have indicated, the Bible is the complete story, or pattern, of man in the earth. And throughout most of his history, Man has remained self–centered, egocentric, nationalistic, argumentative, vindictive, and warlike. Thus it was necessary for Israel to pass through all these experiences, nurturing the spirit of Truth, until this pattern was eventually overcome.

Through it all, no matter how man conceived Him to be, God never changed. His Spirit remained the same, one of peace, love, mercy, and justice for all, willing that no soul perish.

## *Joshua and the Heathens*

The study of the Gentiles, or heathens, draws several strands together which thread themselves through Cayce's philosophy and enable us to see the war against them in the light of God's Love. When the Bible class studied the genealogy of the Gentile nations (Genesis 10), Edgar Cayce stated a premise which was followed throughout the rest of their study:

> "The Sons of Japeth and Ham were called the Gentiles. Although they were akin to those who became the Jewish race, their beliefs, positions, and places of activity were quite different. The genealogy is given (Genesis 10) so that we might have the background of the various groups that are mentioned later. It is a most interesting study to follow each line as it is recorded, and see what happens to each.
>
> "We see certain ones were supposed to be destroyed, others were not to be destroyed at first but eventually, after they were given an opportunity to learn a lesson from the experiences through which they were to pass. They were to view the activities of the children of Israel and recognize, of themselves, that their own brothers or kinsmen (the descendants of Abraham) had chosen another way of living. They were to draw comparisons between the standards of each and the results of living up to those standards.
>
> "Some were sun worshippers, some moon worshippers, others animal worshippers, etc."

Edgar Cayce saw a metaphysical meaning in the history of these tribes. Each name carried a meaning, he said, and if a history of that tribe (or name) were followed from its beginning to its end a message would emerge with definite significance for our lives today.

A case in point can be drawn from the Amalekites. According to the Arabians, Amalek was descended from Ham, the son whose seed was cursed by Noah. Yet most traditions agree that Amalek was the grandson of Esau, that son of Isaac who sold his birthright for pottage.

Amalek translates as "valley dweller" or "he that licks up (or consumes)." The Amalekites are a kind of archenemy of Israel. Whenever they are mentioned in the Bible it is in connection with raids, blood-shed, and violence. They were the first nation to make war on Israel This battle occurred immediately after the Exodus at Rephidim, when Israel was at its weakest. The object of this raid, one authority states, was to capture the well which had miraculously appeared for Moses at Horeb, and demonstrates how completely the Amalekites disregarded God's will and purposes.

According to the Unity Metaphysical Dictionary, the valley symbol-izes the subconscious mind. As "valley dwellers," Amalek and his de-scendents signify *lust*, a force which is warlike and destructive in nature and, when established in the animal forces of the subconscious, is the begetter of destructive and rebellious appetites and passions.

Amalek's father was Eliphaz, meaning "God is Strength, God is Fine Gold." Thus, says Unity, desire at its origin is good and of God; but when it is misdirected by the carnal man it becomes lust (Amalek).

Thus it is easy to see why Moses pronounced a perpetual war on Amalek, and why Samuel later commanded King Saul to completely annihilate them. Metaphysically, they are an ever-present threat and enemy to the Spirit within.

Although it is always difficult to tell when a man or prophet is speak-ing out of his own mind, or when God is speaking through him, Edgar Cayce felt the pronouncements against the Amalekites must have been according to God's will because Israel was later punished for not carry-ing out this order. The following represents some of his thinking on the Amalekite question:

"Do you think God today tells anyone to go and kill people? Let's get a practical, personal application of this. We understand that it is God's purpose to make the earth His footstool. Consequently, whatever stands in the way of that purpose must eventually be eradicated. The character of the Amalekites at that time was such that they were unclean beasts before the Lord. This was because of the manner in which they con-ducted themselves toward their own people as well as their servants by conquest. Thus these people who were living in the Promised Land were abominations. God's People, those who professed Him above all other gods as the one and only God, could not be trusted with the Amalekites. If they were to be established in the land promised to them, the Amalekites would have to be eliminated. There was too great a risk of contamination if they were permitted to survive. Even under the best conditions, it is a great task to keep a large number of people in line. The presence of the Amalekites threatened everything that had been accomplished thus far.

"The Amalekites seemed always headed in this direction. They were the first to war against Israel after the release from bondage . . . Their utter destruction was prophesied then. The only way this prophecy could not have been fulfilled was if the Amalekites repented and changed their ways. But they did not.

"It has been said that God will not always wink at the wickedness of a nation. There will come a time when it has to pay, just as it will with America . . . No nation gets by with anything any more than an individual does. We have to pay every whit.

"Some individuals, and even nations, may be Amalekites today. That influence, that desire of the Amalekites rules in certain sections. When we light a match we can see the flame until it burns out. But even when we no longer see the light, the radiation continues. We know the good we do lives on. So does the evil, in so far as it is allowed to be an active influence through our so-called Amalekites."

The Kenite tribe points up another lesson. Whereas many tribes were to be destroyed, this one was spared. The Kenites are thought to have been Midianites who went with Moses and settled in Canaan. They remained friendly with Israel and were protected by them.

According to the Metaphysical Dictionary, Midianites signify thoughts of contention and strife. The Kenites, as a branch of this family, thus stem from the carnal or sense level of man's thinking, yet possess a degree of judgment, discrimination, and activity for good. The Kenites, as a level of consciousness, retain something lacking in the "nations" (or thoughts of man) that must be destroyed.

When Cayce discussed the Kenites, he drew a lesson from their consistency and pacifistic nature. These attributes were godlike and merited salvation.

"Even to the last of Jerusalem, the Kenites were never destroyed. Always they were living among those who were marked for destruction, but they always escaped. The Kenites were nature worshippers. It was from these people that Moses received his education about nature. Moses never forgot the Kenites. Often he reminded Israel about them.

"They never fought with anybody. Individuals, such as the woman who overcame Sisera (Judges 4), performed feats against a common enemy, but the tribe as a whole never took up arms. Whatever they were, they were pacifists. They lived among the people, but were not of them. Their great virtue was consistency. They lived what they believed.

"When it was known the Amalekites were to be destroyed, the Kenites departed from them. They were given the opportunity to escape." (2 Samuel 15:16)

The Amalekites and the Kenites represent two types of pagans, and yet in Israel's relationships with both, God's love is manifested, at least according to Edgar Cayce, who looked for and was able to see deeper patterns in this story.

Tribes like the Kenites, who possessed an element of purity in their beliefs, had the basis to recognize the higher element of Spirit manifesting through the Israelites. Those who made use of their opportunity to cooperate, convert, or in some manner change to their way of thinking and living were brought into new spheres of activities.

Several Life readings indicate the presence of "heathens" of different tribes who recognized and cooperated with the purposes of the children of Israel. It is interesting to note that the spiritual awakening which resulted from this contact with the Israelites under Joshua led to later incarnations among the Hebrew people.

Reading 5177-1 describes a Canaanite who "followed with the admonitions and the conversations kept between Moses and the Canaanites" and who made "closer relationships with the sons of Ephraim." This Canaanite in her next incarnation was a daughter of the high priest Zerrubabel during the rebuilding of Jerusalem after the Babylon captivity.

Another Canaanite, a seeress, "caused its own people to make agreements with the leader entering into the land." (3645-1) The entity "grew to understand and accept the teaching of Joshua." In her next life, she incarnated as the daughter of King Hezekiah and fled to England during the Assyrian invasion.

There is an interesting reverse pattern in these two readings. Their lives among the Jews was at a time when heathens were invading the land.

Reading 3479-2 describes a Hittite who "became a companion and an associate of those peoples who came into the land." She accepted their truths and tenets and was of the Moabite family from which Ruth descended. Following this experience, she incarnated in Laodicea at the time of Jesus and was active in the establishment of the early church.

Another Hittite (5343) had a period of gaining and losing. She was among the Hittites who made peace and joined with the people of the tribe of Judah. She gained when she applied spiritual law, but lost when she "persuaded those to undertake the material things" of her people. Perhaps "the material things" refers to self-indulgent pagan practices. In her next life, she incarnated as the wife of a French crusader, "dramatized all her hardships," and suffered the karma of the chastity belt.

## Joshua and Reincarnation

In the choice then, let it ever be according to that principle set by Joshua, and yet never given full expression to—although being a man chosen of God, spoken to directly in those preparations for activities of men among themselves in the creation of law and order, morals and health, and relationships with others as ever set forth by Joshua—"Others may do as they may, but for me and my house, we will serve the Living God." Not a dead past, but a living God. For as He gave, He is God of the living, not the dead. 3350-1

There is no greater enemy to spiritual growth than selfishness. Selfishness is the father of all sin. The source of all our energies is from the Spirit, and if our impulses are used only for self-gratification, ultimately a soul will dissipate its energy and lose its divine birthright. The readings indicate the earthplane is the plane of Application, the testing place for the soul's use and understanding of its knowledge of God. Only by application does our understanding become assimilated and integrated into the soul-mind and body. If a soul dissipates itself too greatly through a long-standing pattern of self-indulgence and gratification over a series of lifetimes, it may eventually lose the ability to manifest in the earth, and thus create a serious obstacle on the long road back to the Father.

All that are in the earth today are thy brothers. Those that have gradually forgotten God entirely have been eliminated, and there has come . . . the period when there will be no part of the globe where man has not had the opportunity to hear, "The Lord He is God." 2780-3

The disciplines in the law of Moses were aimed at halting self-indul-

gence. Yet everything Moses forbade was being practiced by the inhabitants of the Promised Land. (Leviticus 18:27) The prohibitions covered
sodomy, incest, homosexuality, and child-sacrifice. The Ten Commandments were aimed at other temptations: stealing, lying, oppression, dealing falsely, abandonment of the infirm and elderly, injustice to the poor,
cannibalism, child prostitution, mediumship, wizardry, and intimida-
tion of strangers.

When Joshua took command over Israel, he inherited a compact,
enthusiastic, and disciplined body whose stringent life in the wilderness forced a great degree of asceticism upon them.

Canaan, unlike the Wilderness, was fertile and fruitful, with native
religions abounding with fertility rites and other sensual practices. Many
of the pagan religions had no other purpose than celebration of the
carnal senses. These rites not only posed a threat to Israel's purpose, for
the Israelites would easily be tempted by these unfamiliar practices, but
they were also a threat to the pagans themselves in the large picture of
spiritual growth and evolution. By participating too extensively in a
pattern of activity on a lower plane of awareness, a soul can become
completely trapped in that state of consciousness and remain indefinitely unaware of any higher consciousness or ideal.

Thus, Death is a necessary experience, resulting from man's separation from God, as this reading tells us:

> [As] man's development began through the laws of the generations in
> the earth; thus the development, retardment, or the alterations in those
> positions in a material plane. And with error entered that as called death
> which is only a transition—or through God's other door—into that realm
> where the entity has builded, in its manifestations as related to the
> knowledge and activity respecting the law of the universal
> influence . . . For in the comprehension of no time, no space, no
> beginning, no end, there may be the glimpse of what simple transition
> or birth into the material is; as passing through the other door into
> another consciousness. Death in the material is passing through the
> outer door into a consciousness in the material activities that partakes
> of what the entity, or soul, has done with its spiritual truth in its
> manifestations in the other sphere.                                    5749-3

Many of the pagan lines were remnants of the pre–Adamic creation
which had survived the Flood. Their physiognomy showed what the

soul desired to express or experience in the beginning. The giants, for instance, had superhuman physical ability, but lacked spiritual awareness. They were intent upon increasing their material strength, without thought of its spiritual source. By projecting into the animal kingdom in the beginning, a genetic code was created which preserved these forms in a physical way and were adopted by souls who were at that level of development.

By eliminating these lines, or races, from the earth, Joshua was doing a service to these souls that they could not do for themselves. In their next incarnation, the giants were forced to take on bodies that were the result of the Adamic creation.

Thus Edgar Cayce's understanding of reincarnation enabled him to see the positive aspects of the pagan casualties in Israel's warfare, such as Amalekites and giants.

"Perhaps by killing these people physically, spiritually Joshua was releasing their souls for greater opportunities, which they would not have had in the flesh. Jesus tells us, 'Fear not them which kill the body, but are not able to kill the soul; but rather fear him who is able to destroy both soul and body in hell.' (Matthew 10:28)

"No doubt those individuals were already in hell, not knowing right from wrong, having come down from the mixture of thought-forms with the animal kingdom. To kill their bodies and release their souls was a merciful act."

His discussion of the Amalekites turned to the subject of death, dimensions of consciousness, and salvation.

"When every purpose of an individual is to do evil, then the only opportunity the soul has is to be taken *out* of its condition—which means death. In that case it is not unmerciful.

"Then, who are we to judge? To be absent from the body is to be present with God. From the life and teachings of Jesus, it would seem there is just as much development in other realms of consciousness as there is in the earthplane—possibly more. The test is in our own physical consciousness. If we continually fail to meet the test, He will not always bear with us.

"Death does not necessarily change the purpose of an individual. It merely gives the soul another opportunity.

"If it had been true that wholesale killing of evil individuals could wipe out sin, then the Flood would have overcome sin. God promised He would never cut off all flesh by the waters of a flood. This was not the way. The evil influence cannot be overcome by physical means. It has to be overcome by a change in the heart of man.

"Thus we begin to understand the reason for the coming of God's Son into the earth, to show how man must overcome sin within himself, which was the original cause of physical death; thereby overcoming death itself by his own spiritual—not physical—evolution."

These readings speak of spiritual evolution through the law, or teachings of Joshua.

We would turn again to . . . that declaration [Joshua 24:15] as made by Joshua, which has become a part of the awareness of each and every entity at times during the sojourns in the earth; partaking of the earth, yet becoming less and less earthly-minded.                         2072-4

Let the bases of thy study be the last admonition by Moses, by Joshua, when there were those applications in the spirit of truth, though erring often, of the children of the Law of One. These do, if ye would show self thy abilities to become one with the strengthening force.     3476-1

## Joshua and the Genetic Code

Cayce's dating of the Exodus at 5500 B.C. places the life of Joshua several thousand years earlier than is supposed, although many scholars believe the Book of Joshua is composed of legends of a much earlier activity. Cayce's date pushes all these events back into a dim and distant era concurrent with the mythological men and monsters which the readings say roamed the earth.

The age before the Flood was an era of occult projections. The rebellious Sons of God, misusing their creative energies, had used the physical world as the negative polarity for projections of mental and spiritual forces. This brought about the manifestation in the material world of their own spiritual distortions and thought–forms.

The Flood destroyed the majority of these creations and marked the end of this era. Yet many remnant lines, or races survived. (Perhaps the elusive Abominable Snowman and the Sierra giants are survivors.)

To the Adamic race and its leader was given the responsibility of eliminating all the corrupt and distorted thought-forms and mutations which exist in the mental, physical, or spiritual worlds of men.

## *We Are the Promised Land*

The real Significance of the war with the pagans can only be made by finding its application to the inner man.

Man values his material accomplishments and those proven principles which bring him success. Thus the divine pattern had to be manifested in the outer world, in the arena of time and space, by proving its ability to conquer enemies, build kingdoms, and ensure immortality and success.

By establishing a pattern of conquest, victory, and superiority in the outer world, man would eventually realize this same force could be applied to the inner self with the same results.

Man's (or an individual's) own inner conflict with the forces of good and evil, of the Spirit with the World, is personified through the history of Israel, with the Spirit triumphant.

In the Revelation of St. John, the symbolism is primarily from the Old Testament, yet everything John experienced was a projection from his inner self, as the following tells us:

> For the visions, the experiences, the names, the churches, the places, the dragons, the cities, all are but emblems of those forces that may war within the individual in its journey through the material, or from the entering into the material manifestation to the entering into the glory, or the awakening in the spirit . . .                    281-16

Just as the readings indicate that the Garden of Eden and the Temple are symbols of Man's body, the following intimates that the Promised Land is another.

> . . . know that in thine own body, thine own mind, there is set the temple of the living God, and that it may function in thy dealings with thy fellow man in such measures that ye become as rivers of light, as fountains of knowledge, as mountains of strength, as the pastures for the hungry, as the rest for the weary, as the strength for the weak.
> **281-28**

To possess this "Promised Land" we must become it. And this we can only do by conquest of the enemies within which are worldly and self-ish.

**Hence, at this particular period when there are changes to be wrought, ye have work to do. For ye have been made conscious of the fact that all have fallen short of their duty, and that if they would bring the earth to be a place in which even their own offspring would live, they must learn to search for their God. And they must put away those gods of the Sidonians, those gods of the heathen, gods of self, gods of gratifying of flesh; and crucifying the flesh—in mind, in body, in spirit—show thyself worthy of being given the opportunity to express thyself to others.**

**3645-1**

The body is the Temple—and we are the Promised Land! Only by putting all other "gods" aside can we complete the pattern.

**Then, in the study of self, there is the recognition that there are forces outside of self, there are forces and influences within self. The true-God forces meet within, not without self. For when there are altars builded outside, which individuals approach for the interpretation of law, whether it be physical, mental, or spiritual, these are temptations. It is concerning such that the warnings were given to the peoples. Though the entity or others may say, "Oh that's the old Jewish conception of it," but be ye Jew, Gentile, Greek, Parthenian, or what, the law is One—as God is one. And the first command is, "Thou shalt have no other gods before me."**

**3548-1**

## The Entry into Canaan

Armed now with new insights and understanding derived from the Cayce philosophy, we return back to the Jordan and the story of the crossing. Tradition states that only two men over the age of twenty-one who left Egypt entered the Promised Land. They were Caleb and Joshua, the two spies who gave the favorable report. The Life readings give no indication which disproves this tradition. In the following, though, we find a woman whose experience spanned the Exodus cycle.

In both the past and the present, her name had been Hannah:

... we find [the entity] during that period known as the return of the
peoples to the Promised Land from that land of bondage as the peoples
were led from the pilgrimage into the Promised Land. As has been
recorded, few that were of the age of accountability entered in the
Promised Land. The entity then, again in the name Hannah, left Egypt
and entered in the Promised Land; in the household of those that settled
in their division of the land about Bethel. In this experience the entity
gained, for though the hardships of bondage—as well as those of the
following through the various experiences in the journeys—the entity
held to that ideal that that had builded the promise, in this particular
people, in this particular period.

In the present, this and other sojourns—or travel—are of special
interest to the entity, and while others wonder often at the falling away
of the peoples under the various experiences and the various trials that
arose, to the entity these are easily—or more easily—understood than to
many. In this application in the present, the abilities to counsel with, to
reason with, the cheeriness of an often counted slight rather makes for
a variation in the experience of those whom the entity contacts, and a
mother to all.                                                    404-1

Although Hannah crossed over, this woman stayed on the other side.
A Hebrew widow was told in her reading she had been a Reubenite, a
member of that tribe which chose as its inheritance land that was not
part of the promise. (See Numbers 32 and Joshua 1:12–15.)

Before that we find the entity was again among the chosen peoples, as
they entered into the Promised Land.

The entity and its sojourners then remained upon the opposite side
of the Jordan, for the entity was among the daughters of Reuben; and
the entity then, of course, was among those that were born in the
wilderness, yet came under those activities of the teacher, the leader,
and the peoples that aided in the services for its own particular group
about the setting outs for those in the way that made for the leadings
of those that had their portion of the service in and about the tabernacle.

Then, the entity was of the daughters of Reuben, but among those
that were aiding in the establishing of those influences that became a
portion of that service.

Hence the entity was joined unto one of the sons of Levi, yet remained with her own people in the period when there was the preserving and the establishing of the lands in the Promised Land; during those periods of Joshua's life.

The name then was Eliesa . . .

(Q) Can you explain the periods of extreme doubt that come, though innately I must believe?

(A) . . . It was innately seen in those experiences when among the daughters of Reuben, in those activities when the men of war and the younger men were aiding their brethren in the establishing of the activities of the chosen people. Fears and doubts then arose. These have been a portion of the entity's experience through its sojourn. Yet, as in those experiences, as were the messages to the leaders from Joshua, "Let others do as they may, but for me and my house, we will serve a living God." . . .

Is it then any wonder that doubt and fear still at times remain a portion of the entity innately, and a portion of that development sought?

Yet if the body will put into the activity those truths presented even then, there may come more and more the answer of those promises that were given of old, "When ye call, I will *hear!* and that right speedily— if ye be my children, I will be your God." These are promises, as from the beginnings of the experience of man meeting his own self. Yet, as He gave, "Though the heavens and the earth pass away, those promises shall not fail" to maintain and to bring harmony and peace into the experience of those that will draw nigh unto Him.                1144-2

## The Parting of the Jordan

*. . . the waters of the Jordan shall be divided, the waters that are flowing down from above shall pile us as though they were in sheepskins, one beside the other.* (Joshua 3:13)

Three times in the twentieth century earthquakes have dammed the Jordan. In 1927 and 1924 severe quakes stopped the flow of the river for twenty-four hours by shoring tons of soil from the embankment. In 1806 the lower reaches of the Jordan near Jericho were dry for twenty-one hours due to the debris of an earthquake. The Arabs record a similar incident in A.D. 1267.

Some scholars feel that the Jordan crossing is only a myth or legend inspired by these natural phenomena. Others feel comfortable with it as the logical explanation, while others will settle for nothing less than divine intervention and the cessation of all natural law.

A similar problem exists for the Red Sea crossing, or "Reed Sea" depending upon the translation. The Suez Canal now covers what is a probable location for the crossing. The existence of fords can actually be traced along this waterway, making it credible that the flight from Egypt could have taken place there.

Near the north end of the Gulf is the site where early Christians assumed the miracle to have happened. Strong northwest winds occasionally drive the waters at this extremity so far that it becomes possible to wade across. In Egypt the prevailing wind is from the west, yet the Bible consistently mentions the east wind, which is typical of Palestine.

Miracles are not devalued because they can be explained by natural phenomena. The miracle is not how it happened, but when! The mystery and wonder is that when the faithful needed a strong wind or an earthquake, it happened. Time and Space become servants of Ideal and Purpose if they are one with the Lord's. The readings assure us it is true that "the stars in their course will fight for thee." (Judges 5:20)

In all the Life readings for Exodus cycle, not one reference is made to the Red Sea, whereas at least two mention the miracle of the Jordan. If, as is supposed, Edgar Cayce was reading the subconscious minds of entities and recalling from them those experiences which had made the deepest impression and carried the most influence, it is curious that the Red Sea miracle, considered one of the most significant and dramatic episodes in Jewish history, is never found among these memories.

The Red Sea is discussed in one reading (*Search for God* series) as a metaphysical symbol used by the teachers of Israel.

> **. . . *all* must pass under the rod, even as was given by those teachers that as Moses and the children passed through the sea they were baptized in the cloud and in the sea; as an example, as an omen, as a physical activity of a spiritual, a physical separation from that which had been builded in their experience as the sojourn in Egypt.          262-60**

Although the reading indicates it was also a literal event in time and space, it is not found among the personal experiences in the Life readings, as the Jordan crossing is. A possible explanation might be that it was not as dramatic as commonly assumed. If it was due to prevailing winds, or exposed fords, perhaps the escape was overshadowed by later events such as the theophany on Mount Sinai, the manna, the years of wandering, and the rebellions, all of which are mentioned in individual readings. Winds are not as dramatic as earthquakes.

The following reading suggests the dramatic and literal nature of the Jordan crossing, and reveals a dynamic and unusual Israelite of that time.

Before that the entity was among those peoples in their march from bondage to freedom.

And this will ever be a seeking in the experience of the entity—freedom—freedom—from all forms of counsel—freedom from all directions. And those who make demands, will to the entity, in many respects represent tyrants.

Do not let those upon whom the entity depends for advice and counsel for judgments be so reckoned by the entity. Let them ever know, too, the law is perfect—if ye know the law.

The entity in that experience was born in the wilderness and thus among those who journeyed into the Promised Land seeing, knowing much about those activities, especially when dissensions arose in those periods when Korah was destroyed. The entity knew then much of the activities and preparations when there was the entrance into the Promised Land, knowing and hearing much pertaining to the crossing of Jordan, also the walls of Jericho. All of these were a part of the entity's physical awareness.

Hence mysterious unseen, unexplained physical conditions are not mysteries to the entity but are a part of the consciousness of those who attain to a certain awareness within themselves.

Hence the entity as has been indicated is not only "sensitive" but intuitive, as to spiritual, as well as the purely emotional feelings of body and mind. Hence this will present to the entity at times problems, as to whether judgments arise purely from the moral and spiritual law or from the purely emotional influences of the body itself. Then in the name Jeheuthel, the entity was an associate of the younger brother of Caleb; becoming one in power for the direction of many when the tabernacle was set up in Shiloh.

The name to the entity means much, if and when analyzed in self.

2905-3

## *Twelve Stones*

When the feet of the priests bearing the Ark of the Covenant touched the river, the waters began to rise up "in a great heap." (Joshua 3:15-16) The priests stood in the riverbed until all the people passed over. When the crossing was complete, Joshua bid twelve men, one from each tribe, to pick up a stone and carry it to Gilgal. At Gilgal the stones were placed as a memorial to the miracle of the crossing, the first monument in the Holy Land.

A hint of the significance of these stones is seen by the space devoted to them—a whole chapter in the Book of Joshua. (Chapter 4) From Joshua himself we learn their meaning:

*And he said to the children of Israel, "When your children shall ask you in time to come, saying, 'What is the meaning of these stones?'*

*Then you shall explain them to your children, and say to them . . . So that all the peoples of the earth might know that the hand of the Lord is mighty, and that you may worship the Lord your God forever." (Joshua 4:21-24)*

One cannot study Cayce's Bible without coming to realize the organic structure and unity of the Book. The Bible is a book of patterns for man's unfoldment which are fulfilled through cycles of experience. The cycles repeat themselves; but as an individual grows in awareness, or "unfolds" he perceives the patterns of life on an ever-broadening field of consciousness.

Although Jacob, when he had his dream, slept on a stone (Genesis 28:18), and set up a pillar of stone (Genesis 35:14), and Moses wrote the law on tablets of stone (Exodus 28:11,12), it isn't until Joshua that we have twelve stones.

Jesus spoke of himself as the "cornerstone" and quoted Psalm 118: "The stone which the builder rejected has become the head of the corner." But Jesus was not referring to himself as a man, but rather to his spirit, or the consciousness he had obtained. This was the same consciousness which was in Peter, enabling him to see Jesus as the Messiah, or a son of the living God. This was the consciousness Peter was in when Jesus said to him, "You are the stone, and upon this stone I will build my church." (Matthew 16:18)

**(Q)** What is the Holy Church?
**(A)** That which makes for the awareness in the heart of the individual . . . The Church is never a body, never an assembly. An *individual* soul becomes aware that it has taken that Head, that Son, that Man even, to be the intermediator. That is the Church . . . What readest thou? "Upon this I will build my church." What church? . . . here ye may find the answer again to many of those questions concerning the Spirit, the Church, the Holy Force that manifests by the attuning of the individual, though it may be for a moment. He asked, "Whom say men that I am?" Then Peter answered, "Thou art the Christ, the son of the living God!" . . . He said to Peter, "Flesh and blood—*flesh* and blood—hath not revealed this unto thee, but my Father which is in heaven!" Heaven? Where?

Within the hearts, the minds; the place where Truth is made manifest! Wherever Truth is made manifest it gives place to that which is heaven for those that seek and love truth! 262-87

In verse 5, Joshua tells the men to "take up every man of you a stone upon his shoulder." It is significant that this same soul who tells his men to take up a stone, or burden on their shoulders, and cross into the Promised Land, later tells his followers to pick up their cross and follow him into the Kingdom of Heaven. The pattern stays the same, just occurring at different levels of awareness and indicating the level of development which has been attained.

One of the central symbols in the Old Testament is the Temple built by Solomon. Twelve is a number representing wholeness, completeness, and is thus a foundation number. The twelve stones which Joshua carried in were set in Gilgal and became the first memorial, or holy place, established by the children of Israel in the Promised Land. Symbolically, this might be said to be a "seed" action. Joshua was laying the foundation for Solomon's Temple. As the rest of the Bible unfolds it centers around the building and rebuilding of the Temple, with the final understanding that the body is the Temple.

The readings also indicated the functions of the physical body could be divided into twelve activities, each of which could be related metaphysically to the name and nature of one of the twelve tribes. Each of the twelve stones represented a tribe of Israel, and the name of each tribe carries its own vibration and significance:

... there is that as may be said to be the literal and the spiritual and the metaphysical interpretation of almost all portions of the Scripture ... In the interpretation of the Name, then: Each entity, each soul, is known—in all the experiences through its activities—as a name to designate it from another. It is not only then a material convenience, but it implies ... a definite period in the evolution of the experience of the entity in the material plane ... For what meaneth a name ... All of these have not only the attunement of a vibration, but of color, harmony; and all those relative relationships as one to another.

281-31

Although there are many parts and divisions within man, the purpose of life is to become One, and to be one with God.

... remember, it has been given that the purpose of the heart is to know *yourself* to *be* yourself and yet one with God even as Jesus, even as is represented in God the Father, Christ the Son, and the Holy Spirit; each knowing themselves to be themselves yet *One!*   281-37

Thus the twelve tribes, whether literally as parts of a nation, or symbolically as functions of the physical body, or metaphysically as experiences or levels of activity or consciousness, must all become as one in order to fulfill the holy pattern.

(Q) Please explain the twelve names which represent the twelve tribes of the children of Israel.
(A) The same as [the twelve ways, the twelve openings, the twelve experiences of the physical to all ... the twelve purposes as represented by the activities of the openings to the bodily forces for their activities ... ] the twelve understandings; or the approach to *Israel*, the seeker—all seeking not then as the expression of self but as one in the Holy One!   281-37

Although we might say that twelve stones find their fulfillment in the Temple, and then in the understanding that the body is the Temple (of which the awareness of the Christ, or God's Love, is the cornerstone) there is one last stone to consider, and this is the white stone that appears in the final book of the Bible.

*To him who overcomes . . . I will give him a white stone, and on the stone*
*a new name written, which no man knows except he who receives it.*
(Revelation 2:17)

Just as the Christ is the cornerstone, the white stone appears to be
the capstone in the process of building and transformation of the self as
seekers of God, or Israel!

**Then in the end, or in those periods as indicated, it is when each entity,
each soul has so manifested, so acted in its relationships as to become
then as the new name; white, clear, known only to him that hath
overcome. Overcome what? The world, even as He . . . Then the
interpretation is that they *have* overcome, they *have* the new name,
they *have* the manna, they *have* the understanding, they *have* their
relationships as secure in the blood of the Lamb!** 281-31

The Book of Joshua and the action of entering the Promised Land are
extremely important in many respects. Not only did the series of miraculous and dramatic events of the Entry set the tone for the next
phase of Israel's unfoldment, but Joshua laid the foundation for a symbol which can only find its fulfillment in man. Peter, who achieved this
understanding, urged all Seekers to the discovery.

*If you have tasted and found out that the Lord is good. The one to whom*
*you are coming is the living stone, whom men have rejected, and yet he is*
*chosen and precious with God; You also, as living stones, build up*
*yourselves and become spiritual temples and holy priests to offer up*
*spiritual sacrifices acceptable to God through Jesus Christ.*
*For as it is said in scriptures, "Behold I lay in Zion, a chief cornerstone,*
*approved, precious; and he who believes on him shall not be ashamed."*
(1 Peter 2:8-6)

## *Baptism*

The readings tell us that often bodies of water provide a natural
creative stimulus for many individuals, and that places of activity in
past lives can stimulate memories and emotions if an individual should
return to them.

We find this suggestion given to one individual:

**These [creative urges], then, will find their greater expression near bodies of water, and near those environs where the entity's activities in the earth's plane have been a portion of the entity's experience.**

**649-1**

Perhaps the same spot where Joshua commanded the priests to "stand still" in the Jordan while the children of Israel passed over (Joshua 3:8) was the place where he, as Jesus, "stood still" when John baptized him. If it was, then the vibrations Joshua had put there and the subconscious associations Jesus had with it aided in the attunement which brought the vision of the dove and the voice saying, "This is my son with whom I am well pleased." (Matthew 3:16; Mark 1:9-11; Luke 3:21-22) Certainly the spoken message could be applied to the two lives!

It was the same experience on a new level of meaning.

## Circumcision of the Nation

The rite of circumcision had not been observed throughout all the years in the wilderness, yet it was the first ordinance which Joshua observed. This was a bold and dramatic action. With one command, Joshua put all his people in the same vulnerable position as Hamor and Shechem had been. (Genesis 34)

Edgar Cayce commented on the significance of this act:

"There is no reference to the Lord calling Joshua's attention to the law of circumcision, but it was the first thing he did in the Promised Land. He put himself, his army—the whole nation—in a position where a mere handful could have defeated the whole purpose. Joshua was doing what he knew was God's will, and the people were not molested.

"According to the best of his understanding, Joshua was attempting to put himself in the right light with the people, Jehovah, and his own conscience.

"Of course, the weakness of man is the strength of the Almighty. The very fact Joshua risked such a thing among thousands and thousands of people proved he recognized God would take care of the situation."

## The Cessation of Manna

*And the manna ceased on the morrow after they had eaten the grain of the land; neither had the children of Israel manna anymore; but they did eat of the produce of the land of Canaan that year.* (Joshua 5:12)

"Hidden manna" is a metaphysical symbol for mental and spiritual energies which nourish the Seeker after God. To this manna there is no end. It is part of our "daily bread." (Matthew 6:11; Luke 11:3) The manna which fed Israel is also "a representation of the universality as well as the stability of purposes in the Creative Forces as manifested to a group or a nation of peoples." (281-31)

There was also a physical manna, and was the central part of the Israelites' diet for forty years. The day they entered Canaan, this manna ceased and the children of Israel began to eat of the game and produce of the Promised Land.

There is an aspect of this which is easily overlooked. With the change in diet, dental care became a problem. A need for dentists arose—and this entity was the first!

Before that—the greater period of activity of the entity in the earth—the entity was among the sons of Eleazer and of the priesthood; among those born in the wilderness and one taken when journeying over Jordan. Of this the entity will never lose hold entirely, in its experiences in the earth.

The entity was active when setting up the settlings of the land, in the care for the mouths of individuals who for forty years had tasted little other than manna or the flesh of quail. But with the variations in the diets, this became a study of the entity. And it may be said that among the children of Israel the entity was the first dentist, as would be called today, or one caring for the welfare of the peoples when they settled around Shiloh.

Hence, as we find, an interest in diets, an interest in the spiritual things . . .

The entity in that period was also interested in the character of water, the elements constituting same, those things soluble in water and those acting as an irritant or restrainer, or those causing through radiation those conditions in soft tissue of mouth, gums, throat, or digestive tract.

Then in the name Ersebus, the entity excelled; not only in the administrations to the people in his abilities to care for his own group, but as a teacher, as an instructor. 3211-2

## Jericho

Modern archeological excavations indicate Jericho could be the oldest city in the world, originating in the nomadic world 9,000 years ago. Archeologists suggest that, as early as 6000 B.C., the residents of the Jericho area banded together to form what could be termed a civilized community.

Cayce's date of the Exodus, 5500 B.C., and modern science's date of Jericho tend to support each other. Edgar Cayce lectured his students on the following topics about Joshua and the Jericho campaign.

"The name of the king of Jericho is not mentioned. Kings then were only great tribal leaders who owned people in a particular area. Jericho was one of the strongest places in Palestine, one of the few which had great walls built around it. From the standpoint of material strength and defense methods, Jericho could have defended itself for years. The people could raise within their own walls all the food they needed, and had enough materials to live indefinitely without seeking outside help.

"Why do you think the spies sent by Joshua went first to Rahab's house? This is a beautiful illustration of human nature. Rahab was a harlot, and anyone who wanted to find out things of a spying nature, would go to such a place first. It is the same today.

"Rahab later became the mother of Boaz, who married Ruth. Thus she is the great-grandmother of David, and part of the line through which the Savior came."

According to rabbinical traditions, Joshua married Rahab and fathered many daughters but no sons. According to the rabbis, Rahab later incarnated as Hannah, mother of Samuel.

On the plain of Jericho, Joshua had a startling psychic experience. (Joshua 5:13–15) Edgar Cayce described it and its significance:

"No doubt Joshua had gone alone to Jericho, to observe the surroundings. This doesn't mean he didn't accept the spies' report, or that he distrusted them, but he wanted to know for himself.

"When the vision appeared, he didn't attempt to run away. Immediately he wanted to know whether it was friend or foe.

"Joshua must have been seeing his other self, his real inner self. Notice that the man did not take sides with Joshua or with his adversaries.

Rather he pointed out that, as captain of the hosts of the Lord, he stood for the RIGHT. We might say this was the personification of Joshua's conscience, which was not warped or swayed in this or that way. First and foremost he had the real purpose to do the will of God.

"What a difference it would make if all wars could be led by leaders like Joshua, who fought for the Right according to God's viewpoint rather than his own. He stood aside and watched himself pass by. Have you ever done that—seen yourself as others see you, or rather, as God sees you?

"This vision was a fulfillment of the promise in Exodus 23:23, 'For mine Angel shall go before thee.' It was Joshua's own guardian angel, his higher self."

Edgar Cayce's familiarity with the divine and its effects upon human consciousness produced new understandings and fresh insights from familiar Bible stories. Have you ever wondered how the seasoned veterans of many campaigns felt as they began their march around Jericho? Cayce discussed this with his Bible students:

"Most of the young men had been soldiers with Joshua. They had fought all their battles with him as their leader. What must have been their thoughts now as they prepared to take the strongest city in Palestine by marching around it and blowing horns? After the miraculous Jordan crossing, they must have had absolute confidence in Joshua's leadership. They must all have believed, otherwise they could not have accomplished what they did.

"The people had to remain quiet, not making a sound, until Joshua told them to shout all at once. This caused a great power to be generated. A certain vibration was created. Perhaps in the same manner as when Jesus' disciples shouted at his triumphal entry into Jerusalem. The Pharisees wanted to rebuke the disciples, but Jesus answered, 'I tell you that, if these should hold their peace, the stones would immediately cry out.' (Luke 19:40)

"If you know the right vibration, you can put out a fire with a fiddle. The same principle is behind the fact that when people march across a bridge they have to break their step, otherwise the bridge would collapse from the vibrations."

Jericho figures largely in the readings that follow.

In an unusual reading for a twelve-year-old boy, only two past lives were given. In the most recent incarnation, the entity had been a friend to several apostles, and from his notes came many portions of the New Testament gospels. In his other life, he was a leader in the march around Jericho.

> Before that the entity was in the Promised Land when there were those gatherings of the peoples from the Holy Land.
>
> The entity was among those born in the wilderness that entered in with Joshua the leader.
>
> The entity then was in the families of Aaron or the tribe of Levi; not a high priest but a lesser priest to whom there was given the mission of sounding the call to worship, and the entity led those groups about Jericho; being among the first to enter that fallen city. This has ever been a favorite story of the entity. Hence these activities—the trumpet has ever been a favorite instrument but the reed will bring to the entity a greater accord or attunement to the needs or the use of same in the meditating periods for the entity—in interpreting the temperaments or moods for the experiences of the entity.
>
> The abilities of the entity are for a leader as to information, from that period. Now it may be put into order as a reporter, a writer of events; and especially sports or those of that nature as would have to do with such activities. These may be a part of the entity's experience.
>
> The name then was Jubeel. 3183-1

The parents of a three-year-old boy were told their son had marched around Jericho—and also was among the first to enter:

> . . . the entity was in the earth during those periods when there was the choosing of the individuals who were to bear the rams' horns when there was the marching of the children of Israel in the wilderness, after the setting up of the Tabernacle and the ordaining of the priests; when individuals were set to perform certain offices.
>
> The entity was among those who marched around Jericho. This was the high point in the experience or the unfoldment of the entity, as Abajalon; for he was among the first of those to enter the city when the walls came down.
>
> In the experience the entity was a leader, a musician, a director, a historian. For he was also the scribe to Joshua when there was especially

**the drawing of lots, in those activities that followed Jericho. 2922-1**

This reading describes an experience of one of the enemies—an entity who was inside Jericho when the walls came down.

... the entity was in that land when there was the return of the peoples to the Promised Land from exile, and the entity among those who resisted the return to that land under the leadership of him who crossed into the land. The entity then in the name Rahai, and the entity was among those who defended the walls of Jericho when it came down; and the entity has in the present experience that innate feeling as regarding the children of Promise, see?                                    2734-1

## Achan's Trespass

When they were ready to circle Jericho for the seventh and last time, Joshua announced to Israel they were to spare Rahab and her family, and were not to confiscate any "devoted things." All the spoil was intended for the treasury of the Lord.

*But the children of Israel committed a trespass in the devoted things; for Achan, the son of Carmi, the son of Zabdi, the son of Zerah, of the tribe of Judah, took some of the devoted things, and hid them; and the anger of the Lord was kindled against the children of Israel. (Joshua 7:1)*

Following their victory over Jericho, the children of Israel went out to do battle against the men of Ai. As this tribe was small in number, Joshua sent only three thousand men against them—and was defeated! The cause of the defeat is definitely placed on the weakness of Israel rather than the strength of the enemy.

*And the Lord said to Joshua . . .*
*"Israel has sinned, and they have also transgressed the commandment which I commanded them; for they have taken some of the devoted things, and have also stolen, and lied, and they have hidden them among their own stuff." (Joshua 7:10-11)*

The transgressor is found to be Achan, the son of Carmi. Not only had he broken God's commandment concerning Jericho, but he had lied and stolen as a result of it. Achan's trespass was a sort of "psychic infection" in the body of Israel. Just as in the physical readings a major illness was often traced to some form of misalignment in the body, so too did Achan's activity throw the whole body of Israel out of its attunement with God.

Edgar Cayce's lesson to the Bible class was as follows:

"According to profane history Achan's wife wanted to 'get into society.' She persuaded him to take the forbidden things. It seems almost unbelievable that one man's sin could affect a whole nation, but the same is true today. The more purified a people become, the more prominent the sinners. One drop of ink will discolor a whole glass of water.

"Joshua realized Achan's sin could destroy the people. The destructive thought which entered had to be nipped in the bud. Achan had to be put to death, as a lesson to all.

"The prince of this world is the devil, and he has his moments with most of us. When those moments overpower us, and are able to influence God's elect, then we will be destroyed—either according to man-made law or our own. Remember Judas. He committed suicide after he understood what he had done.

"When the trouble arose, in order to locate the source of the problem, the people prepared themselves through prayer and meditation. We don't try this very often, but it is a sure way of getting at the seat of any turmoil that may arise. We think we believe this, but we seldom practice it."

In 1943, a young Illinois housewife was told she had been Achan's daughter—and felt the punishment unjust!

**Before that we find the entity was in the land when the children of Promise entered into the Promised Land, when there were those whose companion or whose father sought for the gratifying of selfish desires in gold and garments and in things which would gratify only the eye. The entity was young in years and yet felt, as from those things which were told the entity, that a lack of material consideration was given the parent. The name then was Suthers.** 5366-1

When Achan's trespass was confirmed by uncovering the hidden spoil in his tent, Joshua ordered him to be stoned, then burned with the loot. (Joshua 7:20–24)

*And they raised over him a great heap of stones which remain to this day.
So the Lord turned from his fierce anger. Therefore the name of that place
is called Valley of Achan, to this day.* (Joshua 7:26)

Although by modern standards, this punishment seems excessive,
these people were living their faith. Achan's trespass was a violation of
a command which had proven itself to be divine among them. This
trespass led to unnecessary defeat and slaughter of their own people.
Excessive or not by our standards, we see punishment as having a ben-
eficial effect on the moral consciousness of an associate of Achan.

**Before that the entity was an associate of Achan (not a companion),
that one who partook of the beauty of physical things for selfish purposes.**

**These brought doubts and fears. These have ever been hard to
understand by the entity, the things brought about because of those
disturbances giving to the entity an ideal and an idea as to morals, as to
associates, as to things not ordinarily found—yet the entity can rarely
find words to give expression to same.**

**Throughout that period the entity gained. Learn to apply those
tenets as taught, as may be gained from that experience, in the life
today; and being true to thyself ye will not be false to others. And as ye
treat thy fellow man ye are treating thy Maker.**

**The name then was Asbythen.**                              **3578-1**

The purification achieved its desired effect. The children of Israel were
once again aligned with Creative Force. In their next encounter with the
children of Ai, they were victorious.

In this reading we find an entity with whom we might easily identify.
She had been present at the fall of Jericho and those activities around
Jericho, which would include the punishment of Achan. She had seen these
events, been part of them, yet never understood their significance. How
many great spiritual events are occurring around us today that we fail
even to see much less to learn from and make application in our own lives?

**Before that the entity was in the Promised Land, in those periods when
there was the entering into the Holy Land.**

**Though the entity was among those born in the wilderness, it was
acquainted with and aware of those leaders of that trek from Egypt to
the Holy Land, and had a knowledge of the law. Though the entity was**

close to those who were to administer same, the reckoning which came from those who partook of things when there were the activities around Jericho the entity never, *never* interpreted in its own experience.

And such routine still becomes at times a drudge. But the very activities of the entity, as an associate of the wife of Eleazer, in the preparation of those oils and the incense for the service, give the entity's present abilities in the preparing of compounds of such natures. These have not in the present been made compatible with the experience there, in those activities about Shiloh, where the entity lived during that latter sojourn.

The name then was Adajoniah.                                    2900-2

## Treaties with the Pagans: Joshua Deceived

*And when the inhabitants of Gibeon heard what Joshua had done to Jericho and Ai, they worked subtly, and prepared provisions, and laid old sacks upon their asses, and wine skins, old, torn, and patched; They put on old shoes, or bound their feet with sandals, and dressed in old garments; and all the bread of their provisions was dry and mouldy.*

*And they went to Joshua to the camp at Gilgal, and said to him and to the men of Israel, "We have come from a far country; and therefore make a treaty with us." . . . Moreover they also said to Joshua, "This bread we took hot out of our ovens on the day we came forth to go to YOU; but now, behold it is dry and mouldy. And these wineskins were new, and behold, they are worn out; and these our garments and shoes were new, behold they are old because the journey was very long."*

*And the men took of their provisions and went away, and the Israelites did not ask counsel from the Lord.*

*And Joshua made peace with them, and he made a treaty with them to let them live; and the princes of the congregation swore to them. (Joshua 9:3-6, 12-15)*

This clever ruse by the Gibeonites ensured their survival, although when Joshua discovered the deception he relegated them to a servile position as gatherers of food and drawers of water for his congregation. (Joshua 9:27) When five pagan kings banded together to retaliate on the Gibeonites, the Gibeonites called upon Joshua to honor the treaty and defend them. This occasioned the miraculous battle when the sun stood still. (Joshua 10:1-14)

The crafty Gibeonites and Joshua's reactions drew out these comments from Edgar Cayce:

"Here we have one instance where Joshua disobeyed the command given by Moses. There is nothing to indicate that he was punished for this, except the fact that having made a promise, his conscience held him to it, even though later it proved to be his people's downfall.

"From the very beginning, God's command had been that all those in the Promised Land were to be destroyed; the children of Israel were not to make peace with any of them . . .

"Heretofore, whenever a problem of this kind had come up, Moses *and* Joshua went to the Lord with it, and asked what to do. This time Joshua failed to do that. So far as we know, he was not rebuked for it, though he realized later he had made a mistake. Several hundred years later those same people with whom Joshua made peace rose up and became the thorn in the flesh of the Israelites.

"Why Joshua wasn't rebuked for this weakness as Moses was, we cannot say. Nothing is said about what he was to lose by it. Having made the league with these people, Joshua remained true to it, even though they had been insincere and used trickery to persuade him. He took them at their word."

Cayce found another lesson in Joshua's reaction.

"Most of the old patriarchs possessed a quality that we do not—patience; at least they manifested it more. When analyzing the spiritual attributes that God first manifested in the world, we come to Time, Space, and Patience. Apparently they are far apart, but those who have learned patience know that there is no time or space.

"We find patience manifested in Abraham, Isaac, and in Jacob, and especially Joshua. We do not find reference to a single instance in which Joshua lost his patience. Perhaps he used bad judgment at times, but he didn't lose patience."

In February, 1944, a thirty-five-year-old school teacher was told he had been a Hittite. The reading indicates he may have had a hand in trying Joshua's patience.

**Before that the entity was in the Holy Land when there were those**

gatherings of the people from other lands. Ye were among the natives, but ye were "smart" as it were, for ye were among those who used Joshua to make peace—for ye were among the Hittites, in the name then Jebel.

It is well to be subtle, but don't fool yourself—and you know you're not fooling yourself, even when you fool others. But ye used this to good account for the material gains. Did ye use it as well for the spiritual gains? "Not by might and power, but by my spirit, sayeth the Lord." This learn in all of thy undertakings. 3689-1

The entity remained "smart" and his ability to get ahead extended into his succeeding lives. In Rome he gained power by associating with Julius Caesar. Cayce warned him he would have his own Brutus in the present if he didn't learn to trust his Creator. In his most recent incarnation, he had been a Forty-niner in California. He was smart enough to find the gold, but lacked wisdom in how to use it.

Thus there are karmic patterns he must learn to undo that stem back to his deceptions with Joshua.

## *Other Covenants*

Although Joshua was interdicted by Moses not to spare any tribe, the readings indicate that, in addition to the Gibeonites, compacts and agreements were made with other tribes. Many reasons have been given, both literally and metaphysically, why all the tribes weren't destroyed; however, Edgar Cayce advanced a suggestion to the Bible class which was logical and probable:

"For some reason, many groups were not destroyed. Later, Joshua condemned himself for allowing this condition to come to pass. Of course, they attempted to make slaves of the unconquered people, but it was not always possible to do this. Perhaps these people were gifted in trades which the Israelites thought necessary for their own welfare. For instance, the Israelites had no experience mining or refining gold, iron, metal, or brass. They had worked in Egypt with these after they had been prepared, but knew nothing about their preparation. Perhaps this is why certain groups were spared. The children of Israel were acquiring knowledge in forbidden ways, and they paid the price for it. Later, the very groups they preserved were their own undoing."

In 1940, a young man was told he had been among the Jebusites. Perhaps his abilities as a herdsman and in animal husbandry ensured his survival:

Before that the entity was in the Palestine land, during those periods when there were the hordes or numbers of people entering under the leadership or direction of Joshua.

The entity was among the Jebusite peoples who made agreements with those peoples; hence dwelt among them, because of their *possessions* of the land. Yet because of the agreements or compacts made between the two, the entity was a herdsman—or the keeper for those who had great herds through the land of the valleys, in those portions of that land.

There we find that in the keeping of the entity's activities great help came to many from the material standpoint, and great help came to the entity through the mental and physical relationships with those people, because of their activities in relationships to Creative Forces; and their *moral* actions brought better influences in those groups to which the entity belonged. The name then was Jezeel.                                  2322-2

Just as five kings united in war (Joshua 9, 10), apparently other tribes united to make peace. In reading 2998, a young man was told he had been a leader in this attempt and caused Joshua "to falter."

. . . the entity was in the Holy Land, when those groups of people were entering from the Egyptian land.

The entity then was among those who made overtures for a united effort in making peace with the leader of those groups, and thus—as termed by some—caused even Joshua to falter.

Yet these abilities make in the present for that ability to make peace, and to make for organized effort where the spirit of the law, rather than the letter of the law, may be applied in its relationships and its dealings with others. The name was Jabeliel.                                  2998-2

## Division of the Land

Bible scholars and critics generally agree on the historical validity of the person Joshua, but disagree on the extent of his accomplishments. Traditionally, Joshua is considered to have conquered all the Promised

Land except for a narrow strip along the eastern sea coast in one single, concentrated campaign. Few consider this to be historical fact. They also think the allotment and occupation of the conquered districts in orderly sequence also has to be abandoned as unhistorical. These views are based upon archeological evidence and a comparison with the Book of Judges which shows the invasion of Canaan was carried out through a series of successive campaigns over a long period of time, often suffering serious reversals.

The archeological evidence is hard to refute and a historical or literal level would suggest Joshua did not perform in his lifetime all the conquering and unifying that is attributed to him. However, stripping away all the myth and legend, the experts still agree Joshua was a great and gifted leader.

But whatever mark he may have left on the material world, the readings would assure us, is only a dim indication of his real effectiveness and accomplishment on the mental and spiritual planes. This is why all the myth and legends collect around his name.

Things happen first in Spirit before they are sensed by the Mind or seen in the world. The material world is a shadow of spiritual truths. Thus, the readings tell us, whatever the finite mind observes in the material world is already a past condition in the spiritual planes. Man is ever observing in the present what has already taken place. (3744-4 and 900-24) This is an unsettling notion, but one that leads us to see how, in the real sense, Joshua did all that is attributed to him. If the Lamb was slain before the foundation of the world (Revelation 13:8) when the soul of Jesus made his offering in the spiritual world (262-57), then, before Israel ever crossed the Jordan, the Promised Land had already been conquered and the inheritance apportioned. It was already a past fact in the mind of Joshua. In mind and spirit he had done everything necessary to ensure its appearance in time and space.

God doesn't look on things from the physical standpoint, as we do. Though it may take a long time to appear, He never forgets that there was a time when souls, or a soul, made all the overtures and activities necessary for keeping the faith. For several hundred years after David's death, God said many times, "I will do this for my servant David's sake." This was because that soul, like Joshua, implanted in his relationships with his fellow men something that was representative of God's influence in the earth.

The following readings show several entities who were involved with the dividing of the new land and establishing its boundaries.

Mr. 4052 was told he had made a strong effort to keep the people in touch with their spiritual leaders.

> . . . the entity was in the Holy Land where the entity was with the mighty groups of people who thronged from the Egyptian land. The entity was among those who were in authority, in the name Othiel and was the child of Dan.
>
> Thus, northernmost portions of the land or boundaries have a particular call to the entity. The entity was among those who kept quite a balance between the united efforts of those peoples when once settled, in keeping in touch with those in spiritual authority at Shiloh.
>
> 4052-1

Mr. 3203 was told he had been an Edomite who assisted the Israelites in marking out and dividing the land. His activities then carried over as special interests in the present.

> Before that the entity was in the Holy Land during those periods when the children of promise entered. The entity was one in authority in the land, being of the children of Esau or Edom. Hence we find those various differences as arose.
>
> But the entity was among those that became aware of the activities that had been indicated through the service rendered a people by the two faithful patriarchs Joshua and Caleb.
>
> Hence the entity joined with those forces, those influences . . .
>
> In the experience the entity advanced. For, through those efforts in the latter part of its sojourn, the entity aided in specifying and marking out the land marks for many of those varied groups of the varied tribes, as the land was divided.
>
> Divisions and subdivisions of cities, then, of states, and their boundaries became of special interest to the entity, as these things are applied in the daily life of various groups in various portions of any land.
>
> 3203-1

Mr. 3001 was kin to the discredited rebel Korah, which delayed his acceptance by those who were in authority. This rejection bore bitter fruit. In his next life, the entity had had a compelling desire to make himself known among his brothers. As Benaiah, he rose in authority during the time of Solomon. Due to his lack of consideration and the stress he put upon the people, he added to those influences which caused his people to rebel and gradually lose their understanding of God's ways.

> Before that the entity was in the land when there were those journeyings into the Holy Land.
>
> The entity was among those of the tribe of Levi that were acquainted with, and of the family of, those that rebelled. Though the entity himself was not lost in the destruction of the sons of Korah, the entity became so awed and so evilspoken of in many quarters that it was in the latter portion of the entity's sojourn before he was wholly accepted into the activities that brought the distributing of the gifts of the cities, or of the activities, to the children of Levi.
>
> In the city near Ramah did the entity then dwell, in the name Keldebah. The entity gained much, for it attempted to apply those tenets that had become a part of the activities—in the latter portion of its sojourn.
>
> And those experiences in the present—material gains are little, unless the mental and the spiritual are in accord with same.        3001-1

## Caleb and His Family: The Present

When a Jewish business man requested a reading for his three-year-old son, he had no idea he was adding another chapter to Edgar Cayce's story of the Old Testament.

Cayce, who never recalled a word spoken during a reading, often experienced a recurrent dream of entering a great hall where he was handed the soul's record. During this reading, Cayce dreamed it again, but with an unusual variation. Upon wakening, he said:

> "It was the cleanest record I've ever experienced. The book is the cleanest, and yet I had never thought of any of them not being perfectly clean before."

As the reading progressed, it became clear why the records were so clean. The child was described as "an old soul, and an Atlantean," one that could "not only make for a development for self but for the world." A highly developed mental and spiritual nature was one of the outstanding influences in the entity's makeup, the reading continued.

An incarnation was described during the gold rush era in California in which "the entity gained through the experience and never lost hold upon self in that experience." In the preceding incarnation at the time of the Roman Empire, the entity governed portions of Greece, Turkey, and the Holy Land, and gained materially and gained mentally. And in the life before that, the soul made its greatest mark as the hero of Israel, the mighty Caleb—who is consistently described as "filled with the Spirit." (Numbers 14:24, 32:12; Deuteronomy 1:36)

> The entity was *one* of the two that were twenty-one when they left Egypt to enter the Promised Land.
>
> Hence the entity was ever looked to as one to be counseled with, as one to be looked upon as a leader, as a sage in Israel; Caleb, then as the companion of Joshua, with the children of Judah that made for the cleansing of the land for that which became the Holy City; that has meant, did mean so much in the experience of the people as a people and of the world; that has had, does have so great a mental influence upon the world today, as it ever will.
>
> For as then the entity founded same, its purposes, its desires, its activities were in the law of the living God, that enjoined all those who would to draw nigh unto Him.
>
> And in Him is the defense for every ill, for every disturbance that may arise in the experience of the entity or any individual in a material world.
>
> Too much might not be said respecting the entity's activities during that particular sojourn. Much may be read concerning same; and well, then, that the training of the entity include those admonitions of Moses, the leader of the entity then, and of Joshua, the companion of the entity.
>
> For those laws are ever those things that in the experience of individuals in the material world make for a fortress of strength, as they did for the entity in that sojourn.                                  1292-1

An interesting family situation is developed from the mother's questions:

(Q) What associations has the entity had in the past with his present mother [1294], and when?
(A) The mother was then the daughter of Caleb!

(Q) What should be the proper association in the present?
(A) Much as then. Not that the mother takes guidance from the child or the developing entity. But the day will arise when this will be as the experience. For the entity is one of a dictatorial nature; not as a dictator but as a counselor.

Hence their attitude should be that of love as shown in not merely affection or sentiment but as purposefulness in holding to the truth of the associations of a soul, of an entity, with the Creative Force—God.
1292-1

The next question shows the father had been one of the spies who gave out the unfavorable report. Thus there will be a sensitive area in the present father–son relationship.

(Q) What association in the past with his present father [1291], and how may they mean the most to each other in the present?
(A) . . . In the land of the returning or journeying from Egypt, the present father was then a companion of the entity—among the spies that spied out the land.

Hence we will find in their associations there will arise periods in the present when the entity will doubt its own parent's direction. Yet if these are kept aright they will be made to be more of a helpful experience to both.
1292-1

The next answer is interesting and emphatic.

(Q) What type of nurse would be best for this child?
(A) One that is patient, long-suffering; but most of all one that knows the *law!* Not of the land, but of God!
1292-1

## Caleb's Daughter

From the above question, 1292's mother learned she had once been her own child's daughter. In her own reading she was told she had been Ach-sah, whose story is found in Joshua 15.

As the conquering, settling, and division of the land continued, the portion which Moses promised to Caleb remained unconquered. In order to encourage his warriors to battle with those remnants of the pre-Adamic creation, the giants of Hebron, Caleb offered the hand of his daughter Ach-sah to the spoiler of Keriath-sepra. (Joshua 15:15-17) Othniel, Caleb's brother, took the city and won a bride.

> Before that we find the entity's experience that becomes the greater of its activities . . .
>
> The entity then was the daughter of a leader, Caleb, that brought such a report of the land to all those travelers, those peoples of promise, those chosen that were to give to the world the basic principles for their moral and spiritual life.
>
> Then entity was born in the wilderness, and was given in marriage when there was the conquering and the activity of the father's people in the taking and settling of the lands about the Holy City.
>
> Then in the name Ach-sah, and the companion of the entity in the present was then a son of Benjamin—but not the one to whom the entity was wed. This brought in the experience some doubts, some miscomprehensions. And yet throughout the experience the entity gave to the peoples the ideals of a life of purposefulness, even though the edicts of the fathers overruled the hearts of the women in those periods.
>
> Yet these arise in the experience of the entity at times in the present sojourn—that as the heart longs for, as is seen in the experience—as may be attained even by the seeking, the knocking, the working towards those directions, if used properly may become helpful influences; but if they are used as self-indulgences, they become stumblingblocks to many.
>
> In the experience the entity finds from that sojourn that the laws as pertaining to the relationships of individuals in the marital life, those as pertain to holdings as may be said in the material life, become as much in the manner as the entity entertained during those sojourns. Though it brought the disturbing forces in the present, they may be made to become those influences that may bring peace and harmony. 1294-1

The reading adds a poignant touch to the story of Caleb and Ach-sah. The man she was not permitted to marry in that life became her husband in the present.

> (Q) When in the past have I been associated with my present husband, and what should we mean to each other's development in the present?
> (A) In these we find two outstanding experiences, and yet both were not consummated in the wedded life.

> In the previous, lovers—but never man and wife.
> In the wilderness, lovers—but never man and wife.
> Hence there should be in this experience rather the fulfilling, and the deeper feeling that may be held between each that their love-life, their associated life, should mean more than even to others. Not as lording, but rather as fulfilling a longing.
> And this has been experienced by each.[17]                    1294-1

No doubt, as one of the unconvinced spies, her lover was unacceptable to Caleb. Evidently there was at least one Israelite girl who suffered the same fate as Ach-sah.

> Before that the entity was in the Holy Land when there were those periods of journeying into the land and settling there.
> The entity then was a real character, as the entity was in that position as the daughter of Caleb who was given to his brother's son for taking what was then Hebron.
> The entity then set an example, as did the household of Caleb, as did the household of the husband, among those people through those people following the death of Joshua. And the entity was among the first of those leaders of the groups that kept, as it were, the house in order.
>                                                                3564-2

## Caleb's Family: The Past

A young female vocalist was told she had also been one of Caleb's daughters.

> Before that we find the entity was in the Holy Land when there was the entering into the Holy Land of the children of promise. The entity was among the daughters of one Caleb, one prompted to the activities which brought the entity Caleb with his household into prominence and to the Promised Land. The entity was then one given to song, and the psalms which later became parts of the activities of the children of promise were portions of the experience of the entity.

---

[17]In the case files at Virginia Beach, Gladys Davis has recorded the husband died six months after the reading was given.

Not that it is to be given wholly to psalm singing but these should be
the basis of the purposes of the entity in its teachings and its contribution
to the home.                                                          5356-1

This member of Caleb's household also made strong, positive contributions to the welfare of Israel.

Before that the entity was in the Holy Land when the people were
gathering from Egypt. The entity was among those about the Holy City
that later became the place of David's activities. For the entity was in the
household of Caleb who settled in Hebron and the holy areas of that
particular land.

There we find that the entity was given to good works towards the
preparations for activities of those dedicated to the priesthood.

Thus the entity's activities of being as a teacher, as an instructor, as
a healer through nursing, through caring for those in need of close
attention, may enable the entity to find the greater outlet for itself; as
a nurse, a teaching nurse and instructing nurse in the welfare either of
the young or the old—as a companion for shut-ins.

These activities may at times appear to become very tedious, very
tiresome, yet the joy ye may bring may build all of that which may
produce peace and harmony in the life of the entity.

The name then was Adyar.                                              5018-1

A prominent Protestant physician and surgeon was told he had once
been the grandson of Caleb.

Before that we find the entity was in the Holy Land. For the entity was
among those who were of the peoples of promise born in the wilderness,
and thus entered with its families and with the leaders into activity in
Jerusalem. For the entity was the grandson of Caleb who was given
Hebron as his portion of inheritance for the report given when sent into
the Holy Land to spy out same.

The entity then aided in the establishing of those activities that later
made for the choice by the son of Jesse as a place where a house of God
might be built.

The entity then was an herb physician, in the name Ardyeh. In the
experience the entity gained. The entity has gained from same in the
present, and yet has learned and may learn the more that the personality

and arousing hope in the mental body may contribute the greater to the ability for the entity to gain the confidence of and through same be the greater channel of help to others. 5083-2

## Source Material for Scripture

Under the directorship of Joshua, Israel experienced a high point in its history. It was from events in this period that later portions of Scripture were drawn.

A young boy was told he had been a student under Joshua; later, an associate:

Then in the name Jarpar, the entity's activities were in relation to the keeping of records of the various happenings that were to be recorded for the instruction of the people later. These became a part of the activities from which the writers of Judges (and they were many) and portions of Samuel obtained their material—those records that were kept during that period when the activities were set by Joshua in the early settlings and dividing of the land.

As indicated in the writings of the record kept, the entity was accredited with the writings of the peoples of that day. The entity is still a student of certain groups, certain classes, certain characters of writings that indicate happenings in groups of people or nations. 4035-1

Activities during this time were also source material for the Psalms of David.

. . . the entity was among those who entered into the Promised Land, and saw those days and periods of the establishing within the land of those that had been promised that activity.

The entity then found joy in the expressions with those that aided in the establishings of those periods when, later, from the very writings of the entity the Psalmist chose much that was set to music.

For the entity was an encouraging one to the leader, Joshua, in the experience; in the name then Shumeman, and was of the daughters then of Judah.

In the experience in the present from that sojourn there arises that which makes for a harkening within self to that which is of praise to a holy purpose, a holy desire. 1035-1

And there failed not one of the good things which the Lord had spoken to the house of Israel; all came to pass. (Joshua 21:45)

Joshua inherited a compact and enthusiastic group which had been purified through the trials in the wilderness. The forty years of testing and tribulation were necessary to purge the evil, or negative influences out of the soul of Israel. The ones who died in the wilderness were the rebels. Those who survived kept to God's purposes and will.

Perhaps those souls who were with Moses in Egypt had come in with Adam in the beginning, and in bondage because of karmic patterns built through their fall. Thus the period in the wilderness presented them opportunities to reestablish their relationship with the ideal they held in the beginning.

The wilderness-born "second generation" is characterized by their responsiveness to Joshua, and by their great accomplishments after their entry into Canaan. The gates of reincarnation were closed to souls with a low, or negative, vibration. Except for Achan, the spirit of Satan—which is rebellion, or selfishness—was banished from Israel during Joshua's time. Only those who had "the desire and purpose to glorify the Father" (281-16) were granted the opportunity to establish themselves in the Promised Land.

The following reading describes an outstanding life which epitomizes the spirit of that wilderness-born "second generation," and provides a synopsis of this most outstanding and influential period.

**Before that we find the experience of the great understanding, of the greater influence in the present, and from which there may be builded much of that in the present for not only the enduring influences in the material activities but in the mental as well as the spiritual influences.**

**When there was the journeying of the children of Israel through the wilderness, the entity then was among the children of Judah, born of its parents in and about that land of Sinai when they journeyed there.**

**The entity was under those periods of journeying, under those periods of activities when there were the turmoils and strifes that arose, and the activities that brought about the purifying as well as a leaving off of those things that had brought doubt and fear.**

**For remember, the journeyings at the period were for the purpose that those who had spoken evil of the land to which the promises had been given to the forefathers, for the indwelling there for their prepa-**

ration for a purpose, might be expended and not able to enter in.

Then when the days arose for the preparations, after the periods of mourning for Moses, with whom the entity was acquainted—and acquainted with much of those activities, the entity—just before the crossing over the Jordan—was wedded by those in authority for such, as the leaders and counselors.

For according to the activities, or owing to the activities of the mate, the days for becoming the wife or consummating the wifehood were postponed. For the mate in that experience was among those who, because of representing its tribe for the carrying forward of the undertakings, occupied their place in the line of march.

Then there was the miracle of the parting of waters, and the wonderments as adjourned with the days for becoming the wifehood, and the undertakings with the march about Jericho; and then the friendships and the undertakings when there was the defeat at Ai.

For the entity was a friend of Joachim, who made those peoples to sin in that experience.

O the lessons that the entity gained there! and the beauties and the teachings! Though it was not privileged as a great teacher, the entity gave much counsel during the rest of its sojourn in that land—through its activities when finally parceled with its family about the places where the Tabernacle was left.

And remember that thy body is indeed a shadow of that Tabernacle! For as it was there He promised to meet thee, so now—as in this present day—thy body is indeed the Temple where He has promised to meet thee!

Then as He has given to those of thy understandings, it is neither in this mountain nor yet in the Temple in Jerusalem but Lo within thine own heart, thine own mind, that He meets thee for that awakening!

And when He becomes thine indeed in truth, ye indeed walk with Him, ye talk with Him. For as He has promised to bring to thy remembrance all things, so—as ye commune with thyself, in seeking to be a channel through which blessings may come to others, without the thought of self—ye may, even as ye did as the daughter of Shulemite, and in the name then Marabaa, give to all ye contact, day by day, *hope* and *faith* and *cheer!*

For as He gave, the whole law is to love the Lord thy God with all thy heart and mind and body, and thy neighbor as thyself.

Then as ye practice, then as ye manifest those things that are as the fruits of the spirit, so do ye attune thyself.

For know, as ye learned by the admonitions of Joshua (yea, thy Lord!), it is because of failures that sin lieth at the door.

Search then. For as He has given, "Seek and ye shall find; *knock* and it shall be opened unto you."

*Who* will open? Where will it happen? *Within thine own conscience!* For *there* He has promised to meet thee!                    1595-1

# The Book of Judges

*The* Book of Judges is presented as a history, in chronological sequence, of events from the time of Joshua's death to the birth of Samuel. Scholars agree that the Book of Judges, as accurate history, has no historical value.

The episodes in Judges, presumably, are major highlights of events occurring over a long period of Israel's history. If Cayce's dating of the Exodus as 5500 B.C. (reading 470-22) is correct, the period of Judges could span over a thousand years.

The book enshrines some of the great heroes of Israel and demonstrates that the fortunes of Israel depended upon their acceptance or rejection of God's purposes. Rebellion against His laws led to oppression by pagan nations. Repentance and acceptance resulted in deliverance.

These brief historical accounts provided Israel assurance of God's presence among them:

> **While there is the consideration given to all those influences that are a part of man's experience, as signs, as symbols—and while these do have their place—they are not other than *assurances* to the mind of man of God's presence with, and direction of, those choices made by individuals**
> **2803-2**

The Judges of Israel were ministers, preachers, and interpreters of the law, arbitrating in the differences between their own people and their neighbors. Usually they were influential only in a small area. Under times of crisis or when confronting extraordinary events, such as meeting a common foe, the tribes banded together. Then the tribal leaders ruled as a group with great authority over a large section of the land. When conditions changed and things returned to normal, the leaders disbanded and returned to their home areas.

Samson was influential only in a small area, yet because he was such an important and unusual person, a large part of the history is devoted to him. Other judges are mentioned as being rulers over all Israel, yet no other details are given.

The threat to Israel from pagan nations did not always affect the entire land. Often it was just a tribe or two under stress. The significance of a great leader, or judge, derived from his abilities in getting the other tribes, not directly threatened, to rally to the defense of their brothers.

## *Deborah and Barak*

The Song of Deborah, Judges 5, is the most important source of historical detail for this era, and the earliest extant one. Interestingly enough, in the Cayce readings, Deborah and Barak supply the most significant body of information relating to this portion of history.

Deborah was a prophetess and a judge. Not because she was a warrior, but because she could see and interpret visions.

After twenty years of captivity by the Canaanites, held captive by Sisera and his horde of iron chariots, the people once again were ready to fight. But they needed a leader. The people came to Deborah for advice. Through her abilities as a prophetess, Deborah was able to see Barak as the leader. However, Barak would not accept this responsibility until Deborah assured him she would stand by him with guidance from the Divine.

On April 12, 1939, a young Protestant man obtained a Life reading. In it he was told:

> **. . . indeed, there is a path cut out for thee—the gods have directed that ye will have the opportunity to show forth thy worth.        1710-3**

Shortly after this comment, this challenging statement was made:

Hence, the needs for each soul, each entity to have a standard, an ideal by which the patterns of the life, of its associations with its fellow man, may be drawn.

*And these are in* Him, *as they were through thy experience in those periods when ye fought against Sisera.* [Italics added.]     1710-3

The reading then described a past life experience as Barak:

. . . we find the entity was active in the Palestine land during those periods when there were the judges that arose in Israel.

There we find the entity was associated with the only one of those judges who was a woman.

Hence women have played and will always play an important part in the experience of the entity's life; and the entity will be directed by many, yet—as in that experience—carrying out those directions through the influences for activities in given directions, *free* from those conditions that would bring questions into the own conscience of self as in relationship to same.

As the entity gained there, we may find the application of self in the present through those fields of service in which the activities of others as related to state and nation may and will become a part of the entity's experience.     1710-3

In the question and answer portion of the reading, the young man, then twenty-four years old, was advised to wait until he was twenty-eight or twenty-nine to marry. Three years later, a young Protestant woman, who had been recommended by this man, obtained a Life reading in which she was told:

. . . the entity was in the Promised Land, during those eras of the Judges in the land.

The entity then was that prophetess who enabled Barak to bring freedom to those peoples. While the associations and companion were of another group, the entity chose Barak as the leader of God's forces in the delivery of the peoples from Sisera and those hordes that were making those people in that period as slaves.

Read oft the song, then, of Deborah, as thine *own* composition, as thy tribute to man, to his efforts when guided by the divine as indicated there.     2803-2

Gladys Davis, Edgar Cayce's secretary, noted in this case file that the young woman related that she had often read the Song of Deborah and had received great help from it.

**Thus in thy present sojourn, first apply or establish self as to thy ideal— as may be gained from the study of the Song of Deborah, as may be applied in the study of the Master's words to the woman at the well, and of those He gave to His disciples in that walk to the garden—in the 14th to the 17th of John.** **2803-2**

The young man and woman were contemplating marriage. Evidently a great soul attraction existed between them, due to this experience as Deborah and Barak. She asked:

**(Q) What are the past associations with [1710] and how may I help him for the mutual mental and spiritual development of each.**
**(A) Establish a home together!**
   **As to the associations (that mean anything), these were in the Palestine experience during the period of the Judges.** **2803-2**

Cayce advised marriage within the year. Following his advice (and their own inclinations, to be sure) the young man (now age twenty-eight, the age Cayce indicated would be the best period in his life for marriage) and the young woman were married on January 9, 1943, four months following her first reading.

On April 8, 1943, they secured a joint reading on their lives as Deborah and Barak. Mrs. Cayce gave the following suggestion to the unconscious Cayce:

**You will have before you the entities [1710], born February 26, 1915 . . . and [2803], born January 21, 1919 . . . You will give a biographical sketch of their experience as Deborah and Barak in Palestine, the period of the Judges; giving specific and definite information as to their activities and associations; together with the influences and urges prominent in the present from that sojourn and how they are to be met in the present. You will advise them regarding these activities and the urges and influences pertaining to their mental and spiritual development; answering the questions they submit regarding their experiences and associations. You will go into these thoroughly and give definite**

information that may be easily understood, paralleling the associations then with the present associates and activities.

Edgar Cayce: Yes, we have the records as indicated through these channels, as well as that which is a part of the record of the judges of Israel.

As indicated there, they each had their definite activities; Deborah as the elder in the experience, and the prophetess—thus raised to a power or authority as a judge in Israel; to whom the people of the various groups, of that particular portion of Israel, went for the settling of their problems pertaining to their relationships one to another.

With the periods in which the peoples of the adjoining countries made war upon Israel or that part of same, the people then appealed to the entity Deborah—in the capacity as spokesman, for the spiritual and mental welfare of the peoples, to select one or to act herself in the capacity as the leader in the defense of the lands.

Then did the entity Deborah appoint or call Barak to become the leader in the armed forces against the powers of Sisera. These are the outstanding portions as presented in Holy Writ.

As to the activities—these, as may be interpreted from same, were close in their associations, in their respect one for the other as to their abilities in given activities respecting the defense of the principles as well as the lands of the peoples.

Deborah, as given, was much older in years in the experience, and a prophetess—being a mother and the wife of one of the elders in that particular portion of Israel.

Those activities together, then, were as related to the mental, the spiritual, and the material welfare of the peoples as a whole.

As to the activities of Barak in those periods—there was something like some twelve years variation in the ages. Barak was also a family man, of the same tribe—though not of the same household as Deborah. Their activities, then, brought only the respect one for the other in their associations, their dealings and relationships with others.

In paralleling, or in the application of the lessons as may be drawn from those experiences in the material plane—these in the present make for more than the purely material attraction one for the other. For, the mental and the spiritual become not only a part of the heart or soul of each, but of their relationships as dependencies one upon the other, that are to be taken into consideration.

To be sure, there are latent urges in the experience, or in the consciousness of each; yet these—as related to this experience in the present—if they are but stressed in their dealings one with another, in their relationships one to another, in their activities and relationships with others—will ensure their own joy, their own happiness, their own well-being physically and mentally, and will also keep them in that straight and narrow way that is pleasing to the consciousness within that brings the awareness of being at-one with the Creative Forces—in relationship to activities one with another, and with those with whom they may come in contact from time to time.

Then, keep that experience well in mind, as to what each contributed in the experience to the welfare of the other, as to their dealings with and the effort to keep those awarenesses in the experiences of others, as to the promises of the Creative Forces, or God, to those who would seek to serve Him.

Beware that there is not the attempt on the part of either to dictate to the other, but rather in a singleness of purpose may they, together, make manifest in their own experiences that consciousness that was manifested by those promptings through that experience.

Ready for questions.

(Q) As given, [1710's] activities in the present may become as a service related to state and nation. What type of activity is indicated?
(A) Depending upon the application of self. In those directions in which the promptings carry the entity in relationship to same.
(Q) About when should [1710] expect a change to take place?
(A) When he prepares for same, and as he prepares for same.

This does not indicate that he is going to be a lord or judge or principal or the like, but the contribution such as was made by Barak—which was not as an authority over anyone, but as a director, as a leader for a *principle*, a purpose, an ideal—*under* and *through* the direction of a servant of God!

Get the difference in these. This is not applying to materiality, not applying to material things, but to that having to do with the basic principles of why and how men think and act, in their home, in their relationships to their fellow man!

This is spiritual, *not* material.

(Q) What causes the fears and nightmares [2803] experiences when left alone at night, and how may she overcome this condition?
(A) This should be considered in the material or the physical approach. But if there is the paralleling of that which prompted the individual

entity in that experience to call Barak to lead—out of reason, not in its own family—nor in its own household, nor its own brethren, nor its own husband—it will be seen how that criticism was brought at the time. Parallel same for an experience if there were to be such activities in the present, and we will see there is an innate fear when not in the protection of that choice made, see?

Then, the way and manner to overcome—it is not a physical thing but a psychological. Know in whom you have believed, and that the faith is not in the man alone but in the principle for which he stands—as the love manifested or expressed for an ideal brought forth in the relationships manifested in the present.

And with these understandings, these interpretings—in *whom* is the trust to be made? In [1710], or in God? In thyself and thy relationship to God, or the fear as to what somebody will say?

(Q) In what relationship, name, and activity was [1710] associated with his sister, [1523], and what are the urges in the present?

(A) We haven't [1523] in Deborah and Barak! We have had relationships indicated in other experiences in the world—shall we go to those or shall we conclude this?

We are through.                                                    1710-11

The laws of soul attraction that brought these two souls together also were in effect in their first-born child.

Perhaps, as the psalmist, he composed the music for the Song of Deborah.

Before that we find that the entity was in the Holy Land during those periods when there were those judges in the land, and especially in that period when those activities of the present mother brought judgments to the people as the prophetess (Deborah), and when the present father (then Barak) was a friend of the entity. It was in that period when, as a psalmist, the psalm of praise was given for the leader and for the peoples of that day. The entity, then, in the name Pithlar, led in the praises—not only of Barak but all the leaders and those who held close to a worship of the holy influences in man's activities.

In the present the entity will find, then, that groups, crowds, throngs, will be those things which will tend to direct, to aid or deter from the fulfilling . . .                                                    5398-1

Another entity was told, in the era of the judges, she had been Deborah's sister:

> Before that we find the entity was in those periods when there were those judges in Israel, when there was one chosen of the entity's own sex who was the interpreter for Barak. The entity was then a sister of the one who aided in keeping the children of Israel in the way of the Lord, and the entity gained from the experiences that which brings within its powers in the present of memory, of vision, of color, as of pictures of places, of scenes of peoples who were of its sister through that experience.
>
> The entity was then in the name Shammar. 5367-1

## *The Song of Deborah*

This verse in the Song of Deborah refers to an actual spiritual law, applicable in the lives of all:

*The stars fought from their courses; they fought from heaven against Sisera by the river Kishon.* (Judges 5:20)

> . . . as represented in the leaders of old . . . if thou art true to thineself, the stars in their course will fight for thee; but if thou art upon those ways that make for question marks here as to thy veracity, thy sincerity, thy ability, as to thy consideration of each and every one in the proper sphere that touches each proposition coming before self, then—as it were—the moon and sun are set upon thy efforts, and the darkness of trouble and discord arises from those seeds of uncertainty that bring distressing experiences in the activities of all. 257-162

How accurately does the history of Israel demonstrate this law!

## *Gideon*

The next great deliverer after Deborah and Barak is Gideon. (Judges 6, 7, and 8).

> Study as to why Gideon chose God. Analyze as to what temporal things brought into his experience. 4047-2

Joshua and Moses, and most biblical characters, carried every problem to the Lord. But very few tested themselves upon receiving an answer as Gideon did. (Judges 6:17) He wanted to make sure he wasn't fooling himself, Cayce told his students.

Gideon had a vision that it would not take a lot of fighting men to overcome the Midianites. Victory with a few men rather than a great horde demonstrated the power of the Lord rather than the might of Israel. The unusual procedure was effective.

After his fabled victory, the men of Israel begged Gideon to rule over them. He refused these monarchical overtures, but requested a donation of gold from each man. Gideon melted the gold and had it cast into an ephod. After Gideon's death, Israel returned to Baal worship and "did not show kindness to the family of Gideon for all the good that he had done to Israel." (Judges 8:35)

## *Abimilech*

Abimilech was a half-breed son of Gideon. This son was the opposite of his humble father. After Gideon's death, Abimilech staged a bloody rebellion and slew Gideon's seventy natural sons. Whereas his father ruled only over four or five tribes, Abimilech tried to establish himself over the whole of Israel. With great cruelty, he put down any opposition to him.

It is quite a surprise to find Abimilech appearing in a Life reading given for a middle-aged Ohio minister:

Before that the entity was also in the Holy Land during those periods when there were the judges in Israel. The entity then was among the many sons of a judge in Israel, when there had been those changes that brought disturbing forces to the whole peoples—Abimilech.

The entity acted in the capacity of one setting about to establish its own truths rather than those pertaining to any particular group. This brought disturbing periods to the entity, and was not a gaining in spirituality nor in the mental, even though it was a gain in the material.

These at times appeal strongly to the entity, for there comes occasionally the reverting to those expressions by Gideon as to the manners and means in which the words of truth might come directly from the Maker himself.

These are things to be studied by the entity so as to make application.

Whom will ye serve? Self? Or thy fellowman, as ye may know the
creative forces the better?                                    3411-1

## *Jephthah's Vow*

The story of Jephthah, a mighty man of the Manasseh tribe, follows the
bloody history of Abimilech. He is the next great deliverer after Gideon.

Jephthah was sired by a Gileadite and a harlot. Thus he was a social
outcast, and turned to banditry. His outlaw band grew in daring and
strength. When the Ammonites gathered to make war on Israel, the
elders of Israel sent for Jephthah. Evidently they felt he could do more
than anyone else, Cayce observed.

Jephthah had a psychic experience, Cayce said. He was moved by the
Spirit, enabling him to achieve a great victory. His zeal was so great that
he made an irrevocable (for him) vow to God. Perhaps, being an outcast
since birth, he felt a great need to establish himself as a patriot and hero
above all others. Perhaps his life among hardened, lawless people made
him ignorant of what God requires.

*Then Jephthah came to Mizpeh to his house, and behold his daughter
came out to meet him with timbrels and with dances; and she was his only
child; besides her he had neither son nor daughter. (Judges 11:34)*

Jephthah had made a solemn, but rash vow, to the God he worshipped, and thus felt unable to retract it. The consequences of that act,
a human sacrifice, still have a subconscious effect on at least two individuals. The evidence is found first in a Life reading for a one–year–old
baby:

Before that the entity was in the Promised Land when there was the
experience of Jephthah's daughter, with the return of the father as the
leader of the groups that defended the right.

The entity then was a companion of Jephthah's daughter. Thus the
sorrow that came. Thus the joy that came from a rash vow.

Thus, it is necessary that there be consideration by those directing,
controlling the unfoldment of this entity's mind, as to rash promises, rash
vows, and the stress be put in the sincerity of purpose, truthfulness of
ideals—that must be founded, for the entity, in the promises of the
Christ.

**The name then was Leieh.**
**In that experience the entity had sorrow brought by the sacrifice of**
**its best friend. Thus a portion of the life was clouded. Not so in the**
**present, if the purposes and ideals are set correctly for the entity.**
                                                                    **3089-1**

The second reading was for a twenty–eight–year–old housewife who, in a previous life, had been a daughter–in–law of Noah:

**After that [experience on the ark] the entity appeared in the Holy Land**
**during those periods of the Judges in Israel, and in that period of what**
**is oft spoken of as Jephthah's rash vow.**
**    The entity was a close friend of Jephthah's daughter offered as a**
**human sacrifice to that overzealousness of an individual entity, who**
**used his powers for material gains and strength, and yet accorded those**
**judgments of Truth; causing this entity, Judyth, to become disturbed,**
**distraught, and to lose much of that which had been the impelling**
**force.**
**    Hence the making of rash vows brings individual activities that yet**
**disturb the entity, as to why individuals vow this or that and then,**
**because they change, the entity can never exactly connect them with**
**truth or sincerity. These bring disturbances for the entity. Yet the entity**
**itself gained.**                                                  **3653-1**

## Samson

Because his name means "child of the son," Samson is another of Israel's heroes whom many believe to be purely a mythological figure woven from the tapestry of earlier myths. However, one modern writer calls him a peasant hero in an era which roughly resembled the American frontier, a rustic with great strength and little brain, who derived equal pleasure from tricking his adversaries, subduing ferocious beasts, and conquering women.[18]

The 281 series of readings contain lengthy and difficult discourses upon the relationship and effect of spiritual energies to the growth and development of the physical body, especially how the mental and

---

[18]Webb Garrison, *Strange Facts About the Bible.*

physical activities of the parents affect their offspring during the period of gestation.

In one lesson, Samson and his parents are used as illustrations.

In anatomy books, only the physical body is considered or studied, yet the mental and spiritual aspects have their influence and effect. To illustrate the importance of mental attitude and its effect, the reading turned to Manoah.

**When Manoah sought with his whole desire and purpose that there might be the blight taken from his associations among his fellows, he, with his companion, prayed oft; and then the visitation came. (Judges 13)** **281-49**

At first Manoah was unable to conceive of being visited by an angel, but when he and his wife became convinced that the apparition was real, then conception followed. The inrush of energy through the mind and body of the parents from their change of consciousness and faith definitely had its effect upon the offspring.

**The prayer of Manoah and his companion was answered by the visitation of a heavenly figure, in the form of a man; which was not conceivable by the husband—yet when satisfied of same, and the wife—Mahoa[?]— conceived, the entity physically—physically—was the greater tower of strength. Yet as indicated that strength lay in the hair of the head of the individual. What gland caused that activity of such a physical nature, as to be the determining factor in that development?**

**As is indicated, the thyroid is within the body so placed as to have that influence.** **281-49**

The thyroid is the seat of the Will, according to the reading, that gland through which energies pass into the physical body from centers (or chakras) outside the body which enable the individual to hold on to and carry out decisions, ideals, purposes, etc.

Samson, because of his physical strength and prowess, became enamored of his own body, and thus became negligent in the spiritual and mental aspects of the thyroid (or will).

**Here this is illustrated in Samson, a lad who grew to manhood with the unusual strength and power, the ability to cope with exterior forces and**

influences that were beyond the understanding and comprehension of his associates. Yet his ability to say no to the opposite sex was nil—his ability not to be influenced by the opposite sex was nil—because of the desire for the gratification of those activities which were of a glandular nature within the body.                              281-49

# The Book of Ruth

*The* Book of Ruth, with its serenity and gentleness, is a pleasant oasis amidst the civil wars, anarchy, and warfare throughout the time of the Judges.

The significance of this book, apart from its refreshing view of domestic life and its testimony to love and faithfulness, is in its relationship to what later became the Royal Family. Ruth became the great-grandmother of David.

Ruth and Naomi in their lifetimes were poor and simple. Ruth's marriage to Boaz elevated their social standing, yet they were never conspicuous until David ascended to the throne. During his reign, the family folklore, probably an "oft-told tale," was preserved in written form.

The story is simple, told unembellished and innocently.

Elimelech, his wife Naomi, and their two sons move into Moab while a famine is raging in Judah. The two sons marry Moabite women, Ruth and Orpah. However, during their sojourn in Moab, both Elimelech and his two sons die. After ten years Naomi returns to Judah, accompanied by Ruth who has vowed faithfulness to her and to her God. Orpah, the other daughter-in-law, elects to remain in Moab.

Although Naomi is bitter about her misfortunes, upon her return she is blessed. Ruth, while gleaning in the fields of Naomi's kinsman, Boaz, is noticed by this prosperous and influential landowner. He is impressed both by the beauty and devotion of Ruth. Shortly they are married.

Their first child is a son, Obed. Obed begets Jesse. Jesse is the father of David.

Following the Book of Ruth, the Old Testament begins to center chiefly on the family of David. Boaz was part Canaanite (descended from Rahab of Jericho, Joshua 2:1) and Ruth was a Moabite. Outside blood, then, was an integral part of the chosen family of a chosen nation. As David is viewed by Christians as a foreshadowing of the kingship of Christ Jesus, this blood mixture is also seen as representing Christ's authority over all nations.

In many ways the Book of Ruth is a foreglimpse of The Christ as represented in Jesus. The actual genealogy from Boaz and Ruth leads to the physical birth of the man Jesus. Yet what is more important, the Spirit expressed by Ruth and Boaz anticipates the same Spirit so perfectly expressed in Jesus. Perhaps this gentle little story, more so than the martial dramas and tense, emotional episodes of the Book of Judges, bespeaks of the still, small voice within. It carries the same message as "Feed my lambs, feed my sheep."

The following readings, a lovely collection, revolve around the events in the Book of Ruth.

## Boaz

On July 16, 1927, a successful, young Norfolk businessman was told he had been Boaz.

> In the one before this we find in one that was made known in the lands of the day when the entity rose to position, power, wealth, in the name Boaz, and the entity then brought much good to the peoples of that day, especially in the reclaiming of lands for those oppressed, or for those who had lost same, through the laws of redemption of lands that were taken for debt or for the reason of exile, giving especially to the peoples through that offspring that brought David in the land—and the entity gained through this experience, as there was much to the tenets followed, and expressions of action by the entity through the experience. In the urge as is seen, is that especially toward real estate—for the entity wrote the first advertisement for sale of lands in this age . . .
>
> In the abilities then:
> We find these are many—for in the field of law the entity would have done well. In the application of that as Boaz the entity may do better.

In either the entity will find that first self must be conquered, and that knowledge of self, and the principles of the creative energies of force or power must be directed in that channel that builds for the betterment of others. Bettering not in the way of lasciviousness nor in the desires of flesh. Rather in the building of that that is as character and personality in others, and in applying these the entity will bring—through those channels that guide the forces of the universe—those conditions that bring to the entity the knowledge of the life well spent, in proclaiming the day is at hand for all to acknowledge Him, the Giver of all good and perfect gifts, and in that law as was set by Him, give—give—to others that, that each and every man love God—keep self unspotted from the world.                                                                      2694-1

In January, 1941, a, forty-four-year-old Jewish widow was told she had been related to Ruth through her marriage to Boaz. The spirituality of Ruth deeply influenced this woman, who, as a close companion, aided in bringing new interpretations of the old order.

Before that the entity was in the land of promise during those periods of turmoils, when there were the judges in the land; when, because of the famines, the associations had brought about periods of unrest.

But with the return of Naomi and Ruth, and with the wedding of Ruth with one of the entity's own peoples, we find that the entity became a companion—mate to Ruth in her preparation and the bringing about of the new interpretation of the old order in the land.

Hence the entity became in the position not of one holding a grudge, nor yet of one holding to a worshipfulness, but rather one who did worship the purposes, the aims, the sincerity in the character Ruth; and her offspring were cherished, nourished, and taught by the entity.

Thus the school, the home school, the home training, the home activities, the home surroundings were a part of the entity's activities through that sojourn; not exactly as might be termed of State, for it was much more personal than the name would indicate.

The entity's activities were as an interpreter of spiritual law, a trainer in the mental environ, and a creator of material and home environ.

We find that these same characters of activity and characteristics are a part of the entity's better development in the present experience.

The name then was Sen-Doer.                                                459-12

The widow then questioned Cayce about a prediction:

(Q) Some time ago a prophecy was given, that she [459] would be to this day and age what Ruth was to her day and age.
(A) In the son it's being fulfilled. Will that service as in the proper way, the proper carrying on of the efforts of that one in the way and manner as has been determined in self. Then fill that, considering all angles of the development of that one upon whom the mental will fall . . . Stay steadfast in that as has been given, in making thine son one as a messenger to many peoples, even as David did of old.[19]          459-1

A Protestant housewife was told she was also related to Ruth through marriage. She had been the sister of Orpah, Naomi's daughter-in-law who remained in Moab. This entity followed Ruth and was deeply influenced by her spirituality. It is interesting to note, in this reading, that Ruth apparently never forgot those who were the less fortunate, as she once had been:

Before that the entity was in the Syrian or Moab land, to which the children of Judah had gone when they sought relief from the famine of the land.

The entity there became acquainted with Naomi and Ruth; being then a sister of Ruth; only learning of the needs and that to which one should attain, to bring hope, help, and happiness which comes from conviction of living freedom of experience for purposeful, helpful activities in those with whom the entity was associated, after there were the associations that brought about the conviction of Ruth.

The entity then became a helper in the household of Ruth and her husband; being, then, as might be said, the upper or first maid to the offspring of the sister; seeing then the fields that were harvested not only for the material sustenance of the family but for those also not so fortunate as to be the owners of the land.

Hence the fruitfulness of brotherly love, kindness, and those things that have been a part of the entity's experience.

Then the entity was known as Opahelm; not closely related, but related to that other sister, or sister-in-law, who rejected those truths of

---

[19]Her son obtained a reading, see 1856-1. His profession is listed as writer, actor, and teacher. The reading indicates psychic development and a desire to serve.

which Ruth was convinced and turned again to the husks of self-gratification.[20]　　　　2519-8

Although the whole city rejoiced when Naomi returned to Judah, apparently the relative who had taken over her property did not.

This reading was given in January, 1944, for a middle-aged Methodist career woman:

> Before that we find the entity was in that known as the Holy Land when there were those activities in which Ruth and Naomi returned to Naomi's own household. The entity among those, or of that household whose husband refused to release or to give the activities or the home to Naomi. These were periods of disturbance to the body and with the happenings which followed, when Ruth became the companion or wife of Boaz, the entity then was railed on by its neighbors. This made for demands and of belittlings in the experience.
>
> In the name then Shulah.　　　　5098-1

Two days after the above reading, a teen-aged girl was told she had been a Moabite woman who had befriended Ruth and Naomi, and later became a close friend to Obed, Ruth's son.

> The entity was then among those who were of the Moabite land and yet, becoming friends with Naomi and Ruth, came into the group activity in Judah, and thus the entity later was acquainted with the forefathers of Jesse and David. For the entity was indeed a friend to Obed, the son of Ruth, the associate who brought those activities to an understanding individual whom God loved.
>
> So act, then, in thine activities in the present that this may be said of thee—not merely by thine own acclamation but by what others see—that ye contribute to the welfare of keeping God's word before others.
>
> 　　　　5384-1

A spiritual development expressed through intuition and dreams was

---

[20]The "husks of gratification" so emphatically referred to makes a very interesting tie-in with some rabbinical traditions about Orpah, Ruth's sister-in-law. She is claimed to be the mother of Goliath. The rabbis say that after making a pretense of accompanying Ruth and Naomi, she returned and led a very profligate life. She bore four giants, including Goliath, all of whom were of uncertain paternity.

earned by a young Virginia housewife during a past lifetime as a Moabite who became a part of the household of Obed.

Before that the entity was in the Moab land, or that close to the east portion of Jordan, where the activities of Ruth and Naomi became a part of the experiences of the entity, and from which the entity gained much of that which finds expression in the intuitive or dream forces of the entity in the present.

For, as Naomi and Ruth returned to the land of their nativity, so also did this entity—as Samoah; and joined with those who were later raised in power through one of the family, becoming a part of the household of Obed, the son of Ruth. Thus the entity was in close relationship with Ruth; and the entity lost and gained, lost and gained through those varied activities.

Thus, from that sojourn, we will find again in the present the abilities of the entity for writing of verse or song, and the depicting of the activities of individuals in the *extremes* of their experiences in the material world . . .

(Q) What was the significance of the two series of dreams I had a few years ago, in each of which I apparently lived another life?

(A) Study that as indicated and we will find that ye saw into those experiences especially with Naomi and Orpah and Ruth, and into those experiences in the hills of Judea.

These are the periods, as indicated, when the entity goes to the extreme. Keep that balance.                                                    2175-1

Although Moab and Judah were traditional enemies, ceasing in their differences only in times of natural catastrophes and famine, when political and religious differences were forgotten, many Moabites settled in the household of Ruth and Obed, and held positions of great authority and responsibility.

This Virginian, twenty-nine years old, was the overseer for Obed:

Before that the entity was in the Promised Land, during those periods when there were the activities in which there were the settlings of the people in that land—and the activities in associations with others in the lands adjoining same.

It was during the latter days of the judges in Israel; for the entity then was among the Moabite people—Malchor in name.

Through those associates with Naomi, Ruth, and Orpah, the entity came again into the lands of the children of Judah; and was acquainted with those in the household of Obed, for the entity was then a companion of the present companion.

Thus those various activities as related to crops upon the farms, as the distribution of the products of same, were the experience of the entity through that sojourn in its aids to the householders, or—as would be termed in the present—the greater landowners.

For, the entity then was the overseer for Obed.     2301-1

One of Ruth's most eloquent expressions occurs when she pledges devotion to Naomi and the God of Israel:

*And Ruth said to her, "Far be it from me to return from following after you, and to leave you; for where you go, I'll go; and where you dwell, I will dwell; your people shall be my people, and your God my God."* (Ruth 1:16)

The quote and the spirit it represented were used by Cayce to counsel a woman who was having difficulty with her marriage. This tribute to Ruth and her example is a fitting note for this gentle chapter in Edgar Cayce's story of the Old Testament:

(Q) In what way can I help David overcome certain difficulties and in what way can I help myself with my difficulties?

(A) In the way and manner as we have just indicated. By living the life to fill the married purpose in the experience one of the other. It cannot, it must not be a one-sided affair. Have the perfect understanding—what has been given by that as an ideal, who became the mother of the channel through which He came materially? "Thy God will be my God, thy people shall be my people!"     1722-1

## Summary

The following readings draw lessons from Genesis, Exodus, Deuteronomy, and Ruth:

Begin and read in Genesis 1:3, and see that it is to thee *Light*, the light of men, even that one who is the Christ Consciousness.     3660-1

Take Exodus 19:5. To be sure, it is interpreted by many here that the Creative Forces or God are speaking to a peculiar people. You were one of them. Why not, then, today? Although through the years your name has been changed, the soul is the same. Hence this is, as it were, spoken to thee.

Then take the 30th of Deuteronomy, where there is the admonition as to the source, that it's not from somewhere else, but it is within thine own self. For that influence of the Creative Force is so near, yea closer even than thy own hand!

Then analyze that, reading in connection with same all of the story of Ruth as to her sincerity. And if it needs to be, those companionships may be drawn from thine own activities, and the fear of what may be in the future will fade as the mists before the morning sun.

For in the study of these, not merely read to know them, but get the meaning of universal love, not attempting to make it personal but universal. For God is love and, as ye go about to manifest same in thy conversation, ye may find the true meaning of love.

Study also astrological subjects, not as termed by some, but rather in the light of that which may be gained through a study of His word. For as it was given from the beginning, those planets, the stars, are given for signs, for seasons, for years, that man may indeed (in his contemplation of the universe) find his closer relationships.

For man is made a co-creator with the Godhead. Not that man is good or bad according to the position of the stars, but the position of the stars brings what an individual entity has done about God's plan into the earth activities during those individual periods when man has the opportunity to enter or come into material manifestations.

In the study, forsake not, of course, the true way and light. As is given from the beginning: God said, "Let there be light," and there was light, and that light became, and is the light of the world. For it is true that light, that knowledge, the understanding of that Jesus who became the Christ, is indeed thy elder brother and yet Creator, Maker of the Universe; and thus are ye a part of same and a directing influence.

Then, as ye practice His principles ye become aware of same. And these are first: "Thou shalt love the Lord thy God with all thy heart, thy mind, thy soul, and thy neighbor as thyself."                5124-1

# Man Crowned King

*The* Book of Ruth closes one era, the Judges. Samuel opens another—
the Monarchy.

The great prophet for whom the Book of Samuel is named dominates
this early period. Like Moses, Samuel revolutionized man's awareness
of his relationship to God. With Abraham, man's concept of God became a personal thing. Moses enlarged upon this awareness with rules,
ritual, and laws regulating man's approach to God, yet keeping the approach personal and individual. Samuel, as organizer of the new kingdom, introduced "a new form, a new character of a determining factor
between the peoples and the worship of the living God." (1521-2)

This new factor might loosely be called "politics." The Israelites rejected God, a spiritual principle, and turned to man instead. They put
their faith in a material principle. With this change came many problems to tax the soul.

If souls in their separation from God and through their evolution
have "demanded" leaders, then those who rule us now come from the
natural law of cause and effect. Because of the confusion and chaos
from the Fall, souls have sought for and demanded order and stability
and invested other souls with power and authority over them in order
to insure it. From this early development have come myriad traditions,
laws, ethics, philosophies, and religions concerning the extent of man's
power and privilege over his fellows.

If "politics" is the intervening factor between us and our worship of God, what is our relationship to our leaders? Are they doing God's Will? What if they are not? And how are we to know? What should we do if they are not? Haven't they come to us because we have, like the early Israelites, "demanded" them, and must accept them even if their views and philosophies contradict our own ideals and beliefs?

As we begin to awaken to God and search for Him while in a material world, earnestly desiring to live according to His law, we find an almost paradoxical teaching voiced at times in the readings. We are told unless we can live according to man's laws we will never be able to live with God's laws. Yet the readings also impress upon us that conscience is the supreme factor and that the Spirit itself is above all law.

The laws of the land are between us and the laws of God. We have demanded and put "Caesar" between us and God. These are "intervening factors" between man and his worship of God. Above all the soul desires to be one with the Father, and only the divine spark illuminating personal conscience can lead an individual to make choices in accord with the desire of the soul.

Souls in their separation created "Caesar" and therefore must render unto Caesar. But how much is Caesar's and how much belongs to God? And how are we to discern and divide?

These are questions which did not exist until Israel institutionalized its government. Under the judges, Israel was ruled only by leaders who were directly inspired by God for an immediate situation. Their authority ended when either the spirit left them, or the task for which they had been raised was fulfilled.

However by institutionalizing power, political factors emerged and are still with us today.

## *Israel Chooses*

The Cayce readings tell us the Bible is the story of man, representing the pattern of his development in the earth from the beginning to end. Thus Israel's change from a theocracy under the judges to a monarchy under Saul and David is fraught with significance. It is a crucial phase in the unfoldment, yet also part of a recurring pattern.

The original attempt to bring souls back into the Light was by crystallizing their thought-form projections into God's manner of expressing Spirit. This was carried out through the Adamic race which manifested in the earth in five places at once. But the attempt failed. In time the whole thought of man was to do evil, or to put his own self-interests and gratifications above God's Will.

Thus a new plan became necessary: to raise up a peculiar people who were set aside for a purpose; an individual line to carry out God's purposes and establish His Name in the earth; a Name, as the readings state, by which *all* men might be saved.

The new plan began with Noah, who was "perfect in his generations," and established through Abraham.

Thus it became imperative from the beginning that the descendants of Abraham look for and depend upon guidance and strength from the One Source, God, and manifest His Spirit in the earth.

From the days of Noah to the days of Samuel, Israel governed itself as a theocracy. The theocracy of the Judges was a perfect system for spiritual growth. Like a democracy, it afforded equal opportunity to all for expression and responsibility. Anyone could be used by the Spirit if he lived in accord with the spiritual principles which had come to Israel as a heritage and a birthright. Under the theocracy, in times of great crisis or need, certain individuals, often unknown "least members of the smallest tribe," came to the fore and were accepted and recognized as being divinely inspired. Whether shepherd, priest, prophet, or outlaw, they were able to rally the tribes and organize them for a common purpose.

However demanding this method was, it had proven itself time and time again since the days of Noah. As long as Israel looked to its Source and had confidence in its directions, the great men were divinely inspired, and thus material examples of the Spirit in action, working through men.

It could be said, because the Edgar Cayce readings encourage all to depend upon God, that he was counseling in the ways of a Theocracy.

## *Like all the other nations (1 Samuel 8:20)*

The Throne is one of mankind's oldest and most universal symbols. It is a symbol of stability and order, one of man's most profound and basic needs. Thus the Throne begins to dominate this period of Israel's unfoldment, and reflects their concern and desire.

One of the inescapable truths with which the Edgar Cayce readings confront us is that the source of all our problems is from within rather than without.

The Israelites were no doubt dismayed by their shifting fortunes. Joshua was the first and last judge to unify Israel and give them a strong central government. He made them "master of all they surveyed," and the memory must have haunted them. Since his day, Israel remained a loose confederation of strongly independent tribes who, at times, had nothing more in common than a belief in God.

Plagued by bitter internecine war and the threat of slavery to pagan nations, the Israelites wanted stability. But the fault was not in their theocracy, which had preserved them through the centuries while other nations more rich and powerful rose and fell, but in the people themselves and with their own failure to live in harmony with God's laws.

Perhaps the Israelites were tired of being a "peculiar people" who relied upon Unseen Forces. Maybe they felt the need to get better organized in order to carry out God's Promises. And maybe they were just getting greedy and restless.

When the Israelites became adamant in their demand for a king, Samuel warned the people that their desires were sinful and prophesied the painful consequences of their petition. But Israel cried out, "No, we will have a king over us, that we may be like all the other nations."

Samuel at first thought the people were finding fault with him, but when he inquired of the Lord, God said, "Harken to their voices for they have not rejected you, they have rejected me."

The choice before Israel was whether to put their trust in material things or in spiritual forces.

In *Politics of Hope*, political scientist Linda Quest gives a lucid and concise distillation of a political philosophy derived from the Edgar Cayce readings.

> "In one reading (3976-8) we are told that it is typical of men to regard power as the necessary precondition for everything. Man's way is to accumulate power—money, fame, numbers—before attempting anything and to regard the lack of power—especially the lack of monetary power— as a reason for delay and inaction. The human tendency is to regard oneself as powerless and ineffective unless backed by elaborate funding, prestigeful endorsers, or numerous supporters.
>
> "This is a mistaken approach, Cayce tells us. We should, instead, start where we are, take in hand what we do have, apply what we know, not find fault, not find excuses, not put off action until tomorrow. (633-5)

Those who look upon monetary conditions as a measure of success look in vain. (2897-4) Rather, we should fill the place where we are—and the Lord will open the way. (607-2) Thus, ten may save a city, even a nation, from destruction or may keep the world intact." (633-5)[21]

Although Dr. Quest is defining a political philosophy for today, the definition is applicable to Israel. Under the monarchy Israel did become organized, and by the time of Solomon it became the wealthiest, most powerful and influential nation in the earth at that time. Yet the very success caused Israel's decline. To maintain the pomp and luxury of the court put a severe strain on the common man who paid the taxes. The inequalities which burgeoned in this climate led to resentments, suspicions, and hatreds between classes. The leaders became accustomed to luxury and blinded by material things. Few were the kings after David who looked forward to a spiritual kingdom. Too many looked backward with covetous eyes on the splendor of the past and sought to wrest whatever wealth they could from their brothers.

After the death of Solomon and the division of the kingdom, Israel steadily declined and made only half-hearted attempts to search for God. Only a few brief respites of unity and stability followed in the centuries between Solomon and the very lowest point in Israel's history, the destruction of Jerusalem, the sacking of the Temple, and national servitude in Babylon.

One wonders if the wealth, luxury, and power of the kingdom were a necessary part of God's plan. However, these are things for which man yearns, and thus the fulfillment of these desires (and the consequences) became a necessary experience in the overall plan.

That is the pattern for man, Cayce tells us, as long as he sets his heart on material things. Truly did Israel become "like all the other nations."

---

[21]*Politics of Hope*, A.R.E. Press, 1971.

# The Birth of a Prophet

*And it came to pass, in due time Hannah conceived and bore a son and called him Samuel, saying, "Because I have asked him of the Lord." (1 Samuel 1:20)*

**For this, then, is in every birth—the possibilities, the glories, the actuating of that influence of that entrance again of god-man into the earth that man might know the way.**     **262-103**

Every experience recorded in Scripture can become a personal experience, and nowhere is this shown more beautifully in the readings than in the counseling to mothers.

To articulate the concepts in the readings regarding motherhood two new terms have emerged: "Psychic Motherhood" and "Soul Attraction."

## *Psychic Motherhood and Soul Attraction*

"Psychic" means "of the soul." Psychic forces, the readings tell us, partake of both the mental and spiritual selves and manifest, when conditions are met, through the physical body.

The concept of "psychic motherhood" involves all levels of the self, body, mind, and soul. The view the readings take of motherhood involves concepts relating not only to the reproduction of the physical being, but to the propagation and perpetuation of the best mental and spiritual qualities in a family, race, or nation.

"Soul attraction" is stated simply in the principle of "like attracts like." There are many souls who are in other dimensions of consciousness outside the earth's sphere. After the Flood, souls could enter into the earth through the natural channels supplied by the sexual union of man and woman.

Since the Fall, when spiritual energy became sexual energy, the descendants of Adam were dedicated to the purification and restoration of man's creative potential.

The readings spoke of the sex urge as being both sacred and a privilege:

> Train *him*, train *her*, train *them* rather in the sacredness of that which has come to them as a privilege, which has come to them as a heritage; from a falling away, to be sure, but through the purifying of the body in thought, in act, in certainty, it may make for a people, a state, a nation that may indeed herald the coming of the Lord.          5747-3

Conception can take place purely through a physical act. The channel which results from this union may attract to it a soul in a low state of spiritual development. Proper dedication will attract a soul in a more advanced state.

> Man was given the ability to create through self a channel through which the manifestations of spirit might be made manifest in a material world. As is observed in such, there needs be first that of desire, purpose. It is known as a fact that this may be wholly of the carnal or animal nature on the part of even one, and yet conception may take place; and the end of that physical activity is written in that purpose and desire.
>
> Then it is evident that there is the ideal, as well as the partial or whole carnal force, that may be manifested or exercised in and through such activities—as to bring a channel of mental, spiritual, and material expression in the earth.
>
> The ideal manner, first, is that there may be a channel through which the spirit of truth, hope, divine knowledge and purpose, may be made manifest.          281-46

The Cayce readings offer a wealth of valuable information on the preparations for parenthood. Physical, mental, and spiritual exercises and disciplines were prescribed. The readings emphasized holding positive mental attitudes before and during pregnancy.

The ideal condition is where there is union of purpose between husband and wife.

> Thus the greater unison of purpose, of desire, at a period of conception brings the more universal consciousness—or being—for a perfect or equalized vibration for that conception. **281-46**

By holding the proper ideal and purpose, and with definite expectations of the type and nature of the desired child, prospective parents can, to a large degree, attract to them the type of soul they desire.

In speaking to a five-month-pregnant woman, Cayce said:

> The attitude . . . is *beautiful!* And this held, it becomes as that of old—the remembrance of the Creative Forces in their activity with that body that presents itself as a channel for the expression of a soul into the material world . . . *Hope* for, *see*, the son of thine own body becoming as an expression of the love of the heavenly Father in the experience of those that would make His ways their ways; and we will find that such will be the experiences . . .
>
> (Q) Do I understand that the sex of the child is a boy?
>
> (A) As has been given, *desire, look for*, a son. **1102-3**

Another young woman, 457, became very interested in the concepts of motherhood as given through Edgar Cayce, and obtained a whole series of readings on them. In May, 1943, she requested a reading regarding mental and spiritual preparation "for the creation and best development of a child." This was the tenth in a series. Cayce responded:

> In giving information, or in answering questions respecting mental and spiritual attitudes, all of these should be approached from *this* basis of reasoning—especially as preparations are made in body, mind, and spirit for a soul's entrance into the material plane.
>
> While as an individual entity [457] presents the fact of a body, a mind, a soul—it has been given as a promise, as an opportunity to man through coition, to furnish, to create a channel through which the Creator, God, may give to individuals the opportunity of seeing, experiencing His handiwork.

Thus the greater preparations that may be made, in earnest, in truth, in offering self as a channel, is first physical, then the mental attitude; knowing that God, the Creator, will supply that character, that nature may have its course in being and in bringing into material manifestation a soul. For, in being absent from a physical body a soul is in the presence of its Maker.

Then, know the attitude of [the] mind of self, of the companion, in creating the opportunity; for it depends upon the state of attitude as to the nature, the character that may be brought into material experience.

Leave then the spiritual aspects to God. Prepare the mental and the physical body, according to the nature, the character of that soul being sought. 457-10

A very high ideal was found in another young woman, not yet married, who asked:

(Q) What is the foundation for my great desire in the present life for a child, to give to the world an offering through a son that would be dedicated to God?

(A) It answers itself . . . Retain same, for in the end this must bring to self a knowledge that all channels, all vessels of a physical body, may be consecrated in such a manner to those of the spiritual forces as to bring forth that seed in due season, in and through those channels to which they became dedicated to that service. 288-29

Prospective parents must make necessary mental and spiritual preparations to fulfill the high office their sexual union makes available to them. Union of purpose through a spiritual ideal results in a more perfectly balanced offspring in the spiritual, mental and physical aspects.

To illustrate the rich possibilities of motherhood, Cayce referred several young women to the example of Hannah and Samuel.

## *Hannah and Samuel*

Hannah is revered because she is the mother of the first great prophet of Israel.

Samuel was an unusual and highly developed soul who appeared at a critical and difficult stage in Israel's spiritual development—during the transition from rule by judges to rule by kings. He was born during a period of spiritual darkness. At the time of Samuel's birth, "the word of the Lord was precious in Israel; there was no open vision." (1 Samuel 3:1) This condition existed, according to Edgar Cayce, because no one was offering himself as a channel through which the Spirit could speak.

> In thy reading (for ye are a greater interpreter of books, of writings of others), have ye not wondered why in the sacred writings it is said that God no longer spoke to man in visions or dreams?
>
> It is because man fed not his soul, his mind, upon things spiritual; thus closing the avenue or channel through which God might speak with the children of men.
>
> For, only they who believe He is may make manifest that as a reality in their experience . . .                                                    1904-2

At a time when the word of God was scarce, Samuel received direct guidance. Samuel was recognized early as a prophet of the Lord. Even as a young boy, his words were declared throughout all Israel.

Samuel was the last judge of Israel and the first of the great oral prophets. The Cayce readings state Samuel established a School of Prophets based upon the teaching of Melchizedek. (254-109) The readings locate this school at Carmel (2520-1), although references in the Bible might indicate there were other centers at Ramah, Bethel, Jericho, and Gilgal (1 Samuel 19:20; 2 Kings 2:3, 5; 4:38).

As judge, Samuel was sole director of Israel's welfare from the death of Eli, his predecessor as high priest, to the coronation of Saul. Although not of the priestly tribe of the Levites, Samuel functioned also as the high priest.

He was priest, judge, and prophet in one. Thus Samuel holds a unique position in Jewish history. The synthesis of roles and responsibilities held by Samuel is seen by many commentators as a spiritual foreshadowing of Jesus Christ who represents the final fusing of priest and king.

Thus, at a critical and crucial time in Israel's development, when a great choice was made which was to affect the history and the destiny of this nation dedicated to God, a soul appeared who was equal to the task before it. Without the prayers and dedication of the mother, Hannah, perhaps this incarnation would not have been possible.

## *An Example*

The opening chapter in the first book of Samuel relates the circumstances of the birth of Samuel.

Elkanah, of the tribe of Ephraim, had two wives, Hannah and Pannah. Pannah bore her husband many children, but Hannah, the wife he loved most, bore Elkanah none.

Elkanah was a religious man, and once a year he went to the temple at Shiloh and offered sacrifice. Pannah, because of her fruitful womb, taunted and ridiculed Hannah because Hannah was sterile. Compassionate Elkanah tried to calm his favored wife. But Hannah could not be consoled.

After many years of being provoked and irritated by Pannah, she went to the temple. From the abundance of her grief and the bitterness in her soul, she wept and lamented while she prayed, supplicating the Lord for a son. She vowed if she conceived she would give him to the Lord.

Eli, the high priest, observed the weeping and wailing woman and thought that she was drunk, but after admonishing her and hearing her story, he assured Hannah her prayers would be answered. In a short while they were and Hannah was faithful to her vows.

In several instances the readings recommended a study of the story of Hannah. In one reading dedicated solely to information which would help parents develop in their children a complete and integrated expression of the psychic, or soul, forces, Cayce stated in the opening passage:

**Well that such rules as were given by Hannah or Elkanah be observed, that there is the consecration of those bodies.**          5747-1

Several aspects already discussed under "Psychic Motherhood and soul attraction" can be discerned in the story of Hannah.

The love relationship between Hannah and Elkanah would suggest they shared more nearly a union of purpose and ideals. Like Sarah, Rebekah, and Rachel, Hannah experienced a long period of barrenness. Thus there was a long period of preparation, dedication, and desire. Hannah set forth her reasons for conception. Finally, conception was viewed as a gift from God and reverenced as such.

Cayce counseled Mrs. 1968 about the need for mothers to prepare for the entry of souls who could meet the difficult and crucial years in the national history which lay ahead. A similar parallel could be drawn to Hannah and Samuel, and the critical role he filled in a tumultuous and troubled time.

The reading advised a study of Hannah. A lesson on purpose follows:

> Thus, as has been indicated and as should be, the entity may in this experience be the mother of those who may fill high places; and there needs be that those who fill high places in the present, and the more so for the days to come, be well grounded in the law of the Lord. For it is perfect and will convert the souls of men.
>
> So in the application of self in the present:
>
> Study first to show thyself in body, in mind, in purpose as one seeking to be a channel of blessings to others, keeping self unspotted from the world, condemning none; and as ye do this, ye may become that channel through which help, understanding, yea, many, many individuals may come to know the Lord. Remember, as ye apply self, read, study how Hannah dedicated herself in body, in mind and gave, not by word, but by activity as well, her son to the glory of God.
>
> As ye practice, as ye apply this in thy experience, ye may set thy face so that thy prayers, thy supplications may be heard, and He will not withhold any good thing from those who seek His coming. Thus, may ye apply in this life thy purposes to become the mother of those who may bless the nation.                     1968-10

Hannah is also an illustration of consecration as well as purpose. Mrs. 457, in one of her early readings, asked:

> (Q) I received a message that next spring I should do my duty in letting a soul incarnate through me. If so, should conception take place now or in the spring?
>
> (A) Conception should take place when thy body and thy mind, thy companion and his mind, are purified in the light of the desires of thine heart through the exercising of the offices committed into thine keeping through the giver of life who manifests through the sons of men the glories unto God, even as in the Christ. Then, whether this be in December, March, or May, when thou hast opened thine mind, thine soul and purified thy body, let *Him* call His own into being through thee!
>
> For, does He prepare the body? Hast thou read how that Hannah

blessed not only her household but her peoples and the world by the prayer that her offspring might come from and be a joy unto the Lord all his days?

Dost the Lord prepare the way? Who will say nay?                    457-3

For another, Cayce hearkened to Hannah as an illustration of preparation:

Too oft individuals are too prone to look upon conception or childbirth as purely a physical condition. Rather should it be considered, as it has been from the beginning, that life—[or the] sources of life—is from one source. Oft those who may yearn within their material minds for children are indeed blessed, if they were to consider all the environs to which a soul—entity would have to become accustomed.

Remember how Hannah prepared herself, and how others—as Mary—prepared themselves. There are many recorded, and there are many others of which nothing is heard, and yet there was the long preparation. For God is to each entity, individual. He must become Father-God. For as the Master indicates, "Our Father." He has become this to those who seek to be a channel through which God may bring life for a purpose.

Then make thyself a channel, physically, mentally, spiritually. To be sure, law applies. For in the beginning of man, in His becoming a living soul in the earth, laws were established and these take hold. But

lose not sight of the law of grace, the law of mercy, the law of patience as well. For each has its place, especially when individual entities consider and seek, desire, that they be channels through which life, God, may manifest.                    2977-2

## A Time of Stress

What are the ideal conditions for bringing a child into this world? The answer must be found in the ideal and purpose for which conception is desired, in the inner state of the parent, rather than in any external circumstance. Again, Hannah is a lesson. When she conceived, she was surrounded by those in her own household who taunted and ridiculed her.

For a young woman who had doubts about having children because of material circumstances, Cayce gave the following counsel:

**The fact that there has been in the experience of this entity and its companion the mind of doubt, because of material needs and because of mental aspects as may have been or might be a heritage physically, has delayed or prevented such activities. Remember, there is an example of such in the Scripture that the entity would do well to study, to analyze; not merely as a historical fact but the attitude not only of Hannah but of those about the entity who doubted the purpose.**

**Then, in that same attitude as that entity may this entity in that way bring those activities as may best endow self, as well as the offspring, to be a messenger, a channel to the glory of God and to the honor of self.**

**457-10**

Not only were there conditions of stress for Hannah in her own household, but also in the nation and the world about her.

The Philistines were firmly settled along the coastal plain of southern Canaan, and were intent upon the conquest of all Canaan. From their sweep through Asia Minor they had wrested the secret of iron smelting from the Hittites, the first iron founders in the world. Thus, the Philistines were a well seasoned, experienced, first-class military machine, equipped with weapons far superior to those of Israel. (1 Samuel 13:19–20)

The priests of Shiloh could offer little or nothing for the uplift and edification of the people. God spoke no longer in dreams or open vision. Hophni and Phineas, the sons of Eli the high priest, were notorious profligates who reviled and abused the women of the congregation and forced offerings from the men.

In further counseling Mrs. 457, Cayce described a similarity of needs in Hannah's time and in the present:

**(Q) Is it right to [bring] a child into being in a world such as we have today, even though it may never know a normal life but only one of war and killing and anger and hate?**
**(A) The doubt as created in self, from the very asking of such a question, may be answered best in considering the attitude, the conditions which existed in those people's minds and activities at the period given as an example. If that does not answer, then to this entity it cannot be answered . . .**
**(Q) Should I read any books for my spiritual development besides A Search for God?**

(A) Read the Book of all books—especially Deuteronomy 30, and Samuel—considering especially the attitude of Hannah, the conditions, the circumstances which existed not only as to its relationship to its husband and to other companions, but as to the needs for spiritual awakening in that experience—which exist in the world and the earth today.                                                             457-10

Obviously taking the lessons of Samuel and Hannah to heart, in her eleventh reading 457 asked:

(Q) Hannah turned over her first son to a priest to bring up. Is that feasible today or should I try to bring him up in the way of God myself? (A) This must be dependent upon the body itself. The conditions and circumstances surrounding such today are not the same as in those periods. But there may be those administrations, or the giving over of the body at those periods such as Samuel was given, for complete education; which is indicated in certain types of schools that are organized throughout the land in the present.            457-11

## The Shadow of Jealousy

Both Samuel and Eli, his teacher, shared a similar fate regarding their children. Eli's sons were notorious. Samuel's first prophetic message was about the destruction these two sons had brought upon the house of Eli. Samuel's sons were not of his character either. They perverted justice and took bribes. The Israelites grew increasingly disturbed by the fact that, after Samuel's death, they would be judged by these two sons. This provided the people with a reason—or excuse—for demanding a king.

"So often we have seen cases where the parents were good, Christian people, who did everything they could to bring up their children properly and yet they turned out badly," Edgar Cayce said to his Bible class. "Why? The answer, or an example may be found in the experience of Hannah and Samuel."

The answer is found in the information in the readings regarding "psychic motherhood." Not only do the ideals and purposes affect the character of the child, but also the attitudes and emotions of the parents, especially the mother.

**Then, know the attitude of mind of self, of the companion, in creating the opportunity [for a soul to manifest]; for it depends upon the state of attitude as to the nature, the character that may be brought into material experience.** . **457-10**

**It is known as a fact that [the desire] may be wholly of the carnal or animal nature . . . and yet conception may take place; and the end of that physical activity is written in that purpose and desire.**

**Then it is evident that there is the ideal, as well as the partial or whole carnal force, that may be manifested or exercised in and through such activities—as to bring a channel of mental, spiritual, and material expression in the earth.** **281-46**

The 281 series of readings, devoted to an interpretation of the Revelation of St. John and healing prayer, contains a section devoted to "psychic motherhood." In the forty-seventh reading in the series, Cayce traced the connection between Rachel's feeling of superiority throughout her period of gestation and young Joseph's haughty attitude toward his brothers. In the same series Hannah was also used as an illustration of the negative consequences inherited by the son from the wrong attitudes of the mother.

**When Hannah desired that there be an expression that God, the Universal Consciousness, had not forgotten that there were prayers and alms offered, was there wholly the lack of selfishness? or was there the shadow of jealousy?**

**Then we find there was the promise of the dedication and the purposes, that this expression would be wholly given to the Lord, ever. Yet it brought into being an entity, though dedicated as few—yea, as none other individually—to the Lord—unable of himself to give that in expression which would keep his own offspring in the *same* vibration [of dedication]!** **281-47**

Edgar Cayce amplified this concept in his lectures to the Bible class:

"Although Hannah made a promise to the Lord and kept it, we can see quite a bit of selfishness in her first prayer. [1 Samuel 2:1-10] Her greatest desire was not that she should bring a prophet into the world, but that she should be given a son in order to silence those who were taunting her. She was filled with jealousy toward Elkanah's other wife. Even in her song of thankfulness, we can see her attitude of rebuking those who had acted arrogantly toward her. Outwardly she was saying, 'See what the Lord has done,' while inwardly, no doubt, she was exalting in her triumph over Hannah.

"This is a human trait, of which we all are guilty. But we can see the effect of this in Samuel's life—in his inability to control his own sons."

Selfishness entered into Hannah's prayer, and it might be said that a certain amount of self-centeredness existed in Samuel. He was the superior soul Hannah longed for, and Samuel kept to those things in which he excelled. His primary preoccupation was with God and the nation. Perhaps it never occurred to him that he should give the same attention to the needs of his family.

The Cayce readings stress the importance of *balance*. All aspects of life—God, man, and family—should be considered as One. The first commandment indicates perfect love is when God, neighbor, and self are loved equally.

While setting a high standard for his children, Samuel failed to give them the proper attention and instruction. Thus a reaction set in. As is so often the case, the children not only lacked the desire to live up to their father's standards, but rebelled and did exactly the opposite of everything he wished.

The failure, or inability, of Samuel and Eli to direct their sons (an experience of countless parents) raises a question of spiritual training. When should it begin? Cayce pondered this with his students.

"We wonder why it was that Eli's sons and Samuel's turned out so badly, when they themselves lived the best they knew and tried in every way to do the will of God and fulfill their offices as priest and prophet.

"Perhaps it was because Eli and Samuel did not start soon enough with their sons' spiritual development. Possibly this should have begun before their birth. This we would gather, even from Hannah's experience."

The foundation for this philosophy was expressed in a reading nine years before this discussion took place in the Bible class. In June, 1932, a reading was given "How to Develop Your Psychic Powers." It was requested by Edgar Cayce himself in preparation for a lecture for the first A.R.E. congress.

Study as to how Hannah consecrated the life of her son to the service of Jehovah, how that he was under the influence of the law in every respect and tutored by one who was unable to (or did not, at least) tutor his own. What was the difference? The consecration of the body yet unborn! When would one begin, then, to teach or train children? Many months even before there is the conception, that the influence is wholly of the Giver of good and perfect gifts. 5752-2

Leave *then* the spiritual aspects God. 457-10

Although his inability to pass on his sense of purpose and dedication to his own sons may appear as a failure or shortcoming in Samuel, Samuel did fulfill the purpose for which he incarnated into the earth. He was a true prophet and judge. Under his influence, Israel threw off the yoke of Philistine domination. Samuel paved the way for the organization of the kingdom under David. This, perhaps, was his main mission. Yet one cannot discount the importance of the School of Prophets which he founded. It exerted a tremendous influence upon the rest of Israel's history, and eventually became the Essene movement.

Thus it can be said confidently, Samuel did the will of God, even if his sons did not. Mrs. 457, in the eleventh in her series on preparing for motherhood, was obviously referring to the example of Hannah in the 281 readings, when she asked:

(Q) Where is the first failure which brought about such men as Samuel and Isaac . . .

Edgar Cayce interrupted her in mid-question, and retorted:

(A) . . . Not a failure; it is being wholly in accord with God's purposes with the individual. Man expects to have God to work according to man's idea as to when. God takes His time. 457-11

Her next question was a resumption of the first.

(Q) Was it in the original conception of Samuel and Isaac or in their upbringing afterwards?
(A) As has been indicated, these were dedicated to the Lord, God. *His* time is not man's time. This is indicated in the birth of Isaac, also in the

birth of Samuel. For there is little or nothing that changed the pathologi-
cal effects in the life or experience of Hannah after the birth of Samuel.
It was purely, then, a physical condition. But having dedicated, having
promised those things to God—God's promises to man, in God's own
time—these were fulfilled. The same as they were with Samson, as well
as with Isaac and Samuel.                            457-11

## Mother of the Prophet—Hannah Reincarnated

On January 22, 1938, a young couple obtained a Life reading for their
week-old daughter. The father was deeply involved with the study of
metaphysics and is author of several books on the spiritual life. The
father's background and the information in the child's Life reading suggest the attraction of kindred spirits.

The reading stated the child was exceptional and described several
important incarnations. In the opening passage, Cayce gave the first
surprising intimations of its past lives.

Also it is indicated that the entity is one of a very *determined* nature, one
that will go to extremes oft—or there is the inclination—to have its *own*
way.

One that will be inclined to judge, gauge, or measure its activities in
every phase of experience by the material gains or material accomplishments of the entity.

Hence the spiritual lessons, the spiritual natures and inclinations *must*
be developed; though from the activities of the entity in the material
plane one from the material angle would wonder how, *why* the entity
could *ever* be material-minded in the present! when it was a prophetess
as Anna, when it was the *mother* of the *prophet* as Hannah! . . .

When the records here as we find are considered, the name should be
Mary Hannah or Mary Anna; as this *has* been the name of the entity that
is expressed or manifested in this body . . .            1521-1

New and subtle dimensions of interest accrue when Life readings
contain incarnations of personages who are familiar to us either through
secular or religious history. A study of history shows how an individual
affected the development of a state, a nation, or mankind, while the
reading shows the overall understanding the soul has of the Spirit, and
shows how the soul developed in lives preceding its advent into history,

and the wisdom in which it spent its energies in succeeding lives.

Reading 1521-1 is an unusual one in that it contains three lives which are preserved in our literature, and demonstrates a continuity of moral and spiritual development. In her previous life she had been Ann Boleyn, the second wife of King Henry VIII and mother of Queen Elizabeth, " . . . or that one who lost in its attempt to hold to those forces and influences that would hold to its religion and its moral life"; in the life before Ann Boleyn, she had been Anna the prophetess (Luke 2:36-39) who suffered in mind and body for a spiritual ideal; and before that she had been Hannah, the mother of Samuel.

In the opening passage, Cayce warned the parents that 1521 would have tendency to judge its activities by the material gains or accomplishments it would bring. Cayce warned the parents again about her materialistic strain as he described that notable incarnation as Hannah:

> . . . we find the entity was in the earth during those periods when the children of promise were in the lands of promise, when the preparations and the settlements and the changes had been wrought.
>
> And though there were those individuals and groups who forsook the counsel of Joshua and Moses, the entity then—as Hannah—made overtures for that promise; and it was *that* entity [Samuel] that was *hoped*, that was visioned, that might have been a part of the experience! And yet it may be the guiding force of *this* entity through this sojourn, if there are those activities of those about the entity in the matter of the spiritual guidance that this entity may be dedicated to the spiritual laws and not material things alone.
>
> As Hannah the entity gained throughout in those activities. And though ever looked upon by those in a material experience as one apart, one separate, the entity gained the experience of knowing that God in his heavens does take thought, does take cognizance of the prayers, of the supplications, of the activities of an individual that are in accordance with the manner and way the individual prays.
>
> To that experience may the entity harken for its great awakening.
>
> 1521-1

## *Two Spiritual Guides—Elkanah and Samuel*

A spiritual guide is an unincarnated entity who is acting as a benevolent influence in the safeguarding and development of a soul in the earth. The readings indicate that souls who are "in–between" earthly lives, act as "guardian angels."

The readings also speak about souls who have never incarnated into the flesh, who project mental and spiritual forces into the earth for the uplift and benefit of man. These are spoken of as "the hierarchies" or "guardians of the Realm."

Elkanah, Hannah's husband and father of Samuel, was designated as a spiritual guide for a forty–six–year–old business executive.

(Q). Please give name and history of highest spirit guide assigned to my wife and me?

(A) These had best be sought in self. Not that these may not be given, for they are present with thee in thy activities; but "What is thy name?" that has been sought by others, and as the answer came then, "What meanest these experiences in thy life?" so may the name come to thee, even as it did to Elkanah as he offered the sacrifice, as he offered meat— for he is thy guide.

(Q) Has he any instructions as for our contact with him?

(A) Seek and ye shall find. Put into application that thou knowest day by day, for it is line upon line, precept upon precept, here a little and there a little that ye gather together those forces that make for the greater material manifestation of those influences in thy daily experience that may bring thee to the consciousness, to the understanding of those forces that would aid thee.

For, as has been given, when thou hast shown in thine heart thy willingness to be guided and directed by *His* force, He gives His angels charge concerning thee that they bear thee up and prevent the stumblings that come to the sons of the Creative Forces in and among the sons of men.

Hence keep—keep—true to self and to that thou knowest, for the way is open before thee. Seek rather to show thyself as one worthy of acceptance to the God-influence that is shown in man's experience through the manifestations of His Son in the earth; for He is thy guide; *He* will show thee the way. His brethren, His brothers in the activities in the earth, may show thee thy way.

(Q) What is the sign of His presence?

(A) The circle with the Cross; these make for the sign that all thou hast heard is fulfilled in Him.                                   423–3

In the Life reading for 1521, an intimation was given that Samuel was acting as the spiritual guide for 1521. A second reading was given eighteen months later. Although requested for physical reasons, the reading elaborated on the spiritual relationship in the present between Samuel and the baby. The reading suggests the continuity of an enduring spiritual relationship and ends with a prophecy that infers the child might again be the mother of a prophet.

> . . . a drop more often than one drop, you see; and this would be given about twice each week . . . This as we find . . . will purify the glandular system as to resist adverse influences; combined, of course, with those directions under that influence as may come from Samuel—through the prayer.                                              1521-2

During the period of pregnancy, Edgar Cayce had a conscious vision of the expected child being a male. The next question was asked about the change in sex.

> (Q) Is the soul which is/was hoped might come in the place of this entity, and as a male, that which was Samuel, the son of Hannah?
> (A) As indicated, as outlined, the prayer to and through the guiding force of Samuel will aid in the help to Samuel's mother.
> (Q) If so, is this the soul which will aid the entity and to which the entity can pray for guidance?
> (A) As just indicated. This has been indicated before; it is indicated here.
> For, as some would have it, the hierarchies are not unmindful of the developing of souls through the experiences in the earth. Hence such is not *out* of the ordinary, but the natural spiritual development in and through the very association and the prayer and care of those to whom such a soul is entrusted.
> For, as has been indicated, there is—to be sure—something of a choice of the entity seeking expression. In the material world and materiality, it is more often trained or convinced away from its natural spiritual import. For, is it not for spiritual development that each soul enters? and not merely for mental *or* material or physical?
> For in the pattern, which is the way and the manner, we find that these phases are ever considered as one; yet the Mother [Mary] kept these and pondered them in her heart.
> What meaneth this? save as to that injunction which would be given

to every parent: Ponder well the expressions that arise from the
emotions of a developing child; for, as has been forever given, train them
in the way they should go and when they are old they will not depart
from the way.

(Q) Explain why the change of entity and the change of sex took place,
between the time when a son was indicated through this channel, on
September 23, 1937, and the birth of the child.

(A) This, as has been indicated, was given that there might be the greater
opportunity for the developing of the entity Hannah *under* the direction of Samuel, with the aid *and* direction of thought by the parents. This
was deemed by the seeker as the channel for expression.        1521-2

The last answer ends with a clairvoyant's prediction:

(Q) What is the mission of the entity in this experience?
(A) That the glory of the Father in the Son may be the more magnified
in the lives of those the entity meets.

As the entity brought into the experience of a peoples a new form,
a new character of a determining factor between the peoples and the
worship of the living God, so may the entity in this experience bring into
experience—through the preparation of its body, its mind for the
creating or bringing into conception—an activity that may, *as* the son
then, again revolutionize that relationship of man to the awareness of
his relationship to God.

For the offspring of this entity will anoint a holy one!        1521-2

The closing statement raises an intriguing possibility. The soul has, as
Ann Boleyn and Hannah, been a mother to those who have filled high
places. The reading suggests this pattern will repeat itself. Perhaps
Samuel will incarnate through her again in this life.

There is an interesting footnote to this prophecy in the case file. On
July 26, 1965, 1521 reported in a letter to Gladys Davis Turner, Edgar
Cayce's secretary, that she was the mother of a precocious sixteen-
month-old boy. "Even allowing for the natural prejudice of parents," she
wrote, "it is clear that he is an unusual child . . . He stands up for his
own rights and goes his own way . . . He remembers everything . . . He
is a constant source of amazement to us and all who meet him."

She reported three years later she had given birth to a second son.

# The Story of Saul

*If,* as the readings suggest, the Bible is the story of the unfoldment of Man in the earth, each phase in this pattern is advanced, not by the evolution of the people as a whole, but through individuals. Evolution, the readings tell us, is not a collective phenomenon, but occurs on an individual basis, through the gradual overcoming of self.

God created souls to be companions and co-creators with Him. His relationship with His children was always meant to be personal and direct. But as souls separated, they put many things between them and their creator. In the beginning, the first temptation was to partake of the tree of knowledge. Self-indulgence and complete disregard for spiritual laws brought on the Deluge. At Babel, the Sons of God turned again to material things, which resulted in the dispersion of tongues, a further fragmentation of the original oneness.

Now, at the time of Samuel, Israel was entering a new phase in their involvement with materiality. They were again being tempted with material things.

Reading 440-4 states that the highest psychic realization which can come to man is "that God, the Father, speaks directly to the sons of men." Direct experience and personal contact and guidance from the Highest is the cornerstone and foundation upon which the nation of Israel was established.

During the Exodus, the Israelites were content for Joshua and Moses to meet with God and relay His messages. They were willing to listen, but when the time came to apply those truths by going in and possessing the Promised Land, they lacked that confirming and energizing contact with the Spirit which comes through direct experience. They balked and were terrified, and a long period of wandering began.

Now once again, Israel lacked the confidence to leave destiny in God's hands. They wanted a man to rule them, a king who would "go out before us and fight our battles." (1 Samuel 8:20)

In the broadest sense, the figure of a king symbolizes the universal and archetypal Man. Any man may properly be called a king, when his life reaches its culminating point. Thus, the first king of Israel, a nation which symbolizes the story of man, was given a unique opportunity. In a new era of evolution, he could set the ideal and hold a light which would establish a model of man's own potential.

The Monarchy was part of God's Plan: a natural development if the people had been patient. David would have arisen to weld Israel into one whole, supplying it with its greatest impetus for immortality throughout the national history. The whole experience with Saul could have been avoided had not the monarchy been forced into premature birth.

Yet, beginning with the episode between Sarah, Hagar, and Abraham, the history of Israel is filled with forced issues with God.

The readings tell us the fruits of an act can rise no higher than the source from which they emanate. Rather than waiting for a king to be given them "in God's own time," the people demanded one of their own. The source of their demand was not founded in the Promises of the past, but in their fear, greed, and unbelief in the present. These seeds reaped their own harvest. Saul, like the people who demanded him, did not transcend his own human nature.

Only by the deepest devotion and use of his will power could Saul have set the example which Israel needed held before them. Yet the two features which Saul needed most were exactly those lacking, as a Life reading will show us.

## "Head and Shoulders Above the Rest"

The threat posed by the eminently well-organized and powerful Philistines created in at least one Israelite couple, Kish and Methulabah, the parents of Saul, the desire for a son who would be their nation's deliverer.

Kish and Methulabah prepared themselves mentally and physically before conception took place. This had an effect on the developing embryo. The result was shown in the physical stature of Saul who was "head and shoulders above the rest." (1 Samuel 10:23)

Although his mental and physical attributes came as a birthright through the parents, Saul, later in life, used these endowments selfishly:

> . . . in those relationships borne by Kish and Methulabah, when there were the preparations for the individual entity that was to be king over that chosen people. We find that the preparation of the parents, mentally and physically, was such that there was an elongation of activity in the endocrine system of the pineal [in the embryo] so that the stature of the entity then was of a different type, a different nature, and the mental and spiritual so balanced and coordinated that through the experience of the entity there was a physical and mental development equaled and surpassed by few.
>
> Yet the *application* of the entity of those opportunities was personal; so that what was individually personified of the mental and spiritual of the entity's sojourn was then of self in its *latter* analysis.        281-49

Saul was conceived in righteous desire, yet was unable to hold to his own religious convictions.

> Neither is it easy to understand the illustrations used from the life of Kish, who conceived through righteous desire a son, a channel chosen for a manifestation of material power in a material world; given through the choice of the Maker Himself, and yet the *individual* in his personal relationships defied even that which had been prophesied by himself
>
> 281-51

The destiny of an individual is not determined by the forces of heredity and environment but, as the readings stress, through the use of his Free Will in relation to his development of the God–given abilities which are latent and manifest in his soul.

> Then, it is not that the entire life experience is laid out for an individual when there has been received that imprint as of the first breath or the spirit entering the body as prepared for activity in the material world. For, again, choice is left to the individual, and the personality—as to

whether it is the laudation of the ego or cooperation with its fellow men, or as a consecration to the service of the Creative Forces in its material environs.                                                                        281-49

Thus the following is a succinct summation of the life of Saul.

(Q) Is the following statement true or false: Saul, the son of righteous Kish, in the latter part of his life chose evil. It was the exercising of his own choice rather than environmental or hereditary conditions.
(A) Correct.                                                            281-54

## The Leader They Deserved

It is a familiar principle in politics (and metaphysics) that "the people get the leader they deserve." No man rises to power save that he speaks to the collective needs and beliefs of the majority he governs.

One reading tells us Samuel introduced a new factor in the relationships between the people and their worship of God. This new concept is expressed by Samuel in 1 Samuel 12:13-15. It indicates the people bear the responsibility for their leaders. The power still rests with the people. Their relationship is still directly between God and them. But now there is an "intervening" factor.

If the people do good, the king will do good. If the people are evil, the king will not rise above it. Yet, if the people want to do good, and the king refuses, then the people have the right to change him. A new factor of conscience and responsibility is laid upon the people.

On November 27, 1923, a young Oklahoma oil promoter obtained a physical reading from Edgar Cayce. In the reading, the man was described, in part, as follows. Is this "the leader they deserved?"

One spiritually high-minded. Physically weak in developing much of that condition. One given to do a great deal towards [the] uplift of man, when used properly. *Not always done.* One given to control men through the mental. Not always controlled properly. One given to create a balance, and to find the equalizing forces with the masses. *Not always used properly.*

Be better physically, mentally, if this were kept in the straight and narrow forces than [it] has been at times.                              221-1

The accuracy of this reading inspired the man to write Edgar Cayce, requesting a Life reading. In the second reading, three weeks following, the young man was told he had been Saul, Israel's first king! Although the opening passage is a description of the present state of the entity's development, much that is in it is applicable to Saul. This Life reading is among the earliest given by Edgar Cayce

> Edgar Cayce: Yes, we have the body, the conditions here, and the records as has been made, and as will be made, both in the present and past and future . . . All is not good, yet in many phases of earth's sphere, known as success, this individual will rise high, yet ever those of the wandering forces, as gained from the influence of the Mercury and Neptune forces, will be in this entity's doing and undoing . . . Saturn and Mars afflicting, Moon's forces being earth's spheres. Hence the entity's ability to handle those forces in nature that come from earth's storehouse, and any of the elements of this nature become the speculative forces for financial returns to this body in the earth plane . . . One with the affictions of the forces as given in Mars and Saturn will and does make one slow to wrath, but subtle in the ultraextent in carrying out purposes, good or bad.
>
> One that in the greater development will find moments, hours, years of sublime forces entering in with the great vision of Venus and Jupiter forces, yet holding these rather as ideals than making of these forces a reality in his own experience.
>
> Those of the Moon and Sun's forces we find working as antagonistic in the development of financial forces in Mercurian elements, yet one that will oft times have within his grasp the higher influences of financial force in [the] earth plane.
>
> As to forces with the will as established in self, the entity would do well to keep in that straight and narrow way that leadeth to life everlasting, giving of itself in the moments and hours of the Jupiterian force as is found in the next five months . . .                    221-2

Although in later years in other readings, (5148-2 and 281-48) Cayce attributed Seth (Genesis 5:3) and Benjamin (Genesis 35:18), respectively, as earlier incarnations of Saul, in this Life reading neither of the two is mentioned:

> In the personalities of the individual we find as obtained from these conditions:

Before this we find this portion of entity in that of the Grecian age when the fall of the government was under the rule of the idealists and the materialists became the ruling force of the day. This entity, as then, was the leading force in the minority at the time; hence was often referred to as the weakling of the day.

In that before we find the entity as that of the leader [Saul] as chosen for the first king in and with the chosen people, and was the herder as sought the lost animals of his father when appointed as the leader.

Hence we find in this present sphere those elements bringing through in this personality and individuality those as in this:

In the first the one chosen of the higher elements. Hence ever those forces about this entity where, though all others fail, this one may, through direct self-control, gain those forces of the higher and highest realms in the present plane.

In the second that force as is manifested in the great thoughts and ideals builded about self, yet ever just beyond carrying those to execution. May be done by sheer will and by adhering to those immutable laws that give self the insight of the forces that lend to the upbuilding of all force relative to the higher elements.

In stature from that of all force, as is given, ever has the entity been under the influence of Mercurian elements.                221-2

When the Bible class reached the appropriate place in their study of the Book of Samuel, Edgar Cayce quoted extensively from this reading in one discussion. When he concluded with the lessons from the reading, he summed up with the following comment:

"This individual, as you can see from the above, has a very brilliant mind and is very capable, yet lives by his wits, trying to 'outsmart' the next guy.

"If he continues in this direction, he will come up against a brick wall, and have to start all over again, because—by the natural, spiritual laws of the universe—he must comply with the laws of love and universality of purpose.

"Some of us take a long time to learn by experience. We must hit rock bottom before we realize we are headed in the wrong direction."

## Saul's Past Lives

Few things happen by chance. No man rises to authority over a nation except by "the grace of God." (5142-1) Any man who is in a commanding position above his brothers has earned that privilege and responsibility by developments in past lives.

As a soul, Saul had been bound up with the ideals and purposes of Israel from the beginning. If the readings are correct, this soul had also manifested as Seth and Benjamin, experiences which, no doubt, prepared him for the privilege of being Israel's first king.

While in the clairvoyant state, Edgar Cayce must have observed an unusual panorama of history. Time and again the readings create subtle and sensitive connections between widely separated happenings. Yet when they are pointed out, the clarity of repeated patterns are discerned.

Thus we find Seth, the third child of Adam and Eve and *first* in the pageant of lineal descent, reincarnated as Saul, first among the monarchs of Israel.

There was no self-seeking as Seth. The entity continued his line and successfully advanced the Adamic influence on the earth. As Saul, he was given a similar opportunity, but failed.

This reading draws the lesson:

In giving the interpretations of the records here, there are those experiences in the earth which stand out beyond others, not beyond the present which may be attained, but beyond some others. These may answer questions for some, as to why individuals apparently are so far advanced in one experience and then fail so miserably in others. Self enters in and is ever present. For there is continually, as is set forth in the admonitions of the lawgiver, set before thee today, now and every day good, evil, life and death. Choose thou.

Consider for the moment . . . how that God himself chose Saul as a goodly king, head and shoulders above his fellow men, his countenance that was indeed kingly and gifted with prophecy; and yet he allowed himself because of an exalted physical position to forget his humbleness before God, even as there had been in his experiences in the earth before, in those days as a son of Adam, who had been given that privilege of being the channel through which the chosen of the peoples were to be Abraham, Isaac, and Jacob.                                    5148-2

Throughout the reading for 221 (Saul), Cayce called the entity to the greater use of his will and for exercising direct self–control, in order to gain "those forces of the . . . highest realms in the present plane." Beneficent astrological influences fill the mind with sublime vision, yet the thoughts and ideals built by self are "ever just beyond carrying out."

The lack of desire to make the spiritual manifest has long been in the makeup of this soul. It was this vibration in Jacob and Rachel that attracted the soul in its incarnation as Benjamin.

**The material love was just as great [as when Joseph had been conceived], the satisfying of material desire was completely fulfilled; yet it lacked that desire to *bring* such as was wholly a channel through which the *spiritual* was to be made manifest. But it was a channel that *eventually* brought the material made manifest in Saul, an incarnation of Benjamin.**                                           **281-48**

If Saul had been Benjamin, then he was the same soul whom Jacob spoke of as "a ravenous wolf." (Genesis 49:27)

Although Saul brought certain weaknesses and shortcomings with him in his material incarnation, when he was anointed by Samuel he became a changed man, as the prophet foretold. God "gave him a new heart." (1 Samuel 10:9) However, Saul soon reverted to old habits.

Edgar Cayce saw a hidden significance in the familiar story of Saul's first meeting with Samuel. (1 Samuel 9)

"Saul came to Samuel through the law of material things. His first request from Samuel was material in nature. He wanted Samuel to tell him where his father's asses were.

"Throughout his life, Saul never failed to recognize that Samuel *could* give him the information he sought, but he did fail to use it for the glory of God.

"The spirit of the Lord fell upon Saul, and he prophesied. But only for a short while. The rest of the time he continued to seek his own ends."

What Saul prophesied has not been recorded. Apparently he was flooded with those sublime forces and vision which are, as in the present, "ever just beyond carrying to execution."

**. . . and yet the *individual* in his personal relationships defied even that**

Edgar Cayce drew more lessons on Saul for his Bible class.

"If you are once convinced in spirit, or by the Spirit, then God is with you. If you are able to continually hold to that, nothing can go wrong. But if you forget and entertain the spirit of evil, then you know, as Jesus said, 'Your Father is one who can be touched by your infirmities.' Yes, and he can also be touched by your hardness of heart and your negligence.

"We are co-creators with God. Saul had been ordained. He prophesied. He had been convinced in spirit, but he did not hold to it.

"Saul merited the opportunity which was given to him, just as all those who are in power today have earned the position they occupy. What an individual does with his opportunities is between him and God. Nothing can separate you from God's love except yourself.

"We think certain people are destined for certain things. *Everyone* is destined at some time to be a Caesar, to be a Jesus, to be a devil if that's what he wants to be. Everyone has the opportunity to make choices. It is always up to the individual.

"It has been said when the pupil is ready, the teacher appears. If it takes ten lives to accomplish a spiritual purpose, what does it matter. What difference does it make? The main thing is to keep on trying—which is what Saul failed to do!"

## The Sin of Saul

The words of Paul to the Hebrews are applicable to Saul:

*For it is impossible to restore again to repentance those who have once been enlightened, who have tasted the heavenly gift, and have become partakers of the Holy Spirit, and have tasted the goodness of the word of God and the powers of the age to come, if they then commit apostasy . . .* (Hebrews 6:4-6)

When Samuel anointed Saul as king, Saul became a changed man. He was filled with the Holy Spirit and prophesied. After receiving the Spirit, he united Israel against the Ammonites, who were threatening the brother tribe of Ephraim. So caught up in the Spirit was he after this victory, he took no credit to himself, but acknowledged it totally as the work of God. So complete and all-possessing was his experience that there was no room within him for vindictiveness or malice toward the Israelites who doubted and despised him. (1 Samuel 11:12-13)

Yet Saul, after partaking of the fullness of the Spirit, failed to produce further Spiritual fruits.

> **And, as has been given by the lawgiver of old, think not who will descend from heaven to bring you a message; for, Lo, it is already in thine own heart. It is thyself, thy inner self, thy soul self. Think not who will come over the waters, nor over the seas to bring a message, for it is with thee already.**
>
> **To be sure, these may be encouraged, abetted, kept in line; but it is within self that this must be accomplished. Then if it is used to that of self-indulgence, self-gratification, self-attaining for that of self alone, it becomes sin—even as the sin of Saul.**                          **2995-1**

## Saul's Decline—The First Mistake

Shortly after his inspired victory over the Ammonites, (1 Samuel 11) and his magnanimous example of forgiveness, (1 Samuel 11:13) Saul began to show the pattern that would characterize the rest of his reign.

Saul was in the position to set a new ideal for man in his spiritual evolution, and in the second year of his authority he failed his first test. (1 Samuel 13)

After a successful engagement with the Philistines, Saul called for Samuel to prepare a burnt offering. Samuel set a period of seven days as preparation for the ritual. During that time the Philistines began to amass their forces again. Many of the Israelites began to panic and desert. Those who remained with Saul began to waver. But the time of waiting had not passed, and Samuel did not appear. On the seventh day, Samuel still had not come, and Saul in order to prevent further defections offered the sacrifice himself, thus violating the law of Moses and usurping the sacrosanct privilege of high priest.

Just as he finished the sacrifice, Samuel appeared and rebuked Saul for failing to honor God's laws. This had been a crucial test. Had he proved himself, the Lord would have established Saul forever (13:13). Samuel put Saul on notice that God had chosen a new man, "one after his own heart." (13:14)

Edgar Cayce, who was keenly aware of the importance of attitudes and emotions, saw other indications in this story of Saul's weakness:

"How very much this reminds us of situations in our own lives today. We begin to get panicky and can't wait long enough for the Lord to work through us. We try and figure out a way to do it ourselves. Saul had a good excuse from the material angle. The people were becoming scattered and going home, so he had to hold them by asking for a sacrifice to be brought. He told Samuel he didn't want to go ahead, but forced himself to do it for fear there would be no one left to fight.

"Samuel rebuked him, and from that time on Saul could not take any more rebuke or criticism. He continued to feel his own self-importance more and more, and to exercise his authority more and more arbitrarily."

## *Saul's Rash Vow*

Saul's second mistake was almost a tragic one for his son Jonathan. This episode is recounted in 1 Samuel 14.

Jonathan and his armor bearer engaged the Philistine garrison at Michmash in a night attack. The Philistines, caught by surprise, retreated, thinking Saul's army had attacked. Saul, roused by the sound of battle, marshaled his troops and led them into combat. At the onset he issued a senseless order that, on penalty of death, all his men abstain from eating until he was completely avenged on the Philistines. It would mean almost twenty-four hours without food. Jonathan, unaware of this command, late in the day ate a honeycomb.

When this news was brought to Saul, he found himself trapped by his own rash vow, unable to retract it and loath to carry it out.

The situation is similar to the story of Jephthah (Judges 11), but with a different ending. The people recognized God had been with Jonathan, and stood up for him against Saul. They wouldn't allow Saul to repeat Jephthah's tragic mistake.

"Perhaps Jephthah's daughter could have been saved," Edgar Cayce said, "had the people responded in the same way." This shows the people were beginning to think for themselves, Cayce said, and had remembered what Samuel told them—that they could make the king do what was right.

Although Jonathan escaped an early death this time, he died a young man in battle with Saul. Saul's actions eventually destroyed his whole household.

## *The King's Son*

Two weeks after the reading for the oil promoter who had been King Saul, a successful Dayton, Ohio, real estate broker obtained his Life reading. In it he was told that he had been Jonathan, Saul's son, whose friendship with David has been a model of honor and loyalty throughout the ages.

The reading tells us that his life as Jonathan was one of several in which the entity experienced sudden death.

> **We find in those forces as has been manifest in the entity's sojourn upon the planes that there have been several sudden deaths, or removal. Hence, the innate feeling that is exhibited that some such condition might possibly happen in the present.** **4219-3**

It also comments on the positive developments in the use of his will.

> **. . . the will with the present entity's development will go far to assist in presenting this entity wholly and acceptable unto Him who giveth all things . . . Keep the body fit, that the will and the soul forces may manifest, for the body means much to all who contact same . . .**
> **4219-3**

Then with the characteristic briefness of these earliest Life readings, Edgar Cayce described three unusual and outstanding incarnations:

> **As to the personalities as expressed, the individuality as brought from those before:**
> **The one before this we find in that of the king's son, and the counselor and friend of the shepherd king when the shepherd became king—Jonathan.**
> **In that before, we find in that of Poseida, when Alta ruled the earth's forces, and was then in that [name] of Aramus.**
> **In the one before, we find in the early dawn when the forces showed the Sons coming together for the Glory of the earth's plane.**
> **In the personalities as shown in the present it is in the first [experience] that of the love of sincerity.**
> **In the second, and in that the life [was] lost in the volcano eruption; in that we find the present forces of judgment of structural forces.**

**In the next, the friendship of those who are the faithful to any cause that is just.** **4219-3**

Edgar Cayce made these additional remarks about Jonathan to the Bible class.

"Jonathan was a God-fearing man. Evidently he must have been conceived and born during the early days of Saul's reign, when Saul was still consecrated. We might say Jonathan's mother was a God-fearing woman who later lost favor with Saul through some disagreements with his plans. When Jonathan was pleading for David, Saul lost his temper and called him, 'Thou son of the perverse, rebellious woman.'

"Jonathan was not selfish or egotistical. He realized Saul was not carrying out Samuel's directions. This fact, with David's character, established a bond of friendship that was out of the ordinary. David, when he was acclaimed a hero, still proclaimed his loyalty to Saul. This drew Jonathan closer to David."

## The Third Mistake

The third indication of Saul's poor judgment is recounted in the 15th Chapter of the first book of Samuel.

Samuel ordered Saul to completely exterminate the Amalekites, thus fulfilling an injunction which had been in effect since the time of Moses. Saul defeated the Amalekites, but he did not completely carry out Samuel's command. He spared King Agag and the best sheep, cattle, and spoil for a sacrifice. Although Saul's intentions may have been good, he demonstrated again, by hedging on Samuel's instructions, he would not hesitate to put his will above God's will, his way above God's way.

To sacrifice is noble, though its intent was probably selfish. After the sacrifice, Saul and his warriors would have enjoyed a great feast on the best parts of the "burnt offerings."

Samuel's reply to Saul is one of the clearest indications of what God desires: the sacrifice of self-will, rather than anything external:

*And Samuel said, "The Lord is not as well-pleased with burnt offerings and sacrifices as with one who obeys his voice. Behold, to obey is better than sacrifices, and to hearken, than the fat of rams."* (1 Samuel 15:22)

Or as said in a reading:

**For, He has given, no sacrifice is acceptable save as of the *desires* of self to be one with Him.** 531-5

Other Amalekites must have survived, for they are reported to have raided the town of Ziklag in David's absence. (1 Samuel 30) They weren't completely destroyed until the time of Hezekiah. (1 Chronicles 4:43)

## *"Music Hath Its Charms"*

The mental unbalance taking place in Saul keeps revealing itself more and more distinctly as his reign continues. The most transparent example is with the "evil spirit" that began to possess him. The need to exorcise it brought David into Saul's life.

> *But the Spirit of the Lord departed from Saul, and an evil spirit from before the Lord troubled him.*
> *And Saul's servants said to him, "Behold, your servants are before you; Let them seek out a man who can play well on the harp; and when the evil spirit is upon you, he will play with his hands, and you shall be well."* (1 Samuel 16:14-16)

Edgar Cayce talked of David's music:

"The evil spirit was perhaps nothing more than Saul's guilty conscience. After David's anointing, (1 Samuel 16:1-13) no doubt Saul—though knowing nothing of it consciously—became uneasy. He had a feeling something had gone wrong. In other words, he had the 'blues'! And David's playing chased them away. It made him forget he was out of tune.

"Even then Saul could have repented. But, as so many of us do today, he hardened his heart. We seek outside things to chase our 'blues' away, when what we need to do is to keep them from coming. We can do this by doing something constructive which will counteract those influences, or vibrations, around us which are the results of our own wrongdoing.

"Saul was so egotistical. The thing he was fighting was his own self and self-will. David's music brought back to Saul the consciousness of better things. Having once been aroused to the divine awareness within, one can, at some moments, easily approach the same awareness. The music quieted Saul's anger. In those moments, Saul was able to forget what he was losing."

We find this advice about music in one reading:

> . . . whenever there are the periods of depression, or the feeling low or forsaken, play music; especially stringed instruments of every nature. These will enable [one] to span that gulf as between pessimism and optimism. 1804-1

> *And Saul said to his servants, "Provide me now a man who can play well, and bring him to me."*
> *Then one of the young men answered and said, "Behold I have seen a son of Jesse the Bethlehemite, who is skillful in playing, a man of war and prudent in speech, a handsome man, and the Lord is with him."*
> *Wherefore King Saul sent messengers to Jesse and said, "Send me David your son; he will be useful to me." (1 Samuel 16:17-19)*

These comments about mental unbalance and self–government are applicable to Saul.

> (Q) What relaxation [is] best for the body, in addition to that given?
> (A) Just that! Changing of the mental status is ever the builder, mental and physical. That as the mind dwells upon is builded. When one overtaxes one portion to the detriment of another, an *unbalancing* must ensue. Keep much in the manner as has been given, as regarding diet, exercise, work, perseverance. Be consistent in all thou doest, and when thou hast conquered self thou mayest be able to govern another. He who approaches for mercy, grace, and counsel may not have aught against his brother, but must be able to appreciate and understand that he already has in hand. 257-53

## The Giant Killer

David's first residence at the court of Saul was only temporary. He returned to Bethlehem and tended his sheep. Possibly ten or fifteen years passed between his first summons to play for the king and the battle with Goliath.

From Cayce's notes:

"When David was anointed, apparently he had no idea he would be king someday. He felt he had been anointed for some special task he was to perform for King Saul.

"For years the Israelites had been fighting off the Philistines, and now they were about to give up. All the army felt none could defy Goliath. It was useless to try. They were about to give up. Then, because he had the right purpose and knew God was with him, David put an end to the war with one shot from his sling. This shows us what power there is in the smallest and most insignificant weapon, if our purpose is set in the Lord."

## Two Souls Knit

After his victory over Goliath, David was summoned by Saul to recount the battle for him. David described his victory for the court, and when he finished, one of the most remarkable and memorable events of the Old Testament followed.

*When David had finished speaking to Saul, the soul of Jonathan was knit to the soul of David, and Jonathan loved him as his own soul.* (1 Samuel 18:1)

The Edgar Cayce readings demonstrate time and time again that our response and reactions to many individuals stem from "karmic memories." These "memories" are stored in the subconscious mind as emotional patterns which have been created by past associations in former lives. When old friends, lovers, enemies, or comrades encounter each other anew, the "memories" are released as spontaneous emotions. Similarly, the subconscious responds when "like confronts like." People who hold certain values and ideals find themselves drawn to their own mental and spiritual kind.

In Life reading 4219 an incarnation as Jonathan was given. Cayce described the earliest experience of the soul at the time of Genesis 1, " . . . when the forces showed the Sons coming together for the Glory of the earth's plane." (4219-3)

Familiarity with this first experience of Jonathan's inspired this unique interpretation for the Bible class:

"It is very unusual to find the expression that the soul of Jonathan was 'knit' to the soul of David. No doubt their souls had been knit in purpose from the very beginning, or from the time of the creation of souls.

"This would account for their instant kinship."

## *A Disdain for Intrigue*

Mr. 221, who in his Life reading was told he had been King Saul, was described as being "subtle in the ultraextent of carrying out purposes, good and bad." This trait is in evidence in Saul, and Edgar Cayce charted its course.

Saul's first reactions to David, like Jonathan's, were also favorable.

"Like Jonathan, Saul was also 'taken' with David after his victory with Goliath. David had become a great hero in one day, and the least Saul could do was to recognize what he had done and show appreciation for it. It wasn't until later that Saul realized David was going to replace him. He knew it long before David even suspected it.

"When all the people, including the king's own servants, began to honor David, and the women sang his praises, Saul became very jealous. We seldom feel this emotion unless we feel some lack within ourselves. Perhaps Saul was jealous because he knew David was more deserving of praise than he. When we are sure of ourselves there is no cause for jealousy.

"Saul's jealousy preyed upon him, and he began to plot against David's life. If a small canker is not discouraged, it can grow until it becomes ungovernable and takes possession of the whole being.

"Saul was the best spearsman in Israel. He could cast a spear within a hair's breadth of any target. Yet he was not able to kill David. According to his own interpretation, the Lord had deflected his hand. Whenever Saul came to himself, he was sorry he had sought David's life. But soon afterwards his jealousies were rekindled.

"When Saul failed the first time, his next emotion was fear. In order to feel secure, he began to placate David, and offered him his eldest daughter, Merab, in marriage. This was a tremendous move on Saul's part. Judging by David's reaction, we could only say he did not think himself suitable (socially) to be the king's son-in-law. It just did not make sense. David's reaction must have made Saul feel powerful again. He gave

Merab in marriage to Adriel, the Meholathite.

"When Saul discovered Michal was in love with David, it pleased him. This was another opportunity to undo David. Saul was very sly this time. He used his soldiers, and let them persuade David that the slaying of a hundred Philistines would make him worthy of being a king's son-in-law. David must have loved Michal. It wasn't hard to convince him. He went out and killed TWO hundred, twice the number required. Saul had been sure David would be killed. Having made this stipulation, Saul was forced to give Michal to David.

"Instead of helping Saul with his plans, Michal was in love with David and ready to defend him. David now the king's son-ill-law, was in social rank a prince, and was ever more a threat to Saul—or so Saul felt—and he became more and more afraid."

Approximately a year after the Life readings for Saul and Jonathan, a young traveling salesman, a resident of a small town near Dayton, requested a Life reading. It was given on February 26, 1925. In it, the young man was told he had been Jonathan's armor bearer.

The armor bearer figures in only one episode in the Old Testament, that of the remarkable victory over the Philistine garrison at Michmash. (1 Samuel 14:6-15) No personal features are given about the armor bearer in this account. Indeed, not even his name is recorded. Yet Cayce's description of the entity helps to build an intuitive picture about the nature and character of this anonymous biblical character.

Whereas Saul was "subtle in the ultraextent" in carrying out his purposes, we find in this entity a disdain for intrigue and underhanded techniques. Possibly this could have resulted from a life-time of first hand experiences in the court of Saul.

After the suggestion by the conductor of the reading, Edgar Cayce began:

**Yes, we have the entity and its reaction in the present sphere with the Universal Forces as are exhibited in the physical body in the present earth's plane . . . we have in this body . . . the influences that make a very remarkable personage in the present plane, for we have one that truth, the ennobling influences, that are latent in every act of the entity. One also that the truth is paramount with the entity. One that the love of home and of connections are always in the actions of the body, yet there enters some of the adverse conditions through these [astrological**

aspects] . . . One who will give much influence in the rule to others, when guided, guarded, and directed in the proper channel.

One sensitive of nature, yet noble in thought and act. One timid in manner, yet one capable of reaching heights in expressing that in which the body is well founded in and believes the truth of.

One that has little to do with intrigue and underhand operations. One that thinks less of self should [he] allow [himself] to be misled, or drawn into such intrigues. Hence the purpose must ever be that never of self-condemnation, but rather relying on those elements that would make the sure and the paramount issue of life. Then one that should not place too much confidence in others. While this is not of a fault, yet the nature of this entity finding there was fault loses faith in self. Hence the greater forces should be exercised in placing that faith, that confidence, that purpose, in Him, the Giver of All Good and Perfect Gifts.          2888-2

Cayce foresaw a brilliant career in real estate if the entity would re-new his contact with the person he had known as Jonathan, who was now a land broker in nearby Dayton.

As to the abilities of the entity in the present earth's plane, with the ennobling influences, with the forces as lead the higher elements as an exhibition of the forces manifest, these should be, and would be, made a success in following that of real estate salesman, and this may be accomplished through some with whom this entity once was associated in times past, as we shall see.          2888-2

Cayce then described 2888's most recent past life, as the secretary to Lord Baltimore in Maryland. Then, in the preceding incarnation:

. . . we find in the days when the rebellion was in the hand of the king, the first king, in Israel, and we find the entity then the armor bearer to Jonathan and in the present plane we find this personality: That of the innate desire to defend that which is a principle in the mind and heart of the body. In this relation we would find these experiences which would develop this entity in present earth plane would be under the influence of him who represented that entity then, for [he] is in this sphere at present.          2888-2

Cayce then described an Arabian incarnation in which the entity

learned the worth of land and property, and ended with a recommen-
dation.

**Hence the abilities to compile these two forces [to advise and estimate],
and with that of Jonathan's bring about the success in the real estate
forces of today.** **2888-2**

Concluding the reading, Cayce gave this counsel:

**Then, to use and apply this as given, keep first the faith in Him, the Giver
of All Good and Perfect Gifts, knowing that the physical body is the
temple of the living God, and present same holy and acceptable unto
Him, which is but a reasonable service, for in service to man the greater
service is offered to God.**
**We are through.** **2888-2**

## In Pursuit of David

As a psychic, Edgar Cayce was never able to recall a word he spoke in
trance. And while in trance, he responded only to the questions which
were asked him, often by strangers concerned only with their bodily
ills. But the Tuesday night Bible class gave Edgar Cayce the opportunity
to speak freely, philosophize, interpret, and expound upon the thing he
knew and loved best—his Bible. As a young lad, Cayce had been drawn
to the Book, and its mystery and fascination never diminished for him.
He was able to take the Bible, and all the aspects of life it contained, and
interpret them on the basis of his own life experiences. And many and
varied were the psychic and spiritual experiences in his life which he
could draw upon.

But nowhere in the class are two characters more delineated than
David and Saul. And nowhere in the Bible class does the story come
closest to a dramatic narrative than when Edgar Cayce tells the story of
Saul's pursuit of David.

The story begins with 1 Samuel 19 and continues through to the
death of Saul.

Saul has already tried to impale David once with his javelin, and
failed, and plotted unsuccessfully to have him killed in battle. David has
become the king's son-in-law, and a soul-brother to Jonathan, and, due
to his succession of victories over the Philistines, has been growing in-

creasingly popular with the people. Thus, the "evil spirit" vexed Saul, and he issued a proclamation:

*And Saul told Jonathan his son and all his servants that they should kill David.* (1 Samuel 19:1)

Cayce discussed the relationship between father and son.

"When Saul began plotting against David, Jonathan, as the prince, felt he could influence his father against his plans. Having once been anointed, and having experienced the spirit of the Lord, Saul could, occasionally, be appealed to. Jonathan appealed to the good in Saul, reminding him of all the wonderful things David had done for him and his kingdom. Temporarily Saul tried to live up to the best within himself. He knew deep within that he was at fault, not David. But Saul was wishy-washy. His own selfish desires got the best of him.

"He openly proclaimed that he sought David's life. This caused great consternation to the people who loved David, yet felt they must follow their king. Perhaps the people, at this point, began to regret that they had demanded a king."

David fled to Ramtha, and Saul followed. At Ramtha, Saul encountered Samuel with a company of prophets. Face-to-face with the venerable sage, Saul abandoned the chase, stripped off his clothes, and prophesied.

Although Saul began his reign with the reputation as a prophet, there was a lack of sincerity in this experience which Edgar Cayce detected.

"Everyone who came into Samuel's presence began to prophesy. No wonder the people began to question themselves whether Saul was really a prophet, or to be considered one any longer."

Neither David nor Jonathan understood why Saul was so intent upon David's life. Neither of the men knew of any offense or crime of which David was guilty.

The following day was the feast of the new moon, a holiday banquet for Saul's warriors and dignitaries. David knew he would be missed and that Saul would ask about him. David decided to use this situation to test the temper of the king. Jonathan agreed to his part in the plan, a

simple ruse through which David could have his worst suspicions confirmed or allayed.

For Edgar Cayce, it was a lesson on "to tell the truth":

> "We find many instances where David saved his life by evading the
> truth. It shows his cautiousness. He treated poison with poison. Saul,
> knowing David was anxious to return to his own people, had forbidden
> it. David, then, used this to mislead Saul. Perhaps the purpose justified
> his actions. Some people feel it is best to *always* tell the truth, regardless
> of the consequences.
>
> "We do know if we say or do anything against our higher self, or our
> own conscience, it is wrong. In this instance, David's lie hurt no one.
> What is wrong for one person can be right for another, depending upon
> the purpose behind the act.
>
> "Jonathan agreed to David's plan. He didn't really believe Saul would
> kill David."

Because Saul became enraged when he heard he had gone home to
offer the traditional yearly sacrifice with his family, David knew his life
was in jeopardy. David fled, beginning his life as a fugitive from Saul.
His first stop was in Noh, at the house of Ahimeleck, a priest. This time
David practiced another deception, but with disastrous results for the
priest and his family.

> *Then David came to Noh, to Ahimeleck the priest; and Ahimeleck was*
> *afraid at meeting David, and said to him, "Why have you come alone, and*
> *no man with you?"* (1 Samuel 21:1)

> "Ahimeleck had every reason to be afraid. News of Saul's anger had
> spread throughout the country. Saul had published several edicts against
> David. But David misrepresented himself. He said the king had sent him,
> which was the truth in one sense, since he was fleeing from Saul. But he
> gave the impression to Ahimeleck that Saul had sent him on a mission of
> importance. The priest didn't know whether David was there on busi-
> ness or not.
>
> "According to the custom, the bread of the tabernacle, which David
> asked for, should have been destroyed. No one was supposed to have it.
> Because there was nothing else to give him strength, David persuaded
> the priest to give him the hallowed bread—not just enough for himself,

but for the many men whom the priest assumed were with David.

"We see how powerful Saul and David had become. The priests listened to them rather than standing firm in the laws of God in which they had been trained.

"Later Ahimeleck and all his household were killed for just this conversation with David."

David's next encounter was with Achish, king of Gatha.

*And David arose and fled that day from fear of Saul, and went to Achish the king of Gath.* (1 Samuel 21:10)

Edgar Cayce detected elements of David's statesmanship in this episode.

"The servants of Achish had heard the songs praising David. They thought he was actually the king of the Israelites. Consequently they questioned his unprecedented appearance among them. Then David pretended he was insane. He knew they would let him go if they thought he had lost his reason. He would be of no consequence to them.

"David was quite a diplomat!"

While Saul moved in on the house of Ahimeleck and massacred its inhabitants, David fled into the wild country of Arlam. There he was joined by every man who was in distress, in debt, or discontented, about four hundred in all.

Only one priest of eighty-five survived the slaughter Saul had ordered for Ahimeleck. Abiathar, Ahimeleck's grandson, escaped and joined David. When David heard about the massacre, he took the blame on himself. He realized the whole tragedy could have been avoided if he had not been so overconfident. He didn't try to excuse himself, but accepted the fault as his. He promised Abiathar protection.

Although David was a fugitive, he retained his loyalty to Saul and Israel. Whenever a threat or danger was posed to an Israelite town or settlement, David and his men went to its rescue.

Edgar Cayce called David "the original Robin Hood."

*Then they told David, saying, "Behold, the Philistines are fighting against Keilah and are robbing the threshing floors." And David inquired of the*

*Lord, saying, "Shall I go and smite the Philistines and save Keilah?" And
the Lord said to him, "Go and smite the Philistines and save Keilah." (1
Samuel 23:1-2)*

Cayce asked:

"In what way did David communicate with the Lord? Abiathar was a
priest who used the ephod to enquire. Or David may have received his
own answer from the voice within. All the Israelites knew the body was
the temple, and that God had promised to meet everyone in his own
temple. If we inquire, if we enter within, the answer comes. Moses' last
admonition to the people had been that they be guided by the still small
voice within.

"Perhaps the answer came to David as a voice, in a vision, or just a
feeling: The main thing to realize is that David inquired and received an
answer.

"When his people appeared doubtful, David inquired again, just to be
sure he was right in marching against the Philistines. Two hundred more
of the men of Judah joined him in the fight, and they saved Keilah. Yet
there were those among them who would turn David over to Saul if the
right opportunity arose. David discovered this by inquiring through the
ephod. He and his men then fled into the wilderness."

For a man seeking information about buried treasure through a psychic reading, Edgar Cayce pointed him to the same source which David
and other seekers obtained their guidance.

**(Q) Will it be the proper time to go now?**
**(A) As has been given, such decisions are to be directed by that within
self that answers to the influences or forces from without—but the
answers and directions must come from within; rather than by any
helping hand.**

**Rememberest thou all that has been given as to the manner in which
the individual finds self? Did Moses receive direction save by the period
in the mount? Did Samuel receive rather than by meditating within his
own closet? Did David not find more in the meditating within the valley
and the cave? Did not the Master in the mount and in the Garden receive
the answers of those directing forces?**

**These as directions, these as omens, these as signs *only*, and the**

**direction from the inward closer walk with thine inner self and thy
purposes and thy desire.** **707-6**

Saul and David are a study in contrasts, and nowhere is the difference more clearly emphasized than in what each felt God had called
them to do.

When Saul was advised of David's victory at Keilah, and that David
was still in the city, Saul felt, because he had an opportunity to kill
David, that God was on his side again.

> *. . . and Saul said, "God has delivered him into my hands; for he has shut
> himself up by entering a town that has gates and bars."* (1 Samuel 23:7)

Time and again, in his persecution of him, David had the opportunity to destroy Saul. But he wouldn't do it. He felt that the Lord had
something more special for him to do than to kill the king and take his
place.

Advised that he had been betrayed by citizens of Keilah who were
sympathetic to Saul, David and his men took refuge in the wilderness
forests of Ziph. There they were visited by Jonathan.

> "Jonathan came to David in the forest, and strengthened him in his
> faith. This was the first time David realized he was going to be the king.
> Jonathan told him he would be, and that he, Jonathan, would be next to
> him in power, and that Saul knew all this.
>
> "Jonathan knew David was God's chosen vessel. He knew it by the
> way David conducted himself, and by the way the people loved him.
>
> "David escaped to the wilderness of Ziph, and the Ziphites took ad-
> vantage of the situation to gain favor with Saul. Just as Saul was closing
> in, a messenger arrived with news of an invasion of Philistines. The
> Philistines knew a house divided could not stand, and they were work-
> ing hard to establish a stronghold in Israel.
>
> "We wonder if the message, which allowed David to get away, had
> been sent by Jonathan."

After pursuing the Philistines, Saul resumed his hunt for David. However, this time God delivered Saul into David's hands.

> *. . . and Saul went into the cave and lay down there; and David and his*

*men were staying on the slope of the cave. And the men of David said to*
*him, "Behold, this is the day of which the Lord said to you, 'Behold, I will*
*deliver your enemy into your hands, that you may do to him as shall seem*
*good in your sight.'" Then David arose and cut off the skirt of Saul's robe*
*stealthily.* (1 Samuel 24:3-4)

Once David cut Saul's skirt, he felt it was wrong. He called to the king
from a high hill and begged his forgiveness.

> "David could never get over the fact that Saul was God's anointed. He
> regretted cutting the skirt, and made obeisance to Saul. For the first time,
> he asked his forgiveness.
>
> "Saul melted in the face of David's humility. You see, Saul *knew* what
> was right. He recognized the godliness David presented to him through
> his humility. But Saul was unstable. When he was left alone, his jealou-
> sies and fears overtook him.
>
> "Aren't we like Saul? We can be swayed emotionally at times, and
> vow to make great sacrifices and do big things. But when it comes right
> down to our daily life, we fall back into old habits and think first and
> foremost of our own desires.
>
> "Notice Saul exacted a promise from David, which he kept. Saul did
> not keep his."

The exchange of promises gave David a brief respite from the chase.
In the intervening time, until Saul again renewed his relentless pursuit,
Samuel died (25:1) and David met and married Abigail, the rich young
widow whose husband David had been ready to slay for personal reasons. (25:2–44)

Cayce felt Nabal had pricked David's ego by not giving him the same
recognition he was used to receiving from everyone else.

> "After Abigail came to him, David began to realize what he had almost
> done. He was going to slay Nabal and all his house because of personal
> anger. It had not ever occurred to him to inquire of the Lord first. He
> realized what a great sin would have been his if Abigail hadn't come to
> him first.
>
> "She was very smart, no doubt already in love with David, or, at least
> a great admirer. When she returned home she must have told Nabal what
> she had done in such a way that, with his physical condition weakened

from over-indulgence, it produced heart failure."

Following this interlude, the Ziphites again informed Saul about David's location. Saul returned to the wilderness of Giboath once more, and while Saul slept, David had his second opportunity to slay the king.[22]

*So David and Abishai came to the people by night; and behold, Saul lay asleep in the path, with his spear lying on the ground . . . Then said Abishai to David, "Your God had delivered your enemy into your hands this day; now therefore let me smite him just once with this spear which is on the ground, and I will not smite him the second time."* (1 Samuel 26:7-8)

This episode occasioned a philosophical reflection by Edgar Cayce on the subject of attitudes toward tyrants.

"Abishai wanted to kill Saul. He felt it was too good an opportunity to pass by. Yet David wanted to protect the king. He still respected Saul as God's Anointed.

"There is a fine line of distinction drawn here. Considering that none are in authority save by the power of God, just what should our attitude toward tyrants and dictators be today who, so far as we can see, have no fear of God inside them. We can always turn to the example of Jesus. The Romans in his day were attempting to overrun the world and enslave all the conquered nations. Did Jesus raise an army and stand up to his oppressors. He could have done so, and won. Yet he showed a better way.

"David was aware of this same spiritual law. He said to Abishai, 'As the Lord liveth, the Lord shall smite him; or he shall descend in battle and perish.' The wicked will perish by their own hands. Or, if you give them enough rope, they'll hang themselves. Saul eventually died on his own sword.

"Let us remember, it is only justifiable to destroy life when the whole intent and purpose of that life is to do evil. Saul had many good qualities.

---

[22]Because of their many similarities, many commentators feel the two episodes of chapters 24 and 26 are the same event. Yet Edgar Cayce felt differently. He based his opinion on the fact that David sent spies out to confirm the rumors that Saul had renewed the chase (26:4), indicating he did not at first believe Saul had broken his promises and come out against him.

Many times he repented and, for short periods, tried to overcome his own personal ambition and jealousies.

"Today, when we look at leaders who are responsible for so much suffering, we sometimes feel that their destruction would be a blessing for mankind. Yet who are we to judge? The leaders are not solely responsible. If there had not been the need and desire by the majority, that leader could not have risen to power. But there must come a purging. Those who live by the sword, die by the sword. Those who trust only in the strength of their weapons, must one day be overcome by their own wrong actions.

"As David indicated, time will tell. We must not allow our hearts to be filled with hatred for those who are attempting to rule by force. We should make every effort at keeping humble, in readiness to be directed by His will. Remember, there is no such thing as a coincidence. There is a reason for everything that happens to us, around us, and in this world."

After this episode, David reentered the territory of Gath. He wanted to escape to a land where Saul had no jurisdiction. In Gath, he would no longer be considered a threat by Saul.

But time had run out for Saul. Samuel was dead. David was still popular. The Philistine armies were amassing for another battle.

In this last battle, Jonathan was slain and Saul died on his own sword. David had been tried and tested, and had proven himself equal to Samuel's expectation—"a man after God's heart."

## Saul and the Witch of Endor—Spirit Communication

Saul knew for some time that he had marked out a dark future for himself of death and defeat. Yet, like all men, he hoped this destruction could be avoided. After the death of Samuel, there was no longer a prophet in Israel. Like Saul, many of the Israelites had abandoned their traditional religion. Many worshipped pagan deities. There was no longer anyone to whom Saul could turn.

*And when Saul inquired of the Lord, he did not answer him, either by dreams or by fire or by prophets. Then Saul said to his servants, "Seek me a woman who has a familiar spirit, that I may go to her and inquire of her." And his servants said to him, "Behold, there is a woman who has a familiar spirit at Endor." (1 Samuel 28:7)*

Edgar Cayce drew a distinction between "diviners" in the Bible and those who had familiar spirits. A "diviner" was one who sought to be directed by the spirit of Truth; in the highest sense, one who continuously sought to do God's Will. One with a "familiar spirit" was a medium who allowed himself to be possessed by departed entities who were themselves still in a state of development (or regression).

Throughout the Old Testament, mediumship was never commended. It was prohibited by Mosaic Law, and later condemned by the prophets. Throughout their history, Israel was always directed in its seeking to go to the highest source, the spirit of God which could be found within.

Saul, who began his reign with a spiritual awakening, seldom followed the promptings of the Spirit. He who never heeded Samuel when the prophet was alive, troubled him for advice after he had died.

*And Saul disguised himself and put on other raiment, and he went to the woman by night; and Saul said to her, "Divine for me by the familiar spirit, and bring up for me him whom I shall tell you."*

*Then the woman said, "Whom shall I bring up to you?" And he said, "Bring me up Samuel . . . "*

*And the woman said to Saul, "I saw gods ascending out of the earth . . . " And she said to him, "An old man is coming up; and he is covered with a mantle." And Saul perceived that it was Samuel . . .*

*And Samuel said to Saul, "Why have you disturbed me to bring me up?"* (1 Samuel 28:8-16)

The Cayce readings show how closely connected the unseen and seen worlds are. Spirit communication is an authentic phenomena, yet it was warned against and never recommended as something to be sought after.

**(Q)** . . . is it possible for an ego itself either receding through what we call interstellar space, or existing on another [plane of consciousness] to so keep in touch, or so be aware of little finite details on the earth plane, as to guide in detail . . . one whom that ego may choose to guide?

**(A)** That is correct; this is possible, but the care must be taken by such an one that they be guided in that contact from one receding through stellar space, by the same desire as is made manifest by one so receding and seeking to aid . . . for when one is misdirected, we may find such an example in the seeking of the king to be guided by him, who annoyed him while the desire called up the old man, and the answer: "Why disturbest thou me, know [ye] not there has already been created the lasciviousness of desire earthly, in the activities, that at destruction is already before thee." Study that, see? 136-83

A warning was given to a group who desired to experiment with and record psychic forces.

. . . those who accredit or seek or desire other sources . . . the more oft they will be found to be such as those that are patterns or examples in Holy Writ; namely an excellent one—Saul, the first king. Here we find an example of an individual seeking from the man of God, or the prophet, information to be given clairvoyantly, telepathically (if you choose to use such terms); and we find the incident used as an illustration that may be well kept to the forefront in the minds of those who would prompt or check or record such experiments. 792-2

There are many ordinances regarding mediumship throughout the Bible. Spirit communication and mediumship were topics under frequent discussion in the Bible class. When the class reached the point in their study where Saul, in his desperation, turned to the witch of Endor, Cayce used the opportunity to present his views on spirit communication.

"Many people feel that when a soul passes from the earth, it becomes all-wise and can counsel those who are still here. But, as the tree falls, so does it lie. Samuel did not have any greater power nor any greater wisdom because he had passed over. He rebuked Saul, and repeated what he had already told him.

"'Why has thou disquieted me, to bring me up?'

"This rebuke from Samuel should be the answer for us today. When a soul leaves this earth plane, it has work to do in other realms of consciousness. Unless it is an earthbound soul—and certainly we do not wish to seek guidance from an earthbound entity—it is finished with the cares of this world for the present.

"Our answer should be—it is not right to seek communication with departed entities.

"If we seek to be guided by the Christ, we can accept the messenger He sends, whether it be in the form of a loved one, an angel, or a stranger.

Saul had not heeded Samuel's counsel when he was alive. How could he expect Samuel to advise him differently, just because he had passed from the earth plane?

"When Jesus was transfigured on the mount, Moses and Elijah materialized at his side, and talked with him about the things that were to happen. This experience was a natural consequence of His attunement with God, and came as an assurance.

"We may all have similar experiences if we seek first the kingdom of God. But we should never go out of our way to seek it through familiar spirits."

Several years earlier, the philosophy in this lecture was first expressed in reading.

Then, how may one determine in one's own experience as to the value or the reliability of information that may be given through any channel that may propose to be, or that may be said to be, of a psychic nature . . .

"Try ye the spirits," ye have been admonished; and they that testify that He has *come*, that bespeak such in their activities, are of *truth*.

Then, they that bring to each soul—not comfort, not as earthly pleasure, but—that which is *spiritually constructive in the experience of a soul, are worthy of acceptance* . . .

What sought Saul? For his own satisfying of his conscience, or for the edification of that which might bring truth? Because the soul of Samuel had entered into that inter-between did not change one iota the position that Saul bore with constructive influences. While the *channel* might be questioned, the source—and that received—was truth! For it came from the source that had already warned Saul. **5752-5**

# 16

## King David

### *Abner*

*With* Saul's death, there was nothing to hinder David's rise to power. He had always been popular with the people. Now he was certain to gain ever more popularity, influence and power.

> *Now there was a long war between the house of Saul and the home of David, but David grew stronger, and the house of Saul became weaker and impoverished.* (2 Samuel 3:1)

The Bible records an incident which seems a decisive factor in ending the war. Abner, Saul's general, remained loyal to Ashbashul, Saul's son, and supported him as king over the tribes of Israel, while David ruled over the tribe of Judah.

After two years of Ashbashul's reign, Abner changed his loyalties.

> *And Saul had a concubine whose name was Rizpah, the daughter of Ana; and Ashbashul said to Abner, "Why are you going in unto my father's concubine?"*
>
> *Then Abner was exceedingly displeased at the word of Ashbashul, and Abner said, " . . . I show kindness to the house of Saul . . . and have not delivered you into the hand of David, and yet you charge me with iniquity*

*concerning a woman. So do God and more to Abner, if I do not perform what the Lord has spoken to David, even so will I do, to transfer the kingdom from the house of Saul, and to establish the throne of David over Israel and over Israel from Dan to Beersheba."*

*And Ashbashul could not reply to Abner, because he feared him.* (2 Samuel 3:7-11)

Cayce philosophized on the significance of this episode:

"What a little thing it takes to change the whole course of a man's life, or even a nation's. Ashbashul's faultfinding changed the whole course of the Israelite tribes. It aroused Abner to action. There had been a lull between the Philistines and the Israelites, and Abner was having a quiet time.

"He determined to translate all his energies into helping David become king. Abner knew about the prophecies concerning David. He probably felt it was going to happen anyway, and he might as well have a hand in making it possible.

"Abner still had great influence over the people, and he used it to urge them to accept David as king. He knew David could have made himself king, even before Saul's death, and that he hadn't chosen to do it."

On February 8, 1939, a Life reading was given for a teen-age Protestant boy. In the opening preamble, he was described as "a natural leader, a natural politician, making for, then, even in little details, the activities in which the purposes and intents will be carried out." The parents were also warned their son was "very susceptible to the fair sex." Then, an incarnation as Abner was described:

. . . the entity was among those who were close to the king who was proclaimed after Saul—or a friend of, a companion of David; and raised to one in power—yet the experience became both an advancement as well as a retardment. For the entity allowed self, and the power of self, to become as the greater influence.

The name then was Abner.

Yet as for power, as for influence, as for the musical forces, as for the thrusts, as for the directing powers and forces among men, this is a great force and influence in the present experience.

Hence again, God and right, God and faithfulness, God and truth is to be the motto of the entity in all of its relationships.

Hence the spiritual side of the nature of the entity is to be impressed and directed. And have no instructor, no director that is not well grounded in *spiritual* things!                                          1815-2

The Life reading laid the foundation for Cayce's final assessment of this significant figure in Israel's history.

"Would Abner be called a good man? Perhaps Abner could be described as a good military leader, and a good moral man; though he never quite understood what it meant—as David did—to rely entirely upon the Lord."

## *"A Man After God's Heart"*

The instability of Saul's relationship to God is a fine contrast to the sturdiness which David shows in his. The stature of David is measured in several ways in the readings. He was described as an example for man as a man, and yet the readings also reach out and touch upon his metaphysical and cosmic significance. We also find him among those who contributed to the development of the Christ.

For without Abraham, without Moses, yea without David, what need could there be that Melchizedek, that Enoch, or Joseph, or Joshua, should again come in the flesh? fulfilling all?

Have ye fulfilled all? When ye have, ye are One with Him . . .
                                                            1158-9

David's name is the only one included in Cayce's list of those who developed the God-relationship which is not an incarnation of the soul Jesus.

. . . activity toward the proper understanding and proper relationships to that which is the making for the closer relationships to that which is in Him alone. Ye have seen it in Adam; ye have heard it in Enoch, ye have had it made known in Melchizedek; Joshua, Joseph, David, and those that made the preparation then for him called Jesus.          5749-5

The significance of David's name is measured by its meaning. All who are named David share in its vibration. Cayce chose to call a friend by his middle rather than given name.

(Q) Why is this body so often referred to as David, rather than Edwin David, in psychic readings as given by Edgar Cayce?
(A) The development of the entity is rather in that vibration of David than of Edwin, for these two conditions are with the vibration in the names; Edwin, meaning that of a peacefulness, defender of peacefulness, carrying both the condition and implied forces from same. David, rather that of the gift from the higher forces, or a Son of the Father. One, especially, endowed with gifts from higher forces.          137-13

As a model for man, and as one that was to set an ideal, King David made full use of his talents. He was a well-rounded personality, versatile and gifted, who could claim equal fame as a soldier, statesman, poet, composer, and musician. And yet, as this reading indicates, he is an example of humility.

Who, having named the name of the Christ, has become conscious of that He represented or presented in the world? As the records have been handed down that Abraham represents the faithful, Moses meekness, David the warrior yet humility, so the Christ represents Love; that all may know that He hath paid the price for all.          262-56

As an example for man, one of David's greatest attributes is in his ability to celebrate. When he was sorrowful, he prayed; but when he was joyful, he danced and sang and played, giving praise and thanksgiving for the glories of God.

Throughout his life he remained keenly aware of Nature. He was attuned to the beauties in all forms and walks of Life. He was able to see God manifesting in everything!

Then, play as well as work. Relax as well as keep taut. So, through the mental abilities of the body, be as appreciative of the finer things of life as of material success. Be as capable of appreciating the beggar with a God-given voice as would bring tears of appreciation of love of man for man or woman, or of the appreciation of the beauties in nature, as appreciative of the man with a million, able to wield a power and influence of a nature that shows and belies of self-aggrandizement of power. Be, through the mental abilities, so as to be appreciative of that in art, or beauty in a picture, or beauty in nature. Let these, as they did to thine own peoples—even thine prophet, thine servant David, as he declared in, "The glory of God is made manifest! Even the heavens declare His glory and the firmament showeth His handiwork"; for fame and fortune often take wings and fly away—but one appreciative of the beauties in nature, in the abilities of His handmaid, in the might of Him that serves in song or dance, or the piper, these also declare His glory— and, as these be appreciated, so may that as may be given in this world's goods, in power, in might, in moneys, in position—so one may know how, through what channel, one may serve . . . These are but little things in the eyes of many. These, by their very foolishness to many, confound the wise. These but make contentment that makes one seek and seek for knowledge of Him that gives the gifts in life; for He be the God of the *living* whom thou servest, and material things are but dead— and are dead *weight* when one has not attuned self to the beauties in every field that makes manifest.

*Even* the toad is as beautiful in the sight of the Creator as the lily, and he that heedeth not the little things may not be master of the great things, for he that was capable of using the talents in the little way was made the ruler over *great* cities.

Keep thine body fit. Keep thine mind attuned to beauty.    257-53

Because David was faithful with the little things, he was able to handle the great matters. Rabbinical traditions state, as a shepherd, David treated his sheep tenderly, with loving care. Therefore God said, "He understands how to pasture sheep; therefore he shall become shepherd of my flock, Israel."

Although David grew in his ability to master all aspects of life, there were many times he was not able to conquer the desire to sin. He was tempted in many ways and succumbed often.

One of David's most remarkable gifts was his ability to take criticism. When Saul sinned and Samuel admonished him, Saul hardened his heart; whereas when Nathan rebuked David, David listened. When he was in error, David acknowledged it and blamed no one else for his shortcomings.

In June, 1937, David was cited as an example worthy of study for A.R.E. members assembled at their sixth annual congress.

Using the experience of David the king as an example, what was it in his experience that caused him to be called a man after God's own heart? That he did not falter? that he did not do this or that or be guilty of every immoral experience in the category of man's relationship? Rather was it that he was sorry, and not guilty of the same offense twice!
Well that ye pattern thy study of thyself after such a life!   5753-2

## The Pattern of a Life

Although there is little said in the readings about the life of David, in the Bible class Edgar Cayce dwelt on it at length and in detail. Saul and David were a study in contrasts, and Cayce drew many lessons from their variations. Saul is an example of a man at war within himself, unwilling to submit to the Spirit which had awakened him. This led to madness, self-destruction, and the termination of his house.

David's life witnesses to a remarkable spiritual growth throughout.

Edgar Cayce identified with both Saul and David, for he presented the two men in a believable, compassionate, and understanding way. Yet Cayce identified closely with David, as if he found in the king a model for his own life: a man who knew both weakness and strength, gifted in unusual ways and destined to fulfill a peculiar service.

Edgar Cayce's lectures on David reveal remarkable gems of insight and spiritual understanding which reveal a very unusual character— but whether the person is David or Edgar Cayce, the reader will have to decide.

Although the lectures are valuable, perhaps this reading gives us the key to the greatest similarity between Edgar Cayce and King David.

Study as to why David is called "a man—man—after God's own heart." Not that he was free from fault, but that his purposes, his hopes, his fears were continually submitted to God. And remember, as he gave, "That which I feared has come upon me."   4047-2

## The King

*And David perceived that the Lord had established him king over Israel, and that he had exalted his kingdom for the sake of his people.* (2 Samuel 5:12)

David was crowned king at a unique time in world history. The stage was set for the rise of Israel, and David took full measure of the opportunity which was given him.

In the southwest, the Egyptian empire was in decline. In the east, the Assyrian and Babylonian empires which, centuries later, would take Israel into bondage had not yet arisen. On the highway between these two world centers sat the new kingdom of Israel. In a few short years David led the development of an insignificant nation into the single most powerful kingdom in the earth at that time.

David was twenty-three when he was crowned king over Judah, and thirty years old when he was made king over the twelve tribes. David's first act as king was to make the home of Melchizedek, priest of the Most High, his capital. Jerusalem was among the cities which had remained unconquered by Joshua. It was an impregnable fortress, the stronghold of the Jebusites. It was a strategic city, centrally located on the trade-routes of the world. After establishing "the city of God" as his capital, David's next act was to bring the Ark of the Covenant into the city.

Although there is an obvious military and political significance to these acts, there is also a mystical, or metaphysical meaning which supersedes. The strategy which David followed to establish and unite his kingdom is similar to a pattern of spiritual understanding.

David, perhaps more than any king of Israel until Jesus, understood the kingdom was first a spiritual one, which had to be built in the heart and mind of individuals before it could ever manifest outwardly. David, because he had done it within himself already, was able to bring the pattern of a heavenly kingdom into the earth.

Jerusalem—"the city of Melchizedek"—symbolizes a state of consciousness from which all men should rule, and make their capital, and return the Ark of the Covenant (knowledge of the laws) to it. Then, as David did after subduing all his enemies, we can begin planning for the Temple (which is the body).

## *The Death of Uzzah*

The Ark of the Covenant had been abandoned, possibly for fifty or sixty years. Saul had never paid any attention to it, especially since his break with Samuel. And Samuel had not insisted that he should.

The Ark had not been in the tabernacle since the day Hophni and

Phineas carried it into battle with the Philistines, and it was captured. (1 Samuel 4) No doubt the tabernacle itself had gone into discard and deteriorated greatly, especially the outer coverings.

Following the conquest of Jerusalem, David chose twenty thousand men from all the tribes of Israel. He declared a national celebration and a great ceremonial procession, as they set out to return the Ark of the Covenant to the City of God. However the great procession was marred by the death of Uzzah, an unexpected event which, in the countless generations that have followed, has caused men to speculate, ponder, and attempt to interpret its real significance.

*And when they came to Nachon's threshingfloor, Uzzah put forth his hand to the ark of God, and took hold of it; for the oxen shook it. And the anger of the Lord was kindled against Uzzah; and God smote him for his error; and there he died by the ark of God.* (2 Samuel 6:6-7)

Several traditions have grown out of the attempt to rationalize Uzzah's death. Why should a good man die for attempting to do a good deed? One rabbinical school holds that Uzzah was being punished for relieving himself too near the ark. However, both the readings and the Bible class took note of this event, and supply insights into the happening.

Reading 440-16 describes Mount Sinai as being " . . . electrified by the presence of the God of the people and ohm of the Omnipotent to such an extent that no living thing could remain on same, save those two [Moses and Joshua] . . . " In Moses' time, the people still had a knowledge of electricity which probably had been handed down from Atlantis. In David's time, this knowledge was all but forgotten.

Research now indicates the Ark of the Covenant was a type of electric capacitor capable of producing an electrical charge of 500 to 700 volts. The Ark was made of acacia wood, lined inside and out with gold; or, two conductors separated by an insulator. The garlands on either side may have served as condensers. Insulated from the ground, the Ark is said to have given off fiery rays, acting like a Leyden jar. The capacitor was discharged to earth through the garlands. To move the Ark, two golden rods were slid through the rings attached to the exterior.[25]

---

[25]According to Maurice Denis-Papin, quoted in *Secrets of the Great Pyramid* by Peter Tompkins (New York: Harper & Row, 1971), p. 278.

In the Bible class, Edgar Cayce discussed the possibility of death by shock:

"The indication is that Uzzah only tried to steady the ark, to prevent it from falling. Apparently his purpose was good. There is no later reference to this except by Paul, who calls attention to the fact that one even in his lack of understanding suffered death. It could be that the vibrations were so high that they brought death by shock, just as if he had touched a live electric wire.

"The ark had never been on a cart before the Philistines captured it. The priests always carried it on their shoulders. We might say our relationship to God is a personal thing. We can't put it on a new cart and have someone else haul it for us. Uzzah should have known better than to ever let it be put on the cart. If the oxen shook the ark, that in itself should have warned them it wasn't the right way."

While in the clairvoyant consciousness, Edgar Cayce drew on the illustration of Uzzah to answer the following question:

(Q) Please explain the veil within the Holy of Holies.
(A) . . . as that given by the Master, "These I have spoken in parable lest they see and are converted." What meaneth this?
   That those individuals' times, purposes, intents, had not been completed or sufficient unto where they would be stable in their use or application of the glory or the opportunity or the factor itself.
   So with the veil in the Holy of Holies, which might not be entered save by him who had been dedicated to the office of representing or presenting the purpose, the mind of the people as a whole—and *then* only after consecrating himself for that period or act of service . . . What brought death to him that put forth his hand to steady the Ark that, in *order*, sat behind the veil? That which had brought to that individual material prosperity, laudation among his brethren; yet the soul had accepted all without dedicating his body, his mind, his purpose to that service—breaking through the veil to accept and yet not showing forth that which was in keeping with those commands, those promises. For it had been said and given, "He that putteth forth his hand *beyond* that veil shall *surely* die!"                                            262-94

Be not overanxious; for he that is overanxious, even, is as Uzzah . . .
   Remember Er, Uzzah and Malchus?, how their curiosity brought to

them that period of night when that they had builded must be accounted for.  262-72

## *Bathsheba and the Sorrows of David*

Perhaps one of David's greatest disappointments was that he was forbidden to build the Temple of God. He had been told by a prophet that he could not build the Temple because he had "shed blood abundantly" and waged great wars. (1 Chronicles 22:8) Although He helped David completely subdue the Philistines, the Moabites, Syrians, Ammonites, Amalekites, Edomites, and all the other neighboring nations, God, in His wisdom knew a man of war could not, or should not, build His Temple.

If David built the Temple, there would be too much bitterness among the defeated nations toward David's God. In Solomon's generation much of the pain and horror of those wars had been healed and forgotten.

Perhaps another meaning might be read into this injunction. David, as a man who had waged war and shed much blood, had no hesitation about instigating the virtual murder of Uriah the Hittite in order to conceal his own adultery with Bathsheba. His bloodletting had hardened his heart to such an extent that he was able, as one reading says, "to forget himself" and go to a shocking extreme to get his own ends.

A young Hebrew woman, in her reading, was told that following her incarnation as the daughter of Hur and a helper to Moses and Aaron she had reincarnated at the time of David:

> . . . the entity was in the Holy Land, or the Promised Land; as the children of Judah gathered to proclaim their confidence, their faith in David the king, who worshipped God in a manner such that it was given, "a man after mine own heart." Not that he failed not, but not guilty of the same offense twice, and gave credit ever to God—not to self; the *glory* to God, the weakness acknowledged in self, but the glory to Him.
>
> There we find the entity was a handmaiden to Bathsheba, in those periods when she became the companion to David—under those periods of disturbance when there was the forgetting of self and Uriah was slain; when, as Nathan declared, "Thou art the man." [2 Samuel 12:7]
>
> The entity then was that assistant or companion to the body guard of David, in the name Shelah. The entity gained from those experiences; *learned* much from the sorrows of Bathsheba, as well as of David.

And in the present through the abilities to help others, who find great sorrow in their lives from incidents, accidents, or even from premeditated efforts to take advantage of situations, the entity may counsel with those of her own sex as well as those of the young, in preparing them for meeting the vicissitudes in life's highway.

In the experience the entity gained through the greater part of the sojourn. Well may the tenets of the 1st, the 24th, and the 90th Psalms become as a part of the entity's meditation, in seeking for that at–onement with that *only* which brings peace in self and in the experience or associations with others, as of an at-onement with that Creative Force or God.                                                    2796-1

It is not clear when in David's reign his adultery with Bathsheba took place. As a chronology the sequence of events in Scripture are not historical.[24] The promise to David of an eternal throne is recounted in chapter 7, and takes place at a time "when the king dwelt in his house and the Lord had given him rest from his enemies." Yet in chapter 11, which tells the story of Bathsheba, Israel was at war, besieging Rabbath, a strong Ammonite fortress.

We learn from reading 601-5 that it was not until after his marriage to Bathsheba that there were "favorable periods" for the spread of David's influence over his people and the neighboring nations. Therefore the kingdom could not have been established before.

The same reading states Bathsheba was David's favorite wife. In the Bible, such passages as 1 Kings 1:11–31 suggest Bathsheba had great influence with the king, and that this was recognized by his counselors. Indeed, she may have been "the woman behind the man" whose love and wisdom may have been an essential source of strength and inspiration for David. She may have had a greater influence on the destiny of the emerging kingdom than is normally supposed and greater importance than just as the mother of Solomon.

Whatever blessing may have flowed from Bathsheba, his alliance with

---

[24]That the Bible is accurate history in terms of chronology is a notion that dies hard. The Edgar Cayce readings, such as on Genesis, show the symbolic rather than literal nature of the narrative in which a day, a year, or an epoch can be covered in a single sentence without comment or notice taken of it. This attitude toward time remains throughout the whole book. Even the synoptic gospels cannot be declared chronologically accurate. The earliest Christian writer to discuss the origin of the gospels, Papias (about 140 A.D.), stated explicitly that Mark wrote "not in order."

her also occasioned some of David's greatest misfortune and sorrow. "Only in the matter of Uriah the Hittite did David displease God," said Edgar Cayce, "and for that he had to pay heavily." Because of it, the goodness David established did not continue.

Shortly after the adultery with Bathsheba and the death of Uriah, Nathan, the next great prophet after Samuel, was called to pronounce a fearful sentence on David—"The sword shall never depart from your house forever." (2 Samuel 12:10) David reaped a punishing karma from what he had sown—the effects were almost instantaneous. The child of their union died. David's daughter Tamar was raped by her brother Amnon, who in turn was murdered by their brother Absalom the beautiful. Absalom then led a rebellion against his father which caused him to flee from Jerusalem. Before Absalom was slain by Joab, he publicly violated all David's wives, which requited what David had done secretly to the wife of Uriah.

From the time of his adultery onward David's otherwise glorious reign was marred with unceasing trouble—all of which had been revealed to Nathan.

An elderly Kansas woman was told in her reading that, preceding an incarnation in Palestine during the time of Jesus, she had been in the court of David as a nurse and instructor to David's children. Nathan's pronouncements had a life-long effect upon this teacher of young Solomon:

> . . . the entity was again in the Holy Land, among the maids or helpers to Bathsheba, the queen of the king David. The entity was active in those periods when there were the questionings and the admonitions delivered to the king by Nathan. These made a great impression upon this entity, then Abjada, making for a keeping closer not only to the tenets but to the spirit of the law through those activities. And as there grew to be those changes wrought by the educating of those that were to rise in power, the entity aided there.
>
> Thus children, children's activities, games, directions, cards, any form of books that may aid children in arousing to an active mind that needed, may be a part of the life experience and the work of the entity in the present.
>
> The entity gained throughout, for it caught the vision and it applied the message in those activities with the training of Solomon through those periods of the early childhood.                    3361-1

## David's House

As David rose in power, establishing himself over the surrounding nations, many of the kingdoms began to send tribute and gifts to him. The most notable is Hiram, king of Tyre, who furnished cedars, carpenters, and masons as David built his house. This was the beginning of a lasting alliance between the two kingdoms that extended through Solomon's reign.

It is interesting to note that David, whose chief desire was to build the Temple, was allowed only to build his house. Solomon, who was the builder of the Temple, spent less time on it than he did in the construction of his palace.

On May 10, 1944, an owner and manager of a rest home was told she had been a decorator for the homes of these two monarchs.

. . . the entity was in the land now known as the Holy Land, and among those who were of the children of Judah, during those periods when there were the establishings in the city where the great Temple was built.

The entity was then acquainted with David and Solomon, as a contributor both to the decorations in the Palace of Bathsheba and in the house of the king in Solomon's period.

In the name then Rahalab, the entity gained through those activities because of the counsel, not merely in regard to the preparations in finery.

Thus the entity is at home with the lowly, as well as those in authority or in higher places. Use, don't abuse, those dependencies which arise from the associations in those periods.                                   5082-1

## The King's Daughter

On August 1, 1934, a stately Jewish woman obtained her Life reading, and another memorable page in Edgar Cayce's story of the Old Testament was added.

We have an account in the Bible of two children who were born to David and Bathsheba: the child who died as punishment for their adultery, and Solomon, the heir to David's throne. Yet reading 601-2 describes a third, and most memorable child—the king's daughter.

The first intimation appeared in a reading requesting physical help. Cayce began his diagnosis in the customary manner with an analysis of the blood, and then broke it off immediately to say:

> So many things that have rushed in, from the activities or relations of this
> entity in one experience in its activities in the earth, almost overpower
> all the rest. She was a daughter, you see, of David. The body should wear
> the seal of same at all times; the crown or the vase with the crown of the
> king in same.                                                      601-1

Cayce then returned to his diagnosis of the body. A question at the
conclusion of the reading brought out these additional responses.

> (Q) Is there any other information that may be given this entity that
> would be of benefit at this time?
> (A) As we have indicated, the seal should be worn at most times about
> the body; the king's seal. The cup with the king's crown upon same.
> Either in the form of cameo or other stones. Any stone in which it may
> be; not as a charm, but rather as that which comes with the lineal activity
> or descendant, and the influences that come about; for the soul—or
> entity—was indeed the king's daughter.                              601-1

Three weeks later the first of two Life readings concerning this life
were given.

> . . . we find (wherein much is made manifest in the present sojourn,
> present activities) the entity was during the reign of that ruler, that king
> of the Hebrew people who had been called for a purpose in a Promised
> Land; and among the daughters of David was the entity numbered; and
> among the daughters—or the daughter of Bathsheba that lived; hence
> a close relationship, and only mentioned once in the Scriptures—and
> only in a portion of so much that has been left out.
>
> So, the entity was a sister of Solomon—that also rose to the beauty of
> the pomp and power. This brought into the experience of the entity all
> those glories of the two kingdoms; for the entity was among those that
> were favored, not only of the people but of those that came for
> counsel—as the people of many nations—to receive, in those associa-
> tions and relations, words of counsel from the preacher or the teacher
> in Solomon, and those greater in the Psalms of David.
>
> Hence many of these have been to the entity the songs wherein there
> has come within self much that has lifted up, especially in those instances

when it is said, "I was glad when they said unto me, we will go into the house of our God." In this Psalm the entity led often in the meetings of those that counseled for the aid of those that would purify themselves for the services in the various activities. However, as is known, the mothers and daughters were forbidden much of the activities then.

In the name Sheluenmehei, the entity gained much in the experience, and aided the father during those days when Absalom the beautiful rebelled; during those days when darkness came to the peoples through the various changes wrought by the political forces and powers.

Innately from the experience does the entity view and judges well as to political influences, yet keeps aloof in part from interfering or changing much in same. What might be given of the experience of the entity during that sojourn!

In the present, though, is seen the very movements or activities, and the associations and relations; the aid and help that the entity not imposes, but graciously offers in its services to others, which has endeared itself to many of those whom the entity has been only as an acquaintance, or more so to those whom the entity has shown itself a friend. For indeed in the carriage and in the naturally innate forces does the entity show itself to be a daughter of the king among kings!

601-2

The Books of Samuel appear to be almost eye-witness accounts of the reigns of Saul and David. Chronicles contains much material, often word for word, found in other books of the Bible. However in 1 Chronicles, which recounts events in David's reign, everything doubtful and offensive regarding him and his house is omitted. He is presented as being primarily preoccupied with the organization of the Temple services.

The husband of Mrs. 601 obtained a Life reading, and Cayce placed him among the sons of Abner, and a suitor in that life to the daughter of Bathsheba. This reading also indicates that it was not until after the rebellion by Absalom that the accumulation of materials and organization and preparation for the Temple began:

... we find the period was when David, the shepherd king, the beloved, ruled the land; and when wars were little, and no more were those activities of ... Absalom making for the disturbing forces in the experience.

The entity then was among the sons of Abner that made overtures to the daughter of the king, or the daughter of Bathsheba. For the entity then rose to favor with the king, and was active in establishing—with the individuals and peoples nigh unto the land, in Tyre and Sidon—the preparations of the poles of cedar, the posts of cedar, that were to become the timbers in the Temple.

*These* were the activities of Ajalon, the son of Abner, and the son-in-law of the king.

In the experience the entity was greatly active in bringing about the relationships of those peoples that supplied much for that service in the temple, where the king had purposed in his heart to dedicate a place, a house, to the worship of Jehovah—God.

The entity gained much in the experience, and in the present from same the entity finds that whether the associations are with those within or without the own faith—if they are true to their purposes—they are as One! In this has tolerance come, through those experiences and in the application of that in the present—so that this has grown to be a part of the entity's experience.                                          619-5

## The King's Son-in-Law

In the second Life reading for Mrs. 601, we are told Sheluenmehei was betrothed to the prince of Tyre, and that the marriage was the foundation for the lasting alliance between Tyre and Israel. Apparently her present husband (619)—whom Cayce described as the king's son-in-law—married another of his many daughters.

From the historical aspect, the following is one of the most illuminating readings given for this period:

Gertrude Cayce: You will please give in detail the life history of this entity's appearance in the earth as Sheluenmehei, the daughter of David, and the associations of that period . . . You will answer the questions that may be asked concerning that period . . .

Edgar Cayce: Yes, we have the entity, the inquiring mind and the soul-mind of the entity now known as [601]—now, and the experience of the soul-entity as Sheluenmehei, the daughter of Bathsheba and David.

In that experience we find, after the death of the child when there was the first coition with Bathsheba, the wife of Uriah, and the king, in the next change was the birth of Sheluenmehei—meaning, a reproach has been removed.

The entity then grew up under the conditions that were the more favorable during those periods of the spreading influence of the king, not only with the peoples but with the nations thereabout.

The mother being the favorite of the king had those advantages that might be accorded one in that position; being an accomplished harpist, or what would be the harp today, and that endeared the entity to the king.

With the changes that came with the rise to power of Joab and his associates Manasseh, Anahasia [?], and Haliel [?], these sought the hand of the king's daughter Sheluenmehei in the connections with the taking of the strongholds of the Philistines; but with the coming of Haran son of Hiram, of Tyre and Sidon, the king's daughter became the bride that cemented the friendships with Hiram who furnished the cedars and the building materials for the king's house.

With the change by that association there was brought the greater development for the entity during the period, and the associations in that period with one in the own household in the present—the present daughter—made for a contribution to the developing conditions for the whole. The relations then were rather the friendships, for the daughter was then that of the Anias[?]—or the brother of Joab's wife's daughter, but not of those peoples.

As to the soul development of the entity during the experience: As there has been the close relationships with the king's activities, the law, the psalms, these became a portion of the entity's experience.

Being in an environ that was so changed from that in Jerusalem and that in Tyre, there were brought many longings—and many of those periods when the entity or the soul finds expression in the music. And in the present there are those feelings that when there is that type of music that bespeaks of the longings of home, of the temple, of those changes that may come in the experience of a soul, strikes a chord in the entity that may be recognized as an awareness of those longings for the hills, the home in Jerusalem . . .

With the changes that were wrought in the experiences of the entity during the rebellions among the king's sons, when first the conditions arose from Tamar's (a sister, or half-sister) being despoiled by her brother, this made for the change in many of the associations; yet the daughter continued to visit with those of the king's household.

With the rebellion of Absalom, this brought turmoil and strife, and the attempt on the part of the daughter to come to the aid of David as he fled from Jerusalem; and with the battle won, the daughter then collapsed (being heavy with child) at the news of the death of Absalom; yet being succored or aided by the king, suffering then in body for a period, and with the birth of Huel, the second son of Haran's that became the king after the death of Hiram, the mother—or the entity— then joined or slept with the fathers; coming, as has been seen, in a later experience in the earth.                                601-5

## Absalom's Rebellion

Absalom's rebellion was the most grim and shattering experience in David's life. It was his gravest crisis, and the considerable importance of the rebellion is indicated by the amount of space allotted to it in the Bible, from chapter 13 through 19 in 2 Samuel.

The rebellion divided David's kingdom, caused the defection of some of his advisors, led to the death of his daughter (601), and his son, and, at the end, completely crushed his spirit and broke his heart. And all this had, in some way, been foreseen by Nathan. (2 Samuel 12:10–11) David was a totally different man after Absalom rebelled.

Four Life readings refer to Absalom's rebellion in such a way to indicate it was a turning point in David's reign. 601-2 indicates that the spiritual light which was growing in the minds of the people under David's leadership became obscured, and " . . . darkness came . . . through the various changes wrought by the political forces and powers." 619 and 476 show that there was a new thrust of activity when " . . . no more were those activities of . . . Absalom making for the disturbing forces . . . " (619-5) and "As peace began to be restored after the rebellions of Absalom, there came to the entity the greater development . . . " (1073-4)

The rebellion was the final cleansing, or karma from David's adultery with Bathsheba, even to Absalom's fornication with David's wives in broad daylight "in the sight of Israel" to requite what David had done secretly to the wife of Uriah the Hittite. No doubt all the family relationships were charged with karmic overtones, but lack of any additional information precludes any further speculation. However, a definite cycle can be discerned from David's adultery and Nathan's pronouncement to Absalom's death and the paralyzing remorse which gripped David.

When David finally was able to overcome his depression and inaction, he initiated the great period of planning and gathering materials for the Temple which Nathan had revealed would be built by Solomon.

"Here we have all the scandal that could possibly be conceived," Edgar Cayce said as the Bible class began their study of chapter 13 of 2 Samuel. This chapter contains rape and murder and shows the background events which led to the estrangement between father and son which eventually culminated in rebellion.

When Amnon raped Tamar, Absalom avenged his sister by murdering his brother. He then fled to Geshur, the territory where his mother's father was king, and stayed there for three years.

All through this time David wanted to be reconciled with Absalom. Joab, David's general, knew this and also saw a dangerous situation developing with the people who favored Absalom. Perhaps Absalom even then was plotting from afar.

Joab made wise use of the woman of Tekoah who, through her subtle parable, softened David's heart. David ordered Joab to Geshur to bring Absalom home.

Edgar Cayce told his Bible class:

"We can understand how Absalom felt it was up to him to slay Amon, and how David naturally grieved when his oldest son was slain. In those days it was permissible for relatives to marry. No doubt if Amnon had gone about it in the right way, David would have allowed him to have Tamar. However, his whole purpose was evil.

"Joab, the leader of the army, understood Absalom; and he attempted to warn David by sending the wise woman of Tekoah. Notice that she is not referred to as a witch nor as a soothsayer nor as one with a familiar spirit. Whatever else she might have been, she was certainly a good actress. However, David recognized Joab as the source of it. He knew that Joab understood how he wanted to bring back Absalom, and now there was a way it could be done and still save face.

"David punished himself by not allowing himself to see Absalom. This was very unwise. It engendered in Absalom a spirit of rebellion."

We can see how the mistake David made in not seeing his son affected the proud, unrestrained, and "beautiful" Absalom. It must have pricked his ego and goaded his pride to be ignored, and he began plotting the overthrow of his father.

For four years he stood outside the king's gate and offered to take the people's side in any litigation that came before the king. In this way he used political issues to insinuate his way into the hearts of the men of Israel. He plotted, and his conspiracy grew. Soon the majority of the people were on his side.

When Absalom sounded the alarm which signaled the rebellion, his army outnumbered David's, and David was forced to flee Jerusalem.

David, who was much more spiritually conscious than Absalom, refused to fight over an essentially political issue. In a similar vein, it was the same as Jesus refusing to defend himself against his accusers or to resist the way of the cross. David even ordered Zadok and Abiathar, the two priests who joined him in his retreat, to carry the Ark of God back to the city and to remain with it.

Cayce's remarks stress David's spiritual understanding:

"It became necessary for David to flee Jerusalem. Absalom's army was several times larger than his, and he didn't want Jerusalem destroyed. He had been preparing to build the house of the Lord, and he knew why he was not being allowed to build it. From this time on, David attempts to atone for his sin, instead of fighting back. It was not his intention to hurt his son. On every occasion when he might have done harm to Absalom, he wriggled out of it. He ordered the Ark back to the city. He realized the battle was one for material power, and did not pertain to the spiritual life. So he was running away so that the beloved city would be spared, and not destroyed for purely material reasons."

During the flight from Jerusalem, an episode took place which to Edgar Cayce revealed the key to David's true greatness. During the retreat, at Beth-hurim, Shimei, of the house of Saul, came out and followed David along the side of the road, throwing stones and cursing the king. Shimei shouted angrily that Absalom's revolt was God's way of requiting David for the blood of Saul.

David's soldiers were incensed at this Benjamite's impudence and asked permission to cut off his head.

David's reply was characteristic. It indicates more than just his unwillingness to blame others for his troubles. He had not forgotten Nathan's prophecy. He understood this misfortune was in some way connected with his own shortcomings, when he said:

*What is it to me and you? Let him curse. It is the Lord who has told him to curse David. Who can say to me, Why has this happened? . . . Let him curse; for God has bidden him.* (2 Samuel 16:10-11)

Cayce saw David's character revealed by this response:

"David felt that whatever came, came for a purpose. If we could only learn that lesson today! Misfortune is not for our undoing, but to make us strong. If we can accept it in that fight, it becomes a steppingstone and not a stumblingblock in our greater (spiritual) development. If we hold to the good, we can always do something about our problems. *It was because David was able to hold to such an attitude that it can be said of him, 'he was a man after God's heart.'*

Ahithophel, one of David's most advanced counselors (2 Samuel 16:23) elected to stay with Absalom. Hushai, another trusted advisor, also remained in Jerusalem, but retained his loyalty to David and acted as his agent.

This was Edgar Cayce's lesson:

"Hushai was a very wonderful secret agent for David. Absalom never suspected that Hushai was acting in David's best interests. Being of the nature to seek material position and power, Absalom could understand how Hushai would join with him because he was the stronger. But the fact that Hushai could remain true to David regardless of David's weak position was beyond anything Absalom could understand. This is a good example of how all things work together for good to those who love the Lord.

"David followed Hushai's advice and moved his army across the Jordan, where the people were sympathetic to him. They hadn't fallen under Absalom's spell."

From the other side of the Jordan David mounted his campaign. Once the battle was engaged, David was victorious and Absalom was slain. Although David asked that Absalom be spared, Joab felt the only decisive way to win the battle was to kill him, which he did.

David's deep depression and prolonged sorrow following these events show how deeply he was affected.

David's sons grew up selfish and unrestrained, at least we see this from the examples of Amnon, Absalom, and Adonijah. Indeed if his approach to Adonijah was typical ( . . . *at no time did he rebuke him, saying, Why have you done so?* [1 Kings 1:6]), David must have been the prototype of the ultra-permissive parent.

With the rebellion over, David went through a period of deep soul-searching and introspection as he reviewed the wreckage in his household and his kingdom. Edgar Cayce felt David's extreme reaction was from a sense of personal guilt:

> "David continued to be sorrowful over Absalom's death. This was unusual. When his and Bathsheba's first child died, he ceased to mourn when there was no longer anything he could do. Perhaps he had a guilty conscience, and felt he could have prevented things from turning out as they had. He was beginning to realize he had failed to raise his children properly. If he had, this kind of thing could not have happened. He felt the whole thing was an outgrowth of some failure on his part.
>
> "David was indulging in self-pity. Joab brought him back to his senses. He made David realize he was responsible for the future welfare of the kingdom. The whole nation looked to him for guidance."

With David's return to Jerusalem, he began the great work of planning and preparing for the construction of the Temple, which was not to be built in his life-time. Like Moses, David advanced the great purpose and cause of Israel, but did not live to enjoy the fruits of his greatest labor.

The great work helped take David's mind off the past. By putting his energies into the organization of the Temple, David brought healing to himself, his house, and his nation.

In this reading, a Jewish opera singer was told she was a grandchild of David's, the daughter of Adonijah, the son who rebelled when David was near his deathbed:

> . . . we find the entity was in the land now known as the Holy Land, during those periods when the shepherd king was in order—or ruled.
>
> It was during those periods when turmoil and strife arose through the rebellions within the household of the king—or David.
>
> The entity then was among the daughters of Adonijah, who was among the first of the sons of David.
>
> As peace began to be restored after the rebellions of Absalom, there

came to the entity the greater development as it joined with the sons and daughters and the folk of the king to make preparations for the establishing and the building of the house of the Lord.

Hence we find within the entity's innate experience a reverence for those things that have been blessed even by man, or that have been dedicated . . . to that he worships as the spirit of truth and hope in his relationships to Creative Forces.

Songs create a reverence, or those things of the nature that tend to make for a reverential inspiration—or blessings, or prayer.

The entity was among the first to set the Twenty-fourth Psalm to music, or that which is now called a portion of the Twenty-fourth Psalm. For the entity enjoyed the music of the grandfather upon the harp.

In the name then of Besne-berea, it may be said that the entity gained; especially in the latter part of its sojourn . . .        1073-4

## Footnotes to an Era

It is said that the most perfectly written lines in the English language are, "O my son Absalom, my son, my son Absalom! would God I had died for thee, O Absalom, my son, my son!" (2 Samuel 18:33) They ring with the same compassion, sadness, and love as Jesus' words, "O Jerusalem, Jerusalem." (Matthew 23:37; Luke 13:34)

For Mrs. 601, Cayce used the verse as a lesson on love:

(Q) How can I help those nearest and dearest to higher development?
(A) In pointing those principles as held innately and manifestedly in self, that what ye do unto thy fellow man is that by which ye will be judged before the Throne. For when an unkind thought, an unkind deed is done within the mind—or the soul-mind of an entity—it builds that which makes for the interference with the will and desire of the spirit association within self; or the conscience will smite thee.

Then, in aiding others; just being kind, showing forth that love as the entity heard: "O Absalom, Absalom, my son Absalom! would God I had died for thee!" This will bring, as the entity says same to self, a change in the feelings as respecting what love—*love*—means.        601-5

Another description in Mrs. 601's reading supplies an additional important footnote to this era—the king's seal!

## The King's Seal

Edgar Cayce described a gift from King David to his daughter in Tyre.

The seal that the entity wore then, as the gift from the king, should ever be about the body. This we would give in some detail:
A cross; each prong being the same length, you see. Cut as a shadow box in its making. On the cross, the rosette of the king. In the center of the rosette a raised figure; or plane, and on this plane this figure: Draw a seven. Draw it! In the front raise the upper line of the seven, see? In front of this line draw a mark slanting towards the right; heavy, and slanting almost straight down. On the back side of the seven a line leaning towards the seven, you see, just a little space from same. This, of course, represents the Hebraic characters of the cabalistic intent or import; meaning El Yah[?]-God Preserves!                               601-5

In connection with the seal, Cayce made a prophecy.

(Q) If possible, please give information as to where I can find a design of King David's seal, which it was suggested that I should wear?
(A) Make as has been indicated. It will one day be uncovered in Jerusalem.
(Q) Of what would it be best for it to be made?
(A) Either ivory, coral, or gold; or ivory inlaid with gold; or gold with the raised figure of the rosette and the letter.
(Q) Is there any further advice that would be helpful to me at this time?
(A) Much may be given. These we would think and ponder over. Keep these close in the heart.                               601-5

## A Brother to Solomon

A reading for a young Alabama man adds another portrait to the gallery of David's sons. Apparently this one, like the others, was a disappointment. The reading began in an interesting manner, pointing to a lesson:

For what a body-mind, a soul-mind does about or with the knowledge or understanding that it has makes for development for that soul. For some beautiful comparisons may be drawn from the entity's own experiences in the earth. For, while the entity was an associate or a brother to Solomon in an experience, what one did with his knowledge and understanding and what the other did with his understanding made for quite a difference in each one's position in that experience and the [following] sojourns of each soul in other experiences.　　476-1

The reading indicates David was unable to impress his own spiritual understanding upon this son who, under the reign of Solomon, became a tax gatherer or assessor in his commercial enterprises.

. . . we find the entity was in that period when David was ruler in the Promised Land, and among David's sons we find the entity's activities—Ajalon. These we find in a contention again, though reasonable to many; yet to self the activities brought not the use of the knowledge obtained through the counsel of the father (earthly) as to become wholly acceptable—either in the spiritual or the material things in the experience. There were contentions with Absalom, who won the hearts of the people, and associations with the sister of Absalom in an unethical manner. The associations with that son who became the ruler, and known as the "wise one," brought rather both mental and physical development to the entity, yet in the spiritual or soul forces rather a standstill—or non-development, as seen in the next experience.[25] In the application of self in the present experience, however, that sojourn may be said to be that one which may influence the entity in the present to a greater degree. For, the activities may be turned into fields—not of a political nature, neither wholly commercial, yet that deal with both—where gatherings of sales or taxes may be in the experience of the entity, from the purely material sense, the activities in which the greater strides or successes may be made. As to what the entity may do respecting its soul or spiritual development depends upon the application of the knowledge and understanding, and as to whether or not the trust and the ideal is put in these influences that may guide, guard and keep the soul in the way of the Lamb.

Hence as an assessor, a tax gatherer, a statistician, in such fields of activity, the entity may find the greater successes in the present . . . for the entity's material development　　476-1

---

[25]About the time of William the Conqueror and the Norman Invasion, the entity incarnated "with a grudge" which made him "a natural leader," but for destructive rather than constructive purposes.

# 17

## The Golden Age of Solomon

*Under* Solomon Israel reached the apex of its glory. The Spirit manifested more fully in the affairs of men than it had ever done before. Wealth, Culture, Power, and Worship all flowered in an Age of Peace. Yet a few short years after his death, Solomon's Temple and Palace were sacked, the first of many times. Its brief existence has raised the notion that the real purpose for the glories of Solomon was to hold up an assurance, a preview of the glories of the millennial reign of Christ.

We know that the reign of Christ has always existed, but begins individually, with the discovery of the Christ within. It is a spiritual law, however, that before entering into any new dimension of spiritual understanding, we will be tried and tested in our faith. Before entering the Promised Land, the children of Israel were tested in the wilderness. On the threshold of the Golden Age, the people were tested under Saul. As in the wilderness, they were confronted with a mass of conflicting forces and urges and given the opportunity to choose whom they would serve. Saul and David are like the brothers Cain and Abel, or Jacob and Esau—representing the two principles of worldliness and self-gratification as opposed to selflessness through service and the seeking of Truth.

Those like Jonathan, who grew to understand why Saul was rejected, learned why David was accepted.

God chose David because David chose Him. Saul could not overcome his own self-interests, while David tried to keep God's Will first and foremost. By choosing David the people were choosing God. When a sufficient number followed the young king, they were cooperating with God's Plan of redemption by becoming "a helpmeet with Him in bringing that to pass that all may be one with Him." (281-16) Those who lived with David and were loyal to his purposes laid the foundation for the Golden Age, the greatest epoch in Israel's unfoldment since the time of Joshua.

## The Kingdom Within

As a symbol for possibilities and potential in man's experience, the Golden Age of Solomon is equally as vital and inclusive a symbol as the Garden of Eden or the Promised Land. It exists outside time and space as something which can be looked back upon in history as an assurance, and forward to as an experience. From the Cayce readings we have the understanding that, like all other symbols in the Bible, this unprecedented "Golden Age" can be related a state of mental and physical development with a spiritual equivalent which can be experienced on the inner-planes of consciousness.

Solomon made two enduring contributions to Israel: its wisdom literature and its Temple. Yet Solomon only completed that which David had begun. By building the Temple, Solomon was putting into material form the spiritual perceptions of David.

When David turned over the plans and patterns for the Temple to Solomon, he acknowledged that the Spirit had guided him in all the work. (1 Chronicles 28:19) God himself designed the Temple. Like the Ark of the Covenant and the Tabernacle, the Temple conformed to a pre-existent spiritual pattern which had been received through revelation and inspiration.

David's willingness to be led by the Spirit guided him to the highest possible conceptions about architecture, music, and ritual worship. All was according to God's purpose and his plan of Redemption. This brought into manifestation a material image through which man could eventually come to understand himself. For the Temple represents the Body, the glorified body of Man. There is a pattern within Man which Man may awaken to and experience—the Temple of the Living God where nothing within is less valuable than silver and gold.

**Draw from those activities the fact that the body–physical is indeed the**

Temple of the living God, just as much as the Temple in which there were the material sacrifices offered. So there may be mental and material sacrifices offered and experienced in the present, if the needs would be met for the building of the determination to fill the purpose for which each soul enters a material experience. 2054-2

. . . the understanding that there must be—and would be, through the very expression of that Being in the earth—the understanding that the law was written in the hearts of men, rather than upon tablets of stone; that the Temple, that the holy of holies was to be within. 587-6

The Temple became the focus in this reading:

Thy body is indeed the Temple of the living God. Hold to that. By might and main of the mind, attempt to make the best, the most beautiful, the most acceptable Temple according to thy concept of a living Christ Consciousness. Hold to that. Let no one, in any manner, take that from you.

Then apply, in an expectant manner, those measures which will aid the body-forces to create within self those influences necessary for this building of the body to a beautiful Temple to thy God. 2968-1

. . . ye that have seen the light know in Whom thou hast believed, and know that in thine own body, thine own mind, there is set the Temple of the living God, and that it may function in thy dealings with thy fellow man in such measures that ye become as rivers of light, as fountains of knowledge, as mountains of strength, as the pastures for the hungry, as the rest for the weary, as the strength for the weak. 281-28

Nothing in Solomon's Temple was less valuable than silver and gold. What a suggestion this is as to our true worth when we become Temples of the Living Spirit.

And, as the entity has learned in the present, the body is indeed the Temple, and that the pattern given in the mount is that pattern of the individual entity or self as it is set up and hedged about, and yet is the place where man meets his Maker. 3129-1

. . . the body is indeed the Temple of the living God and must be

considered and treated as such . . . a channel through which greater
help, greater means of expression of self in the present may be brought
into being.
For it is *there*—in thine own Temple—as He gave—that He has promised
to meet thee!                                                        1598-1

## Portrait of a King

Solomon's reign begins with a vision and a promise.

*Then the Lord appeared to Solomon in a vision by night; and God said
to him, "Ask that which I should give you."*

*And Solomon said . . . "O Lord God, thou hast made thy servant king
in the place of David my father; and I am but a little child; I know not how
to go out or come in among thy people, whom thou hast chosen . . . Give
therefore to thy servant an understanding heart to judge thy people and
to discern between good and bad; for who is able to judge this thy so great
a people?"*

*And it pleased the Lord because Solomon had asked this thing. And the
Lord said to Solomon, "Because you have asked this thing and have not
asked for yourself riches, neither have you asked the lives of your enemies
nor have you asked for yourself long life, but have asked for yourself
wisdom to discern judgment; Behold, I have done according to your words;
lo, I have given you a wise and understanding heart, so that there has been
none like you before you, neither shall any arise after you like you.*

*And I have given you that which you have not asked, both riches and
honor, so that there Shall not be any among the kings like you all your
days.*

*And if you will walk in my ways, to keep my statutes and my
commandments, as your father David did walk, then I will lengthen your
days."*

*And Solomon awoke; and, behold, it was a dream.* (1 Kings 3:5-15;
see also 2 Chronicles 1:7-12)

"No fairer promise of true greatness, or more beautiful picture of
youthful piety is known in history." Modern critics dismiss this story as
a romantic myth. Yet in Edgar Cayce's own life he had a youthful experience which bears marked similarities to young Solomon's. The incident was one of Edgar Cayce's most cherished memories, and is related

in full in *There Is a River*, the biography of Edgar Cayce by Tom Sugrue, and retold for children in *The Vision and the Promise*, by Vada Carlson.

**Edgar Cayce became an avid reader of the Bible in his early teens, spending hours alone with it, totally immersed in its contents. One day while reading the book outdoors in a special lean-to he had constructed in the woods behind the family house, he became aware of a strange presence. He looked up and saw a woman standing before him. The sun was bright and his eyes could not focus quickly after staring at the pages for so long. He thought his mother had come to bring him home for chores.**

**The woman spoke, and the young Cayce knew the voice did not belong to his mother, or anyone else he knew. It was like music, he said, soft-spoken and very clear.**

**"Your prayers have been heard," she said, and then posed the same question as was asked of Solomon: "Tell me what you would like most of all, so that I may give it to you."**

**He had just finished reading about the vision of Manoah from the Book of Judges. He saw the outline of wings in the woman's shadow. He was frightened. This was an angel! He tried to speak, but no words came out. Scenes of Jesus and his disciples flashed across his mind. Then another shock! He heard himself talking.**

**"Most of all," he stammered, "I would like to be helpful to others, and especially to children when they are sick."**

**Suddenly the woman was gone. She was no longer there. He looked at the spot where she had stood, trying to see her in the beams of light, but he was all alone.**

Not long after this experience, the vision was confirmed. Cayce discovered he had the ability to put himself to sleep, and while in this self-induced trance state, able to diagnose physical illness. Shortly after this discovery, he was asked to help a five-year-old girl, Aime Dietrich, who had been seriously ill for three years. Her parents had been told she could never be healed. In trance, Cayce described the source of her illness and prescribed treatments. The parents followed the recommendations and the child recovered her health. This was the first of thousands that confirmed the young boy's vision and the promise it contained.

This experience was one among many which demonstrated through his own life the hypothesis he advanced as a student and teacher of the Bible—that everything recorded in Scripture is capable of being experienced. Or, as said in one reading:

**Condemn no one. Love all. Do good. And ye may experience it all.**
**281-30**

Cayce accepted Solomon's experience as authentic. He could relate it to his own, and thus was spared the necessity of seeking elaborate explanations or rationalizations.

When it came time to discuss Solomon's vision in the Bible class, Cayce drew upon views created by reflections on his youth.

"Solomon expressed humbleness. He realized he was completely new at the business of receiving guidance from God. Also, his had been a rather sheltered life. He had been protected and had not accomplished great things like his father had done when still a young man.

"None before Solomon requested such a thing, and none after him has been given the same unique opportunity as he had. Solomon was given a choice, just as everyone is. How we use that choice is completely an individual matter."

Although Cayce apparently was born with a love for God and a desire to serve, he never consciously set out to be a psychic. It wasn't until he reached middle-age that he made psychic diagnosing a full-time and life-long work. From the age of thirteen, he had been guided, led and shown—often unwillingly—how that youthful vision would be fulfilled.

That acquired wisdom is reflected in his next comment.

"If the Lord appeared to us today, would we understand our place among our friends, our neighbors sufficiently, to know what ability we had which could best serve them? If not, whose fault would it be? Not the Lord's, but ours. God always knows what's best—but it is necessary for us to know also the best manner in which we may serve.

"Solomon made a wise choice. We also could make that choice, by asking not for ourselves, for long life or riches, but that we might have judgment to deal with the problems with which we are faced."

## Another Dream

Two years after Edgar Cayce made his decision to engage full-time in psychic work, he dreamed he talked to King Solomon. An interesting tradition in Jewish lore is that anyone who dreams of Solomon will be given wisdom.

The dream occurred in December, 1925, shortly after Cayce completed the decisive move to Virginia Beach, Virginia, the location his own readings had stated would be the most conducive for his work. The interpretation reveals how deeply Cayce searched for wisdom, and also contained a warning.

**(Q) Tuesday night, December 15, or Wednesday morning, December 16. Dreamed of talking with King Solomon.**

**(A) In this we find the entity in that manner and way in which the inmost forces of self seek the wisdom that is given to him of whom it has been said, "None shall rise that in physical will be mightier in wisdom than he." In this seeking, then, we find that attunement that should be used by [the] entity in seeking out those ways to carry on the work as has been set before same; being wise in every way, without the weaknesses of the flesh as were in that entity, see?** 294-53

## Pages of Wisdom

Three thousand proverbs and 1,005 songs are attributed to Solomon. (1 Kings 4:32) His wisdom ranged from the mysteries of life to everything known about the animal, vegetable, and mineral kingdoms. So schooled was Solomon about the natural world, legend states he was able to communicate with animals. When judging a case, he knew instinctively which party was guilty and did not need the presence of witnesses.

Is such a life unobtainable in the present day? Even the legendary Renaissance men could not match the accomplishments of this genius. But we may find parallels in Cayce's life to match Solomon.

Cayce's more than 14,000 psychic readings preserved and on file in Virginia Beach attest to his ability to tune in to an Infinite source of knowledge and wisdom. The subject matter in these discourses comprises thousands of topics and touches upon all aspects of Man—his spirit, his soul, his God, his mind, and his body. Just as Solomon's reputation in his day drew earnest seekers from all walks of life to query the king, the unerring accuracy of the Cayce readings draws researchers and seekers from all parts of the world to Virginia Beach. Thousands of individuals from all walks of life have found in the Cayce material practical and applicable as well as astounding truths which have enhanced the quality of their lives.

Cayce's sensitivities are also part of the lore that surrounds his life. His abilities to see and read auras made him an unnerving judge of character. He was a conscious telepathist and clairvoyant. Although there are no stories about him talking to animals, his ability to see and communicate with departed entities is well-known.

However, with all his accomplishments and gifts, the impression one receives from Edgar Cayce is not of a great intellect or gifted genius. His conscious wisdom is shown through spiritual sensitivity applied to practical matters. He cloaked himself in an aura of humility, and all his life strove to be "a common man."

While Cayce may not be a particularly good example of a genius, Solomon is not an archetype of spirituality.

Solomon towers over his reign and projects himself as its most important figure. With so much genius attached to his name, one may feel awed by the shadow he casts and diminished by our own feeble ability to match any of his accomplishments. Edgar Cayce will never be considered the most important aspect of his own legacy, for he completely subordinated himself to the Source which flowed through him. His work in no way diminishes a man, for it continually holds up the promise, "Greater things than these you can do if the Spirit is allowed to work through you."

## Solomon Goes Astray

Solomon's vision contained a promise of wealth which, when it came true, must have exceeded the dimensions Solomon himself might have imagined. Solomon's wisdom made him one of the richest men in history; while Cayce's enabled him to live a sparse life with the consolation of faith that his daily needs would be met.

Yet Edgar Cayce knew the temptation that prosperity brings. The wisdom came again from personal experience.

"How was it that Solomon went astray, having been given an understanding heart and deserving such a gift? Perhaps it was the same old story, 'The woman Thou gavest me—*she* persuaded me.'

"Very few people can stand prosperity and Solomon was not one of the few. We can understand from his life what Jesus meant when he said it is easier for the camel to pass through the eye of the needle than for a rich man to enter the kingdom.

"In the beginning of Solomon's reign, he approached God always with the statement, 'I remember what you did for my father David.' But after many years of worldly things, his heart was drawn away from God. Too many riches, too much wine and women made it harder and harder for Solomon to hold to his ideal."

In the worldly sense, Edgar Cayce never knew financial security. Although this lack occasionally disturbed him, it was a greater concern to his friends and associates than it was to himself. One reading indicated that at one level of the mind, Edgar Cayce was withholding the flow of abundance from him. The financial stress resulted from "an innate fear in self" regarding his ability to withstand the temptations prosperity would bring. A Life reading also indicated the condition was karmic, stemming from a past life in which Cayce had misused his psychic abilities for material gain.

Edgar Cayce realized in his later years that had he been financially successful in his youth, he might possibly have abandoned spiritual work altogether, and certainly would not have obtained the purity of purpose and ideal his poverty imposed upon him.

Ultimately Solomon lost his hold not only on his own faith but on his people as well.

Although Cayce in his lifetime never really knew wealth, power, or renown, except in a very limited way, the indication is that he was faithful to the end, and thus earned his crown, a crown of lasting life. (James 1:12, Revelation 2:10)

## The Courts of Solomon: They Were There

## Asaph—The king's seer in the matters of God (Chronicles 25:5)

It would be peculiar indeed if the soul who, as one reading states,

(5322-1) supplied the purpose for the whole Bible to be written; who caused the line of Israel to come into existence; who had been Adam, Enoch, Melchizedek, Joseph, and Joshua, was not reincarnated during the Golden Age of Jewish history. It does not seem likely that this soul who had experienced every phase of the national development would by-pass the opportunity to experience its highest achievement and further its glory.

Yet the Edgar Cayce readings say little and offer scant clues. When asked about the important incarnations in the development of Jesus, we find no reference to this period.

> **(Q) Please list the names of the incarnations of the Christ, and of Jesus, indicating where the development of the man Jesus began.**
> **(A) First, in the beginning, of course; and then as Enoch, Melchizedek, in the perfection. Then in the earth, of Joseph, Joshua, Jeshua, Jesus.**
> **5749-14**

But when asked which incarnations of Adam were the most significant in terms of the world's development, we find a slightly amended list, with the name of Asaph appearing on it.

> **(Q) Please give the important reincarnations of Adam in the world's history.**
> **(A) In the beginning as Amilius, as Adam, as Melchizedek, as Zend, as Ur[26] as Asaph, as Jeshua, Joseph, Jesus.**
> **364-7**

The second, and only other direct reference by name to Asaph, is found in reading 364-8, as Cayce again enumerates the incarnations of Jesus.

---

[26](Q) In the Persian experience as San (or Zend) did Jesus give the basic teachings of what became Zoroastrianism?
(A) In all those periods that the basic principle was the Oneness of the Father, He has walked with men. (364-8)

(Q) In what country, and in connection with what religion or philosophy, did Jesus live as Ur?
(A) Ur was rather a land, a place, a city–and the thought, or intent, or the call was from Ur. Ur, then, as presented or represented in the experience of Jesus, as one that impelled or guided those thoughts in that period, or experience. (364-9)

**. . . as in the periods . . . when He walked with men as the Master among men, or when as Joseph in the kingdoms that were raised as the saving of his peoples that *sold* him into bondage, or as in the priest of Salem . . . Or, as in those days as Asapha or Affa, [or] in those periods when those of that same Egyptian land were giving those counsels to the many nations [as Hermes or Enoch] . . .                    364-8**

Another intimation is found in a Life reading for a person who had incarnated during the time of Joshua and Moses and the period of David and Solomon.

**Hold fast to that thou didst give to thine peoples when thy self, thine inner self, supplied strength not only to the leaders of men—as Moses and Aaron and Joshua—but to that which *became* the strength of the musician [Asaph,] and of him [David] of whom it was said, "the Lord loved him."                    1035-1**

Although these are only scant references and no secondary details are given, it is generally assumed by students of the readings that the Asaph (or Affa) mentioned in the incarnations of Jesus refers to Asaph the choirmaster.

Asaph was the founder and eponym of a musical guild within the priestly tribe of the Levites. Twelve psalms are attributed to Asaph. Thus he has a distinct place among those who are believed to have composed and developed the present collection of Psalms, a list which includes Adam, Melchizedek, Abraham, and Moses.

Under his direction, the "sons of Asaph" prophesied with lyres, harps, and cymbals. (1 Chronicles 25:1) Some traditions give Asaph the title attributed to Heman (25:5), "the king's seer in the matters of God."

It is not difficult to ascertain why Asaph was included among the most significant incarnations of Adam in terms of the world's development. Music is a universal language. Music alone can span the space from the spiritual realms to the spheres of material activity. (3509-1)

**The entity's music may be the means of arousing and awakening the best of hope, the best of desire, the best in the heart and soul of those who will and do listen. Is not music the universal language, both for those who would give praise and those who are sorry in their hearts and souls? Is it**

**not a means, a manner of universal expression? Thus, may the greater**
**hope come.                                                    2156-1**

One of the most widely recognized effects of music is its ability to change moods. Despair, depression, and hopelessness can be lifted through music into faith, hope, and inspiration. Music can also reach into the deeper areas of the soul and awaken intuitive knowledge of who we are, where we came from, where we are going.

Descriptions in the Life readings for this period indicate many came from all parts of the world to hear the inspired interpretations of the psalms, songs, and poems of David and Solomon. Stimulated and imbued with new consciousness and understanding, presumably these visitors returned to their native lands and shared the message with their neighbors.

Thus Asaph's influence upon world religion began in his own lifetime and has continued to the present. Today, the only part of the Old Testament familiar to many Christians is the Psalms. This is also true in other world religions.

As valuable as music is in changing moods and altering consciousness, the description of the Temple dedication indicates Asaph may have known another use and schooled his musicians in the art of raising vibrations for an epiphany.

*And it came to pass, when the priests were come out of the holy place (for all the priests who were present there entered into the holy place; also the Levites, who were the singers, all of them of Asaph, of Heman, of Jeduthun, with their sons and their brethren, being arrayed in white linen, having cymbals and psalteries and harps, stood at the east end of the altar, and with them an hundred and twenty priests sounding with trumpets);*

*That the trumpeters and singers were as one, to make one sound to be heard in praising and thanking the Lord; and they that lifted up their voices with the trumpets and cymbals and instruments of music, and praised the Lord, saying, "For he is good; for his mercy endures forever;" that then the house was filled with a cloud, even the house of the Lord, so that the priests could not stand to minister because of the cloud; for the house of the Lord was filled with the brightness of his glory.* (2 Chronicles 5:11-14)

## Solomon's Sailor

The undisputed genius of Solomon was in the field of trade and commerce. He recognized the commercial possibilities in Arabia before anyone else, and knew fantastic riches would follow the man who could organize the trade of the early world.

The Phoenicians were the great sailors of this period. The pact between David and Hiram of Tyre continued into the reign of Solomon. This alliance enabled Israel to profit from Phoenician shipbuilding and navigational personnel and experience.

Hiram and Solomon sent out regularly scheduled trade missions that took up to three years to accomplish. Cyrus Gordon in his book *Before Columbus* asserts that the quest for metals, stones, and valued materials such as ivory and special woods impelled the great merchant kings to launch expeditions to the ends of the earth. Gordon states that the Semitic IBRZL meaning "land of iron" most likely is Brazil.

In his book, Dr. Gordon puts forth an impressive array of archeological, linguistic, and cultural evidence which points to the existence of an extensive prehistoric maritime trading empire in which the cultures of Asia, Europe, and America enjoyed widespread contact with each other. Thus the Phoenicians no doubt inherited a legacy from the Minoans who in turn had benefitted from the advancements of an earlier civilization. Dr. Charles Hapgood in his *Maps of the Ancient Sea Kings* also sees evidence in his studies of ancient maps of a superior prehistoric maritime empire whose maps were copied and recopied and in use through the time of Columbus.

Edgar Cayce's descriptions of Atlantis include expeditions which were sent to all parts of the world, to points as widely separated as Mexico and China, in vehicles which included airships and submarines.

Dr. Hapgood and Dr. Gordon indicate the technology of this empire was not completely lost, but preserved and passed down in one form or another from a period of at least 6000 B.C. The Cayce information suggests an even older period and a more advanced civilization than the two scientists are willing to acknowledge. *The Critias* of Plato suggests the priests of Egypt preserved the knowledge of Atlantis which was transmitted through the priests and initiates of the ancient religions.

No doubt the knowledge of sea routes and lost continents were preserved with the esoteric lore. This information must have been communicated to Solomon. Indeed, the readings would suggest the Israelites had access to all the knowledge of the world.

The Minoan, Phoenician, and Greek empires all maintained a policy of establishing colonies to look after the commercial interests of the homeland. Solomon settled Israelites at key points beyond Israel's borders. We may assume, with Dr. Gordon, that Solomon followed this same policy in all parts of the world. Later these colonies may have played an important role in offering places of refuge for the "lost" tribes during the invasions from Assyria and Babylon.

Although Israel, in the main, is a land–loving people, three tribes are described as navigational: Dan, Zebulon, and Asher. (Genesis 49:13 and Judges 5:17) They must have played an important part in the organization of Solomon's trading fleet. The fleet was manned chiefly by Phoenicians, but comprised other nationalities as well. Greeks were a great seafaring people and some researchers, like Cyrus Gordon and Manly Hall, see in their myths about voyages to unknown lands to the West evidence of contact with the American continent.

The following describes a Greek who joined Solomon's fleet and later rose to a favored position in the court. On November 27, 1942, a New York City book publisher was told:

> . . . the entity was in the Grecian land, when there were those rumors of those activities in the Holy Land, as called; when the son of David was made king; when those ships of Hiram, the ships of the new king began to ply the waters about the land.
>
> The entity then joined in those activities, that there might be the adventure of seeing, of knowing, of experiencing the stories or tales that had become as hearsay to that awakening people.
>
> The entity became as one favored, eventually, in the court of Solomon, and thus first understood those deeper intents and purposes that must prompt individual activities in material adventures in relationship with things, conditions, experiences.
>
> Then the entity was gifted in making those pronouncements, those announcements of the king during portions of Solomon's reign.
>
> The name then was Persus. In that experience we find there was the development of those things that are innately a part of the present consciousness of the entity; character, strength of body, of mind, the interest the entity experiences in all those influences that develop body; athletics, food values for body building, those things for mind building. All of these are a part of the consciousness from that experience.      2834-1

## The Wise One

This age of wisdom covered all realms of knowledge, both esoteric and exoteric. Few times has so much light shown through so many in such a small area. Solomon's legendary genius derives in a large measure from the creative court which surrounded him. Genius, spirit, and talent clustered around the king. The mark of a great leader is determined by his counselors.

In this reading an actress was told she had been a friend of Solomon's. As a wise counselor in his court, her intuitive knowledge added to Solomon's renown:

**Before that the entity was in the "city beautiful" during those activities and periods of the wealth of the world, the renown of that phase of ability, that were a part of the experience of that era; during the reign of King Solomon.**

**The entity then was a close companion of, and an interpreter for the king. For, through the activities in which there was the interpreting of the law, the interpreting of poetry and songs of the period, the entity induced the friendships in many of the other lands.**

**Then the entity was in the name Jethebeth, *and* a companion of that king. From same in the present we find there are those experiences and feelings that may be as dreams, or those visions that have been a part of the experience, in the formulas that have been the attempt of the entity at times, to turn to the innate self.**

**In the true way may the entity find much, for the entity answered for the king even to that princess that came to question Solomon during that period.** **2598-2**

## Two Apshas

As did knowledge and commercial wealth, music and ritual worship also reached their culmination in this period.

Three musicians of this period appear in the Life readings. Two of the three were given the same name—Apsha. Apsha was the eponym of the musical guild within the Levites. His name and its variants may have been common, perhaps indicating title or rank.

Solomon's majestic Temple crowded out all the other cults and shrines in Israel. The lofty services and imageless worship of an Unseen

God were an effective stimulus upon the inmost reaches of man, coun-
terbalancing the immediate appeal to the sensually gratifying pagan
cults. Trained musicians were skilled in the use of music to lift man's
consciousness.

A young and gifted musician obtained Life reading 5056. He was told
in pre-Adamic Atlantis he had been "a real musician on the pipes and
reeds," and in the following incarnation, during the days of Solomon,
was trained for Temple service. However, Solomon had a different use
for his skills.

**Before that we find the entity was in the activities in the Temple of
Solomon in Jerusalem when there was the choosing by David of those
who were to be prepared for the service of music in the Temple which
was yet to be built. David chose young men and they were given the
physical as well as the mental and spiritual training through the activities
in the preparations in the school as had been undertaken or begun by
Elijah in Carmel.**

**Thus the entity in the name Apsha was among those who were in the
Temple service when the activities were begun through those periods of
Solomon's reign. Those were the periods when there was the great
amount of what today would be called notoriety, or during those
periods when the Queen of Sheba visited Solomon, the entity was
chosen as the one to make music for Solomon to make love by, to the
Queen.                                                              5056-1**

In his next life, the entity studied music under St. Cecilia, the patron
saint of musicians. Music became a source of sexual stimulation for
5056, and he became enamored of the saint and desired her physically.
Music was forgotten, and, being rebuffed, he eventually destroyed himself.

The second Apsha is found in a Life reading given for an eleven-
month-old child on September 8, 1941. The entity is described as among
the chief musicians in the Temple. This Apsha held to the purpose of using
music to attune the mind for worship. The influence of this life carried
over into his next—as Franz Liszt. The great Hungarian pianist and composer again was a leader in expressing the spiritual qualities of music.

**Before that the entity was in the earth during those periods of the
preparation and the accomplishing of the setting up of the music in the**

Temple that was planned by David and completed by Solomon.

The entity was an associate then of both David and Solomon, being among the chief musicians for setting the psalms to the order of preparation for the various instruments upon which there would be the music for services in the temples. And the psalms of David as well as the songs of Solomon were a part of the entity's experience, in their preparation, as well as the psalms and the musical activities in which the entity engaged.

Then the entity was in the name Apsha. In the experience the entity gained. For there were those attempts ever to keep the activities in the service such that they appealed to the minds of those who would come to worship. Also there were the constant attempts to attain or gain favor with those in authority, and to impress upon them—in the various ways and manners—the needs of their being leaders, as individuals, in the spiritual and mental attributes as well as the material.

Here, too, will be the needs for the instructions to the entity through the formative years, by those upon whom the entity is dependent for an environment in which there may be kept the spiritual, the mental, and the material experiences well balanced in the activities throughout the developing years.                2584-1

## The Dreamer

Perhaps the only appropriate note to end upon is with a dreamer and her memories. *Mind is the Builder*, as the Cayce readings so often remind us; and without dreaming, the mystery and splendor of the higher truths could never enter into the mind of man.

Divisions, boundaries, limitations blur and alter as we awaken to the Divine Within. The Seen and Unseen are unable to be separated. The point of demarcation between imagination and fact cannot be found. As Consciousness becomes spiritualized, all becomes One.

The third musician in the readings was a court entertainer. A middle-aged New Hampshire widow was told:

. . . the entity was in the holy city, or Jerusalem, during those periods when there was a great splendor indicated in the activities; during the reign of Solomon.

The entity was among the entertainers—a musician—in the royal palace.

**The love of indolence, the love of quiet, the abilities as the musician as well as the love of the mystery and the splendor that goes with the dreaming of same, are all a part of the experience. The entity gained, the entity lost, the entity gained throughout that period of activity.**

**Then the name was Rhouel.** 2576-1

"It has not yet entered into the mind of man those glories which God has prepared for those who love his ways." The purpose of the Bible is to put into man's mind an understanding of God's Love and man's relationship to it. The Cayce readings are rich with vital, living concepts about the variety and depth of man's inner nature and his spiritual potential. We begin to see what the Throne of David and the Halls of Solomon tell us about our own souls.

Indeed, the Cayce readings, correlated with the Bible, do allow man "to dream."

# Part Three

## From Solomon's Glories
## to the Birth of Jesus

*And it shall come to pass afterward that I will pour out my spirit upon all flesh; and your sons and your daughters shall prophesy, your old men shall dream dreams, your young men shall see visions; And also upon the servants and upon the handmaidens in those days will I pour out my spirit. . . . And it shall come to pass that whosoever shall call on the name of the Lord shall be delivered; for in mount Zion and in Jerusalem shall be deliverance, as the Lord has said to the remnant whom the Lord has called.* (Joel 2:28, 29, 32)

In the days of old, when there were those developments of man as to his attempts to understand his relationships to the Maker, warnings were given again and again as to what would be the experiences of individuals who professed one thing and lived another, or who attempted to use amiss that which was given them. And these came to pass in the experiences and in the generations of those peoples so directed.

These came about in the manners indicated, though not always at the times or periods as had been felt or expected by individuals. For, oft such expressions are found in dealing with such, that "his day and generation has not been completed," yet in a little while there comes the opportunity.

Then there came that period in man's activity in which it was proclaimed that no longer it would be in this temple or in this mountain that there would go out the message to the people, or to their gatherings here or there, but lo it would be written upon their hearts—so that the old men should dream dreams, the young men should see visions, the maidens should proclaim the acceptable year of the Lord.

**3976-25**

# Foreword: World Affairs and the Bible

. . . for they [periods of history] will be seen to come in cycles . . . for, as in energy, there is seen the relativity of space and force as is begun, and as same continues to vibrate, that one law remains. Whenever it vibrates in the same vibration, it shows as the same thing. That's deep for you, yes.                                                                    254-47

O, ye say, this is not new! Neither is thy present disturbance, nor thy presence hope, nor *anything!* For, even as He said, "There is nothing new under the sun." What is has been, and will be again.     3976-27

From 1930 through 1944 a remarkable series of twenty-nine clair-voyant readings was given by Edgar Cayce on world affairs.[27] Significant portions from these readings are included in this volume for the additional clarification they give on the meaning of the Bible. These readings offer a psychic's commentary on a turbulent and shattering era, interpreting the causes of war, depression, and civil strife, with prophecies of earth change, revolution, and economic upheaval, and with predictions and promises concerning the rise of a new order and a new age based upon universal, spiritual happenings.

---

[27]These discourses are catalogued under the case number 3976 in the Edgar Cayce readings.

In short, the readings discussed the latter half of the twentieth century as a time of "testing" and a passage through the complete Old Testament cycle or "the latter days" with all its threats, warnings, promises, and hopes. The network of global events of the thirties and forties and the forecasts Cayce gave for this period were reviewed and revealed as the effects of man's compliance or rejection of two basic spiritual ideals: *We are our brother's keeper* and *love of neighbor as of self.* The one unchanging law and principle, the one source, foundation, and resonating factor in the story of man is "thou shalt love the Lord thy God, thy neighbor as thy self." This is the basis of all spiritual law. (3976-14)

The words of the Old Testament prophets, which Cayce voiced, stressed, and paraphrased in the world affairs readings, are still valid because the cycles and patterns of man's history are unchanged. The language of his readings are replete with quotes from the Old Testament, as if Cayce in his clairvoyant consciousness could only suggest the significance of our contemporary history by its relativity to the Bible. The Old Testament pattern was repeating itself. Why? Because man had not yet learned fully to love his brother.

Yet for those who can learn to love, even through an era of destruction, of suffering and pain as the effects of man's selfishness sweep over the earth, a new age is promised, a new testament, a new covenant is offered as it was then and is now and will forever be.

# Introduction: The Coming Is from Within

*In* the Old Testament, men waited for the coming of a messiah. Today, Christians look for the return of the Christ. It is the same hope, the same waiting, a deep yearning for the same experience—*Completion*—the time when our earthly trials and tribulations end and all God's promises are realized and complete.

But how, we might ask, will the Lord come to those who await His Coming? The Edgar Cayce readings stress the inward experience.

The real coming is not when He returns, but when we do. God never left us. He is as much present as He ever was in the Bible days. His laws and covenants are eternal. "If ye will be my people, I will be your God." Christ said *He* would be with us always (Matthew 28:20), therefore He never went away. Man has wandered from the realization of His Presence, thus has lost one of the most precious birthrights God has given.

The Old Testament, in its most universal meaning, is the story of a fulfillment and a promise by God—to bring a blessing to all mankind. The soul we know as The Christ took it upon Himself to be that blessing. Through all His incarnations in the earth He reflected the ideals of service and self-sacrifice, manifesting the love and power of God until He was so at-one with the God-within that it became inevitable that men accept Him as the savior and messiah. He had the abilities to demonstrate and prove His Sonship—and thus, to show us ours.

Yet the Jews did not accept Jesus as messiah, for the promised age of

peace did not follow His coming, as prophesied. Some Christian thinkers say it will be the Christ of the Second Coming, the resurrected and
glorified Christ that will be the messiah acceptable to the Jews, for a
thousand years of peace shall follow His coming.

The Cayce readings stress that Jesus is the savior in that He set the
example and pattern by which all humanity can know the experience
of the Christ, the messiah, abiding within.

What bars us from this realization? What are the biggest distractions,
the greatest obstacles? It is in the Bible, it is the story of man—these
must be overcome: selfishness, fear, hate, jealousy, lack of faith, lack of
love. As seekers after God, we struggle with the same influences and
forces as did the Israelites in their efforts to develop the pattern for a
perfected humanity. We confront daily the same temptations and illu-
sions as Jesus did in all His incarnations, whether as Adam, Enoch,
Melchizedek, Joseph, Joshua, Jeshua, or Jesus.

What is a savior? Someone who can make God's love real to another.
And how do we make God real to another? By first knowing Him ourselves, as this reading indicates.

From the world affairs series, we find:

> **As to the material changes that are to be as an omen, as a sign to those
> that this is shortly to come to pass—as has been given of old, the sun will
> be darkened and the earth shall be broken up in divers places—and *then*
> shall be proclaimed—through the spiritual interception in the hearts and
> minds and souls of those that have sought His way—that *His* star has
> appeared, and will point the way for those that enter into the holy of
> holies in themselves. For, God the Father, God the teacher, God the
> director, in the minds and hearts of men, must ever be *in* those that come
> to know Him as first and foremost in the seeking of those souls; for He
> is first the *God* to the individual and as He is exemplified, as He is
> manifested in the heart and in the acts of the body, of the individual, He
> becomes manifested before men.** 3976-15

An earlier reading in the same series tells us how to find Him: by
looking within. The reading speaks of a process and the direct experience of knowing.

> **Seek first to know within self that which has prompted thee, and when
> thou hast set thine house in order, when thou hast made thine peace**

with thine own conscience (that would smite thee, if ye will look within your own heart), then may ye find the answers that will come to every soul that seeks. For, as He has given to those of old, He is the same yesterday, today, and forever. Think not as to who will ascend into heaven to bring down comfort and ease to thine own aching heart, or who will go over the seas to bring that which may be of a recompense within thine own experience, but lo! ye shall find it in your own heart!

Thus has the lawgiver given, and thus has He said who has set the way to make the intercession for man: "I will not leave thee comfortless, if ye will seek to do my biddings." 3976-14

We are living in Bible times, for all time is God's time—and all life is, in its essence, spiritual.

The readings make it extremely clear how relevant the Bible is today. When passages were recommended for Bible study in the readings, often the counsel was to read them " . . . as if the writer, as if the Father was speaking direct to the entity, to self!" 1231-1

Know that these words are speaking to self, and that they are from the living God. 3406-1

This is the divine speaking as to the self. 5241-1

The Cayce readings can help us, not just to a knowledge of the Christ, not just to a stronger belief and faith in Christ, but to the experience of the Christ, of being a Christ—Christ on the inside, as a part and portion of the individuality and personality of our being—as well as knowing the universality of the Christ "without."

The Only Begotten Son of God is a Spirit—the Christ Spirit, the Christ that is within every soul. From this Spirit, our universe, our world, and all created things have come into being. It was the Spirit of the Christ in the hearts and minds of the Children of Israel that guided them through the long years of their history—and it is this same Spirit beckoning us, calling to every soul to complete and fulfill the pattern. When mankind can reach this point, all wars of every kind shall cease, no tears will flow, and joy and harmony shall reign everywhere.

When the Christ was fully realized and manifested in the physical life of the man Jesus, one phase in Israel's long commitment was finished—man had a Way, a star, a light to guide him—but until men and women everywhere have developed their own spirits and *MAN* is the Messiah, Israel and the Christ's work will never be complete.

Until we know the fullness of His spirit within us, we are Old Testament figures living out our chapter in the search for Truth. The Bible is not a finished piece of work. We are still completing its meaning. When we reach the state when we are transformed and "made anew" through our unity with God, then the old concepts of heaven and hell, God and man, good and evil, will pass away. There will no longer be questions about the meaning, purpose, or relevancy of the Bible. It will have fulfilled its purpose, its function in us—and we will be a new chapter, a new testament to its meanings.

# 18

## Solomon's Sins

*Part* Two ended on the high note of Solomon's glories. Part Three really begins with a study of the sins of Solomon. A subtle lesson was underscored by Edgar Cayce in a lecture to the Bible class.

> "Solomon put heavy taxes on the people he had conquered. Later, when Rome rose to power, the Jews reaped this karma by having to pay tribute to Rome. It seems that Solomon, being well-versed in the history of his people, would have understood the spiritual law too well to become guilty of the same persecution practiced by pharaoh."

In the first part of his reign, Solomon was faithful to the commission David had given him. (1 Chronicles 28:6, 20), but in his later years he went beyond the moral and spiritual limits which constrain a good leader and stepped into those areas that make for tyranny and despotism.

Solomon was the wisest ruler in the world, yet one of the most greedy and ambitious. He was the father of many injustices and his administration fostered dangerous principles. Indeed, the weight of gold talents he received in one year—666—becomes in the Book of Revelation the symbolic "code number of the beast." (1 Kings 10:14; Revelation 13:18) This "code number" as interpreted by Edgar Cayce indicated that a person who served "the beast of self-aggrandizement, self-indulgence, self-glorification" had his days "numbered"—they were not eternal like the soul; but with a beginning and end, like a man. A man marked with the number 666 "lacks that consciousness of God and God alone directing." (281-34)

Like many leaders who are uniquely prepared and singularly outfitted for a special role and purpose, Solomon found the excitement and pleasure of material life more than he could withstand, and did not realize his own inner spiritual resources.

Edgar Cayce spoke of it to the Bible class:

> "Solomon's religious ancestry and training had given him the basis for a strong life. His own request at Gibeon and his zeal in the worship of God foretold a vigorous religious career. But, though he built the temple, and in the prayer attributed to him, he expressed some of the loftiest sentiments of a man thoroughly zealous in his worship of Israel's God, his career did not fulfill his early resolves. The polytheistic worship introduced by his foreign wives into Jerusalem and his faint and ineffectual opposition to their request that their gods be shown respect led to his moral and religious deterioration."

Ultimately, as Cayce told his Bible class, Solomon lost hold upon himself, his religion, and his people, and Israel began its decline. The whole nation lost its consciousness of God The ruling class—the leaders and policy makers—were rich and self-satisfied. The people were angry, frustrated, and burdened. One of the men responsible for this condition is found in the Life readings—Benaiah.

## *Benaiah*

Benaiah figures prominently in the reigns of both Solomon and David. With Abiather, he was David's most trusted counselor, and accomplished three noteworthy exploits worthy of mention in Scripture. (2 Samuel 23:20-23; 1 Chronicles 11:22-24)

Benaiah was loyal to David and distinguished himself in military affairs. When Adonijah attempted to usurp Solomon's throne, Benaiah sided with Solomon in proclaiming him king. He put Adonijah, Joab, and Shimei to death, and succeeded to the supreme command of Solomon's army.

In the Life reading for a New York textile executive, Benaiah is described as the entity's most outstanding incarnation. The reading begins:

In giving the interpretations of the records as we find them here, these are not all pretty, from some angles; but these we choose from same with the desire and purpose that this information may be a helpful experience . . .

From a particular sojourn we find the greater part of the characteristics that are manifested in the present; that in the period when the entity was the leader of, or friend to, Solomon. For the entity then was Benaiah. 3001-1

The influence from exposure to foreign cults and royal visitors is echoed in the entity's present interest in comparative religions and philosophies, and his desire for knowledge. We find him also a "hard taskmaster," a phrase which carries the mind back to the Exodus:

Hence those inclinations or tendencies; for the individual or tendencies; for the individual would not be called a religious man, and yet there is the adherence to—or the desire for—information, knowledge, or that in which the entity interests self—in comparative religions, comparative philosophy, comparative things having to do with the mental and spiritual influences in the lives of men. Yet it also makes the entity a hard taskmaster.

The entity is very decided as to its views. Once having set itself as to its views on any proposition—whether a material, a mental condition, or about things, about people, or in any form—it takes a lot to change him! This is a real stubbornness at times, though the entity is very sure this is not true.

But if the entity will analyze itself, it will be seen that this was not only the outstanding appearance of the entity, but also from same come the greater characteristics. 3001-1

This description of the present entity, 3001, applies equally to Benaiah.

The astrological aspects as may be indicated have little to do with this entity . . . these are far in the background to [in comparison] the characteristics of this special appearance of the entity in the earth.

Hence it makes of the entity a good leader—if there is the choosing of the spiritual import—a good director; one in whom—when the word is given—one can put one's confidence. Yet others might say just the opposite—unless in complete agreement with the ideas of the entity. But innately and deeply, the entity is honest—though isn't always honest with self; honest more with others than with self. 3001-1

Cayce described an incarnation preceding Benaiah, also in the Holy Land, but during the time of Joshua. He then was kin to the discredited rebel Korah, and this delayed his acceptance by those in authority. Perhaps this rejection created the desire to be "remembered" which manifested in his next life. Cayce described the urge, as the reading continued:

But ye have a soul, a mind, a body, and the Lord thy God is One! But who is thy God? Thyself, thine own interests? as they were considered during that period when ye would make of thyself one to be remembered. Well if the entity could forget what he caused his own people to bring into their experience, that led them gradually away from the way, away from the Father-God! 3001-1

Because of the existence of certain compulsions, Cayce gave the following counsel:

But look, listen! Better stop those things of making or forcing thine own inner self to thine own self. True, thy measurement to others is the manner in which ye treat thy Maker. But thy judgments—are they in keeping with the law? that if ye cause thy brother to offend, ye are worse than the infidel?

Let that which was the directing force in the law keep thy ways, thy directions, and ye will find ye will come into a closer, better understanding of the purposes of life, and find greater joy in same. 3001-1

The great material glories of Solomon's reign were built upon a weak foundation of heavy taxation and forced labor, over which this entity had been "a hard taskmaster." The charge that Solomon was "a greedy and relentless autocrat," whose despotism created feelings of social injustice and class hatred, is echoed in the following. Just as the desire for knowledge has remained with Mr. 3001 since the days of Solomon, so, too, have the anguished cries of the people.

... the entity was in that land and during the period when Solomon, the son of David, was king of Israel; when the entity, as Benaiah, was raised to one of authority, one of power, and yet one who brought to himself—while in the material plane gratifying experiences, and wonderments in the mental—those judgments that must be corrected in the present.

Be well if the entity would analyze and study especially the life of that leader of the peoples, as to how servitude was brought about, as to how the various groups—as to classes—became a part of the experience through much of the activity of the entity in that period; and the lack of the due consideration or stress put upon man's relationship to Creative Forces in that experience. 3001-1

The reading contains a yardstick for Mr. 3001 to measure his mental and spiritual growth. Perhaps this advice could be applied equally well to Solomon:

What gains the man if he gains the whole world and loses his own soul? or what can the man give in exchange for his soul? For, the purpose of the manifestation of individuality in the earth is to be to the glory of God, not to the gratifying of self, nor of that ego, nor to be well-spoken of. To be well-spoken of is beautiful, but is this of self or to the glory of the Creative Force? 3001-1

## Coronation and Rebellion

*And Solomon slept with his fathers, and they buried him in the city of David; and Rehoboam his son reigned in his stead.* (2 Chronicles 9:31)

The lack of sensitivity to the needs of the people shown in Solomon and Benaiah was passed on to Solomon's son and successor, Rehoboam—and resulted in the tragedy of rebellion, secession, and civil war.

The assembly for Rehoboam's coronation was at Shechem, the one sacred, historic city within the province of the ten tribes. Before the coronation, the assembly requested reforms in Solomon's policies. The old men, who had seen the evils of Solomon's course, advised Rehoboam to yield to the people; but the young princes, accustomed to the pleasures of a brilliant court, were not willing to modify a policy that yielded to them such large privileges. The reforms would reduce the royal exchequer and its power to continue the magnificence of the court.

Apparently Rehoboam had no spiritual understanding, Cayce told his Bible class. Rehoboam took advantage of his material power, but never considered the privilege he had of serving the people in a spiritual sense.

The young princes urged Rehoboam to increase the revenues, and Rehoboam consented. The counsel was callous and selfish:

*Thus shall you speak to the people who have said to you, "Your father made our yoke heavy, but make you it lighter for us;" Thus shall you answer them, "My little finger is thicker than my father's thumb. And now whereas my father laid a heavy yoke on you, I will add to your yoke . . . "*
(1 Kings 12:10)

The advice of the young princes gave rise to this revealing interpretation in the readings:

**Things that are of the spirit must arise from the spiritual promptings; things that are material arise from the material promptings. What seek ye? Remember, my children, those examples shown thee. What spoke the Lord? Know ye not that where thy burdens have been as those of the finger, they shall become as thick as the thigh? Know ye not that those that seek material things must in all things pay the price of same?**

**254-85**

The world affairs readings carefully delineate the eternal and unchanging causes of all disturbance between men. Hostilities and animosities between men stem from one basic and fundamental principle: Man forgets God and, in the forgetting, loses sight of the fact that he is his brother's keeper.

In Solomon's reign, many one-sided advantages accrued to the royal house. Under Solomon's hand, with "hard taskmasters" such as Benaiah, the unified kingdom of David began to dissolve from within. Even in Solomon's lifetime, Jeroboam, who was later to play such a commanding role in the impending revolution, "lifted up his hand" in revolt. (1 Kings 11:26)

Yes, we have . . . those problems which have brought about the upheavals and the wars, the distrust, the jealousy, the hate existing today.
These are the result of man's forgetting God, and that which truly
represents man's sincere attempt to worship, honor, and glorify a living
God.

For this may only be done in the manner in which individuals, states,
nations, treat their fellow man. For, as ye do unto others, ye do to thy
Maker. And when those activities are such as to dishonor thy fellow man,
ye dishonor thy God—and it brings all of those forms of disturbance that
exist in the world today. 3976-28

One of the central teachings in Genesis is that we are our brother's
keeper. The world affairs discourses stress this fact. The following inter-
prets its import. Revolution is the leveler. Only love can prevent it:

. . . just as indicated . . . we *are* our brother's keeper.

Then if those in position to give of their means, their wealth, their
education, their position, *do not* take these things into consideration,
there must be that leveling that will come.

For unless these are considered, there must eventually become a
revolution . . . and there will be a dividing of the sections as one against
another. For these are the leveling means and manners to which men
resort when there is the plenty in *some* areas and a lack of the sustenance
in the life of others.

These are the manners in which such things as crime, riots, and every
nature of disturbance arise—in that those who are in authority are not
considering every level, every phase of human activity and human
experience . . .

Then those who are in power must know that they *are* their brother's
keeper, and give expression to that which has been indicated in "Thou
shalt love the Lord thy God with all thy heart and mind and body, and
thy neighbor as thyself." . . .

But when there becomes class or mass distinction between this or that
group, this or that party, this or that faction, then it becomes a class
rather than "thy neighbor as thyself."

For all stand as *one* before Him. For the Lord is *not* a respecter of
persons, and these things *cannot* long exist. 3976–19

Isaiah forecasted social revolution, based on the same principle:

*The foot shall tread it down, even the feet of the poor and the steps of the needy.* (Isaiah 26:6)

**For those who are hungry care not as to the source of strength or power, until there is the fulfilling of that desired.**
   **Unless there is, then, a more universal oneness of purpose on the part of all, this will one day bring . . . revolution!**                **3976-24**

An earlier reading in the same series repeats the warning:

**And there *cannot* be one measuring stick for the laborer in the field and the man behind the counter, and another for the man behind the money changers. *All* are equal—not only under the material law but under the *spiritual*.**
   **And *His* laws, *His* will, will not come to naught!**
   **Though there may come those periods when there will be great stress, as brother rises against brother, as group or sect or race rises against race—yet the leveling must come.**                **3976-18**

The laws are not new. The results are not new. The pattern remains unchanged. From the beginning, man has been instructed to love. Although the command to "love your neighbor as yourself" is considered new, it is one which man has had from the start. According to John (1 John 3:11), it is just another way of saying "We are our brother's keeper." The law, which Israel had before them always was simply stated, reaffirmed, and amplified by Jesus.

Rehoboam took the self-serving advice of his young counselors, which resulted in the rebellion of the ten tribes and the beginning of a history of civil war, heartaches, suffering, tragedy, and the ultimate degeneration and effacement of both kingdoms.

## To Your Tents, O Israel!

Divine revelation is an eternal process and, like the Creation, still continues. The Bible is a mirror of the processes of growth and change, and bears witness to man's progressive discovery of the truth. Thus we discover that *all time is one time*, and that the Bible contains patterns that emerge in our own lives.

The material aspects of Solomon's reign were the most transient part of his glory, yet the most blinding to the carnal mind. And it is still the same today. The lust for material things blinded his successors and kept them from seeing their true spiritual purpose. Thus, in the cycle following Solomon, there was a steady rise in the prophetic voice with its insistence on repentance, preparation, and purity.

The changes which took place after Solomon's passing are part of the process of spiritualization. The disturbances following Solomon were the preface to a new order and understanding among men, completed in the master Jesus who obtained Christ-consciousness and fulfilled the biblical pattern in its entirety.

As in Solomon's day the "old order" had to pass away for new forms and consciousness to emerge. Cayce told his contemporaries in a world affairs reading:

> It is also understood, comprehended by some, that a new order of conditions is to arise; that there must be many a purging in high places as well as low; that there must be the greater consideration of each individual, each soul being his brother's keeper.
>
> There will come then about those circumstances in the political, the economic and the whole relationships where there will be a leveling—or a greater comprehension of this need . . . For His ways will carry through. For as He gave, "Though the heavens and the earth may pass away, My word will *not* pass away."                3976-18

All the promises in the Bible are conditional. There is an "if" clause attached to everyone, including those to Solomon. However, because Solomon had so blatantly failed to honor his part of the covenant, changes became necessary that prove "God is not mocked" and that His words are words of power and truth.

The secession of the ten tribes was according to God's judgment. It was the way through which the "old order" would be changed, the high brought low, and the low exalted. Each new age in the evolution of spiritual consciousness is prefaced by the breaking up of conditions which are blocks and barriers to the light. Conditions around us are ever working toward the fulfillment of God's word.

When Rehoboam would not listen to the people, they answered the king, saying:

*"We have no portion in David, neither have we inheritance in the son of*

*Jesse, to your tents, O Israel!"* (1 Kings 12:16-20)

The rebellion marks the beginning of the final phase in the Old Testament story.

With the loss of the ten tribes, the royal tribe of Judah would be made weak, and in its weakness would regain its true strength—by its need for God. The ten tribes, forming now a separate and independent kingdom, would constitute a "new order" with new opportunities.

The prophet Abijah had foreseen Jeroboam as the man with the necessary qualifications to lead the new kingdom. To Abijah, and others of the ten tribes, Jeroboam was the logical choice because, as the young rebel who had lifted up his hand against Solomon, he possessed, if nothing else, the courage of his convictions.

A leader was present whom the people felt could meet their needs. This is ever true, and a fulfillment of a spiritual law.

**And then there should be, there *will* be those rising to power that are able to meet the needs. For none are in power but that have been given the opportunity by the will of the Father—from which all power emanates.**

**Hence those will be leveled with the purpose, "My word shall *not* fail!"** **3976-18**

# Jeroboam, King of Israel

*The man Jeroboam was a mighty man of valour.* (1 Kings 11:28)

Jeroboam was promised as sure a house as David's, but the promise was conditional. His house would be stable only "if" he walked in the ways of God. (1 Kings 11:38)

No doubt Jeroboam had been conditioned and prepared through experiences in past lives for the opportunities and responsibilities of his new career. He was put in a unique position. Like Saul he was the standard bearer in a new age. He was a model for the new kingdom. Things would be made better or worse according to his choices.

Jeroboam was given his chance because he answered to the needs of the people. There was an authenticity to his call which made it divine. He felt the injustice and unrest, thus the spirit of God's purposes could work through him, magnifying the leadership qualities he possessed.

*Many are called, but few have chosen,* Cayce once told the Bible class. Not *are* chosen, but *have* chosen—for the call comes to every soul. What is a "call"? A practical and working definition is suggested in an early world affairs reading. Basically, it is the willingness of an entity to choose to be used "as an instrument of good for the saving of the good in human principles"—a call to which all can harken and apply in every phase and all relationships of daily living.

**First the choosing of those who would give self in holy communion with this one purpose and, making self right with God, choose to be used as an *instrument* of good for the saving of the good in human principles; for, as is seen, as has been given, the world awaits the coming of those who will proclaim the day of freedom from the bonds of those who would role, either through prestige or through political influence, see? Then ones so chosen by their fitness—as will come through such communion—will be the first to begin.** 3976-4

The readings indicate we are "chosen" if we choose. We have a "call" if we but listen. The Spirit bids all to follow, and the closer we draw to the Source the more we will be able to manifest its attributes—psychic and spiritual forces. The Cayce readings make it clearly evident, whether we are conscious of the fact or not, that we can and are, by our moods, attitudes and convictions, creating the spiritual, mental and physical environment of our worlds.

By harmonious co-operation with the divine, our souls are opened by the Spirit which activates and magnifies those talents and abilities within, which will enable us to fulfill our purpose. By following these creative impulses, we develop skills, abilities, and understandings which lead us into greater spheres of activity and responsibility. In future incarnations we are drawn to situations where we will have the opportunity to use that which we have developed.

Like Jeroboam, we will all have the opportunity to be standard bearers. But unlike Jeroboam, pray that we may resist the temptations that make us fall and pervert the purpose of our call.

**Let him that is weak of mind or heart not take the handle, for he that ploweth and looketh back is worse than the infidel.** 3976-4

## Jeroboam's Fall

**In [this entity] there is seen the abilities of the use of power and of principle, yet that inner self must be made over again, as it were, in that oneness of the purpose as has often been set in self . . . for before each there is set a way, and in that way is set a light. Veer not from same!** 3976-4

All power or authority comes from God. Because Jeroboam had been responsive to the needs of his brothers, he was raised to authority. However, "few does power not destroy." (3976-13) Once in power Jeroboam determined to retain his position no matter what the cost.

His guile is shown immediately. When Rehoboam returned to Jerusalem and was crowned king over Judah, he assembled his men of war to fight against Israel. However, the prophet Shemaiah spoke out against his intentions, saying that the division of the tribes was God's work and that the tribe of Judah should not wage war against its brothers. (1 Kings 12:22-24)

Rehoboam obeyed the prophet and disbanded his men. By accepting God's word, Rehoboam had unconsciously provided a non-violent solution to the disunity. The Israelites still had strong mental, emotional and spiritual ties with Jerusalem, especially the temple. They desired to return to the city to worship. Perhaps in this desire the differences could have been settled or overcome, and the nation united again, if Jeroboam hadn't interfered. Jeroboam saw, in the desire of his people to return to Jerusalem to worship, a strong threat to his independent authority. Rather than lead the people back to worship, and risk losing his temporal crown, Jeroboam instituted worship of the golden calf and built altars for the burning of "the sandalwoods of Egypt." (See 274-10)

*And Jeroboam said in his heart, "Now the kingdom will return to the house of David; If this people go up to do sacrifices at the house of the Lord in Jerusalem, then shall the heart of this people turn again to their lord, even to Rehoboam king of Judah, and they shall kill me . . . " So the king took counsel, and made two calves of gold, and said to all Israel, "It is too much for you to go up to Jerusalem; behold your gods, Oh Israel, who brought you up out of the land of Egypt."* (1 Kings 12:26-28)

Cayce gave his analysis of this section of the Book of Kings to the Bible class:

"Jeroboam may have started with a good purpose, but it didn't last long. He used politics to get power. He took advantage of the people's unrest and made himself popular. In other words, Jeroboam was the lesser of two evils. They were in that consciousness now that a king was necessary to them, and Rehoboam had failed."

The readings commented on two sources of Jeroboam's corruption; first, his counselors:

> Look upon those that were called into service as was Saul, the son of Kish; as was Jeroboam, the son of Nebat. These came by the divine call from out of their brethren and were endowed with that which would make for such a manifestation as had not before been seen in the earth. Yet counselors of these made them but laughingstocks to the nations roundabout. 254-85

Second the ever-present evil of self-indulgence. This practice may have started during Jeroboam's exile in Egypt. (1 Kings 11:39)

> What did Jeroboam, that he made the children of Israel to sin, but to offer rather the sandalwoods of the nations or the Egyptians that made for the arousing of the passions in man for the gratifications of the seeking for the activities that would satisfy his own indulgence, rather than the offering of those things that would make for the glory of the Lord's entrance into the activities of the individual! 274-10

The world affairs readings contain the statement: that when "selfishness is the prompting attitude"; turmoils and strife follow as a natural effect. (3976-17) Another reading states:

> *Rather* does man—by his compliance with the divine law—bring order out of chaos; or by his *disregard* of the associations and laws of divine influence, brings chaos and *destructive* forces into his experience.
> 416-7

The spirit of selfishness characterizes Jeroboam as king, and this vibration was perpetuated in all the leaders who followed him, creating in their wake a national history filled with regicide, revolution, counter-revolution, pogroms, and persecution, ceasing only with their effacement through conquest and captivity by a foreign power.

Many were the kings who were "valiant in the ways of the earth," but, as Jeremiah states, knew little of the ways of the Spirit. (Jeremiah 9:3) Men such as Omri and Baasha were brilliant military leaders, and others like Jeroboam and Ahab were gifted political strategists who "did right" in terms of self-preservation and increasing their power base.

They did that which seemed right at the moment (Romans 6:21), and often their efforts were successful for a short time, but seldom for more than a generation. The end result was death, decline, and change. With all its efforts toward self–preservation, Israel could not save itself.

A recurrent refrain echoes through all the dynasties of Israel. All the nineteen kings "walked in the sins of Jeroboam" and "made Israel to sin."

Jeroboam was another Saul, but no David rose up after him to offset his influence. The sin was violation of the first commandment.

> For, the first law that has been given to man from the beginning is: "Thou shalt have no other gods before me." And when man has faltered, has altered . . . that command that has come to man throughout the ages, then there arises that which creates those things that are the fruits of the evil influences that are in the earth. Such as: hate, jealousy, avarice, and the like. These make for the creating of those conditions in all walks of life for power, for position, for the love of money and that it will bring in its associations in the lives of individuals . . . For, with that command has come ever that to which mankind may expect to find himself reduced when he has forgotten that which is his *first* duty, and the second which is likened unto it: "Thou shalt love thy neighbor as thyself."
>
> Then, this condition has been the experience in the greater portion of the whole nation, the whole world. For that is the experience of the individual that makes for the creating in his environs, his surrounding, of that which breeds strife, that which breeds hate, that which breeds malice, that which breeds selfishness. **3976-14**

## Jeroboam and the Man of God (1 Kings 13)

Sometime after his eighth month as king, Jeroboam was burning incense at his altar when he was approached by a prophet who spoke out against him. The man of God had come from Judah to warn Jeroboam that unless he changed his inner purpose, men's bones would eventually be burnt from his altar. Jeroboam was beginning to lead the children of Israel astray, and God was trying to warn him.

Jeroboam was incensed at the prophet and put up his hand (perhaps the same one he lifted against Solomon) to strike the man of God, and as he did, the arm withered. The angry king instantly became fearful, and implored the prophet to heal his hand.

Cayce made a wise observation, as he lectured on this episode:

> "Notice that Jeroboam did not entreat his own god, but asked the man of God to entreat *his* god. If he had asked for the strength to change his heart, to do the right, no doubt the future would have been entirely different. He only asked for his hand to be restored—apparently so he could carry on his evil doing in the same way he started."

A similar note is struck in a world affairs reading:

> **Let each and every soul call on not their god but the One God!**
> **3976-26**

When people sought physical help, often the readings asked why the individual wanted to be healed. All illness comes from sin (misapplication of spiritual laws), the readings stressed. If the purpose for the healing was only to enable the entity to carry on in the same life-style that had brought on the affliction, it could be better for the person to suffer until he had a change of heart and learned the lesson of his pain.

A reading on healing prayer tells us:

> **And if thy life is disturbed, if thy heart is sad, if thy body is racked with pain, it is thine bungling of the laws that are as universal as Life itself.**
> **281-27**

Life is of God, and only by seeking God can we come to know the purpose for Life. "Those He loves, He chastens and purges," the reading states, that we may produce fruit worthy of our Creator.

The instant healing did not change Jeroboam. He continued to "bungle" his opportunity to be a spiritual leader. Perhaps if he had not been healed so readily, he would have remained in awe and fear of the Lord, and the course of history would have been changed.

Although this chapter may seem like an interlude in the general context of the story, it contains important lessons, to which the Cayce readings add an additional richness. The story does not end with Jeroboam, but leaves him standing at the altar and follows the man of God on his way home.

## The Prophet

Jeroboam implored the prophet to come to his home to eat with him, and so he could give him presents. The prophet replied emphatically:

*"If you give me half your house, I will not go home with you, For so it was charged me by the word of the Lord, saying, 'Eat no bread and drink no water, nor return again by the way you came.'"* (1 Kings 13:8-9)

The prophet headed home by a different route, but his journey was interrupted by another prophet, an old man, who had heard what the man of God had done. The old prophet invited the younger man to his home for food and drink, but the prophet refused. The old prophet then responded that "an angel spoke to me by the word of the Lord" to invite him to bread and water at his home.

The young man accepted, and dined with the old prophet. Suddenly, during the meal, the old prophet stood up and cried out, "Because you have disobeyed the word of the Lord and have not kept the commandment he commanded you, your corpse shall not rest in the sepulcher of your fathers."

The two men finished their meal. On the way back to Bethel, the prophet was attacked by a lion and slain.

In the Cayce library there are several remarkable readings for individuals with great psychic abilities. Among the most interesting is one given for a six–year–old Rhode Island child. The boy was told that in a previous incarnation he had been the man of God who warned Jeroboam and in a succeeding incarnation had been the great psychic whose conversation is told in Acts 8:5-23.

Although the story of the two prophets is one of the most unusual and enigmatic in the whole Old Testament, with meanings that are not easily reached, perhaps this reading and Edgar Cayce's commentary will add new insights. The reading began:

**Yes, we have the records here of that entity now known as or called [4087].**

**As we find, there are great possibilities but there are also great problems to be met with the training and the direction for this entity through the formative years.**

**For as we find this entity has more than once been among those who were gifted with what is sometimes called second sight, or the super-**

activity of the third eye. Whenever there is the opening, then, of the lyden [Leydig] center and the kundaline forces from along the pineal, we find that there are visions of things to come, of things that are happening.

Yet in the use of these through some experiences, as we will find, the entity is in the present meeting itself. For the entity was the prophet who warned Jereboam. Read it! You will see why he is not to listen at all of those who may counsel him as to the manner in which he is to use the abilities that have been and are a portion of the entity's experience; but to trust in Him who is the way.                                      4087-1

The old prophet's ability to change the young man's mind about God's message is an indication of a larger weakness in the entity that is being met and must be learned in the present—to be true to his own inner guidance and counsel, and not to be led astray by others, no matter how well-intentioned.

Cayce's commentary to the Bible class could be included as an interpretation of the reading:

"The other man was also a prophet, or had been. How do you suppose he fooled the man of God? So often, even the best of us are fooled by flattery. The old prophet didn't say God had spoken to him, but an angel. Perhaps it was a fallen angel. At any rate, the man of God listened to what another had to say, rather than remaining true to what he had been told himself.

"No matter what someone's else's command is, or how conflicting it may be with ours, it is up to us to carry out *our* orders. This old prophet was a channel for evil, perhaps unintentionally, just as the serpent was for Eve when it said, 'Ye shall not surely die.'

"The same old prophet who led him astray became the channel for the message of doom.

"The old prophet's gesture of repentance was seeing that the man of God received a prophet's burial. He recognized his part in the man's fall from grace, and was sorry. A man of God was very rare in those days, and he wanted some congenial company—someone who could talk his language, as it were.

"This demonstrates how necessary it is for us to watch our every move, to be sure that our prompting is of the very highest source; else we, too, may lead someone astray."

The reading describes how the entity turned aside:

. . . the entity was the prophet of Judah who was sent to Jeroboam to warn him, and who brought about the withering of the hand, and also the healing of same; *yet turned aside when faced with that in which the mind said, "A more excellent way."*

The reading continues, with valuable counsel to the parents:

There are no short cuts. What God hath commanded is true. For the law of the Lord is perfect and it converteth the soul.

Here the parents have a real, real obligation. They have a real, real opportunity. So live in self that thine own lives may be an example to this entity through its formative years. So teach, not let it be given to someone else—so teach for it is thy responsibility, not the priest's, not a teacher's, not a minister's responsibility, but thine. Don't put it off. Don't neglect, or else ye will meet self again.

In the training let it first begin with self, as with the entity [4087]. Joseph he should be called. Let the training begin with that indicated in Exodus 19:5—"If thou will harken to the voice, He hath a special work, a special mission for thee—but thou must harken to the voice within, that ye present thy body as a living sacrifice, holy and acceptable unto Him, which is a reasonable service." For they who have been called, who have been ordained to be messengers have the greater responsibility; not as a saint—for there is more joy in heaven over one sinner than ninety and nine who are so-called saints, or those who are themselves satisfied with that they do.

Then study that interpreted in Romans. Ye will find it is not from somewhere else, not from out of the blue, not from overseas, not from before the altar. For thy body is indeed the temple and there he may indeed meet his Maker. There indeed may he meet himself. There indeed may he open the door of his own consciousness so that the Master may walk and talk with him.

Do not discourage, do not encourage the visions—until the first lessons are learned.

Then there will be the needs that thou, as well as others, take heed to the warnings this entity may be sent to give. 4087-1

## *The Kingdom of Judah*

If the history of the kingdom of Israel (the ten tribes) reflects the inevitable consequences of selfishness, the kingdom of Judah, while sharing many features in common, reveals the fruits of spiritualization. Both kingdoms warred with each other, knew bitter internal strife, followed false gods, and were conquered and made captives by foreign nations. But the kingdom of Israel became "lost" while the kingdom of Judah preserved its identity and fulfilled its purpose for being in the earth. Man must remember *who* he is, and complete *his* purpose—which is to be *one* with God.

If Cayce's premise is correct and the Bible is the story of man, and its history contains the pattern or process of his complete unfoldment, a meaning must be assigned to the disappearance of all but one of the twelve tribes. Ten are "lost," swept from the stage of the apocalyptic drama; and Benjamin, the only other royal tribe, is absorbed by Judah and gradually loses its separate identity. Of all the great numbers in Israel, only Judah remains, and that is reduced to a remnant. And it is those few who, at the end, complete the pattern.

God is a consuming fire, a purifier, purging the drosses in man, cleansing the soul from all that separates it from Him. Judah was purified by Fire which, according to Isaiah, was "the light of Israel," and its flame was "his Holy One." (Isaiah 10:17) "Behold," the prophet writes, "I have refined you, but not with silver; I have purified you in the furnace of affliction." (Isaiah 48:10)

Jesus, who was the crown of Judah, "learned obedience through the things he suffered." (Hebrews 5:8; 262-56, 262-82)

Judah passed through "the furnace of affliction" and came out of captivity in Babylon with "a will to mind the things of God."

Perhaps this pattern of rejection and selectivity, as once large numbers are consistently worked down and reduced to a handful, and then to one, should emphasize to man how much he has filled his body, mind, and soul with a clutter that prevents him from seeing the purity he should treasure most highly; and how much the flame of the "Holy One" has to burn away before that vision is gained.

A reading tells us:

> **. . . what is the will of the Father? That no soul should perish! And *all* will be—all *are*—tried so as by fire. The fires of nature are what? Self-indulgence, self-glorification.** 3976-23

## *The Story Begins*

During the first eighty-five years of the new kingdom, Israel was rent with revolution and regicide. During most of the same period, the kingdom of Judah experienced continued stability and growth.

Solomon's worship of "earthly forces" (900–428) had made its deteriorating effect upon the national consciousness and had begun a cycle of decline. However, two morally and spiritually responsible kings, and their prophets, working with and through a believing populace, were able to "keep the spirit alive" and reverse the downward trend.

The kingdom of Israel had nineteen kings, representing four dynasties. With the exception of Ahab, whose wife Jezebel tried to forcibly implant Baal worship as the state religion, each king practiced a form of religious toleration, which allowed a multiplicity of cults to flourish. As Israel became populated with an astonishing variety of "gods," its spiritual life became hopelessly fragmented, and deterioration became inevitable. The nation lacked a loyalty focus for the highest aspirations of its people.

But Judah possessed the temple and the tradition that it was the royal and chosen tribe of God. It had a point of unity, a spiritual focus for binding all the mental, spiritual, and emotional energies of the people. Whereas Jeroboam could not risk a spiritual revival for fear of losing his hold upon the people, Judah could not afford to be without one. Their only hope as a "chosen" people was to lose themselves in a whole-hearted search for God's will. Thus, as the children of Judah strove to fulfill the "if" clause in their covenant, we find them much more creative, imaginative, inventive, and bold in their worship, and in the application of their faith in many challenging situations, with astonishing—but predictable and promised—results.

## *The Downward Kings—Rehoboam and Abijah*

Rehoboam reigned seventeen years and followed the ways of Solomon and not David. In Rehoboam's fifth year as king, the children of Judah had drifted so far from their understanding of God that they lost His protection. Jerusalem was invaded and the royal palace was sacked. Just twenty years after its dedication, the temple was desecrated. The prophet Shemaiah informed the king and his princes that the destruction was the result of their forsaking God.

Abijah followed Rehoboam, and ruled three years. "He walked in all the sins of his father, and his heart was not perfect . . . like the heart of David." (1 Kings 15:3)

Although Rehoboam repented sufficiently after Shemaiah's rebuke to turn away "the wrath of God" (2 Chronicles 12:12), and Abijah had enough faith to march against Jeroboam when outnumbered two-to-one (2 Chronicles 13:3), neither monarch could offset Judah's rapid decline. All Solomon's pomp and glory withered instantly.

The condition was neither karmic nor predestined. One man whose "heart was perfect" could have offset the trend. Judah needed not another Solomon but a David.

One reading asked:

**Why then the turmoil in the world today?**                    **3976-24**

The answer was basic:

**They have forgotten God! Not that it is merely a karmic condition of a nation, of a people; for, know ye not that the prayer of one man saved a city?**                                              **3976-24**

The solution is unchanging, with the same answer found both in the Bible and the readings.

**(Q) What can we do to counteract such serious [future trouble]?**
**(A) Make known the trouble—*where it lies; that they who have forgotten God must right about face!***                    **3976-26**

## The Upward Kings—Asa and Jehoshaphat

**. . . though in hardships, though in trials, though in tribulation, there was found by the entity that those who seek the Lord while He may be found—and have a workable knowledge of His desires toward men— may have that as is builded-in in a material position, whether it be fame, fortune, social, or what . . .**                              **1733-2**

The downward trend was reversed by Asa, who listened to his prophets and "remembered" God.

The prophet Azariah went out and challenged Asa at the beginning of his reign with this warning:

> *"Hear me Asa, the Lord is with you for ever and ever; if you seek Him, He will be found by you; but if you forsake Him, he will forsake you."* (2 Chronicles 15:2)

Cayce spoke briefly but wisely on this counsel to the Bible class:

> "The prophet assured Asa that the Lord would be with him as long as he sought God, but if he forsook God then God would forsake him. This truth is constantly before us. As Jesus said, we are gods in the making." [John 10:34]

Rehoboam and Abijah were intent upon emulating Solomon, while Asa looked back to David. Asa "did right in the sight of the Lord, as did David his father." (1 Kings 15:11) The new king's heart "was perfect with the Lord his God all his days." (1 Kings 15:5) He inherited great problems, but was able to solve most of them by setting an example and drawing the people back to a greater reliance or dependence upon the spirit.

> *And he said to Judah, "Come, let us pray before the Lord God of our Fathers."* (2 Chronicles 14:4)

Thus we find in a world affairs readings that this is a good practice for any nation.

> **Yet, as we find, if there is the turning of every man and woman to the thought of God, then we may solve every problem. For it is not by mere thought, not by any activity other than the moving force [of God] within each entity, each body; and when more of patience, more tolerance, more thought of others is advanced and kept in the heart of the individual, this lends that power, that influence, that force for good.**
>
> **Ye are to have turmoils, ye are to have strifes . . . [How to] meet same? Only that each soul turn not to self alone and cry for strength, but that each soul *live* in such a manner that there may be the awakening to the needs, the purposes, the causes for the nation coming into existence! 3976-24**

Asa began strengthening his people by uprooting the pagan practices which had led Judah away from the spiritual ideals of David.

> . . . no government, no nation, no state, no city, no family—yes, no individual—is stronger than the weakest habit; the destructive forces that may in any way or manner at any time undermine if they are self-purposing.
>
> But if the ideas and the ideals are rather that each should be, each *will* be, each purposing to be, a channel for presenting brotherly love, kindness, patience, long–suffering, just being kind . . . we will find more and more that there will be drawn the greater dawn of *every form* of helpfulness, hopefulness, in the experience of an individual, a family, a state, a city, a nation.
>
> Not that there may not be those things that have been so well presented as in the days before the flood; they were married, given in marriage; there were the reckless, there were the saints. As in those days before the end may come, these may be ever *just* the same.
>
> But man being a creative nature, man being endowed with divinity within self, may work that to his own undoing or to his own glory in the Father, the Son and the Holy Spirit that worketh in and through those according to that purposed in their hearts.                    3976-17

Opposition to Asa's reforms must have been strong and fierce. Pagan worship had made its inroads even into the royal family. The queen mother worshiped foreign cults and must have influenced Asa's father, Abijah, in the dangerous course he followed as king. In spite of her son's reforms, Maachah continued in the pagan cult until Asa was forced to depose her. The unseating of Asa's mother (2 Chronicles 15:16) suggested to Cayce that Asa's spiritual commitment superseded the natural ties of flesh and blood—or, as Jesus said, "Who is my mother, my father or brother? He who does the will of God." (Matthew 12; Mark 3)

The episode drew out a commentary on human nature for the Bible class:

> "Why would Asa be a good king, whereas Abijah, his father [2 Chronicles 14:1], had been an evil one. Asa took advantage of the opportunity to study the law and tried to fulfill it. Abijah sought only his own personal interests.
>
> "Asa paid attention to the teachers, and those who on certain days

read the law. Others paid no attention. Human nature hasn't changed one whit since Adam! Will it have to change? What is human nature? When Jesus was in the garden and betrayed, He reminded his disciples, 'I have the power to call a legion of angels.' Certainly it was very much against human nature not to do it. He had the ability to come down from the cross, even in the hour of suffering. Certainly He could have done that, when He had the power to raise himself from the grave. But He deliberately allowed His body to die. That is a change in human nature. The natural thing would have been self-preservation. Yes, we must change human nature. We must eventually reach the place where we say, as Jesus, 'I'll pay it all now, and won't have to go through this anymore.'

"Asa went against human nature when he took his mother from the throne because of her idols."

However, as Cayce observed, Asa's "human nature" was not completely overcome.

"But he did not destroy the places for idol worship that had been established by Solomon. Practically on every hill Solomon had allowed high places to be built to the various household gods worshiped by his wives. Asa didn't remove those places. He knew he could not afford to bring on his head the condemnation from all those groups of people. This was a very human reaction. Perhaps if he had undertaken to destroy those high places, he would have received divine help just as the many other leaders had done in the past. Asa missed that opportunity of becoming a great power for good. He might have changed the whole biblical history. As it is, he receives honorable mention due to the fact that he tried to do that which was right in his own household."

Asa was put to the test in another arena. In the bold and creative traditions of the past, he went to war against "a million Ethiopians" with a handful of men. (2 Chronicles 14)

**It is, then, still the challenge to each country, to each nation—that while there is, to be sure, the natural instinct or purpose of self-preservation, it is to be less and less of self and more and more for that which was from the beginning.**                                    **3976-23**

From the beginning, the people had been promised that, if their small numbers were in harmony with God's purposes, they would never be intimidated by larger forces.

**For as has been said of old, If the Lord be with *one* he shall put ten thousand to flight.**                                                    **262-96**

**The Lord is thy strength and thy redeemer . . . And they that keep His ways need not fear. For harm of a *destructive* nature *cannot* come nigh to those that love Him.**                                    **262–98**

Or,

**For, as it has been given, "Yea, though there be only ten just men, they may save the city; they may save the nation; they may save the world."**
**3976-14**

Therefore, Asa prayed:

*Thou art our Lord, thou art the help of thy people; and when thou dost deliver a great army in the hands of a small force, then all the inhabitants of the earth shall know it is good to rely on thee.* (2 Chronicles 14:11)[28]

Asa was victorious and this army was the only one he had to face until the thirty–fifth year of his reign, when Baasha, the "wicked," came up against him. (1 Kings 15) Baasha was the third king of Israel. He had come to the throne through a military coup and by murdering Nadab, Jeroboam's son. Baasha was so wicked that he was not even buried, after ruling twenty–four years. (1 Kings 16)

Cayce's comments about Baasha indicate the spiritual climate among the ten tribes which made a dramatic contrast to the reign of Asa which, for the most part, was contemporaneous:

"The most horrible thing that could be imagined at that time (and possibly in the present) was for anyone not to have a decent burial. From the very fact that Abraham had prepared the special burying place for

---

[28]Lamsa translation.

his family, it had become a matter of principle among the Israelites. Baasha and his house had gotten so far away from the worship of the one true God that even such a material consideration as this was not to be shown. They were not to have a monument to their memory. No descendant could be proud of what they had done. They were to be outcasts, not counted worthy to be buried in consecrated ground. This shows how far they had gotten away from the idea of oneness."

Baasha's intrusion against Judah was unsuccessful. Asa entered into a league with the king of Damascus, which forced Baasha to withdraw. However, to finance this alliance, Asa took gold and silver from the temple treasury.

Although the solution was bloodless and politically successful, Asa was rebuked by his prophet Hanan for relying upon "an arm of flesh" and not keeping his heart "perfect in his worship." Hanan scorned Asa for not seeking to understand "all God's wonders" for "the Lord will fight for you." (2 Chronicles 16)

All that we can ever know of God is within us, the readings state, and our knowledge is gained only by application of the things we already know. They grow as we use them. No individual can ever realize his own potential until he learns to trust wholly in God. We all possess souls, and the soul is "the image of God." What is meant by "His Spirit will work through us?" The full implication is given in Jesus' words, "Greater things than these, ye shall do!" (John 14:12)

Asa was in a position where he could again demonstrate the power and protection of God, if he trusted God against Baasha as he had against "the million Ethiopians." Why he didn't we don't know. It's not given in the record.

Asa was in a commanding position to give an example to his people and to posterity. His faith in the past had been seasoned with prosperity, victory, and blessings. Yet Asa encountered a situation with Baasha where he failed to apply his spiritual insights. The fact that he outwardly depleted the temple treasury to finance his alliance symbolizes the inward fact that he robbed his own soul (his temple) of a vital experience he could have known through the application of his faith.

All the "good" kings of Judah, until Jesus, followed a similar pattern. In certain areas they showed remarkable faith and spiritual development, applying these truths for the benefit of their nation. Yet in other areas they fell short. When the weaknesses of their "human nature" dictated their policies, and not the strength of their souls, their efforts produced short-term and immediate benefits, but to future generations brought bitter fruit.

We are all "kings," and too often our own choices (in terms of the soul) are not best in the long development, although they may be instantly gratifying to the ego and the carnal sense.

Whenever a king made a bad decision (from the spiritual point of view) there was always a prophet to remind him.

## *Good King Jehoshaphat*

Jehoshaphat continued the spiritual and religious reforms of his father, Asa, and "walked in the first ways of David." (2 Chronicles 17:4) The "first ways," Cayce told his Bible class, refers to the spiritual ideals of David which not all David's ancestors followed. He "prayed to the Lord God" and kept all his commandments and statutes. (v. 4) His "heart was strengthened in the ways of the Lord" and he uprooted the altars and high places in Judah. (v. 6) Jehoshaphat took advantage of the peace he inherited from his father and continued strengthening his kingdom with walls, fortifications, and a large standing army. Thus peace, prosperity, and security continued in Judah.

"The Lord God established the kingdom in his hand" (v. 5) and "Jehoshaphat grew exceeding rich." (v. 12)

Jehoshaphat's prosperity, like that of Asa, is not attributed to anything other than the natural consequence of following in the ways of God. (v. 4, 5) This is the same truth which Jesus taught, when he said, "Seek *first* the kingdom of God, and all else shall be added unto you." This is fundamental and should be the basis for all national security. In a world affairs reading Cayce counseled with the same principle:

As has been indicated, if that ideal is *kept* by those who have been and are *in* power, there will be kept a general trend toward greater security, greater economic considerations of the whole, greater peace, greater harmony.

Not that there are not those influences that have gone about to make a beautiful condition an experience as dross, yet wherever selfishness is the prompting attitude there may be expected to be brought turmoils and strife.

Where the purposes are the Prince of Peace, where "*I AM* my

**brother's keeper—***I will* **do the right," these will keep and bring social security, financial security, and** *peace* **of mind to those that propagate same.** **3976-17**

Judah had a tradition and a purpose, and kings with spiritual ideals. The kingdom of Israel, which began in rebellion, lacked that binding force.

The pattern described in this reading is clearly discernible in the leaders of both kingdoms:

**. . . for without the ability to constantly hold before self the ideal as is attempted to be accomplished, man becomes as one adrift, pulled hither and yon by the various calls and cries of those who would give of this world's pleasure in fame, fortune, or what not. Let these be the outcome of a life spent in listening to the divine from within, and not the purpose of life.** **239-1**

Jehoshaphat persisted in rebuilding the spiritual life of Judah. He even enlarged upon Asa's reforms and began sending teachers and priests out to instruct the people in the laws of God—perhaps even in the disciplines of meditation, that art in which the soul's forces are awakened, for in a later battle, Judah is commanded to "stand still" and watch the salvation. (2 Chronicles 20:17)

Cayce commented to the Bible class on Jehoshaphat's new practice:

"This is the first reference we have to the sending of teachers to various parts of the land; not the first emissaries, but rather evangelists to their own people. David was the first to send missionaries. Samuel also made it a point to go from place to place to strengthen the people. He went throughout Israel from Dan to Beersheba. Now, one hundred years after David, Jehoshaphat returned to this custom."

This activity unified the people and strengthened the bonds between them, magnifying the spirit within to such an extent that "the fear of the Lord fell upon all the kingdoms of the lands that were round about Judah, so that they made no war against Jehoshaphat." (2 Chronicles 17:10)

Those who are familiar with the study of vibrations will sense the truth in Cayce's next remark.

"It seems rather remarkable that the 'fear of the Lord' fell on all the heathen kingdoms around Judah, so that they refrained from fighting Jehoshaphat. We must remember, however, that since the days of Joshua the heathen had been afraid of the chosen people whenever they went to studying the law. They had a good healthy respect for God."

Power is made manifest through groups that put their trust in God. There is a corporate nature to miracles that is not overlooked in the Cayce readings. Jesus himself could do no miracles in his home town because of the unbelief. (Matthew 13:58) Priests and prophets are powerless when the spirit is blocked by doubt and fear in those to whom they minister.

As people become allied with a common goal or ideal, the more power they are able to generate and manifest—the more God's spirit can flow through them. The promise, "Where two or three are joined together in my Name, I am in the midst of same," is God's law.

Or:

**For as the people of each nation pray, *and* then live that prayer, so must the Spirit work.** **3976-23**

## *Ahab, Jezebel, and Jehoshaphat*

Jehoshaphat followed in the ways of God, and wealth, power, and renown came as a natural consequence. As be grew "exceeding rich" he was not distracted from his spiritual ideals, but the wealth did afford temptations that led him to join forces with Ahab.

Ahab was the son of Omri, who founded Israel's fourth dynasty by slaying Zimri who had become king by murdering Elah, the son of Baasha who had come into power through his assassination of Nadab, the son of Jeroboam who "made Israel to sin."

Ahab was the son of Omri, and is introduced to the Bible story with these details: that he did evil above all those who went before him; that he wasn't content to equal the sins of Jeroboam but had to compound the evil by marrying Jezebel. (1 Kings 16:29–34)

Bible scholars disagree on Ahab, whether he was a weakling, completely dominated by Jezebel, or a strong military genius like his father who shared the same evil disposition as his wife. Cayce called him "a changeable man."

But most commentators agree upon Jezebel. She is one of the strongest female characters in ancient history, self-centered, autocratic, and determined. She has become a personification of evil. The wild license of her life became a proverb in Israel. (2 Kings 9:22) Long after she died her name remained as a by-word for all that was loathsome; in the Revelation it is given to a church in Asia Minor, suggesting a combination of fanaticism and profligacy. Jezebel used the absolute power of her royal office to eradicate the knowledge of God and replace it with the worship of Baalism, a religion which appealed chiefly to the desires of the flesh.

Ahab inherited Omri's invincible stronghold "Samaria," a strategic fortress in the highlands of Samaria, and a strong army to go with it. The Assyrians were beginning their ascendancy into history. A cruel and ruthless people, eager for conquest, they began marching beyond the borders of Mesopotamia, intent upon world conquest. Political superpowers and ambitions of global dominion seem to be an integral part of the "latter days" cycle. The emergence of Nazi Germany, equally as savage and barbaric as the Assyrians, was the backdrop against which the world affairs readings were given.

Ahab was also threatened by his traditional enemy, the king of Damascus, perched along his northern border. Edom, Moab, and the Ammonites were additional problems. And Ahab's own kingdom was torn with unrest as Jezebel tried to forcibly implant her Phoenician religion on the Israelites, and was opposed by Elijah.

For most of his reign, Ahab was an unabashed pagan, practicing pagan rites, including child-sacrifice. During the last three years of his life, he was brought to repentance through the stern pronouncements of Elijah. (1 Kings 21) Ahab was forced to realize what his own repeated violations of moral and spiritual law had worked upon him.

Sometime during these last three years, Jehoshaphat made his overtures to Ahab. Conditions were favorable for an alliance. Jehoshaphat was rich and powerful. Ahab possessed a strategic fortress. They faced a common threat. Jehoshaphat was religious, Ahab repentant.

As the class studied the Book of Kings, Cayce commented on Jehoshaphat's move toward reconciliation:

> "Although Jehoshaphat might not have been in complete sympathy with Ahab, he—being king of Judah—wanted to cooperate with the king of Israel. He knew that their strength lay in unity."

When the class reached the same episode as recorded in Chronicles, Cayce was more specific.

> "This is where Jehoshaphat started on the downward path. When he was rich with worldly goods, it went to his head—he had to join up with somebody who might increase his power."

Ahab welcomed the move and invited Jehoshaphat into an alliance against the Armenians who were threatening him.

Cayce noted that Jehoshaphat's response to Ahab reflected the same spirit as Ruth's. (Ruth 1:16)

*And he answered him, " I will go up as you do; and my people are as your people; and my horses as your horses; and we will go to war."* (2 Chronicles 18:3, 1 Kings 22:4)

Before embarking on the campaign, Jehoshaphat asked Ahab to inquire of his prophets. All four hundred promised success.

Cayce, with his insights into human nature and spiritual processes, told this story to his class:

> "Ahab had repented to such an extent that he listened to the advice of certain prophets. Evidently the four hundred he consulted were not the very best, for Jehoshaphat apparently doubted their advice—or tried to seek further. Then Ahab told him of another prophet, Micaiah. But, because this prophet never said anything good about Ahab, Ahab wouldn't listen to him. So many of us are like Ahab in that respect. We won't listen when someone tells us something unpleasant, even though it may be the truth.
>
> "Jehoshaphat insisted on consulting Micaiah; evidently be had a premonition of the things that were to be."

A messenger was sent to summon Micaiah, and bring him to court. The messenger encouraged Micaiah to speak "pleasant" words and "prophesy good." However, when asked by the king, Micaiah predicted that the children of Israel would lose their king and become "as sheep without a shepherd scattered on a mountain."

When Ahab blurted his irritation about this message, Micaiah revealed the full extent of his vision:

*" . . . I saw the Lord sitting upon his throne, and all the host of heaven standing on his right hand and on his left. And the Lord said, 'Who shall entice Ahab, king of Israel, that he may go up and be slain at Ramath-gilead?' And one said 'I will entice him after this manner', and another said, 'I will entice him after that manner.'*

*"Then came out a spirit, and stood before the Lord, and said, 'I will entice him,' and the Lord said, 'With what?'*

*"And he said, 'I will go out, and be a lying spirit in the mouth of all his prophets.' And the Lord said, 'Go out and do according to what you have said.'" (2 Chronicles 18:18-22)*

Cayce's insights continue.

"This is the complete vision of Micaiah, indicating that all four hundred prophets had been misguided and that their information was false.

"The type of spirit that Micaiah describes is common to spiritualistic séances; they're always ready to be used as messengers. Perhaps this is not an exact description of what actually happened, but Micaiah explained it in a way that the people would understand.

"Zedekiah, one of the four hundred, slapped Micaiah and sarcastically asked him, 'Which way went the spirit of the Lord from me to speak to thee?' In other words, he was making fun of Micaiah. Micaiah reminded him that he could find the answer within himself, when he sought the spirit of the Lord.

"Evidently Zedekiah had not lived what he preached. His messages from God (as he called them) were colored by Ahab's own material desires. Zedekiah was seeking favor with the king by not telling the truth as he received it. Consequently, after continuing this practice over a long period of time, he was no longer able to recognize the truth.

"Ahab became so furious with Micaiah that he put him in bonds, on bread and water, 'until I return in peace.' If he did return it would be proof the Lord had not spoken.

"We hear no more of Micaiah, but he certainly must have been released when his prophecy came true in every detail."

*How shall I entice a man to his destruction?* A rephrasing of Micaiah's vision might be answered with: "Surround him with those who tell him only what he wants to hear." The heart of man is basically selfish—and selfishness leads to destruction. If a man refuses to be corrected by those who know the truth, he inevitably walks toward his own collapse. No one has to plan it for him.

The subsequent scene shows that Ahab was not immune to Micaiah's presage. Inwardly he must have known it was the truth, yet believed he could escape his fate by a clever ruse. Edgar Cayce studied the emotions of the men—and the law!

"Ahab tried to play it safe by disguising himself, so no one would know he was king. He advised Jehoshaphat to wear his royal robes, knowing the Syrians would think Jehoshaphat was king of Israel and follow him. Jehoshaphat must have felt pretty sure about Micaiah's prophecy to take the chance he did. He was a good man. He dressed in the robes and tried to lead the Syrians away from Ahab. But no man can escape his destiny—or keep from meeting himself. A chance shot hit Ahab, one not even intended for him. This reminds us of what Jesus said, 'He that attempts to save his life shall lose it.'

"Ahab's death was the end of Israel's glory. His son, Ahaziah, was such a weakling that he soon lost his foreign possessions. Moab revolted immediately."

## *Last Words on Ahab*

Elijah's last words to Ahab foretold the complete destruction of his house. The evil acquisition of Naboth's vineyard brought forth the grim prophecy that Ahab's posterity were to be "plucked out" one by one. (1 Kings 21) Two years after Ahab's death, his son, King Ahaziah, suffered a fatal fall from the palace balcony and died in bed. Jezebel and the remaining sons were slaughtered by Jehu (the son of Nimshi), an insurgent with a divine call whom Elijah had designated. (2 Kings 9:30–37; 10:1–18)

Cayce's last words on Ahab reflect his understanding of the principles of soul-attraction and karmic involvements found in the readings, and sound a note of compassion for Ahab as well.

"After Ahab had done all the evil that could be imagined (being stirred up by Jezebel), he repented. His repentance was sincere, else God would not have stayed his punishment.

"Ahaziah, Ahab's son, became king, the one who was to reap in his day the punishment that had been delayed for Ahab. Some might get the idea Ahab's punishment was reaped entirely by his son. Ahaziah reaped only the reward for his own sins, for Ahab—being so evil, and having such an evil wife—could only have attracted a son who was completely evil, who was meeting his own sins from some other past experience.

"On the other hand, perhaps the greatest punishment Ahab could have was to see his son suffer. That is the way most of us are—we would rather suffer ourselves than see those we love hurt.

"Ahab must have suffered greatly while anticipating all the sorrow that was to come, and mental distress is often worse than physical; but, because of his change of heart, there was peace to his people during the rest of his lifetime."

## *Jehoshaphat Rebuked*

Like Asa, his father, Jehoshaphat had to bear the rebuke of his prophets. As he returned home, victorious in battle, successfully concluding the alliance with Ahab that was to end the eighty-five years of intermittent fraternal warfare between the two kingdoms and begin an era of fifty years of peaceful co-existence, Jehu (the son of Hanan) announced to Jehoshaphat that the Lord was angry with him for joining with "the ungodly" and loving those who "hated the Lord."

The king must have instinctively known his prophet was correct. Jehoshaphat did not lash out or react from the level of his "human nature." He accepted the rebuke, and took a renewed interest in the spiritual life of his kingdom. He began instructing the judges, priests, and Levites that their activities should not be for man but for the Lord. As Jehoshaphat became immersed in his social, political, and religious reforms, his awareness and confidence grew in the Spirit. When a new threat appeared from a mighty coalition of Moabites and Ammonites, he was sufficiently cleared of his human tendency for "ungodly" alliances to face the enemy alone and through prayer.

All the men of Judah assembled in the temple court, "with their little ones, their wives, their sons, and their daughters," (2 Chronicles 20:13) while Jehoshaphat led the congregation in prayer.

Commenting on this episode, Cayce reminded his students that the succeeding miracle of deliverance was corporate in nature, the natural outcome of an integrated group consciousness.

"Jehoshaphat offered a very beautiful prayer which, because of its sincerity and the sincerity of the people who also were seeking, brought immediate results. Always when everyone in a group seeks the Lord at the same time, something happens. If we could just remember that and try to act on it more often, our lives would be much more sane and fruitful."

Because the Spirit manifests through man's soul, Jehoshaphat's prayer aligned his and his people's consciousness with the soul-forces within. Fears and doubts were removed as the god-within was attuned to the God-without. The vibrations were raised to such a high level when Jehoshaphat concluded his prayer, asking that "God show himself," that a mighty spirit rose up in Hazaiel, a priest, who spoke with strength and power, saying, "Be not afraid, the battle is not yours, but God's." (2 Chronicles 20:15)

Hazaiel instructed Judah to go to the battlefield and "stand still," which indicates they were to take time to quiet their fears, calm the mind, and attune to the God-force and "wait for the salvation of the Lord."

When the people first demanded a monarchy, Samuel reminded them that the king would always be an expression of the spirit of the people— if they did evil, the king would be evil. If they wanted to do good, the king would follow suit. If he didn't, they had the right to change him.

The presence of a believing populace, "husbands, wives, and children" praying with the king indicates why Asa and Jehoshaphat were "good" kings. The collective faith and prayers of a seeking people must have had a strong, unseen influence on both Asa and Jehoshaphat, keeping them on the path in spite of their human failings.

The law is eternally valid. Cayce saw it in action in his day, as this reading describes:

**What, think ye, has caused or did cause that meeting of the democratic countries, or the democracies and the totalitarian states? [Treaty of Versailles, June 1919?] Was it because of the wisdom of the men that met, or that either of the four there had their own way? Rather was it not the prayers of the mothers and the fathers of each nation represented there, that there might not be that destruction of human life which would be the natural outcome of open conflict?**

**3976-23, June 13, 1939**

## *One Besetting Sin*

However immersed Jehoshaphat became in the social, political, and religious life of his country, he could not cure himself of his one besetting sin—alliances with "the ungodly." After Ahab's death, Jehoshaphat initiated a maritime pact with Ahaziah, Ahab's successor, and was soundly condemned by the prophet Eliezer. (2 Chronicles 20:35–37) Ahaziah's reign was brief, lasting only two years. He was succeeded by his brother Joram. When Joram came into power, he asked for Jehoshaphat's help against the king of Moab. Although Jehoshaphat had been rebuked for his alliances with Ahab and Ahaziah, he accepted Joram's request and set out on an expedition that would have cost him his life had it not been for Elisha. (2 Kings 3)

After a seven-day march in the wilderness, the expedition was ready to perish for lack of water. Joram, troubled by his conscience, felt the situation was requiting all for their sins. The godly Jehoshaphat calmly asked that a prophet be found who could give guidance. Elisha was nearby and volunteered. Elisha said he would not give aid to the king of Israel, but Jehoshaphat was worth saving. Elisha called for a minstrel, and while he played, the prophet entered into deep meditation and envisioned an unusual strategy which proved successful.

Although there was a materialistic aspect to Jehoshaphat's alliances, Cayce saw spiritual overtones as well. In speaking of Jehoshaphat's last battle, he commented:

> "When Joram came into power, the first thing he did was take a census, to see how many fighting men he had. Then be besought Jehoshaphat to join forces with him as he had done for Ahab. Jehoshaphat's answer again reminds us of Ruth. That's why he was called the great Jehoshaphat. He tried to unite the divided kingdoms, so they would again be as one. However, the kings of Israel did not have the same ideal. They wanted unity for material reasons alone. They did not consider the spiritual advantages or God's original purpose."

Cayce summarized the life of this great man with a few brief comments and lessons:

> "Jehoshaphat was a good man; he made peace with Ahab, and later with Ahaziah, and did everything that was right; except he, too, failed to

take away the offerings in the high places. No doubt this had become an impossibility as far as any one king is concerned. Every now and then we have this statement to remind us that no matter how good the king was, '... nevertheless the high places were not taken away.' One especially good thing Jehoshaphat did was to get rid of the remnant of the Sodomites, which his father Asa had failed to do.

"It seems that Jehoshaphat's only besetting sin was evil associations. He did all right as long as be sought God and stayed away from evil companions. But, immediately when he became associated with those who did wickedly, he was drawn from the correct path. Many of us are like that today. It's easy to be good when it is all smooth sailing; when everyone agrees and swims along with us. But when we come up against an obstacle such as people of prominence who disagree with us, we feel weak and unstable. We don't stick to what we believe, regardless."

# Elijah and Elisha

## Ahab, Jezebel, and Elijah

*Introductory* details are given in the Bible about Ahab and Jezebel. Ahab did evil above all those before him, built altars to Baal, served idols, added to his abominations by child-sacrifice, and provoked the Lord to more anger than any of his predecessors. (1 Kings 16:30–34)

Jezebel came from a prominent family. She was a Phoenician princess, the daughter of Ethbaal, king of the Zidonians. But Elijah appears in the story without warning or introduction. The Bible only notes where he came from—Tishbeh, the location of which is uncertain.

Elijah is the archetype of the Hebrew prophet, strong, courageous, unable to compromise with sin, terrible in his denunciations. He appears in Israel when the nation has passed the point where self-preservation is possible. Abijah, the prophet who anointed Jeroboam, had the first grim insight into Israel's national destiny. He predicted that the new kingdom would be "uprooted and scattered" and be no more. (1 Kings 4)

The spiritual deterioration which had taken place under Solomon, coupled with Jeroboam's example, proved too powerful an influence for the ten tribes to overcome. None of Israel's kings had the moral, mental, or spiritual development to offset the national trend that was set, apparently, in Jeroboam's lifetime.

The kingdom was doomed because of the path it chose to follow, and

Ahab and Jezebel were a natural part of the fabric. Although Jezebel forced Baalism on the people, it had been a popular religion even before her lifetime. The sensuous rites of a fertility cult were forever distracting the Israelites. But the Spirit had not given up. Elijah was called to be the counterthrust to Jezebel, putting before a backsliding and wayward people the knowledge and power of the One God.

## *Edgar Cayce on Elijah*

Edgar Cayce's acceptance of reincarnation enabled him to be an able interpreter of the law of karma, or cause and effect. His psychic sensitivities brought deep spiritual insights into all phases of life, and he took this understanding to his study of the Bible. His approach in the Bible class was almost deceptively casual and very low-keyed. His pragmatic and "homespun" delivery shows the influence of the rural Kentucky farmland where he was born and raised, but the spiritual laws which undergird each lesson are universal and eternal, reflecting his own highly perceptive and developed sensitivity.

When he discussed Elijah and his bitter conflict with Jezebel, he did not highlight the dramatic elements of the story, or stress the struggle between good and evil, as so many commentators have been led to discuss and expound upon so profoundly and so well. His lectures reflect rather his concern that the Bible study be rooted in the experiences of everyday life. Thus he chose as his lesson the weaknesses of Elijah and his fears, and how the Lord was trying to make him strong, something the students knew was happening in their lives too.

Elijah shows great strength and unswerving conviction when dealing with Ahab or fighting against Baalism. He first appears in the Bible directed by God's word to forecast to Ahab the coming of a drought in Israel. The Lord then instructs Elijah where to go for the duration of the drought, where he remains in hiding for three years, coming out only when it is time to announce the end of the plague.

Elijah summoned Ahab to gather together all the people of Israel and all the prophets of Baal to the top of Mt. Carmel for a test. He challenged the prophets of Baal to prove their god was superior to Jehovah, but not before he rebuked the Israelites for "limping with two different opinions."

He denounced the people for forsaking God and chastised them with his boast:

*"I, even I only, remain a prophet of the Lord."* (1 Kings 18:22)

Elijah challenged the priests of Baal to prepare a ritual sacrifice, a burnt offering, but with no fire. Elijah would do the same, and each would call upon their god to answer with fire. The god who answered would be the true God.

The priests of Baal prepared the altar and prayed and called to Baal all day, with no response. By evening they had begun to cut and slash themselves with knives, hoping to get Baal's attention with their pain and mortification. All their efforts were futile and Elijah truly enjoyed their frustration.

When Elijah prepared his altar in the evening, be had the altar, the offering, and the wood soaked three times with water. He ordered a trench dug around the altar and filled with water. Then he called to Jehovah, who answered him with a great fire that consumed the altar, the offering, the wood, and even "licked up" the water in the trench.

The people were convinced with this demonstration. Elijah ordered the prophets of Baal seized. Not one of the four hundred escaped. They were taken to the brook Kishon and killed.

Apparently this was all done in the presence of a powerless Ahab. The test on Mt. Carmel coincided with the end of the drought. Elijah said to Ahab, *"Go . . . for there is the rushing sound of rain . . . Mount your horse, and get down before the rain stops you."* (1 Kings 18:41, 44)

Up to this point we have an inspiring and unparalleled story of one man's faith, courage, and unswerving loyalty and trust in his God. No hint of fear or weakness is present.

Ahab rode swiftly to Jezreel and arrived ahead of the winds and the black clouds which brought a driving rain, and reported immediately to Jezebel. When she heard of the happenings on Mt. Carmel and the loss of her priests, she dispatched a messenger to Elijah with a proclamation that she would have his life "about this time tomorrow."

Elijah's reaction has fascinated students of the Bible ever since:

*And Elijah was afraid, and he arose and fled for his life.* (1 Kings 19:3)

## A Woman's Wrath

He fled for one day with his disciples, and then, apparently to be able to travel faster, he left them behind and continued for another day alone.

What was he running from? It wasn't death he feared, for that night he prayed, "Lord, take away my life." He was afraid of Jezebel!

"Elijah was a prophet who could stand up to four hundred priests," Cayce told the class, "but he couldn't face the wrath of a woman." He escaped Jezebel's revenge, but he eventually had to face that woman again, Cayce suggested, and met that fear within himself in a later incarnation as John the Baptist!

It is not surprising that Cayce saw in the relationship between Elijah and Jezebel a karmic pattern which he assumed was something brought over from previous incarnations. His assumption that Elijah later incarnated as John the Baptist was based upon a biblical prophecy, support from a reading, and the testimony of Jesus. This enabled Cayce to see the karmic entanglement continued in a New Testament setting. He told his class:

> "In the last chapter of Malachi we are told, 'Behold, I will send you Elijah the prophet before the coming of the great and dreadful day of the Lord.' (Malachi 4:5) In the 11th of Matthew we have Christ's testimony concerning John, 'For this is he of whom it is written, Behold I will send my messenger to prepare the way before thee! . . . and if ye will receive it, he [John] is Elijah, who was to come.'"

The connection between Elijah and John is stated in reading 262–87 and repeated in 3054–4, and drawn most clearly in 1158–6:

**Did not John come as the voice of one crying in the wilderness and in the spirit of Elijah? Yet he *was* Elijah.                                    1158-6**

The readings instruct us that what are normally considered hardships, and difficult problems in life, in reality give us chances to overcome our limitations and present opportunities for soul growth. If Elijah was subject to fear of women, or a woman, Jezebel offered him the greatest "opportunity" for overcoming it. His devotion to God should have supplied the strength to surmount his weakness. But in John we find the same fault:

**For even in Elijah or John we find the faltering, the doubting. We find no faltering, no doubting, no putting aside of the purpose in the Master Jesus.                                                                        3054-4**

Harmony with God's spirit, which is the universal spirit of love, patience, and mercy, leads to grace, and in grace all karma is erased. Self-will, rather than God's will, is the source of all our hardships.

The absence of God's command, ordering Elijah to slay Jezebel's prophets, impressed Cayce. This intimated to the seer that Elijah may have been acting on his own initiative, rather than performing God's will, thus building a negative karmic pattern. Cayce asked his class:

> "Was Elijah commanded to kill the prophets of Baal? It is not indicated that he was, but he did. Evidently a personal animosity was involved, which Elijah had to meet at a future date—perhaps as John the Baptist."

Elijah's mockery and great delight over the frustration and failure of the prophets of Baal are other indications suggesting deep-seated personal and emotional drives which may have colored and misguided his directions from high spiritual life.

Cayce assumed Herodias, the wife of Herod, was a later incarnation of Jezebel. When she ordered the beheading of John, she obtained her revenge and the karmic wheel completed a full cycle. Cayce philosophized to the class:

> "Jezebel's threat was to take Elijah's life on the morrow. She intended just that, but sometimes it takes us several hundred years to realize our tomorrows.
>
> "Eventually Jezebel had Elijah's head cut off, as she promised she would."

## Another Karmic Lesson (1 Kings 2)

The final episode in Elijah's struggle with members of Ahab's family drew additional commentary by Cayce on the possible basis of a karma sown by Elijah which was reaped by John.

When Ahaziah, Ahab's son and successor, fell from his balcony and was severely injured, he sent messengers to the priests of Baal for a remedy. The messengers were turned back by Elijah who told them to instruct the king that he would never rise from his bed, but would die in it. The messengers returned and reported to Ahaziah. Ahaziah recognized Elijah from their description and sent them out with orders to bring the prophet to him.

When the messengers arrived with the summons, Elijah's response was unprecedented. He did one thing at which he excelled—called down fire! and the messengers were consumed.

Cayce saw the effects of this coming back on John.

"It is hard to understand Elijah's actions with the messengers of Ahaziah. It appears as if he was afraid of going to Ahaziah and was using his power wrongly when he called down fire to consume those men. We can't conceive of this being God's way. Of course we have no way of knowing Ahaziah's purpose in sending for Elijah. He may have wanted to put Elijah to death. Or Ahaziah may have intended to beseech the Lord, through Elijah, to give him another chance. Anyway, we can be sure Elijah had to meet his acts. The time came when, as John the Baptist, he was put to death and no one, including Jesus, saved him from it. Jesus could have, but John was meeting himself. From our previous studies, we have learned that the meeting of self sometimes requires death itself.

"In other words, it was necessary for John to die this way in order for him to have the awakening he needed. Remember, Jesus said that the least in the kingdom was greater than John, because John was not aware of his own purpose even though he had prophesied about the purpose of others.

"John was expecting Jesus, whom he had proclaimed as the Savior, to save him from physical death. But it was through his death that John met and overcame his own shortcomings. That, for John, was his cross—at that particular period; just as we each today have our individual crosses to bear. No one can save us from them, but if we try to understand WHY we have them, and seek the aid of the Christ, they become easier to bear."

The basis for this interpretation is found in 3976–27, a world affairs reading:

. . . even as He gave to that one who had announced by the authority of the prophets, "Behold the Lamb of God that taketh away the sins of the world," who comes to bring peace into the hearts of those who seek to do righteousness in the earth. And yet because he had fallen into that answering as of self to fears within, he began to doubt—as apparently no measure was being attempted, outwardly at least, to relieve him of his bonds; and he asked, "Art thou He that was to come, or shall we look for another?" The Master's answer is the judgment of today, even as then. There was not the Yes or No answer, but "Go tell John that the sick are healed, the poor have the gospel preached, the lame walk, the blind see." 3976-27

The episode with Ahaziah's messengers is the last recorded act in Elijah's life, but not his final appearance in Scripture. Malachi prophesied his return as John the Baptist. But even after John's beheading, Elijah reappeared with Moses on the mount of transfiguration (Matthew 7:3) to discuss with Jesus how holy powers "might be entrusted into the keeping of men and women everywhere." (1809-1) The presence of Elijah on the mount of transfiguration was a message in itself to the onlookers, indicating "that they, too, would become as messengers to a waiting world." (262-87)[29]

## The Still Small Voice

*And behold, the Lord passed by, and a great and strong wind rent the mountains and broke in pieces the rocks before the Lord; but the Lord was not in the wind; and after the wind an earthquake; but the Lord was not in the earthquake:*

*And after the earthquake a fire; but the Lord was not in the fire; and after the fire a still small voice.*

*And when Elijah heard it, he wrapped his face in his mantle and went and stood at the entrance of the cave.* (1 Kings 19:11, 12)

Elijah's flight to escape Jezebel lasted forty days and forty nights and took him to Mt. Sinai, the holy mount where Moses talked to God. Here, in the recesses of a cave, Elijah confessed his fears to God: "They seek my life, to take it away."

Meditation, dreams, and prayer are the means by which man attunes

---

[29]Moses' part on the mount of transfiguration was to talk with Jesus about "what manner of means there would be for the bringing of the awareness and consciousness into the hearts and minds and lives of the children of men" and "what the death, the passing on the cross might mean." (1809-1) Moses' presence meant to those apostles who were present "a definite undertaking which set them apart from other peoples." (262-87)

his consciousness to God and gets to be on speaking terms with his own soul. While meditating in his cave, Elijah had the deeply moving vision about the forces of nature and the still small voice, a spiritual experience which must have changed the course of his life.

Spiritual experiences, as universal and elemental as Elijah's, move on many different levels, and, to the person who receives them, bring new insight and vision into all aspects of life. In other words, Elijah was not only being confirmed in the truth about God, but was also being told something about himself. Dreams and visions from the divine come, as the readings tell us, not only for inspiration and revelation, but for correction and guidance.

No doubt Elijah was seeing himself in this experience. His demonstration on Mt. Carmel and his action against Ahaziah's messengers are revealing, and indicate Elijah set great store in his own psychic abilities. He had the power to perform "great wonders" and to call down fire.

In the Revelation, the disciple of love, John, writes that it is within the power of the beast (or carnal man) "to perform great wonders" to such an extent as to even "make fire come down from heaven on earth," which beguiles men and causes them "to make an image to the beast." (Revelation 13:13)

The "beast" is the symbol for the lower nature of man, the unruly emotions, and might even include psychic power that is not spiritually directed. Cayce suggested, as we have seen, that Elijah may not have been entirely spirit-led in his actions against the priests of Baal, but acting through personal animosities. Those who can perform "great wonders" inevitably set the examples which influence others in forming their concepts of God. If the example set indicates that God is the phenomenon rather than spirit, or consents to the wholesale murder of unbelievers, this makes for an "image to the wild beast," rather than the still, small voice.

Elijah must have gone deep into the soul to have the experience he did. Perhaps his revelation brought to his mind that he was closer to the true spirit of Jehovah when he gently filled the widow's cruse and quietly restored her son (1 Kings 17:9-24) than when he challenged the priests of Baal or called down fire on Ahaziah's messengers.

We find this interpretation in the readings:

**Think not, even as He, to do some great deed that would make the welkin ring throughout the earth. Rather *know* it is the little line, the**

little precept, the little lesson given into the lives and experiences that brings the awareness into the hearts and souls of men and women; that consciousness of the *nearness* in the still small voice within.

For as proclaimed of old, it is not in the thunder or lightning, it is not in the storm, it is not in the loudness—but the still small voice within!

So as ye write, so as ye talk, so as ye love—let it be in meekness of spirit, in *purposefulness* of service, in an activity and an eye single to the *glory* of the Father through those that are His children.     1472-3

The same principle is restated in this reading:

For know, it is not the great deeds one performs that make for the building of hope in the hearts and minds of those you meet, nor the mere satisfaction of a self-aggrandizing experience; but it is that which *creates* hope—that which makes for the expression of patience, long-suffering, grace, mercy and truth! *These* are the things that build into the hearts of men, *everywhere*, harmony and peace and hope!     1574-1

Elijah learned a great lesson. The truth he encountered must have upset and challenged some of his set opinions. God is the spirit of truth, while men are hedged in, prejudiced, and blinded by their emotions. Only those who seek, through meditation, to attune the conscious mind to the God-within through periods of silence, like Elijah, can overcome the limitations of the self and gain the greater understanding of their souls.

Cayce's presentation to the Bible class rested with this lesson:

"The elements obeyed Jesus. They were used by Him; yet these are the things of which man is most fearful. However, we are reminded again and again that it is the still, small voice that can do the most, not only in our physical selves but in the effect we may have, or may make, upon the lives of others, according to the purpose of those who stop and listen.

"Our relationship to God is bound to be individual. It becomes a personal thing for us to know God, and we can only know Him by answering the still, small voice within."

## The School of the Prophets

Those who studied the Cayce readings were well acquainted with the religious sect in Judaism called the "Essenes" long before the discovery of the Dead Sea Scrolls. Several decades before the discovery at Qumran, the Life readings described in great detail the practice, beliefs, purposes, and many of the personalities who were involved in this prophetic and mystical cult to which Joseph, Jesus, and Mary belonged.

Describing the Essenes at the time of Jesus, one reading states, " . . . their purpose was of the first foundations of the prophets as established, or as understood from the school of prophets, by Elijah." (254–109)

The site of the school of prophets, as well as the later Essene center, was on Mt. Carmel.

> . . . in Carmel—the original place where the school of prophets was established during Elijah's time.          5749-8

This reading indicates by inference that the occult was studied by the prophets:

> . . . these were called then Essenes; and those that were students of what ye would call astrology, numerology, phrenology, and those phases of that study of the return of individuals—or [re-]incarnation . . . [and] that certain periods were a cycle . . .    5749-8

Both the Essenes and the School of Prophets grew from the same roots.

> . . . the group we refer to here as the Essenes, which was the outgrowth of the periods of preparations from the teachings by Melchizedek, as propagated by Elijah, and Elisha and Samuel. These were set aside for preserving themselves in a direct line of choice for the offering of themselves as channels through which there might come the new or the divine origin, see?          254-109

This reading, although describing an incarnation at the time of Jesus, states specifically what Elijah taught, and infers what his approach may have been:

> The entity was closely associated with the priests who were active in the Carmelian area, where there had been the early teachings established

years ago by Elijah, Elisha, Samuel; that taught the mysteries of man and his relationships to those forces as might manifest from within and without.

The entity then was among the sages who chose the young that were to be set apart as channels through which that blessing might come to the world [the Divine Birth] . . .

*These brought at times periods when the entity needed long periods of meditation, and the setting aside of activities necessary to induce the submerging of the physical to the spiritual in its relationships to materialization.* [Italics added]          2520-1

This extract, also from the New Testament period, offers additional insight into the original practice of the school of prophets:

. . . the Essenes . . . cherished not merely the conditions that had come as word of mouth but had kept the records of the periods when individuals had been visited with the supernatural or out of the ordinary experiences; whether in dreams, visions, voices, or what not that had been and were felt by these students of the customs, of the law, of the activities throughout the experiences of this peculiar people—the promises and the many ways these had been interpreted by those to whom the preservation of same had been committed.          1472-3

It is not certain when Elijah established the school of prophets. Until his experience with the still, small voice on Carmel, he believed, and had boldly asserted before God and his fellow man, that he was the last remaining, and only, true prophet in Israel. (1 Kings 18:22; 19:10, 14) Certainly the school couldn't have been established before this.

The readings describe the earmarks of a genuine spiritual experience:

Seek experiences not as experiences alone but as purposefulness. For what be the profit to thyself, to thy neighbor, if experiences alone of such natures rack thy body—owing to its high vibration—without being able to make thee . . . a better neighbor, a better individual in every manner? These be the fruits, that it makes thee kinder, gentler, stronger in body, in mind, in purpose to be a channel through which the love of God . . . may be manifested in the world. Not as a vision, an experience alone.          281-27

A spiritual experience is necessarily humbling to the carnal ego, but strengthening to the soul. Although Elijah testified that he was the last and only prophet in Israel, he learned through the still, small voice that there were seven thousand others in Israel who "had not bowed to Baal." (1 Kings 19) Elijah was not alone.

The experience on the mountain altered and broadened Elijah's vision, renewed his courage, calmed his fears, and added a new dimension to his ministry. It would not be the only time a vision has changed the course of a great man's life. Perhaps by becoming aware of the other seven thousand "good men" in Israel he was inspired to seek out the faithful and begin the school of prophets.

Although Elijah saw the wind, the earthquake, and the fire, it wasn't until he reached the still center of the soul that he received guidance. He was told to go down from the mountain and back into the world and anoint Hazael as king over the Syrians, to raise up Jehu to replace Ahab, and to seek out Elisha and accept him as his student and successor to his prophetic office.

Although there were always prophets in Israel—Abraham himself is given the title—from this time on they begin to rise like a fresh current of living water in a polluted stream: Elisha, Isaiah, Joel, Jeremiah, Hoshea, Amos, and others less known, and some completely anonymous.

Although the presence of so many gifted seers can be explained as a purely spontaneous happening born out of the stress and trauma of a national decline, it is interesting to consider that this waxing prophetic impulse was channeled and directed through a school headed by Elijah.

A Georgia woman was told that in a previous incarnation she had been "the daughter of that prophet" and was exposed to all the activities of the period.

**Before that the entity was in the Holy Land among those of the household of the prophet during the period of Ahab's and Jezebel's rule in the land.**

**The entity then was the daughter of that prophet,[30] in the name Adah. The entity knew trials, the entity knew the wrath of those**

---

[30]Edgar Cayce, in his correspondence, expressed the opinion that the "prophet" referred to in this reading was Obadiah (see 1 Kings 18:3).

surrounding the entity and those periods of turmoils and wickedness among those in high places. Yet the entity kept the faith through the period.

The entity was acquainted with the activities of Jehu and the entity's sister.

The entity kept the faith and saw the fulfilling of the prophet's words about Ahab, Jezebel, and those people of that day.

Hence the prophecies as well as the promises throughout the Book have meant and do mean much to the entity.          4065-1

## Edgar Cayce on Elisha

And it came to pass when the Lord was about to take Elijah up to heaven by a whirlwind . . . Elijah said to Elisha, Ask what I shall do for you before I am taken away from you. And Elisha said, Let a double portion of your spirit be upon me. (2 Kings 2:9)

Elisha was able to receive the boon because he fulfilled the conditions which Elijah put about it.

*And he said, "You have asked too much; nevertheless, if you see me when I am taken from you, it shall be so to you; but if not, it shall not be so."* (2 Kings 2:10)

Then came the test:

*And it came to pass, as they still went on and talked, behold, there appeared a chariot of fire and horses of fire, and separated the two; and Elijah went up by a whirlwind into heaven.*

*And Elisha saw it and he cried, "My father, my father, the chariot of Israel and the horsemen thereof." And he saw him no more.* (2 Kings 2:11, 12)

Was this the death of Elijah? his translation? (as with Enoch, Genesis 5:24) or a transfiguration, like Jesus' on the mount? (Matthew 7:2, Mark 9:2) Whichever it was, it marked an end to the dramatic ministry of Elijah and the beginning of Elisha's.

Cayce drew a few lessons from the prelude to the ascension (2 Kings 2:1-8), and offered his reasons why as a demonstration of the spiritual forces in man, it could be considered the "high point" in the Old Testament. He told his class:

> "We have a lesson in perseverance in Elisha. He would not give up. Evidently the school of prophets had predicted that Elijah would ascend, and fifty sons of prophets—that is, students, the same as Elisha—followed Elijah at a distance, hoping to see the ascension when it took place. Elisha didn't mingle with them, but stuck close to Elijah, refusing to be left behind. It was necessary that he be consistent and persistent.
>
> "Here, possibly, is the high point in the Old Testament. Together these two individuals were capable of generating the most powerful force that had ever yet been manifested in the flesh."

The chariot arose, and Elijah threw down his mantle. When Elisha picked up the mantle and put it on his shoulders, he received the "double portion." Thus began the ministry of the man whose miracles are second only to Jesus'.

## *Elisha*

In a remarkable reading for a four-year-old child some astounding information was given. Three outstanding incarnations were described. If the reading is correct, the entity who had been Noah, or " . . . that one to whom was entrusted man's advent into the world," was also the same who later incarnated as Elisha. The influences of that prophetic life were described for the parents:

> . . . the entity was that one upon whom the mantle of Elijah fell—who in his material activity performed more unusual acts, or miracles, that are only comparable with the Master himself.
>
> The entity then as Elisha brought into the experience much that was of the unusual in expression.
>
> So in the present, in the experiences of this entity, there may be expected just as unusual expression; as those coming to the entity to receive the blessings from the handkerchief, the photograph even, or those things that the entity may touch or bless . . .
>
> Here we may see a demonstration, an illustration of that which has been indicated or intimated through these channels, as of a *perfect* channel being formed for the advent of an entity-soul that would bring

blessings to all—*if* there is the directing of the developing years . . .
Do not allow the entity, in the first ten to twelve years, to get away from the spiritual truths in the Old and the New Testaments; not as an ism, not as a cult. For it will be easy for a cult, an ism, to be formed about the entity and its prognostications. But rather let it be as one glorifying the truths that are promised in the thirtieth of Deuteronomy, and in the fourteenth, fifteenth, sixteenth, and seventeenth chapters of John. These impress. Accredit the entity's abilities to these sources. When there are questions as to the source from which the entity obtains its information, agree that it comes from the infinite. For these are the developments. 2547-1

Cayce's lessons to the Bible class reveal a great admiration for the prophet.

"No other character in all the Bible, other than Jesus, performed so many miracles as Elisha, or was in the midst of so many unusual happenings. Practically every type of miracle we can imagine was performed by Elisha. We don't credit this to any special thing in Elisha save as a 'double portion' of Elijah's spirit, or because Elijah's mantle fell on his shoulders.

"Except where he cursed the children and they were eaten up by the bears, he was one of the most consistent of all prophets in the Old Testament. He never, never refused help to anyone, and never asked for or accepted anything for himself. If it hadn't been for that one thing with the children, it seems as if he would have been perfect."

The incident with the children occurred shortly after Elisha received his "double portion" of spirit, and is recorded in 2 Kings 2.

. . . *and as he was going up along the way, there came forth little boys out of the city and mocked him, saying "Go up, you bald head, go up, you bald head."*
*And he turned back and saw them and cursed them in the name of the Lord. And there came forth two she-bears out of the forest, and tore forty-two of the boys.* (2 Kings 2:23-24)

Just as the readings enabled Cayce to see the karmic pattern from Elijah to John, the readings also enabled him to look back upon a cause and effect relationship between Elisha and Noah. He told the Bible class:

"Remember, Elisha was a reincarnation of Noah, as indicated in the readings. He made good all the way. The only activity that seems uncalled for was the cursing of the little children who made fun of his bald head. How quickly human nature reacts! These incidents give us a glimpse of the human nature of these individuals and shows how much God has to overlook. If we realize this, it should be easier to overlook faults in others and not condemn them, thus glorifying God the more.

"We recall that Noah cursed his own grandson, apparently for just such a minor offense. The human nature in the individual hadn't changed one iota from the time of Noah. We can easily imagine that these children might have been reminders of that other day when he had warned the people about going into the ark and they made fun of him. Sometimes, no matter how good we try to be, we lose ourselves for the moment and in anger undo what it has taken us centuries to build. That is the human trait we must overcome.

"It is a consolation that such holy men, in direct contact with God, fell down occasionally. No wonder we fall by the wayside. That's the price we pay by being in the flesh."

## Misuse of Power

The readings always counseled individuals seeking power—whether it was psychic, spiritual, economic, social, political, or whatever—to know their ideals and be sure of their purpose. When Elijah left in the whirlwind, he didn't "leave" his spirit, but gave Elisha a technique, or tool, to open up his own spiritual centers. When Jesus ascended, he didn't take his spirit with him, but said, "My spirit I leave with you." The spirit is everywhere. It does not come and go. Elijah's mantle was the material means which enabled Elisha, through his faith, to attune to his soul's forces. Jesus gave us His promise that through faith in His word we would be able to raise our consciousness to the divine within and do "greater works." (John 14:12)

Perhaps when Elisha received his "double portion" he was not well-grounded in his responsibility for its constructive uses. Being so newly (and suddenly) invested with such a large amount of psychic energy, when the children laughed, he reacted with his human nature and abused his gift.

A reference to Elisha, and a philosophy about power, is developed in this reading for a lawyer, who was seeking to develop his psychic abilities to gain an advantage in the stock market:

Look at those . . . money powers of the earth. And look at what their bodies, minds, and souls are today! Are ye willing, then, to pay such a price?

Are ye willing that such shall be thine *own* temptation? that ye are to build within thine experience that which will give thee, in thine own personal self, the right to say Yea and Nay to thy brother in want here and there?

Are ye willing to take, rather, that of knowledge—as Elisha, thine *own* helpmeet oft—and . . . use same in such a manner as that the lowliest, yea those in authority, yea thy fellow man that ye meet day by day will call thee blessed?

Or is it *power* alone ye seek?

As to the manners then—these ye *must* determine within thine *own* consciousness; and these ye would weigh well with thy purposes through this material experience.

For know, ye *are* constantly meeting thine *own* self! Not that an individual is not to be endowed with purposes, desires, and the like in relationship to his fellow man—or to conditions of every nature whether they be social, economic, political, or what not. But for what purpose are these positions chosen by thyself?

Are ye to keep well-balanced? Are ye to keep the influences and the activities in those directions in which ye may know ever that thy purpose is that the glory of the Father-God is to be daily manifested in thy dealings with thy fellow man?

Or are ye to become a lord, a god within thine own right; that ye may say to this one, "Go," or to this one, "Stay," and he doeth it? 826-9

# 21

# Bad News for Judah

## *Jehoram, Ahaziah, and Athaliah*

*Jehoshaphat* cemented the alliance between Judah and Israel through the marriage of his son, Jehoram, to Athaliah, Ahab's daughter. Although Jehoshaphat did much that was "right" in the sight of God, he was soundly rebuked by the prophets for his besetting weakness for "ungodly" alliances. His alliance with Israel may have been brilliant politically, but it eventually resulted in Jezebel's daughter sitting on David's throne, with nearly fatal consequences for the Davidic line.

Jehoram was as dominated by his wife as Ahab had been by her mother. When Jehoram became king, he became an advocate of Baalism and a persecutor of those who opposed him. His first act was to order the murder of his six brothers.

The sixty years of peace and security which Judah enjoyed, through the moral and spiritual leadership of Asa and Jehoshaphat, soon dissolved as Jehoram began forsaking and forgetting God. Edom revolted and the Philistines and Arabians invaded the country. Jehoram lost all his sons in the fighting, except one. After an eight-year reign, Jehoram died of a horrible disease—"his bowels fell out." (2 Chronicles 21:19)

Ahaziah, the surviving son, succeeded his father and ruled for one year until he was slain by Jehu, who had been designated by Elijah, and anointed by Elisha, to purge the evils of the house of Ahab from the land.

Jehu extinguished the house of Ahab from Israel and began a new dynasty. And Athaliah was intent upon establishing her dynasty in Jerusalem.

With Ahaziah's death, Athaliah became the queen of Judah, and her first act was to order the murder of all her sons and grandsons.

The prophets were vindicated who had rebuked Jehoshaphat. The dangerous consequences of his alliances had come full cycle. But, because God is a universal consciousness, and a part of His mind is in every soul, Athaliah's plans were thwarted. Jehoshabeath, the daughter of Jehoram, was inspired to move swiftly and courageously. She concealed one of Amaziah's young sons, Joash, and kept him hidden for six years in her bed chambers while Athaliah reigned. After six years, Joash was taken out of hiding and crowned in the temple by Jehoiadah, the high priest and husband of Jehoshabeath. Athaliah was overthrown and the Davidic dynasty reinstated.

## *Satan Bound, Satan Loosened*

In Revelation 20, Satan is cast into a great pit and chained for a thousand years, and then loosened "for a season." This prophecy, the readings tell us, is symbolic of cycles which come in man's experience. The anti-Christ spoken of by John in the Revelation is nothing other than the spirit of hate, which breeds strife, selfishness, egoism, contention, and other fruits which can take possession of individuals, groups, and masses.

**The devil, or "Satan," is the spirit in man which is in rebellion against God's laws of love, joy, obedience, kindness, and long-suffering. This devil has no strength except through man's weakness.** **281-16**

Many times was "Satan bound" in the Old Testament. When the Israelites were strong in their search for God and had a will to live according to God's laws, the devil was powerless. Under Joshua, the people suppressed their rebellious spirit and worked long and hard for constructive ends. Under the moral and spiritual leadership of Ahaz and Jehoshaphat, the "devil" was kept in chains for sixty years, only to be let loose through Jehoram's bad conduct.

In his weakness Abraham was almost deceived into destroying his only son. If he had, the plan of salvation would have been thwarted.

Absalom's rebellion almost destroyed David's kingdom before it was established and its principal work—the temple—begun. If it had, the whole pattern of spiritual revelation would have been upset and delayed. Because of Jehoshaphat's "one besetting sin" Athaliah sat on David's throne and used the opportunity to destroy his heirs.

The jealousy of Joseph's brothers, Saul's gloomy moods, Absalom's pride, and Jehoshaphat's alliances were all avenues through which the destructive forces could move: and would have been successful had they not been overturned by faith.

The readings indicate that the "devil" is always kept in chains as long as men seek to do God's will first and foremost.

> **Thus is Satan bound, thus is Satan banished from the earth. The desire to do evil is only of him. And when there are . . . those only whose desire and purpose of their heart is to glorify the Father, these will be those periods when this shall come to pass.**
>
> **Be *ye all determined* within thy minds, thy hearts, thy purposes, to be of that number!**                                          **281-37.**

## Jehu: the Corruption of a Call

> *Then Elisha the prophet called one of the sons of the prophets and said to him, "Gird up your loins and take this flask of oil in your hand and go to Ramath-gilead;*
>
> *And when you get there, look for Jehu the son of Jimshi, and go in and make him arise up from among his brethren, and bring him into an inner chamber;*
>
> *Then take the flask of oil and pour it on his head, and say to him, 'Thus says the Lord, I have anointed you king over my people Israel.'*
>
> *Then open the door and flee, and do not tarry."* (2 Kings 9:1-3)

In the world affairs readings, we find another startling lesson in Edgar Cayce's story of the Old Testament. Hitler was said to be in the same position, relatively, toward the Jews as Jehu, another Old Testament dictator with a "divine call."

**(Q) Is Hitler psychically led?**
**(A) Psychically led; for the understanding of psychic is that the relationships between the mental activities and the source and the spiritual**

influences are being directed, or *are* directing, the physical activities of the body. Hence it may be said that he is psychically led, for he is called for a purpose as has been given; not only in the affairs of a nation, but as in the affairs of the world. And he stands much in the position as did Jehu, as regards that people that *think* themselves oppressed.

**3976-13 November 4, 1933**

The name Hitler is now a "proverb and by-word" for inhuman cruelty, megalomania, barbarism, and fanaticism. It is hard for the modern mind to think of Hitler as anything but the ultimate incarnation of evil, yet reading 3976-13 implies that even then (1933), Hitler had the opportunity to fulfill a divine call. The reading states this overtly and through the association with Jehu, who had been "raised up" by Elisha (1 Kings 19:16) and anointed by Elisha (2 Kings 9), two of the greatest psychics of the Old Testament.

Like all souls, Hitler had the ability to choose between good and evil. The reading tells us he could have brought "light to the world," and states he was "psychically led" and "called for a purpose." The reading also declares that his policies were "initiated . . . from spiritual sources" and "gained through deep meditation." Clearly, in these respects, he shares much in common with many of the Old Testament leaders.

From the cosmic level of consciousness from which Cayce drew his information while giving a reading, the seer described Hitler as an entity of force, power and destiny:

It would be well that each interested in the policies, and in which is the directing influence in the life of the dictator or of Hitler, study that which has been the impelling influence in the *man*—as a man, in the mind as it acceded to power; *for few does power not destroy, as men. Yet this man, unless there is material change, will survive even that.* [Italics added] **3976-14**

Indeed, the Old Testament prophets, such as Elijah and Elisha, must have sensed and seen the presence of a similar power and destiny in the men they selected and supported for carrying out God's purposes in the earth. Yet they prophesied and supported only with the conditional "if." We have no record as to the prophecies and conditions laid out for Jehu, but we do have Cayce's warning on Hitler.

**If the power is held in that line as it has been directed in the present . . . there will rise a new ideal in the hearts, in the minds of the people.**

**If imperialism among the people is kept in abeyance, great may be the rewards to this peoples, this nation . . .** **3976-13**

Although this reading was emphatic about Hitler's opportunity to fulfill a divine mission, the association in 1933 with Jehu was, for a student of the Bible, grimly prophetic.

## A Reign of Terror

"Unimaginable horror and loathing . . . merciless butchery, reeking with blood . . . a dreadful nightmare, a lurid picture of brutality and horror."[31]

These words of a Bible scholar describe Jehu's rise to power as depicted in the ninth and tenth chapters of 2 Kings—yet how easily could they be the words of a contemporary historian applied to Hitler.

As more and more question marks arose about Hitler's rise to power, a question was asked in a subsequent world affairs reading of 1935.

**(Q) Explain the relation between the information just given regarding Germany and the changes for this year, and the information already given through this channel on Hitler.**

**(A) Read that, my children, that has been given; that there was the destiny for the man, if he did not allow imperialism to enter in—and it is entering. Hence must be called into question.** **3976-15**

Was Jehu psychically developed as the readings imply Hitler was? If so, then both men were open to a deeper source of unconscious vitality, energy and charisma which made them "chosen" leaders. They were subjective channels of a higher force. How they used—or allowed that energy to be used—becomes the personal responsibility of that soul.

**(Q) Why is it that apparently Hitler is making a mistake in initiating policies that seem to be antagonizing the world? (4 Nov. 1933)**

---

[31]*Interpreter's Bible*, Abingdon Press.

(A) Because the world has as yet not understood wholly Hitler's policies. For these are initiated rather from the spiritual source; and the world is very material-minded, and oft understands little of spiritual direction or dictation. But they must come to understand, unless there is more injection of the imperialistic influences . . .                    3976-13

A destiny called into question—*the corruption of a call.*

If Cayce's clairvoyance is trustworthy, at some point between 1933 and 1934, the time between the two world affairs readings 3976-13 and 3976-15, Hitler's "call" became irrevocably corrupted as "imperialistic" forces rather than his own psychic, or "inner" guidance began to dictate his policies.

Hitler was presented with choices between spiritual direction and imperialism, and did not overcome the temptations to abuse and misuse the power that his guidance delivered to him. If pure religious motivation was detected by Elijah and Elisha in Jehu, it, too, became corrupted in his bloody rise to power. What Jehu's obstacles and stumbling blocks were, we don't know. We only know his heart was not pure in the Lord, and, as king of Israel, he "walked in the ways of Jeroboam, which made Israel sin."

It is a challenging task to rethink our position on Hitler to include the view taken toward him in the readings—as difficult as it has been for generations of Bible scholars who have had to reconcile Jehu's methods with God's plan. Although we can't know the inner-condition of the heart and soul of these two dictators, we do have a means of judging. "By their fruits ye shall know them." Hitler's legacy bespeaks the darkness of the imperialism which possessed him. Jehu fulfilled, in part, the purpose for which he had been called, but did not remain loyal to the spirit which had raised him.

And so it is written of him:

*Thus Jehu wiped out Baal from Israel. But Jehu did not turn aside from the sins of Jeroboam the son of Nebat, which he made Israel to sin, the golden calves that were in Bethel and in Dan. And the Lord said to Jehu, "Because you have done well in carrying out what is right in my eyes, and have done to the house of Ahab, according to all that was in my heart, your sons of the fourth generation shall sit on the throne of Israel."*

*But Jehu was not careful to walk in the law of the Lord God of Israel with all his heart; he did not turn from the sins of Jeroboam, which he made Israel to sin.* (2 Kings 10:28-31)

## The Great Tribulation—
## Cycles and Patterns and Prophecy Fulfilled

Jehu was raised as the fulfillment of a prophecy—to complete the destruction destined for Ahab's house, and to purge Israel of Baalism— a religion all too frequently attractive to the Israelites. Perhaps, in the Old Testament sense, Hitler was also raised as a "rod of chastisement" who, possessed by the power given to him, went too far.

How difficult it is for us to fathom the working of spiritual forces as they manifest through the physical and mental expressions of men. There is ever-present in the story of man the Old Testament necessity of purging and cleansing until the conditions laid down in the first commandment can be met—the unqualified and universal love for God, neighbor, and self.

**(Q)** Analyze Hitler's attitude toward the Jews. (November 4, 1933)[32]
**(A)** When the *character* of those that have received, in a manner, their dictations—or the dictates of the activity of the director in affairs—is considered, then it will be understood how that this is but that dictation which was given of old; and how that those peoples though they *were* called—have wandered far afield, and their rebelliousness and their seeking into the affairs of *others* has rather brought *them* into *their* present position.

Read they not that which has been given? "When ye forsake my ways

---

[32]In 1878, Rabbi Hile Weschler wrote these words of warning: "Although there were enemies of the Jews at all times, it is our time which has created an anti-Semitism of a thoroughness which has never existed before . . . One wants to destroy the Semitic element lock, stock and barrel . . . and ruin the Jews so radically that their atoms will never be connected and resynthesized."

After twelve years of Nazidom, these words are not surprising–but written sixty years before Hitler, they are genuinely clairvoyant. (See *The Reluctant Prophet*, by James Kirsch, Sherbourne Press, Los Angeles, 1973, Ch. 4.)

Rabbi Weschler's analysis of the cause–the Jews' own spiritual apathy–and the purpose of the tribulation–to accelerate the advent of the Messiah–agrees in intent with Cayce's interpretation in 1933 of "Hitler's attitude toward the Jews," as given above.

Clearly the law as perceived by Moses (Deut. 31:16-21) and later by Jeremiah is still in effect, as it ever will be.

ye shall be scattered, ye shall be without those things that would bring
ye into the knowledge—until that time is fulfilled."

Hence that attitude that is assumed is rather a fulfillment of that
prophecy that has been made, and is the beginning of the return that
must come throughout the earth.                 3976-13[33]

## A Lesson on Power

What a warning and lesson should Hitler—and others, such as Jehu
and Jeroboam—be to those who seek material power to implement their
ideals.

A warning was given to a group of men who saw in Edgar Cayce an
unparalleled opportunity to use his psychic capacities to form and guide
a world organization to "control finance, railroads, oil and steel industries, newspaper and news syndicates and shipping industries," using
the "power and influence gained thereby . . . for the upbuilding of mankind." In a sense, to establish "The Kingdom of God" on earth.

The warning on power given here not only applies to the lessons of
the Bible, but embraces all souls of all religions in every nation in all of
time:

> . . . such conditions have been the dream of many an individual; and of
> many with much more material power and prestige than those as would
> consider such at the present. Same was the idea of Alexander when be
> sought to conquer the world, yet the tenets of the ideal were forgotten
> in the desires of the flesh, and while the principles as set forth in the mind
> and heart of the man as the student under Plato and Archimedes, and
> Aurelius and others, the man became so gorged by the greed of power
> as to become the loathsome body—as it passed to its reward for the use
> of the power as given into the hands.     3976-4, February 11, 1927

Idealism may direct the mind of a leader to the source of power
within and give the words and concepts which inspire many to follow—
but what happens when one accedes to power and temptations multiply? How difficult it is to be a David, and how few there are in the

---

[33]For additional information, see "Cayce on the Holocaust," by Rabbi Yonassan
Gershom, Cayce reading report 378-50.

world—and only one Christ in history! Or, as has been said, elsewhere, "what does it profit a man to gain the whole world, and lose his own soul?"

## Joash—the Halfway King
### (2 Kings 11, 12; 2 Chronicles 22:11; 23; 24)

Joash did that "which was right" in God's sight "all the days of Jehoiadah, the priest," his guardian and protector. Under Jehoiadah's guidance, Joash ordered the temple restored. A collection box was built through which donations were received to finance the project. The people were drawn back into the spiritual life of Judah by contributing to the temple restoration. Each person was called to do his part in strengthening and rebuilding the spirit of the nation. Their true defense was to always return to the original purpose for which the nation was brought into existence.

But after the death of Jehoiadah, egotism again showed itself in Judah. Joash permitted himself to be worshiped by the princes of Judah, thus turning them away from true spiritual worship. When Zedekiah, Jehoiadah's son, censured Joash, Joash had him killed.

Judah began to get a forecast of the great tribulation ahead, as their spiritual unity began to ebb. Joash's grandfather, Jehoshaphat, was a king and spiritual leader. With a small army he had defied "a million Ethiopians." (2 Chronicles 14) With Joash, conditions were reversed. Hazael of Damascus came against Joash's troops with a small army and was victorious. (2 Chronicles 24:24) Joash lacked the spiritual attunement within which insures victory, but he did possess the gold and holy things which had been brought to the temple. Joash turned Hazael away with the hallowed objects of the temple and gold from the treasury paid as tribute.

Joash was assassinated by his own servants, as an act of revenge for Zedekiah.

Although Judah made a continuous effort to keep the Spirit alive, there was never the ability to put aside "the sins of Solomon." Selfish instincts, material gain, and lack of vision were never completely cleansed from the national spirit, and Judah drifted into a decline.

During Joash's reign, Joel prophesied. He foresaw the impending disasters, but also beyond, to the end of the bitter cycle, and gave Israel (or man) one of its great assurances.

*"And it shall come to pass afterward that I will pour out my spirit upon all flesh; and your sons and your daughters shall prophesy, your old men shall dream dreams, your young men shall see visions; and also upon the servants and the handmaids in those days will I pour out my spirit."* (Joel 2:28)

Both kingdoms faced dark days, unrelieved by any hope except through those who trusted God and were preparing for the coming judgment. In Cayce's day, the same "latter day" cycle of tribulation leading to purification was building. We find in a world affairs reading Joel's prophecy as counsel to those who were to pass through the dark night of world crisis:

Thus it will require—yea, demand—that there be an expression on the part of each as to that given 3,200 years ago: "Declare ye today *whom ye will serve!* As for me and my house, we will serve a living God."

If there is sufficient, then, of those that will not only declare this in mind and in purpose but by deed and word of mouth, there may come then an enlightening through that which has been promised of old; that the young men shall dream dreams, the old men shall have visions, the daughters or maidens may know the spirit of truth—yea, that all may come to the greater knowledge of the indwelling of the Prince of Peace.

**3976-26**

# 22

# New Light

## *Uzziah*

**When** Amaziah became king, he slew his father's assassins, but permitted their children to live, thus honoring the law of Moses which said that every man should suffer for his own sins, and not the children for the sins of their parents, or the parents for their children's sins. Amaziah listened to those prophets who stressed a literal application of the law. Amaziah did "what was right in the sight of the Lord" but "not with a perfect heart."

Joash and Amaziah were basically good kings, sufficiently aware of spiritual forces, yet not stable in their ideals. Thus, through their reigns, Judah kept sliding into a decline.

However, King Uzziah renewed the light and drew the people back to God. He did that "which was right" in the sight of God, "according to all that his father David did." "He prayed before the Lord" and was the student of Zechariah, priest and prophet, who instructed Uzziah "in the worship of the Lord."

The fact the biblical writer recorded that Uzziah was a student of Zechariah indicates that it was noteworthy and important. Ritualistic worship dates back to the days of Moses. (Jethro, Moses' father-in-law, was adept in ritual sacrifice: see 1266-1.) Through sacred ritual, the initiates in the priesthood could attune to higher dimensions of the spirit, or soul-forces, and manifest greater degrees of psychic energy and consciousness than ordinarily possessed by man.

Uzziah must have been an able student. He conquered the Philistines and the Arabians, and received tribute from the Ammonites. He refortified his country, reorganized and re-equipped his army, and personally engaged in agricultural pursuits. His success as king and commander-in-chief made him the ruler over the largest realm in Judah since the disruption of the kingdom.

Yet his strength became his weakness. Uzziah must have been sufficiently impressed with the office of the priesthood and the knowledge of Zechariah to want to be a priest himself as well as king. Uzziah usurped the privileges of the priesthood, and judgment was swift. While burning incense at the altar, Uzziah was struck with leprosy and forced to live his last years in a leper's house.

Cayce philosophized with the Bible class on this point:

"Why do people today who blaspheme God's word, or do wicked things, not meet their punishment as suddenly as many of those who were in authority at that time? They were in that stage of evolution where quick judgments came. Then it was 'an eye for an eye, a tooth for a tooth.' Today, though we may not agree with it or look at it this way, because of Christ's advent into the world, God is more merciful. We are under the law of mercy and not judgment. Our punishment is longer in coming, but more severe in the end. When we are shown over and over again, and still sin against the Holy Spirit, there's no forgiving, there's no getting around the law of cause and effect.

"In the olden days, they were quick to pass judgment on themselves— so judgments came quickly. This is a thought concerning it, at least."

## Jotham and the Prophetic Voice

Jotham ruled during Uzziah's confinement as a leper, and succeeded him after his death. The year King Uzziah died, a momentous event took place, the effects of which are still reverberating on the skein of time and space—Isaiah achieved a cosmic awareness and, baptized by the Spirit, began his ministry. (Isaiah 6)

Personal spiritual experiences are perhaps the most profound and overlooked factors shaping and molding man's history. The quiet corners where individuals meditate, or a bed where revelation or guidance has been received through a dream, has been the place where many of the great movements and institutions which have affected our destiny have begun. Or, as one reading tells us:

**The beginning of all great institutions, of all great things, is first in the mind of individuals who are in touch with infinite forces.     254-31**

The Bible itself, another reading tells us, is the greatest collection of psychic experiences in the world. Not only does it describe a variety of phenomena, but also tells what individuals did about their experiences. The Bible is a witness to the worth of the individual spiritual experience, and its cumulative value when it is lived and applied. Abraham was only a merchant's son until he heard a voice and acted on it. Isaiah would have been soon forgotten if, as the cousin of Uzziah and grandson of Joash, he had valued only his royal blood and not his soul.

Many names remain with us from this period because of their spiritual beliefs and actions. The prophetic voice was rising in Judah and Israel, and with it came a new tension and struggle. It was the conflict between priest and prophet. Internalized, it represents the struggle within self between intellect and intuition.

Jotham did right like his father, but did not remove all the high places. He inherited a strong government and defeated the Ammonites, who paid him immense annual tribute. But the increasing corruption of the north kingdom began permeating Judah, as seen in the words of Isaiah and Micah. Hosea refers to Judah under Jotham as lacking in purity of life and worship.

## *Ahaz*

Ahaz followed Jotham. Cayce described him to the Bible class:

"Ahaz started out right, with high ideals and purposes; but, like so many, his environment got the best of him."

Ahaz yielded to the glamour and prestige of the Assyrians in religion and politics.

When Pekah, a murderer and usurper and eighteenth of the nineteen kings of the north kingdom, appealed to Ahaz to join him and the Syrian king in a league against Assyria, Ahaz turned to Assyria for help.

He stripped the temple of all the silver and gold and sent it as a present to the mighty Tiglath-pileser III, who was preparing to attack Palestine and Syria. Tiglath-pileser accepted, and did not invade Judah, and relieved Ahaz of his troublesome neighbors, Israel and Syria.

Ahaz journeyed to Damascus and swore homage to the Assyrian king and his gods. When he returned to Jerusalem, Ahaz rearranged the temple trappings and the services to conform to Assyrian standards.

However, Assyria had an enormous appetite. Tiglath-pileser was not content with one payment from Ahaz, but returned and demanded—or extorted—more and more tribute. The payments drained Judah of its resources, and Ahaz' policies, which were influenced by his weaknesses, fears, and lack of faith, took the people farther and farther from the true understanding of the Spirit. His policies were strongly opposed by Isaiah, who counseled the king to rely upon God. But Ahaz could not find it within himself to do so.

Cayce made a summary of Ahaz' reign; he told the class:

> "On the whole, Ahaz' government was disastrous to his country, especially in its religious aspects, which is—or should be—the main consideration in every country. When there is a decline in the religion of a country, a decline in political power soon follows, although it may appear to prosper in a greater measure for a short time.
>
> "When we come to Hezekiah, Ahaz' son, we will see that a large part of his reforming work was aimed at undoing the evil Ahaz had wrought."

Ahaz' manipulations with Assyria yielded immediate blessings, but inwardly, his policies worked a greater curse. They led to a continued deterioration of the kingdom, and proved what all man's political, military, and economic maneuvers do—that God is not mocked!

An interpretation in a world affairs reading strikes this note about a contemporary situation (June, 1939).

> **Then ye ask, "What is to be the outcome of England and France in their efforts to join hands with Russia as an encirclement of the totalitarian regime?" These, so long as they are in keeping with God's purposes with man, will succeed. When they become active for self-preservation without the thought or purpose of their fellow man, they must fail.**
>
> **So it is with the endeavors of Germany, Italy, Japan. As they attempt to preserve their own personalities, their own selves, without thought of**

their fellow man, they may succeed for the moment, but "God is not mocked," and whatsoever a man, a country, a nation sows, that it must reap . . .

Then, rest not on those things that become as quicksand about thee, but on the true, the tried arm of God. For the earth is His, and the fullness thereof.                                                                       3976-23

# Good King Hezekiah

*King* Hezekiah is best known for his moral and spiritual leadership, and for his association with the prophet Isaiah. Under his reign, Judah returned briefly to a pure form of worship, based upon the prophetic guidance of Isaiah. Isaiah's visionary policies were, in the main, adhered to by King Hezekiah in matters of state. Jeremiah records Hezekiah listened to Micah as well. (Jeremiah 26:18, 19)

These were days of great upheaval and stress in Israel and Judah. Hezekiah saw Israel swept away by the Assyrians who ravaged the land and ordered the mass deportation of its people. While Hezekiah was king, tens of thousands of Israelites were violently taken from their homeland and resettled in foreign lands, and their places filled with conquered peoples from other areas. This was Assyrian policy, and its intent was to destroy national consciousness and break the will of the people.

With the exception of Samaria, all Israel was under Assyrian control. Nine years later Samaria was taken. Hezekiah, too, lost part of his kingdom to the Assyrians. He was a tribute paying vassal because his father, Ahaz, had voluntarily submitted to Tiglath-pileser.

In these darkest days, Hezekiah was a great light—for he "trusted in God" so that "after him there was not one like him among all the kings of Judah nor among those who went before him." He did that which was right, just as his father David had done. (2 Chronicles 29:2) "He held fast to the Lord and turned not aside." (2 Kings 18:5, 6)

In a deteriorated kingdom, Hezekiah returned to the one tried and true defense—spiritual reform. Hezekiah's first act as king was to order the repair of the temple, which had been closed during the reign of Ahaz. He reorganized the services of the priests and Levites, and cleansed the house of the Lord and all the vessels in it, which had been thrown away, purifying them. When everything was sanctified and set in order, Hezekiah gathered the rulers of the city and went to offer sacrifice. A sin offering was made, the sins of the people were rolled back through the releasing of the scapegoat. Offerings were made while the people sang praises to the Lord and worshiped. The offerings were so abundant the priests had to ask the Levites for help.

Hezekiah rejoiced with his people—the Lord had preserved them, the house of the Lord was in order! Hezekiah's effort, with Isaiah, was to center the collective consciousness of the people on the Lord.

Cayce told his class:

"Hezekiah was a righteous man and knew the wrath of the Lord would not be turned from Judah until the people turned again to God."

The temple was the great binding focus between the people and God. Hezekiah's next step was to involve the people of both kingdoms in his reforms and renewals. He sent messengers throughout Israel and Judah, asking the people to come to Jerusalem to keep the Passover. The Passover had not been observed on this scale for many years. News of its revival brought scorn and mockery by some, but many people responded. A great crowd gathered, and the Passover was celebrated with great solemnity and rejoicing as had not been seen since Solomon's days. The crowd which assembled for the Passover was so large the priests could not minister to them. And many of the people ate the Passover feast who had not been cleansed according to Mosaic law.

The need for the Passover was greater than the need to observe the law. The situation led—or forced—Hezekiah to trust a spiritual intuition: that the spirit was greater than the law. When Hezekiah saw the Passover was violating the ritual law, he prayed beautifully:

*"Lord, pardon everyone that prepares his heart to seek God, the Lord God of his fathers, though he be not cleansed according to the purification of the sanctuary."* (2 Chronicles 30:18)

Thus he added to an evolving consciousness.

This same prophetic understanding is shown by Samuel, when he rebuked Saul: "To obey is better than to sacrifice, to harken better than burnt offerings." (1 Samuel 15:22)

Cayce offered the nation this same counsel in a world affairs reading in 1939:

> Then, there needs be that not so much be set as to this ritual, or this form, or the other, for any given peoples or any nation, but rather that the individuals in each nation, *everywhere*, are to turn again *to* the God of the fathers and not in self-indulgence, self-aggrandizement, but more and more of self-effacement.
>
> For as the people of each nation pray, *and* then live that prayer, so must the Spirit work.   **3976-23**

In an interesting Life reading for a Russian jeweler who had been a craftsman who worked on the restoration of the temple for Hezekiah, we find the same counsel regarding spiritual understanding.

> Before that we find the entity was in the land now known as the Promised Land, during that particular period of Hezekiah, the king in Judah, who opened again the house of the Lord of those peoples.
>
> And the entity—as Jabin—was a worker in metals; being among those peoples given the privilege and authority (notice those words) to restore the utensils pertaining to the worship, and the activities especially in the courts of the temple; restoring the censers upon which incense was burned.
>
> Hence, in the present there are not only the abilities to work in metals—as of gold, silver, brass and the like—but the knowledge of the value to bestow upon odors, and certain activities pertaining to the burning of incense . . .
>
> As were the promptings of those activities directed by the entity in that sojourn as Jabin, know that the intent and purpose must be for the worship of—because of the faith in, and the promptings of the heart and mind and soul—toward—a living God! Not alone to reach a certain effect, through affecting certain poses or conditions in the relationships and activities of self toward others, or the prompting of others as to shortcuts to attain certain results in their material affairs.
>
> To be sure, the law is, "They that receive a prophet in the name of a

prophet, receive the prophet's reward." Yet, as indicated in that given above, both may fall in the ditch and be far, far from living and being wholly acceptable unto Him, who *is* the Giver of all good and perfect gifts! 2077-1

The Passover celebration drew the people together into one body as they had not been since David's time. After the feast, they went out and broke down the images and cut down the groves and smashed the altars on the high places. The whole nation was seeking for God as one people. Their unity was necessary, for the people were soon called to face the awesome threat of Assyria.

Hezekiah had been successful in his wars against the Philistines, driving them back as far as Gaza. He retook all the cities lost by his father and conquered others belonging to the Philistines. Hezekiah was aided in his campaign by Isaiah, upon whose prophecies he relied, venturing even to revolt against Assyria by refusing to pay the usual tribute. Hezekiah came under Isaiah's influence only after a hard struggle with certain ministers, who advised him to enter into an alliance with Egypt. The alliance was not acceptable to Isaiah. He saw it as a deviation from trust in God. He advised Hezekiah to rely upon God and no one else.

Eight years after the fall of Samaria and the mass deportation of the Israelites, the fourteenth year of Hezekiah's reign, Assyria marched against Judah, conquering many cities. An Assyrian victory monument bears this inscription: "Sennacherib captured 46 strong cities and carried away captive into Assyria, 200,150 captives of the men of Judah."

When Sennacherib invaded, Hezekiah lost his faith. He acknowledged his fault (in not paying tribute) and parleyed with Sennacherib for a new treaty. The Assyrian imposed a new levy of three hundred talents of silver and thirty of gold. Hezekiah was forced to take all the silver in the temple and from his own treasury to pay it, even to "cut off the gold from the doors of the temple."

After receiving the tribute, Sennacherib sent a large army under three of his generals to besiege Jerusalem. Rahshakeh, the leader, called upon Hezekiah to surrender. He mocked Hezekiah for his hope in Egypt and made an effort to inspire the people with mistrust in Hezekiah's reliance upon God.

This disastrous turn of events must have turned Hezekiah back to God, or made him realize there was no hope or help except from God. In this trial, Hezekiah kept the faith. He took the letters with the Assyrian terms to the temple and laid them open before the Lord and prayed for the deliverance of Jerusalem.

While Hezekiah poured out his soul in the temple, Isaiah received God's word and carried it to the king. Sennacherib would not invade, Isaiah promised, but would be forced to return "by the way that he came" and would not trouble Jerusalem again. (2 Kings 19)

Isaiah's prophecy was quick to be confirmed. Sennacherib was forced to withdraw because the king of Ethiopia was marching against him. That night, the "angel of death," through the agency of a plague or an infection, destroyed the whole Assyrian army. Sennacherib returned home in shame and was murdered by his own sons while praying in the house of his gods.

The threat passed. Judah was released for the time being, and, re-lieved and inspired, they gave all the credit to God.

## *"They Were There"*

The cruelty of the Assyrians is legendary. However, in this Life read-ing we find one with a quality of mercy. A reading for a young society matron mentions Sennacherib and places the entity among the Assyrian royalty:

> . . . we find the entity was in the land now known as the Persian, when there was the arousing of the peoples for the influences which were a part of that experience in the land when Sennacherib and the peoples were overcoming the Jewish forces.
>
> There we find the entity was among those of the household then of the ruling forces—or of the ruler himself.
>
> Hence we find those things of pomp, of power, of wealth, of all the activities that went with the period, were a part of the entity's experi-ence.
>
> The name then was Shedeli. In the experience the entity gained, for the entity showed mercy to those who were under the entity in the periods when the helpmeet and those of the entity's people became rulers over those of the land.
>
> And in the present it may be said that this was one of the greater virtues—the patience the entity has with those who are in a more menial position, or who are in the social status beneath the entity's position.
>
> **1752-1**

In this reading, Cayce described for a Jewish girl her experience as an Assyrian captive:

> . . . we find the entity was in the land during the reign of Hezekiah, when the peoples of promise were taken into captivity.
>
> There we find the entity was under the material hardships, and forgot not its own tenets and teachings that were given in the early part of its activities in the holy city and its environs there.
>
> Thus, in the name Vistula, the entity's activities in those new environs, new scenes, among new faces and new activities, brought great experiences of development.
>
> Yet little hates, petty malices, the desire for freedom, arise from these experiences.
>
> One may be free indeed in thought, though the body may be bound in chains; and be much more free than those who are chained by their own consciousness in those things which are in keeping with the ideals in the material as well as mental and spiritual life.
>
> These understandings the entity must gain through the abilities to curb self, in being too quickly outspoken when little resentments arise. For this once gained, the entity may again come to know much of those experiences that were gained even in the lands where foreign activities, foreign associations, foreign purposes, even foreign worship in the spiritual things, were roundabout—yet the heart kept singing all the while the purposes of the living God.
>
> And these should be aroused, and held to—"Let others do as they may, but as for me and mine, we will serve a living God." Let these be as frontlets upon thine eyes, as those influences upon thine hands—yea, as that above all that would govern thy speech and thy activity! Thus ye will find that peace, that harmony, which is beyond price—and may indeed be called blessed by many!
>
> For then ye *live*, rather than just profess, thy relationships to thy Maker!                                                                      1669-1

A Pennsylvania man was told he had been one of Hezekiah's soldiers taken as hostage by Assyria–and found God!

> Before that the entity was in the Holy Land, when those activities were being broken up by the order of the king when the people had so belittled themselves by gratifying their own selfish desires and had

forgotten the ways of the Lord; and, as the warnings had been given, they were carried away into captivity.

The entity was among those of the soldiery at the time of Benaiah, when the soldiery of Hezekiah was carried away.

In the foreign land the entity remembered. Hence in the present there are the periods when the entity becomes retrospective and it brings discomforts, yet a joy. For ye will still recall that the promise is, "Though ye be far away, if ye call I will hear."

Then turn ye to Exodus 19:5 and begin—and find self. Then turn to Deuteronomy 4 and again read those warnings that are a part of thy experience from that sojourn, and a part of thine own headstrongness in the present.

From that experience the entity learned to write. For, as Benaiah, the entity was educated in the schools of those lands where the entity was taken as hostage.                                             3528-1

## Hezekiah, Figs and Babylon

During the Assyrian siege, Hezekiah fell dangerously ill with Job's affliction—boils—which Isaiah diagnosed as fatal. All illness comes from sin, the readings tell us, and Hezekiah's was due "to the pride of his heart." (2 Chronicles 32:25)

Hezekiah wept bitterly and prayed earnestly to live, reminding God how righteously he had lived "before pride exalted his heart." As Hezekiah poured out his soul in prayer, Isaiah heard the answer as he walked through the temple courts. Hezekiah had fifteen years added to his life because of the sincerity of his prayer. Perhaps Isaiah was even given guidance on the cure—a fig poultice, which he applied to Hezekiah's boils, and the king recovered.

Those who are familiar with the Cayce readings are aware of the efficacy of his "home remedies" and the variety of poultices he pre-scribed, which include everything from grapes and onions to castor oil and turpentine—all of which have amazing healing properties when applied in right combinations to specific illnesses. A poultice of figs and warm milk was recommended a few times for gum and tooth infec-tions. Apparently it was an old remedy used in dentistry. An ancient manual of veterinary science dating from 1500 B.C. recommends a fig poultice for horses suffering with swollen heads and sore noses. The healing properties in figs for combating certain types of infection were recognized by people in the ancient orient, and used by Isaiah to cure Hezekiah.[34]

Many of Cayce's remedies are as ancient as man, dating back to biblical times and beyond, and, like Isaiah's poultice, consist entirely of ingredients supplied by nature. But these external means are only aids and not the source of healing. According to the readings, the healing must come from within. The outward means—whether physical, mental, or spiritual—act only to stimulate, awaken and coordinate with the individual's own latent healing forces. Cayce made a cogent perception on Hezekiah's recovery. He told his students:

> "Hezekiah was cured of his boils by a poultice of figs. No doubt the infection was spreading, and the poultice was necessary—but the spiritual seeking and awakening had to come first."

## Hezekiah and the Babylonian Preview

The kingdom of Israel was destroyed by Assyria, and Judah fell to the Babylonians over a century later. Assyrian dominance continued for another eighty years after the death of Sennacherib until the brutal empire, beset by Scythians, Medes, and Babylonians, fell and Babylon gained mastery. Isaiah had the first clear insight in the Babylonian ascendancy years before it happened, and knew what it held in store for Judah.

The first mention of Babylon in the Bible, an advance notice of the future history, is contained in the story of Hezekiah's sickness. After his recovery, the king of Babylon sent ambassadors to Hezekiah to congratulate him on his return to health and to inquire about the miracle. The real purpose for the visit was to ascertain if an alliance with Judah would be advantageous for his own kingdom in his struggle against Assyria.

Hezekiah received the Babylonians eagerly and escorted them through his temple, the palace, and the armory. Hezekiah showed the ambassadors that he was a man of great importance and not to be despised. His boils had been healed, but his "pride" had not. The lesson had been forgotten.

---

[34]Werner Keller, *The Bible as History.*

Isaiah rebuked Hezekiah. He read in the king's behavior a distrust in divine power. Hezekiah repented, but it was not enough to turn aside that which Isaiah had foreseen.

*Then Isaiah said to Hezekiah, "Hear the word of the Lord: Behold, the days are coming when all that is in your house and that which your fathers have laid up in treasure to this day shall be carried to Babylon; nothing shall be left for you, says the Lord.*

*And of your sons that shall issue from you, whom you shall beget, shall they take away; and they shall be eunuchs in the palace of the kings of Babylon." (2 Kings 20:16-18)*

Was this punishment for Hezekiah's sin—or a condition which had been steadily building because Judah continually wavered between trust in God, and looking to outside forces for support? Judah's decline into captivity and servitude could have been avoided had the people and leaders looked steadily to God and followed the inner guidance of the still, small voice which is so easily overlooked amid the emotional upheavals of the day. Hezekiah, although a great example of a God-trusting man, allowed "external" events to alter his vision. Few of his descendants even matched his development, and all—until Christ—remained in that state of consciousness—and confusion—of wavering between turning within and looking without, a state of mind we find ourselves still in today.

## *The Growing Darkness—Manassah and Amon*

When Hezekiah fell ill, he was without an heir. The Davidic dynasty was again in danger.

During the fifteen years which were added to his life, Hezekiah's son, Manassah was born. Manassah had the longest reign of any of the kings of Judah, and it is considered the most wicked. He spurred a reaction to Hezekiah's reforms and reintroduced all the pagan cultic worship. The Assyrians regarded Judah as a conquered and tribute-paying province, and in their inscriptions refer to Manassah as a vassal king.

According to Chronicles, Manassah was brought in chains to Babylon by the king of Assyria, where he repented and was restored by God to his throne. But in Kings nothing is said of his change of heart, rather three deplorable details of his reign are stressed: the free adoption of foreign cults, the religious reaction which followed his reign, and the bitter persecution of the prophets.

Amon, Manassah's son, was twenty-two years old when he began his reign and ruled two years, following in his father's footsteps. "Amon forsook the Lord and followed not in the ways of the Lord." Though he ruled in a critical time, little is known of his reign.

If the story is true in Chronicles about Manassah's repentance in Babylon, the lesson was lost on Amon. Manassah humbled himself, acknowledged that the Lord was God, and prayed to return to Jerusalem. When he did, he led a different life. He built a wall about the city of David, removed the strange gods, repaired the altars in the house of the Lord, offered sacrifices, and commanded Judah to serve the living God.

Cayce commented on Amon to the Bible class:

"Evidently the lesson his father learned did Amon no good. He was about seventeen years old when Manassah experienced his change of heart, and this is a hard lesson to learn by observation. Amon trespassed more and more until his servants conspired and slew him, and made Josiah king."

The endeavors of the prophets to establish a pure form of religion were, for a short time, successful under Hezekiah; but a reaction set in after Hezekiah's death. Both Amon and Manassah followed the popular trend in re-establishing the old Canaanite cults. For many decades, those who sympathized with prophetic ideas were in constant danger.

## The Last Great Light—Josiah

Josiah was eight years old when he became king, and ruled thirty-one years. He did that which was right and walked in the ways of David, turning "neither to the left nor right." (2 Kings 22:2)

Three momentous events occurred under Josiah: Jeremiah began to prophesy; lost books of the Law of Moses were discovered; and Josiah inaugurated the great reformation which marks an epoch in the religious history of Israel, and insured the preservation of a remnant:

. . . yet only in Josiah was it given to again approach even the threshold of the understanding as was necessary for the deliverance of a portion

of the peoples, even sufficient to keep the natural lineage of the
promised one.                                                    900-428

In his eighth year, Josiah began to seek God, and in his twelfth, he
purged Judah of the images, groves, and high places. In his thirteenth,
Jeremiah began to receive the word of God and had the vision concerning his purpose. (Jeremiah 1) In his eighteenth year, Josiah began repairing the house of the Lord, and the book of the law was found.
Josiah became greatly alarmed that the calamities (2 Chronicles 34)
threatened in the law for non-observance of its commands, would come
upon him and his people. This inspired the great reformation.

Solomon's example of tolerance to pagan practices, and his stress on
luxury and privilege, created deteriorating inroads and were blinding
to man's spiritual consciousness. Despite the determined efforts of the
good kings and inspired prophets, the persistent stain of selfish desires
and evil purposes in the national moral and spiritual fabric would not
be cleansed. Asa, Jehoshaphat, Uzziah, and Hezekiah, and prophets like
Elijah, Elisha, Isaiah and Jeremiah kept the knowledge of the spirit from
being lost entirely. By giving evidence of the effect of the Spirit in their
lives, they advanced the consciousness.

Without them, there would not have been the hope, the fortitude,
and the inspiration to encourage Judah to place its faith in an unseen
force, a spirit that "did not think like men," yet had promised through
David an eternal throne and a future king. The history of Judah shows a
consistent and continuous effort to keep this spirit and understanding
alive.

In Josiah's time, the effort bore fruit. The understanding was preserved, insuring that there would be a remnant with enough devotion
and conviction of the spirit to pass down their understanding through
the next one hundred years of national trauma, captivity, deportation
and servitude.

## The Countdown Begins—the Last Kings

Following the death of Josiah, Judah's decline was rapid. The people
anointed Jehoahaz to replace his father. Jehoahaz was not first in the
order of succession, but popular with the people. Perhaps, as Edgar
Cayce suggested, he was the most likely spiritual successor to his father.
His reign was brief—three months. Necho, pharaoh of Egypt, invaded

Judah and carried him captive, never to return. Necho installed Eliakim, Jehoahaz' elder brother, on the throne, and changed his name to Jehoiakim. Judah was under Egyptian domination and paid a heavy tribute.

Nebuchadnezzar invaded Palestine, entered Jerusalem, and compelled Jehoiakim to pay tribute to Babylon. After three years, Jehoiakim rebelled and Nebuchadnezzar returned, and took Jehoiakim back to Babylon in chains and fetters.

Jehoiakim died after an evil reign of eleven years. It was he who slew the prophet Uriah "and cast his dead body into the graves of the common people." (Jeremiah 26) Jehoiakim was also the king who impiously destroyed Jeremiah's scroll of prophecies and threw it into the fire as it was being read to him. (Jeremiah 36)

Jehoiakim was so despised by his people that when he died he was buried "with the burial of an ass, drawn, and cast forth beyond the gates of Jerusalem." (Jeremiah 22:19)

Jehoiakim's son, Jehoiachin, reigned only three months. He was scarcely on the throne when Nebuchadnezzar returned and took him, his mother, his servants, captains, and officers captive and sent them to Babylon. The treasures of the palace and the sacred vessels of the temple were taken also. Jehoiachin remained in prison in Babylon for thirty-six years. When Nebuchadnezzar died, his son Evil-merodach released Jehoiachin and gave him an honorable seat at his table.

Nebuchadnezzar gave Jehoiachin's crown to Mattaniah (son of Josiah), whose name was changed to Zedekiah.

Zedekiah was the last king of Judah and the youngest son of Josiah. He was a full brother to Jehoahaz, who was carried captive to Egypt by Necho.

The eleven years of Zedekiah's reign are notable for the steady decline in Judah's power, and for the desperate efforts of Jeremiah to avert the coming disaster.

Zedekiah was a weak king, pliant and yielding readily to the influence of any advisor, whether prince or prophet. At times he would listen to Jeremiah, and at others follow counsel that was in direct opposition.

In the fourth year of his reign he journeyed to Babylon to swear an oath of allegiance to Nebuchadnezzar. But the Egyptian king persuaded Zedekiah to break his oath.

Zedekiah rebelled, in spite of Jeremiah's counsel to submit to the inevitable "yoke of slavery" as the judgment of God and a lesson to be learned. The revolt brought the Babylonian army back to Jerusalem. Jerusalem was taken, plundered, and burned; its best population deported to Babylon as captives. As a result of his conspiracies and as punishment for his rebellion, all Zedekiah's heirs to the throne were slain before his eyes, then he was blinded and taken to Babylon as a rebel prisoner.

The Jewish kingdom perished. Israel ceased to exist as an independent nation. Zedekiah lived out the rest of his life in a Babylonian dungeon. Although Zedekiah's punishment was severe, Cayce gave a compensating view to the Bible class:

"It seems horrible that Zedekiah, although an evil king, should have to suffer, first by seeing his sons killed before his eyes, then his own eyes put out, and spending the rest of his days in a dungeon. Although no more evil than many of the other kings of Judah, be had a prolonged suffering, while many others 'got by' with a horrible but sudden death after a life lived in luxury.

"While it appears Zedekiah's was the greater punishment, and that sudden death would be easier—and more merciful—we can only judge from the outward appearance. God looks on the heart. Perhaps it took years and years for those other kings to become adjusted to their state after passing from this earth, or they may have had to pass through periods of suffering, as Dives in the parable of Dives and Lazarus. (Luke 16:19-31)

"Suffering in the material sense, such as Zedekiah's, can make us spiritually strong within. Zedekiah needed strength. He had been so wishy-washy throughout his reign. As the son of Josiah, he no doubt knew what was right from wrong, yet didn't have the courage of his convictions. Through his remaining years, though in a dungeon, he could review his life and build up strength for a nobler effort the next time he returned to earth.

"In other words, Zedekiah met his karma in that particular life, while some of the others did not."

# The Lost Tribes and the New World

*The* kingdom of Israel fell over one hundred years before Zedekiah was taken to Babylon and Jerusalem destroyed. Judah had made a consistent effort to keep the Spirit alive, but could not overcome its own selfish spirit. Thus, the day of judgment was delayed, but not circumvented.

The people of both kingdoms continually disregarded the warnings of their prophets. The School of Prophets, begun by Samuel, and given its greatest impetus under Elijah, was turning out individuals familiar with higher states of consciousness and knowledgeable about the laws of cause and effect, or karma. The prophets knew how to "tune in" and receive from God. They were able to see the pattern in their people's choices and gain spiritual insights as to where it would lead.

The people were given opportunity after opportunity to reform, but did not. Instead of remaining true to the original inner convictions, they turned to the unrestricted and more sensually pleasant way of life they saw around them. Consequently they were ignoring divine law. Nothing could save them, but themselves. They deliberately brought about their own destruction by rejecting God.

One of the rewards from the Cayce readings is to see new dimensions added to famous Bible characters, through actions which are unaccounted for in the Bible. When the north kingdom fell, the Israelites became victims to the cruel Assyrian policy of being violently driven

461

from their homeland and deported to foreign lands. The aim of these uprooting tactics was clear: To destroy the sense of nationalism and to break the people's will to resist.

When the kings and people of the north kingdom were taken, they were absorbed into the population of foreign lands and never emerged again in history, and the fascinating question of "the lost tribes" arose. All investigation into what became of the ten tribes, until recently, has revealed nothing.

However, the Cayce readings indicate that King Hezekiah, under the guidance of Isaiah, may have given his support to a program of migrations and resettlements into parts of the world untouched by Assyrian power. And one of those lands was America!

In one reading, Cayce was asked:

**(Q) How did the lost tribe reach this country [America]?**
**(A) In boats.** 5750-1

The lost tribes are being found. Although the question of where they went has never been settled, modern archeology is shedding new light on this old question, and the findings are supportive of statements made in the readings ten and twenty years earlier.[35]

Recent discoveries indicate the presence of Jewish voyagers to American soil several thousand years ago. This growing evidence confirms yet another unusual chapter in Edgar Cayce's Story of the Old Testament and brings new insight to these statements by Isaiah:

*. . . the mighty men of the nations have broken down the branches . . . its shoots spread out, they are gone over the sea.* (Isaiah 16:8)

*"I will set a sign among them, and those who escape I will send among the nations, to Tarshish, Pul, and Lud . . . To Tubal, and Javan, and to the islands afar off that have not heard my name."*[36] (Isaiah 66:19)

When it became obvious that Assyria was the engine of destruction

---

[35]See Cyrus Gordon, Ph.D., *Before Columbus.*

[36]The locations of the places have never been determined.

the prophets had foreseen, and its path of conquest could not be turned aside, the prophecies began to be taken more seriously. But for many, it was too late. The ones who escaped were either the adventurous, or those with deep-seated spiritual motivations who felt a need to preserve their heritage and religion.

A young mathematics teacher was told in 1940 that she had been one of the adventurers:

> Before that the entity was in the English land, but during the early periods of those journeyings of the peoples of Hezekiah's reign—during the time when the children of promise were carried into captivity.
>
> The entity was among those voyagers who fared forth seeking out other lands.
>
> Hence the love of adventure, the love of strange places, strange environs; and the desire to study various activities when there may be indicated as to the source or cause of individuals thinking or acting in given directions.
>
> Thus we find the abilities as the mathematician, or even the abilities as a nautical director; for the entity might easily have become either an aviatrix or one who would sail boats by the stars or by the compass or by those things considered rather as a *man's* direction—though the entity has the more oft (in those sojourns that have an influence in the present experience) remained in its present sex.
>
> The name then was Zenbeuen. In the experience the entity gained, for it was the seeking for freedom as well as for the preservation of those tenets and truths which brought the entity's desire to seek out other lands, and the putting of same into activity—and the setting up of the stones in the forms of circles for altars.
>
> Hence we find that symbols at times mean much to the entity, or the study of same.                                                      2205-1

A young teen-ager was told in 1944 he had been a leader in the search for new land:

> Before that the entity was in the land of the present nativity [United States] in the early periods when those came into this land from the separations or divisions of the peoples in the periods of uprisings in the Holy Land.
>
> Then the entity was among the leaders in such activities.

Thus we will find activities of the unusual nature in the seeking out of strange places, strange things, will be a portion of the entity's innate and manifested nature. Don't let these wander too far afield. 4084–1

The readings describe two important Jewish colonies; one in England and another in the southwest United States. There are indications of a settlement in the South Seas (1253–1), in Peru (1159–1), and "the central portion of Ohio," during "the early period of the Mound Builders." (1286–1)

Other traditions would indicate other locations as well. This extract describes the course of one migration:

. . . during that period as would be called three thousand years before the Prince of Peace came, those peoples that were of the lost tribes, a portion came into the land; infusing their activities upon the peoples from Mu in the southernmost portion of that called America or United States, and then moved on to the activities in Mexico, Yucatan, centralizing that now about the spots where the central of Mexico now stands, or Mexico City. Hence there arose through the age a different civilization, a *mixture* again. 5750-1

## The American Colony

The two following readings describe the colony in the American Southwest.

A reading for a Pennsylvania model and showgirl contains an important note about her purposes as a priestess in that spiritual center:

Before that the entity was in the own land of nativity during the early settlings; not America as known in history, but when there were the activities of those peoples that were dispersed by the carrying away of the children of promise into captivity.

The entity was among those born to those who escaped across the waters into what is now the southwestern portion of the entity's present native land [America].

There the entity came in contact with those who were a part of the Atlantean civilization before it was broken up, and the entity was made a priestess—as in keeping with a combination of the old Mosaic teachings and those of Ax-Tell and the children of the Law of One.

The entity gained throughout the experience. For its purposes, its activities were not only for the betterment in the daily activity but for the building up of body and of mind by and through the application of spiritual laws that coordinate the physical manifestations in a material body. The name then was Zes-Zeun.     2540-1

A New Jersey librarian was told she had been among the newborn in the colony:

Before that the entity was again in the land of the present nativity during those periods when activities were set up or established in the Southwest, by those who had journeyed from other lands when the ten tribes were carried away.
  The entity was among those children born in that land, now a portion of Arizona and New Mexico. These portions of the land appeal in many ways to the entity—the wide open spaces, and yet there is a desire for home, for security, in mental as well as in spiritual as may apply in material things.
  The entity became a teacher, one after whom the young modeled, and things pertaining to such direction should be a part of the present experience of the entity.     3513-1

Reading 4129, given in December, 1925, also mentions America, but no specific location is described.

. . . in the days when . . . the peoples of the Promise came to the foreign shores in now America, the entity then . . . came as the mother in the first of those peoples. Then in the name Ibeois, and the entity developed much in that plane and gained much spiritual understanding of the developments of people . . .     4129-1

## The English Colony

The most important center for the escaping Jews was in England. The site which drew them has a long history in the metaphysical and spiritual traditions of the world. The migration to England took the Jews to the legendary Druid center, the site of Stonehenge and future location of the first Christian church, settled in England by Joseph of Arimathaea in the first century, and later the fields of King Arthur's castle of the Holy Grail. This important spiritual center was active before the Jews arrived and has continued to exert a profound influence and mystery on man into the present. The readings enhance the legend.

Somerset is clearly described as the center where the royal family, the descendants of Hezekiah and Zedekiah, settled, joining with the children of Israel who had foregathered. The connection between Stonehenge and the altars built by the Jews is not clearly spelled out in the readings, but references suggest some connection.

In 1944, a young Pennsylvania teen-ager was told:

> Before that we find the entity was in the English land in the early settlings of the children of Israel who were foregathered with the daughters of Hezekiah in what is now Somerland, Somerhill, or Somerset. There the entity saw group organizations for the preservation of tenets and truths of the living God, just as those admonitions would be for the entity in the present as it begins that social service with children.
>
> Preserve the law of the Lord. For it is perfect and it converteth the soul. Not, then, by might or power but by His word, saith the Lord of hosts.
>
> In the experience the entity gained, for it helped in establishing aids to the children of the period in making better homes, in making better relationships in the abilities to care for selves, and as vocational activities . . .
>
> The name then was Ruth.                                                  5384-1

Altars as well as homes were established:

> . . . the entity was in the Holy Land when there were those breakings up in the periods when the land was being sacked by the Chaldeans and Persians.
>
> The entity was among those groups who escaped in the ships that settled in portions of the English land near what is now Salisbury, and there builded those altars that were to represent the dedications of individuals to a service of a living God.
>
> Thus the entity aided in giving the records and teachings that may help others in the present, in giving to others that helping hand—who may be as a record keeper.
>
> The name then was Mayra.                                                 3645-1

A 1938 reading for a missionary writer tells that not only the religious laws were preserved, but also the economic laws. Dan, the tribe with a seafaring background, and Judah, the royal tribe, combined efforts:

> . . . when there was the breaking up of what has been in our memories or histories given as the taking of the ten tribes, or their dispersing.
>
> The entity then was among those who came into the land now known as the English, and was of those peoples who were the children of one faithful in many ways—being a portion of those descended from the children of Dan and those who had been with Caleb in Bethlehem.
>
> Then the entity was of both those tribes, but entered into the activities in the land for the preservation not only of those manners of worship, those manners of preserving lives, but of the economic laws that h`ad been a part of the experience of those peoples who were the fathers of the entity then—in the name Zedekiah.
>
> In the experience the entity gained, but in the latter portion lost. For the signs, the symbols came to be rather as the purposes than that for which they were brought into being.
>
> Thus the entity failed in that portion. But the entity had a helpful, developing experience in all the manners of health, of sanitation, of diets. 　　　　　　　　　　　　　　　　　　　　　　　　1598-1

A Minnesota housewife had been one of Hezekiah's grandchildren who went to England. In time the center was absorbed, but it left its stamp upon the nation:

> Before that the entity was in the English land during those periods when there was the breaking up of the tribes of Israel.
>
> The entity was a granddaughter of Hezekiah the king, and among those who set sail to escape when the activities brought the rest of the people into servitude in the Persian land.
>
> Then the entity was among those who landed and set up the seat of customs as indicated in the altars built near what is now Salisbury, England. These were the early traditions carried into those activities.
>
> The name then was Elemeshia. The entity gained in the ability as a leader, in the ability to influence others, the ability to control the activities of individuals in such a way as to make for the forming of moral habits and ideas in their material experiences. 　　　　　　　3590 -1

Apparently the migrations stretched over a long period of time, like an underground railway. Another member of the royal family is found in a 1940 reading:

Before that the entity was in the land now known as the English land, during the very early developments there of a people who were a part of the tribes that had been dispersed with Hezekiah's being carried into captivity in the Chaldean land.

The entity was the younger of the queen's household that came into the England land—the name Ariel. In the experience the entity aided its companions, those of its own household, of its own families or tribes—as they were known in those periods—to establish homes, places of refuge, places for the protection of individuals as well as groups, when hardships or turmoils would arise in their experience.

In the present we find the desires, innate and manifested, and the channels or outlets through which the greater awareness and consciousness of the abilities to aid may come—in advice with, and in counseling with, others. 2109-2

The re-establishment of the altars for worship was an important consideration.

The entity was with those people who sought refuge in what is now the English land, and in and about what is now Somerset. The entity was with the groups who had come from even the temple watch in Jerusalem, who established the outer courts or the temple for individual service and activity, as well as the altars which have long since been torn away and yet there are evidences of these having been set up in a form of a court and an inner court for the admonitions and the directions and encouragements to peoples who would learn the Lord.

The name then was Puella. 5276-1

Altars are again mentioned in this reading from 1944. A South Dakota woman was told:

. . . the entity was in the English land during those periods when there were the activities from the daughter of Zedekiah, the king, whose activities were cut short and then prolonged by Nebuchadnezzar. There was the founding of those activities in the English land in and about those places where the stones were set up as the altars. These were to represent the tabernacle. These were enlarged upon and these were those experiences of the entity, and thus all forms of mysticism, all forms of occult science, occult influences were a portion of the activity; as the holy of holies, the ephod, Urim, and Thummim; all of these were parts of the entity's experience.

The entity then was in the present sex, in the name Judith. The entity guided the interpreting of the worship in the forms which set up discarding blood sacrifice for those as of fruits, yet blood by those that were of another form of same in its activities. Thus relationships which were and are a part of man's experience became abhorrent to the entity in its present period of development. 5259-1

With the dispersion and the wandering, the Israelites were given new opportunities to establish the seeds and fruits of a universal consciousness. A Jewish man was told:

Before that the entity was in the English land during those periods when there were those journeyings into that land from the Holy Land, when the children of Hezekiah prompted many of those even in authority to leave the Holy Land because of Nebuchadnezzar's activities.

The entity was young in years when it came into the coasts of England where altars were set up to tie up the meanings of "The Lord thy God is one." The building up of this thought makes no bonds, no slaves among any peoples.

The name then was Jeheuh. The entity gained greatly.

Hence the abilities to meet with its fellow man, to control through its personality; that is, being what it is truly and not just to be seen of men but to be seen of its Maker. 3581-1

The female members of the royal family were actively engaged in the work of resettlement. "The daughters of Hezekiah" are mentioned throughout, probably as a guild. The following describes a daughter of Zedekiah:

The entity was of the daughters of Zedekiah, and among those who— through the activities of some of the children of Benjamin, Judah and Dan—came to the Isles, and began the establishing of an understanding that the mysteries of the ages that had been handed down to the priests—in the judgment of the records given by the prophets and sages of old—could or might be established in such a form, such a manner as to ever present—to the peoples who looked upon same—a reminder of the promises of Divinity to the children of men—even in their weakness!

Then the entity was in the name Zeurah, and a prophetess—yea, as one given in the understanding of the influences of the seasons, of the years, of the signs as set in what ye call the zodiac, in what ye call the various phases of man's experience.

Hence the entity gained, yet set—as it were—a temptation in the way of others; in that the *symbol* became to mean more than that for which it had stood!

Man is three-dimensional in his aspects and study of what he finds within and without, and as to its source and its end—yet of the moment and not the whole. For know as of old: "Know, O ye people, the Lord thy God is one!"                                      1580-1

One male of the Davidic dynasty also survived. Apparently he escaped the punishment meted to Zedekiah's heirs. He went to England, worked with his hands, and developed spiritually. In 1939, a young Jewish boy was told:

Before this we find ye—as the grandson of Zedekiah—made for those activities in the land now known as the English, where—with those of thy peoples—ye set up the attempted activity in that land.

There ye went, not a priest but rather as a teacher, a workman with thy hands; as a leader, as a director—in the name then Zeruben.

In the experience ye gained, for ye established freedom of individual activity, yet united in one accord for the common good of all in the material relationships.

The weaknesses of forcing the purposes, the issues, became manifest during the experience; yet these *grew* by the tempering of self *for* the greater purposes to be those lessons that ye may apply in this present experience.                                      1856-1

## *Ireland*

The Irish have a long-standing tradition that Jeremiah, the prophet, came with the remnant of the royal tribe of David and established a settlement in Ireland.

This reading speaks of an Irish colony. In 1939, an incarnation as Zedekiah's granddaughter was described for a six-year-old girl:

> Before that we find the entity was in the land now known as the Promised Land, during those periods when there was the breaking up of the land under the king who was carried away captive into the Persian land.
>
> There we find the entity was a granddaughter of that king, Zedekiah, in the name Zelka; among those peoples who escaped from the activities under Nebuchadnezzar's forces and took ship for that now known as Ireland.
>
> There we find the entity was among those who set up or established a part of a settlement in that land. Hence then of a hardy people, those accustomed to things that would have to do with the out-of-doors . . .
>
> In the experiences then we find the entity developed through those activities, bringing about the greater longings for places and activities where there might be the better mental and spiritual interpretations of those things that had been handed down to its peoples as customs, as things that happened in the varied ways and manners as legends of its peoples, legends of its leaders, its kings, and those who went not to stand before—those of the powers of the south and the east and the north and the west. All of these are latent within the experience of the entity in the present sojourn.                                    2005-1

## On the Altars of the World

Wherever the scattered people went—America, Mexico, England, or Babylon—they established altars. Although this extract describes altars in Yucatan, it is the premise behind the activities in all the newly settled lands. The work has always been to lead souls back to the universal consciousness.

> The altars upon which there were the cleansings of the bodies of individuals (not human sacrifice . . . ), these were later the altars upon which individual activities—that would today be termed hate, malice, selfishness, self-indulgence—were cleansed from the body through the ceremony, through the rise of initiates from the sources of light, that came from the stones upon which the angels of light during the periods gave their expression to the peoples.                                    5750-1

# Judah in Babylon

*When ye forsake my ways ye shall be scattered, ye shall be without those things that would bring ye into the knowledge—until that time is fulfilled.* **3976-13**

The Israelites were called to establish the kingdom of God on earth, but where the kingdom was to be built, and how, was frequently misunderstood. Only a few, like David, knew it had to start from within.

As time passed, more and more of Israel's energy, thought and emotion was devoted to the material aspects and preservation of the kingdom, and less and less to its original spiritual intent and purpose. As the people became more enmeshed and involved with the outward forms, they lost sight of the inner principles through which the kingdom had come.

As captive slaves, Judah finally found the time to do that which it had failed while free—to find God.

The Cayce material tells us that wherever we are, in whatever condition we find ourselves, is the place we must begin to search for God. Judah had a multitude of opportunities in a variety of changing circumstances to search for and know God. As a free nation and in days of plenty, they gradually forgot and forsook those creative and spiritual principles which had formed and shaped the nation under Joshua, the Judges, and David. By forgetting God, they forgot about their souls and lost sight of the only power that could perpetuate the nation.

Although occasionally they were called back to the light by prophets and kings to enjoy renewed strength, vitality, and prosperity, they ultimately degenerated all the resources which had been given them. They were called to the light, only to drift back into the darkness. Over and over again the nation repeated this cycle, sliding ever closer to the final tragedy and national trauma when the "day of reckoning" arrived. They had misused and abused everything that had been entrusted to them, now everything was taken away—everything except God.

The captivity was caused by the same disregard that had brought on the deluge:

> . . . the deluge was not a myth . . . but a period when man had so belittled himself with the cares of the world, with the deceitfulness of his own knowledge and power, as to require that there be a return to his dependence wholly—physically and mentally—upon the Creative Forces.
>
> **3653-1**

A Jewish businessman was told in his reading that he had been among "the sons of Moses," a direct descendant, and that the spiritual lesson of the captivity was not lost on him.

> The entity gained through this experience, for those waitings, those openings of the hearts of the peoples in an alien or foreign land, brought many lessons to the entity, that service to man is the highest service that may be rendered to the God. This the entity has lost in, somewhat, in the present, yet is there that bond ever present that self must be in touch with that upon which one may lean, not only in dire circumstances, but in joys, in pleasures, in hardships, in trials . . .         **426-2**

In captivity the Jews were forced into introspection and re-evaluation. They had time to question their direction and, aided by great prophets like Daniel, Jeremiah, and Ezekiel, awaken with humility and obedience to the Spirit and to their service to man.

Although the seventy years of captivity was a time in which the traditions and religious experiences of the past became "hearsay" (2305-2), and much was neglected by the teachers and interpreters of the law (2444-1), and a great deal of drunkenness or dissipation prevailed among the Jews who were favored with high positions in the court (1096-2), there was also that important "remnant," that immeasurably valuable handful, who kept clear of all these influences and searched for God.

It was the people who entertained the spirit of God within who had the most influence on their captors. Deep calls to deep, the psalmist said, and spirit to spirit. Both the Chaldeans and the Jews were sons of God. As the Jews reawakened to the universal spirit of the Father–God in them, it drew out a response from the same spirit within the Chaldean, and later the Persian, so that all could work together for the fulfillment of God's will—that not one soul should perish. Thus Jeremiah counseled the captive Jews in Babylon not to resist the bondage, but to "seek the peace of the city" where they had been taken and "to pray for it." (Jeremiah 29:7) Only by finding God in the place where they found themselves could they ever become at-one with His spirit and agents of His will.

## The Highest Service

If service to man is the highest service to God (426-2), and the greater service to man is "awakening an individual to the consciousness of that presence which may abide within" (2787-1), as slaves the Jews were in a unique position to serve. Through their long and highly developed relationship with the creative forces, with the added impetus given through David and Solomon, the nation had much to give in the fields of wisdom, art, and science.

Some vivid accounts of the *spiritual* service are found in the Book of Daniel. Several Life readings of this period give additional insights into the ability of the "slaves" to lift the consciousness of their captors.

## An Account of Slavery

Nebuchadnezzar recognized the superiority of the Jews, and ordered the flower of the population to grace his court.

*And the king spoke of Ashpaz the chief of his eunuchs, that he should bring some of the children of Israel, of the royal families and the nobility, youths without blemish, handsome and skilful in all wisdom, endowed with knowledge, understanding learning, and competent to serve in the king's palace, and to teach them the letters and language of the Chaldeans.* (Daniel 1:4)

The following reading amplifies this text as it describes the experience of a Jewish maiden in the courts of Babylon:

Before that we find the entity was in the land when the children of promise were among those who were carried away captive.

There we find the entity was among those of the then Chaldean or Persian land, during those periods when there were the activities under Nebuchadnezzar; and there we find the entity was among those whom the lords of Nebuchadnezzar's army had besieged.

Thus we find the entity coming into those activities in which persecutions were not exactly the nature, because the entity became a slave, for the slaves in that experience were those who were learned in the arts or in what ye call science, or in what ye call beautiful speech or poetry or art, or *all* of those things. For that was thought by those to be rather only the work of those who had the time or the period to devote to such study.

Again, then, we find the entity gave expression in song, in music upon the harp—not in the shape of the harp known today, but the harp of the period, that was much in the shape of a butterfly wing.

But the longings for the hills of its native land, the songs for those periods of sacrifice, the songs for those periods of rejoicing—all brought to the land that which eventually—through its evolution in the hearts and minds of those peoples—brought redemption *for* the entity's people, that came again in the much later periods to its own land again. The entity did not see the land—it in the material plane knew little of that which brought such about, yet deep and innate within self is felt, from the activities, the *joy* of being good—not only because of its innate abilities but the harmony as created within the very *being* itself, and the great abilities that may arise in the experience of those who *practice* such in their daily life.

The name then was Estha—of the peoples led away by the first of the armies of Nebuchadnezzar *from* the regions about Jerusalem—and of the daughters of Rechab. 1934-1

As can be imagined, not all slaves enjoyed their position. The following reading pictures a young Jewish beauty forced into "abhorrent" activities by her captors:

Before that we find the entity was in the land now called the Persian, or a portion of India or Mesopotamia and those portions of the lands to which the chosen peoples were taken as captives—or in bondage.

Hence the entity was of those that were close in the household of Zedekiah, the king carried into Babylon.

Because of the beauty, because of the abilities of the entity, it found favor among the leaders of the soldiery and thus was protected; but became—by force, not by choice—as a pawn among those leaders. Thus it was forced into activities that were abhorrent to the individual's self in the experience.

Yet from the *mental* forces the entity gained.

As to the activities from that sojourn, we find in the present the love of ease; the abilities to find grace or favor—many of these come from those experiences; as does the love of soft things, the delicate things close to the body—and yet the knowledge of [what] all these imply is as an innate force in the experience.

The name then was Shasdacha.                    1522-1

The readings make it clear that every incarnation is influenced and conditioned by the lives which preceded it. It is the biblical law of "what ye sow, so shall ye reap." Although the two entities above were in the collective karma of their nation, both knowing slavery, their individual experiences were diverse and unique, the result of activities begun in former lives.

In the preceding life, both entities had incarnated in Egypt during the same period; [1934] gained spiritually as an instructor in "artistic manners and forms" for use as home decorations and temple services. The good vibrations set up in that life influenced her opportunities and experience as a slave in Babylon.

In Egypt [1522] ministered to the sick and afflicted in hospital service, but as she rose to position and authority, turned to self-indulgence and "brought for itself that of condemnation." The bad vibrations of her Egyptian life were encountered karmicly through those "abhorrent" activities inflicted by the self-indulgence of her Babylonian captors.

Although our local, national, or world communities may be building karmic conditions which will be met on an inevitable "day of reckoning" our experiences within the pattern need not be traumatic nor bitter. When Jesus spoke of the great tribulation of the "latter days" he urged his disciples to pray and avoid the things of the world which burden the spirit in order to be "worthy to escape" from those things which were bound to happen. (Luke 21:34–36) These two readings, in the great cycle of the last days of the Jewish monarchy, show the universal and timeless validity of doing good.

## Daniel

Among the most memorable events during the captivity are found in the Book of Daniel and revolve around the experiences and visions of the prophet for whom the book is named.

Reading 3976-15 contains a clear indication that Jacob and John the Beloved were incarnations of the same soul. The reading states that this entity is "one beloved of all men in all places where the universality of God in the earth has been proclaimed . . . " No figure in the Old Testament is more beloved than Daniel. Comparisons between the Book of Daniel and the Revelation reveal a similarity which strongly suggests Daniel as another incarnation of John. (See the visions of the beasts, prophecies of the latter days, and compare Daniel 8:15–19 with Revelation 1:17; 22:8.) Jacob, Daniel, and John—the dreams and visions of these three beloved figures have guided, shaped, and opened man's consciousness to the glories of God.

In the first chapter of Daniel, the prophet takes a stand:

*But Daniel resolved that he would not defile himself with the king's rich food, or with the wine which he drank.* (Daniel 1:8)

This reading tells why.

**As has been given of old, when the children of Israel stood with the sons of the heathen, and all ate from the king's table, that which was taken that only exercised the imagination of the body in physical desires—as strong drink, strong meats, condiments that magnify desires with the body—this builded, as Daniel well understood, not for God's service . . . he chose, rather, that the everyday, the common things would be given, so that the bodies, the minds might be a more perfect channel for the manifestations of God; for the forces of the Creator are in every force that is made manifest in the earth.** **341-31**

## Daniel and Nebuchadnezzar

How can anyone interpret a dream when its contents are not known? This was the task Nebuchadnezzar put to his astrologers, magicians, and sorcerers after his spirit became troubled by a dream. (Daniel 2) He refused to divulge the dream, and promised riches and reward to the one who could tell him the dream and its meaning, and death to all if an interpretation was not forthcoming.

This was a difficult task, but not an impossible one. According to Edgar Cayce, the Chaldeans were the first people to give psychic readings. (3744-1) They began about 4000 B.C., the reading asserts, and were given as a means to assist the flow of the life-giving forces of soul and spirit to and through the physical body—a description which applies equally as well to the Edgar Cayce readings!

Apparently the psychic arts were lost to the Chaldeans by Nebuchadnezzar's time, approximately a thousand years later, for there was no one among his wise men who possessed the psychic sensitivities to meet the unusual situation created by Nebuchadnezzar.

Edgar Cayce was often asked to interpret forgotten dreams. Instances of this are found frequently in the 900 series, and in other readings as well. Other times, when dreams were written out and submitted for interpretation, Cayce elaborated upon the forgotten elements of the dream which had not been recorded. The reading would often stimulate instant recall by the dreamer who then was able to confirm the accuracy of the interpretation.

In a reading devoted to the subject of "psychic phenomena," Cayce discussed his own ability to gather information while in the psychic state:

In this [trance] state the conscious mind becomes subjugated to the subconscious, superconscious, or soul-mind; and may and does communicate with like minds, and the subconscious or soul force becomes universal. From any subconscious mind information may be obtained, either from this plane or from the impressions as left by the individuals that have gone on before.                                3744-2

Speaking of the trance state again, in another reading we find:

. . . in this body [Cayce] lying here, we find all life in suspension; only

portions of the higher vibrations in accord with those vibrations that
communicate with the universal forces. 900-10

Apparently Edgar Cayce was able to achieve the same attunement
with the universal as Daniel.

The decree that all the wise men of Babylon would be slain included
Daniel and his companions. Daniel besought the king for an appoint-
ment, then he returned to his house and, with his friends, prayed that
God would reveal the dream and its meaning.

That night while Daniel's conscious mind and physical body were in
that state of "suspension" called sleep (or deep meditation) his subconscious and superconscious minds were in attune with the universal
forces, and he received the vision. Apparently he attuned his mind to
the subconscious mind of Nebuchadnezzar and the impressions his
dream had created upon it.

Daniel went to Nebuchadnezzar and recounted his dream and its
meaning. Daniel's accuracy is confirmed through Nebuchadnezzar's reaction:

*Then King Nebuchadnezzar fell upon his face, and did homage to Daniel,
and commanded that an offering and incense be offered up to him. The
king said to Daniel, "Truly, your God is God of gods and Lord of kings,
and a revealer of mysteries, for you have been able to reveal this mystery."
Then the king gave Daniel high honors and many great gifts and made
him ruler over the whole province of Babylon and chief prefect over all the
wise men of Babylon. (Daniel 2:46)*

## *The Fiery Furnace*

Daniel was either an able teacher or among a group in an advanced
state of consciousness. When Nebuchadnezzar built an enormous statue
of solid gold and ordered all the officials of his kingdom to bow down
and worship it, Shadrach, Meshach, and Abednego refused. The king
was enraged and threatened the men with death in a fiery furnace.
The men were unshaken, and answered:

*"O Nebuchadnezzar, we have no need to answer you in this matter. If it
be so, our God whom we serve is able to deliver us from the burning fiery
furnace; and he will deliver us out of your hand, O king. But if not, be it*

*known to you, O king, that we will not serve your gods or worship the golden image which you have set up."* (Daniel 3:16)

The men were cast into the furnace, and were not consumed. They walked about singing and praying with a fourth person whom Nebuchadnezzar discerned through the flames. (Daniel 3:25) Apparently it was a total absorption with the God–consciousness which worked the miracle of deliverance, as the following reading will indicate.

A dream reading was requested by a young Jewish stockbroker with pronounced psychic ability. The reading was the eighty–eighth in his series. In the preamble, Cayce said of the dreamer:

In the dreams as are seen as presented to this entity, more and more come those visions of that in which and through which the entity may gain for self that insight into that full consciousness of the strength that lies from within, when once attuned to that consciousness that brings those lessons, those experiences, to the body-conscious mind through the subconscious forces of the entity, and the entity may gain in mental, physical, and financial manners from same. Ready for dream. 137-88

A dramatic dream with an obvious parallel to the fiery furnace was submitted.

Evening of September 30, or morning of October 1, 1929. A direct comparison between the essence or heat energy in fire and the essence or human energy of Man. Both seemed one and the same substance or force. I, or someone, jumped into the fire to prove this oneness. Someone else thought that I or the person who jumped in the fire to indicate that the force of my inner self and the outer world are one and the same force or God, was crazy. The person in the fire seemed to have a peculiar expression, but felt no pain.          137-88

The answer gives an insight into men of the fiery furnace.

The entity sees, visions, here is an experience that is as one of the lessons as proof to the entity of the oneness of all force, energy, or what not, varied in its various aspects, and the entity in studying same, and the effect upon the individual, gains an insight into the lessons as would be studied by the entity—for, as is seen, all energy set in motion becomes an applied force in its application, and, as is seen, when one universal law, whether of human energy or of that in an *element*, as is created by the energy meeting those laws through the combustibility, as is called fire, then we see how that only at a different angle does each present itself to the consciousness of man, and man making self, then, in the at-onement with the forces, is able to overcome or demonstrate the whole oneness, yet man, conscious of the other variations in the one force, feels the burning pain, and not the at-oneness.                 137-88

The miracle of the fiery furnace had an indirect effect as a spiritual service. Like Daniel's revelation, it brought Nebuchadnezzar to the point of conversion.

*Then Nebuchadnezzar came near to the door of the burning fiery furnace and said, "Shadrach, Meshach, and Abednego, servants of the Most High God, come forth, and come here." Then Shadrach, Meshach, and Abednego came out from the fire. And the satraps, the prefects, the governors, and the king's counselors gathered and saw that the fire had not had any power over the bodies of those men; the hair of their heads was not singed, their mantles were not harmed, and no smell of fire had come upon them.*

*Nebuchadnezzar said, "Blessed be the God of Shadrach, Meshach, and Abednego, who has sent his angel and delivered his servants, who trusted in him, and set at naught the king's command, and yielded up their bodies rather than serve and worship any god except their own God. Therefore I make a decree: . . . for there is no other god who is able to deliver in this way."*

*Then the king promoted Shadrach, Meshach, and Abednego in the province of Babylon.* (Daniel 3:26-30)

Daniel in the lion's den (Daniel 6) may be explained by the same principle. Daniel's awareness of God's presence was so all-pervasive that he saw the lion as a creation of God rather than the wild, fearful creature men have been conditioned to seeing. Thus he and the lion were at-one with the same spirit and no harm came to either.

## Nebuchadnezzar's Madness and the Tree of Life

The fourth chapter of Daniel consists of a letter which Nebuchadnezzar had circulated throughout his kingdom. It is the account of his madness which possessed him for seven years, rendering him as a "beast of the field" and the dream which had previewed this condition and the interpretation which Daniel had accurately ascribed to it.

Nebuchadnezzar had several dramatic examples shown him of the power of God manifesting through man. He recognized the spirit and had awakened to it himself by showing mercy and forgiveness, yet he could not turn away from the self-indulgent pleasures of his court life, nor from the ego-centered imaginations of his own mind. The same conflict had driven Saul to madness and led to the death of pharaoh who had hardened his heart after witnessing the increasing manifestations of Moses' spiritual power.

The Tree of Life in Genesis 2 is a symbol of man's soul in true attunement with God. In the Revelation, the Tree of Life symbolizes the soul, or entity, whose purposes are rooted in the spirit of the Christ. (281-37)

In Nebuchadnezzar's dream, he saw a great tree growing in the midst of the earth:

*"The tree grew and became strong, and its top reached to heaven, and it was visible to the end of the whole earth. Its leaves were fair and its fruit abundant, and in it was food for all. The beasts of the field found shade under it, and the birds of the air dwelt in its branches, and all flesh was fed from it."* (Daniel 4:11-12)

An angel intrudes in the dream and hews the tree down, and proclaims:

*"Let his mind be changed from a man's and let a beast's mind be given to him and let seven times pass over him."* (Daniel 4:16)

The angel then declares the purpose for this is to teach men that the Most High rules the kingdoms of men and gives it to whomever He wills.

Daniel was to the point in his interpretation of the Tree.

*"It is you, O king, who have grown and become strong."* (Daniel 4:22)

The downfall portended in the dream came from separation and

Nebuchadnezzar's true lack of understanding as to the real source of his power and ability. His ego, his passions and desires, brought on his downfall and his madness. After seven years, he experienced a complete change in consciousness and a new understanding. He was a little bit closer to being the true "tree of life" which never falls.

*"At the end of the days I, Nebuchadnezzar, lifted my eyes to heaven, and my reason returned to me, and I blessed the Most High and praised and honored him who lives forever; for his dominion is an everlasting dominion, and his kingdom endures from generation to generation . . .*

*At the same time my reason returned to me; and for the glory of my kingdom, my majesty, and splendor returned to me. My counselors and my lords sought me, and I was established in my kingdom, and still more greatness was added to me. How I, Nebuchadnezzar, praise and extol and honor the king of heaven; for all his works are right and his ways are just; and those who walk in pride he is able to abase."* (Daniel 4:34-37)

The counsel in this reading applies equally to Nebuchadnezzar's experience.

**So will He, that is the Maker of Heaven and earth, He that is the uprising and the down-sitting of all mankind, bring to thy life and thy experience that necessary for thy greatest development—and peace and harmony within self will be the result, if thy purposes, thy desires, thy labors are spent in the activity for others, rather than attempting to justify ideas of any moral, physical, or mental relationships.**

**Know that truth and honor need no justification; rather the glorifying of same only is righteousness in the sight of thy Maker.          2061-1**

This queen of Nebuchadnezzar's learned a lesson by observation.

**Before that the entity was in the Persian land, during those periods when peoples were brought in as chattels, or as servants, from other lands. For, the entity then was one of the royal family, being the wife of the king during that experience; knowing then much of the madness of Nebuchadnezzar, as well as of the sojourns of the peoples under bondage.**

**Those were periods that will be expressive in the present experiences of the entity; that those things of material security, that are of the**

worldly nature, are the less secure than friends and spiritual peace—spiritual peace from knowing that there is that activity in the relationships to individuals, no matter what their position in life may be—that ye should do to them as ye would desire to be done to thee if circumstances were altered, or reversed.

Those lessons learned then by the entity, even from those who were servants to the entity, may be those that may keep the balance in the experiences through this present sojourn . . .

The name then was Sczeldhardi. In the experience the entity suffered mentally, the entity was exalted materially, the entity sought gratification of self's own indulgences; and yet in the later portion the entity gained through trouble, turmoil, and the deposing of the powers—with the madness of the companion.                    2468-1

## Captives and their Masters

The great service of spiritual awakening was performed in less dramatic ways than the events recorded in Daniel. The Jewish slaves as they searched for and awakened to the Spirit had a subtle but lasting effect upon their Chaldean captors, as several readings testify. The presence of the spirit was over all. The following describe the various awakenings and manifestations of the spirit in the lives of those who lived in Babylon through this period.

Jewish slaves played a role in the spiritual awakening of this Chaldean. Although in authority, this entity felt uneasiness in his soul as he looked upon the conquered peoples:

Before that the entity was in the Chaldean land, during those periods when there were peoples gathering there from other lands.

The entity then was one close in authority to those who ruled in the land, during the period of Nebuchadnezzar and those closely following same.

Hence we find that the entity enjoyed the blessings, or curses (dependent upon their use), which the natural sources and resources had to offer. Yet the entity was not wholly pleased with the happenings, because of the social environs as well as the lack of harmony—in those periods—in the mental and spiritual development of the peoples.

The entity then heard many mournings of a people, and of many peoples of varied lands—and combined what may be called the true

oriental music (or the mourns) with the joys of those who put their trust
wholly in, and looked for, redeeming force and power.

Then the name was Helzonput—the entity gained, lost, and gained;
gained in the very desire to keep the helpful influences in the minds of
those with whom the entity came in contact, so as to bring joy and
harmony; lost in the turning of these influences for self's own gain, and
in the exerting of same for self's own indulgences.

But from that sojourn we find in the present that great abilities arise
from deep within, to wield a power of might, as well as the still small
voice of love and hope.                                          2132-1

A Jewish housewife was told that as a young captive she kept her
faith:

. . . when the entity's peoples were being carried away into captivity by
the Persians, or by Nebuchadnezzar and his horde and hosts.

The entity was among the younger people who were thus carried
away, yet its sincerity of purpose in keeping its tenets as to its relationships to Creative Forces, or those things that had been taught by those
of its own household, brought hardships—but harmony—by the very
influence of such in the experience, though in a strange land.

The name then was Elkan.                                        2061-1

This reading speaks of Chaldean cruelty and a lesson to be learned:

The entity was among the leaders of Nebuchadnezzar's forces, in the
name then Xerteiun.

In the experience the entity made for that which finds expression in
the present; as to its politics, its home, its business being as separate
things in the life.

But know the truth of that which was taught by those priests whom
ye heard of old, and those upon whom you made many stripes for the
announcing of their faith (or had it done) that "The Lord thy God is
One!" Know that their law is true. While life and death are the
opposites, they are constant companions one with another. Only the
destructive forces know death as lord. Only spiritual or creative forces
know life *as* the Lord. Know *ye* the Lord!                    1432-1

The spiritual influence from the Jewish slaves formed deep-seated spiritual insights for this Babylonian leader—with results which helped later to free the captive people. In 1940 an Austrian housewife was told:

Before that the entity was in the Chaldean land, during those periods when a people became as servants, as chattel of that land *over* which, *through* which, the entity had influence and power.

For the entity was of the household of one Beltzadader, a leader of one of Nebuchadnezzar's armed groups.

There the entity gained greatly in its abilities to apply some of those tenets gathered from those who became servants to the entity through a portion of that experience.

And the entity applied same in its relationships or dealings with others—not as to what might be termed its court or social life, other than in a general manner; yet the purposes, the intents, the activities of the entity then—as Shalazur—were those tenets, those principles that years later made for the creating of that which *freed* a peoples, under those determinations and activities of Xerxes; also at those periods of the return of that people who had taught much to the entity, through those tenets and principles of the young, who had been instructed in that law which is universal—"As ye would that men should do to you, do ye even so to them."

It is simple in words, yet so deep in its meaning, so far-reaching in its application in every phase of human experience! For it is the opposite of greed, avarice, hate, and that which makes people afraid.  2170-1

This princess was aided in her natural spiritual development by her Jewish slaves.

Before that the entity was in the Chaldean land, during those periods when there were other lands brought under submission—politically.

The entity then was a princess in that land. Yet, coming under the care of some of those that were as but slaves, the entity gained by that association.

Abilities as a danseuse, abilities as an artist, abilities as a musician, arise from the entity's application of the tenets gained in the youth, in the meeting of the problems in the court during those periods of activity— even in the court of Nebuchadnezzar, the king in Babylonia. Though the entity was of the Babylonians, it was not as those of the legends; of Babylon but not a Babylonian. For, the entity applied its abilities not to excite or to satisfy the selfish appetites, but rather was known for its beauty, its grace, its dependability in developing body and mind to those of the beauties rather than the low, the mean things as may arise from gratifying appetites.

The name then was Schardezrah. And this was one of the great material experiences of the body-entity . . . For there were the purposes, the desires for the manifesting of beauty and grace among those with whom the entity constantly came in contact through that sojourn.

It is well to use those promptings in this present experience.

2559-1

Although one of Zedekiah's daughters (1580) and two grandchildren (1856, 2005) escaped to England, at least one daughter went to Babylon and worked for the release of her people. A young Virginia housewife was told:

The entity then was among the princesses of the Jewish peoples, or of the daughters of Zedekiah, who was carried into the Babylonian land; becoming associated with those who were in authority during those periods when there was the re-establishing of that people, in the Persian and Chaldean land . . .

Then the entity was in the name Esmara, and the entity aided in establishing among its own peoples that desire which later found expression before those in authority for the return of the peoples to the worship and the rebuilding in the Holy City.

In the experience, then, the entity gained the greater concept as to how to be, and not to be, the more helpful in all environs, in whatever might be the activities or the associations.          1857-2

# 26

# Liberation

## *Belschazzar and the Fall of Babylon*

*The* Babylonian empire scarcely outlived its founder, Nebuchadnezzar. The empire lasted seventy years, exactly coincident with the seventy years of captivity, over which Nebuchadnezzar reigned forty-five. Approximately twenty-five years after his death, the mighty empire collapsed under Belschazzar.

Shortly after Daniel interpreted "the handwriting on the wall" (Daniel 5), Babylon was taken by Cyrus the Great and supremacy passed to Persia.

The dissipation among the ruling class led to decay and weakness, and for Belschazzar created karmic knots which have yet to be untied.

A reading for a young musician began with an analysis:

> Many peoples are doubted by the entity. Many are weighed in the balance of mental ability by the entity and found wanting. Truly might it be said of the entity, as is seen in one of the experiences, that *"mene mene tekel upharsin"* to the entity ever stands before the entity; for to this entity the handwriting was *real*—being the king in power and ruler at that period. **4609-1**

## Dreams and the Fall of Babylon

Unusual events surround the fall of Babylon. The handwriting on the wall was part of a precognitive prologue. Nebuchadnezzar's dream of the tree with the gold and silver bands around the trunk, also interpreted by Daniel, was another preview. (Daniel 2) Until the seventeenth century, Babylon was unsurpassed for its beauty, art, science, and power. Thus it was the most precious and imaged as "gold" in Nebuchadnezzar's dream. The Persian regime which followed this was strong and glorious, but fell short of Babylon's glory. Thus it was represented as "silver," a precious metal but inferior to gold.

The conqueror of Babylon, Cyrus, was also a soul of destiny, and unusual dreams surround his birth. When Cyrus' mother was still a young girl and a virgin, her father had a dream in which he saw a stream of water flowing from his daughter that flooded the whole Asian continent. During her term of pregnancy, Astyages had another vision. In the second he saw a vine growing from his daughter's womb that overshadowed Asia. The Magi interpreted both as portends of the destiny of his daughter's child—Cyrus the Great.

In 559 B.C. Cyrus began a revolt against the Median empire. Through a series of brilliant campaigns, he was able to unite many disaffected elements among the Medes; and in 540 he marched against Babylon.

The conquest of Babylon itself was unprecedented in the military annals of the orient. The city was taken without bloodshed, struggle, or the loss of life.

A clay cylinder of Cyrus' describes what took place:

*As I entered Babylon in peace, and established my royal residence in the palace amid jubilation and rejoicing, Marduk,[37] the great lord, warmed the hearts of the Babylonians toward me, while I for my part devoted myself daily to do him reverence. My troops wandered peacefully widespread throughout Babylon. In all Sumer and Akkad I let no man be afraid. I concerned myself with the internal affairs of Babylon and all its cities. The dwellers in Babylon . . . I freed from the yoke that ill became them. I repaired their houses, I healed their afflictions . . . I am Cyrus, king of all, the great king of the four corners of the earth.*

---

[37]Marduk was the chief Chaldean god.

With this triumph, Cyrus became master over western Asia, establishing an empire that stretched from India and Greece to the borders of Egypt.

In contrast to the brutal patterns of conquest and subjugation by the Assyrian and Babylonian kings, Cyrus' swift and brilliant rise to power was unmarred by atrocities and unusual violence. Whereas the Assyrians and Babylonians deported conquered nationals, Cyrus let them go back home.

The Bible pictures Cyrus as an enlightened king. His achievements reveal a man of broad and universal vision, an admirable and attractive figure among the despots of the ancient oriental world.

The author of many humane policies, Cyrus respected all religions. He honored the gods of Babylon, repaired their temples, and restored the cult statues. He followed a similar policy in Egypt.

In 538 B.C., in the first year of his regime, he fulfilled the vision of Isaiah, who had foreseen Cyrus a century earlier (Isaiah 44:28, 45:1), and the prophecies of Jeremiah, when he authorized the return of the Jews to Palestine and made arrangements for rebuilding the ravaged temple in Jerusalem.

One reading reminds us that the spirit of Christ is eternal and a part of every age:

**Ye have seen His Spirit in the leaders in all realms of activity, whether in the isles of the sea, the wilderness, the mountain, or in the various activities of every race, every color . . .          5749-5**

The Spirit of Christ moves through all men in all nations at all times to bring to completion God's cosmic plan of redemption and salvation. Cyrus, king of Persia, contributed to that plan. By releasing the Jews he was not favoring a nation but giving a blessing to all mankind.

## The Court of Cyrus

An elderly Virginia housewife, a Christian Scientist, was told of her life as Cyrus' queen. The reading alludes to the universality of purpose in Cyrus—that there might be "the good of all."

**Before that the entity was in the Persian or Babylonian land, when there had arisen the desires upon the part of Cyrus that there be given the**

opportunity for the varied groups over which he had become the power and might, to manifest in their *own* ways and manners; that it might be to the good of all.

The entity then was the queen, Amasmam. In the experience the entity gained greatly by its aid and help to those who were allowed, under the edicts as directed by the king, to return to the Promised Land and there to rebuild the worship which to them had become—then—merely a thing of which they had heard.

Thus the entity was in close association with Zerubbabel and those of his household—Nehemiah, who was a favorite of the entity during his service at the court, and who has been a part of the experiences of this entity in associations through activities in the earth more than in that experience alone.

The entity brought a helpful influence toward the educating of those who were to interpret the law, and to make same accessible.

Thus we find the abilities of the entity in the study of various groups, cults or isms, denominations, political and economic forces as may relate to groups or to states or to nations. And the entity's counsel in such is not to be passed over lightly.

In this experience, then, through its abilities as a speaker, a lecturer, a writer upon such subjects, the entity may bring that measure of service in which there may be *again* much given to others in their search for God—even as this was the motive prompting the entity's interest in these activities through that particular sojourn.

Yet also from that sojourn there is the urge for pomp, for having one's own way, for being in authority, and those influences that make for the feelings at times of superiority in so many little material things that are to be curbed in the entity's present experience.

Thus there has been brought many a trial to the physical influences or activities, through the stubbornness—rather has it been self-will, and not intentionally has the entity been dictatorial or stubborn. 2523-1

This reading supplies an interesting dimension to the Bible story. A young Alabama woman was told she had been Cyrus' daughter. This princess fell in love with Nehemiah, the great Jewish hero of the later period. Cayce counseled the former princess on the meaning of love as he interpreted her experience:

Before that the entity was in the Persian land in those experiences when there were the preparations for the return of a peoples to build a city to their God.

What, who, where is thy God? Just as ye experienced, as ye saw as the daughter of Cyrus who issued the decree to bring about these changes in the lands. These were disturbing for ye knew not how to apply. Yet they answered to something within thy activities then, in the name Purcelus.

It may be said that the entity gained, for there was the attempt to apply the teachings of those individuals. For, the entity then was very much in love with the cup bearer to the king, Nehemiah. And yet kept separate, kept aloof because of the religious as well as social conditions in the experience.

Remember, true love knows not barriers of any kind that are only of man's creation. For man is the co-creator with the builder and the maker of the universe, and yet creates conditions, positions, thoughts, that often turn and rend his own self. These were builded through the experience because of social positions, but the entity gained. For it learned a lesson of patience, as well as the abilities to sing and to play—if it would—and to dance well.

All of these have their place in the experience, but use them to the glory of God the more often, rather than for the mere satisfaction of the social or body emotions . . .

As the daughter of the king, the most powerful king in the earth at the time, and one called of God to set the house in order for those who felt themselves superior even to the king and yet were subject to him, ye found within thine own self abilities that are still latent. Do not dissipate them, but use them to the glory of God.         3351-1

This woman was told she not only aided those who encouraged the king, but also knew the rebuilding must start from within.

The entity then was among those peoples that aided in persuading the king who gave helpful advice and counsel to Zerubbabel, encouraging the hearts of Ezra and Nehemiah.

For the entity then was that one or as one who had not neglected the counsel of these who had given, "Keep these laws upon thine heart; bind them upon thine forehead; teach them to thy children that they depart not from the Lord."

Hence the entity was as the mother of those who would remember, bringing to those that were the leaders the encouragement necessary; not only for the trials of the passage but encouraged them in building in their lives and hearts and associations as one to another the remembrance of that which had been given, "Separate yourself if ye would become as those that would know the Lord and His ways!" And as these activities went forward, the entity gave the blessings to those, though not seeing the city nor its rebuilding herself.

Then in the name Esdrus.                                              1290-1

## Babylon Symbolizes Self

If, as the readings suggest, the story "from Abraham to Christ" in a blueprint, or pattern, of mental unfoldment (281-63) and the whole Bible, from Genesis to Revelation, is the complete story or pattern of man in the earth, demonstrating all his potential within for good and for evil, then Babylon, appearing near the end of the completed pattern, holds meaning and significance. Babylon has great importance in the Old Testament, and is a primary symbol in the Revelation of St. John, that last and most enigmatic book of the New Testament which Cayce believed held the key to the meaning of the whole Bible.

Both John and Isaiah prophesied the destruction of Babylon. Although Isaiah's pronouncements were directed toward the historical city, and John's were warnings for the early Christians, both prophecies were directed at the same condition—the selfishness of man.

Babylon represents a condition of consciousness, a state of mind and being. The city symbolizes the ideal of earthly pleasure and excesses of every kind, including misuse of the occult. It is the symbol of man led to a false awareness through the pursuit of selfish desire.

The dirge of Babylon which Isaiah sang for the city (Isaiah 47) can be applied equally well to any world-weary individual.

> *Your knowledge and your wisdom have misled you, and you have said in your heart "I am, and there is none else beside me."* . . . *You are wearied with the multitude of your thoughts.* (Isaiah 47:10, 13)

An interpretation was asked of the Babylon of the Revelation.

(Q) Does Babylon symbolize self?
(A) Babylon symbolizes self.

**(Q) Does Revelation 18 give some idea in symbols of the effect of the fall of self—[or] selfishness?**
**(A) It does.** 281-36

In an earlier reading, Cayce was asked to interpret the fall of Babylon as described by John in the fourteenth, seventeenth, and eighteenth chapters of the Revelation. Because it is a pattern of *every* soul's experience, the answer is included here.

Babylon represented the individual; those periods through which every soul passes in its delving into the varied mysteries that are the experiences of the carnal-mental, the spiritual-mental forces of the body; and, as viewed from that presented, may come to the knowledge only through the cleansing that is shown must come to those that would be saved from the destructions that are given there. 281-16

It is by purification and cleansing of the inner self that man can escape the destruction to his spirit created by selfishness. Only by returning to God can the soul be liberated from the accumulated burdens of earthly lives.

Babylon collapsed under the weight of its own self-indulgence, to fall to Cyrus, a universal liberator. Cyrus gave all the captive nations an opportunity to serve the gods they worshiped.

Israel was presented with a choice. They could remain in Babylon, plying the merchant trade which had made them wealthy, and retain their positions of influence and authority—or they could return to their Holy City, devastated Jerusalem, and build it anew.

Israel had followed the laws of God and accumulated the wealth of the world and knowledge. Now, if they were to continue following God, they must, like the rich young man in Jesus' parable, divest themselves of their earthly attachments. Their earthly ambitions led them into Babylon, a symbol for the egocentric, carnal-minded level of consciousness that holds the soul captive in the earth and its pleasures.

Only a handful, a remnant, stimulated and awakened by the Spirit, went back to Jerusalem to rebuild and complete the purpose which brought the Adamic race into the earth.

This ambition was not for any of man's earthly desires. It was no longer for riches, for the fame and renown of any particular nation, tribe, or individual—but for God alone, for His Spirit and the validation of His promises and protection. The purpose was spiritual, as it had been from the beginning. They were returning to the Holy City, the first ideal, to rediscover and obtain that original and permanent state of consciousness which souls knew before the fall. Jerusalem symbolizes man's effort to rebuild that condition while in the flesh.

## The Resurrection

A Cayce reading makes the startling statement that without the resurrection the whole purpose of Jesus' life "would have been as naught." (5749-10) The experience would have counted for nothing. A challenging concept, but true! Many holy men before and after Jesus have preached the kingdom of God and performed great miracles, but none has risen from the dead to be the answer to all man's needs and questions.

The resurrection is equally significant in the Old Testament.

In Ezekiel's famous vision of the dry bones (Ezekiel 37), the Lord was calling His people out of the graveyard of Babylon to the new life in the Promised Land. Unless the spirit could resurrect His people from the spiritual death, the whole purpose, the whole history—and the Bible itself—would have been lost, and the story of men would be incomplete.

In whatever way we may be dying—to whatever degree we may have already died—God's words are clear, "Unless I can restore you to life, I am not the Lord."

*Then he said to me, "Son of man, all these bones are the bones of the children of Israel, who said, 'Our bones are dried and our hope is lost; we are completely gone.'*

*Therefore prophesy and say to them, Thus says the Lord God; Behold, I will open your graves and bring you up out of them and bring you into the land of Israel. And you shall know that I am the Lord, when I have opened your graves and brought you up out of them,*

*And I will put my spirit in you, and you shall live, and I shall place you in your own land; then you shall know that I am the Lord; I have spoken it, and I will do it, says the Lord God." (Ezekiel 37:11-14)*

# Return from Bondage

*Evidence* is so scarce for this last and most critical, and crucial, phase of the Old Testament history, that one authority writes: "We are in the direst need of information as to the history of the Jews in the Persian period, and every scrap of material that promises help ought to be treasured and put to use."[38]

The two short books of Ezra and Nehemiah are the principal sources of information, and the authenticity of these books is seriously argued by Bible scholars. Most agree that Nehemiah is authentic history, but many dispute all claims to the reliability of Ezra.

The importance of this period is enormous. It is the last important period of revelation and activity between the Old Testament and the birth of Christ. It was the events in the Persian period that led to the restoration of the Jews in the Holy Land, a necessary precondition for the coming of the Christ.

No arguments can be settled until conclusive evidence is uncovered which will be acceptable and "treasured" by scholars. Until then, those who accept the readings as a reliable source of information will have graphic and illuminating insights which confirm, and conform to, the historical outline presented in the Bible, enriched with a lustrous por-

---

[38]*Interpreter's Bible*, Abingdon Press.

trayal of personalities, events, issues and controversies.

A surprising amount of the biblical incarnations in the readings fall into this period. Perhaps this was because of the relative similarity between that period and the present, with the great need to restore and rebuild spiritual ideals in a world threatened to be overrun and overcome with the effects of evil.

## Problems with the Readings

A large number of incarnations in the Life readings fall into this obscure period and supply considerable details, yet also raise serious questions which may delay their acceptance by scholarly minds. Perhaps the most difficult problem in dealing with their credibility is the consistent view taken that many individuals were active throughout all three returns. It is generally assumed there was a lapse of over one hundred years between the first return under Zerubbabel and the second and third under Ezra and Nehemiah. Thus, orthodox dating would make these individuals well over a century old.

Modern theologians feel that the first return granted by Cyrus was led by Sheshbazzar (Ezra 1:11) and was unsuccessful, and occasioned Zerubbabel's return years later during the reign of Darius. If this assumption is true, then it would put the three returns closer in time and make the "overlapping" expeditions in the readings credible. Yet the readings themselves adhere to the orthodox chronology.

The only way to have a basis to accept the view suggested by the readings of hale and hearty individuals over a century old still engaged in the work of rebuilding Jerusalem is to find an acceptable means to extend the lifespan of these individuals.

The Bible indicates that man's life in the beginning spanned centuries. The life was "nearly a thousand years" and gradually shortened "first from a thousand to a hundred and twenty, then to eighty" because of man's desire for self-gratification. (3976-29) Thus man can reverse the pattern. Our present life-span of seventy years is self-imposed and arbitrary, and can be extended indefinitely by living in harmony with certain creative principles. Dr. Josef P. Hrachovec, an expert on aging at the University of Southern California gerontology center, recently stated that all men have an inborn potential for living a century or longer. Dr. Hrachovec claims proper diet and exercise, and learning how to control emotional pressures, could enable modern man to stretch his life-span "like a rubberband." Another expert, Dr. Roy M. Hamlin, a research psychologist, says that if an individual feels needed and is willing to work, he can and will retain his competence and live longer, up to 120 and 140 years old. These contemporary insights suggest the possibility of hearty individuals active under the regimes of Zerubbabel, Ezra, and Nehemiah.

The readings also give no support to another popular view growing among biblical scholars that Nehemiah's return actually preceded Ezra's. The picture created by the readings follows in outline the structure presented in the Bible. Scholars feel there are too many contradictions and unresolved questions in the Ezra–Nehemiah narrative, and in order to reconstruct the true picture, transpose and interpolate chapters from Ezra to Nehemiah and vice versa. The readings fill in many of these questions and seeming contradictions, showing why Nehemiah had to follow Ezra, thus resolving many of the issues and sparing us the necessity of revision.

All the evidence is not in which would validate the readings' descriptions of this obscure Ezra–Nehemiah period, or discount them. But for now it presents a fascinating and complementary picture to that in the Bible, with descriptions of events and issues that will broaden our orthodoxy.

## *A Religion Based on the Dictates of Conscience*

The true significance of this return and rebuilding is impossible to contain in definitions. Three of mankind's greatest boons are rooted in this period: the national life and character of the Jew was preserved; it made possible the birth of Christ; and gave us the Bible. Without that handful whose spirit "God had stirred," it is unlikely we would have had any or all of these three. To evaluate what these three events have contributed to man from then to the present is to appraise the significance to this period.

The purpose for the return was stated in a variety of ways in the readings: to rehabilitate a destroyed purpose, a destroyed ideal (257-201); or, as "a definite mission, a definite purpose," by people who were called by God to establish His name in a definite and given place (454-2); and who were to complete the activity that would cause man to take thought of the spiritual forces in the earth. (510-1) The most frequently stated purpose was to "re–establish a religion based upon the dictates of conscience." (1201-2, 1210-1, 1285-1, 1638-1, 2545-1)

Only by man becoming aware of his own soul can he complete his spiritual evolution. The Israelites kept to their commitment to advance the spiritual understanding of man through the awareness of the inner light, or God-within. Thus, they had to re-establish an approach to God based upon the understanding of the "inner-self" or soul and its relationship to its source.

To prove this concept, they had to put it into application, reconstructing that which had become only "a hearsay to most" (2305-2): They were called to preserve "the tenets of old" and to bring forth that which could create and renew the purposes in the hearts and minds of those that would know their relationship to God. (1825-1)

This is the concept most affecting and influencing us today. Where do we stand in relation to our "conscience," to the prompting of our own souls? Do we honor it, or disregard it? How true are we to our spiritual convictions, and moral insights, and ethical standards? What do we value more than our own personal worth?

By becoming aware of our own souls, the inner light of the divine spark, we will be guided into all manner of truth and to the ultimate realization of who we really are, and what God has implanted within. But the voice of "conscience" must become strong, and obeyed despite all the hardships, turmoil, misunderstanding, and opposition which one will receive while in the earth, staying true to that sure and trustworthy guidance. This is a discernible experience in the rebuilding.

**For His love faileth not to sustain those that put their trust in Him. And though He slay thee, though He break thee as flax upon the wheel, though He bestir thee to the depths of despair, know thy Redeemer liveth-and thou shalt see Him, and He shall purify thee in those things that thou doest that are lovely unto thy fellow man.**      **378-18**

## Adam Reincarnated: Jeshua—Leader of the First Return

The final Old Testament incarnation of the soul who had been Adam, Enoch, Melchizedek, Joseph, Joshua, and Asaph, the readings state, was Jeshua, the high priest who, with Zerubbabel, led the first return, and was responsible for the ecclesiastic leadership in the community and directed the rebuilding of the temple.

Jeshua's name heads the list of those who came with Zerubbabel

(Ezra 2:2). He, with the priests and Zerubbabel, rebuilt the altar (Ezra 3:2) and revived the feast of Booths (Ezra 3:4) and all the festivals sacred to the Lord. (Ezra 3:5) (The feast of Booths had been instituted by Joshua and had not been observed since his time. Cayce noted in the Bible class that it was no coincidence that Jeshua revived this feast, since he, as Joshua, had been the one to inaugurate it.)

Jeshua also directed the work on the house of the Lord. (Ezra 3:8). He and Zerubbabel rebuffed the mixture of people when they first attempted to join the work. (Ezra 4:3) He was one who was "stirred up" by Haggai and Zechariah to renew the rebuilding after fifteen years of delay. (Ezra 5:2) Jeshua's sons head Ezra's list of those who had taken foreign wives. (Ezra 10:18) He and his sons also head Nehemiah's list of the interpreters who were able to make the law understood by the people. (Nehemiah 8:7)

The readings add to the accomplishments of Jeshua: He was active in translating, classifying, and codifying the laws, putting them into the language of the people. As a translator, he rewrote the Scripture from Genesis through Nehemiah. Teaching, reading, writing, and translating the law so that it could be acceptable and understood by the learned priests as well as the lowly day laborer, with all the different tongues and dialects the returning Jews brought back to Jerusalem, must have resulted in an enduring development in Jeshua to make himself understood.

With this background, it is easy to see how, in his final incarnation as Jesus, this soul had the ability to astonish the priests as a callow child of twelve, able to draw large masses to him as a man and to renew and revitalize those he had chosen.

As Jeshua, the soul completed that development which enabled him, in his next incarnation, to become the Savior of man. The understanding of the Jeshua–Jesus connection also adds new import to Zechariah's visions concerning the high priest.

In its historical setting, this vision in which a heavenly court absolves Jeshua of all iniquity and changes his "filthy garments" for clean apparel signifies the divine sanction for the ecclesiastical authority of the high priest in face of doubts of a returned exile for the office. It also signifies his jurisdiction over the temple.

But what is it also saying about the *soul* of this entity who was so near to that state of purification and perfection which he reached as Jesus the Christ? What does it also say about Zechariah's own awareness (on a different level of consciousness) of the *true* identity of Jeshua? Zechariah's vision is:

*Then he showed me Jeshua the high priest standing before the angel of the Lord, and Satan standing at his right hand to harm him.*

*And the angel of the Lord said to Satan, "The Lord rebuke you, O Satan; even the Lord who has chosen Jerusalem rebuke you. Is not this a brand plucked out of the fire?"*

*Now Jeshua was clothed with filthy garments, and stood before the angel of the Lord.*

*And the angel answered and spoke to those who stood before him, saying, "Take away the filthy garments from him." And to him said, "Behold, I have caused your iniquity to pass from you, and I will clothe you with good raiment."*

*And he said, "Let them put a clean mitre on his head and clothe him with good garments." And the angel of the Lord stood by.*

*And the angel of the Lord charged Jeshua saying,*

*"Thus says the Lord of hosts: If you will walk in my ways and keep my commandments, then you shall also judge my house and keep my courts, and I will grant you to walk among these that stand by.*

*Hear now, O Jeshua the high priest, you and your fellows are marvelous men: Behold I will bring forth the rising of the sun upon my servant.*

*For behold the stone that I have laid before Jeshua; upon one stone shall be seven facets; behold, I will open its gates, says the Lord of hosts, and I will remove the iniquity of that land in that day.*

*In that day, says the Lord of hosts, every man shall invite his neighbor under the vine and under the fig tree."* (Zechariah 3:1-10)

The second vision of Zechariah is fraught with even more significance, both temporal and cosmic, concerning Jeshua's destiny. A coronation is envisioned.

*This word of the Lord then came to me: "Take from the returned captives Heldai, Tobijah, Jedaiah; and go the same day to the house of Josiah, son of Zephaniah (these had come from Babylon).*

*Silver and gold you shall take and make a crown; place it on the head of Jeshua, son of Jehosadak, the high priest. And say to him thus says the Lord: Here is a man whose name is Shoot, and where he is he shall sprout,*

*and he shall build the temple of the Lord.*
*Yes, he shall build the temple of the Lord, and taking up the royal insignia, he shall sit as ruler upon his throne. The priest shall be at his right hand, and between the two of them there shall be friendly understanding.*
*The crown itself shall be a memorial offering in the temple of the Lord in favor of Heldai, Tobijah, Jedaiah, and the son of Zephaniah. And they who were from afar shall come and build the temple of the Lord, and you shall know that the Lord of hosts has sent me to you. And if you heed carefully the voice of the Lord your God all this shall come to pass.*"[39]
(Zechariah 6:9-15)

## The Last Life

As Jeshua, the soul who had been Adam, Enoch, Melchizedek, Joseph, Joshua, and Asaph, collected and organized the many strands of activity he had begun in the earth.

A brief analysis will show how true this statement is, made by Edgar Cayce:

> . . . from the very first of the Old Testament to the very last even of Revelation, He is not merely the subject of the Book, He is the author of the greater part, having given to man the mind and the purpose for its having been put in print. 5322-1

As Jeshua he aided the people in their return to the original purpose and ideal he had brought with him as Adam. As Enoch, he had given blessings and recommendations (2072-4) and warned against the flood. Thus he insured the preservation of a remnant who were "perfect in their day and generation" and whose spiritual and mental advances were leading factors in civilizing mankind. (2627-1) As Melchizedek he had initiated Abraham into God's new plan after the flood. Melchizedek also wrote Job (262-55) and other teachings which were used by Samuel and Elisha to found the School of Prophets (254-109). The prophets kept

---

[39]Slightly amended from *The New American Bible* (New York: P. J. Kenedy & Sons). A footnote in *The New American Bible* for this passage points out that Jeshua is not the one crowned in the vision, but the Shoot. This would indicate the Shoot represents the Spirit, or the Christ itself, upon which the crown is to be placed. In his next incarnation, Jesus was that *Shoot*.

Israel from being completely destroyed. In Babylon the School of Prophets was discontinued, but revived under Ezra (2444-1) Jeshua must have been instrumental in reactivating the School of Prophets which preserved and practiced the esoteric and mystical concepts given by Melchizedek. The School of Prophets became the Essene sect within Jewry, through which, as the readings show, there came the virgin birth of Jesus.

As Joseph he had preserved his people again; and as Joshua he had conquered and settled the Promised Land, insuring the place where the divine drama would be staged. Several centuries later they still possessed the arena Joshua had obtained for them.

As Asaph he had been in charge during the days of David, and founded the guild of Levitical singers and musicians who lifted the people's consciousness with praise and thanksgiving. As Jeshua led the people in the effort to rebuild and restore their way of life, he was aided by the sons of Asaph (Ezra 3:10), musicians skilled in attuning the minds of the people to spirit within.

As Jeshua, the entity interpreted, translated, and rewrote the whole Bible as it had been lived and recorded since the beginning. All the strands, the threads, were gathered together, and Jeshua was responsible for organizing and collecting them, putting them into a working whole.

The people he had been leading and serving had passed through the experiences of the world. They had been tested, strengthened, purified, chastened, and purged. They were returning back to God and to a service in His name. Jeshua had passed through it all with them.

All that remained was the final return as David's heir—the Savior.

# 28

# The First Return

*Zerubbabel* and Jeshua were the leaders of the first return. Zerubbabel was appointed by Cyrus as governor of Judah. Although Zerubbabel is generally considered to be a direct descendant of David, the readings describe him as a priest, which would make him a Levite and not of the household of Judah. Perhaps Cyrus was more willing to trust a priest than a former member of the old ruling family. Cyrus did appoint one of Zedekiah's direct descendants as a record keeper and gave him a place in the first return. (See 1120-1)

Because so little is known of this period outside the Bible, the rebuilding is said to be a monument to the anonymous individuals, the forgotten men and women who worked, amid so many dangers and hardships, to reconstruct that which had been lost, which was to be the hope, the light of the world.

Zerubbabel, Jeshua, and 42,360 Jews, 7,337 servants, and 200 singers, with 5,400 vessels of gold and silver, set out across a forbidding and hostile terrain to resettle their devastated and depopulated homeland. The contribution they made is unrivaled. Through the Life readings we are given valuable glimpses of their story.

A reading for a ten-year-old boy tells of his experience as an interpreter of the spiritual and mental motivations of the Jews as they set out on "that unusual journey" from Babylon to Jerusalem:

Before that the entity was in the Persian land when there were those edicts by the individuals in authority, when there was the allowing of the peoples of the Holy Land to return and build the city and the temple.

The entity was among those given authority to aid with those peoples active in their return. Thus the entity, it might be said, was the one given authority by the Persian king to go with Zerubbabel and those peoples, as they prepared for that unusual journey.

Thus again we see reasons for the interpreting in the entity's experience of those lands, in this particular sojourn.

The entity aided much, and the interpretation of those promptings of the spiritual as well as the mental laws through that period made for developments in those forces that will be the greater urges in this particular experience.

The name then was Zeldezer.                    2890-2

Many of the prophecies throughout the Bible can only be realized and fulfilled through a search for, and love of, God. Jeremiah had prophesied, in the name of the Lord, " . . . I will give them a heart to know me . . . and they shall be my people and I shall be their God when they return to me with their whole heart." (Jeremiah 24:7) Now the time was fulfilled.

This next reading speaks of that determination. In April, 1931, an eleven-year-old girl was told:

The entity was then among those of the first peoples to return, during that period when Zerubbabel led the peoples back again. Little thought, little care, little attention was taken by those people in that land as to whether foes were without or within, but with an eye–single to return to a service of a one source, and one force, was uppermost in the minds of those who journeyed; and the entity was as a companion to those of the priests that led the peoples back—not the high priest, but those of the priests' household and in those of the ones that were the enterers into the outer courts in the new established forces. The entity gained through this experience, in the name Pleneheai . . . for trained in the beginning, added to by precept and example, the entity served in bringing aid, succor, counsel, understanding, to those in the way—and in the re-established homes.                    2668-1

Perhaps the second return under Ezra was even more unusual than the first under Zerubbabel. Ezra was a great reformer who was "ashamed" to ask for a Persian military escort. He felt God's protection was sufficient and should be impressed upon the people. Thus he passed· through the same hostile territory with great treasures, armed only with his trust in God.

An experience as a guide and hunter for those of the first return was recalled by Edgar Cayce in this reading:

> There the entity was active as an aid to Zerubbabel; not as a priest but rather as a guide. For the entity had been a hunter and thus aided in carrying on those activities through even hostile lands when the great amount of booty or of things had to be cared for in order to make the various offices of the priest become again effective. The entity acted in the capacity of taking care of these.                3268-1

A Jewish writer and housewife was told she had been a daughter of Zerubbabel. The reading mentions Ur, which reminds us that land of captivity was the same land from which Abraham had been called and sounds a note, again, about the purpose of the return:

> . . . we find [the entity] in that land when there was the return from the wanderings, and the walls of the temple were rebuilt, and as Zerubbabel led the peoples from the Ur and from the Chaldean country—the entity among those that made for the *betterment* of the understanding influences of the peoples as a chosen peoples, as a people with a definite mission, a definite purpose, called of the Divine to establish the name in a given place, a given purpose, to a *waiting* world. In the experience, many hardships. In the name Zephaniah, and the daughter of Zerubbabel,  •
> the entity led many to a better understanding of *God's*-Jehovah's-relationship to His people; making much then, of the hangings of the new temple, and especially brocades have a peculiar fascination to the entity from this experience; and blue and gold are the colors the entity seeks to find often in their varying shades—as does the pomegranate, and the hangings of gold in pomegranate folds, make for an interesting thing to be handled by the entity . . .
> *Write* of self in Jerusalem, and it will be a masterpiece! Take this as the basis, when a people *cried* unto their God in Chaldea—even in the *abundance* of the land, and in the aid as came through the little things; of a bewildered people, raised to power—and self, with the pater, or

father, led those again into the land of desolation, and raised up the temple and its court, and its hangings. A *beautiful*—wonderful—condition! Self will lose self easily in this.                     454-2

A Jewish woman from New York was told that as Zerubbabel's niece she had been a strong entity whose ability to bring order out of chaos made her beloved among her people. Cayce, again, reiterates the purpose for the return:

Before this we find the entity in that land now known as the Persian or Indian, but rather then the Chaldean or Assyrian land, when a peoples were in exile from their Promised Land, and when there were made those overtures to those in power that there might be the return of these peoples to their native land, and to those activities that were to cause— and that have caused—thought of the spiritual activity in the earth.

The entity, as a niece to Zerubbabel, in the name Lexlia, gained in favor, gained in power, not only with the rulers in the Chaldean land but in the counsel that was given to those that—with the Zerubbabel and the high priest's command—brought those peoples into the Promised Land; aiding in setting to work those as the classifications of their own abilities in the various fields of activity necessary in that land, bringing order out of chaos in the eyes and in the minds of many; and thus in the physical experience endearing self to those that were to again carry on to that whereunto a peoples had been called in a manner to present in the experiences of their lives their concept of the Creative Forces in their experience . . .

In the present the concepts of authority are founded most upon that *innately* gained in that sojourn, yet at the same time making for the appreciations of the activities of others that in their own development must meet their *own* problems.                     510-1

Another Jewish woman, a thirty–eight–year–old widow, was told that, like her forefathers in the Exodus, she was torn between the comforts of captivity and the hardships which come while earning freedom.

Before that the entity was in the Promised Land, during that period when there was the returning to the rebuilding of the temple, the reestablishing of the faith of the fathers in the land.

The changes that were wrought brought into the experience of the entity the hardships, the longings for things as they had been and as they might be under the varying circumstances, or as before they had been separated from the worldly aspects to consider the spiritual future of its peoples.

But in service—as the entity established with the daughters of Zerubbabel, or as one of them—in the name Abijah—the entity gained materially, mentally, spiritually.

So may the entity gain in this present experience, in the re-establishing of self in those ways which are not past finding out. For, those who search to know may find Him. 2401-1

## Altars and the Home

. . . the highest of man's achievement in the earth—the *home!*
480-20

. . . the home is the nearest pattern in earth (where there is unity of purpose in the companionship) to man's relationship to his Maker. For it is ever creative in purpose from personalities and individualities coordinated for a cause, an ideal 3577-1

Zerubbabel's chief mission was to resettle the homeland and re-establish the way of life which would allow the expression of the deepest spiritual instincts of his people. He began the reconstruction of the temple building and revived the priesthood. Another important effort was directed toward the home life and the family unit, especially the children.

The love of family has been one of the strongest elements in Judaism since the time of Abraham. Thus, as the Jews returned to their devastated city, re-establishing homes and home life became a concern of the first order. The family was the basic unit which would insure survival and continuity of purpose.

Home altars, as symbols and reminders of sacrifice and devotion to God, were considered a necessary part of every home, as this entity was told in her reading:

. . . when the edicts of the king in the Persian land made it possible for the return of the children of promise to the Holy Land . . .

We find the entity was among those who came with the earlier portion, or under Zerubbabel. And while there were periods of turmoil, periods of anxiety, there was builded the greater service in the temple and its activities—in the closer associations with those who would establish the home first, as might be called, or the altar in the home.

And these brought into the experience of the entity then, as Shumel, the great abilities of creative forces as to the establishing of home, the establishing of associations with others in their aids to build better environments for children, for the teaching of others for activity in individual service—as in vocational training and activities.        1872-1

This entity, born in captivity, found deep meanings in the home, an answering to the longings of the soul.

The entity was among the first of the peoples that came again under Zerubbabel to the Holy City, and of that people; though, to be sure, was born in exile.

Home—home—has become as a portion of the entity's experience that is latent and finds ever and anon the expression of same in the desires of the inner self to see or to know, to feel the security of some place, some surrounding in which that may be felt as a part of the whole self.

Not so much as the religious thought or purposes during the experience, for the *entity* was rather interested in the purposes for freedom!

And this is a portion of the entity's experience in the present . . .

Then the name was Judith.                                        1082-3

A Protestant housewife was told that as Zerubbabel's daughter-in-law, she had made impressive contributions for the welfare of the children:

Before that the entity was in those activities when there was the returning of the children of promise to the Holy Land; when there were the preparations for the renewing of the service in the temple.

It was when there was the re-establishing of those activities there under Zerubbabel and Ezra and Nehemiah. All of these were acquaintances of the entity, but Zerubbabel was the closer relationship, for the entity was his daughter-in-law.

The name then was Jephtha. In the experience the entity set the example for the mothers in that period, by the establishing—in the homes of those who returned to the city—the teaching centers for the children, for the making known of the awareness of the law as well as the ordinances, as well as the (meanings of those things which had) been established by Aaron and Moses and the earlier priests . . .      910-4

Home life is mentioned again in the experience of this outstanding life:

. . . as Zerubbabel set out for the long journey again to the city in the hills there in Jerusalem, the entity was among those of that company; and with the entering in aided in the setting of the home life again to the ordinances of the homes as of old . . . and the entity aided much in giving to those peoples an understanding in the preserving of that *innate* in her peoples as to the *necessity*—in the material law as well as in the moral law—of preserving of self in cleanliness as well as in godliness; the preserving not only of the letter of the law but the spirit of the law. And truly, indeed, it may be said of the entity then, as Ashai, that the people under her aid builded with a *will*; for they *minded* the things that pertained to God.

In the experience the entity gained throughout; though there were hardships of travel, though there were hardships of privation during the early portions of the experience. Yet in the latter portion there was not only the satisfaction of seeing the restoring of the worship in the city and in the temple, but the satisfaction of seeing her own peoples raised to places of accomplishments in the affairs pertaining to the king and the city again established there.

There comes to the entity in the present, in the periods of the deeper meditation, those things that take hold upon the offices pertaining to temple service. These have at times been ruthlessly trod upon by others; and it has brought in the experience of the entity much that has made for a longing and a loneliness deep within.      872-1

## The Great Conflict

Religious differences are the swords of men. Man's evolution in the earth is to bring him to the understanding that he is his brother's keeper. That consciousness is absolute, eternal, unchanging, and without beginning or end. "Thou shalt love the Lord thy God, with thy whole heart and mind, and thy neighbor as thyself" is not only a commandment, but it is the spirit of God Himself, which, when applied and understood, makes man one with Him.

No matter what our backgrounds and past may be, all must eventually realize our oneness with God and our fellow man. But, the readings point out:

> . . . more wars, more bloodshed have been shed over the racial and religious differences than over any other problem! These, too, must go the way of all others; and man must learn—if he will know the peace as promised by Him—that God loveth those who love Him, whether they be called of this or that sect or schism or ism or cult! The Lord is *One!*
> **3976-27**

Not all the 42,000 Jews who went with Zerubbabel followed him to Jerusalem. Many settled in cities along the way, or returned to their ancestral home sites. Only a small number actually settled in Jerusalem to begin the work.

In the seventh month of the first year, Jeshua and Zerubbabel summoned the people from all their settlements to gather in the Holy City for the dedication of the altar. (Ezra 3:1)

The next milestone was the laying of the foundation for the temple. This was accomplished in the second month of the second year, and occasioned another memorable celebration.

> . . . *the priests stood up in their vestments with trumpets of rams blowing with them, and the Levites, the sons of Asaph with large trumpets, to praise the Lord according to the ordinance of David, king of Israel.*
> *And they sang and praised in unison, giving thanks to the Lord for he is good . . . And all the people shouted with a great shout when they praised the Lord because the foundation of the house of the Lord was laid.* (Ezra 3:10-11)

The beginning of the work was promising, but as it progressed it attracted the attention of the "outsiders," and the great problem which characterizes this whole period began—strife created from racial and religious differences, the "great conflict" found most frequently in the history of man.

The "outsiders" are those ever–present people who don't think like we do, who are of a different race or cult or creed, who have different problems and needs from ours. The "outsiders" are everywhere, omnipresent, and found on every pathway that leads us back to God.

The "outsiders" in this case were the mixture of people who were the result of the intermarriage between the Jews who were left in the land and the settlers imported by the Assyrian and Babylonian kings. (See 2 Kings 17:24–31)

The Assyrian king had allowed the foreigners he brought to Palestine to be instructed by Jewish priests, so the new residents would be familiar with the local god. As a result of their instruction and intermarriage, the mixed people recognized Jehovah, but also worshiped their own idols. Thus they were not "pure" in their religion.

Intermarriage was forbidden in the law of Moses, and the reformers returning from Babylon were intent upon establishing the pure form of their traditional religion. The mixed people desired to join in with the work, which they considered a part of their heritage, but were refused.

*But Zerubbabel and Jeshua and the rest of the chiefs of the fathers of Israel said to them, "You have nothing to do with us to build a house to our God; for we ourselves together will build a house to the Lord God of Israel, as Cyrus, king of Persia, commanded us." (Ezra 4:3)*

The mixture people had enjoyed privilege and position under the Assyrian and neo-Babylonian regimes, but now that the Persians controlled the territory, their circumstances were changed. The Jews promised to be the new ruling class under the Persians. Perhaps it was the political rather than the religious factors which motivated the mixture people to join with the Jews, and inspired the rebuff from Jeshua and Zerubbabel. Whatever the cause of the rejection, the results were predictable—resentment and hostility.

*Then the Gentiles of the land weakened the hands of the people of Judah, and terrified them that they should not build, and hired objectors against them to frustrate their purpose all the days of Cyrus king of Persia, even until the reign of Darius. (Ezra 4:5)*

As time progressed, the emotional climate intensified. Because of their efforts to frustrate the purposes of the Jews by blocking their efforts to rebuild, the mixture people—later known as the Samaritans—became hated and mistrusted with an intensity that endured to the time of Jesus, four hundred years later.

Any opportunity for large-scale unity was destroyed. The divisions and differences between the two groups became set and settled into hard and durable molds. And out of the fracture came a new group, a new denomination, a distinct people, a separate nation—another label—*Samaritan*—to separate men.

The Samaritans remained well-versed in the law of Moses and the prophets, but differed in their interpretations. They kept to the days, the seasons, and the moons of Jewish law. The real dividing factor was the place chosen for worship. (993-5) They chose as their holy place the mountain where Jeroboam had established his altar. (1 Kings 12:23, 29; 262-9)

As the readings state, the most important factor in worship is not the place, the name, or any other external forms in the way you worship. The most important factor is the purpose of the heart. This determines whether your religion is constructive or destructive. Israel is not a physical nation, but a spiritual pattern and consciousness. True religion should not be limiting and exclusive, but all-embracing and encompassing.

Many of the mixed people were sincere in their purposes, while many among the Jews were misguided in their judgments.

The Life readings show a deteriorating relationship between the mixed people and the Jews which intensified as the rebuilding continued. This reading suggests the existence of a friendly climate in the earliest days of the rebuilding. A Massachusetts man was told:

> **There we find the entity was with Zerubbabel and those peoples returning to the Holy City.**
>
> **The entity made for friendships with many of the natives and with the conditions surrounding, in the name then Abjadel; being in associations with those in authority, being in connection with those put in places of confidence and hope.**
>
> **Yet the entity held not altogether to those tenets, and there came a period through which much disturbance arose owing to the conditions and hardships that were brought about.**
>
> **Meet them then in the present, in the way in which the greater promise may be fulfilled—"If ye will abide with me I will abide with thee."**

And remember the new commandment, "Love one another." Not in a possessive manner. O that all would learn that *love* is all-embracing, and *not* merely possession! 1816-1

An English chiropractor and naturopath was told of her experience as one of the mixture people. She worked in the spirit that would unite the diverse elements.

. . . the entity was among those peoples that had been left in the land when there were the activities in the exodus of the main body, or of that peoples.

For the period covered years and years. Yet when there were those activities under the supervision of Zerubbabel, the priest, and Nehemiah and Ezra, the lawgiver and the priest and the active service, the entity persuaded many of her own peoples—that were called later the mixed races, or the peoples that were hated later by their own brethren—to become closer affiliated, closer associated with the spiritual activity in the lives of the individuals.

Thus the entity builded in that experience not only in the material but in the mental and the spiritual activities.

Thus may the entity build in the experiences of others in all the various thoughts in which the entity has delved and thus contact not the differences but rather that which is co-ordinant in the principles, the teachings of many varied sects and activities of others.

These are a part of the entity's experience in the present in contacting many that are of various faiths, of various cults, of various beliefs, or various tenets.

These, then, if the entity will find that common ground upon which all may meet for a *goodly* purpose, will be as the experience of the entity then—in the name Shulmean, which made for that development mentally, spiritually, materially. 1397-1

An English welfare investigator was told she had struck the note that led to class and caste distinctions between the two groups.

Before that we find the entity was in the land now called the Promised Land, during the periods of the returning of the children of promise from the Chaldean land.

There we find the entity was among those peoples who came with

Zerubbabel, and of those who aided in extending the activities to help others.

The entity was among those who refused its own brethren (though of a different cult in the experience) from joining; and thus making for periods when there was too great a consideration of class or the acknowledgment of all being of one purpose.

The name then was Hannah. In the experience the entity gained, the entity lost and lost; gaining in the abilities to meet the circumstances which arose; losing in forming too great a class distinction and producing great hatred during those experiences . . .

Hence in the present we find that the greater service may be in aiding those who are as new arrivals in a strange land, or enabling individuals to become acquainted with or accustomed to new surroundings and new environs, as well as enabling those of every nation and every tongue to meet upon a common ground of service to *one* God.       1897-1

This individual, as a priest and an authority, worked to establish better relationship between all groups, so that distinctions between class, race or office would be minimized.

The entity was in the authority of the builders, yet given in service for the preparing and the attending of the sacrifices that were prepared during those experiences.

Hence a priest, and of the household of the Levites—and a close association with Zerubbabel, though not of the same house—in the name then Zepheniath.

In the experience the entity made for closer associations with those that were in the agricultural activities, with those that were as the merchants and the tradesmen; and these made for the great stresses that were brought upon the activities of the entity in associations with those that were left in the land aforetime when there was the carrying away to captivity. But the entity made for the better relationships, and these give the abilities for the making of closer relationships and closer undertakings between the laborers and those in authority.       1442-1

## The Work Stops

Cyrus was seldom home to personally hear and settle the disputes and intrigue in the courts between the Jews and their adversaries. He was spreading his empire in other parts of the world until, in 530 B.C., he was slain in battle. Cambyses had been appointed by Cyrus as regent of Babylon. With Cyrus' death, Cambyses became king. He ordered all work on the temple and the walls around the city stopped, and dispatched a large army to see that his edicts were obeyed.

The Jews actually made very little progress on the temple or the refortifications of the city for over one hundred years. When the temple was built, the elders, who had seen the original temple structure, wept over its insignificance. Whenever the Jews would start to work on the wall, their more powerful neighbors would either bluff them off by force, or intrigue to get orders from the Persian court to halt the work.

Cambyses' order led to a fifteen-year shutdown on all the rebuilding, during which time the Jews were confronted with dangers and hardships from hostile neighbors.

Application of spiritual lessons in this trying time led to a greater vision for this woman:

**Before that we find that the entity was in the land when there were those returning from captivity to the Holy Land.**

**There the entity was of those peoples who came with Zerubbabel, and among those in authority; being the companion or wife of one who served in the holy temple in that experience.**

**Thus we find that the entity was among those bearing the hardships of material activities, yet enabling such to give to the generations of that experience, as well as to those to follow, the greater concept of the relationship of man to the Creative Forces, and how that such activities are reflected in the influence or force which directs the individual in the relationships to the fellow man, as well as to the ritualistic forces combined in the services throughout the activities in the holy temple and holy activities . . .**

**The name then was Susannah.** **2054-2**

Afraid of their opponents and blocked by legal sanctions and political forces, the work did not advance until Haggai and Zechariah began to stir up the spirit in the people with prophesy. Inspired and exhorted by the two prophets, Jeshua and the people began to labor again. They took the first step, knowing it was the right one, but not always sure where the next was going to lead.

Haggai and Zechariah not only preached but labored. They continued working in spite of the opposition and threats by the neighboring people and government officials who came to question them on their rights.

The dispute grew and went up to higher and higher levels of government as the Jews persisted in building, until finally the matter reached the court of Darius, the new king of Persia.

To settle the complex issues, Darius ordered a search for Cyrus' decree which gave authority to the Jews. Darius is remembered by historians as a great administrator, and the Persians were famous as record keepers. The original decree was found. When it was discovered, Darius ordered that nothing should stand in the way of the work. He also decreed—and this was a bitter reversal for the Gentiles—that the expenses of the reconstruction be taken out of the tribute and taxes he received from that area. The opponents were going to finance the work they had opposed! Anyone who frustrated these purposes, Darius decreed, would be put to death! (Ezra 5, 6)

As the readings so often and well advised, "Take the first step, and the next will be given." Or, as Edgar Cayce told his Bible class, if we listen and hold to what we believe, and disregard what others may say, God will provide a way. By taking the first step and resuming the work, the way opened, which not only allowed the temple to be completed but brought unexpected benefits in royal patronage and support.

One of the prophecies of Haggai, which encouraged and strengthened the heart of the people, was interpreted in the readings:

(Q) Please explain Haggai 2:7, "And I will shake all nations and the desire of all nations shall come; and I will fill this house with glory, saith the Lord of hosts."
(A) In the interpretation of that spoken by Haggai or any of the prophets, take into consideration first to whom the message was being given. Yet know that any message that bespeaks God's dwelling in the heart or in the temple of man is to the individual a lesson now, today. Here we find, however, from the literal interpretation, that a wayward people had forsaken their temple worship, where they had been appointed to meet with the living God. For there alone they had heard the words, and there alone they had received the instructions as of old. And the interpretation was that these should be turned again, as they were only a few years later, in how that even those that were called the heathen were shaken to the core and *granted* the people again to

establish the desire of their heart in rebuilding the temple. As ye have received from Him, "The day cometh when neither in Jerusalem nor in this mountain shall ye seek or desire to know the Lord, for ye will find Him in thine own heart, in thine own conscience; and if the desire of thy heart will be that the temple of thy soul (the image of thy Maker; the soul—not the body—the image of thy Maker) shall be renewed in Him, thou shalt be able in self to know that . . . and the way that thou shouldst go." 262-64

Several Life readings give us examples of individuals who helped soften or "shake" the heart of the kings of Persia. In this reading we find a peacemaker and an advocate for the Jews:

Under the leadership of Zerubbabel did the entity return to the Holy City. And as there were those attempts to rebuild the temple and the walls, we find the king called on the entity to act in the capacity as a mediator between the peoples of that individual land and those who had returned for the re–establishing of the land.

In the present we find abilities from that sojourn; for with Nehemiah, Ezra, and the rest of those in authority, the entity—as Zerubbabel—made for much help and strengthening during those turmoils that were brought by those because of the refusal of the priests to join with the Samaritans in that labor.

Hence we find the entity in the present is inclined to oft be in the midst of turmoils in secular natures pertaining to truths that bear rather upon the individual and those of a city, of a nation, a people, as to what must be the final outcome of their activities.

Know, here again, as in those experiences, there must be the turning to the universal law and not to those of such a secular nature that the individual rather than the masses would be considered.

Hold fast then to ideals that are a part of every soul's development.

*Again* we find the entity being fitted to deal with conditions in which buildings, as pertain to many natures, become a part of the experience.
1797-1

In this we find a Persian who favored the persecuted peoples and acted as a go–between in the royal court:

Before that we find the entity was in that land now known as the Persian, during those periods when there were the activities of those peoples who had brought the Jewish people under bondage.

The entity, though of the Persians, was rather inclined towards the persecuted peoples, because of the associations with some of those in those activities; for the entity then married a Jewess!

This, to be sure, brought disturbing experiences, yet the abilities of the entity to later act in the capacity of an interpreter of and for Zerubbabel; as well as becoming closely associated with Nehemiah brought not only the places of responsibility but of judgments necessary in aiding those peoples when they began their return to the Holy Land.

Hence we find the entity acting in those capacities as among the helpers to those persecuted.

In the present we will find the entity will become the defender always of those who are persecuted, or any that might be called the "underdog."

Thus we find that innate need for the manifestation more of, "If you would have friends, be friendly; if you would find love, love your fellow man."

Remember the greater commandment as given by Him, who is Lord of Lords and King of Kings, "Love ye one another, even as I have loved you."

The name then was Eleaza. 2030-1

## Other Conflicts

In addition to the problems with the "outside" groups, the Jews became divided by conflicts within their own ranks. Questions arose concerning the amount of taxation and who should pay; problems between laborers and those in authority grew up, and class and caste distinctions began. The conflicts were inner in nature, stemming from selfish motives at war with constructive ideals.

This entity, a Russian Jew, was told he had experienced an inner conflict in those days as the desire for earthly gain warred with his spiritual instincts:

The entity then was among those peoples who aided in the first upbuilding of the temple activity. And many of those things that became as of hearsay, as of tradition, as of the gatherings of those things that made for the activities as they were renewed, came through the hands of the entity then—in the name Adajar.

In the experience the entity gained; and the entity lost when those things that were turned into that for self-indulgence were such that privileges were sold to individuals for conveniences and satisfying of forces within self—these eventually brought destructive forces in the experience.

Hence we may find in the experiences of the entity in the present those periods when duty and the religion, earthly gains and the law of the innate self, clash. But hold fast to that which is the law of One, that ye may know in truth—as has been given—that house, that temple, that soul that finds itself divided against itself becomes one of turmoil. And what gaineth a man though he gain the whole world in fame or fortune and hath lost his own rest, his own peace, his own soul?      1232-1

A young Jewish student was warned that her spiritual growth had been retarded in past lives by predominant carnal desires. The source of the problem began in Jerusalem:

The entity then among those who assisted in setting up the temple worship for the peoples, and the entity gained in that experience through the application of self in and for the benefit of many, yet losing in turning same to that of the selfish motive of over loving in the flesh. In the name then Abidiha, and the entity finds the urge, as is seen in the present, of having the ability to keep those who would make love afar, unless the entity desires the use of the individual. This may be used to excess, and to entity's undoing. Beware of same.      480-1

This reading describes the conflict of a priest torn between selfless service and self-indulgence. He lost his battle and discredited not only himself but the office of the priesthood as well. A young Jewish merchant was told:

There we find the entity was among the priests of Zerubbabel, in the name Eljah. In the experience the entity gained, the entity lost. When the activities were such as to make for the greater developments for the whole peoples, well. When there was the use of the office as well as the social affiliations turned into self-indulgence, these brought periods of debasement—not only of self but of the office itself.

And remember, these are but experiences that must be met in thine own self. For an individual through varied experiences in the earth is constantly meeting himself.

Those abilities as an interior decorator, those abilities to choose hangings for draperies or the like, are innate from those experiences— as are the mental urges to *doubt*—because of self's own abilities to analyze others and their emotions. This does not indicate, because the emotions of an individual may be analyzed, that the individual's real purpose or desire is as open as a book—even to one so gifted as self in the interpretations of the emotions of others.

Use these abilities, then, as well as the indications given, for a greater spiritual awakening, that the material and mental purposes may arise from the results accomplished within self and self's own development, *through* the aid to others.

For, know, ever: What ye are speaks so loud, seldom is there heard what ye say.                                                        1950-1

Here we find conflicting emotions warring within a musician. A young Jewish boy was told, following his experience as a rebel in the Exodus, he had incarnated in Jerusalem:

Before that we find the entity was in the days when there was the rebuilding of the walls of the Holy City, when Nehemiah and Ezra returned to the Holy Land.

The entity was among those who were of the trumpeters about the wall, as well as for the announcing and calling of those for service as defenders as well as those that ministered justice to the peoples during those periods.

There we find the entity gained and lost, and gained; gained when the application of self was in those fields of service for the greater good of all; lost when in the activities self-indulgence and self-aggrandize-ment became the order of self's relationships with others.

Hence the warnings again that may be given regarding music, as well as its relationships especially to those of the opposite sex.      1881-1

# 29

# The Second Return

## *Esther and Vashti*

*The* temple was completed and dedicated in the sixth year of Darius, who had authorized its building.

It is interesting to note that Darius is considered to be the one who established Zoroastrianism as the state religion of Persia. Zoroaster emphasized in his teachings the individuality of man and his responsibility toward the universe in which he lived. The religion stressed moral dualism, that the *Good* God created everything true, wholesome, positive, and constructive while all that is false, immoral, and ugly was the work of the Evil Being. Men must choose to ally themselves with either good or evil, and in the afterlife would be rewarded in heaven or hell according to their actions on earth. Zoroaster saw that good would ultimately triumph over evil, but the task rested with man and depended upon his will and resources. The one great command of Zoroaster was that man must fight for good.

Perhaps Darius saw the *Good* God working through the Jews, and with this in mind, gave his patronage and support to their effort.

The readings indicate his successor, Xerxes, was equally absorbed in the events of Jerusalem. This reading suggests why:

**The entity may be said to have been the counselor then to the king,**

Xerxes; that there might be not only the satisfying of the king's longings for knowledge but that there might be tried out the experiment that those people might proclaim again that which was a portion of their traditions during those experiences. 1297-1

## Esther

Xerxes succeeded Darius as king over the empire, and during his reign Esther became queen. Esther's enthronement occurred around 478 B.C., approximately twenty years before Ezra returned with the second expedition to Jerusalem.

The Book of Esther, many scholars feel, is unhistorical because no records outside the Bible have ever been discovered which confirm the story. According to the Bible, had it not been for Esther and her kinsman Mordecai the Jewish nation would have been completely annihilated 500 years before Christ. If one accepts the biblical version, Esther is not just a moral tale but a description of a very important event in a crucial epoch of Israel's history.

The readings indicate Esther is based on historical fact. Three principals from the Book of Esther are found among the Life readings—Queen Esther herself (1298), Queen Vashti (1096), who is a central figure in the opening chapter, and Haman (1273), who, as the king's prime minister, allegedly plotted the genocide of the Jews (Esther 3:6) and was hung on the gallows he prepared for Mordecai. (Esther 7:10)

The Cayce readings agree in general outline with the story presented in the Bible, but differ in emphasis. As Cayce told his Bible class:

"We must remember the book of Esther was written by a Jew, so we have only the Jewish side presented."

A beautiful divorcee was told in her reading that she had been Vashti, Ahasuerus' queen, and was advised to write a book about that incarnation. She was told to analyze the Book of Esther, and then "give that of Vashti's version." (1096-1)

The woman obtained three additional readings, rich in historical detail, to secure material for her book. The second in the series supplies background information leading up to the banquet and Vashti's dethronement. (Esther 1)

The reading tells us that with the liberal policies of the Persian kings and their interest in their conquered peoples, there was a great deal of freedom and activity in the royal court among the nationals to secure favored positions with the king. Vashti was an adherent of Zoroastrianism, and represented the regions near India. In the political manipulations and maneuvering, the Jews made an issue of the fact that Vashti was without children, and used it as a means to oust her from the throne.

As there came the experience that Vashti failed in becoming the mother, as had been expected for those activities that were to keep the house or the sons of Ahasuerus upon the throne, then there became more and more the cries from the Jewish peoples that were in the court as counselors or as reporters of the activities that dealt with the service and the actions of those peoples.

More and more came the insinuations of the lack of the interests on the part of those that were in authority in the relatives or relations of Vashti, through the periods of the wars with those in both the northern and in the southern lands, or in the southeastern lands, that *had* brought more and more of the turmoils of a religious thought.        1096-2

To counteract this, Vashti turned to Haman. The reading continues:

Hence there arose to power, through the activities of Vashti, that one indicated in some records as Haman; and there began then the activities through this as an individual to change the thought, to change the ideals, to change the ideas of the king as respecting these. And yet there was still the harkening of the king to those that made the declamations that no heir was upon the throne.        1096-2

In the opening chapter of Esther a great feast is described. The drinking and the revelry was uninhibited and unrestrained. There was no ban on the amount one could drink. It was the king's command that everyone should do "according to his pleasure."

Ahasuerus came to the throne in the early twenties, and was not an uncouth man; yet—with the ease of the conditions and surroundings being lauded by the princes of the various charges over which the counselors came—he became rather what would be termed in the present as a dissipated man.        1096-3

After seven days of self–indulgence, the king commanded his eu–nuchs to bring Vashti before his guests to show off her beauty. But Vashti did the unexpected and unpardonable—she refused! The king, who considered himself a god whose orders were never to be ques–tioned, "was very wroth and his anger burned within him." The princes at the feast argued that not only was the king offended, but they and all the people as well, for the queen had set an example of disobedience to her husband. Lest their own authority be held in contempt, the princes insisted Vashti be deposed. The king obliged and a new queen was selected.

**And there were those periods of the abuse of self [the king], in the drunkenness, the dissipations in the activities by those influences not only from the Indian land but from the Jews and those that had attempted to make for those periods of the changing of the king's ideas.**

**Hence Vashti was *ordered*, not by her own but by the *Jewish* people, to appear at the banquets to display *bodily* charms—as were those of the Jews, and those of the Indians in their dance at the court.**

**With the refusal of Vashti (and this was only in the early portion of the twenties—in age—of Vashti), then there came the choosing of those that were to take the place of the queen.[40]**

**Hence we find, as would be termed in the present day, there was *proclaimed* a beauty pageant of the young women of the land.**

**1096-2**

If it was not the overt intention of the Jews to have the deposed queen replaced by a Jewess, it became the result. Esther was chosen from among all the beauties of the empire to be Ahasuerus' new queen.

*So Esther entered before King Ahasuerus into his royal house . . . And the king loved Esther more than all the other women, and she obtained grace*

---

[40]All time is *one* time, the readings tell us, and the patterns of our past lives continue in the present. We are continually reliving the same experience until new spiritual patterns are established. Mrs. 1096, who was very attractive and appeared much younger than her years, related that she had been married twice and divorced once. Her first marriage was to a well–known real–estate developer whom she felt had been Ahasuerus (Xerxes), since the cause of their divorce came through his insis–tence that she appear nude before his guests at a large party.

Her second husband was told in his reading that he had been Haman.

*and favor in his sight more than all the other virgins; so that he set the royal crown upon her head and made her queen instead of Vashti.* (Esther 2:16-17)

## Queen Esther

When another beauty, a career woman and student of metaphysical thought, requested a Life reading, an incarnation as Esther was given. The advances made in that life were described as well as the sacrifices.

The entity then was Esther to Ahasuerus, close with those activities that have made for that upon which a peoples have worshiped not the individual but the purposes as wrought in the heart and activities of an individual, as directed by a man of God—Mordecai!

These brought in the experience of the entity the closer concept of the ideals, and yet the very act and fact that the entity itself enjoyed not those privileges of seeing the re-establishing of the temple, or the peace offerings to the inner self before those altars, brought longings and dreads in the experience of the entity—that find in the present that longing for an expression in some manner in which the application of that which has been gained may be the more individual and not so much national—yet national in its scope; which may be brought by the entity's application, as was done in those periods—by its writings of that which prompted those beseechings that a people be allowed to worship according to the dictates of their own conscience. For there the entity learned tolerance, which so few possess in any experience in the earth!

Selflessness is the greater tolerance. For when self seeks exaltation, beware!                                                                 1298-1

Her lack of a personal form of worship was not the only denial and sacrifice Esther made as queen. A follow-up reading describes another one:

(Q) Is there a karmic link between myself and [5766]

(A) In the activities when the entity was queen, then this entity was as one who opened the doors, who was as the guard, who was as the one caring for the queen in those experiences.

(Q) Did I once hurt him emotionally?

(A) Not so much hurt as a disregard of the affection shown. The difference in the position after the entity was made queen caused more of the hurt.

(Q) Why has he had such an emotional effect upon me, stirring me to such depths. I find him almost distasteful at times after a short contact, yet a glimpse of him often leaves me deeply stirred, and extremely lonely, why? Was he ever a knight or warrior? His carriage seems to bring haunting memories, and a sort of pride back to me, why?

(A) Look at the conditions that must have existed then; being almost betrothed to the entity, then suddenly being made queen, causing the difference in the positions. Hence this is natural that the entity allows self to become emotional over the variations in the positions at present.

1298-3

## *Haman Reincarnated*

Six months after the Vashti readings were given, a third cameo was added to the Esther–Vashti drama. Her new husband obtained Life reading and was told he had been Haman, Vashti's loyal advocate.

From the intense self–centeredness which Cayce attributes to that incarnation, no doubt, came his reputation as the arch–enemy of the Jews. It never served his purpose to favor them.

Before that we find the entity was in the Persian land during those experiences when Xerxes or Ahasuerus[41] was upon the throne, during those periods when turmoils arose according to the activities of Ahasuerus in the dethroning of the queen.

The entity then was overzealous in its own personal gains, in the name then Haman, which came to be to a portion of those experiences as a byword; yet to those peoples that were in authority from what would be termed today the educational and the purposeful view, of high estate.

In the material things the entity lost; again in the mental and the soul and the influences for the greater development, the entity gained.

Beware in the present of the egotism of self becoming a stumbling block. Use rather as a constructive force, and we may find not only will

---

[41]Xerxes is the Greek name, Ahasuerus the Persian or Jewish name for the king.

the material, the harmonious mental and the greater soul development arise from those associations of those experiences there, but those activities that may be as a part of the entity's sojourn or activity in the present. 1273-1

## Esther in Power

With Esther's rise to power and the establishment of Mordecai as prime minister, the position or security of the Jews with the Persian kings was firmly established. These readings speak of Jews raised to authority through Esther's influence.

. . . we find the entity was in the land about the peoples of promise in a strange land, during those periods when there was the raising of Esther to a position of power.

And *again* there were those activities with the Persians . . . and the rising of power, and the falling away of power of the Persian king.

The entity then was among the chosen peoples, and a *relation* to not only Mordecai but to Esther also, and came into a position of power as one that would supply not only to its own peoples but to those of the king's household, to those of the king's consorts, the entertainments, the actualities of the experiences, of the interpretation at times of the

law, the applications in those experiences that brought the closer relationships of the entity's own peoples to the king and those that were in authority.

There we find the entity gaining and losing. In those same activities that made for understandings and interpretations, because of power, because of fear of those influences that would be wrought, the entity became self-indulgent, and lost for a portion of those experiences.

The name then was Carolieen. 1193–1

This reading describes another relative raised to power:

Before that we find that the entity was in the land through the periods when the children of promise were under bondship to the Persian king, Ahasuerus.

There we find the entity was among the offspring, or household, of Mordecai—who became to the peoples of that time and place as a lord, as a prophet.

For, through the influences as may bear upon the entity even in the present, Esther brought those places of position and power to the kinsmen of Mordecai and of herself, when she—Esther—became queen.

Thus we find that in the present experience the entity may find fame and position in high places bringing to the entity in the present, even as then, those inclinations for quite questionable influences in the thoughts of self as well as others.

The name then was Te-huran.                                                    1646-2

Cayce's philosophy of the unity of men through the oneness of God created a point of view which was objective and universal. As much as he loved the Bible and the Old Testament Israelites, he was not blinded to their faults. With Esther's rise he commented on the characteristic pattern in the use of her power.

"Esther is lauded as a great savior of her people, a sort of martyr to the cause. Still, we notice that after she gained power with the king, she caused the same destruction to others that she had prevented for her own people."

## But What of Vashti?

Throughout Edgar Cayce's Story of the Old Testament the Life readings have added many new heroes, personalities, and spiritual lessons and examples to the Bible story. Queen Vashti is added to this gallery.

Vashti is an example of integrity and morality. Like Tamar (Genesis 38; reading 1436-2), Vashti refused to compromise her soul by yielding to man-made edicts.

Why did Vashti fail to present herself at such a condition or period? It was not only because of the political influence of those that had been placed in power, and the pitting of the friendships as one against another, but because of the moral attitude owing to the religious trend as a follower of Zend.[42]                                                    1096-2

---

[42]Zend, according to the readings, was a Persian incarnation of the soul who later became Jesus. Zend, the readings state, was the father of Zoroaster.

Esther is one of the honored women of the Bible, yet Vashti deserves equal prominence for her integrity and the example of equality she gave to women.

In the fourth and final reading in the Vashti series, Edgar Cayce evaluated the Vashti incarnation and its significance.

> This entity came into an experience during those early activities of Ahasuerus, or Xerxes as called by the Grecians, that there might be during those experiences a fulfilling of the promises that had been made to a peculiar people . . .
>
> In that experience, though belittled by those that were in a development of a *personal* ego, those activities of the entity filled a parallel with that universality of love in holding to that which made for the elevating of the activities of others to that which cries aloud in its seeking for expression—that all souls, men *and* women, stand as *one* before that Universal Consciousness, that Throne of grace, of mercy, that has brought the souls of men into materiality in body, that there might be an awareness more and more of *their* relationship—yea, their kinship to that *source* of right, justice, mercy, patience, long-suffering, love.
>
> Hence the entity in that particular experience found itself in that position of championing the cause of those that had through the timidity of the activities from the expressions been kept in that way of woman being the weaker vessel. Yet in the very activity there came to the forefront that expression which found its *crowning* when the virgin gave birth to Him who became the Savior of men!
>
> In those surroundings of egotism, then, in those surroundings of faults and fault-findings, the entity *gave* to those peoples, to the world, a concrete example of the *freeing* of the souls of those that, though in body they be joined to those in power or authority, seek—their individualities, their souls, their entities seek and make expressions in a material world! **1096-4**

Cayce told the woman that her present incarnation was for the same purpose she had served as Vashti.

> That it *again* may give expression to the *freedom* of the soul even under the laws that have been made by man, for these be not the laws of the Universal Love . . .

> The ideas will come, naturally flow through self . . . through the ideas and through those expressions that will naturally arise—that which will *free* man! . . .
>
> And that man and his companion as from the beginning must stand as *one* before not *only man's* made law but as they do in God's holy law! . . .
>
> (Q) How may my book bring clarification in the minds of many regarding that period of Vashti?
>
> (A) As indicated, as held by the traditions of a peoples who have through their very urges kept alive rather the abasement of woman's position in the relations, in the activities as subservient to the orders of men, the entity may use those activities in the present to give expression to that variation that is thrown off now as having been a yoke that was set by man's vanity, not God's purposes!                     1096-4

Vashti was twenty years old when she was chosen queen, and reigned for eight years. (1096-3) After her fall from favor, she was given to a friend of the king's as a companion. (1096-2) The change was a belittling experience for Vashti and created an influence still present in the entity that causes her to question those who have dedicated themselves for an active service and do not separate themselves. (1096-3) Even after her fall, she still was presented with choices.

> When another was chosen and the entity was to become demoted, there came the choice for those activities that held to the purposefulness of self—in keeping self in accord with those that were the moral laws of the entity, rather than enjoining with those things that might bring for the entity a position or pleasure for a season.                     1096-1

She died five years later.

> Only at the age of thirty-three did the entity depart that experience, through those activities that came about by the destruction of those that clamored against those peoples raised to authority by those that supplanted Vashti in the experience.                     1096-2

## *Ezra and the Second Return*

Those who accept the authenticity of Esther as a historical event, dispute whether Esther was actually made a queen, or given an honored place in Xerxes' harem, because no records have yet been discovered which indicate that Xerxes had a Jewish queen.

Whatever her position was, it gave the Jews great prestige at court. Esther remained an influential person in the palace when both Ezra and Nehemiah went to Jerusalem. Approximately twenty years after Esther became queen—about sixty years after Cyrus' first edict—the second return to Jerusalem got under way, led by Ezra.

Xerxes was succeeded by Artaxerxes who, as Esther's stepson, was also favorably disposed toward the Jews. It is generally assumed that Ezra held a high position in the court, perhaps as the king's advisor on Jewish affairs.

While Zerubbabel and Jeshua returned to Jerusalem, Ezra remained in Babylon where he earned the reputation as a greater scholar and interpreter of the law. The first return was devoted to the temple rebuilding and reviving the priesthood; the second period was dominated by Ezra's interpretation and application of the law and its effects upon the people.

Ezra was a devout reformer and strict interpreter. His approach was legalistic and exclusive; he was a "purist" in his commitment to his religion.

Conditions in Jerusalem were not rising to the expectations of the Jewish leaders, and apparently Ezra felt the situation merited his presence in the city.

*For Ezra had set his heart to seek the law of the Lord and to do it and to teach in Israel statutes and judgments.* (Ezra 7:10)

Although Ezra's intentions were clear, Artaxerxes' motives were not, at least to one of his counselors:

**The entity was among those of the Persian or Chaldean land who became imbued with that causing the individual ruler, not an adherent of that faith, to issue such edicts; whether to be popular with the subjects and in following Cyrus' edicts or whether motivated by the seeking of those in authority as priests and scribes in the city of the king, when there were those requests for the prayers of the children of the king.                                         2940-1**

Artaxerxes approved Ezra's request to return to Jerusalem. In addition to being given the responsibility of instructing Israel in the laws of God, the king also gave Ezra sweeping authority to levy taxes, take tribute, and appoint judges and governors throughout the region. Artaxerxes also gave great treasures to Ezra from his tribute and out of his own household to be used for the refurbishing of the temple and as purchase for needed supplies.

Because of his scholarship and devotion to the law, Ezra was looked upon as its representative and chief example. He took his position seriously, and lived not just with tenets and ritual, but with a serious and practical application of the prophetic ideal, both in Jerusalem and on his way there.

As he set out on his journey, Ezra felt it incumbent upon him not to ask for a Persian military guard. He was "ashamed" to ask for a military escort because he had said to the king, "The Lord is with those who seek him for good." (Ezra 8:22) If Artaxerxes looked upon the Jewish activity as a religious experiment, as his father Xerxes did (see 1297-1), the sight of unaccompanied Jews marching across a hostile, and in parts lawless, territory with a great amount of booty must have created rich philosophical speculation.

Ezra was living what he believed. He trusted the revelations of the prophets, and was doing what he knew was God's will. Although he could easily have been annihilated, or at least humiliated by Bedouin outlaws or village chieftains, after a four-month march Ezra and his people arrived safely in Jerusalem.

## Ezra in Jerusalem

When Ezra and his troop arrived in Jerusalem, the princes came and informed Ezra of the conditions in the land, emphasizing particularly the vast amount of intermarriage between the Jews and the people of the land. Ezra was overwhelmed and aghast. This strict and literal interpreter of the law was stunned and shocked by this terrible news and "sat speechless" until the ninth hour, while those who were "diligent concerning the word of God" assembled around him and gave their interpretations and versions of the situation.

After hearing all their views, Ezra was moved to pray for mercy. The law of Moses forbids intermarriage, and violation of this law had been Israel's undoing in the past. Ezra felt the grace God had 'shown by permitting a "remnant" to survive, in spite of the great sins of their ancestors. The opportunity to rebuild, Ezra believed, was now jeopardized by this great sin.

## *Reforms*

Ezra's prayer was long and infused with the strength of sincere conviction. Although he himself was not guilty, he included himself in the petition as he prayed for God's mercy and forgiveness. Perhaps his inclusion of himself among the sinners added to the strength of his prayer, which made such a deep impression on the leaders and people who were present.

When Ezra arose from his knees, he had made his decision. Only by breaking up the foreign marriages could he get at the seat of the sin. The people were asked to repudiate their foreign wives. When many did not, Ezra took drastic measures to separate the mixed couples. A committee was organized with the laborious task of investigating all the cases in the land. The investigation was carried out over a period of three months, and met with division and opposition in some quarters. But many were moved to join with Ezra and his reforms.

During the Babylonian captivity, many Jews had intermarried with Chaldeans, and then Persians. The peasants, who had been left in the land to care for the vineyards and trees (2 Kings 25:22), had taken foreign wives. Those who had remained in the land had seen the temple destroyed and national unity broken and had become prey of the pagan peoples. Many of them had given up all hope of any restoration. These people had children and grandchildren.

Now they were being asked to repudiate their wives and exclude their loved ones from the Jewish community. The human anguish and heartache in Ezra's harsh policies cannot be measured. The testimony in the Books of Ezra and Nehemiah indicate this hard line met with some success, but other testimony (Nehemiah 5) shows it caused great hardships. Many were aroused to a new vigor and dedication in observing the prophetic ideals, but it also caused a dispiriting and a demoralization of a large number.

Edgar Cayce made an enlightened observation to the Bible class about Ezra's reforms.

"He was a learned man, who had been educated in a foreign land while in captivity. When he came home he began to make application of some of his knowledge, but as applied to the letter of the law according to the old records he found. Ezra didn't try to modernize the terms of the law to fit the changed environs. Some of his strict rules of conduct were, no doubt, as strange and foreign to the people of that day as some of the rules of the Puritans would be for us now, in our modern times. Naturally, this caused trouble."

This reading bespeaks of the hardships of personal experience, yet spiritual development also, from that edict.

**In the one before this we find in that period when there the entity was among those who labored in the rebuilding of the wall . . . The entity gained in the greater portion of this experience. Hence that peculiar phase of religious fervor that has permeated the being of the entity, or the body-being in the present; faltering oft, as it was in that experience, through the various activities as were brought as for the contentions as arose in marital relations, as the contentions arose in that experience through the sojourns with individuals where the relationship had brought, did bring for that experience, that made for separations under conditions and circumstances that brought trials, tribulations and ordeals to the body. In the name Myriah.**

**In the present experience from this, we find added *with* the fervor of religious thought, sacredness of certain relationships with individuals, and those—to the entity—that break their word, or their bond with others, are as those that would do bodily harm to others. Hence the moral, religious, and the *filial* relations of the entity, are high—and oft have they received *in* the experiences those of desecration.    2141-1**

## Lost Records Found

Ezra's great interest in the law and his interpretations which characterized this period could, in part, have stemmed from phenomena described in the readings, but unaccounted for in the Bible—the discovery of "lost" records in the temple ruins. The effect of these discoveries cannot be measured, but the impact must have been catastrophic. Individually, as the Life readings will show, the study of these records affected, and changed, many lives. Historically, it must have added to Ezra's determination that the law should not be just hearsay or tradition, but something to be applied and lived, leading to the great emphasis on translation and interpretation during the Ezra–Nehemiah period. This part of Edgar Cayce's Story of the Old Testament begins with the woman who discovered the lost records:

> Before that we find the entity during those periods when there was the returning to the Holy Land.
>
> It was during the return of the second group, when the activities of Ezra and Nehemiah made for the greater gatherings of the peoples that would return to the worship in the Holy City.
>
> The entity then was among those that were very close to those that served as a portion of the temple activities.
>
> Thus it came to be the more interested in the redecorations, the rehabilitations of the hangings of the temple; as they went about the repreparations.
>
> And to the entity may be accredited the discovering of the portions of the writings that were later transcribed by Ezra.
>
> For the entity *cleaned* in the temple when they were discovered. Is it any wonder in the experience that there is continued to be unfolded to the entity, in its seeking for that which is the pearl of great price in the experiences of others in their attempts to make for the greater manifestations of the love of the Father as shown to the sons of men?
>
> The name then was Rebekka.                                              1456-1

The lost records, apparently, had to do with conduct regarding the priests, as seen in the following. The study of these rules added to the spiritual climate, and changed this entity from within.

> . . . when the first of the groups returned to the holy city with Zerubbabel. The entity was among those, being a companion to the priest, Eleazer.
>
> The entity then was in the name Juduth. The entity was one who helped prepare again the priestal robes for the people in that first period of preparation, taking from the records which were again discovered there, and thus the entity brought to self, brought to the many, a greater knowledge of the closeness of the Father-God to man in this new period of activity.
>
> Thus in the present, not overzealousness of the Lord, or the word of the Lord, but the innate ability of being pleasant, of being consistent, of being in that place of not finding fault with others. This is a lovely

experience and don't be afraid, there's not but few that have that consciousness as ye have in thyself. But don't abuse it, don't misuse it! For it is of the divine.                                              5241-1

Because of the many groups which had been scattered in foreign lands, as well as the Jews who had remained in the Holy Land and intermarried, and those who were in Babylon, a variety of languages and dialects were spoken. In order for the law to be understood, it was necessary for it to be interpreted. Children born of the mixed marriages spoke the language of the mother, which was a dialect of the Hebrew tongue. The Moabites, Ammonites, and Edomites were akin to the early Hebrews, and spoke different Semitic dialects. Nehemiah and Ezra both were opposed to the mixed marriages and the departure from the Hebrew tongue.

Yet the readings describe a great effort to put the law into the language of the people as well as to coordinate all the history and records into the Hebrew. A dual activity is described in this reading:

There the entity was as the *companion* of the scribe, Ezra; making those activities which brought into the experiences of the young what might be called the re-establishing of the school—that had been a part of Elijah's experience on Mt. Carmel.

For, the entity aided those who set about to make the copies of the law, the interpreting of same into the language and into the dialects of that day.

Hence the entity made for advancements throughout that experience, *as* the teacher then, in the name Luenar.

In the present application from those activities, the entity will find that *easily* there will be recalled much of those things that were as ordinances—especially that had been neglected by those who were teachers *and* interpreters through their period of exile; and as to those things and activities which had been a part of same.        2444-1

The new discoveries led to a closer study of the law. The study created in this entity a firmness of conviction, which brought her into conflict with the authorities.

The entity was then among those who aided in the establishing of the original activities of the priest, and the entity was one among those who

> worked upon the garments of those who ministered in the temple.
> In the name then Marian, the entity was given to the building up of the body, mind, and soul and failed not in its administrations to the many offices; though questioned even by the scribe of the period and Nehemiah, as he later appeared on the scene, but the entity's help brought conclusion to the activities as the law was studied the more closely by the entity, as well as the associates.      4055-2

The intense study of the discovered records led to unexpected benefits for several entities who were involved in this important work. Talents for linguistics, interpretation, translation, and ability to work with groups of diverse backgrounds were carried into the present incarnation.

A reading for a Tennessee housewife describes her life in Jerusalem:

> The entity came with the last group, or those portions under Nehemiah; known to those leaders, Ezekiel, Ezra, and those that became the greater active in the recording of the records.
> And we find the entity then, though in the opposite sex from the present, was among the scribes and translators of those activities during that experience; and associated with those in the temple as well as in those activities that gave the ministry in the teaching, the interpreting, the changing of the law as befitted the language of the day.
> Hence we will find in the present the entity is a good linguist, one easily able to learn or to interpret other languages. The associations of the entity with peoples of various tongues will be a part of the experience. Yet the letter of the law and the spirit of the law not only of man but of God becomes a reckoning, or an experience or a judgment to be made by the entity in this present experience . . .
> Then the name was Shulemite, of the tribes of Judah *and* Benjamin combined; for the entity made for an advancement, development, materially and mentally and spiritually during those experiences.
>                                                          1499-1

A reading for a one-month-old child shows where his abilities lie.

> There the entity was as an aide to Jeshua, as well as Ezra, in the interpreting of the law to the language of the peoples of that period.
> Hence we find the entity will be inclined to language, and especially

the study of same; an excellent reader, an excellent interpreter of the
old and the new writings. These will be the natural inclination of the
entity.

The name then was Eloieh.                                        2498-1

This reading shows another talent related to language stemming from
this period. A California woman was told:

The entity was among those who were the early births in that land, and
in the household of Ezra, the scribe, as his daughter by Athelie—and the
name of the entity through that sojourn was Astedoth.

The entity aided much in the interpreting of the parchments or scrolls
that were found, translated, and written for the peoples of the period.

Thus the entity in the present would find the abilities to write—even
yet[43]—of those things, conditions, and experiences which would enable
individuals and groups to see and to foster and to cherish the better
experiences in their activities through this material plane.     2305-2

Any new discovery can, as the Lord's Prayer says, "lead us into temptation" or "deliver us from evil," depending upon our use and application of the knowledge.

This entity, of the first return, saw the law discovered and heard it
interpreted. He gained a great vision mentally, but lost spiritually when
he tried to force his vision on others. A present-day student of Theoso-
phy was told:

. . . the entity was in the Promised Land when there was the return from
the land of the Persians and with Zerubbabel the entity came into the
Holy City—saw the desolation, and the raising up of purpose in the
hearts and minds of individuals through the experience; and saw and
heard the interpreting of much of the law as was discovered among the
ruins of the temple.

Hence the entity through the experience became one well-grounded,
materially, in ritual and rote for a purpose of purifying body and mind,
as same was designated or dedicated for any individual activity for many.

---

[43]She was eighty-two years old at the time of her reading.

The entity gained, the entity lost through that experience—as Adonajahem. For as the entity gave and let others give also, it gained. As it attempted to impel or to prevent those not so endowed with the broader vision from their class or environ, or by the heritage of the environs in a strange land, the entity lost—as it hindered others.

1703-3

## *Footnote to the Lost Records*

One great phenomenon which has occurred throughout man's spiritual evolution is the uncovering of "lost" and forgotten information. An undisclosed amount of ancient wisdom is embedded in the earth in a variety of forms. It remains hidden until man is ready for its discovery.

The Cayce readings describe a secret chamber near the feet of the Sphinx, as yet undiscovered, which contains the history of Atlantis and the teachings of the Law of One. When these are brought to light and interpreted, they will revolutionize man's religious concepts and his view of the past. Yet the readings intimate that only an initiate in the knowledge of the One God can unseal the chamber (5750-1), and will, when mankind needs and is ready for the information it contains.

In Joshiah's time, the lost books of Moses were discovered because Judah needed them in order to "preserve a remnant" to keep the lineage of the Promised One. Under Ezra, when Israel was again zealous in its desire for God, lost records were again discovered, almost as a symbolic show of God's presence.

The Bible itself was a "lost" record, except for an educated handful, until the invention of the printing press. When the masses in Europe began to get pages and fragments—seldom the whole Bible itself—translated into their spoken tongue, it created a revolution, and a vast reorientation in religious beliefs.

The earth, with the storehouse of hidden knowledge it contains, is an outward expression of man's own subconscious mind, which, as the readings tell us, contains all the wisdom of the universe and a record of all our experiences as a soul. The Christ has promised to bring to remembrance "all things from the foundations of the world." Thus, new discoveries are brought out of the depths of the mind by the spirit of God, supplying what information we may need from day to day.

## Ezekiel in Jerusalem

The influence of Ezekiel and his prophecies is widely recognized as an essential factor motivating and inspiring the tiny remnant to rebuild and rededicate itself to God. His unique contribution to the history of prophetism lies in his manifest interest in the temple and the liturgy, an interest unparalleled by any—including Jeremiah, who was also a priest. His influence on the postexilic religion was enormous. He has been rightly called "the father of Judaism."

His first prophecies prepared Israel for the destruction of Jerusalem, and his later ones held up the promise of salvation through a new covenant and the conditions which were necessary to obtain it. The exiles were the only hope of Israel's restoration, once the allotted time of exile had been fulfilled.

However, the readings suggest another dimension to Ezekiel's involvement with the postexilic community which is unaccounted for in the Bible or in any biblical traditions.

The readings refer to Ezekiel as a leader of one of the returns. (1732-2, 1759-1) Readings 1434-1 and 1499-1 indicate that it was the second return, with Ezra. In a reading for a child we find:

> The entity [was] among those who ministered to the needs of the ailing and the sick, and was the physician in this period to Ezekiel—who led this return. In the name Zedkahi, and the entity gained and lost through this experience—gaining in the application of self to those who labored in the cause; losing in the selfish stand as taken against those who persecuted the builders—and brought to self condemnation for self in the attitude assumed.                                759-1

Whenever there is a threat or a danger menacing, there is also a greater Presence available which can overcome it. Ezekiel, as a teacher, instructed his scribe how to avail himself of that Presence:

> In the one before this we find [the entity] in those days when the walls of the Holy City were being repaired under that direction of Ezekiel, and the entity coming in, then, from that of the king in exile, and was then the assistant to Ezekiel, as the scribe, and the entity gained in that plane, for under the tutelage, the power of the force as was manifest in Israel, the entity assisted much to those who labored on the wall, who

defended the helpless from the invasions of those who would hinder. Then in the name of Abidda, and the urge in the present is that closeness as is felt to all things sacred . . . 257-10

Another follower of Ezekiel is described here:

. . . when the peoples of the Promised Land returned to that land from the exile, and under the leadership of Ezekiel did the entity return to the Holy City, and among those of the household of Zerubbabel. The entity gained through this experience; giving self much in service of those who labored in the restoring of the Temple and in the aiding of those who gathered of the worldly goods to make same possible, both from the house and lands of Artaxerxes and also of the lands about the Holy City, being of the household of those that warred with Sanballat during this rebuilding. In the name Corienl, and there were many that called the entity blessed during that experience. 1732-2

One individual who was told he had been "a messenger to all the realm" during the Creation cycle in Genesis, in his next incarnation was very close to another messenger—Ezekiel—and later was Jude, the brother of Jesus.

In the one before [the Jude incarnation] we find in that of the one calling the chosen people from the Assyrian lands to the building again of the walls of the Holy City, and this entity in that of the armor bearer for Ezekiel. 137-4

## Ezekiel's Vision: Ancient Astronauts and a Flashback to Atlantis

And, remember, man—the soul of man, the body of man, the mind of man—is nearer to limitlessness than anything in creation. 281-55

Because man is a soul, and the soul is nearer to limitlessness than anything that is, the theory, popular today, that ancient astronauts came in spaceships in the early days of man's evolution to educate and guide him in planning new civilizations, is no longer necessary to explain the existence of highly advanced prehistoric civilizations with superior and highly sophisticated technologies and theologies.

Man's first existence was a soul, a spiritual being in the image of God, and, according to the Edgar Cayce readings, his first contact with the earth plane was in this condition. The material plane became, for spiritual man, a laboratory into which he could project and experience his own creative abilities. The contact with materiality gradually sapped his energies, distracted him, tempting him to further separate from his spiritual estate. The more materialized and encased in dense, gross three-dimensional forms the soul became, the greater was the atrophy of creative ability and loss of awareness and memory. Man devolved until he reached his lowest point, and then began the slow ascent upward, back to his spiritual source.

A soul is eternal, and through the fall in spirit, has need of regeneration through the process of many incarnations in the earth—a process and an opportunity sanctioned by a merciful God of infinite love.

Who were the ancient astronauts? *We were!* Superior beings also came with blueprints for a new civilization, and then depart. *They're still here!* We are those ancient civilization builders, the legendary scientists, technicians, astronomers, priests and poets, and spaceship commanders of fabled prehistoric civilizations. Our abilities are not "lost" but forgotten and lie within, waiting to be awakened through the realization of our full creative potential.

If this is an explanation of the past, what explains the present? Are the UFO sightings today a form of visionary experience, the results of a psychic dislocation in the Collective Unconscious, as suggested by Carl Jung? Are they purely fabrications and hallucinations? Or, literally, "men from outer space"? Are they, perhaps, fellow souls, who are experiencing life in a different dimension of consciousness—our sons, daughters, brothers, parents, friends, and neighbors who have walked upon this earth but are now in the "inter-between" and no longer bound and limited by the flesh?

These questions serve as a prologue to a discussion of Ezekiel. Ezekiel is one of the most mysterious of the major prophets. His prophecies, advices, and exhortations provided much of the inspiration and determination of the Israelites to rebuild, yet little of what he said and did is studied outside the seminary. But one portion of his experience is widely known and cited most often as evidence of extraterrestrial contact with visitors from outer space. (Ezekiel 1)

*And I looked, and behold, a whirlwind was coming out of the north, a great cloud, and a flaming fire and a brightness was round about it, and out of the midst of it there came as it were a figure out of the midst of the fire. Also out of the midst of it came the likeness of four living creatures. And this was their appearance: they had the likeness of a man.* (Ezekiel 1:4-5)

Was Ezekiel visited by men from outer space, as a popular theory suggests? Or were the great, flashing spinning wheels of his vision (Ezekiel 1:15-21) a glimpse, while in an altered state of consciousness, of the chakras of his astral body, as suggested in esoteric traditions? Was the vision purely a hallucination, or a fabrication, as gathered from the rationalistic, materialistic point of view? Several levels obviously apply.

From one Edgar Cayce reading, we have an indication that the symbology, or the experience, could have been drawn from memories of an earlier incarnation. In a Life reading, we find this description:

**Before that we find the entity was in the Atlantean land, during those periods particularly when there was the exodus from Atlantis owing to the foretelling or foreordination of those activities which were bringing about the destructive forces.**

**There we find the entity was among those who were not only in what is now known as the Yucatan land, but also the Pyrenees and the Egyptian.**

**For the manners of transportation, the manners of communications through the airships of that period were such as Ezekiel described of a much later date.** 1859-1

Another clear indication of Atlantis-derived symbology appears in the prophecy against Tyre. (Ezekiel 28:12-15) The references to Eden and the conditions described by Ezekiel clearly have their parallels in the Cayce readings on Atlantis, the site of Eden.

If the Spirit was reaching into Ezekiel's mind to articulate its message—why would it not activate—in a prophecy of destruction—the memory of the greatest destruction, Atlantis, and overlay it on his message to Tyre?

Ezekiel attuned himself to the great storehouse of God's Memories, the Akashic Record, and the symbology and prophecy which flowed through him was channeled for the benefit of his and all future generations, each to find, in its multi-leveled meanings, the revelation that speaks to the soul.

Yet the study of "memories" does not exhaust the possibilities. Another interpretation in the readings suggests Ezekiel's vision may have been from his own subconscious (or superconscious) mind with a message, in part, as a warning to himself.

For a man with pronounced psychic potential whose development had been guided through a number of readings, Cayce gave the following interpretation of this dream:

> **Dream: An aeroplane rose in the sky trying for height, and for height only. Aeroplane came to a sudden and disastrous stop. Starts its sudden crash for the earth, leaving a wake of flame from fire. Plane seemed to be in the vicinity of Mt. Washington, a light mountain in the White Mountain Range . . .**
>
> **Edgar Cayce: This, we find, is the emblematical condition as was given to Ezekiel, as found in [the] last half of first and second chapters, as called. This, we see, pertains to the mental of the individual body [137]. And the altitude, or heights, in the place, we find showing the place where there might be the giving of popularity through such manifestation [of psychic ability]. The sudden descent and the blaze of fire is of the destruction that it would bring to self, if the popularity were the thought in mind, and in [the] expression to the populace or peoples. This, then, is as the warning that would come to the one who would attain great heights in the psychic forces as obtained through such manifestations.** 137-10

## Breaking Down from Without

The renewed interest in the law and the discovery of the old records engendered great mental activity, leading to the formation and implementation of new interpretations and policies. The great problem was the race question, which potentially was the most destructive and explosive issue challenging everyone.

Although Ezra's policies were harsh and uncompromising, his approach was needed to convince the people of the importance of their heritage and purpose; yet, at the time, his policies created great upheavals which almost destroyed the community itself by dispiriting and demoralizing a large segment of the populace.

God creates, not by bringing about uniformity, but by creating diversity which then requires a greater degree of integration.

God unites, and evil divides. Selfishness and egoism made reconciliation difficult, but reconciliation was the one prerequisite for survival. Reconciliation requires that each side give up something in order that reconciliation may take place. This takes place when enough people will be guided by the Spirit within, which is forever seeking unity, harmony, and brotherhood.

Ezra injected a necessary element into the struggling community, and Nehemiah, who followed him, became the reconciler. Thus the work progressed as an organic whole, with each individual making his contribution.

The most destructive adversary (from without) was Sanballat, the principal resister who, with Tobiah the Ammonite and Geshem the Arabian, is mentioned in the Book of Nehemiah. The self-righteousness of the priests, who refused the mixture people's joining in the beginning, was also spiritually harmful in its effect upon others.

This life indicates the effects of the rejection:

> The entity was among those who had been left in the land, and was that one who with Sanballat sought for a consideration among those efforts attempted.
>
> Because of the refusal of those in authority, there came distresses and disturbances, and those attempts to placate the activities. Again there were the attempts to establish in the mountains the worship as had been proclaimed by other teachers.
>
> Hence there were the doubts and fears of those who were self-righteous. Thus in the present we find the entity is one who within himself dislikes self-righteousness, and who becomes wary of those who by might or power would proclaim or *induce* others to be forced under their rule or their guidance.
>
> The name then was Joseph. 2167-1

This reading describes the discord in one of the "mixed" race:

> The entity was among those who grew up in the land—those who were not taken away, and the entity joining with those in the return was pulled many ways; for having been once a consort in Sanballat's group (not personally), the entity found much that brought consternation in the material affairs, yet harkening most to those spiritual instincts and gaining something of the spirit of those who would rebuild . . . the

entity became an extremist, pulled from one to the other—even as is seen in the present, often halting between two opinions; yet in presenting any condition, position, thing, person, place, or time that the entity has set self to do, this entity does! In the name Bennahi.     1915-1

This one was left in doubt and confusion:

The entity was among those peoples who chose to come with the first under Zerubbabel, yet the entity was not wholly of the Jewish or Hebrew blood. And these very influences made for confusions when the entity made overtures or associations with the friends and associates of Sanballat or those who had been left in the land and known later as the Samaritans.
     This among the entity's own close associates caused confusion and disturbance.                                               1523-4

Another indication of a disrupted family is shown in 2344-1:

Before that the entity was in the Chaldean land, when there were the gatherings of those under the king to be returned to the land of promise.
     The entity's companion sought rather to remain, and yet under the supervision or counsel of the friends as related to Zerubbabel, Ezra, Nehemiah and the leaders in the return, the entity persuaded him to join with those who did return. And this brought to the entity some doubts as respecting these conditions, when turmoils arose with the neighbors in that land.
     Hence we find the entity then was being halted between two ways, yet in the application of self in those manners that made for the unifying of the purposes—even under the stresses of the occasions, the entity found peace and happiness. The name then was Uslar.     2344-1

Life reading 2153-3 shows more turmoil for one close to Zerubbabel:

The entity then was among those close in the household of those who directed that activity, under the direct lineage of Zerubbabel, of the Levites—and thus of those of the priesthood.
     In the beginnings the entity aided much, but with those disputations which arose regarding others who are descendants of those left in the land, the entity sided more with those [the descendants]; and thus

brought disturbing forces in its experience, and . . . rebellion . . . The
name then was Esdreldia. 2153-3

## *The Resisters*

. . . each individual must stand according to that he has applied—and
not according to class, or heredity. In other words . . . merely being in
power, or power alone, does not always make right. 1638-1

. . . for innately the entity is spiritual minded, but being blinded by
those of power of possession, of the abilities to say "Come and he
cometh," these may be turned into those of destructive forces for the
entity. 1234-1

The principal opponents of the rebuilding were Sanballat the Samaritan (Nehemiah 2, 4, 6), Tobiah the Ammonite (Nehemiah 4, 6, 13),
and Geshem the Arabian (Nehemiah 6). Although Ezra must have encountered difficulties with these men, he makes no mention in his writings of them or any source of trouble which led to the breakdown of
the work. Nehemiah, on the other hand, designates who the chief resisters were, and pinpoints other problem areas, such as the merchant's
disregard of the Sabbath law and intermarriage. (Nehemiah 13)

Sanballat, Tobiah, and Geshem made every effort to stop the rebuilding, conspiring even to kill Nehemiah, who they also accused of rebellion against the king of Persia. (Nehemiah 4)

Although Ezra's hard-line policy may be criticized, it was done with
a positive purpose in mind, enabling him to make an enduring contribution to the welfare of mankind.

Those who resisted had only destruction as a goal. Sanballat's name
appears frequently in the readings for this period, indicating he was the
most formidable antagonist, the one whose "destructive forces" impressed themselves most strongly on the minds of the people. His rejection by Ezra and Nehemiah must have been galling to his ego, and
created a party factionalism within the Jewish ranks. (Nehemiah 13)
One of Jehoiadah's descendants, the priest who had been Joash's guardian, was the son-in-law to Sanballat. (Nehemiah 13:28) This son-in-law
was Eliashib, a high priest, who also gave a place to Tobiah the Ammonite in the court of the house of the Lord. (13:7)

The following reading speaks of the destructive purposes of the resisters. In an early Life reading, we find the armor bearer to Sanballat.

The entity then among those who resisted those that builded, being in that [name] of Sanbad, the armor bearer to Sanballat—and the entity lost through this experience, for those that builded builded in a purpose. Those that resisted did so for the satisfaction of the self and for the power that might be given to self through that of destructive forces to man, and that the builders represented. Bringing to self destructive forces through aggrandizement of selfish interest. The urge as is seen from same, that of mistrust in some that build toward selfish motives, even though the appearance is good.                    165-2

This reading suggests the devastating effect Sanballat had upon the people.

. . . as the wife of a brother of Zerubbabel . . . the entity aided then in making for strengthening of purposes in the hearts of those who labored under such circumstances that brought fear and trembling, owing to the various causes roundabout, the activities of the sons of Sanballat and the peoples without the gates and the peoples that were left in what later came to be known as the mixed races—those of the Samaritans.
                                                              1033-1

This one again indicates the seriousness of Sanballat's threats. As "the wife of one of the Korahites":

The entity gained through the associations and relations, giving much to those peoples that were so tempted by those peoples roundabout who under Sanballat and his kind tempted, and tempted, those that would serve . . . The entity in the latter portion of that experience became a teacher and an aid to the establishing again of the schools for the prophets . . .                                              2118-1

## Breaking from Within

The readings indicate that Ezra's hard line almost caused the rebuilding to fail. His attitudes toward intermarriage led to upset and turmoils among a great many of his people, even among the pure-blooded, not all of whom agreed with his policies. In other areas his strict interpretations clashed with the perceptions of others and led to additional dis-content, and a siphoning of energy into conflicts, when unity was desperately needed.

Eventually, under Ezra's regime, the work had to be stopped because the people were "discouraged or disheartened" because of "the rebellious forces roundabout" and from "turmoils and quarrels from within." (2006-1)

A reading for a Polish rabbi describes an incarnation as Zerubbabel's son, and an episode which brought to a halt the labor on the walls. The entity was rebuked by Ezra, and he rebelled:

> . . . we find the entity was in that period when there was the return of the children of promise from captivity to the rebuilding of the walls of the city, to the rebuilding of the temple itself.
>
> Then as Zuekide, the son of Zerubbabel, the entity labored at the rebuilding; and was set as one of the sons who kept and gathered the tax that was to assist in the re-establishing of the temple service.
>
> The entity then, being overzealous as to those activities, was rebuked not only by those under Nehemiah but those in the second return—as Ezra.
>
> Hence those things recorded as of Nehemiah's and Ezra's writings have in the entity a feeling of insecurity, insincerity; for the rebuke was deep to the entity. For had not the entity felt that those who were able to pay *should pay* for those who were *unable* to pay?
>
> Hence the *innate* feelings were higher even than the priesthood; and the entity was banished, becoming among those that—as it were—followed from afar. Yet the entity aided mightily with its bodily strength in building up the city, in building up the walls roundabout.
>
> No wonder, then, that these have a peculiar feeling for the entity; yet at times one of repulsion, and again the feeling that there are those things mightier than the walls which bespeak the efforts of man in those directions to set up that which may be sustaining as a monument—that should be builded rather as the lowly Nazarite gave, "Not in this mountain, nor in this city; rather in the hearts of men, should the God of Israel be worshiped." For He has given, as through this entity then, [that] there is not required silver nor gold nor only sacrifices; but there comes the call that ye be just and patient and long-suffering with thy fellow man. For *these* bespeak the words of Jehovah rather than those that require this or that rule.

*And it was because of such a rebellious force of the entity that they ceased to labor on the walls, until Nehemiah came.* Yet with a mighty labor did the entity give of the strength in that experience . . .

*Hold fast* to that thou didst gain before the altar in the temple; that God loveth mercy and justice rather than ritual or might; that being patient, being kind, being gentle is more precious in the sight of Jehovah than the offering of many sacrifices or the giving of bounty, or the requiring of this or that of the law itself. For who is the law? He that loveth mercy and justice, or he that ruleth in the thunder or in the might? *God* is a God of love!

These things gave forth the entity; these ring true in the experience today. [Italics added] 991-1

Those who made a big show of proclaiming and interpreting the law were under close scrutiny by this entity. Their example created dissatisfaction, which added to the breakdown of the community:

Under Zerubbabel did the entity first enter, and also under Nehemiah did the entity labor. In the name Gehgin. The entity gained through this experience, yet the religious experience of the entity during this experience was not altogether satisfactory to the entity; for the lives of many as leaders, the lives of many as priests, the lives of many of those that waited on those that were of the house, of the temple, were not in keeping with that held *by* the entity as compatible with that they professed. Hence the entity in the present experience, hard to judge, hard not to condemn, hard not to say the life is not so and so; yet the broadness of vision as respecting religious experience is gained through *this* experience. 99-6

The breakdown of cooperation and unity is again suggested in the following:

Before that the entity was in those activities that followed the return of the children of promise to the Holy City, when the activities were brought about by Nehemiah in the third of the drawings upon the crowds.

Then in the name Samantha, the entity became associated with those who labored in and about the temple. The great stresses laid by the varied leaders at that time brought a characteristic to the entity that is apparent in its present personality: when others dispute among themselves the entity chooses its own way and goes along without considering any. And these are the periods when the entity is misinterpreted, or judged on the one hand as knowing much more than it gives expression to, and on the other hand as being not just exactly in the same line that it would pretend in thought.

These are the experiences. Not as faults, but as misapplication at times of a virtue that is apparent from the experiences through that particular period when the entity contributed to the welfare of others as a nurse and as a physician. 3478-2

In a reading for a young soldier we find a reference to conflicts between the priests. Apparently there were differences over ritual and worship, as well as the mixture people:

In the activities the entity saw those disputes that arose between the priests of one class and those under Ezra and Zerubbabel and Jeshua.

Hence in the present we find those questionings as to ritualistic activities of any particular faith; yet the entity in its contribution to the welfare of the peoples in that period united much of the efforts; not only of those who had been left in the Holy Land but those disputations that arose because of the mixing of the races—or of the peoples of the land with the children of those returned from captivity.

The name then was Adonjhed. In the experience the entity was a looker-on, as might be called, and yet a contributor to the welfare and the activities of peoples—as indicated in the universal consciousness of the entity . . . 2940-1

Help came from an unexpected source. It was not a priest or religious leader who responded, but a civil servant, a citizen—Nehemiah—who was touched and stirred in his heart. Nehemiah was the king's cupbearer, and was one in whom the king had absolute trust and confidence. Poisoning was, and still is, common in the orient. Therefore, the cupbearer had to be the most trusted official in the king's retinue. The Persian rulers, being despots and lavishly wealthy, had many enemies. No one, not even members of his family, could be trusted.

The cupbearer was also one of the few with whom the king could be intimate. Persian kings lived in complete isolation. Not even the queen or his children could approach him without being summoned. The cupbearer could come freely into his presence, and was one of the very, very few who could be personal with the king.

Thus, when the king observed Nehemiah's sad countenance and asked about his depressed mood, Nehemiah was able to speak freely.

*" . . . why should not my countenance be sad, when the capital city of the kingdom of my fathers is in ruin, and its gates have been burned with fire."*
(Nehemiah 2:3)

The king responded to Nehemiah's concern, and granted him all he asked to carry out his mission: military force, supplies, and royal authority.

And the third expedition was underway.

# 30

## The Third Return

*The* Book of Nehemiah opens with an account, by emissaries from Jerusalem to Nehemiah, of the deplorable situation in the Holy City:

*" . . . Hanan, one of my brethren, came, he and certain men of Judah; and I asked them concerning the remnant of the Jews who were left of the captivity and also concerning Jerusalem.*

*"And these men whom I asked said to me, 'The men who escaped captivity, behold they are in the city, dwelling in misery and reproach; the wall of the city also is broken down, and its gate has been burned with fire.'"* (Nehemiah 1:2, 3)

Commenting to the Bible class, Edgar Cayce made the following observation:

"The men gave Nehemiah a sad report concerning the work in Jerusalem. Whether this great affliction had come because of Ezra's strictness regarding the marriage law, or from the disputes which had arisen with the people roundabout, we do not know . . .

"We wonder if being such a great moralist didn't redound to Ezra's harm in the end. However, he must have felt what he was doing was right. Most of us at times choose wrongly, but if we are willing to acknowledge it and ask God, we can be sure of having the correct way pointed out."

## *Nehemiah Reincarnated*

The amazing consistency and cohesiveness of the entire Cayce material is again found in Edgar Cayce's story of Nehemiah. In a reading for an elderly businessman, still alert, active and aggressive at seventy-six, an incarnation as Nehemiah is described. In the reading we find these qualitative descriptions about the entity in the present, all of which stem from his expressions in former incarnations:

> One that knows most of the time what it desires, and sets about to gain same . . . one democratic in its ideas and the freedom of thought, the freedom of activity, the freedom of choice—and that the answer must ever be within the individual self to give the reason for this, that or the other choice of activity in its experience . . . One tender-hearted in its dealings . . . One inclined to give credit where credit is due . . . One that must ever keep romance as a part of its everyday experience.
>
> 1767-2

Leadership ability was acknowledged.

> . . . the entity is considered as the leader and the director in many an undertaking of every nature or character. A natural builder of character . . .
> 1767-2

The character and nature of an entity, or soul, varies little from incarnation to incarnation. Change and development are builded "line upon line, precept upon precept" not just in one lifetime, but over many. Thus the consistency of this soul is shown throughout—a uniter of diverse loyalties, and a respecter of the individual conscience. As Nehemiah, the entity was a leader and able to unite those who were willing to "work for a purpose."

> Before that we find the entity was again in the activities of the builder, when there was the second and third return of the people of promise from the lands where they had been in exile for so long.
>     There we find the entity was the leader, the lawyer, the soldier, the director—Nehemiah.
>     And if there will be the perusal of those things that are considered as the messages of Ezra, as well as those of the activities accredited to

Nehemiah, we may find much that is responding to something within as to the desires and purposes of the entity even in the present experience.

The abilities as the builder, the abilities as to judge, as to the thought and as to the ability of producers in *any* field of service.

And as the entity then sought to give example to those over which the entity had authority, those who were willing to work, those who would work must be willing to work for the purpose and to work with and never *for* the entity or the individual, but work with, toward the building of something within the mind, the heart, the soul of each entity for the *greater* purpose for which each soul finds expression in materiality!

So from those experiences there are the abilities in the present as the leader, as the director—the ability to listen as well as to give the orders. These are innate and manifested in the experience of the entity.

1767-2

The reading described an incarnation following the Nehemiah experience during the Constantine period when the Roman church began exerting its influence. As a result of his incarnation as Nehemiah in the Holy Land, where law and order and personal conscience were the important underlying issues, the entity saw church and state clashing over whose authority should govern. The entity was able to see both sides in the disputes, but his position was the same as it had been in the past and was in the present:

Yet for the entity, the basis of that taught by Him *is* that the Way, the Truth, the Light may be free for all, and that the choice in the present, as then, must be within the individual rather than that as may be given as authoritative by any group or individual who would act in the capacity of a director. 1767-2

The whole reading supplies the basis for an interpretation of the differences between Ezra and Nehemiah. Ezra enshrined the laws, the rules that should govern man, whereas Nehemiah favored man himself.

Ezra gave the unique and characteristic stamp to Judaism and preserved a nation, and a heritage; but Nehemiah appears to be more representative of the universal spirit, found in Jonah, Ruth, and the early visionary experiences of Abraham, Noah, and Jacob.

Another aspect in this reading, which also demonstrates the total consistency of the Cayce spiritual interpretations, is that each incarnation prepares us for the next. Our future lives are conditioned by our activities in the present.

The atmosphere created by Ezra—divisions and factionalism—could only be resolved by a soul with the ability to unite diverse elements into a working whole.

The Life reading shows that Nehemiah's abilities were developed in a preceding incarnation in ancient Egypt. The Egypt of this period was one of rebellion and upheaval. It was an era of "turmoils, strifes, and divisions." Cayce described the entity's contribution to an unsettled era:

> **In the experience the entity it might be said saved that period of activities for the great work that was accomplished in the land by unifying all those in the political, the social, the religious influences during that sojourn.** 1767-2

The "great work" alluded to above was a reference to the spiritual and religious developments which took place under the priest Ra-Ta, after the civil war and rebellion were settled. Thus, in the following incarnation, the soul was attracted to the Holy City and the Jews, and a similar situation in another important period of man's spiritual advancement.

The reading concludes:

> **. . . the entity may give in this experience, may be in the unifying of the principles of law, order—but under the spiritual and purposeful guidance for each soul to be accountable unto its own conscience to that call which rises from within as to its relationships to the Creative Forces or God, as may be expressed by its dealings with its fellow man.** 1767-2

## Wives, Friends, and Lovers

Nehemiah's personal influence is an essential part of his story. Men worked for and with him because of their love and respect for the man and his goals. The readings add to this picture of his magnetism and charisma.

Cyrus' daughter (3351-1) is described as in love with him. Another individual, a member of the Babylonian court, was told that she had been his "lady friend." (3271-1)

Two wives are also attributed to Nehemiah. The first wife was a

Chaldean, thus making Nehemiah guilty of "mixed marriage."

> The entity was active in that particular portion under Nehemiah, or the one known as or called Nehemiah; for the entity then was the companion or the wife of Nehemiah—in the name Adjaah, being of the Chaldean as well as of the Jewish peoples.
> In the experience the entity gained throughout. While there were periods of turmoils and periods when many anxieties were brought for the entity because of the mixed relations, the entity developed because of the adherence to and the fulfilling of not only the records for the king but for Nehemiah. **1612-1**

While the first wife was of the mixed race, but gained spiritually, Nehemiah's second wife "lost." The tone of this reading suggests she may have been a pure-blooded Jew, perhaps taken by Nehemiah as a conciliatory move toward Ezra's faction.

> Then, the one before this, we find in the return from the captivity in the land to the Promised Land. The entity then in that of the one that was the aide to the one leading the peoples, for the entity then the wife to Nehemiah, and the entity then lost in that appearance, for the desires were to the land and not to the service. This *again* we find is felt in the inner self in the present, that these are the rule—that the head of the house should rule, yet the assistant, or the mate, should have [her] word. **2486-1**

Another woman, a companion in the past, was drawn to this same entity again:

> Then in the name Shelehi, the entity was a companion of Nehemiah— that has been, is, a companion of the entity in the present. **1144-2**

## *The Persian Guard*

The moral and financial support of the Persians is shown in the Bible story, but their actual involvement with the work in Jerusalem is not so clearly indicated. Here the readings throw an illuminating light, adding a universality to the work that is not indicated in the Scripture. Jews and Persians worked side by side. Apparently Nehemiah made full use of a source of help which had been unthinkable to Ezra.

This reading tells of a Persian soldier, an architect, who was drawn into the work because of his admiration for Nehemiah:

The entity then was among those who worked close with Nehemiah, for the entity was of the Persian peoples who aided in the replenishing, having accepted the activities because of the love of the entity for that leader.

Hence as a soldier, as well as a builder or an architect or an engineer, the entity—as Azuriel—was active in strengthening the determinations of many of those peoples who were under the supervisions of that entity through that particular sojourn.                    2162-1

We find in this reading that Artaxerxes' nephew accompanied Nehemiah on his return.

Before that we find the entity was in that land now known as the Promised Land, during those periods when there was the return from captivity to the rebuilding of the walls and the temple in Jerusalem.

The entity then was not of that peoples now called the Jews, but rather of the Persians; being then a nephew of Artaxerxes, and of the household of the rulers of that land, yet so closely associated, so closely active with those forces under Nehemiah that the entity was the representative then of the Persian peoples that went with Nehemiah for those activities in suppressing the influences that had arisen that caused the stopping of the rebuilding of the walls.

So again we find the entity associated in what would be called in the present means, ways, and manners of communications for messages that must be sent to those in authority in Babylon . . .

There may be yet discovered those activities of this entity, Axterern, in the excavations that are being made in portions of what is called Mesopotamia, for the means for preservation of messages—that was a part of the entity's activity.

In the experience the entity gained, because of those promptings of the king to let those peoples go that cried for a means of expression, a means to return to the material activities in a spiritual service to that as was held by them to be the way and means of serving their God . . .

Hence those latent forces that make for the tenderness—as may be called—in the entity's experience; the tenderness of heart, and the willingness to listen to a sad story, the ability to make those expressions of sympathy—not only in words but in deed.     1362-1

## The King's Records

The Persian kings throughout this period showed great interest in keeping informed about events concerning the Jews and the rebuilding. Persian letters and documents are important elements in Ezra and Nehemiah.

. . . the entity was in the Promised Land when there were those edicts given by the Persian kings for the return of those children of promise; that they might themselves establish their *own* worship according to their own ideals.

The entity was an armorbearer to the king; and eventually was sent as one to assist in seeing that those edicts were carried out, and that protection was given to those who labored in a cause.

Thus the entity came into the Promised Land with Nehemiah, with Ezra, Zerubbabel, and those who labored in those periods of activity. From there the entity reported back and forth. There the entity kept the activities in such measures that from one king to another there were the various edicts given that aided those peoples to again establish a place of worship.

The entity gained and the entity lost through those periods of activity. Hate arose because of the attempts within some of those to turn the activities into self's own interest; until those periods when there was the establishing of that necessary for the rebuilding of the wall, in which there were the edicts by the entity that the weapons of defense be kept at hand, as well as the implements with which to repair the wall.
                                                                    1662-2

Another reading speaks of the king's interest:

The entity was among those who came into the Holy City with the activities of Nehemiah, when there were the gatherings rather for the rebuilding of the walls and the making of the covenant or the pacts or agreements with the peoples roundabout. Also there were to be reports made to the king—yes, kings—who had given the decree or who had allowed these peoples to return for their own religious undertakings . . .

1583-1

Another record keeper is described here:

For the entity, though being rather of the Persian than of the Jewish peoples, was among those who joined with the activities for the preservation of peace, as well as the keeping of the records for the king who had given the decree or made it possible for these people to return to their Holy Land to set up again their activity—yet being under the supervision, as it were . . . of the Persians . . .          1539-2

This reading tells an interesting story of a Persian official who overcame the dissipation of court life through the hardships in Jerusalem:

In the one before this we find in that period when there were those returnings of a people to the Holy City, and among or with those under Nehemiah did the entity journey from Chaldea to the Holy City, being among those that directed the movements of the peoples—both as the representative of the king and of the peoples that would replenish, resupply, resuscitate—as it were—the *moral* and material relations of a people to carry on . . .

The entity gained through this experience, and lost and gained; for with the setting out the entity rose to power; with the humdrum that came with the lack of those elements to supply the same surroundings the entity entertained and enjoyed in the king's favor, dissipation came, discontent arose, and the entity lacked [stamina].

With the finding of those relationships in others that brought for a better understanding, though hardships ensued in many ways the entity found self and aided in giving to the peoples much strength to withstand those foes without as well as from within.

The entity was then in the name Cerrabil.          1932-1

## New Policies

Although Ezra and Nehemiah were in agreement on their purposes in Jerusalem, their methods inevitably had to vary. The differences in their character and personality were marked. Ezra was a "religious idealist" and Nehemiah a "practical realist." Whereas Ezra was "ashamed" to ask the king for protection, Nehemiah was willing to use whatever help was at hand. Ezra had a mystical concept—the prophetic ideal—which he was trying to realistically implement. Nehemiah, one feels, was more involved with the human situation and the needs of his fellow creatures. Ezra felt man had to meet and live up to certain preconditions, while Nehemiah accepted those who had the "right purpose" even if their religious or racial backgrounds differed from his.

Ezra was a man devoted totally to his religion, while Nehemiah, it appears, was a political and social, as well as religious, creature.

Nehemiah's approach was practical and logical. He must have evaluated the situation in Palestine and the Holy City, and then requested the king for the necessary authority to remedy the problem areas—even if it meant overriding some of Ezra's dictums.

Nehemiah was empowered to make "covenants and pacts" with the outside groups:

**The entity was among those who came into the Holy City with the activities of Nehemiah, when there were the gatherings rather for the rebuilding of the walls and the making of the covenant or the pacts or agreements with the peoples roundabout.** **1583-1**

The Persian kings were interested in keeping peace in this area, and were concerned with the natives and their reactions to Jewish policies. This individual was to report on the situation:

**The entity was among those who were of the groups that came with Nehemiah, when the walls were to be rebuilded—though the associations of the entity were with the peoples who had come under Zerubbabel and the laborers of those who were in command, or under the direction of Nehemiah as with the priest and with the scribe—with whom the entity was associated because he had received a decree from the king that there should be kept the records of the activities not only of those who were in authority *but as to how well the activities of that people were received by the natives as well as the remnant as had been left in that land.* [Italics added]** **1933–1**

Apparently the king wanted to keep all his subjects as content as possible, as well as allowing the Jews "freedom of expression."

For the entity, though being rather of the Persian than of the Jewish peoples, was among those who joined with the activities for the preservation of peace, as well as the keeping of the records for the king who had given the decree or made it possible for these people to return to their Holy Land to set up again their activity—yet *being under the supervision, as it were, such as the entity represented, of the Persians,* or during those periods of the Medes and Persians. [Italics added]

1539-2

One reading uncovers what might have been a real source of conflict between Ezra and his adherents, and Nehemiah and his followers.

Nehemiah had the legal power to override Ezra in formulating policies to maintain peace. Thus, reading 2970 tells us, when the walls had been rebuilt there was "the *re-establishing* of the relationships with those that had been disturbed because of the intermarriage with the peoples of the native lands." The reading continues, and seems to suggest Ezra, or other leaders, ignored and failed to support these measures: "Yet by those in authority, much of these were set aside, to the undoing—or misinterpreting—of many." (2970-1)

Which is greater—the faith of the idealist, or the wisdom of the realist? This was the crux of a question raised in the mind of this entity as he observed the two leaders and the implications in their behavior:

The entity then was an aide to the peoples as they returned; coming first with Zerubbabel and aiding with those under Nehemiah. There the entity saw under varied activities; the one disregarding the influence from without, relying wholly upon the spiritual promise from within that they would be cared for, yet with the Nehemiah influence the entity saw those activities wherein there was the trusting to the power of might, to the name of the king, to the effect that this must produce upon those lands and peoples through which the first of the bands under Nehemiah passed.

Then in the name Jeel-bached, the entity gained; for the entity held close to those things that became the precepts with those activities under Zerubbabel.

Also the entity saw the greater application of those activative forces that impelled the writer of same to say that the work progressed because they all *had a mind* and a purpose to work, to serve a living God!

633-2

The readings answer the question: *Be true to your own guidance!*

These should be *ever* those influences prompt the activities of the entity in all its relationships, drawing more and more upon the meeting of that great I *Am* Presence, as it was given to the fathers of old, "Whom shall I say hath sent me? *I AM that I AM!*"
When these influences are relied upon, in the experience of him who has set his house in order, then such an one may indeed be guided aright. Do not rely upon the fleshpots of Egypt, nor the places of the high hills, but rather in *humbleness* of purpose serve the Lord; for He is good.
633-2

## A Change in Status

Although Nehemiah is one of the most beloved of Jewish leaders, we find in this entity one who hated him because of "revolutionary edicts" he proclaimed:

Before that we find the entity was in the Holy Land during those periods when there were those returnings from captivity when there were the activities of Ezra, Nehemiah, and Zerubbabel. The entity was among the daughters of Zerubbabel, who entered into the temple service and yet, with the periods when there were the upheavals brought about by the changes when Nehemiah made those revolutionary edicts, the entity swore vengeance. And he who swears vengeance pays even unto the last farthing. So it brought developments, retardments, for when there is jealousy, hate, things that do not make the soul of man free, these bring retardments to an individual in his activities in the earth. The entity was in the name then Adar.
5177-1

Evidently Nehemiah was fearless in his effort to get at the source of the problem—questioning even the highest officials about their policies and activities, including the direct descendant of the royal family. This entity had come with Zerubbabel, and as "royal blood" perhaps he was overzealous in breaking up the mixed marriages:

Before that . . . we find the entity was among those of that period when there was the returning of the children of promise from alien lands to the rebuilding of the walls about Jerusalem, and the temple that was first begun—under Zerubbabel.

For the entity, while not of the priestly family, was rather among the sons of Judah; and in direct lineage of the king that had been carried away captive—Zedekiah.

In the name then of Zedder, the entity's activities were in keeping the accounts of its own peoples as related to the edicts that had been issued by the king of the Persian land.

The entity made for a development in those in many respects; only losing when there became *questionings* under the leaderships as brought by Nehemiah.

Hence we find the entity in its religious turns and religious activities often questions those who are put into authority for delegated activities of church or church relationships to definite activities . . .

In the present the entity may gain much from those experiences by the study of those things presented not only by Nehemiah but by Ezra. For these will, in a great measure, recall to the entity innately; and gradually manifest in the experience of the entity itself those activities during that sojourn.                                                    1120–1

More general discord between Ezra's group and Nehemiah's is indicated here:

With the rebuilding of the temple and those activities under Zerubbabel the entity first came to the land. The divisions or disputations which arose among the second and third groups who returned brought disturbance and disorder into the experience of the entity, yet the ability to plan, the ability to become very staid or set or hardheaded, all arise from the experiences of the entity then as Perthuel.                              5358-1

The change in the balance of power brought with Nehemiah was a welcome one to this entity, who was in disfavor for acting on behalf of the mixture people.

There we find the entity was with the first of the groups under Zerubbabel that came into the land.

There we find the entity acting as the intercessor for those peoples of that later called the Samaritan land, and the attempts to make for those periods when there would be a united effort in the rebuilding.

Losing in the efforts and activities there, the entity lost faith, lost "face" with those leaders—until there were those activities under Nehemiah that brought the greater numbers and the altering as to the relationships of individuals . . .

Hence we will find in the present experience that any building of wall or any activity of the nature holds an interest for the entity; as also does the study of that which will bring *union* out of the devious manners of thoughts of various groups.

The entity will oft be asked to act in the capacity of the peacemaker . . . The name then was Abdjah—of the children of Judah.

1842-1

## Before the Water Gate

In the 1970s, "Water Gate" erupted in our contemporary situation with a tremendous force and impact. Yet "Water Gate" was not new. It appears in the Bible, in a situation of some relative significance to the present.

*Then all the people gathered themselves together as one man into the street which is before the water gate; and they spoke to Ezra the scribe to bring the book of the law of Moses.* (Nehemiah 8:1)

In a prolonged and determined effort of fifty-two days, Nehemiah and his Persian troops, and Jewish supporters, rebuilt the walls of the city, thus insuring its safety, and the safety of the people within, from attack and invasion by the outside resisters. The wall was the practical solution to the problem which was coming "from without." With this work completed, there would be time to turn to the problems within. Internal consolidation and reform were made possible by the reconstructed wall. When the walls were complete, Nehemiah ordered that a genealogy of all the people who participated be recorded.

Following that, the people gathered before the Water Gate and asked that Ezra read them the law. And at the Water Gate the extremes met. The many moods, attitudes, understandings, and misunderstandings that were in the people were gathered in one place.

Based upon his understanding of the psychic material which had been coming through the Life readings, Cayce saw this eighth chapter of Nehemiah as the place where Nehemiah and Ezra "locked horns," though, as he told the Bible class, "it is not recorded that way."

If Cayce is right, and Ezra and Nehemiah did "lock horns," the issue was probably over the interpretation of the law. Up to this time the people had never read or understood the law for themselves, but had been getting other people's interpretations and proclamations. Now they were to understand it for themselves.

*And Ezra blessed the Lord, the great God. . . . Also Jeshua and his sons . . . and the Levites ministered to the people explaining the law; and the people stood in their place.*
*So they read in the book of the law of God distinctly, and gave the sense, so that they understood the reading thereof.* (Nehemiah 8:6-8)

The teachers and interpreters read and discussed each topic until it was understood by those who listened. Edgar Cayce suggested they must have met in small groups where questions were asked and answered until all became of "one mind" and agreed to the sense of the meaning.

It is interesting to note Jeshua's name heads the list of the interpreters. He was the one who had copied and rewritten the biblical history from Genesis through Nehemiah, and was the one whom the readings state was Joshua, Joseph, Melchizedek, Enoch, and Adam.

The people wept as they heard the law read. (Nehemiah 8:9)

Mr. Cayce spoke to his class:

"Why did the people weep? Because they recognized they had gotten far away from the law. It had never been interpreted for them before. They had heard what was considered to be the essence of the law, which had been handed down to them. But now they began to realize that the law was something to live, just as we are having to learn at this time."

After they understood the law, the people confessed their sins and entered into a new covenant. Those who took the oath were recorded. A tenth of the people were chosen by lot to dwell in Jerusalem and the rest in the outlying towns. The temple service was reorganized and the walls dedicated, and a program of vigorous reforms was instituted, such as halting the wanton disregard of the Sabbath by many of the merchants.

The spirit of the community had fallen to a dangerously low ebb. Selfishness had made its deteriorating inroads, dividing and fragmenting the people through a variety of issues and causes until the original intent and purpose for the founding of the nation and its rebuilding had been lost.

> Before that we find the entity was in these periods when there was the return of a chosen people to their land for the reestablishing in the land of promise of a ritual service.
>
> There the entity, with Zerubbabel's handmaids, became a helpful influence. And with the coming then of the priest—or princes—and the prince in Nehemiah, we find the entity lent that aid which made for the helping of those who resisted the peoples roundabout. Not by might, not by power, but by lending a helping hand to those who suffered bodily; aiding in bringing to those a better understanding of that edict which was given by the king for the reestablishing of those services of a peoples in their *own* land.
>
> Then the name was Belenda, and the entity gained, lost, gained through the experience. For being misjudged for the associations with those then as of the heathens roundabout, as termed by those strangers in their own home land, the entity felt within self as being misunderstood and condemned, when innately within self there was known how the protection was brought even to many of those that labored upon the wall, as well as in those that were established.
>
> Yet if the entity will read very closely the sixth and eighth chapters of Nehemiah, it will find much that harkens for an awareness of its presence there.
>
> Hold to those things that make for this ability to be tolerant, even with those that despitefully use thee. For it engenders strife to hold animosities . . .                                                1143-2

The reading of the law and the successful attempt to have the people understand it was the saving grace through which unity and solidarity was achieved. Ezra's interpretations, while good for many, did not speak to the well-being of all. Although a great reformer, Ezra could not unite or rectify the many diverse moods his policies had created. Nehemiah was able to reconcile the extremes and create a new synthesis and harmony out of many diverse elements.

Through the public reading of the law, everybody worked together until they all could agree and get their own understanding. Renewed through this experience, they became unified in their willingness to work for a common goal, a common ideal. Spiritual renewal and reform, which had been so essential throughout Judah's history, worked again to preserve the nation and insure its continuity.

## *At the Water Gate—They Were There*

At the Water Gate, this entity learned the meaning of the law. A psychology teacher was told:

> Before that we find the entity was in that land when there was again the preparation for the return of the chosen to the temple and to the Holy City.
>
> And the entity with Nehemiah and Ezra came into the activities, in the Holy City, from the Persian and Chaldean land; and was an aide to Ezra in the interpreting of the revising of the law as then found.
>
> Thus in the present there is the opening of the understanding as to how the interpretations of tenets are things to be *lived* and not held as tenets or as rote alone!
>
> For as ye have learned, it is even as He—who "went about doing good." The name then was Shes-Beder.                    1529–1

This entity's understanding of the law enabled her to be a peacemaker:

> The entity was among those that were born in captivity, to be sure, yet joined hard with those peoples not only that aided in giving comfort and aid to those that went with Zerubbabel but with Nehemiah in his return with political influence and force.
>
> For then the entity represented not only the law of his peoples but the law as an edict of the king, then changed.
>
> These made for those experiences when it may be said there was the greater development of the entity in a material, in a soul, in a mental experience. For the application of the law as interpreted and read by Ezra in the hearings of the entity, then Abajah, produced in the activities of the entity the making of the first overtures to those about the activities in the city when the temple had not only been rebuilt but when the walls had been rebuilded, that made for peace and harmony.
>
> Hence the entity in its activities while as a law interpreter, as a lawgiver, as a law devisor in ways and means, will ever be in the capacity rather to make peace than to stir up strife among peoples or groups or

nations or states. Thus the activity in that same capacity in the present may bring the greater development, bringing the greater harmony and peace into the experience of the entity in the present.      1285-1

In this reading we find a resister who changed sides:

Before that we find the entity was in the Holy Land, when there was the returning of a peoples to those activities in a rebuilding of the walls, and the repairing of same, and the restoring of the temple.

There we find the entity was among those peoples who warred against that general activity, yet becoming—in the second and third dispensation of the king who made it possible for those people to return—a part of same.

The name then was Abijah, and the entity in the experience was warring with self as to principles; and being under the influences of Nehemiah, the leader, brought an influence for power for good throughout the experience.      1998-1

This entity, of the mixed race, gained from Ezra's interpretations:

The entity was among those who were the offspring of those left in the native land, and hence there was a longing for and yet withdrawing from those of that environ where organization had been attempted.

And thus with the return of Zerubbabel and those activities under Nehemiah, the entity came again into an active service; and yet brought discord through the attempts to unite the efforts of Sanballat with the peoples who had journeyed from the land of bondage—or of outcasts.

There we find the entity learned, little by little, those variations in the law of the period and the experience; and only under the interpretation of Ezra did there come the more perfect understanding for the entity.

Thus we find in the present it behooves the entity to first know self, and know the ideal, and know the sources and the purposes of same; and the abilities for the making of associations with toilers of the soil in all of the phases become the abilities in the present.

Then in the name Eljah, the entity lost and the entity gained.      1946-1

A high note resounds in this reading for an entity of the mixed race who rose above all the turmoils to an honored place in the temple service:

Before that we find the entity was also in the Holy Land, as known in the present, during those periods of the return of the peoples of promise.

Though the entity was of those peoples that remained in the land, it became especially interested because of the activities which followed the intents and purposes of the edict issued by Ezra during those experiences. And as the entity showed itself to be equal to and sincere in its efforts for the establishing of ideals, it was among the very few chosen to become a part of the experience in the re-establishing of the temple and the spiritual worship of those peoples during that experience.

The name then was Belenhi. Though among the Samaritans (as called), and of that people, the entity gave its service to those who made for the establishing and reiterating of the laws pertaining to the service and the activities in the temple, and the activities of the peoples in their replenishing and reactions in those experiences.

The entity gained then throughout.

In the present we find the ability to interpret, the ability as a linguist being a part of the entity's experience, from those *very* abilities as established during the retranslating of much of those things that were a part of the experience.

*And if the entity will review the activities of Nehemiah, Ezra, and Jeshua and Jezreel, much of these will become as an opening door to the consciousness of its abilities to direct, to hold, to maintain a unity where others have failed.*

Thus the entity will be enabled to give even the greater counsel to those just starting their relationships as one with another, and with the *efforts* in fitting themselves into environs and activities in which they have found and do find their experiences entirely different from their earlier periods of activity. [Italics added[                    1663-2

## The Eternal Light

*And God said, "Let there be Light," and there was light.* (Genesis 1:3)

Out of the darkness of chaos and disunity, the people merged into a new totality by searching for the one light that could guide their ways. With the rebuilding of the temple, we find this entity a keeper of the lights. Apparently the temple lights were symbols of the "eternal" light which never fails or grows dim, and shines even in the darkness when man neglects and forgets. The entity, in the present, finds the eternal "inner" light illuminating his visions and dreams.

The entity then among those of the latter peoples that returned under Nehemiah, and the entity then one that kept the lights in the temples in the city, and the first of the lights that might be kept burning without the continued attention were set by the entity in *that* period. In the name Zeruri. The entity gained through this experience, for service in the capacity as the *keeper* of the lights—in the directing forces as was given by Nehemiah, as was given by Ezra the priest, as was given by those in that period—brought an understanding and a knowledge of the associations of *spiritual* forces with *material* forces, and the entity happy throughout the experience—from the leaving of Shushan[44] in Persia (now) to the Promised Land [and] the holy city. In the present, as will be seen, oft does the entity vision, by the various lights and the odors as arise in the imagination, those of the various experiences as in the way through the desert, through the hill land, as well as the visions in the cities, and the dreams of the entity oft partake of those experiences. 2662-1

The great period of rebuilding, with all its struggles, its strifes, its divisions and differences, was completed because the light which all these diverse entities were seeking—Jeshua, Ezra, Nehemiah, Zerubbabel, and the many others—was greater than the darkness which separated them. That same light still shines, able to draw all men into unity and brotherhood, if all men will search for the spirit from which the light proceeds.

## *Back to the Beginning*

Resettling the Promised Land, and rebuilding the temple, made it abundantly clear to the Israelites that the days of the monarchy were finished. Only the inward unity and solidarity of a religious community could guarantee their existence in the face of whatever world and political developments might confront them in the years ahead.

---

[44]The royal residence of the Persian Kings.

Israel was returning back to the beginning. Israel turned its back on politics and great worldly ambitions. The high priest became the head over all Israel. The little community was no longer a monarchy, but a theocracy, as it had been in the days of Samuel, the priest and prophet who warned Israel that their demands for a king were "sinful."

With Persian approval, the law of God became the law of Israel. For two centuries the Persians were the liege lords of Jerusalem. Israel kept apart. Archeology indicates no violent variations during this period. There were no plottings, no machinations, no rebellions. Only an outward quiet or calm, and an inward searching for purpose and direction.

With the rising of Alexander, the Macedonian empire supplanted the Persian. Again, Jerusalem kept free of entanglements and involvement, in a shifting and changing world. Jerusalem was untouched by the invasion of Alexander as be marched on Tyre and Egypt. Indeed a legend exists that Alexander intended to sack and destroy the Holy City, but changed his plans when be realized the high priest of Jerusalem was the same man he had seen in a dream before leaving Macedonia. Alexander turned aside and spared the city. Perhaps this story is only a legend, but it serves to emphasize the fact that as long as Israel kept to the things of God, no harm of any nature would come to them.

There is very little in the sacred writings about the four-hundred-year period between Ezra and Nehemiah and the birth of Jesus. Nothing important happened in outward affairs, nor were there great manifestations or revelations from God.

Yet the peace, the quiet, the unbroken continuity of purpose, over four centuries in this little religious community, enabled a sect within Jewry—the Essenes—to complete the Old Testament by bringing into the earth that which had been in the beginning—a living soul unspotted and unstained by the world, at-one with the light and in harmony with the Father. In the garden, Adam had been a "living soul," innocent of earthly experience. In Jerusalem, he became "a quickening spirit," having passed through, and overcome, all the forces, drives, and temptations that separate a soul from its source.

**Ye say that there were those periods when for four hundred years little or nothing bad happened in the experience of man as a revelation from the Father, or from God, or from the sources of light. What was it, then, that made the setting for the place and for the entering in of that consciousness into the earth that ye know as the Son of man, the Jesus**

of Nazareth, the Christ on the Cross? Did the darkness bring the light? Did the wandering away from the thought of such bring the Christ into the earth? Is this idea not rather refuting the common law that is present in spirit, mind, and body that "Like begets like"? As was asked oft, "Can any good thing come out of Nazareth?" Isn't it rather than there were those that ye hear little or nothing of in thine studies of same, that dedicated their lives, their minds, their bodies, to a purpose, to a *seeking* for that which had been to them a promise of old? Were there not individuals, men and women, who dedicated their bodies that they might be channels through which such an influence, such a *body* might come? 262-61

# Epilogue

## *The Perfect Body*

**The soul looks through our eyes and feels with our emotions. Spiritual awareness is developed through the factors in all five senses. 487-17**

In the beginning, Man was made a living soul. The Garden of Eden is a symbolic picture depicting his first estate. Both the Old and New Testaments tell us we are gods in the making. And Edgar Cayce tells us why—because we possess a soul.

Man lost his spiritual awareness when he became blinded by material things, and self-indulgence. Having lost the original oneness, man would have to gain it back by the use of his free will, expended in the search for God.

Edgar Cayce stressed that it was just as important to understand the Old Testament as it was to understand the New. No one is perfect in the Old Testament. They searched for God, dedicated themselves to Him, tried to the best of their abilities to serve, yet they were enmeshed in all the forces that distract and tempt man, that make him proud, vain, fearful, weak, and wicked; that harden his heart, deafen his ears, and blind his vision. They were in the world, struggling to overcome all its drives, temptations, and distracting influences, yet were never completely successful until the first Adam who led Israel as Enoch,

Melchizedek, Joseph, Joshua, and Jeshua became Christed as Jesus and totally Spirit-directed. Through his life in the earth as Jesus, he gave to Israel (the seeker) a new pattern, a new vision, a new consciousness for which there is found no parallel in the Old Testament.

As with him, the Old Testament is not complete until it is completed within. Mankind is still caught between the drawing pull of the Spirit and the desires of the flesh. While caught in the struggle, we inevitably repeat the Old Testament patterns. As long as we are struggling and seeking, we will find in the Bible some character or situation relative to our state of growth and awareness.

## *The Perfect Mind*

Edgar Cayce tells us that, on the metaphysical level, the Bible from Abraham to Christ can be interpreted as a symbol process of mental unfoldment. (281-63) The spiritual meaning of Abraham is *Call*. (262-28) Christ is the attainment of the Call. If the story of Abraham through Christ is a pattern of mental development, then the Old Testament is the story of the building of the perfect mind—the mind that was in Christ.

Christ-consciousness—perfect awareness—is the crowning development in the pattern of Israel's growth. The growth is contained in two principles Cayce assigns to the word *Israel*.

*All who seek are Israel.* (262-28, 2772-1) The first principle is that Israel seeks Truth. (5377-1)

There is a specialized connation to Truth as defined in the readings. It is described in the "A Search for God" series as "that which makes one aware of the divine within each and every activity." Truth, then, is an awareness of divinity interpenetrating and permeating all phases of life. It is a process of growth, felt on the mental, physical, and spiritual levels of the self, and takes place in each and every individual. (262-81) Truth is an experience, and it is this which Israel is seeking.

The second principle of *Israel* is *Service*. According to one reading, the greater meaning of *Israel* is: "Those called of God for a service before the fellow man." (587-6) Or, as another reading states: "For in Zion thy names are written, and in Service will come Truth." (254-42)

The symbol and manifested reality of these two principles of *Service* and *Truth* is shown in the Christ as he applied them throughout his Old Testament incarnations. These were the building blocks of his messiahship. The people Israel, by attuning to these same principles, created the environment through which this perfect pattern could be wrought.

Like Adam, we all have fallen from the perfection symbolized by the Garden. Like Christ, we must become priests, prophets, and ministers not only for the life and resurrection of our own souls but for the benefit and uplift of all humanity.

Cayce tells us that in order to obtain "the Mind of Christ" we must, in the physical plane, be able to manifest His Spirit. Mind is the Builder, and thus we must ever seek to make our perceptions of spiritual truth physical realities. Jesus himself tells us we must become "perfect" (Matthew 5:48)

To become "perfect" entails a discipline of Mind, for we must learn to increase and expand the dimensions of our awareness from the physical through the mental to the spiritual. As "seekers" heeding our call, we are seeking a deeper penetration into the realm of ideas, to the source and father of all our energies through all the levels of consciousness that separate us from understanding that we are "the divine image" affirmed in Genesis. We are *Israel* as we seek comprehension and a new relationship to those eternal truths and processes which are embodied in the symbology of the Old Testament.

## *From the Garden to the City*

According to the Cayce readings, we were all souls in the beginning—spiritual beings in a spiritual world. This is the Eden we have lost and forgotten. Just as Genesis preserves a memory, the Revelation points to future consciousness, a potential experience for all. The Bible then is the story of man's journey from the garden to the city, from Eden to the New Jerusalem. (Revelation 21:2)

God *gave* us the garden, but man must *build* the city.

The city of Jerusalem grows in meaning throughout the Old Testament story. It was the home of Melchizedek, a spiritual center to which David gave new significance when he established it the capital of his newly emerging kingdom. After Solomon completed the temple which David had planned, he turned his energies to rebuilding and transforming David's city into a place of awesome magnificence and splendor. Jesus enlarged Jerusalem's meaning when—as a symbol—it became the seat of his kingdom—which was not of this world!

All that was temporal and corruptible in Solomon's glories has passed away, but the city of splendor which he created inspired the symbol in the Revelation of the New Jerusalem. Unlike Solomon's city, the New Jerusalem was "a city not built with hands." It was a city not built with the taxes and forced labor a despot exacts from his people, but, like the garden, by the thought of an All-Merciful Creator.

And we find John the Beloved was the first to enter.

## A New Heaven, a New Earth

*And I saw a new heaven and a new earth; for the first heaven and the first earth had passed away, and the sea was no more.*

*And I saw the holy city, the new Jerusalem, coming down from God, prepared as a bride for her husband.* (Revelation 21:1-2)

Both David and Solomon had glimpses of "a new heaven and a new earth." They envisioned things which men had not yet seen in manifested form. When they built, they gave to Israel a new revelation into the nature of God and His relationship and faithfulness to those who call on Him. But, because their vision rested partially on material things, the full understanding did not emerge except through John.

When Jerusalem was destroyed in 70 A.D., symbolically the last vestige of the old materialistic cycle was completed. The destruction was coincident with the emergence of the new understanding that came with the teachings of Jesus, David's heir.

One cycle was completed and another began, structured on the same pattern with the same symbols—the Promised Land, the Holy City, the Temple—but on a new level of consciousness. And those who prepare themselves by building through Old Testament patterns of searching for Truth and serving God were able to receive the New Testament realizations of Oneness and the free flow of Spirit in all phases of Life.

The kingdom of God, the Holy City, and the temple were established in the outer world, now they must be built within.

This is affirmed in this interpretation by Edgar Cayce:

**(Q) What is the meaning of "a new heaven and a new earth: for the first heaven and the first earth were passed away . . . "?**

**(A) . . . Can the mind of man comprehend no desire to sin, no purpose but that the glory of the Son may be manifested in his life? Is this not a new heaven, a new earth? For the former things would have passed**

away. For as the desires, the purposes, the aims are to bring about the whole change physically, so does it create in the experience of each soul a new vision, a new comprehension.

For as has been given, it hath not entered the heart of man to know the glories that have been prepared, that are a part of the experiences of those that love *only* the Lord and His ways . . . For those who come into the new life, the new understanding, the new regeneration, there *is* then the new Jerusalem. For as has been given, the place is not as a place alone, but as a condition, as an experience of the soul.

Jerusalem has figuratively, symbolically, meant the holy place, the Holy City—for there the ark of the covenant, the ark of the covenant in the minds, the hearts, the understandings, the comprehensions of those who have put away the earthly desires and become as the *new* purposes in their experience, become the new Jerusalem, the new undertakings, the new desires.
281-37

# The Relevance and Significance of
# Edgar Cayce's Story of the Bible Today

*In* one reading Edgar Cayce was asked what the highest psychic realization was for man. He answered, "That God speaks directly to the sons of men." Stated simply, the great significance of Edgar Cayce is that for thousands of people he has made this realization possible. The most important discovery an individual can make is that God is within. Like Jesus, we all may know "I and the Father are One."

The Bible is one of the most important legacies given to men. In no other work or record do we have such a vision of the potential and possibilities of which man is capable. The Cayce readings really only amplify and interpret the basic themes, assumptions, and promises expressed in Scripture. What greater promise could come from any teacher or leader than the one given by Jesus, "Greater things than these I do, ye shall do because I go to my Father." Cayce showed, through the example of his life, how this promise might be fulfilled.

Those who knew him remember Edgar Cayce not as a great psychic who possessed a wide range of paranormal sensibilities. The enduring impression was of a deeply spiritual man committed to the path of brotherly love, self–sacrifice, and service, a man infused with confidence and trust in his Creator.

The quest for self–realization and self–development speaks strongly to modern man. The Cayce readings are unique in their vision. There is a cosmic dimension to all men, and a practical means to obtain it. If Jesus was perfect, it was because it is the potential of all men to become perfect.

Edgar Cayce lived as a disciple of Christ's, whose life reflected his belief in the promises of his master. Although hundreds came to listen to his words, and many thousands were given counsel and advice, and his psychic gifts far surpassed that of any living person, Edgar Cayce gently reminded them that they all had equal access to the Source from which his gifts arose.

Equally significant in the Cayce philosophy is that nowhere is the development of psychic power a primary goal. Living in unity and harmony with God's Laws and raising the Christ-consciousness within are the central objectives. The *fruits* of the Spirit—patience, kindness, long-suffering, tolerance, sensitivity to the needs of others—are valued more highly than the *gifts*, which include clairvoyance, telepathy, aura-reading, and other forms of psychic phenomena. Psychic development, the readings show, is the natural outgrowth of spiritual development.

The great emphasis in the Cayce readings is on personal application of spiritual truths. Only by living the truths which are presented to us can we ever experience, understand, or evaluate them.

In a restless, questioning age, when many individuals are seeking new values and life styles, Cayce points us to the Bible, this central piece of literature which bespeaks where the source of our strength, our health, and well-being can be found, and gives us the key for its interpretation. To understand it, we must live it.

What could be more relevant and significant today than the incentive the Cayce philosophy provides for testing out that truth which Jesus taught—that "we are gods," made in his Image.

# Appendix: Edgar Cayce's Bible Class Notes and Lectures

## Looking at Three and Seeing One

*In* the Garden of Eden we find our first symbols of a three-dimensional world, MAN, the Tree of Knowledge and The Tree of Life . . . Then we have Cain the body, Abel the mind, and Seth the soul, representing the three phases of man's whole understanding. There were many sons and daughters of Adam, but the first three become figures of the Body which sins, the Mind which desires to do right, and the soul through which men begin to call on God for help. It was through Seth, the third son of Adam that men begin to call upon the Lord (Gen. 4:26) while the children of Cain were going their own way without thought except for their own indulgence and gratification.

In the day Jesus was offered on the cross, we find three—one who rejected Jesus, one who accepted Jesus, and Jesus himself. We have the world, the flesh, the devil . . . the body, the mind, the soul . . . the Father, the Son, the Holy Spirit. The pattern of three seems to follow throughout.

The same three characteristics in the nature of man have been his stumbling blocks; namely, self-preservation, self-exaltation, and self glorification

The Bible itself is a good example of these three phases. The Book is the Body, the writing of it the Mind, and what it tells us as we read and study is the Spirit or Soul! The influence it bears depends upon how we unfold, or *respond* to the unfolding pages day to day.

If we can get an understanding of the three phases of ourselves being one—the body, mind and soul—just as the Father, Son and Holy Spirit, we can understand what is meant by viewing or accepting things in a spiritual way. All three bodies must be in harmony and coordinant with the Great Triune, of which we are just a shadow.

In keeping with Mr. Cayce's observation of a three-phase Bible in relation to ourselves, we can view the Bible Story through three major phases: the development of the body, the unfolding of the mind, and the consciousness of Spirit.

We can relate the first phase to the creation of the Adamic body as the ideal physical vehicle for the non-physical spirit, or intended companions—spirits of the Creative Source. The Adamic body was first a thought in the Mind of God, designed as a vehicle for the soul and evolved through the processes of evolution. This body allows the soul to experience and explore the denser vibrations of materiality and maintain its relationship to the original Oneness from which it came by honoring its divine nature and following its intuitive wisdom. The soul, a creative spirit possessed of free will and choice as its birthright, can also use the Adamic body purely as a vehicle for sensation, power and pleasures in a self-gratifying way. We have the freedom to make those choices, but we can't escape the consequences, for the laws are perfect and unchanging: what we sow, we reap. There are consequences for every thought, action and intention. And with that choice, we become entrapped in our own outcomes and creations and lose the awareness of ourselves as spiritual beings and continue the ever repeating cycles of loss, separation, crises and catastrophe, as represented by the loss of the Garden and the Great Deluge—and the need for "a way of escape,"—a way to awaken our own inner divinity and find our way back to the original unity and harmony of the One—Home!

## *Bible Class Notes, Phase One— Thought Forms and the Adamic Body*

After the creation of souls, God, through thought, began the process of evolution. All souls were created and were with God before the earth was brought into being. All of us were with Him in the beginning, even as Solomon speaks of being with God, "before his works of old. " (Proverbs 8:22-32)

When Spirit pushed itself into matter, we had thought forms. God brings into being His first begotten son, the Christ, the first one to whom He gives a physical body and gives him dominion over the earth, a privilege denied the thoughts forms. God was giving Himself [as Adam] to bring in the perfect way for the soul to find its relationship to the creative Influence or God, or come to that realization of the Christ Consciousness—the consciousness of being one with Him, as described in the beginning of the world.

Thus, Satan, that Spirit which rebelled in spiritual realm, could only become active through God's physical man *as* that physical man allows him to become active. God did not warn man that he would be tempted. He did tell him to hold to the knowledge he had already been given, and the result would be good.

In our physical body, as man is the last of creation, we are made up of everything that was created before, so we are dependent on upon all that has gone before. Then unless our bodies are in harmony, we will be sick.

In the physical, every organ's holy desire is to reproduce itself. Only when attempting to gratify material desires, does it become sinful [or misdirected—that is, sin is an archery term which means 'missed the mark'—no bull's eye]. Adam and Eve were perfect, made for each other. It was not a sin for them to have each other; it was only when they associated with the thought forms that they became contaminated and ashamed before God.

When they realized they had had associated with the thought forms outside of themselves, they realized they were naked and ashamed. The voice of their own conscience began to disturb them, but they pushed it aside. Even today, it is man's nature to try and forget, or ignore such pricking of conscience.

After Cain [Body] slew Abel [Mind] he went east, outside of the presence of God's kingdom, where there was no conscience. Civilization moves ever westward; Cain went eastward, and built his own environment, his own surroundings.

Who did Cain marry? Unless we accept thought forms, those things outside the presence of the Lord, that are not of the material creation that was part of God, there is no answer.

"Be fruitful and multiply, and subdue the earth" was spoken to the spiritual beings, not to fallen man. After the fall, man became subject to the earth. It was the beginning of his struggle to eke out an existence from the very dust of which he was made and of which the serpent was to eat.

Noah found grace in the eyes of God because he acquainted himself with the things having to do with his relationship to God. Noah was perfect in his generations, which is to say there was no mixing of his parents or grandparents with the sons and daughters of men. Yet we find that even he, later, succumbs to physical temptation.

Although parts of Bible history may seem very profane, within the first few chapters we find basic truths, the foundation and beginning of man's concept of his relationship to his Maker.

## Bible Class Notes, Phase Two— Mind, Faith and Will

When we listen to or act from instincts and urges of the body and ego alone for safety, power and influence or gratification, the urge or compulsion to put self first without consideration of others ultimately and invariably leads to some form of breakdown, deterioration or crisis in our awareness and relationship to the Divine. When our disappointments, losses and suffering awaken us to seek better answers and outcomes, we are at the place of Abraham and the development of Mind in relation to Faith and the constructive use of our Will.

Abraham responds to an inner experience, and acts on it. His is a felt experience that motivates him to move in consciousness away from the past and all that is known, comfortable and familiar to him. As Abraham begins his journey, his movement takes us forward to Jacob/Israel, the truth seeker, Joseph the clairvoyant dreamer, Moses the lawgiver, Joshua the warrior, King David and Solomon, all leaders, each with their faults, weaknesses and imperfections, yet reflecting some stage or phase of the spirit's development in relationship to its physical form and needs of the body, and the soul's desire to know and serve through faith in what the mind recognizes and understands as God.

Abraham accumulates great wealth and prosperity as he journeys following the guidance and direction he receives from within himself, but its origin is from beyond himself. The everlasting wealth that he gathers is through the promise and the knowing that all his descendents, those truly of his spiritual lineage are destined to be sovereigns, the spiritual royalty of many nations.

In the Bible we see the process of building up consciousness of the physical, mental and spiritual bodies from age to age. In Noah and his descendents we find a different kind of man than in the Adamic age. Man is now developing through the mental processes, and the physical temptations are repeated in the mental.

From the very beginning it has been shown us that man has to move out on Faith, first believe that God is, and then act in that manner which makes that faith known. Faith is an attribute of the mind cultivated by use of the will. We don't gain faith by belief alone. Belief is a preparation. Faith comes as we choose to act on what we believe to be true, or in keeping with God's will.

Hence we come back to the spiritual man, Abram, who seeks guidance from within and carries out that guidance, becoming father of the faithful. With Abram, or Abraham, we have the beginning of man's mental self, relying upon the spirituality within, represented by faith, an attribute of the soul.

Abraham became aware of an influence that aroused something within himself, which often prevented him from being influenced by things around him. Whether it was a higher consciousness or a direct voice, we are to determine within ourselves. God is as mindful of us as he was of any of the patriarchs of old, if we will be as faithful as they were.

When we study those experiences of Abraham, we realize human nature hasn't changed. Then we can understand how that Abraham is not merely a character in the Bible, but truly a condition in our whole experience.

## Two Sides of Moses

Through the Old Testament characters, we may see the individual developing through various stages to reach the perfection that Christ represents in our lives. We see ourselves in such characters evolving from the purely materialistic through the mental into the spiritual life as shown in Christ, in whom we may completely know ourselves to be what we are and what we shall be, by his grace.

Moses was afraid at first to look on his higher self. (Exodus 3:6) He was so full of knowledge that it was hard for him to remain in the attitude to receive and have faith in his guidance from his higher self. We find that he often injected his own personal will, enforcing his ideas on the people as law and gospel, which is not ideal. In many of the Old Testament leaders we find the same condition. Many fought battles of material conquest, believing God had directed them, when perhaps the source of their interpretation was merely their own selfish desires.

It is recorded that God lost patience when He saw the people of Israel before the golden calf. Moses is accredited for pleading with God and reminding Him of His promise that in Judah all the nations of the earth would be blessed. This seems strange, because Moses first lost his patience with the people and was so angry that he broke the tablets on which God had given him the commandments. (Exodus 32:19)

We ourselves have experiences today such that we often break ourselves, our bodies, our minds, over things that are just as useless.

We see no such display of temper in Jesus even though from a physical standpoint He was able to do something about such things that were not in harmony with the LAW.

However when Moses realized what he had done, he must have tried to appease his own conscience with the knowledge that he could make himself materially the leader of nations. He also knew God's promise spiritually had been otherwise, and to fulfill his own purpose he must conform to God's purposes. Consequently, Moses must have been pleading, really, with the God-force within, not the all-powerful Creative Force without.

## *Weakness and Sincerity, Sinner and Repenter*

King David had many weaknesses, just as we have. It is said of David that he was guilty of all the sins. Yet, because of his attitude, his belief in the righteousness of God, he was considered a man after God's own heart. How then it is that David is a man after God's own heart?

He was a great sinner, but also a great repenter, never guilty of committing the same sin twice. He always repented and found new ways to manifest an appreciation of God's love. In many of his psalms, we find him pouring out his soul calling on God for mercy and forgiveness.

In seeking to justify ourselves, we might turn to David as an example; yet if we do we should go all the way and be in the same repentant attitude

We cannot claim or possess God's love and forgiveness unless through our belief in him, we are prompted to live up to our belief. It should be a constant source of encouragement to know Jesus Christ takes us where we are today. We are to fulfill the law of love in our own little niche, in whatever place we find ourselves.

## The Inner and Outer as One—
## An Aspect of Mind in Development of Faith

The great Indian yoga master Paramahansa Yogananda described Christ, or Christ Consciousness, as a level of conscious awareness through which we behold all manifested expressions—animal, vegetable, mineral—not as objects, but as projections of divine intelligence. In the second phase of our Three Fold Bible, through Will and application of its faith, the Mind of the seeker continues to unfold and grow into and toward an ever expanding clarity of the Higher Mind and its communications. For those who continue grow and develop their awareness of their Higher Mind and its communication through faith and application of free will and choice, their trust grows through experience and wisdom into an unshakeable understanding and confidence of the benevolence, love and direction of the Higher Sources.

As we continue our journey through the wilderness of physically rooted, self-centered emotional reactions of fear, greed, hate and prejudice, bearing the hope and promise of a Higher Mind, and a more full relationship with God, our Source, each experience of faith applied reveals in some way great or small—line upon line, step by step—that our physical and mental bodies are much more and than a systems of drives and appetites, fears and impulses to be gratified, satiated and endured. Through the body, we may become as aware of the Divine and its purposes as we are aware of ourselves and our souls, but it is a temple in which we communicate with God. Jesus knew that not anything outside—whether in Jerusalem or on the high holy hills—is more sacred than what you are, for your body, the body is a temple.

## The Building of the Tabernacle

We are each a manifestation of something that is spiritual in its concept. Because man is the expression in materiality of spirit, he is desirous always of having something before him as a reminder.

With the realization that we are body, mind and soul, there is also the longing within for the continuation of our own experience.

In addition to the Ten Commandments and an outline of the ordinances, Moses was also given specific directions as to how to build the tabernacle, even what the furnishings were to be. When we look for the metaphysical interpretation of the furnishings of the tabernacle, and the manner in which it was built, we see that it was not only a perfect building but emblematical of our own body . . . which is the temple of the living God. The temple prepared by David and later built by Solomon was a replicate of the tabernacle built in the wilderness.

In a letter to a newly acquired friend and inquiring seeker Mr. Cayce continued with his lessons from a living Bible:

> "No—when we read the Bible as a history we lose the real purpose it seems to me. Do we think of the characters as periods through which we as individuals pass? Then when we read ordinances they are directed to our imagination of unfoldment and not as ritual that was rarely adhered to by any of the people to whom they were given—and when they are taken as ritual it doesn't relieve, merely bypasses a crisis for some individual. It is the spirit not the letter of the law that is so important. The Ritual is a symbol and not an activity—rarely at all." EC Letter to 2072

## Bible Class Notes, Phase Three— Patience, Soul and Spirit

If the reign of Solomon and all its glories represents an aspect of mind or phase of developments, what is there of it that relates to you? A phase or aspect of life when we are at a peak of our development, all our goals met; mentally, physically, financially, and intellectually fulfilled and in the best all around condition possible. We have a knowledge of God and a great edifice as our gathering place for worship and to express gratitude for blessings bestowed.

And yet for all its glories and material expression, the earthly kingdom endured for only a brief moment in time. Shortly after Solomon's passing, due to the unequal distribution of wealth and excess of privilege claimed by the royal tribe of Judah and Benjamin, the remaining ten tribes rebelled and withdrew to form their own nation of Israel in the Galilee while the royalty claimed Jerusalem as its own. This break among the tribes introduced a long, debilitating period of conflict and unrest with occasional times of cooperation between the tribes. This material continued until both the nation of Israel and the royal tribe of Judah were conquered and carried into captivity—and lost generally to history. Judah followed later with the same fate, all lost except for power of God's promises and the enduring memories of what once was—and could be again faith.

There would not again be seen such a glorious kingdom among the Jews until Jesus taught the handful who listened, "the kingdom is within" and John Beloved in the last chapters of his Revelation experienced his kingdom and revealed the unimaginable treasures and wealth available collectively and individually to those who faithfully seek and know "the kingdom is within."

God is faithful to his Promises and rewards those who seek him. If we move toward him an inch, God comes by the mile. Solomon manifested all the earthen and intellectual glories, yet because of his materialism, the seduction of power and privilege kept God from being truly first is his priorities. He made compromises and adjustments to his early vow to seek, as king, the wisdom of God first. Instead he became worldly wise and entangled and obligated through his many political and financially motivated alliances and marriages with foreign women and their gods, and brought the inevitable end.

Solomon gave an enduring example of what is possible through a well-developed consciousness and built its outward expressions. But more, he gave us an everlasting gift through the wisdom and timeless legacy of proverbs and psalms. Solomon represents a phase or potential of the soul's development and expression in the earth, but not yet a perfect or completed one.

We still look forward to the full manifestation of the Christ Light in man, perfectly expressed. There is a foreshadowing and intimation as this third and final phase of the Old Testament story nears it conclusion. Zechariah, a holy prophet and high priest keenly perceives in Jeshua the completion of the perfected pattern. In a vision at the time of the Return to the Promised Land after a long period of captivity in Babylon, Zechariah beholds in a vision the High Priest Jeshua purified, crowned first with a turban indicating high priesthood and then with a gold crown and given the name Branch, "and he will branch out from his place and build the temple of the LORD." (Zechariah 3–10; 6:9-15)

What makes this memorable is that Jeshua, as given by Edgar Cayce, is the final and culminating incarnation in the Old Testament of the first Adam. In his next appearance he returns as Jesus, the second and final

Adam. All through his incarnations in the earth, the Adam/Jesus soul had been preparing to fulfill the role he accepted, as one to find a way to awaken souls to the memory within of who they are and where they came from, and to live in such a way as to provide a pattern and ideal that would lead them back home, back to the original unity and harmony of the One.

Zechariah's vision is multilevel and not time bound. He beholds Jeshua in his current role as high priest, yet the vision simultaneously foreshadows the future. Jesus fulfills his mission and purpose and ascends to be king of heaven and high priest of the eternal order of Melchizedek (Hebrews 7) in an unbroken continuation of his earlier experience as the High Priest Melchizedek.

Malachi is the second prophet from this culminating period, who is given prophetic vision concerning the coming of the Messiah and his messenger. The words of Malachi's prophecy are the last words in the Old Testament. The Holy One is near and his appearance is soon.

*"Behold, I send My messenger, And he will prepare the way before Me. And the Lord, whom you seek, Will suddenly come to His temple, Even the Messenger of the covenant, In whom you delight. Behold, He is coming, Says the Lord of hosts."* Malachi 3-4 (NKJV)

Abraham and Sarah waited many years for the Promise of Laughter to be fulfilled through the birth of their child, Isaac. Jacob also had to wait fourteen years before he would claim Rachael, his beloved, as his bride. Moses could climb the holy mountain with his own strength and determination, but when he reached the peak, he had to wait; there was no way to force or accelerate the process, only to abide in patience and listen to the still, small voice.

With the final prophecies, there is nothing to do but wait.

Edgar Cayce through the readings, his lessons to the Bible Class, encouraged patience as one of the attributes of the soul to be developed. Active waiting is a virtue to be mastered on the path of return to the One.

## Patience as an Attribute of the Soul

To understand patience we must understand time, and the fact that time means much to us and very little or nothing to God. Thus, Malachi could prophecy a Redeemer who in the mind of God was imminent, but in the calendar of man was 400 years away. To wait for this Redeemer through long generations of sin and suffering required patience, and even the faithful were given to doubt.

Patience is the ability to endure the passage of time until we arrive at that place in our minds where there is no time and no space. Then we know that we are with God. *We* need patience when we have reached an awareness of the goal, yet haven't reached the goal. Patience, therefore, is that which helps to carry us toward the goal, and is just one of the many attributes of the soul to be magnified in our lives. These attributes are part of our consciousness or awareness, and when we make application we become conscious of the creative power within.

We must learn not only to have patience with our fellow man, but to have patience with ourselves. Often we become disturbed over our own weaknesses and lose patience with ourselves. Only in manifesting patience can we become aware of the promises made to us by God, as being true in our lives. Too often we look upon these promises as being made merely to those people who lived in that day and age, when in reality they apply to us now, today.

The laws and methods of training the people, as laid down in the Old Testament, are just as applicable in our lives today.

Patience means being positively constructive in the face of pessimism or destructive attitudes, not only by our conversation but by our every act! We ourselves must cultivate patience. It is just like sowing seed for a garden. We each have a different soil, and what is necessary to protect and preserve one type of soil might be wrong for another. We each must be the judge as to how well we are sowing the seed and caring for our own Garden.

## *Cayce's Talks and Letters— Man's Relationship to God*

*[The following is a transcript of a lecture delivered at the Cayce Hospital, Virginia Beach, VA by Mr. Cayce.]*

Please understand that I am not trying to explain your relationship to God. I am only hoping that I will be able to tell you something that will stimulate you to thought.

First it is necessary that we review, as we might say, man's experience in the earth's plane—so far as we have a history of it. The broadest understanding that we can get, I think, is from the Scripture itself. I don't mean that I am going to preach any special theology or give you an idea of what I believe in the theology of the day, or the theology of the past.

It doesn't matter as to what we may claim we believe. What is really worthwhile is what difference does that which we believe make in our lives? What change, what difference, does a belief make that may come into your life? That is the thing people are really interested in. The world does not care whether you believe the whale swallowed Jonah, or whether Noah was in the Ark a whole year or only forty days. What is an individual's belief in those things that have come into his life that have changed his attitude toward his fellow man, or towards his God? This is important.

### PART ONE: FROM ADAM TO ABRAHAM

If we take the history given us in the Bible, we would begin with the first individual that we find had a concept of his relation to God. Who would this first man be? Not Adam. No, for Adam's concept at first was his relationship to his fellow man or his relationship to his mate—if we take it just as an individual. It is the seventh from Adam that we find had a different concept entirely. "Now Enoch walked with God and he was not, for God took him." He was considered by the people of that day as a man with an individuality. First it was known as an individuality or a personality, if we may put it in those terms. It was the personality as manifested in the relationship of one individual to another individual. Enoch, we find, was one who began to consider his relationship to his Creator—call Him by what you will or may—whether the God of the first cause, the God of nature, or the God of the divine. Then we find there is a different concept that begins to move among the people. They are moved in a different way and manner. It changed that man's life.

The next man we find that comes down through history as one who had a definite religious experience is Noah. Now, Noah was a just man. He was a perfect man in his day and generation, but it changed his attitude. Not only did it change the man's attitude as to his relationship to what he worshipped as his God, but as to his relationship to individuals round about him, and it brought a different activity in his life. That is the kind of thing that we are trying to get at; to see how these things change about.

Abraham is the next. His experience brought to the world a great change. He was called out to make of his seed and of his generation a peculiar people, a separate and distinct nation. He was an elderly man without an offspring, yet God spoke to him and made him a great promise. "Now separate yourself from among these people and go out to a strange land which I will give to your seed forever as a heritage. I will make of you a peculiar people, and through your seed will all the nations of the earth be blessed." Abraham harkened to that call. In this very matter there lies for most of us a great fault. Have any of us so lived that we were called to do a special thing? Have any of us so lived that we may be guided by that something from within that will direct us if we would but stop; to harken to "the Voice?" We notice that when this call came to Abraham he heard the call and knew it was not in him that the people were to be blessed, but in the way that he was to act towards his brethren. He was to separate himself from these for a peculiar service.

This idea has grown to seed. This is held against those very people. They separated themselves from others as a chosen people of God. It was to make a nation that Abraham was called, and through Abraham should ALL nations be blessed. Through the acts of this individual, through his understanding and response to the call, were all people to find happiness. But when these people begin to make this promise an individual thing, that "I can sin because I am chosen," they begin to fall by the way.

## PART TWO: JACOB, MOSES AND JOSHUA

Next we come to Jacob. When the day came for Jacob to be taken to his fathers, he called about him his twelve sons and explained to each his faults and virtues. He showed them what each of his sons had built, was building, through his concept of his relationship to Jehovah, and the results it would bring in their lives. All that he told them came to pass.

The next in line is Moses, who is raised up to be a deliverer of his people. Abraham had been told that his seed would be in bondage for four hundred years, and then there would be one raised up who would lead them back to this Promised Land which he, Moses was not allowed, to possess, but which would become the land of his people, God would remain with them as their God if they would remain to Him His people.

Then, this is given in a way and manner that it works from both sides. It isn't that one should set self up and say, it is thus and cannot be any other way—for we find anything may be changed by the will of an individual. There is something that man must do, as well as something that the Creator must do. There is a purpose in life. It is not a haphazard thing.

Now we come down to the days when the Jews went out to the Promised Land. As they wandered through the wilderness they began to think about their own personal relationship to God. They forgot all the hardships through which they had passed in Egypt. Human nature has always been and will always be just the same. As we pass through life we feel that the present is about the hardest time we have ever had, but after a few years have passed we begin to look back on those things, only seeing the things that have come out of this. Why? Why does this happen? There is a cause. When the people murmured and when they asked that they might have a physical God that they might see something that was tangible, they cried to Moses. You speak of the spirit and you are able to go up on the mountain and speak with God. You are able to go up on the mountain and bring us wonderful messages but we don't see Him; we don't hear Him.

We hear only those things that you come back and tell us. We have seen the [pillar] of fire by night and the cloud by day but these have become every day matters. We expect these. Now we want to do things that other people do. We want a God like they have.

They had forgotten they were called out to be a separate and distinct nation. They had forgotten the call that had come to their forefathers and the heritage that they were about to claim.

Throughout all of this Moses maintained his faith in and upheld the God he had come to know through personal experiences. He had heard the call from within. God to him had become a personal God. For the people who fought among themselves at the foot of the mountains God was still the God of war, the God with the big stick who beat off their enemies but would turn on them if they went too far.

Cannot we get this idea? God is a personal God. He is not a God of war or a God of plenty nor even a God of an individual. He is a God of ALL. In all things and our heritage is in Him. We may illustrate this. Just as the earthly parent feels in respect to his own offspring, so may we in our own selves conceive of something that God may feel, must feel, about his children, His peoples here in this world.

It is His purpose that we make ourselves a channel through which His spirit may manifest. He would use us. You may say, well I don't want to be used. I heard a lady say this about her little eight or nine months old boy, "I know his father wants him to become a great artist, but I don't want him to do anything that may be called the work of genius because he will have to suffer physically." She might just as well have said, "I do not want him to give up the desire of the flesh for a spiritual life." To my mind that is a sad condition. What has been the experience of the peoples of this world when they have forgotten that there is a purpose in their passing through this experience in this material plane? That purpose is to make their wills one with the Creator. Let us prepare to be used as a channel that He may manifest through us. Write that down. Get it. It isn't that you are to be bossed over by someone else, for there is nothing in the world that we can do for God. What we do we do for the other fellow, for in so doing we become one with the will of the Father. He has given us control of the physical world that we may use it for helping our fellow man. We may be the channel through which the other fellow, less fortunate than ourselves, may be aided in whatever is needed for him to gain a better conception of his relation to his God.

It would be well if we could remember the decision of the great Jewish leader who said, "Others may do as they may, but for me and my house, we will worship the living God." Daily, we are confronted with problems that require just such a definite stand. Let us remember His promise and be strong.

## PART THREE: SAUL, DAVID AND SOLOMON

We may now trace the history of the Jews on down to the time when the first king was chosen. Saul was raised up to be their king and leader yet he failed to understand that the time had come when the people had developed to the point where God did not desire a sacrifice of animals but of individuals to His cause. David was the next in line and despite the fact that he did many things that we today call sins we may learn many lessons from his attitude toward his God. Saul tried many times to kill him yet always David said, "It is not meet that I should raise mine hand against an anointed of the Lord." It is not right that any one individual should raise his voice against another individual who is doing his service in the manner he feels God has spoken to him. God has never called an individual to lord it over his brother, but always to become the servant of his brother.

Finally there comes the last rise to power. The Jewish nation becomes under King Solomon, David's son, one of the greatest of the time. After the beautiful temple has been built and prosperity comes to the nation the people begin to forget their relation to God, and led by the king they turn to the worship of the physical pleasures of the world. Their fall is near. The period of the prophets follows. Individuals arise who have a vision of what the relationship to God should be, but the people will not listen to them, and the Jews are torn apart as a nation, and scattered to the four winds.

The question has come down to every age, to every individual: What is your relationship to your God? It came to Enoch, to Noah, to Abraham, to Isaac, to Moses, to Joshua, to Saul, to David, to Solomon and it comes just the same to you today. What is your relation to your God? Remember that He is the God of the Living, not of the Dead. Remember that in serving Him you must serve your fellow man. Remember that you must become a channel through which God may work His divine will here on earth. When the burdens become hard to bear and you feel yourself beginning to slip away from the path you know is right, draw nearer to your God and He will draw nearer to you. As a child will come and sit at the feet of its parents, seeking their guidance and advice, asking their help, just so we must approach through prayer the God who is our Father and Creator.

First to know God we must believe that He is. We must seek to find His face. "Seek and ye shall find, knock and it shall be opened unto you." Now in coming to know Him, is it not evident that as we consider and help our fellow man so do we carry out God's work. Our relationship to our God then becomes our relationship to our brother. There is nothing that we can do for God, but there is much that we can do for His Children, His created creatures, and our brothers. As we go about in our every–day work let us remember to lend a helping hand wherever we may, and know that in so doing we are fulfilling the Will of the Creator and coming ever nearer to our God.

# Index

## A

Aaron, 119, 121, 126, 129, 131–132, 140–
 143, 145–146, 149, 151, 153, 162–163,
 165–167, 169, 170–171, 173, 176–179,
 185, 198, 225, 332, 359, 511; breast-
 plate of, 162–164
Abajalon, 225
Abarther, 155
Abatha, 120
Abazeal, 177
Abel, 40, 43, 45, 47, 49, 52, 77, 98, 349,
 585, 587; murder of, 45, 47, 98, 587
Abiathar, 169, 313–314, 342
Abigail, 316
Abigal, 145
Abihu, 164–166, 168–169, 177
Abijah, 169, 189, 384, 395–398, 413, 509,
 571; and kingdom of Judah, 395,
 397–398
Abimilech, 88–90, 253–254
Abishai, 317
Abiram, 173
Abjada, 334
Abner, 323–325, 337–338
Abraham (Abram), x, xxi, 22, 26, 53, 72,
 76, 81–82, 86–100, 108, 113, 117–119,
 121, 124, 137–138, 148, 168, 171, 182,
 197, 201, 203, 230, 267, 269, 292, 297,
 325–326, 359, 400, 424, 432, 443, 494,
 507, 509, 557, 578, 588–589, 594, 596–
 597, 600; God's promise to, 92; Isaac
 and, 86, 88, 93, 97, 118, 230, 297, 600;
 Lot saved by, 95–97; Melchizedek
 and, 81–86, 119, 197, 325, 359, 503;
 Sarah and, 86–99, 292, 594
Absalom, 334, 337, 340–345, 347, 433
Achan, 226–228, 242
Achish, 313
Ach–sah, 237–239
Adah, 50, 424
Adajoniah, 229
Adam, Fall of, xii, xiv, 35, 37–39, 274;
 first reference to, 30; formation of,
 22–24; naming of animals by, 29, 30;
 reincarnations of, 26, 28–29, 31, 40,
 46, 54, 81, 103, 109, 119, 170, 325, 358,
 372, 500, 503, 508, 377; subsequent
 incarnations of, 372
Adamic race, xiv, 22, 30, 32, 43, 53, 83,
 211, 268, 495; five lines of, xiv, 30;
 reason for development of, 32, 43

Adonijah, 344, 376
Adriel the Meholathite, 308
Adyar, 240
Affa, 359; *see also Asaph*
Agag, 303
Ahab, 388, 395, 404–409, 411, 413–415,
 424–425, 431–432, 436; "a changeable
 man," 404; destruction of his house,
 408; and Elijah and Jezebel, 413–415,
 424–425; and Jehoshaphat and
 Jezebel, 404, 409, 413–414, 425; and
 Micaiah, 406–407
Ahaz, and Assyrians, 443–444–, 447–448
Ahazia, and Jehoram and Athaliah, 431
Ahimeleck, 312–313
Ai, 226, 228–229, 243
Ajalon, 338, 347
Ajlon, 176
Akashic record, 9, 545
Allen, Eula, 37
Altar(s), established in English Colony,
 463, 466–467, 469; established by
 "lost" tribes, 471; and the home, 68,
 509
Amalek, 203–204
Amalekites, 149, 197, 201, 203–206, 209,
 303–304, 332
Amaziah, 441
American Colony, established by "lost"
 tribes, 462, 464
Amon, and Manassah, 455–456
Ammonites, 254, 299–300, 332, 405, 409,
 442–443, 538
Amilius, 28–29, 31–32, 39, 44, 46, 49, 60,
 358
Amnon, 334, 341, 344
Ana, 323
Anahasia, 339
Andes, the, 26, 28
Ani, 62
Anias, 339
Animals, in Ark, 66; forming and nam-
 ing of, 29–30; speaking by, 183
Anna, 286–287
Apple, the, 30, 35
Apsha (two entities), 363–365
Aramus, 302
Araaraatt, 56
Arabians, 203, 431, 442
Archangels, 192

Ardyeh, 240
Ark, the, 66–71, 80, 596
Ark of the Covenant, 87, 157, 198, 217, 329–331, 342, 350; brought to Jerusalem, 157, 329, 342; Jordan crossed by, 198
Arlam, 313
Artaxerxes, 533–534, 543, 560
Asa, and kingdom of Judah, 396–402, 409–410, 412, 431, 457
Asaph, incarnation of Jeshua, xv, 357–360, 500, 503–504, 512
Asbythen, 228
Ashbahel, 175
Ashbashul, 323–324
Asher, tribe of, 155, 362
Ashua, 166
Assen-ni, 52
Association for Research and Enlightenment, Inc., ix, xii, xvi–xvii, 37, 167, 200, 271, 284, 327
Assyrians, and Ahaz, and Hezekiah, 444, 447, 450, 452–454
Astrology, 19, 422
Athalia, 431–433
Atlantis, xviii, 9–10, 26–28, 31, 44, 52, 56–57, 61–62, 73, 172, 330, 361, 364, 541, 543, 545;
Adam in, 26, 31, 44; destruction of, 61–62; exodus from, 73, 545; records of, 56–57, 62, 541
Automatons, 52, 60
Azariah, 396

**B**

Baal, 185, 253, 395, 405, 413–415, 417, 420, 424, 431, 436–437
Baalism, 405, 414, 431, 437
Baal-peor, 185
Baasha, 388, 400–401, 404
Babel, Tower of, 77–78, 80, 137
Babylon, xv, 206, 271, 329, 362, 453–456, 458–459, 461, 471, 473, 475–477, 480, 482, 485, 487–491, 494–496, 502, 504–505, 513, 517, 533, 535, 538, 558, 560, 593; fall of, 489–491, 495–496; fall interpreted by Edgar Cayce, 495; and Hezekiah, 453–455; and kingdom of Judah, 473, 475; and symbolization of "self," 494–495
Babylonian Empire, and Nebuchadnezzar, 458, 475, 480, 482, 487, 489, 490
Babylonian mythology, "Tablets of Destiny" in, 162
Balaam, 182–185, 188

Balak, 182–184, 188
Baltimore, Lord, 309
Baptism,
Barak, 246–252
Bathsheba, 332–338, 340, 344
Belschazzar, 489
Belial, 38, 5–47, 52, 59–60, 65, 107, 172; see also Sons of Belial
Beloi, 97
Benaiah, 234, 376–380, 453; as "hard task-master," 376
Benjamin, 103–104, 238, 295, 297–298, 394, 469, 539, 592
Besne-nerea, 342
Bethel, 150
Beth-hurim, 342
Beth-Korah, 150
Bethlehem, 305, 467
Bezaleel, 149
Bible, the Cayce readings and, ii, 158; the chronology of, 333, 498; literal interpretation of, xxii; organic unity of, xx, 217i; as pattern of mental unfoldment, 76, 130, 138, 254, 494, 578; versions of, xvi
Bilhah, 103
Bithiah, 121
Birth, 260, 273, 278, 282–283,; see also Motherhood, psychic Boaz
Body, gold as connecting link between mind and, 27; purification of, in Temple of Sacrifice, 74–75; as temple, 131, 139, 156–157, 160, 191, 212, 218, 310, 314
Boils, plague of, 134
Boleyn, Ann, 287, 290
"Born again," 139
Brazil, 361
Breath, Holy, 23
Buried treasure, man seeking information about, 314
Burning bush, 125, 127, 148, 152, 191

**C**

Caesar, Julius, 231, 299
Cain 37, 40, 43, 45–46, 48–50, 52–54, 59, 65, 77, 133, 349, 585, 587; as result of Fall, 37, 43; murder of Abel by, 45, 587; Sons of, 46, 50, 53–54, 59, 65; see also Sons of Belial
Caleb 170, 172, 212, 216, 235–240, 467; family of, 235–238, 240
"Calling," 127
Cambell, Thomas, 64
Cambyses, 516
Canaan 79, 87, 116, 119, 205, 208, 212,

222, 233, 242, 281; entry into, 119, 198, 205, 212, 222, 242
Canaanites, 201, 206, 246
Carlson, Vada, 353
Carmel, 277, 364, 414–415, 420, 422–423, 538
Carpathia, 26, 28
Cayce, Edgar; on discord between Nehemia and Ezra, 566, 571; on Elijah, 414; on Elisha, 425; on Esther, 523–524, 527, 529–531; on Ezra, 535–537; interpretation of fall of Babylon, 495; and trance state, 353, 479, 133
Cayce Hospital, closing of, 94
Cayce, Hugh Lynn, *Venture Inward,* 199
Cecilia, St., 364
Ceclia, 131
Chaldeans, and psychic arts, 479
Children of the Light, 5; *see also Sons of God*
Chosen people, 19, 395, 404, 597
Christ, xii, xx, xxii, 10, 22, 25, 54, 81–82, 90, 98, 109–110, 137, 145, 153–154, 193–194, 219–220, 260, 277, 325, 349, 371–373, 383, 418, 432, 439, 455, 482, 491, 494, 497, 499, 501, 503, 524, 41, 578, 579, 584, 587, 589, 591, 593; *see also Jesus*
1 Chronicles (book), 304, 332, 337, 350, 357, 359, 375–376, 406, 455–456
2 Chronicles (book), 337, 352, 357, 360, 379, 396–403, 406–407, 409–411, 431, 439, 447–448, 453, 455–457
Churchward, James, 132
Circumcision, 221
Commerce, maritime, 361
Conflict(s), 53, 520, 551, 553; racial and religious, 512, 563; world affairs reading, 512
1 Corinthians (epistle), 94, 97
Cozbi, 185, 187
Creation, xxi–xxii, xxiii–xxiv, 1–15; Cayce's analysis of days of, 11–15; Mind and, 1–2, 20–21; myths of, 26–27
Cyrus, court of, 491; and the first return, 505, 513, 516–518

**D**

Da, 9
Dan, tribe of, 156–157
Daniel, dreams of, 478; and Nebuchadnezzar, 479–480
Darius, 498, 513, 518, 523–524
Darkness, plague of, 135
Dathan, 173

Daughters of Men, 8–9, 52, 60, 64
David, x, xv, 63, 101, 150, 201–202, 223, 241, 259–260, 262–263, 265, 268, 271, 285, 292, 302–308, 310–318, 323–350, 352, 357, 359–362, 364–366, 375–376, 379–380, 383, 387, 389, 395–398, 402–403, 438, 441, 447, 456–457, 470, 473, 475, 504–505, 512, 519, 580, 588, 590, 592, 599–600; Cayce's estimate of, 324–325; Goliath and, 305–307; Jonathan and, 302–303, 306–308, 310–312, 315, 318, 349; as king, 324; Saul and, 268, 313, 315, 328, 337, 349; seal of, 336; Temple and, 332, 33, 337, 341, 344, 350, 364–365, 580
Davis, Gladys, xv, 239, 248, 290
Death as necessary experience, 208; soul after, 208
Deborah, 246–252; Song of, 246, 248, 251–252
Deep sleep" as meditation, 32–33
Deluge (Flood), 55–56, 59, 61–62, 64, 67, 70, 72–73, 76, 291, 586; Atlantis' destruction by, 61–62; Enoch's warning of, 55–56; worldwide myths about, 72
Denis-Papin, Maurice, 330
Deuteronomy, 45, 190–191, 195, 198, 201, 236, 265–266, 282, 427, 453
Devil, the, xxiii, 2–3, 43, 192–193, 227, 299, 432, 433, 585; as Serpent, xxiii, 2–3, 36–37, 59, 177, 181, 182–183, 392, 588; as spiritual rebellion, xxii–xxiii, 2–3, 8
Dictators, David's example and, 317
Dietrich, Aime, 353
Dinah, 105–106
Divine, Awareness, 304; Image, xii–xiii, 579
Diviners, Cayce on, 319
Dream(s), 478; and Daniel, 478–483; and Elijah, 419–421; and Ezechiel, 545–546; and the fall of Babylon, 490–491; interpreted by Edgar Cayce, 545–546; and Jacob, 478; and John the Beloved, 478; and Nebuchadnezzar, 482–484
Dreaming, 143, 365–366

**E**

Earth, subduing of, 21–22, 40, 48, 588
Eden, 23–25, 28–29, 38–39, 52–53, 61, 139, 211, 350, 545, 577, 5769, 585; *see also Garden of Eden*
Edomites, 180, 332, 538; passage of Israelites prevented by, 180

603

Ego, development of, 47
Egypt, xxvii, 52, 55–56, 62, 66, 73–75, 85, 88–89, 106, 111–113, 116–117, 119–120, 123; Atlantean knowledge in, 361; can be left at any time, 137; Joseph in, ; Moses in, 117–136; see also Pharaoh
Eijalu, 157
Elah, 404
Elded, 156
Eleasiah, 150
Eleazar, 185, 188
Electricity, Mount Sinai as charged with, 330; Uzzah's death and, 329–331
Eli, 277–278, 282–282, 284
Eliab, 173
Eliesa, 214
Elijah, 53, 119, 405, 408, 413–417, 419–425, 427–428, 431, 434, 436, 457, 461; and Ahab and Jezebel, 413–417; appearance with Moses, 321; discussed by Edgar Cayce, 414–417; dreams and visions of, 420; and karmic lesson, 417–419; and karmic pattern, 416–417; reincarnated as John the Baptist, and the School of Prophets, 119
Elimelech, 259
Eliphaz, 204
Elisha, 64, 411, 413, 424–429, 433–434; discussed by Edgar Cayce, 425, 427–428
Elkanah, 278, 287–288
Elzjah, 184
Endocrine system, 92, 99, 154, 293
Endor, witch of, 318, 320
English Colony, established by "lost" tribes, 465–466, 468, 470; establishment of Altars in, 466, 468
Enoch, 28, 44, 54–56, 62, 81, 84, 86, 103, 109, 119, 358, 372, 425, 500, 503, 568, 577, 596, 600; incarnation of Jeshua, 28; records of Atlantis preserved by, 56, 62
Enos, 44
Er, 101, 331
Ersebus, 222
Esau, 105, 181, 203, 234, 349
Essenes, 85, 422, 574; and reincarnation, 422; and School of Prophets, 85, 285, 422–423
Esther, authority of, 527, 529, 533; discussed by Edgar Cayce, 524, 530; and Vashti, 523
Esther (book), 524, 527

Ethiopian woman, Moses' marriage to, 170, 173
Eve, creation of, 33, 46; daughters of, 53; as Mary, 39; temptation of, 35, 38
Evolution, 1, 2–5; of animals, 13, 30
Exodus, 112, 118, 141, 143, 176, 210, 212, 223, 245, 291, 377, 508, 522; date of, 210, 223, 245
Exodus (book), 52, 119, 122, 124, 126, 131–135, 137–138, 140, 142, 149, 150–152, 159–163, 197, 201, 217, 589–590
Ezakiai, [?], 121
Ezekiel, 154, 474, 496, 539, 542–546; the father of Judaism, 542; and interpretation of dream, 546; and psychic phenomena, 543, 545; and reincarnation, 542–543, 545
Ezra, 497–499, 506–507, 532, 534; and discord with Nehemia, 566–567; discussed by Edgar Cayce, 535–536; and "lost" records, 536–537, 541; reforms of, 533, 535; return to Jerusalem, 534; and Nehemia, 547, 549

**F**

Fiery furnace, and Nebuchadnezzar, 480–482
Fiery serpents, 181–182
First-born, slaying of, 130, 133, 136
Flood, the 30, 33, 46, 56, 61, 64–67, 70, 77, 208, 210, 274; see also Deluge
"Forbidden fruit," 35; see also Apple

**G**

Garden of Eden, 28, 211, 350, 577, 585; Eve's temptation in, 35–37
Garrison, Webb, 255
Gath, 313, 318
Genesis, ix, xii, xviii, xxi–xxiii, 6, 9–10, 12, 15, 30, 37, 49–51, 55, 67, 83, 265, 333, 381, 494, 50, 543, 568, 579
Genesis (book), xi, xxi, xxiii, 1, 6–8, 10–11, 13–14, 17, 20, 22, 24–25, 27, 29, 32, 36, 38, 41–42, 44–45, 48–50, 52–54, 59–60, 62–65, 71–72, 77–79, 81, 86, 89, 91, 94–96, 100–105, 108, 110, 112, 114–115, 124, 201, 217, 221, 265, 295, 298, 306, 362, 425, 483, 530, 572, 585
Genetic code, 209–210
Gentiles, definition of, 203; Joshua and, 203–207
Gershonites, 175–176
Geshem, 547, 549
Geshur, 341
Giants reported by Moses' spies, 170

Gibeonites, 229-231
Giboath, 317
Gideon, 252-254
Gilgal, 198, 217-218, 229, 277
Gizeh, construction of Great Pyramid at, 55
Gobi, 26, 28
God, Beginning and, xxi-xxiii, 1-14; companionship desired by, 30; direct speaking of, 291-292; as love, xxiii-xxiv; Moses' re-identification of, 118-119; of love, vs. God of war, 201-203; as One, 40-41; purpose of, in creation of souls, 291; *see also Divine Image*
Gold as connecting link between mind and body, 27
Goliath, 305-307
Gomorrah, 96-97, 137; *see also Sodom and Gomorrah*
Good Shepherd, 21
Gordon, Cyrus, 361-362, 462
Graven images, 154
Great Pyramid, construction of, 55-56
"Guardian angels," 288

## H

Hagar, 91, 93, 292
Haggai, 501, 517-518
Hailstorm, plague of, 135
Haliel, 339
Hall, Manly, 55, 362
Ham, 65, 79, 203
Hamor, 221
Hanan, 401, 409, 455
Hannah (entity in Life reading), 213; Hannah (mother of Samuel), 223
Hapgood, Charles, 361
Haran, 339
Haman, 524-525, 528
Hatherpsut, 123-124, 163
Havilah (land), 27
Hebrews (epistle), 84, 299
Hebron, 227, 239-240
Heliopolis (On), 112-113
Heloise, 188
Heman, 359-360
Henriettah, 164
Henry VIII, 287
Hep-Su-Tun, 143
Hermes, 55-56,3 59
Herodias, incarnation of Jezebel, 417-418
Heth, 86-87
Hezekiah, 206, 304, 444, 447-457, 462-

463, 466-469; and Assyrians, 447, 451, 455; and Babylon, 454-455; counseled by Micah, 447; and Isaiah, 447-449; and Philistines, 450; and spiritual reformation, 447-450
Hiram, 335, 339-340, 361-362
Hitler, 433-438; *see also Jehu*
Hittites, 67, 201, 207, 231, 281
Holy Land, God's promise of, 170
Holy of Holies, 157, 331; veil within, 157, 331
Home, importance of,
Homosexuality as due to pre-Adamic experience, 9
Hophni, 281, 329
Horeb, 204
Hoshea, 197, 424
Huel, 340
Human nature, 129-130
Hur, 146, 149-150, 332
Hushai, 343

## I

Immaculate Conception (Virgin Birth),46; of Eve, 33; of Mary, 39
Incarnation(s), and Cambyses, 517; and conflicts within Jewish ranks, 520-525; and Persians, 519-521; *see also Reincarnation(s)*
India, 26, 88, 477, 491, 525
Intuition, 33, 132, 263, 443, 448
Irish Colony, established by "lost" tribes, 470-471
Iron smelting, 281
Isaac, 81, 86, 88, 91-93, 97-99, 113, 118, 121, 203, 230, 285-286, 297, 594, 600; Abraham and, 97-99; birth of twins to, 99-101
Isaiah, 180, 381, 394, 424, 442-444, 447-448, 450-451, 453-455, 457, 462, 491, 494; and Hezekiah, 447-453, 454-455
Ishmael, 86, 88, 91, 93
Israel, 22; meaning of term, 171; renaming of, 108
Ithamar's son, 166
Izhar, 173

## J

Jabal, 50
Jabeliel, 232
Jacob, 86, 297-298, 349; friend of, 104-106; Jacob, dreams of, 478; God's promise to, 201; renaming of, 108; Reuben and, 103-104
Jacob's ladder, 107-109

James, (epistle), 97
Japeth, 79–73
Japin, 171
Jarael, 146
Jared, 181
Jarpar, 241
Jebusites, 201, 232, 329
Jeduthun, 360
Jeheuthel, 216
Jehoahaz, 457–458
Jehoiachin,458
Jehoiadah, 432, 439
Jehoiakim, 458
Jehoram, and Ahazia and Athaliah, 431–432
Jehoshaphat, and Ahab and Jezebel, 404–406; and kingdom of Judah, 409; reformation of, 402–403; and "the ungodly", 409
Jehovah, 118, 125, 140–141, 152, 161–162, 167–168, 221, 285, 338, 4414, 420, 507, 513, 551–552, 597; meaning of word, 125
Jehu, 408–409, 424–425, 431–438; relative to Hitler, 433–438
Jeluen, 190
Jephthah, 254, 301
Jericho, 182, 197, 214, 216, 223–226, 228–229, 243, 260, 277; battle of Jericho, 197, 224, 226
Jeroboam, 380, 384–391, 393, 395–396, 404, 413, 436, 438, 514; fall of, 386; as instrument of good, 385; and the man of God, 389–391; world affairs readings, 380, 388
Jerusalem, as David's capital, 329; David's flight from, 334, 340, 342; destruction of, 202, 271
Jeshua, xv, 28, 84, 120, 358, 372, 500–505, 512–513, 517, 533, 539, 553, 568, 572–573, 578, 593–594; and the first return, 500, 505, 533; reincarnations of, 500
Jesse, 210, 260, 263, 305, 384,
Jesus,x, xii, xv–xvi, xvii, xiv–xv, 2, 6, 10, 18, 22, 24–26, 28, 31, 39, 41, 54–55, 81–82, 84–86, 90, 99, 101, 110, 118, 120, 133, 153–155, 161, 189, 193, 197, 199–200, 202, 207, 209, 217, 219–221, 224, 233, 260, 266, 277, 299, 317, 321, 325, 329, 334, 342, 345, 353, 357–359, 367, 371–373, 382–383, 394, 397–399, 401–402, 404, 408, 416, 418–419, 421–422, 425–428, 477, 495–496, 501, 503–504, 514, 530, 543, 574, 578–580, 583–585, 590–591, 593–594 ; baptism

of, 139; on being born again, 139; as "cornerstone," 217; death on cross of, 40, 42, 182, 399, 419; as first and last Adam, xii; incarnations of, xv, 18, 22, 28, 54, 110, 118, 358–359, 371–372, 578, 594; knows he will be Savior, 39; Light in, xiv, 2, 10; Peter and, 82, 90, 217–218; Romans and, 317; Sermon on the Mount of, 153; three primary appearances of, 84; Way demonstrated in, 193
Jethebeth, 363
Jethro, 124, 148–149, 166, 441
Jeurepth, 80
Jewish refugees, 128
Jezebel, and Ahab and Elijah, 395, 405, 413–417, 419, 425; and Ahab and Jehoshaphat, 404–405; and karmic lesson, 417; personification of evil, 405; reincarnated as Herodias, 417
Jezeel, 232
Joab, 334, 339, 341, 343–344, 376
Joan of Arc, 131
Joash, and kingdom of Judah, 439
Job (book), written by Melchizedek, 18, 85, 119, 503
Jochabed, 121
John the Baptist, 416–419; Elijah reincarnated as, 416–419; and world affairs reading, 418
John the Beloved, dreams of, 478
John (book), xv, 2, 23–24, 35, 81, 102, 248, 382, 397, 401, 427–428
John, Revelation of, xviii, xxii, 211, 283, 494–495, 580, 593; see also Revelation of St. John
Jonathan, 301–303, 306–312, 315, 318, 349; death of,301–302, 318
Jordan, parting of, 214–216
Joseph, incarnation of Jeshua, 28, 84, 358, 372, 578
Joseph, xv, 28, 84, 86, 102–105, 109–117, 119, 132, 147, 193, 197, 298, 325, 358–359, 372, 393, 422, 500, 503–504, 547, 568, 478, 588; as first physical incarnation of Adam, 28, 84, 103, 358, 372, 500, 503, 568
Josephus, Antiquities of the Jews, 56
Joshua, 4, 28, 53, 84, 118–120, 145–149, 155, 170, 171–172, 178, 189, 193, 195, 197–201, 203, 206–210, 212, 214, 217–218, 220–221, 223–227, 229–234, 236, 289, 241–242, 244, 253, 270, 287, 291, 325, 329–330, 350, 358–359, 372, 378, 404, 432, 473, 500–501, 503–504, 568, 578, 588, 600; giants to be slain by,

170; Jesus and, 199; marriage of, 147; Moses and, xxii, 24, 118–120, 146, 149, 171, 178, 189
Joshua (book), 24, 197, 214, 217, 221–223, 226–229, 232, 238, 242
Josiah, and reformation, 456–459
Jotham, and kingdom of Judah, 443
Jubal, 50
Jubeel, 225
Judah, Kingdom of, 393–395; and Abijah, 395; and Asa, 431, 457; in captivity, 394, 455, 457; and Hezekiah, 448, 451; and Jehoshaphat, 403, 409, 432, 457; and Joash, 432, 439, 443; and Jotham, 443; and Rehaboam, 395; tribe of, 393
Judaism, 27, 197, 422, 509, 542, 557
Jude (epistle), 44, 192
Judges (book), 206, 215, 252–254, 256, 301

**K**

Kaballah, Hermes linked with Enoch in, 56
Karma, xviii, 24, 137, 207, 334, 340, 375 494, 417, 459, 461, 477; interpreted by Edgar Cayce, 414; and Zedekiah, 459
Karmic lesson, Elijah, 414, 417; Jezebel, 416–417, 419
Karmic memories, 306
Karmic pattern, Elijah to John, 417, 427
Keilah, 313–315
Keldebah, 235
Kenites, 205–206
Keriath-sepra, 238
Keturah, 148
Killing, by Phineas, in name of God, 185;
    in sixth commandment, 155
Kings, concept of, 270–271
1 Kings (book), 352, 355, 375, 380, 384–385, 387–389, 391, 396–397, 400, 404, 405, 408, 413, 415, 417, 419–420, 423–424, 434, 514
2 Kings (book), 405, 408, 411, 425, 427, 433–434, 437, 439, 448, 451, 455–456, 535
Kish, 92–294, 388
Kohath, 173
Korah, 145, 149–150, 164, 173–178, 216, 234–235, 378
Kotapet, 110

**L**

Laban, 103, 105
Lamb "slain before the foundation of the world," 26, 233
Lamech, 54, 102–103
Laodicea, 206
Lapeth, 70
Laws of the universe, angels as, 193
Leaders, as deserved, 268; should not be judged, 268
Leah, 102–103
Leieh, 255
Lemuria, 28, 67
Levi, 106–107, 123, 141, 145, 149, 164–165, 170, 173–174, 201, 213, 225, 235
Levites, musical guild in, 359, 363
Leviticus (book) 165, 208
Lice, plague of, 129, 134
Lifespan, 62, 63, 498
Life, the Tree of, and Nebuchadnezzar, 482, 483
Light, xxiii–xiv, 2, –6, 10–11, 21, 32, 75, 107–108, 128, 172, 177, 211, 265–266, 340, 373, 386, 434, 441, 471, 500, 572–573, 593
Light, the, xxiii–xiv, 2, 5–6, 10–11, 21, 25–26, 40, 53, 96, 135, 268, 557, 572, 574–575; as of Son of Man, 40, 53, 96, 135
Liszt, Franz, 364
Locusts, plague of, 135
"Lost" records, 536–537, 541
"Lost" tribes, establishment of altars, 362, 462, 464, 468; establishment of American Colony, 464; establishment of English Colony, 465; *see also Ten tribes*
Lot and Lot's wife, 94–95
Love, Absalom's death and, 345; God as, 160
Lucifer, xxiii, 43; *see also Devil, the*
Luke (book), xx, 41, 202, 221–222, 224, 287, 345, 459, 478
Lust, 8–9, 204, 383; *see also Sex*

**M**

Magicians of Egypt, 131
Malchor, 264
Malchus, 331
Male-female beings, 6
Man, evolution of, 41, 65, 75, 511, 543; rebellion of, 8, 245; *see also Adam;* Adamic race, xiv, 22, 30, 32, 43, 53, 83, 211, 268, 495; Man of God, and Jeroboam, 389–390
Manassah, and Amon 455–456

Manasseh, Manasseh, 190, 254, 339;
(associate of Joab), 339; tribe of, 254
Manna, 142, 221; cessation of, 221
Manoah, 256, 353
Maran, 67
Mark (book), chronology of, 221, 398, 425
Mary, 39, 86, 102, 280, 289, 422
Marriage, 34, 45, 147, 166, 170, 238, 248,
259, 261–262, 265, 307–308, 333, 338,
398, 431, 526, 555, 559
Mary, as Eve, 39; Immaculate Concep-
tion of, 39
Matthew (book), 82, 90, 209, 217, 221–222,
345, 371, 398, 404, 416, 419, 425, 579
Meah, 184
Mediumship, 208, 319–320
Melchizedek, xv, 18, 28, 81–86, 103, 109,
119, 197, 277, 325, 329, 358–359, 372,
422, 500, 503–504, 368, 578–579, 594;
Abraham and, 81,3 59, 503; incarna-
tion of Jeshua; 28, 358, 372, 578; Job
written by, 18; as priest, 329
Mercy seat, 158–160, 165
Merab, 307–308
Meribah, 178–179
Methuselah, 62
Michael the archangel, 192
Micah, counsel to Hezekiah, 447
Micaiah, and death of Ahab, 406–407
Michal, 308
Michmash, 301, 308
Midian, 124, 130, 148, 184, 188–189;
Moses' war on, 188–189
Midianites, 124, 185, 188–189, 205, 253
Mizpeh, 254
Mind, Creation and, 12, 76, 578–579; in
post-Deluge era, 76
Miriam, 121, 140, 149, 151, 164, 166, 173
Mississippi basin, 28
Moab, 128, 184–185, 259, 262, 24, 405,
408, 411
Moabite women, fornication with, 259
Moabites, 182, 264, 332, 409, 538
Mordecai, 524, 527, 529–530
Moses, x, xxii, xxvii, 24, 30, 45, 52, 77,
117–194, 197–198, 201–202, 205–206,
217, 237, 242, 291, 303, 330, 359, 419,
437, 441, 474, 483, 513–514, 534, 541,
588–590, 592, 597–598, 600; appearance with Elijah, 53, 321; birth of,
119–120; bones of, 193; concept of
war of, 201, 203, 205; death of, 190,
192; Ethiopian woman married by,
170, 173; Joshua and, 197–199, 201,
203; Kenites and, 205; Pharaoh and,
118, 122, 130, 132, 135–136, 179; at

Sinai, 146, 148, 151–152, 330, 419; in
the wilderness, 141–142, 172, 202
Motherhood, psychic, 273, 278, 282–283
Mount Sinai, 146, 152, 216, 330
Mu, 9, 31, 67, 464
Music, 304, 359–360, 364N

**N**

Nadab, 164–169, 400, 404
Nabal, 316
Nadab, 164–169, 400, 404
Naomi, 259, 261–265
Nathan, 327, 374, 334, 340–341
Nebuchadnezzar, and Babylonian Em-
pire, 458, 468, 487, 489; and Daniel,
480, 482; and dreams, 480–481; and
the fiery furnace, 480, 482; madness
of, 482, 484; and Tree of Life, 482, 483
Nehemiah, 492–493, 497–499, 501, 510,
515, 519–520, 522, 533, 535, 537–539,
547–549, 551–574; and discord with
Ezra, 551, 572–574; and Ezra, 493,
497–510, 515, 519, 522, 533, 535, 537–
539, 547–549, 561; reincarnation of,
556–557
New Jerusalem, 87, 580–581
Nicodemus, 139
Nile River, 28, 120, 133; changed into
blood, 133
Noah, 33, 47, 55, 59, 61, 64–68, 70–73, 80,
86, 201, 203, 255, 269, 426, 428, 588–
589, 596, 600; purity of generation
of, 47
Noh, 312
Numbers (book), 169–171, 173–174, 176–
180, 182–183, 185, 188, 190, 197, 213,
236
Nun, 197–198

**O**

Obed, 260, 263–265
Odenatus of Palmyra, 184
Og, 9
Omri, 388, 404
On (city), 112
On (person), 173
Opportunity, World as, 4
Orpah, 259, 262, 264–265
Othiel, 234
Othniel, 238
Oz, 9

**P**

Pannah, 278

Papias, 333
Parents, failure of, 284; honoring of, 155
Passover, world affairs reading, 449
Patience, 9, 91, 230, 592, 594–595
Paul, 24, 127, 299, 331
Peleth, 173
Pelus, 71
Persians, and incarnations, 557; and third return, 555
Persus, 362
Peter, 82, 90, 217–218, 220; rebuked by Jesus, 90; recognizes Jesus as Christ, 90, 217
1 Peter, 220
2 Peter (epistle), xiv, 184
Pharaoh, 89, 113, 18, 130–132; Abraham and, 89–90; Moses and, 118, 122, 130, 132, 135–136, 179
Pharaoh's daughter, 120, 130
Philistines, 90, 281, 292, 300–301, 306, 308, 310, 313–315, 324, 330–332, 339, 431, 442, 450; and Hezekiah, 450
Phineas, 185, 188, 281, 330
Phoenicians, 361–362
Pishon (river), 27
Plagues, the, 189, 129, 131, 133–134, 136
Plato, Critias, 361
Prayer, power of, 96
Pre-Adamic World, 8
Prodigal Son, xiv
Poseida, 61, 302
Promised Land, meaning of, 220
Prophets, School of, 85, 119, 277, 285, 422, 461, 503–504; and Essenes, 422–423
Prophets, whether God is speaking through, 129, 204
Psalms, 241, 333, 336, 359–360
Psychic arts, and the Chaldeans, 479
Psychic development as outgrowth of Spiritual development, 584
Psychic motherhood, 273, 278, 282–283
Psychic phenomena, and Ezekiel, 496, 542, 544–545
Psychic powers, of Cayce, 284; development of, 284

## Q

Queen of Sheba, 364
Quest, Linda, 270

## R

Ra-Ta, 55, 106, 163, 558
Rabbath, 333
Races, five, 27, 43, 66

Rachel, 99, 104–105, 278, 298; pregnancy of, 103–104
Rahab, 223, 226, 260
Rahai, 226
Rahalab, 335
Rainbow after the Deluge, 72
Rakim, 180
Ramah, 235, 277
Ramtha, 311
Raoul, 105
Reading, dream, and fiery furnace, 480–482
Readings, Cayce's, described, xvi–xix, 498; world affairs, 369–370, 372, 380–381, 383, 385, 388, 390, 397, 402, 405, 418, 433, 435–436, 440, 444, 449; and Ahaz, 444; and Jeroboam, 386, 388–389; and Joel, 367, 440; and John the Baptist, 416, 418; on power, 438; on religious conflict, 59, 512; and revolution, 381–382, 565; spirit is greater than law, 449
Rebekah, 99, 278
Rebellion, Devil as, xxiii, 2–3, 423; Man's, 8, 141, 245; and Satan, xxiii, 432; of ten tribes, 382–384
Red Sea, crossing of, 139, 215
Reformation, of Josiah, 456
Rehoboam, and kingdom of Judah, 394–395; and rebellion of ten tribes, 393
Reincarnation; of Adam, 500–503; in American Colony, 464–465; during Babylonian captivity, 474, 476–477; of Belschazzar, 489; of Benaiah, 234, 377–379; Cyrus' daughter, 492–493; Cyrus' Queen, 491; daughter of Obadiah, 424; of Elijah as John the Baptist, 415–416 ; and English Colony, 466–470; of Esther, 527–528; during Esther's influence, 529–530; and Ezekiel, 539, 542–543; of Hanan, 528; during time of Hezekiah, 449–453; and Irish Colony, 471; of Jeshua, 500, 503; Jezebel as Herodias, 417; Joshua and, 503, 568; and "lost" records, 537; and "lost" tribes, 463; of Man of God, 391–392; and Noah, 426–427; and return to Jerusalem, 505–506; and Samaritans, 514–516; and slavery, 486–488; sons of fathers and, 154; of Vashti, 525–526; and Vashti, 530–532; of Zerubbabel, 494–493, 498–501, 505–517, 519–521, 533, 537, 540, 543, 548, 550–553, 5671, 563–566, 570–571, 573; see also Essenes

609

Rephidim, battle of, 204
Resurrection, reason for, 496
Reuben, 102–103, 150, 173, 213–214;
Reul, 124
Revelation of St. John, xviii, 211, 283,
  494
Revolution, world affairs reading, 383;
  *see also* Rebellion
Rezepatha, 68–70
Rhouel, 366
Righteousness, 98
River, four-headed, 25, 139
Rizpah, 323
Romans, Jesus' answer to, 317
Ruth, ; (book of), 259–260, 267

## S

Sabbath, 154, 549, 568
Sacrifice, of Isaac, 97; Temple of, 74–75
Sahara Desert, 28
Samaritans, 513–514, 519, 548, 550, 572
Samson, 246, 255–256
Samuel, 86, 119, 204, 223, 245, 267, 269–
  270, 273, 276–279, 282, 284–285, 287–
  291, 294, 296, 298–301, 301, 311, 316,
  318–321, 327, 329, 334, 337, 403, 410,
  422–423, 449, 461, 503, 574; birth of,
  245, 273, 278, 286; death of, 316, 318–
  319; Saul and, 298–301, 303, 311,
  318–319, 321, 327
1 Samuel (book), 269, 273, 277, 281, 283,
  292–294, 298, 300–301, 303–306, 308,
  310–319, 330, 449
2 Samuel (book), xxvii, 206, 323–324,
  328, 330, 332, 334, 340–341,343, 345,
  376
San, 358
Sanballat, 543,547–550, 571
Sarah, 86, 89–93, 98–99, 278, 292, 594
Satan, xxiii, 41, 99, 193, 242, 432, 502,
  587; *see also Devil*; and rebellion, xxii–
  xxiii, 2–3, 8
Saul, King, 204, 299, 302, 305–307; David
  and, 302, 305–306; death of, 319
School of Prophets, 85, 119, 277, 285,
  422–424, 426, 461, 503–504; under
  Elijah, 119, 422–424, 426; and
  Essenes, 85, 285, 422–423, 504
Séances, 33, 407
Segualar, 157
Self, symbolized by Babylon, 475
Sen-Doer, 261
Sennacherib, 450–451, 454
Sermon on the Mount, 153
Serpent, the, xxiii, 2–3, 36–37, 59, 177,

181, 182–183, 392, 588; fiery, 181; *see
  also Devil, the*
Seth, 40, 44, 46, 50, 56, 65, 104, 205, 297,
  585; children of, 44, 50
Sex, creation of, 75; "forbidden fruit" as,
  35; ideals and purposes of, 36, 99;
Shammar, 252
Shalmahr, 147
Shebeth, 150
Shechem, 106–107, 221, 379
Shelah, 332
Sheluenmehei, 337–339
Shem, 171
Shemaiah, 387, 395–396
Sheol, Moses' enemies consumed by,
  176–177
Sheshbazzar, 498
Shiloh, 198, 216, 222, 229–, 234, 278, 281
Shimei, 342, 376
Shittim, 185
Shulah, 263
Shulzar, 178
Shushan, 151, 573
Sidon, 338–339
Sidonites, 212
Sidiptu, 123
Sierra giants, 210
Simeon, 106–107, 185
Simon, 82, 201
Sisera, 206, 246–247, 249, 252
Slavery and awakened consciousness,
  475; and Life readings, 476
Sodom and Gomorrah, 96–97
Solar System, creation of, xxi, 13
Solomon, 202, 218, 235, 271, 332–336,
  341, 346, 349–357, 359–367, 375–377,
  379–380, 382–383, 389, 395–396, 399,
  413, 439, 448, 457, 475, 579–580, 587–
  588, 592–593, 599–600; Cayce's dream
  of, 355; greed and ambition of, 375,
  378; sins of, 375, 430; Temple built,
  218
Sons of Belial (Sons of Cain), 45–48, 59–
  60, 65, 172; automatons and, 52, 60
Sons of Darkness, 5
Sons of God, xxiii, 3, 5, 8, 11, 14, 18–21,
  25, 38, 44, 46–48, 52, 59–60, 64, 72–73,
  77, 82, 85, 172, 210, 291; in Amilius,
  29, 31; entry into earth of, xiv, 29
Sons of the Law of One, 49, 59, 73; *see
  also Sons of God*
Sons of Man, 8
Soul, animal associations of, 31; after
  death, 38, 41; evolution of, 11, 13; as
  sexless, xxii–xxiii, 1–2; *see also Divine
  Image*

610

Soul attraction, psychic motherhood
and, 278
Souls, God's purpose in creation of,
Space, 3, 9, 215, 230
Spirit communication, 320
Spence, Lewis, 62
Sphinx, 541
Spirit, Adamic race as expression of, ;
male–female union as means of re-
turn to Oneness of, 75; water as first
materialization of, 18
Stones in Aaron's breastplate, 162, 164
Strange fire, 165–167, 177
Sugrue, Tom, xviii, 353
Sun stands still, 197, 229
Suthers, 226
Syria, 444

### T

Tabernacle, 149, 156, 197–198, 225, 243,
350, 591
Tahi, 121
Tamar, 101, 334, 339, 341, 530
Tanai, 121
Teheru, Princess, 114
Tekla, 113
Tekoah, 341
Temah, 88
Temple, the, 24, 211–212, 218,219, 243,
271, 329, 332, 335, 337–338, 341, 344,
350–351, 360, 364, 543, 580; body as
24; David and 332, 344, 350, 365, 433,
592, 600; sacking of 271; Solomon's
building of, 218, 335, 341, 350, 376
Ten, symbology of, 159
Ten tribes, the fall of 379, 382–384, 393,
400, 413, 462, 465, 467, 592; and
Rehoboam, 379–380, 382–383, 387,
395–397; see also "Lost" tribes
Ten Commandments, receiving of, 153,
156, 208, 592
Tep-Lepan, 115
Terahe, 88
Thanksgiving, lesson of, 144
Thessalonica, 111
Thummin, 163–164
"Things" (automatons), 52, 60
Thought-forms, end of, 72
Thyroid gland, 256
Time, 4–5, 9, 11, 22, 215, 230, 280; as
relative concept, 51
Tobiah, 547, 549
Torah, 118
Trance state, xvii, 133, 183, 353, 479
Trances, Cayce's, xix–xx, 310

Tree of Knowledge, 24, 29, 37, 291, 585
Tree of Life, xii, 24, 51, 482–484, 585;
and Nebuchadnezzar, 482–484
Tubal-Cain, 50, 53–54
Tuesday Night Bible Class, ix, xviii, 133,
147, 160, 310
Turner, Gladys Davis, x, 290; see also
Davis, Gladys
Twelve (number), 218
Two, symbology of, 158
Tyrants, David's example and,
Tyre, 335, 338–339, 346, 361, 545, 574
"ungodly," the, and Jehoshaphat, 409,
411, 4341

### U

Unity Metaphysical Dictionary, 204
Ur, 87–88,358, 507
Ural Mountains, 28
Uriah the Hittite, 332, 334, 340
Urim and Thummin, 163–164
Uzziah, and the priesthood, 442
Uzzah, 329–331

### V

Vashti and Esther, 523–525
Vegetarian diet, 48
Velikovsky, Dr. Immanuel, 143
Versions of the Bible, xvi
Virgin Birth, 33, 504; see also Immaculate
conception
Visions, 69, 132, 143, 162, 211, 246, 277,
363, 367, 392–393, 420, 423, 440, 478,
481, 501, 573; see also Dreams
Vocations, first practitioners of, 50

### W

War, Moses' idea of, 201
Warrior, Joshua as, 199–200, 588; Temple
not to be built by, 332
Water, as beginning of life, 12; as first
materialization of spirit, 18; from the
rock, 179
Water Gate, 567, 570
White Brotherhood, 56
Wilderness, the, 91, 116, 138, 141–142,
156–157, 164, 166, 169, 172–173, 178,
180, 182, 189, 198, 202, 208, 213, 216,
221–222, 225, 228, 238–240, 242, 314–
315, 317, 349, 411, 416, 491, 591–592,
598; Isaiah and, 180
Witch of Endor, 318, 320
Woman, creation of, 33
Word, the, 21–22, 42; see also Mind

World affairs reading(s), 370, 380, 388, 397, 405, 433, 436; *see also Reading(s)*
Worlds in Collision (Velikovsky), 143

## X

Xerxes, 487, 523–524, 526, 528, 531, 533

## Y

Yucatan, 27, 66, 75, 464, 471, 545

## Z

Zadok, 342
Zebulon, tribe of, 362
Zechariah, 441–442, 501–503, 577, 593–594; vision of, 502
Zedekiah, 407, 439, 458–459, 461, 466–471, 477, 488, 505, 566
Zend, 358, 530
Zephaniah, 141, 502–503, 507
Zerrubabel, 206
Zeruba, 130
Zeta-Elda, 136
Ziklag, 304
Zillah, 50
Zimri, 185, 187, 404
Zin, wilderness of, 141, 166
Ziph, 315
Zipohar, 174
Zipporah, 148–
Zoroastrianism, 358, 523, 525

# EDGAR CAYCE'S A.R.E.

### What Is A.R.E.?

The Association for Research and Enlightenment, Inc., (A.R.E.®) was founded in 1931 to research and make available information on psychic development, dreams, holistic health, meditation, and life after death. As an open-membership research organization, the A.R.E. continues to study and publish such information, to initiate research, and to promote conferences, distance learning, and regional events. Edgar Cayce, the most documented psychic of our time, was the moving force in the establishment of A.R.E.

### Who Was Edgar Cayce?

Edgar Cayce (1877-1945) was born on a farm near Hopkinsville, Ky. He was an average individual in most respects. Yet, throughout his life, he manifested one of the most remarkable psychic talents of all time. As a young man, he found that he was able to enter into a self-induced trance state, which enabled him to place his mind in contact with an unlimited source of information. While asleep, he could answer questions or give accurate discourses on any topic. These discourses, more than 14,000 in number, were transcribed as he spoke and are called "readings."

Given the name and location of an individual anywhere in the world, he could correctly describe a person's condition and outline a regimen of treatment. The consistent accuracy of his diagnoses and the effectiveness of the treatments he prescribed made him a medical phenomenon, and he came to be called the "father of holistic medicine."

Eventually, the scope of Cayce's readings expanded to include such subjects as world religions, philosophy, psychology, parapsychology, dreams, history, the missing years of Jesus, ancient civilizations, soul growth, psychic development, prophecy, and reincarnation.

### A.R.E. Membership

People from all walks of life have discovered meaningful and life-transforming insights through membership in A.R.E. To learn more about Edgar Cayce's A.R.E. and how membership in the A.R.E. can enhance your life, visit our Web site at EdgarCayce.org, or call us toll-free at 800-333-4499.

**Edgar Cayce's A.R.E.
215 67th Street
Virginia Beach, VA 23451-2061**

## EDGARCAYCE.ORG